A Picturesque Situation

A Picturesque Situation

MACKINAC BEFORE PHOTOGRAPHY 1615 – 1860

BRIAN LEIGH DUNNIGAN

WAYNE STATE UNIVERSITY PRESS / DETROIT

© 2008 by Wayne State University Press, Detroit, Michigan 48201.
All rights reserved. No part of this book may be reproduced without
formal permission. Manufactured in the United States of America.

12 11 10 09 08   5 4 3 2 1

Library of Congress Cataloging-in-Publication Data

Dunnigan, Brian Leigh.
  A picturesque situation : Mackinac before photography, 1615–
1860 / Brian Leigh Dunnigan.
     p. cm. — (Great Lakes books)
  Includes bibliographical references and index.
  ISBN-13: 978-0-8143-3214-6 (hardcover : alk. paper)
  ISBN-10: 0-8143-3214-5 (hardcover : alk. paper)
  1. Mackinac Island (Mich. : Island)—History—17th century—
Pictorial works. 2. Mackinac Island (Mich. : Island)—History—
18th century—Pictorial works. 3. Mackinac Island (Mich. :
Island)—History—19th century—Pictorial works. 4. Mackinac
Island (Mich. : Island)—Description and travel. I. Title.
F572.M16D965 2008
977.4'923—dc22
                        2007025941

∞ The paper used in this publication meets the minimum
requirements of the American National Standard for Information
Sciences—Permanence of Paper for Printed Library Materials,
ANSI Z39.48–1984.

Grateful acknowledgement is made to the Florence Gould
Foundation and the Ford R. Bryan Publication Fund for generous
support of the publication of this volume.

Designed and typeset by Savitski Design
Composed in Minion and Frutiger
Printed in the United States of America
by University Lithoprinters, Inc.

The people of Mackinac Island were peculiar, and possibly some of them
are still entitled to that distinction.

Reverend James A. Van Fleet, 1882

For all my "peculiar" and very special Mackinac Island friends, past and present,
year-round and seasonal, who have made the place home for me.

Brian Leigh Dunnigan

CONTENTS

Mackinac Suillet 1856.

"Photography had not been introduced into the United States at this time"

On a July day in 1856 Reinhard Wernigk stepped across Mackinac Island's Market Street from the stately Greek Revival home built by the late Judge Samuel Abbott. Wernigk and his wife had come from Chicago to spend that summer as guests of the William Saltonstall family, who rented the mansion from Abbott's brother. Brayton Saltonstall, who was seven years old at the time, later recalled Wernigk as a "Frenchman with a German name" who had emigrated from Paris and set

himself up in the growing Lake Michigan city as a "photographic artist." Brayton's sister, Constance, was impressed that their guest had brought a "fine camera" from Paris, quite a novelty, as she believed that "photography had not been introduced into the United States" at that time.[1]

Across the way, at the corner of what is today known as Hoban Street, Wernigk set up a tripod for his cumbersome device. His intention was to get a "fine view of the Fort." From that spot his perspective was virtually unobstructed. The houses along the unpaved track were still mostly low, dark, log structures of antique, Canadian style, their yards enclosed by palisade fences. Hardly a tree was to be seen. The few larger buildings—the Michilimackinac County Courthouse, the former headquarters and warehouse of the American Fur Company, and the substantial Mitchell and Geary homes—were far enough in the distance so as not to mask any part of historic Fort Mackinac. Wernigk aimed his contraption and proceeded to take the first known photograph of any part of the Straits of Mackinac region.

The Saltonstall children were fascinated and remembered the event clearly many years later. "Photography was in its infancy then," Brayton remarked, and he treasured the picture for the rest of his life as a souvenir of childhood summers on Mackinac Island.[2] Monsieur Wernigk had brought to Mackinac a technology that was already more than fifteen years old, but it had yet to make an impact on the picturesque Straits area. His first photograph could hardly have been better composed. It captures many of the elements that had already begun to transform Mackinac into the recreational destination it

remains today—clear air, dramatic scenery, peaceful surroundings, quaint buildings, and a romantic history and folklore revolving around Native Americans, the fur trade, and past military struggles.

Wernigk was only the first of uncounted photographers who would record their visits to the Mackinac region.[3] Within a decade photography was no longer a novelty at the Straits. By the 1870s it had become relatively common. The 1880s and 1890s saw increasing numbers of professional photographers, some of whom, like William Gardiner, would set up shop on Mackinac Island or in the mainland communities of St. Ignace, Mackinaw City, and Cheboygan, where they regularly recorded aspects of life at the Straits. The advent of simplified, personal cameras at the end of the century set off an explosion of picture taking that continues to be an important part of life and leisure in the twenty-first century. Today, historic photographs depicting scenes of the Victorian resort era or early twentieth-century tourism have largely shaped our impressions of "old" Mackinac.[4]

By 1856 and the first photograph, however, Mackinac was already a well-known spot that had grown increasingly popular with leisure travelers over the preceding three decades. For two centuries before that time, visiting Native Americans, soldiers, missionaries, traders, explorers, and scientists had all found it necessary to record their impressions of the place and somehow pass them on to distant audiences. The usual medium was words, spoken or written in letters, reports, diaries, books, and legal or financial documents. But there were visual options as well. Some who visited, lived, or worked at the Straits of Mackinac possessed the motivation and the skill to map or draw what they observed. Military officers recorded fortifications and topography. Surveyors mapped boundaries. Cartographers defined local geography. Travelers sketched scenery and colorful personalities. The limited numbers of early visual documents that survive provide rare and important glimpses of Mackinac before the age of the camera and complement the many written and printed descriptions of the area. As Daniel Curtiss remarked after a visit in 1851, Mackinac presented much to interest the "pencil-artist, poet, or philosopher."[5]

Therein lies the point of this book—to identify, document, and interpret the visual record of Mackinac before photography began to provide more comprehensive coverage of the appearance of the place and its people. The visual history presented here has been based on an extensive iconography—a collection and study of images—for the years through 1860. By that date, four years after Reinhard Wernigk's first photographic exposure, the Mackinac that is familiar to us through the camera's lens had come into being. Elements of the older days remained—and remain today in many cases—but their context and surroundings had begun to change. The Mackinac of Native Americans and fur traders in bark canoes, fishermen in Mackinaw boats, and soldiers on guard was being reinvented as the resort jewel of the Great Lakes, a role the Straits continues to play today.

Images, whether photographs or the media that preceded them, are important historical documents. Unlike photographs, however, drawn images are entirely subjective and may or may not show what they purport to. In this they are rather more like written accounts. Errors, lies, omissions, or distortions can be transmitted as easily through maps and drawings as by words. The context and purpose of each map or picture are therefore important, and the use of other sources, such as written or printed documents and oral history, to confirm or challenge its veracity is essential. As a result, what follows is not so much a comprehensive history of the Mackinac region for the years to 1860 as it is an attempt to document its visual record and provide context for what these images reveal of life and events at the Straits.

The geographical scope of this study is the Straits of Mackinac, the connecting water passage between Lake Huron and Lake Michigan. It was a location of pivotal importance to exploration, trade, missionary activity, and military affairs in the early Great Lakes. The area encompasses the tips of Michigan's two peninsulas at St. Ignace and Mackinaw City, the islands of Mackinac, Round, Bois Blanc, St. Helena, Green, and the two St. Martins, and the surrounding coastlines and waters. Early maps of the area vary greatly in their coverage but tend to include all or most of these elements.

This study will confine itself to the immediate Straits area, essentially within view of the Mackinac Bridge. Not surprisingly, the focus of the maps and views changes over time according to the centers of human activity in the Straits. The majority of the earliest images depict features of the French-Indian settlement at St. Ignace and the subsequent post at the site of Mackinaw City. Mackinac

Island attracted the lion's share of attention following 1779 and continued to do so until after the Civil War, when the mainland towns began to develop more rapidly and commerce and industry shifted in their direction.

It might be prudent, at this point, to explain the distinctions between the names "Mackinac" and "Michilimackinac" in their many and varied spellings and to define how they are used here. Today, most Americans associate the longer form with the post maintained on the Lower Peninsula mainland from 1715 to 1781. "Mackinac" usually describes the Straits and the island. The same name, ending in "w," is used for a modern mainland town and objects such as the "Mackinaw boat" or "Mackinaw coat." Past custom was not so clear-cut, and "Michilimackinac" was applied more broadly and employed much more recently than is generally supposed. In 1839 James Lanman observed that "Mackinaw proper, as the term is used in modern times, is confined to the island," and maps bear the longer name for the Straits, and even the island, well into the 1830s.[6] The town on Mackinac Island remained the "Borough of Michilimackinac" as late as 1847, and the "Village of Mackinac" was not formed until the following year. As late as 1895, John R. Bailey felt it necessary to title his popular history and guidebook *Mackinac, Formerly Michilimackinac*. Indeed, even today, many Canadians tend to use the longer form. Often, usage was simply a matter of preference. "You see I write the name sometimes in extenso, and sometimes as now abbreviated," Thomas McKenney informed his readers in 1827.[7]

While the meaning of "Michilimackinac" has been disputed, most Europeans and Euro-Americans accepted the translation to be "Great Turtle" or something similar and supposed it to have been a reference to the outline of Mackinac Island.[8] The name was originally applied to the entire region. After the coming of Europeans, their military and fur-trading post was known as "Michilimackinac," and it was so called well into the American occupation, whether in reference to the establishments at the sites of modern St. Ignace, Mackinaw City, or Mackinac Island.

Individual elements of the post of Michilimackinac often bore their own names. "St. Ignace" described a mission. Fortifications were individually christened, such as Fort de Buade and Fort Holmes, though both were elements of the post of Michilimackinac. In 1780 General Frederick Haldimand declared that the new fortress on Mackinac Island should be styled "Fort Makinac," while the post itself would continue to be known as "Michilimackinac."[9] Generally, contemporary usage will be followed here to provide the flavor of past times and to accustom readers to the gradual development of the place-names that are familiar today.

Finding the pre-photographic images of the Straits of Mackinac has meant searching for them in institutions and collections in North America and in Europe. Many are unique manuscript items, prepared for a very limited audience of the artists' friends, colleagues, or superiors. Others made their way into print as

FORT MICHILIMACKINAC, MICHIGAN.

This woodcut, purporting to show early Mackinac Island, illustrated Charles R. Tuttle's *General History of the State of Michigan* (Detroit, 1873). In 1875, Straits-area historian Father Edward Jacker attempted to identify the "old engraving" from which it had been copied. His effort was in vain because the image was a fanciful reconstruction prepared for Tuttle's book. *Clements Library, University of Michigan (Print Division).*

illustrations in books and magazines intended for a wider audience. Regardless, each image illustrated here is accompanied by the information necessary to locate the original for future research. Appendix A is a chronological listing of all identified, pre-photographic Mackinac visuals including those that are too poor in quality to be reproduced and those that are simply duplicates of better examples. This list also includes "phantom" images—those described in written sources but which, if they survive, remain to be found.

If these drawn or printed renderings of the Straits of Mackinac are to be considered effective windows on the historical past, then care must be taken to guarantee that they are, in fact, primary sources. Graphics created at a later time to reconstruct scenes of earlier days are of no use in this respect. Care has been taken, therefore, to ensure that the images reproduced or listed here are primary visual documents drawn by or based on the work of artists or cartographers who actually observed the scene. In some cases, authentic images survive only as later copies because the original art has disappeared or remains to be discovered. Maps and views that appear to have been accurately reproduced have been included here when the original is unavailable.

Regardless of academic concerns about authenticity, research value, and historical importance, the best way to use the maps, pictures, and text in this book is for the sheer pleasure of visiting the Straits of Mackinac of a distant and unfamiliar time. Readers who know and love Mackinac are sure to discern many uncanny similarities between the place and its people of the past and those of the present. The images depict a very real and vibrant locale where events, both noteworthy and mundane, helped shape the history of Michigan and the Great Lakes. These maps and pictures are full of revealing detail, and there is much to be learned by studying them with care. Brayton and Constance Saltonstall must have gazed on Reinhard Wernigk's 1856 photograph with curiosity and even awe. Modern visitors and residents of the Straits of Mackinac can likewise use the visual technologies of the pre-photographic age to explore a fascinating place as it appeared to the people who made the history that is celebrated there today.

The critical starting point in a search for the pre-photographic imagery of Mackinac was the collection of visual materials gathered over the past half century by the staff of Mackinac State Historic Parks. Many of the maps and pictures in this book will be familiar because they have appeared in publications and exhibits produced since the reconstruction and restoration of Forts Michilimackinac and Mackinac began in the late 1950s. This solid foundation to discovering the "look" of early Mackinac was laid by the agency's dedicated, current and former professional staff, particularly the late Dr. Eugene T. Petersen, Dr. David A. Armour, Dr. Keith R. Widder, Steven C. Brisson, and current director Phil Porter. Thanks to them all, particularly Phil and Steve, for ready assistance, hearty enthusiasm, and inspiration.

The labor of finding and documenting the images of Mackinac was greatly eased by an institutional connection with the William L. Clements Library of the University of Michigan. The support and encouragement provided by the university, and particularly the Clements Library's Committee of Management, has been considerable and is most gratefully acknowledged. Also much appreciated are the unparalleled resources of the university's numerous libraries, particularly the Bentley, Hatcher, and Special Collections, that guaranteed that virtually any title was available as needed.

The documentary and graphic resources of the Clements Library and the support and encouragement of its staff, particularly its director, John C. Dann, have been essential to the completion of this project. John backed it from the beginning, offering many helpful insights and enthusiastically presenting the project to the library's governing body. Phil Mason, president of the Clements Library Associates and a distinguished Michigan historian, has been another solid advocate. Clayton Lewis, curator of graphic materials, provided invaluable assistance with photography. Curators Barbara DeWolfe, Jan Longone, Mary Sponberg Pedley, and Don Wilcox offered support and advice. The late John C. Harriman selflessly assisted in many ways in the early stages of the last of many projects on which we cooperated. Other members of the Clements Library staff, particularly Julie Barnes, Janet Bloom, Shneen Coldiron, Laura Daniel, Julie Fremuth, Sakina Kanpurwala, Oksana Linda, Valerie Proehl, and Cheney Schopieray, have also assisted in many ways. Special thanks are due Audrey Williams for her computer wizardry and advice.

Helpful and enthusiastic colleagues at other historical institutions greatly facilitated the process of research and the discovery of new images. Particular thanks go to Len Coombs and Karen Jania of the Bentley Historical Library; David Poremba, John Gibson, and the other professional staff of the Burton Historical Collection of the Detroit Public Library; Bryan McDaniel of the Chicago History Museum; Susan James of the Chippewa County Historical Society; Frank Boles and the staff of the Clarke Historical Library, Central Michigan University; Sylvia Inwood of the Detroit Institute of Arts; the late Sandy Whitesell and Karen Wight of the Detroit Observatory, University of Michigan; John Polacsek of the Dossin Great Lakes Museum; John Magill of the Historic New Orleans Collection; Peter Blodgett of the Huntington Library; Jim Burant of Library and Archives Canada; Michelle Hill, the late Bill Fritz, Brian Jaeschke, and Lynn Evans of Mackinac State Historic Parks; Kay Kays of the National Museum of Wales; Russell Bastedo of the New Hampshire Division of Historical Resources; Robert Karrow of the Newberry Library; Doug DeCroix and Ray Wigle of the Old Fort Niagara Association; Tom House and Carol Marshall of the Olin Library at Kenyon College; Nicola Woods of the Royal Ontario Museum; Nan Card and Gil Gonzalez of the Rutherford B. Hayes Presidential Center; Kathryn L. Beam of the Special Collections Library, University of Michigan; Alan Walker of the Toronto Public Library; Al Aimone of the United States Military Academy Library; James W. Cheevers of the United States Naval Academy Museum; Mary Rogstad of the Vermont Historical Society; and Adam Jablonowski and Peggy Mitchell of the Wayne County Medical Society of Southeast Michigan.

Private collectors shared resources and advice as well, particularly Bruce Baky, Martin and Pat Jahn, James L. Kochan, Richard and Jane Manoogian, Larry Massie, Thomas Shaw, Ken Teysen, and David V. Tinder. And then there were the individual Mackinac historians and enthusiasts, all of whom were ready to share their knowledge and discoveries—Brother Jim Boynton, Dr. Todd Harburn, Bruce Hawkins, Owen Jansson, Patricia Martin, Wesley Maurer, Paul Muldoon, Tom Pfeiffleman, Dan Seeley, Bob Tagitz of Grand Hotel, Tim Todish, and Father Jim Williams. Thanks also to Jeff Dupre of *Mackinac Living* magazine for help with some difficult photography.

Other friends, researchers, and collectors shared knowledge and sources or made helpful suggestions, including Bob Andrews, Edward Boyagian, René Chartrand, John Dunbabin, Dennis Carter-Edwards, Ed Dahl, Scott Hawley, Les Jensen, Kim McQuaid, Helen Hornbeck Tanner, Dr. Edward G. Voss, and J. Martin West.

Turning a manuscript into a completed and attractive book was the doing of the fine team at Wayne State University Press. Many thanks for the hard work and encouragement of Kathryn Wildfong, acquiring editor; Carrie Downes Teefey, production editor; and Jennifer Backer, a very thorough copyeditor. It has been a pleasure to work with them all. Blending text and images into a handsome book was the considerable accomplishment of Mike Savitski of Savitski Design, who applied his unmatched talents to that task and succeeded as admirably as he did with the earlier *Frontier Metropolis*.

Financial support was also an important part of production. The support and encouragement of Barry Adams and the Mackinac Bands of Chippewa and Ottawa is gratefully acknowledged.

It is difficult to understand how any book can be completed without the comfort and support of family members. I am particularly fortunate in this respect to have a wife, Candice Cain Dunnigan, who will read rough drafts, a son, James, who is willing to search the thickets of Mackinac Island for lost boundary markers, and a daughter, Claire, who has been helping with proofreading since she was eight years old. All of them love Mackinac, and I hope they will be pleased with the results of the project they have had to endure for years.

BRIAN LEIGH DUNNIGAN
Easterly, Mackinac Island
August 2006

"The most advantageous post in Canada"

1615–1761

In August 1708 François Clairambault d'Aigremont found himself on the windswept shores of the Straits of Mackinac. He had not seen the place before, but he knew its history and was there on the orders of King Louis XIV to evaluate a situation that greatly vexed the administrators of New France. Michilimackinac had been officially abandoned for some time, its fort stripped of a garrison in 1697, its Huron and many of its Ottawa inhabitants lured to the new post of Detroit

in 1702, and the Jesuit mission complex of St. Ignace abandoned and burned three years later. This once-vibrant entrepôt of the fur trade and center of missionary zeal was a shell of its former self. From the beach of the sheltered bay facing the island of Michilimackinac the French naval commissary could see charred ruins, derelict cabins, fallow cornfields, and tumbled stockades.

Although Aigremont found Michilimackinac greatly declined from what it had been only a decade before, it took him less than four days to recognize its potential. He was convinced that the place was "the most important of all the advanced posts of Canada, both on account of its advantageous position . . . and from the trade that can be done there." The location had much to commend it. Michilimackinac was well situated as the natural resort of the Native American nations of Lake Superior, Lake Michigan, and Wisconsin. The quality of beaver pelts from this northern region far surpassed those trapped in the south and taken to Detroit. The waters of the Straits abounded in whitefish and trout, and the land, though not as fertile as Detroit's, could produce adequate crops of Indian corn. Most important, Michilimackinac was well placed to counter the efforts of English traders on Hudson Bay and, unlike Detroit, was far enough from the Iroquois and their English allies in New York to discourage Great Lakes Indians from deserting to the competition. Only the lack of a French commandant with a garrison of soldiers and official sanction for trade licenses, Aigremont believed, kept the place from regaining its former importance to New France.[1]

Aigremont's four days at Michilimackinac came roughly halfway through the 127 years that France dominated the Straits of Mackinac.

The first Frenchmen had passed through in 1634, and French colors would be seen on the waterway until 1761. During that time the Straits of Mackinac appeared on the map, Michilimackinac became a well-known place-name, and much of the character of the region was established in local culture and tradition. The French confirmed the fur trade as the basis of Mackinac's economy. Patterns of commerce would shift over the years, but this economic dependence would last until the 1830s. The seasonality of the trade in furs perpetuated a durable Mackinac practice, begun by pre-historic Native American inhabitants and adopted, in turn, by the French, British, and Americans. A harsh climate and the annual cycle of the fur trade caused Mackinac's population to swell during the summer months of trading, farming, and fishing and dwindle as snow and ice isolated the Straits and winter hunting beckoned. Tourism ultimately replaced the fur trade, but Mackinac is still a very seasonal place.

Although Native American groups had occupied the Straits for centuries by the time Europeans appeared, the French were the first to record human presence and activity through written records and cartography. Their maps and reports documented many of the native names for places, including "Michilimackinac" itself, and bestowed French appellations on many geographical features—Bois Blanc Island, St. Ignace, and Gros Cap are only a few that survive today. Many more are known by English translations of their French names—Round Island (Isle Ronde) and St. Helena Island (Isle St. Hélène), for example.

Well before the arrival of the French, for seven hundred years or more, the Mackinac region had been frequented by groups of Native

Americans, who established seasonal villages at many locations in the Straits. They were attracted primarily by the abundance of fish in the surrounding waters and, to a lesser extent, by maple trees, whose sap they boiled to make sugar each spring.[2] These peoples left no written records, so evidence of their pre-historic activities comes primarily from archaeology. Early European visitors wrote down and preserved some of their traditions and oral history. Father Claude Allouez passed through the Straits in November 1669 and was the first to leave a written description of the experience. The legend he recounted was particularly appropriate to the area. It was that of "Michabous . . . 'the Great Hare' Ouisaketchak . . . who is the one that created the Earth." According to Allouez's informants, "it was in these Islands that he invented nets for catching fish, after he had attentively considered the spider while she was working at her web in order to catch flies in it."[3]

Allouez was fishing for souls to convert to Christianity, but most of his countrymen had more temporal goals. Faced with an unknown continent, French explorers had begun moving up the St. Lawrence Valley within a few years of founding Québec in 1608. An early animosity with the Five Nations of the Iroquois diverted them from the most direct route up the Great Lakes through Lake Ontario. A more northerly and safer way by the Ottawa River and Lake Nipissing led Samuel de Champlain to the shores of Georgian Bay by 1615. Among his Native American contacts were the people who came to be known to the French as the Huron. Their prosperous agricultural villages occupied the rich lands of the peninsula of Ontario. The Huron were rivals of the Iroquois and willing partners with the French in a trade in furs. By 1634 their villages also hosted Jesuit missionaries.[4]

Farther to the west were other peoples and lands that were described to Champlain but rendered only vaguely on his maps. While it is possible that Frenchmen had penetrated farther into the upper Great Lakes before the mid-1630s, no accounts of their activities survive, and the first explorer to be credited with passing through the Straits of Mackinac was Jean Nicollet, in 1634. Nicollet had been charged with making "a journey to the nation called People of the sea," partly in the hope that he could find his way to the Pacific Ocean. He reputedly reached Green Bay that summer, where, attired in "a grand robe of China damask, all strewn with flowers and birds of many colors," he presented himself to the local Winnebagoes carrying a pair of pistols. Despite the fact that the Winnebago women and children fled at the sight of "a man who carried thunder in both hands," Nicollet was able to conclude a treaty of peace with these people and return to the Huron country. He had not, however, been able to confirm the belief that the western waters offered a route to China.[5]

This early and relatively promising entry into the upper country was soon cut short by events that would influence French activities in Canada and the Great Lakes for the rest of the century. In 1641 the Iroquois, who had fought the French and their allies on earlier occasions, commenced a long series of wars that would displace many of the Native American groups friendly to the French. Iroquois war parties devastated the Huron country in 1648–49 and started them, along with related peoples and an Algonquian group, the Ottawa, on an exodus that would eventually lead to the Straits of Mackinac.

Many of the refugee Huron united with survivors of the related Neutral or Tionontati nation and retreated up Georgian Bay to Manitoulin Island. By 1651 they had moved to the Straits of Mackinac, where they lived briefly before fear of the Iroquois forced them farther west to Green Bay by the following year. Their odyssey continued, leading them through Wisconsin to the Mississippi River and then finally north to Chequamegon Bay on Lake Superior by 1660.[6] There, Jesuit missionaries made contact with them once again in 1665, founding the mission of St. Esprit. In 1670–71 the Huron and Ottawa followed their missionaries back to the Straits of Mackinac. These people established villages around the new mission of St. Ignace.

Where the missionaries ventured, commercial and imperial interests soon followed, or in some cases preceded them. The Straits of Mackinac had presented an attractive spot for commerce as early as the 1650s, and the new concentration of villages provided further opportunities for trade to flourish.[7] By 1688 there was a small but active settlement of *coureurs de bois,* independent traders, who found the location very convenient for business. Louis-Armand de Lahontan observed that year that the position "'tis not inconsiderable, as being the Staple of all the Goods that they truck with the South and West Savages; for they cannot avoid passing this way" when going to the peoples of Green Bay, the Illinois country, and the Mississippi.[8] Canoes brought European manufactured goods to Michilimackinac each summer where they were bartered for furs, which were then taken to Montréal via the Ottawa River route for shipment to France.

Despite the confidence demonstrated by the return of the Huron and Ottawa to Michilimackinac, the wars with the Iroquois were far from over, and military considerations remained paramount. Iroquois forays into the West had been less than successful and had resulted in some humiliating defeats in the 1660s, but they remained a threat. There was also increasing concern that the English, who had taken the colony of New York from the Dutch, would encroach on the French monopoly. In 1683 a military commandant was appointed for Michilimackinac and the upper country. Although he had no permanent force, this officer could draw on the manpower provided each year by the traders and *coureurs de bois.* A more substantial fortification was constructed about 1690. Named Fort de Buade, it held a garrison of regular soldiers.[9]

War had erupted between France and Britain in 1689, and the conflict with the Iroquois was reaching its climax as well, thus explaining the rationale for constructing Fort de Buade. But the presence of soldiers and large numbers of traders was seen by some as having a negative effect. While the Jesuit missionaries railed against the licentiousness and vice encouraged by the involvement of officers and men in the fur and brandy trade, colonial officials had other concerns. By mid-decade a serious glut in pelts had developed and French officials decided to abandon the posts of the West and withdraw the soldiers and traders, who were seen as the source of the problem. The order was given in 1697 and Fort de Buade was left to rot.[10]

Michilimackinac's position as chief post in the upper country was eclipsed after 1701 by a cluster of fortified settlements of French and Native Americans located on the straits between Lake Huron and Lake Erie. Antoine Laumet, who presented himself with the title "Lamothe Cadillac," established Fort Pontchartrain du Détroit with royal permission over the objections of the governor and intendant of New France and the Jesuit missionaries of Michilimackinac. Indeed, his mandate was an exception to the decree that had withdrawn troops and forbidden fur traders from the upper Great Lakes. Cadillac had lost favor by 1708, however, and François Clairambault d'Aigremont had been dispatched to investigate the state of affairs at Detroit and the condition of trade at other locations on the upper lakes.[11] Aigremont had arrived at the Straits of Mackinac fresh from three weeks at Cadillac's post, where he had not been favorably impressed by what he had seen.

Of equal concern were problems that the establishment of Detroit and withdrawal from the upper lakes were supposed to have solved, but in fact had not. Rather than blocking Iroquois and English traders from the Great Lakes fur trade, the closer proximity of Detroit had only aggravated the situation. There were fears that tensions between Cadillac and the Hurons would cause the latter to settle with their old enemies, the Iroquois. And commerce at Michilimackinac had not, in fact, ceased. It had only been driven underground as illegal traders continued to barter with goods, including brandy, forwarded to them by Montréal merchants. Some of this contraband was even carried by the boatmen who transported supplies to the Jesuits, who returned each summer to continue missionary activity among the remaining Ottawa.[12]

Aigremont visited the Straits and made his recommendations during a time of war. A second European conflict with England had commenced in 1702, and it spilled over to the North American colonies. Fighting would continue until 1713, but at least, by the time of Aigremont's journey, the Iroquois were peaceful at last. They had signed a treaty with New France in 1701, the year Cadillac established Detroit. Unfortunately, the abandonment of Michilimackinac had caused French influence to wane among the peoples of the northern lakes. As Aigremont repeatedly warned, a new commandant would have to be appointed and a garrison dispatched to the Straits if French prestige were to be reestablished.[13]

It was some time before his recommendation could be implemented. A number of factors contributed to the delay, including the conclusion of the second war with England in 1713 and a new and very disturbing development at the troublesome post of Detroit. In 1711 Cadillac invited the Foxes or Mesquakies to relocate to his settlement and join the communities of Ottawa, Huron, and Ojibwa. It proved to be a volatile mix, and large-scale violence erupted in the spring of 1712. Although the French and their Native American allies dealt them a grievous blow, the Foxes were not subdued. Instead, they retreated to their homeland in Wisconsin where they would remain a threat for the next twenty years.[14] The long conflict with the Foxes provided a compelling reason to reoccupy Michilimackinac,

The devastating Iroquois offensive of 1648–49 drove many of the Huron and neighboring native peoples on a westward migration that eventually took them to the Straits of Mackinac. The Jesuits abandoned their missions in Huronia, where several priests, including Jean de Brébeuf and Gabriel Lalemant, were tortured to death, as graphically depicted in this 1664 engraving from Du Creux, *Historiae Canadensis*. Missionaries would not reestablish contact with the western Huron until the mid-1660s. *Clements Library, University of Michigan.*

strategically located as it was on the route from Canada to the Fox lands in Wisconsin. The post was well placed to serve as a gathering spot and depot for French forces and native allies. In 1715, while an ultimately abortive expedition against the Foxes was being organized at the Straits of Mackinac, the soldiers appear to have been occupied in erecting a stockade and several buildings on the south shore. Thereafter, until 1781, this would be the site of the fortified village of Michilimackinac.

The new post served much the same purpose as its predecessor on the north shore of the Straits, with a garrison and a commandant to represent royal authority. The Jesuits reestablished themselves at the new location, as did the Ottawa who had not moved to Detroit. The French and Native American populations swelled each summer as licensed merchants and their voyageurs arrived from Canada and Indian trading partners came to exchange furs for goods.[15]

The fortified village remained small in size and unsophisticated in defense until the 1730s, when a major expansion took place. The increase in the area of the fort seems to have been accompanied by growth of its French population, although many of the new houses were occupied only seasonally. It was at this time that the familiar street plan and row house arrangement came into being, a layout that would remain little changed until the site was abandoned during the American Revolution.[16] Unfortunately, no map documents Michilimackinac before 1749, so its early appearance is poorly understood.

The post underwent further important changes in the 1740s. In 1742, responding to the exhaustion of their croplands near the French fort, the Ottawa removed their village and fields to a place called L'Arbre Croche some thirty miles to the southwest on the shores of Lake Michigan. Their Jesuit missionary followed, taking with him the name St. Ignace by which the mission at the Straits had been known since 1670–71. Within a year, the French community and the voyageurs who visited each summer had constructed a new church within the walls of the settlement. It was probably at that point that their parish came to be named for St. Anne, a patron popular with sailors and boatmen.[17] The Jesuit missionary thereafter served both congregations.

Two years later, in 1744, France was once again at war with England. Although Michilimackinac was far from the fighting that wracked Nova Scotia and New England, its garrison contributed to the war effort by recruiting local Ottawa and Ojibwa warriors. Unfortunately, the conflict created a shortage of merchandise that stunted the fur trade at Michilimackinac—only five licenses were issued in 1746.[18] The situation was aggravated by the infiltration of English traders into the Ohio country and the growth of their influence over the southern nations. This sparked uprisings at several western posts in 1747. Both Detroit and Michilimackinac were attacked, resulting in loss of life and destruction of farms and livestock. Several Frenchmen were murdered in the Michilimackinac region, and the post's horses and cattle were driven off or killed.

A plot to surprise the garrison was even discovered and foiled. Warriors entered the fort with hostile intentions and were only "obliged to leave, by ringing the [church?] bell and beating the tap-too . . . and even making some defensive demonstrations."[19] Sometime after 1744 the defenses of Michilimackinac were strengthened, most likely in response to the events of 1747.

Although peace returned in 1748, it provided only a brief interlude. The fur trade recovered, but the Ohio country remained a tinderbox where a continuous escalation of tensions belied efforts in Europe to clarify the indistinct boundaries between the French and British colonies. In 1749 Captain Pierre-Joseph Céloron de Blainville, a former commandant of Michilimackinac, led an expedition down the Ohio River to mark it as French territory. In 1752 a resident of Michilimackinac, Charles Mouet de Langlade, led a war party from the Straits to destroy the Miami Indian village of Pickawillany in western Ohio and expel the English traders there. A year later, a large force of French troops and Canadian militia began to establish a chain of military posts on the portage from Lake Erie to the Ohio River to obstruct English traders and provide a permanent presence in the region. Real fighting exploded in 1754 near the junction of the Allegheny and Monongahela rivers. Although France and Britain would not declare themselves at war until 1756, the shooting had begun.[20]

Michilimackinac seems to have changed little during the brief hiatus of peace. When Ensign Michel Chartier de Lotbinière surveyed the post in 1749, he found only ten permanently established families there. A few years later, sometime around 1755, an unidentified observer recorded twelve to fifteen.[21] Michilimackinac was not the sort of place to grow as an agricultural colony, and the only livelihoods for a French population were the fur trade and fishing. While settlement at Detroit was encouraged and even subsidized in the years between 1749 and 1755, Michilimackinac was seen as unsuitable for much population growth. "It would be very desirable that habitants should be Settled at Michilimakinac . . . and increase the population of the country," the governor and intendant wrote in 1749, but "the poor quality of the soil does not permit of it."[22] Michilimackinac would remain a place for trade for many years to come.

Any hope that Canadians from the St. Lawrence Valley might be enticed to settle at Michilimackinac was soon dashed by the escalating conflict in the West. In 1754, with fighting underway, Captain Michel-Jean-Hugues Péan was dispatched with four hundred men to visit the western posts to consolidate the support of Native American allies. The first real indication of war reached Michilimackinac on August 10 with the arrival of Péan's canoes from Detroit. The expedition found Michilimackinac's stockade mounted with six small cannon and guarded by a garrison of thirty soldiers.[23]

Michilimackinac's flimsy walls and tiny garrison would be of little direct utility in the coming fight, other than to protect the fur traders who gathered there. The leaders of New France were more interested in its influence on the fur trade and the friendship of the Indian nations of the upper lakes. Nearby Ottawa and Ojibwa warriors, as well as peoples as far away as Wisconsin and Lake Superior, were within the orbit of Michilimackinac. During the twelve days Péan's troops camped outside the fort he held three different councils with representatives of sixteen nations, among them Foxes, Outagamies, and Winnebagoes from Wisconsin and even Dakota from the Mississippi River.

Péan made his message clear in the first council, held under the cannon of the fort. "I was sent to you by your Father Ononthio," he said, referring to the governor of New France. The captain had come to solicit their feelings "about pledging yourself to raise the hatchet, and to go with your French brothers to fight the English." In response, all the chiefs stated that "they were, and always would be, ready to march at the order of their Father Ononthio." Presents were distributed, and Péan's small army left for Georgian Bay and Montréal on September 1.[24]

For the duration of the war Michilimackinac would provide warriors to support French and Canadian forces fighting in the Ohio Valley and along Lake Champlain. Ensign Langlade, who had destroyed Pickawillany in 1752, often led them. He fought against General Edward Braddock near Fort Duquesne in 1755 and, two years later, was with the French general Montcalm helping lead over three hundred Ottawa and related peoples from Detroit, Saginaw Bay, and Michilimackinac against Fort William Henry. The western warriors carried smallpox back to their villages that winter, but, despite the deadly sickness and waning French successes, Langlade was able to again encourage contingents from Michilimackinac to go with him to Québec in 1759 and to Montréal in 1760.[25]

At the conclusion of his last expedition of the war Michilimackinac's best-known partisan officer brought home news of the collapse of French arms in North America. Langlade returned to find his commandant, Captain Louis Liénard de Beaujeu, disinclined to accept the capitulation of New France to the English. Sometime in October Beaujeu departed with most of the garrison on a difficult winter march to the Illinois country, leaving Langlade to await the conquerors. Like the rest of New France, Michilimackinac would have a new flag and new masters.

FRENCH COMMANDANTS OF MICHILIMACKINAC, 1683–1761

Captain Daniel Greysolon Dulhut, Troupes de la Marine, 1683

Captain Olivier Morel de La Durantaye, Troupes de la Marine, 1683–90

Lieutenant Louis La Porte de Louvigny, Troupes de la Marine, 1690–94

Captain Antoine Laumet dit de Lamothe Cadillac, Troupes de la Marine, 1694–97

No regular military garrison, 1697–1715

Captain Constant Le Marchand de Lignery, Troupes de la Marine, 1715–19

Captain Louis Liénard de Beaujeu, Troupes de la Marine, 1719–22

Captain Constant Le Marchand de Lignery, Troupes de la Marine, 1722–29

Captain Jacques-Charles Renaud Dubuisson, Troupes de la Marine, 1729–30

Captain Jacques Testard de Montigny, Troupes de la Marine, 1730–33

Captain Jean-Baptiste-René Legardeur de Repentigny, Troupes de la Marine, 1733–34

Captain Pierre-Joseph Céloron de Blainville, Troupes de la Marine, 1734–42

Captain Jean-Baptiste Jarret de Verchères, Troupes de la Marine, 1742–45

Captain Louis de La Corne, Troupes de la Marine, 1745–47

Ensign Charles-Joseph de Noyelles, Troupes de la Marine (acting) 1746–47

Captain Jacques Legardeur de St. Pierre, Troupes de la Marine, 1747–49

Captain François Lefebvre Duplessis Faber, Troupes de la Marine, 1749–52

Lieutenant Louis Liénard de Beaujeu, Troupes de la Marine, 1752–54

Captain Louis Herbin, Troupes de la Marine, 1754–57

Captain Louis Liénard de Beaujeu de Villemonde, Troupes de la Marine, 1757–60

Ensign Charles Mouet de Langlade, Troupes de la Marine (acting), 1760–61

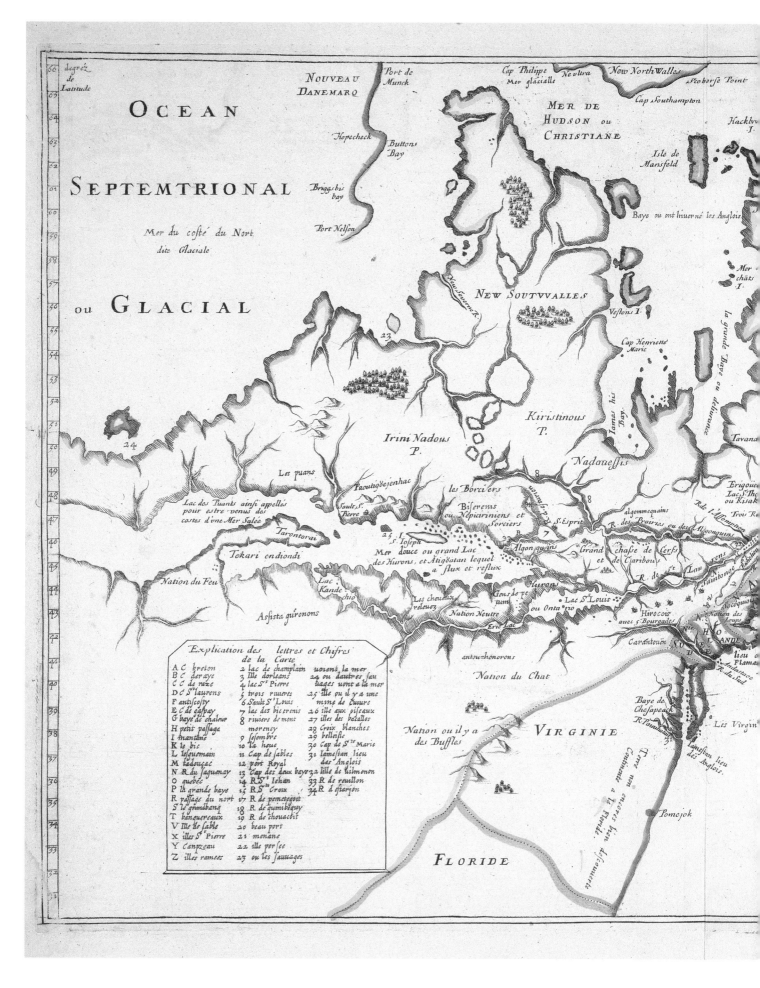

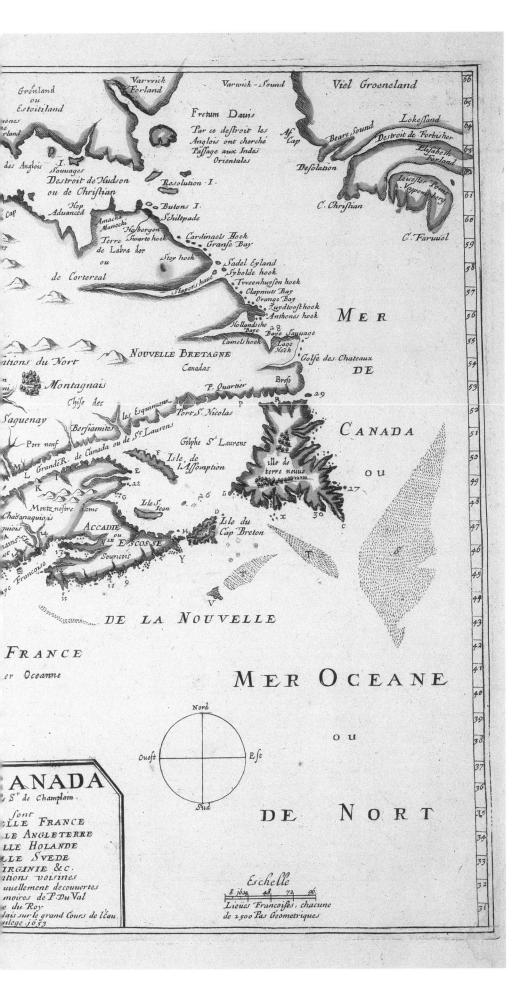

FIGURE 1.1

TITLE: Le Canada faict par le Sr de Champlain, ou sont La Nouvelle France La Nouvelle Angleterre La Nouvelle Holande La Nouvelle Svede La Virginie &c. Avec les Nations voisines et autres Terres nouuellement decouuertes Suiuant les Memoires de P. Du Val Geographe du Roy A Paris. En l'Isle du Palais sur le grand Cours de l'Eau. Avec Privilege. 1653.

AUTHOR: Pierre Duval (1618–83) after Samuel de Champlain (1567–1635).

DATE DEPICTED: 1615.

DATE OF WORK: 1653.

DESCRIPTION: 35.5 x 55 cm. Colored, copperplate engraving.

PROVENANCE: Published by Duval as the first production state of his alteration of the plate originally engraved for Champlain in 1616. Gift to the Clements Library in 2001 by Mr. and Mrs. William G. Earle.

COLLECTION: Clements Library, University of Michigan, Ann Arbor (Map Division, 4-A-12).

There are no beavers in France, and the French come to get them here

Native American storyteller

Father Claude Allouez had labored four years in the missions of Lake Superior and Sault Ste. Marie by the time he passed through the Straits of Mackinac in November 1669. The Jesuit had occupied himself during the long winters in working to convert the Huron and Ottawa who had found a refuge from the Iroquois along the shores of that great lake. But he had also listened at the winter lodge fires to, as he put it, the "legends with which the Savages very often entertain us."

Allouez was on his way to Wisconsin, escorted by two canoes of Potawatomis who had approached him for assistance, not in learning about the religion of the Jesuits but in curbing "some young Frenchmen, who, being among them for the purpose of trading, were threatening and maltreating them." French traders were already established on the western edge of the Great Lakes seeking beaver pelts and offering European goods in exchange. The Indians had given Allouez their understanding of why young Frenchmen traveled so far into the wilderness. Lake Superior had once been a great beaver pond, they said, until their god, Michabous, stomped down the dams that held back the water at Sault Ste. Marie. The beavers fled northward to escape such a mighty hunter. When they arrived at the salty "North Sea," hoping to cross over to France, they found the water too bitter and lost heart. Instead, they scattered across the continent of America. "That is the reason why there are no beavers in France," the Indians told Allouez, "and the French come to get them here."[26]

The trade in furs had indeed been a powerful motivation for French explorers to rapidly penetrate the Great Lakes. By the time of Allouez's journey to Wisconsin, the geography of the region was well-known to the French, only fifty-four years after Samuel de Champlain had made his way to the shores of Georgian Bay. The lakes, rivers, and peoples of the region had appeared on several maps during that time, each reflecting a greater understanding of the country than the last. This gradual unfolding of the water system had, by the 1650s, defined the strait at the place called Michilimackinac.

Samuel de Champlain was the first to put the Great Lakes on the map. From the time of his earliest voyage to Canada in 1603 until his first large map was published in 1612, Champlain explored in the Maritimes and up the St. Lawrence River as far as the later site of Montréal. Although only Lake Ontario is defined on his 1612 map, including an indication of a mighty waterfall at its western end, the cartographer suggested that further large bodies of water lay beyond.[27] Three years later, Champlain undertook a voyage to the country of the Huron and reached the shores of Georgian Bay.

The explorer mapped as he went, and by the time Champlain returned to Québec in the summer of 1616 he had combined his own observations with information obtained from Native American informants. This allowed him to provide a confident impression of Georgian Bay, which he called "Mer douce" or "sweet-water sea." His map also gave a sense of the connection between the upper waters and Lake Ontario and even a tiny representation of what might be interpreted as Lake Erie. Champlain left the most westerly body of water unfinished, presumably in the hope that a navigable passage could be found across the continent.

The identity of this lake, unnamed on Champlain's original map but labeled "Lac des Puants" on the later version of it reproduced here as Figure 1.1, remains open to speculation. Champlain did not see it himself. Is it Lake Superior, as has often been suggested, or is it Lake Michigan? One clue lies on the north shore of this mysterious body of water, where Champlain identified a people he called "Les puans." The French usually applied this name to the Wisconsin group known today as the Winnebago, who lived near Green Bay. If a large river to the east of "Les puans" is interpreted as the St. Marys draining an unseen Lake Superior, then the body of water below could be Lake Michigan. If so, then a strait is suggested connecting it to Georgian Bay and Lake Huron. The question, however, is probably irresolvable.

Champlain returned to France for the winter of 1616–17, and there he apparently entrusted his map of Canada to an engraver to prepare it for publication. A number of factors conspired to keep the map from appearing, however, and Champlain himself was apparently too occupied to see it to completion. By the early 1650s the unfinished copper plate was in the hands of Pierre Duval, a Paris mapmaker, who apparently printed a single proof copy before altering it.[28] Duval then greatly enhanced the old plate without significantly altering its geography. He added the names of additional Native American groups and further notations, including one in the mysterious, incomplete western lake identifying it as "Lac des Puants" after the people shown living on its northern shore. The resulting map (Fig. 1.1) was first published in 1653.[29]

Champlain's days of active exploration were finished by the 1620s. He nonetheless continued to compile information on the country. Exiled to France after the English captured Québec in 1629, he summarized the results of his years in Canada in *Les voyages de la Nouvelle France occidentale, dicte Canada. . . .* (Paris, 1632). The book contained his great map of Canada (Fig. 1.2) with further clarifications of the West as Champlain understood it by 1629. Unfortunately, the area beyond Georgian Bay remains subject to interpretation. The usual reading is that the body of water labeled "Grand lac" represents Lake Superior with the unnamed, smaller lake above

Beavers, hard at work on their dam, as represented in François Du Creux, *Historiae Canadensis* (Paris, 1664). The fur trade would provide the foundation of Mackinac's economy until the mid-1830s. *Clements Library, University of Michigan.*

FIGURE 1.3

TITLE: Le Canada, ou Nouvelle France, &c. Ce qui est le plus advancé vers le Septentrion est tiré de diverses Relations des Anglois, Danois, &c. Vers le Midy les Costes de Virginie, Nouvlle Suede, Nouveau Pays Bas, et Nouvelle Angleterre Sont tirées de celles des Anglois, Hollandois, &c. La Grande Riviere de Canada ou de St. Laurens, et tous les environs sont suivant les Relations des Francois Par N. Sanson d'Abbeville, Geograph ordinaire du Roy. A Paris . . . 1656. [Detail].
AUTHOR: Nicolas d'Abbeville Sanson (1600–1667).
DATE DEPICTED: 1640s.
DATE OF WORK: 1656.
DESCRIPTION: 40 x 54.5 cm. (entire map). Colored copperplate engraving.
PROVENANCE: In Sanson's atlas titled *Cartes générales de toutes les parties du monde* (Paris, 1658), plate 86.
COLLECTION: Clements Library, University of Michigan, Ann Arbor (Map Division, Atlas, W-1-D).

and to the right explained as a misplaced Lake Michigan with "La Nation des Puans" thus properly located in the vicinity of Green Bay.[30]

The key to Champlain's 1632 map identifies "33" as "River of the Puans, issuing from a lake where occurs a mine of pure copper." Number "34," below and to the left, is described in Champlain's text as "Gaston Rapids, nearly two leagues in length, emptying into the Freshwater Sea and flowing from another extremely large lake, which together with the Freshwater Sea makes a 30 days' canoe journey, according to reports of the Indians." The editor of this 1936 translation understandably associated the Gaston Rapids with those at Sault Ste. Marie, and thus the "Grand lac" that they drain must be Superior.[31]

But is there a more logical interpretation? Given the fact that Champlain never visited the region and relied on "reports of the Indians," alternative possibilities suggest themselves. A lake with a copper mine is much more likely to be Superior, and its outlet at "33" is then properly placed to be the St. Marys River. Perhaps it is the villages of the Puans and the rapids that have been misplaced, and the "Grand lac" is actually (and more reasonably) Lake Michigan with a roughly formed Lower Peninsula below and to the right. The "Gaston Rapids" might then be interpreted as the Straits of Mackinac. Its length of "nearly two leagues" (about six miles) is appropriate to that waterway.[32]

By 1650 the French cartographer Nicolas Sanson had clearly differentiated Lake Superior in the north from the more southerly "L. de Puans," which would come to be known as Lac des Illinois and then, finally, Lake Michigan.[33] Figure 1.3 is a detail from Sanson's 1656 *Le Canada*, which shows an even less ambiguous configuration for the four lakes above Niagara Falls. For the first time, Lake Erie, the Detroit and St. Clair rivers, Lake St. Clair, Saginaw Bay, and the peninsulas of Michigan are rendered as recognizable entities. Manitoulin Island appears. There is also some indication of the islands west of Manitoulin and in the mouth of the St. Marys River. And, as in Sanson's 1650 map, a strait is clearly shown connecting Lake Huron with Lake Michigan. Sanson's newer information was in part attributable to the activities of Jesuit missionaries, who had worked in the country of the Huron and neighboring Neutrals since the 1630s.[34] Jean Nicollet's voyage of 1634 might also have had an impact in defining these waters, although both of the western lakes remain incomplete, perhaps in the continuing hope that the Pacific Ocean and China lay just beyond.

The steady improvement in the cartography of the Great Lakes was dealt a setback in the 1640s as the Iroquois struck out against their neighbors and French allies. Their destruction of the Huron in 1648–49 displaced the survivors and ended missionary activity in the West for the next sixteen years. By 1670, however, conditions were right for a permanent settlement at the Straits of Mackinac as the Huron and Ottawa contemplated a return eastward from their mission villages on Lake Superior. A new mission was established at Sault Ste. Marie in 1669, where Fathers Claude Dablon and Jacques Marquette were stationed in the spring of 1670.

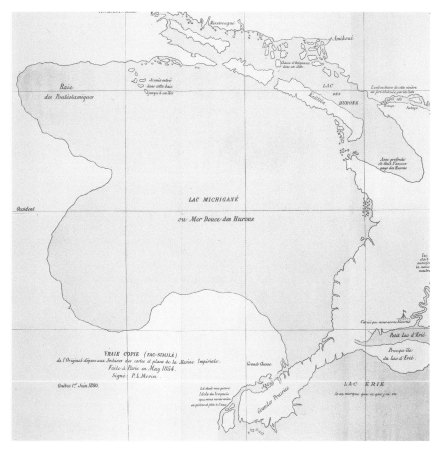

FIGURE 1.4

TITLE: Carte du Lac Ontario et des habitations qui l'environnent Ensemble le pays que M. M. Dollier et Galiné, missionaires du Seminaire St. Sulpice ont parcouru. 1670. [Detail].

AUTHOR: After an 1854 tracing by P. L. Morin of the original map by René Bréhant de Galinée (ca. 1645–78). [Detail].

DATE DEPICTED: 1670.

DATE OF WORK: 1895 from an 1854 tracing of the original.

DESCRIPTION: 36 x 67.5 cm. (entire map). Colored lithograph.

PROVENANCE: The original manuscript map was deposited in the Dépôt des cartes et plans de la Marine et des Colonies. P. L. Morin made a tracing in 1854 from the original map, which had been lost by 1870. A further notation on the 1895 print is dated "Québec 1er Juin 1880," probably indicating another copying at that time. A copy of the tracing was used as the basis for this reduced version published in Gabriel Gravier, *Carte des Grandes Lacs de l'Amérique du Nord dressée en 1670 par Bréhab de Gallinée Missionaire Sulpicien* (Rouen, 1895). Other tracings were also made before 1870.

COLLECTION: Clements Library, University of Michigan, Ann Arbor (Book Division, Map Div. Gr).

On May 25, the feast of Pentecost, the two Jesuits heard the salutes of muskets from the St. Marys River, heralding the arrival of a Sulpician priest, François Dollier de Casson, and his deacon, René Bréhant de Galinée. The pair was on a remarkable voyage that had begun the previous year. Taking advantage of an interlude of peace between the French and the Iroquois, they had left Montréal intent on proselytizing among the Potawatomi of Wisconsin. Rather than follow the Ottawa River route, they had crossed Lake Ontario and wintered on the north shore of Lake Erie. There, an accident caused the loss of their altar service, so the pair decided to return to Canada by way of Georgian Bay. Passing up the Detroit and St. Clair rivers, they were the first to describe those waters in detail before heading north along Lake Huron.

The Jesuit fathers warmly received Dollier and Galinée, who were impressed by the new mission buildings but "saw no particular sign of Christianity amongst the Indians." The pair was soon able to set out for Montréal with the annual flotilla of Indian canoes taking furs to trade.[35] Following their arrival, on June 18, Galinée was encouraged to produce a map of their route, which was later sent to France. It survived into the middle of the nineteenth century, when at least four copies or tracings were made from the manuscript before the original had disappeared by 1870.[36] Figure 1.4 is a detail from Galinée's map as reproduced in 1895.

Galinée's map is of interest for what it reveals of the routes leading to the Straits of Mackinac. His was the first to chart the passage from Lake Erie to Lake Huron in detail. This would thereafter be the southern route to Michilimackinac. The older and more traveled way across Georgian Bay is also well rendered, but the map shows some remaining confusion in the names it gives to different parts of Lake Huron. Here Georgian Bay is "Lac des Hurons," while the waters south of Manitoulin Island are called "Lac Michigané" and then alternately given Champlain's old name for Georgian Bay ("Mer Douce des Hurons"). The open lake was described by Galinée as being "as large as the Caspian Sea," and the entrance to his "Lake of the Hurons" (Georgian Bay) was distinguished by "four mouths"— the passages between the major islands.

Because the cartographer was scrupulous in drawing only what he had actually seen, the map's treatment of the Straits of Mackinac is disappointing. A single notation suggests that Galinée might have caught sight of the islands in the straits, and Les Cheneaux are indicated. Otherwise, the connection between Lake Huron and Lake Michigan ends abruptly as a stub labeled "Baie des Poutéotamiques," a reference to Green Bay and the route through the Straits of Mackinac that Allouez had traversed the previous autumn on his way to visit the Potawatomi there. The cartographic scene was set, however, and the Straits of Mackinac would soon appear on the map in detail.

We erected a chapel there

Father Claude Dablon, S. J.

Around noon on November 4, 1669, Father Claude Allouez and his companions turned their canoes westward from the Detour Passage and entered the waters of Lake Huron, bound for Green Bay on the far shore of Lake Michigan. It was not an easy trip during that season, and Allouez was a working passenger. By evening the wind was against them, and they were forced to camp for the night. The men awoke covered with snow, and they had great difficulty loading the canoes and getting them underway, which they did with their bare feet in the water. Over the coming days the priest and his companions had many occasions to have "recourse to Saint Anne, to whom we entrusted our journey, praying to her, together with Saint Francis Xavier, to take us under her protection."[37]

Despite his discomfort, Allouez was alert to his surroundings, noting landmarks as they appeared. The canoes passed "a great number of Islands to the Northward," and landed the evening of November 5 on "a little Island" (probably Little St. Martin), where bad weather and making ice delayed them for six days. It was November 11 before they could cross to another island (probably St. Martin) and then to the mainland. Allouez took note of the cape at the entrance of Lake Michigan and the "large Island" of Michilimackinac behind and to the east. All of these features would soon appear on the first map to show the Straits of Mackinac in recognizable detail (Fig. 1.5).[38]

The Straits occupied only a small part of the remarkable map (Fig. 1.5) published in Paris in 1672 and tipped into the Jesuit *Relation* of 1670–71.[39] Lake Superior was its focus, but the northern portions of Lakes Huron and Michigan were included to show the new missions established by the Jesuits in the country of the "Outouacs." Prominently labeled on the map was the "Mission de St. Ignace" and, for the first time, the "I. Missilimakinac." In his preface to the *Relation,* Father Claude Dablon reported that the map had been drawn by "two Fathers of considerable intelligence, much given to research, and very exact, who determined to set down nothing that they had not seen with their own eyes." This accounts for the abbreviated coverage of the two lower lakes, although Dablon claimed that the priests had also journeyed over both of them. Their waters, he wrote, appeared more "like two seas, so large are they."[40] The unnamed cartographers are generally accepted to have been Father Allouez and Dablon himself.[41]

The "Jesuit Map" of Lake Superior is astonishingly accurate in its rendering of the largest of the Great Lakes and its connecting waterways. It is particularly so in comparison to the published maps that had preceded it as recently as the mid-1650s (see Fig. 1.3). Allouez had probably gathered much of the necessary geographical information by the time Dablon joined him at the western missions in 1669. The two subsequently circumnavigated the lake and made

In 1672 the Ottawa joined the Huron at the St. Ignace mission. These people would thereafter form an important part of the Straits of Mackinac community. Father Louis Nicolas sketched an imposing and heavily tattooed Ottawa warrior around 1675. His drawing was reproduced in *Les raretés des Indes,* "*Codex canadiensis,*" in 1930. *Clements Library, University of Michigan.*

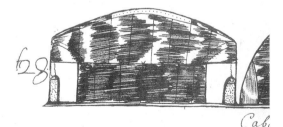

The Huron village at Michilimackinac was made up of bark-covered longhouses, each sheltering several family units. Father Louis Nicolas's circa 1675 rendering of a Huron longhouse shortens the structure. Some measured up to 130 feet in length. *Les raretés des Indes,* "*Codex canadiensis.*" *Clements Library, University of Michigan.*

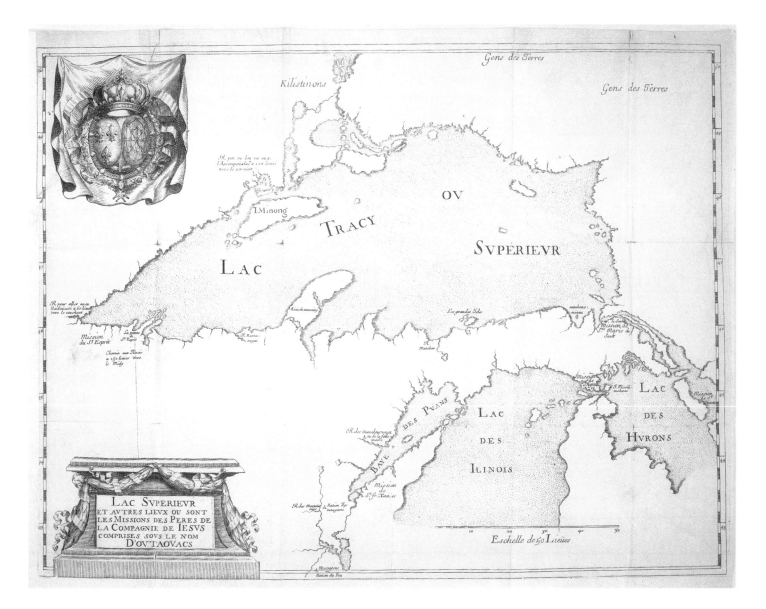

FIGURE 1.5

TITLE: Lac Svperievr et avtres lievx ou sont les Missions des Peres de la Compagnie de Iesus comprises sovs le nom d'Ovtaovacs.

AUTHORS: [Father Claude Allouez, S. J. (1622–89) and Father Claude Dablon, S. J. (1619–97)].

DATE DEPICTED: 1671.

DATE OF WORK: 1672.

DESCRIPTION: 35.7 x 48 cm. Copperplate engraving.

PROVENANCE: Published in *Relation de ce qui c'est passé de plus remarquable aux Missions de Peres de la Compagnie de Jesus en la Nouvelle France, les années 1670 & 1671* (Paris, 1672). The example illustrated here was acquired separately from the Clements Library's copy of the book.

COLLECTION: Clements Library, University of Michigan, Ann Arbor (Map Division, 6-L-5).

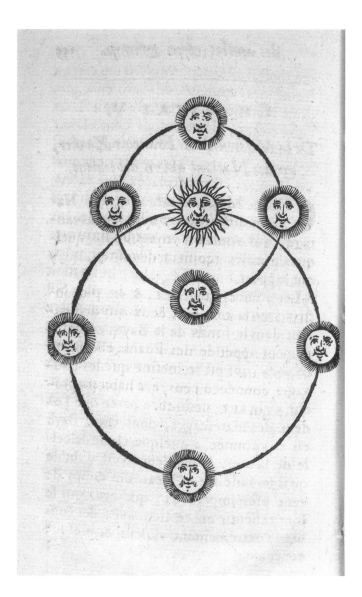

FIGURE 1.6

TITLE: [Figure of a parhelion observed at Sault Ste. Marie].
AUTHOR: Unknown.
DATE DEPICTED: March 16, 1671.
DATE OF WORK: 1672.
DESCRIPTION: 10.7 x 8.2 cm. Woodblock print.
PROVENANCE: Published in *Relation de ce qui c'est passé de plus remarquable aux Missions de Peres de la Compagnie de Jesus en la Nouvelle France, les années 1670 & 1671* (Paris, 1672), opp. 155.
COLLECTION: Clements Library, University of Michigan, Ann Arbor (Book Division, C-RJ-1672-Da).

further observations. It seems likely that Allouez's difficult journey to Green Bay later that year provided details on the route through the Straits of Mackinac and across northern Lake Michigan.

Father Allouez's perspective during his passage probably accounts for the generally accurate but distorted rendering of the main features of the Straits. The north coast is reasonably well treated, with Les Cheneaux Islands, the St. Martin islands and bay, and even the rivers flowing into it shown with some accuracy. The size of "I. Missilimakinac" is far out of proportion, however, especially when compared to the tiny renderings of Round Island and the much larger Bois Blanc. St. Helena Island at the western end of the Straits is also much exaggerated in size. Notably, all six of the major islands in the Straits of Mackinac appear for the first time on this map.

As Allouez's canoe turned into Lake Michigan, Round Island and the low profile of Bois Blanc were some distance to the east, and his poor view of them must account for their insignificance on the "Jesuit Map."[42] The imposing bulk of Mackinac Island was much nearer, and St. Helena would also have seemed large when Allouez passed between it and the Upper Peninsula mainland. Father Dablon later noted, in his *Relation* of 1670–71, that Mackinac Island had "such high, steep rocks in some places that it can be seen at a distance of more than twelve leagues." The priests might also have wished to emphasize its importance. The island's situation "exactly in the strait connecting the Lake of the Hurons and that of the Illinois," Dablon wrote, formed "the key and the door" to missionary activity.[43]

The priests must have sent their map to France sometime in 1671. By that time the Jesuits could boast of five establishments among the Ottawa and Huron of Lakes Superior and Huron and the Winnebago, Potawatomi, and other peoples living along Green Bay and the Fox River. The first mission was St. Esprit at Chequamegon Bay near the western extremity of Lake Superior. Ste. Marie du Sault stood below the rapids draining the waters of Lake Superior through the St. Marys River. On the north shore of Manitoulin Island was the mission of St. Simon. An establishment dedicated to St. François Xavier can be found near the bottom of Green Bay. Finally, situated on the north shore of the Straits of Mackinac, is the "Mission de St. Ignace," honoring Ignatius Loyola, the founder of the Jesuit religious order. In his text, Father Dablon noted that, by looking at the map, "one will gain more light upon all these Missions than by long descriptions that might be given of them."[44]

Dablon had begun the new mission at the Straits of Mackinac sometime toward the end of 1670. His 1670–71 *Relation* notes that this had occurred "during the past Winter, which we spent there."[45] Accounts describing the exact location of the mission are ambiguous, although at one point Dablon specifically referred to "that famous Island of Missilimakinac, where we last winter began the Mission of saint Ignace."[46] He had been told that at an earlier time the Hurons "had lived for some years on the Island itself, taking refuge from the Iroquois," so security might have been a factor in his decision to establish the mission there. A more obvious advantage was the abundance of fish in the Straits and a belief that the island's soil was suitable for raising corn.[47]

The Jesuits found Michilimackinac convenient as well for the access it provided to Native American nations living to the south along Lakes Huron and Michigan. Its location on the primary water route made it possible, Dablon reported, to "instruct these poor people when they pass." As the priest wintered on Mackinac Island he continued to plan for a permanent establishment. He was particularly aware that "the future course of this Mission depends on the resolution adopted by the Savages to return thither."[48]

One advantage of Michilimackinac was the shortness of its winter, at least by the standards of Lake Superior and Québec. Father Dablon claimed that the season did not begin until after Christmas, and spring arrived about the middle of March. An atmospheric event during the winter of 1671 must have been considered a positive omen of the future success of his mission. On January 21 a parhelion, an optical, atmospheric illusion in which multiple suns are perceived, was observed at the mission at Green Bay. Then, on March 16, similar phenomena occurred simultaneously within sight of the missions of St. Marie, St. Simon, and St. Ignace on Mackinac Island. Three suns appeared several times during the day at Michilimackinac, and the illusion took varied forms at the other locations. Indians living near the missions suggested to their priests that the multiple disks represented the sun's wives. At least one of the Jesuits, probably Dablon, seized on the opportunity presented by the appearance of the parhelion. He observed to the Indians that "the maker of all things wished to instruct them concerning the Mystery of the Holy Trinity and to disabuse them by means of the very Sun that they worshipped." The phenomena were unique enough that an unidentified artist made a rendering of the parhelion as it appeared at Sault Ste. Marie, where at one point eight suns were visible. This "Spectacle highly pleasing to behold" was later engraved and included as an illustration in the *Relation* of 1670–71 (Fig. 1.6).[49]

By the spring of 1671, more tangible events were encouraging growth of the mission of St. Ignace, for the Ottawa and Huron were relocating there en masse. Their mission and villages at Chequamegon Bay were located uncomfortably close to a people known to the French as the Nadouessi—the Sioux or Dakota—whose warlike traits were thought comparable to those of the Iroquois. The residents of St. Esprit had maintained an uneasy peace with them, but by the spring of 1671 there was fear of war. The Hurons decided to withdraw to the island of Michilimackinac, while many of the Ottawa went to live near the mission of St. Simon on Manitoulin Island. Dablon made much of the relocation and noted that "in transmigrations of this sort, people's minds are in no settled condition." Father Jacques Marquette, who had found himself assigned to St. Esprit, followed his flock eastward and relieved Dablon at Michilimackinac.[50]

It was apparently at about this time that the disadvantages of the island location became apparent, and it was probably Marquette who moved the mission to the nearby bay (East Moran) on the Upper Peninsula mainland. A chapel was erected there to minister to passersby and to serve the Hurons who had already settled at the Straits.[51] By the time Dablon and Allouez's map was completed and sent to France, the transfer was complete, and the mission of St. Ignace would eventually give its name to a town at the same location.

French missionaries are shown baptizing and preaching to Native Americans on the title cartouche of Guillaume de L'Isle's *Carte du Canada* of 1703. *Clements Library, University of Michigan (Map Division, 4-B-2).*

15

Missilimakinak, where there are two villages of savages

Henri de Tonty

The westerly wind had howled through the rigging for nearly twenty-four hours before the crew of the *Griffon* began to lose hope. Their voyage on Lake Huron had been uneventful until the vessel passed Thunder Bay. Then, as she doubled "a great headland jutting out into the lake" on the evening of August 25, 1679, the wind struck with full force. At first it was possible to tack under reduced sail, but by the next morning the crew had to lower the topmasts and yards in hopes of riding out the gale. The tiny vessel drifted at the mercy of the wind on the open lake, for no one aboard knew any place of shelter. The captain, René-Robert Cavelier de La Salle, feared that his commercial aspirations were undone.

It was at this time, according to Father Louis Hennepin, that "every Body fell upon his Knees to say his Prayers, and prepare himself for Death." Everyone that is, except the pilot, who had a reputation for refusing to pray. He stood defiantly on the deck where all he did was "curse and swear against M LaSalle, who, as he said, had brought him thither to make him perish in a nasty Lake, and lose the Glory he had acquired by his long and happy Navigations on the Ocean." Not long after, to everyone's surprise, the winds began to decrease, the sails were hoisted, and progress was resumed. By the morning of August 27 the *Griffon* was once again sailing easily, pushed by a gentle southeast wind. Later that day she glided into the sheltered bay at Michilimackinac and dropped anchor in six fathoms of water.[52]

From the anchorage, Father Hennepin could see that the vessel lay between two settlements of Indians who had established themselves near the Jesuit mission of St. Ignace. At the south end of the bay was the village of the Huron, while farther to the north could be seen that of the Ottawa. The arrival of La Salle's ship was announced by salutes from its cannon. The first sailing vessel to be seen on the upper Great Lakes created quite a stir in the two villages. Each day the *Griffon* was surrounded by as many as "sixscore Canou's" in which the occupants sat "staring and admiring that fine Woodden Canou as they call'd it." La Salle added to the drama with pomp and ceremony of his own, appearing for Mass in the Ottawa village surrounded by armed men and dressed in a fine scarlet cloak trimmed with gold lace.[53]

The mission of St. Ignace had stood on the shores of Michilimackinac for eight years by the time of La Salle's arrival. Details of its relocation from Mackinac Island to the mainland are scanty, but the move was probably accomplished during the summer or fall of 1671. By that time at least some of the Huron had established themselves nearby, and Father Marquette had erected a chapel.[54] The Hurons had fortified their village near the Jesuit church by the summer of 1672. They were soon joined by the first groups of Ottawa, some of whom had moved from Green Bay, while others came from St. Esprit at Chequamegon Bay by way of the mission of St. Simon on Manitoulin Island. By the time Marquette departed for his famous voyage of exploration to the Mississippi River, in May 1673, the Huron village contained 380 inhabitants, supplemented by a settlement of sixty Ottawa. These numbers represented the expanded summer population, for two hundred of the Hurons had left their village in the autumn of 1672 to spend the winter in their far-flung hunting camps.[55]

The Jesuits apparently built a new and more substantial chapel in 1674, and by 1675 two priests ministered to the growing Native American population of Michilimackinac. Father Philippe Pierson served the Huron and Father Henri Nouvel the Ottawa.[56] Few physical details of their mission complex survive, but the buildings of St. Ignace were probably similar to those described at Sault Ste. Marie in 1670: "a pretty fort, that is to say, a square of cedar posts twelve feet high, with a chapel and house inside the fort."[57] Father Hennepin, who spent the winter of 1680–81 at Michilimackinac, reported only that the chapel of St. Ignace was roofed "with Rushes and a few Boards" and that Canadians had built it.[58]

Other changes were indicative of growth by the time of La Salle's visit. Sometime during 1677 the Ottawa established a second village, probably at Gros Cap on the Lake Michigan side of the peninsula. In November, Father Nouvel moved to a "small bark cabin" situated between the "village of the Kiskakons (one of the four clans of Ottawa at Michilimackinac) and the new village of the outoauaks" and about three-quarters of a league from the main church of St. Ignace. The Jesuits erected a small bark chapel near the cabin and christened it for St. Francis Borgia. It was to be used on alternate days by the inhabitants of the Kiskakon Ottawa village and those of the newer establishment to the west. In August 1679, Henri de Tonty, who visited with La Salle and Hennepin, reported that the Jesuits had two churches at Michilimackinac. The priests themselves described a seasonal population in the three Native American villages of five hundred Huron and as many as thirteen hundred Ottawa.[59]

Although the mission complex at Michilimackinac was not mapped in detail, larger-scale cartography provides some idea of the surroundings of the Straits in the 1670s. Figure 1.7 represents part of the body of work of Louis Jolliet, best known as Father Marquette's companion on his voyage to the Mississippi in 1673. Jolliet compiled a map of the Great Lakes two years later and supported it with more detailed compositions of the individual lakes. Although the east-west orientation of his rendering of Lake Huron shows the influence of

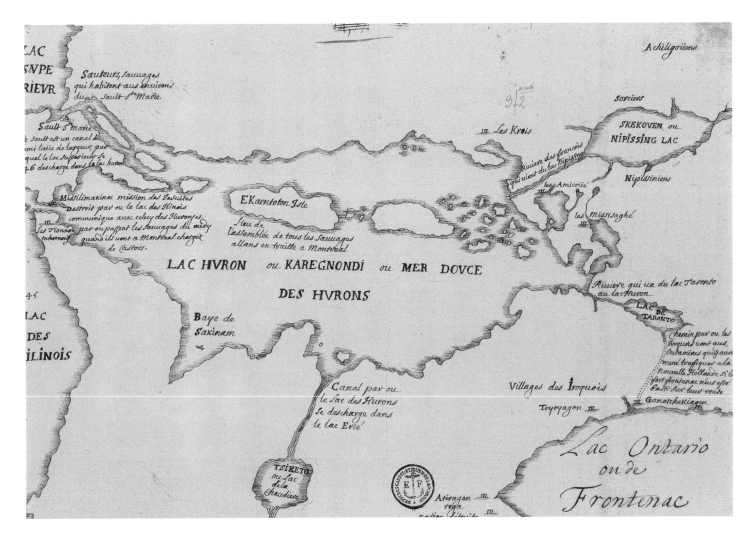

FIGURE 1.7

TITLE: Lac Hvron ou Karegnondi ou Mer Dovce des Hvrons.

AUTHOR: [Louis Jolliet (1645–1700)].

DATE DEPICTED: 1675.

DATE OF WORK: ca. 1675.

DESCRIPTION: Approximately 42 x 50 cm. Pen and ink on paper.

PROVENANCE: One of a series of maps of the Great Lakes drawn by Jolliet for the Comte de Frontenac, governor of New France. Retained in the records of the Ministère de la Marine.

COLLECTION: Service historique de la Défense-Marine, Château de Vincennes, France (Receuil 67, Carte 48).

Although no authenticated portrait of René-Robert Cavelier de La Salle (1643–87) is known, a Dutch engraver offered this impression of his appearance. The image was engraved for Louis Hennepin's *Beschryving van Louisiana* (Amsterdam, 1688). *Clements Library, University of Michigan.*

FIGURE 1.8

TITLE: [Construction of the *Griffon*].

AUTHOR: [Father Louis Hennepin (1626–ca. 1705)].

DATE DEPICTED: 1679.

DATE OF WORK: 1704.

DESCRIPTION: 12.8 x 16.7 cm. Copperplate engraving.

PROVENANCE: This example was published in a Dutch edition of Hennepin, *Aenmerkelyke Voyagie Gedaan na't Gedeelte van Noorder America. . . .* (Leyden, 1704), 43. It appears in other Dutch editions of Hennepin from 1704.

COLLECTION: Clements Library, University of Michigan, Ann Arbor (Book Division, C-1704-He).

Bark canoes provided the primary means of transportation on the seventeenth-century Great Lakes. Captain Louis-Armand de Lahontan studied these vessels, described them in his book, and illustrated the principal types. The Iroquois, he noted, were hindered in their raids by a reliance on flimsier boats of elm bark (top), while the birch bark canoe (bottom) was more seaworthy. Canoes could be portaged around rapids, as shown at top center. From Lahontan, *New Voyages to North-America* (London, 1703). *Clements Library, University of Michigan.*

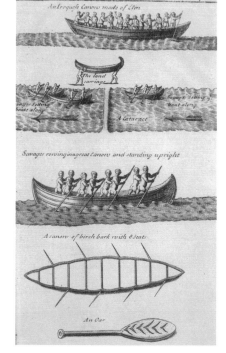

Champlain's earlier cartography, Jolliet demonstrated a better understanding of the northern route to Michilimackinac. He also added comments about the two main Jesuit missions in the region and identified the favorite assembly place for Montréal-bound canoe brigades at "Ekaentoton Isle" (Manitoulin Island).

Jolliet's map of Lake Huron emphasized the importance of the Straits of Mackinac as the channel of communication for Native American nations west of Lake Michigan when they took their beaver furs to Montréal. Details of the islands in the Straits are sketchy, with St. Helena shown at the western end and only a single island to the east. Jolliet identified the location of the Jesuit establishment at St. Ignace, but, oddly, placed the village of the "Tiannontateronons" (the Huron) on the south shore of the Straits. This might have been influenced by the general understanding that "the three Nations now dwelling as strangers on the Bay des Puans [Green Bay] formerly lived on the mainland, to the south of this Island [Mackinac]" during their flight from the Iroquois in the 1650s.[60]

It was into these poorly charted waters that La Salle ventured with his *Griffon* in the summer of 1679. The vessel had been constructed on the Niagara River above the great cataract. This was in the country of the Seneca, westernmost of the Iroquois, but La Salle's enterprise took place during a lull in their warfare with the French. Although the Seneca complained of the French intrusion, and parties of Iroquois frequently visited the shipyard during the winter of 1679 to harass the builders, the *Griffon* was launched in the spring. La Salle sailed for the West early in August.[61]

Relatively little is known of the trail-blazing vessel that appeared in the bay at Michilimackinac later that month. La Salle himself described the *Griffon* only as a craft of forty-five tons, while Father Hennepin recalled her as being a somewhat larger sixty tons. *Griffon* was named for the mythical beast that graced the coat of arms of

Louis de Buade, Comte de Frontenac, who was then governor of New France and La Salle's patron.[62] Contemporary images are even rarer than written descriptions, and the earliest to appear was engraved for a 1704 Dutch edition of Hennepin's chronicle of his travels in North America. The scene (Fig. 1.8) was probably based on the priest's account of the construction of the *Griffon* and shows the incomplete vessel on the stocks near the Niagara River. The topography is entirely imaginary, down to the palm tree symbolizing its exotic locale. The vessel itself is of contemporary form, though perhaps somewhat more Dutch than French, and shipwrights and blacksmiths are hard at work preparing the *Griffon* for her only voyage. In the right foreground a party of suspicious Iroquois confronts a French officer to protest this invasion of their territory. Beyond the vessel, the Niagara River winds away toward the promise of the West and its lucrative fur trade.

On September 12, 1679, La Salle sailed his *Griffon* out of the bay at Michilimackinac and headed west into Lake Michigan, bound for Green Bay. By the time he reached his destination, the season was rapidly advancing. La Salle decided to send the vessel back to Niagara with the pelts collected to date, depositing his remaining stock of trade goods at Michilimackinac for later use. On September 18 the *Griffon* sailed from Green Bay commanded by the pilot with a crew of six men. That was the last any Frenchman saw of her, for she never arrived at Michilimackinac. Indians later told La Salle that a great storm had arisen, and, although the stubborn sailor at first sought shelter, he ignored the advice of the Indians and ventured into the lake again. The warriors watched the *Griffon* "tossing frightfully, unable to make head against the storm" until "they lost it from sight."[63] The "nasty Lake" had claimed the blasphemous pilot and created the first and most durable maritime mystery of the Great Lakes.

An idealized figure of Recollet Father Louis Hennepin (1626-ca. 1705) appears in the title cartouche of Johann Baptist Homann's circa 1718 map of the Mississippi River. *Clements Library, University of Michigan (Map Division, Atlas, W-5-C).*

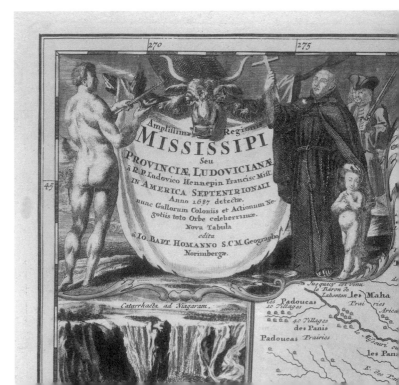

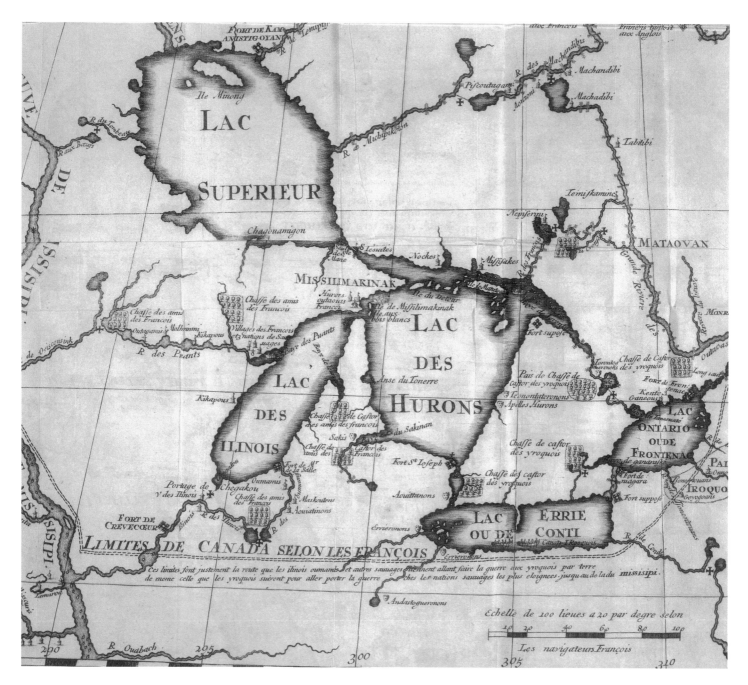

FIGURE 1.9

TITLE: Carte Generale de Canada Dediée au Roy de Danemark Par son tres humble et tres obeisant et tres fidele serviteur Lahontan. [Detail].

AUTHOR: Captain Louis-Armand de Lom d'Arce de Lahontan, Troupes de la Marine (1666–before 1716).

DATE DEPICTED: 1688.

DATE OF WORK: 1703.

DESCRIPTION: 43.5 x 55.5 cm. (complete map). Copperplate engraving.

PROVENANCE: Published in Lahontan, *Nouveaux voyages de Mr. le Baron de Lahontan dans l'Amérique Septentrionale* (La Haye, 1703), 2:1.

COLLECTION: Clements Library, University of Michigan, Ann Arbor (Book Division, C-1703-La).

Certainly a place of great Importance

Captain Louis-Armand de Lom d'Arce de Lahontan

In the spring of 1688 a French cartographer first mapped Michili-mackinac and the relationship of its Native American and French villages. These had become well established in the years since the Jesuits had founded their mission of St. Ignace. The land along the bay facing the island of Michilimackinac had been cleared of trees, and much of this space was filled with cornfields. Michilimackinac was a prosperous center of the beaver trade, and the nine years since La Salle's visit in 1679 had witnessed the growth of a small, seasonal village of Canadian fur traders.[64]

The military importance of Michilimackinac was also increasingly apparent. Although hostilities with the Iroquois had eased during the 1670s, warfare commenced again in earnest in the 1680s. By the middle of the decade there were also signs that the aggressive merchants of New York were casting covetous eyes on the upper Great Lakes fur trade. To better coordinate military activities at Michilimackinac and protect the interests of New France in the West, a military commandant was appointed for the upper posts in 1683. He had no regular force at his disposal but could rely on manpower diverted from the fur trade.[65]

Companies of trained soldiers were also sent to New France in 1683 to protect the colony, and it was an officer of one of those units who would first map the post at Michilimackinac. Captain Louis-Armand de Lom d'Arce de Lahontan served in garrison and in punitive expeditions against the Iroquois in 1685 and again in 1687. The latter campaign led to his appointment as commandant of a new post on the water communication between Lake Huron and Lake Erie. Fort St. Joseph was established in 1687 at the head of the St. Clair River (modern Port Huron, Michigan) to block Iroquois and English forays into the upper lakes. Lahontan reached his post in September.[66]

The captain and his small garrison spent a difficult winter at Fort St. Joseph. In the spring of 1688, in need of provisions for his men, he set out to purchase corn from the Huron and Ottawa of Michilimackinac. Lahontan arrived at the Straits on April 18 and remained until June 2. He then visited Sault Ste. Marie before returning to Fort St. Joseph, which he decided to abandon as untenable. Lahontan evacuated his garrison to Michilimackinac but then set out across Lake Michigan to winter in the upper Mississippi River region. He later claimed to have explored even farther west. Lahontan returned to Michilimackinac in May 1689 and went to Canada a month later.[67]

Following his return to Europe, Lahontan drew on his experiences to produce one of the most widely read books on America produced during the eighteenth century. First published in 1703, it was revised and reissued for more than half a century. As many as twenty-five editions had appeared by 1758.[68] Lahontan's account of Canada, although questionable in some of its details, carried a certain authority, in part because of his maps and illustrations of Native American cultural activities. Central to the book was his *Carte générale de Canada* that mapped the colony from the Atlantic to the Mississippi. It provides one of the best visual summaries of the political situation on the Great Lakes at the end of the 1680s. A detail is included here as Figure 1.9.

Lahontan's cartography is not among the most accurate portrayals of the lakes, particularly its crude rendering of Lake Superior. It is useful, however, for illustrating the disruption caused by the wars between the Iroquois and the nations of the West since the 1640s. Shield-shaped symbols for destroyed villages dot the land and the hunting territories of the Iroquois, and the Indians allied with the French are carefully differentiated. Lahontan recorded improved knowledge of the routes from Michilimackinac to the Mississippi River and the locations of Native American groups in the region. His rendering of the Straits of Mackinac identifies the primary elements that he found there in 1688 and 1689—a mission and village of the French and substantial settlements of Ottawa and Huron. In the Straits itself Lahontan identified "Ile de Missilimakinak" and, for the first time, "Ile aux Bois Blancs."

It was probably during his six weeks at the Straits in the spring of 1688 that Lahontan recorded most of the information on Michilimackinac that made its way into his book. This was also his opportunity to map the settlement, take soundings of the waters between the mainland and the islands to the east, and, for the first time, define in detail the relationship between the primary bodies of land on the Lake Huron side of the Straits. His map of Michilimackinac (Fig. 1.10) was included in the original Hague (La Haye) edition of 1703, and variants of it appear in most subsequent printings.

Lahontan's plan of the settlement clearly shows how the missionaries, the traders, and the Ottawa and Huron had established themselves along the shores of East Moran Bay. He noted that the two Indian villages had, until recently, been built very close together.[69] By the spring of 1688, however, the Ottawa were constructing a new fortified village on higher ground to the north. Lahontan's map shows this situation, with the Huron village depicted at "C" and that of the Ottawa farther up the bay at "E." Stockade pickets and bark longhouses had a limited life span, and it is likely that these villages had already been moved or rebuilt at least once since 1671.

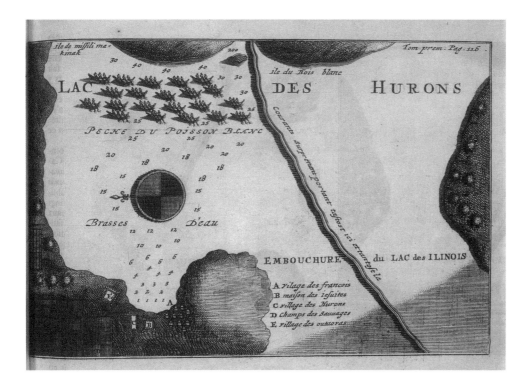

FIGURE 1.10

TITLE: [Michilimackinac].

AUTHOR: Captain Louis-Armand de Lom d'Arce de Lahontan, Troupes de la Marine (1666–before 1716).

DATE DEPICTED: 1688.

DATE OF WORK: 1703.

DESCRIPTION: 10.7 x 16.3 cm. Copperplate engraving.

PROVENANCE: Published in Lahontan, *Nouveaux voyages de Mr. le Baron de Lahontan dans l'Amérique Septentrionale* (La Haye, 1703), 1:116. Beginning with the 1705 edition of Lahontan, the page number at the upper right was altered to 127.

COLLECTION: Clements Library, University of Michigan, Ann Arbor (Book Division, C-1703-La).

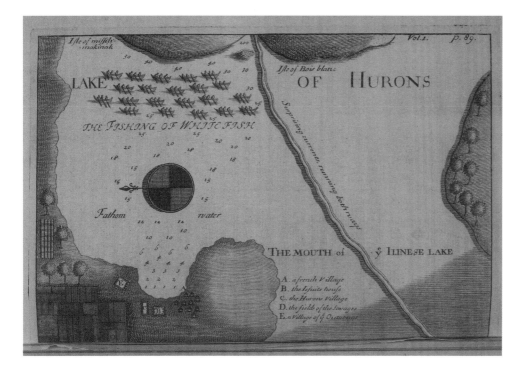

FIGURE 1.11

TITLE: [Michilimackinac].

AUTHOR: Captain Louis-Armand de Lom d'Arce de Lahontan, Troupes de la Marine (1666–before 1716).

DATE DEPICTED: 1688.

DATE OF WORK: 1703.

DESCRIPTION: 10.6 x 16.4 cm. Coppperplate engraving.

PROVENANCE: Published in Lahontan, *New Voyages to North-America* (London, 1703), 1:89. The Clements Library copy includes an additional copy of the map in 2:89. The map also appears in later English editions.

COLLECTION: Clements Library, University of Michigan, Ann Arbor (Book Division, C-1703-La).

FIGURE 1.12

TITLE: [Michilimackinac].

AUTHOR: Captain Louis-Armand de Lom d'Arce de Lahontan, Troupes de la Marine (1666–before 1716).

DATE DEPICTED: 1688.

DATE OF WORK: 1703.

DESCRIPTION: 14 x 8.5 cm. Copperplate engraving.

PROVENANCE: Published in Lahontan, *Nouveaux voyages de Mr. le Baron de Lahontan dans l'Amérique Septentrionale* (La Haye, 1703), 1:116. Reversed image published in pirated editions of Lahontan's book. This plate was reused in editions through 1728. A new but still reversed plate appeared in an Amsterdam edition of 1728 with the page number at the upper left altered to 136 and then, in editions of 1741 and later, to 156.

COLLECTION: Clements Library, University of Michigan, Ann Arbor (Book Division, C-1703-La).

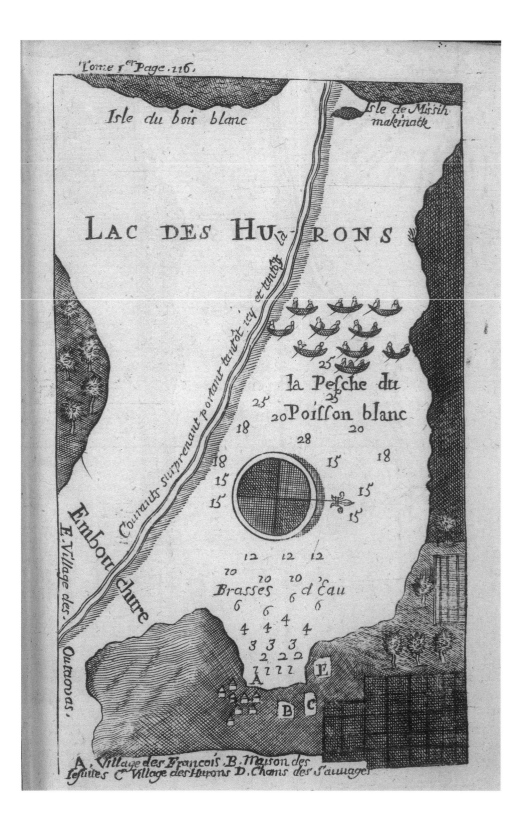

Ile Minong

LAC

SUPERIEUR

Chagouamigon

MISSILIMAKINAK

Piſcoutagam

R de Michipikoton

Souk des Ste Marie

S Iesuites

Nockes

Miſſiſake

Ile de Manitoal

Hurons outaouois Francois

Ile du Detour

Ile de Miſſilimakinak

Chaſſe des amis des Francois

Ile aux obis blancs

LAC

des amis

ncois

mis Malhoinni

Kikapous

Villages des Francois

et 3 nations de Sau

uages

Baye des Puants

Baye de Tole

DES

des Puants

Baye des Puants

Anse du Tonerre

Kikapous

LAC

HURONS

DES

Chaſſe des amis des francois

de Caſtor

du Sakinan

Ap

Sakis

Bay

ILINOIS

Chaſſe de amis des

Caſtor des Francois

Fort St Ioseph

Chaſſe d

des yro

Chegabou

Fort de Mr de la Salle

Portage de V des Ilinois

Oumamis

Chegakou

Oumamis

Aouittanons

Chaſſe des amis des Francois

Maskoutens

Aouiatinons

Ilinois

R des Ilinois

R des

Errieronons

LAC

OU DE

DE CANADA SELON LES FRANÇOIS

Errieronons

es limites font justement la route que les ilinois oumamis et autres sauuages tiennent allant faire la guerre

meme celle que les yroquois suivent pour aller porter la guerre ches les nations sauuages les p

Strong defenses were a necessity in the dangerous environment of the Great Lakes during the Iroquois wars. The Native American villages at Michilimackinac were fortified from the beginning in the Iroquoian manner with an enclosure of palisades. It is possible that their walls incorporated elements of European design as well, for the French were willing to assist their allies. In September 1682, Governor Frontenac suggested that the Ottawa and Huron of Michilimackinac refortify their villages, and he even had plans drawn up and presented to them.[70] In 1683 the two Native American forts were strengthened under the direction of Captain Daniel Greysolon Dulhut, newly appointed to command the upper posts.[71] Whether this work followed Frontenac's plans or relied on Native American–style fortification is not known. Lahontan's map reveals no distinctively European features.

It is likely that the villages were fortified in the manner described by Captain Antoine Laumet de Lamothe Cadillac, who commanded Michilimackinac in 1694–97. "These forts are made of stakes," he wrote. "Those of the outer row are . . . about 30 feet high; the second row inside is a full foot from the first, and leans over the top to support and prop it; the third row is four feet from the second one, and consists of stakes . . . 15 or 16 feet out of the ground." The pickets of the inner row were placed tightly together, while those of the two outer rings had spaces between them so the defenders' fire would not be blocked. The concentric walls described by Cadillac were typical of Native American village fortifications. These incorporated "neither curtains [straight walls] nor bastions, and, properly speaking, it is a mere fence," he wrote. Inside the enclosure, the residents lived in bark-covered, communal longhouses up to 130 feet long, 24 feet wide, and 20 feet tall.[72]

The French settlement at Michilimackinac was clustered at the southern end of the bay. There stood the church of St. Ignace, described by Lahontan as "a little House, or Colledge adjoyning to a sort of Church, and inclos'd with Pales [palisades] that separate it from the Village of the Hurons." The houses of the French traders, or *coureurs de bois*, stood south of the church in a scattered and unfortified village that Lahontan characterized as "very small."[73]

The rest of his plan depicts the relationship of the settlement to the islands of Michilimackinac, Bois Blanc, and Round, the last as yet unnamed. To the south (right) is the tip of the Lower Peninsula of Michigan. Between the mainlands Lahontan identified the strong and variable currents in the Straits of Mackinac that had been reported as early as 1670–71 by Father Claude Dablon. These, Lahontan reported, were unpredictable in their direction and were powerful enough to carry away fishing nets.[74]

Lahontan saved his most enthusiastic comments for a resource that he identified on his map by a cluster of canoes and fishermen. "You can scarcely believe," he wrote, "what vast sholes of white Fish are catch'd about the middel of the Channel, between the Continent and the Isle of Missilimakinac." Despite the produce of their fields, Lahontan believed that the Ottawa and Huron would never have been able to subsist at the Straits of Mackinac were it not for the fishery. He was not the first to enthuse about whitefish, and most travelers who followed him recorded similar comments. "It has one singular property," Lahontan continued, "namely that all sorts of Sauces spoil it, so that 'tis always eat boil'd or broil'd without any manner of seasoning." The Straits held other bounty as well: "Trouts as big as one's Thigh." Fishing was done with both hooks and nets.[75]

Figures 1.11 and 1.12 represent variations of Lahontan's map of Michilimackinac. The first is from the London edition of 1703 with the labels in English. Figure 1.12 was also produced in 1703. Although folded into a book with the same Hague imprint as Figure 1.10, it is a pirated edition, produced in a smaller format. The map is notable for having been copied directly from the authorized edition without the engraver taking the time to reverse the image on the plate. The peculiar result is a map of Michilimackinac printed as a mirror image of Lahontan's revealing original.

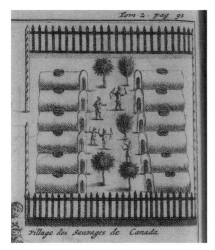

The Native American villages of Michilimackinac were fortified against Iroquois raiders by enclosing the rows of longhouses with a palisade of pointed stakes. Lahontan depicted a similar town in Canada during the 1680s. This detail is from his *New Voyages to North-America* (London, 1703). *Clements Library, University of Michigan.*

Lahontan's map of the Straits of Mackinac emphasized the abundance of fish in its waters. This food source made a large settlement possible at Michilimackinac and remained a staple of the inhabitants' diet well into the twentieth century. Father Louis Nicolas sketched a large whitefish (*left*) about 1675. *Les raretés des Indes, "Codex canadiensis," Clements Library, University of Michigan.*

Michilimackinac should be reinforced with a garrison of trained soldiers

Intendant Claude-Michel Bégon

The quarter century between 1690 and 1715 was a turbulent period at the Straits of Mackinac. During that time, the increased military importance of the post led to the establishment of a French fort with a garrison of regular troops. Then, in a series of setbacks for those who appreciated the value of Michilimackinac, the soldiers were withdrawn in 1697 and fur traders were barred from the West by the revocation of trading licenses. After the establishment of Detroit, in 1701, the Huron and many of the Ottawa inhabitants of Michilimackinac were persuaded to relocate there. During an eighteen-year hiatus (1697–1715) the temporal authority of a military commandant and, after 1705, the spiritual guidance of Jesuit missionaries were exercised only intermittently at the Straits. Both the church and the military had returned to Michilimackinac by 1715, and they would thereafter remain permanent fixtures until the end of the French regime. When the fort, mission, and Ottawa village were reestablished, however, they were at a new location on the tip of Michigan's Lower Peninsula.

Despite the importance of these years in the development of Michilimackinac, they are poorly documented in contemporary imagery. Only a single map of the Straits is known to exist. Fortunately, it is an interesting and useful composite, showing the post on the north shore as it was in the 1690s and its replacement on the south side of the Straits as it developed after 1715. No author is known for Figure 1.13, but the basis of this colorful manuscript map was Lahontan's survey of Michilimackinac as he found it in 1688 (Fig. 1.10). It offered a convenient starting point for an unnamed French cartographer to illustrate the transfer of the post from its old to its new location. The composition is thought to date to around 1717.

This map incorporates most of the cartographic details found on Lahontan's map, including the islands in the eastern end of the Straits and notations describing the whitefish grounds and lake currents. The layout of the original settlement on the north shore is also taken largely from Lahontan, although the author chose to show the Indian villages as unfortified. He also provided additional architectural detail of the Jesuit mission, suggesting a stockade with a building in its southwestern corner. Crop fields are shown, and the area of cleared and cultivated ground must have been extensive by the middle of the 1690s after twenty-five years of occupation.

The most significant addition to the settlement on the north shore is represented by the figure of a European-style fort, drawn in a conventional shape with a bastion at each corner. This is Fort de Buade, named for Governor Frontenac and apparently located in the French village shown by Lahontan. No firm date has ever been

established for the construction of Fort de Buade, although it was not in existence at the time of Lahontan's visit in 1688. By the summer of 1690, however, officials in France were referring to expenses for a fort at Michilimackinac, so it was either in use or its construction was imminent.[76] While the shape of Fort de Buade might be merely a cartographic convention, it seems likely that the French soldiers who constructed it would have incorporated bastions—projecting defensive positions located at each corner of the enclosure. These were employed in most fortifications of New France.

The construction of a fort at Michilimackinac was a logical culmination of events in the upper country during the 1680s. Incursions by New York traders, the constant threat of attack from the Iroquois, and the fear that Michilimackinac and its trade might be lost to the Iroquois and the English all encouraged heightened security. By 1689 Governor Louis-Hector de Callière could describe Michilimackinac as "one of the most important posts of Canada; our entrepôt for the Fur Trade and the residence of the Superior of the Reverend Jesuit Fathers who are Missionaries among our Indians, and which belongs, incontestably to us."[77]

Antoine Laumet de Lamothe Cadillac commanded Michilimackinac from 1694 to 1697, and he later described the post much as it is shown in Figure 1.13. The French fort was located on a spacious, sandy cove (East Moran Bay). "This post is called Fort Du Buade," Cadillac wrote. "The Jesuits' convent, the French village, and those of the Hurons and Outaouas, are contiguous to one another; and all together border on, fill and complete the head of the cove," he continued. The stockades of the Indian villages enclosed rows of bark-covered longhouses, while the French preferred buildings of horizontal logs roofed with cedar bark, a form of construction that would remain common at the Straits of Mackinac well into the nineteenth century. Only the Jesuit church and house were more substantially roofed with boards.[78]

The location of the post of Michilimackinac was considered particularly good. The bay guaranteed a degree of shelter, except from an east wind, and the Straits provided a passage for Indians on their way to Montréal or for French traders bound for the West. The site had an additional security benefit, for, Cadillac noted, no one could pass or approach without being seen "because the horizon is so wide that canoes can be distinguished from the fort as far as the strongest eyes can see."[79]

The advantages of Michilimackinac were not compelling enough to ensure its preservation when a royal decision was made to withdraw from the posts of the West. The garrison was evacuated in 1697, and the traders were ordered to return to Canada. The adjacent

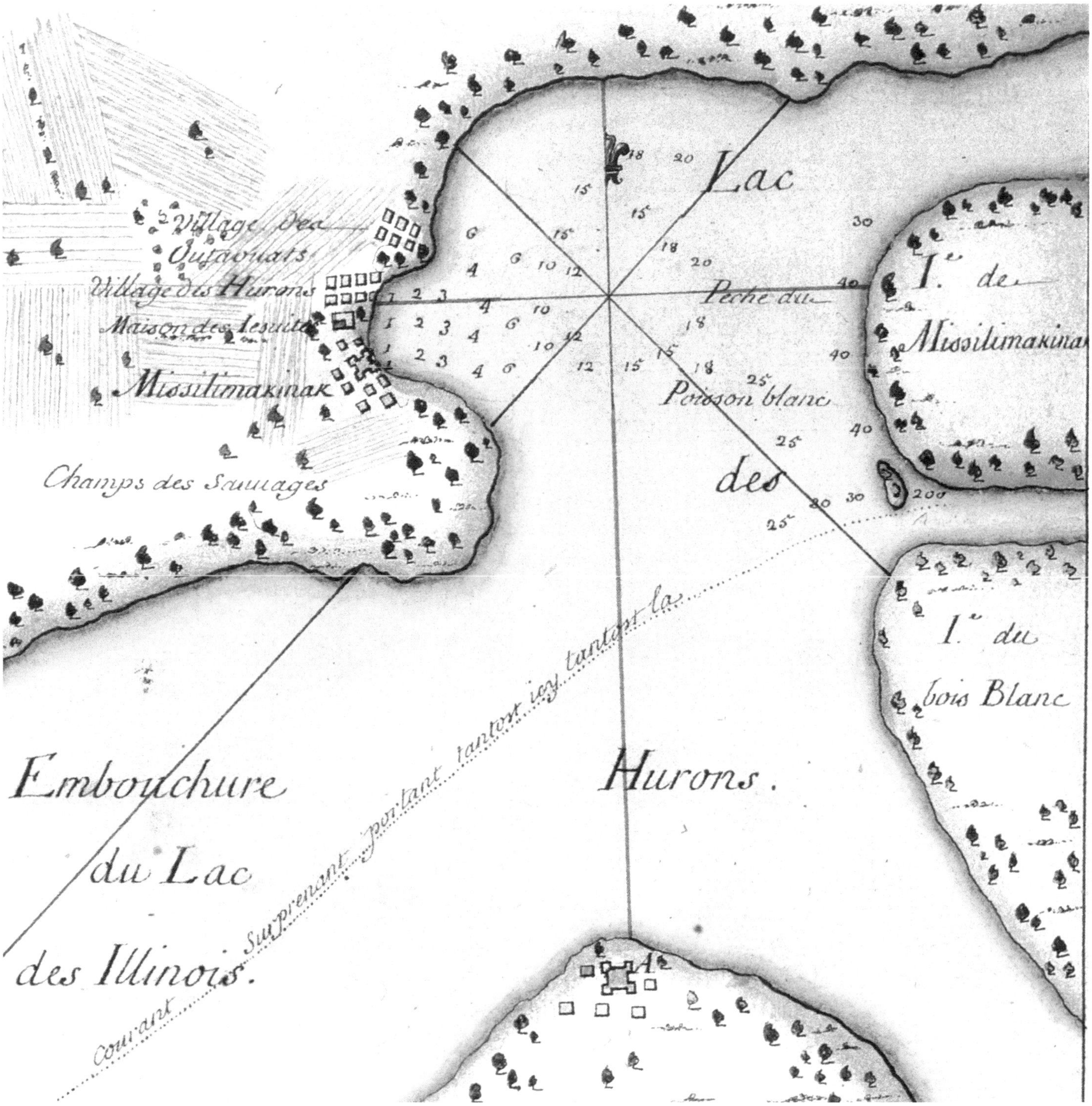

FIGURE 1.13

TITLE: Plan de Missilimakinak avec la description de la route du Missisipi.

AUTHOR: After Captain Louis-Armand de Lom d'Arce de Lahontan, Troupes de la Marine (1666–before 1716). Updated details by an unknown hand.

DATE DEPICTED: ca. 1716.

DATE OF WORK: ca. 1717.

DESCRIPTION: 24 x 18.4 cm. (map only); 24 x 36.5 including title and description. The map is one of four drawn on the same sheet having total dimensions of 50.5 x 36.5 cm. Pen and ink with watercolor on paper.

PROVENANCE: Unknown until acquired by the Newberry Library.

COLLECTION: The Newberry Library, Chicago, Edward E. Ayer Collection (Map 30, Sheet 109). Also commonly cited as Cartes marines, No. 109.

Indian villages remained, however, at least until 1702–3, when the Huron and many of the Ottawa decided to move to Detroit. In the fall of 1705 the Jesuits, having lost the greater part of their mission congregation, "reduced their church, their dwelling and possessions to ashes by fire" and returned to Montréal.[80]

All of this movement might suggest that Michilimackinac was abandoned in the years after 1705, but in fact a considerable community remained. Father Joseph Marest returned to minister at Michilimackinac for part of each summer, and it even appears that Fort de Buade remained standing, at least as late as 1706. The missionary came to visit the Ottawa who had refused to go to Detroit, and in 1706 Marest reported that their community numbered 180 individuals. The traders, of course, had never entirely given up their lucrative business, continuing to operate illegally with the connivance of merchants in Montréal. When François Clairambault d'Aigremont visited in 1708, he found about fifteen Frenchmen doing business at Michilimackinac.[81]

What was lacking, Aigremont complained, was royal authority in the form of a commandant and a garrison. The absence of legal traders also meant that many furs from the region were taken north to the British at Hudson Bay. "It is absolutely necessary," he reported, "to place a commandant at Missilimakinac with a garrison of thirty men and to issue . . . licenses" once again, he wrote.[82] Colonial officials seconded Aigremont's recommendation in 1710 and in subsequent years.[83] The arguments remained much the same, strengthened after the spring of 1712 by the imperatives of a new and particularly violent war against the Fox Indians of Wisconsin.

The conflict with the Foxes finally focused official attention on suggestions to reestablish a garrison at Michilimackinac. An expedition aimed at their Wisconsin villages brought a military force to the Straits of Mackinac during the summer of 1715. Although the operation proceeded no farther, the troops erected a stockade and left a garrison for the winter. Captain Constant Le Marchand de Lignery later claimed to have constructed "a fort for the garrison, with two guard-houses; and a 40-foot house" at his own expense.[84]

As with the establishment of Fort de Buade, the construction of the fort on the south mainland is very poorly documented, and no plan seems to have survived. Chief among the questions surrounding this event is why the post was relocated from its site on the north side of the Straits to a sandy, windswept, and unsheltered point on the south shore. The view of the waterway was certainly more expansive, and it is likely that the soil around the former mission and fort had been exhausted by forty years of intensive corn cultivation. None of the sources provides a definitive answer to this question.

A detail from Figure 1.13 showing the post of Michilimackinac as it appeared in 1690–97 after the construction of Fort de Buade. The colored building in the Jesuit mission compound probably represents the church of St. Ignace.

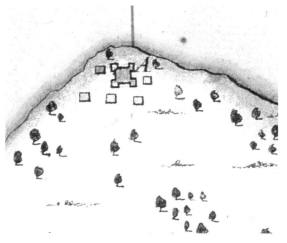

The new post of Michilimackinac is shown soon after its establishment in 1715 on the south mainland in this detail from Figure 1.13. The colored building outside the fort is probably the relocated Jesuit mission church of St. Ignace.

One possibility is that the French soldiers followed the local Ottawa and their Jesuit missionaries to the new location. After the Huron and many of the Ottawa moved to Detroit in 1702–3, the remnants of the latter community built a new village, perhaps on the Lake Michigan shore of the St. Ignace peninsula at or near Gros Cap.[85] Their new fort and houses were badly damaged by fire, perhaps even destroyed, during the summer of 1708. The catastrophe, combined with a need for more fertile crop fields, might have motivated a move to the south shore. This seems to have been accomplished around 1710.[86] Years later, in 1767, British fur trader John Porteous suggested, presumably based on local memory, that the Ottawa had requested that the new fort be built to protect their village on the south shore of the Straits.[87]

Figure 1.13 is the earliest image to depict the new French post, again identified by a conventional symbol for a fort and surrounded by a cluster of buildings. These were probably meant to represent the habitations of the Ottawa or, perhaps, houses constructed by the traders. Details of the new stockade at Michilimackinac are known today only from archaeology, and investigations have discovered no evidence of bastions at the corners of the fort, even though such defensive features were virtually universal at important military posts. The Jesuit mission church, perhaps identified by the single blackened house symbol, appears to have stood outside the west wall of the enclosure.[88]

The reestablished post of Michilimackinac included a new component that distinguished it from the former fort and village. The text with Figure 1.13 reports that there were settled French inhabitants at Michilimackinac by 1716, including even some women. Although a common criticism of Michilimackinac was that its lands were not fertile, it would seem that this did not prevent an agricultural experiment.[89] By 1717–18 Michilimackinac was noted as a place where "some French have settled."[90] Although the year-round population would never be very large, the basis of a colonial community was in place.

French soldiers and Native American warriors, flanked by the symbols of the church and the state, appear in the title cartouche of Nicolas de Fer's *La France Occidentale dans l'Amérique Septentrional* (Paris, 1718). *Clements Library, University of Michigan (Map Division, 1-H-6).*

The situation of Michillimakinac is most advantageous for traffic

Father Pierre-François-Xavier de Charlevoix, S. J.

On June 28, 1721, Father Pierre de Charlevoix disembarked from his canoe on the beach at Michilimackinac. He was not particularly impressed with the appearance of the place. The priest noted that the fort was kept up and that there was a house for the missionaries, his fellow Jesuits. The Ottawa lived there too, but Charlevoix described their habitation as "a sorry village." In general, he thought that the post was "much fallen to decay" since the establishment of Detroit twenty years before.[91]

Perhaps Father Charlevoix's disappointment stemmed from his knowledge of the vitality of the mission of St. Ignace during the late seventeenth century, no doubt gained from reading the Jesuit *Relations* of the 1670s and 1680s. The current state of the mission was certainly not what he thought it should be. The Huron had always been the nation most receptive to Christianity, but they had moved en masse to Detroit. The Jesuits had never found the Ottawa, especially those who remained at the Straits, "much disposed to receive their instructions." By 1721, Charlevoix reported, the missionaries of Michilimackinac were "not distressed with business."[92] Not so the fur traders. Despite some leakage of pelts from the northern Indian nations to the British on Hudson Bay, Michilimackinac "carried on a considerable fur trade," largely because the place was "a thoroughfare or rendezvous of a number of Indian nations." Strategically situated between the three largest Great Lakes, the post was, Charlevoix believed, "most advantageous for traffic."[93]

Charlevoix, like Lahontan, eventually crafted his North American travel experiences into an influential and widely read book.[94] His *Histoire et description générale de la Nouvelle France* appeared in Paris in 1744, complete with numerous maps, including one of the Straits of Mackinac (Fig. 1.14). Although its author, Jacques-Nicolas Bellin, had never visited North America, he was able to compile this map from the many pieces of manuscript cartography deposited in the "Dépôt des Cartes et Plans" of the Marine Department in Paris. Bellin, as "Engineer of the Marine," had access to the cartographic data gathered since the establishment of a French presence at the Straits of Mackinac.

Bellin's map is the most detailed treatment of the area to be found for the years from the relocation of Michilimackinac in 1715 until the end of the French regime in 1761. As such, it says much about the frustrating lack of cartography and plans representing the Straits during that time. The Lahontan map of 1688 and its derivative of circa 1717 (Figs. 1.10 and 1.13) are very useful, but no detailed ground plan of Fort de Buade is known. Nor does a survey of Fort Michilimackinac survive prior to 1749 (Fig. 1.15). It is likely that none was ever drawn, for neither post drew the attention of an engineer, and the commandants presumably had no orders to prepare plans.

Only archaeological evidence survives to give an idea of the appearance of the fort at Michilimackinac. This suggests that, until the 1730s, the defenses were made up of a simple, rectangular stockade protecting a few buildings. The Jesuit mission church appears to have stood outside the west wall, in the direction of the "Mission S. Ignace" noted on Figure 1.14.[95] Michilimackinac was not much of a fortification at the time of Charlevoix's 1721 visit, despite its importance in the ongoing war against the Foxes. Only during the later stages of the conflict were plans drawn for a more substantial and sophisticated fortification to defend French interests at the Straits.

Sometime in 1731 Gaspard-Joseph Chaussegros de Léry, chief engineer of New France, submitted plans for a stone "redoubt" (small fort) to be built at Michilimackinac. Léry, who had served in the colony since 1718, was an advocate of massive, roofed, masonry towers of three to four stories incorporating overhanging or "machicolated" top floors that permitted downward, flanking musket fire. These structures were self-contained forts resembling small castles. Léry had recommended construction of such redoubts at La Gallette on the St. Lawrence River and Sodus Bay on Lake Ontario in 1728, and he completed examples at Fort Niagara in 1726–27 and at Fort St. Frédéric on Lake Champlain in 1737.[96]

Although costly to build, Chaussegros de Léry's machicolated redoubts possessed certain advantages for guarding important, isolated passes like the Straits of Mackinac. The buildings were nearly fireproof and impervious to small arms fire. Living quarters were integral to the fortifications, so redoubts required smaller garrisons than conventional forts. They possessed another advantage in the climate of Michilimackinac. With their indoor defensive positions, there was no fear that "ice and snow covering the artillery on the ramparts" would render them useless in the winter.[97]

Léry's proposal was declined because of the huge expense it would have entailed, and his plans have not been found in the appropriate French collections. Officials in Paris declared instead that Michilimackinac was to remain a "wooden structure, with attention to granting land to those who want to settle nearby." Should settlement progress, they promised, consideration would be given to having a "better fort" erected.[98] The very existence of Léry's expensive proposal, however, suggests that colonial officials believed stronger defenses were needed. Michilimackinac's stockade was enlarged and reconstructed later in the 1730s, enclosing new buildings arranged in a carefully planned, military fashion.[99]

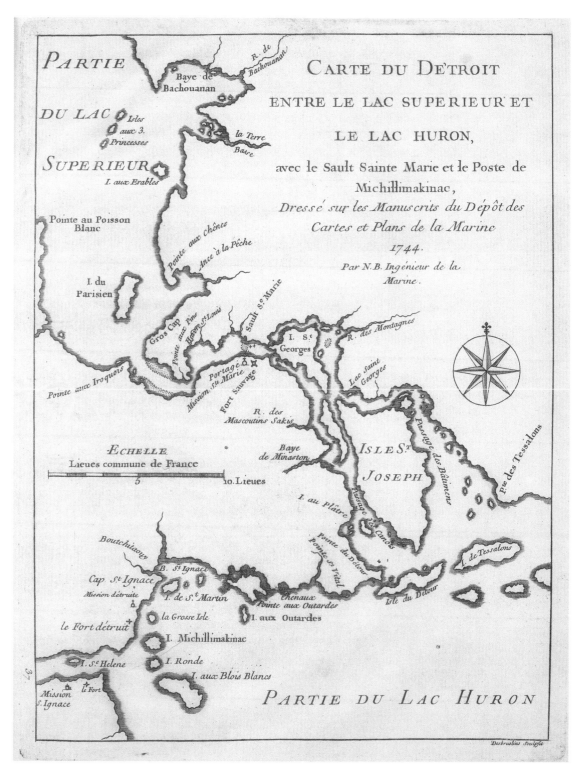

FIGURE 1.14

TITLE: Carte du Détroit Entre le Lac Superieur et le Lac Huron, avec le Sault Sainte Marie et le Post de Michillimakinac, Dressé sur les Manuscrits du Dépôt des Cartes et Plans de la Marine 1744.

AUTHOR: Jacques-Nicolas Bellin (1703–72). Engraved by F. Desbruslins (active 1719–57).

DATE DEPICTED: 1716–42.

DATE OF WORK: 1744.

DESCRIPTION: 21.3 x 16 cm. Copperplate engraving.

PROVENANCE: Designed from manuscript maps deposited in the Dépôt des Cartes et Plans. Published in Charlevoix, *Histoire et description générale de la Nouvelle France, avec le journal historique d'un voyage fait par ordre du roi dans l'Amérique Septentrionale* (Paris 1744), 3:280.

COLLECTION: Clements Library, University of Michigan, Ann Arbor (C2-1744-Ch).

Cost-conscious administrators had found a less expensive solution than a four-story tower overlooking the south shore of the Straits.

Aside from noting the abandoned mission and fort on the north shore, Figure 1.14 gives no indication of other areas of settlement in the Straits. It does, however, place names on nearly all of the islands—and then some. Father Charlevoix's 1721 description was the first to provide any detail about the two easternmost islands. Bois Blanc drew his attention because of its size, "five or six leagues long." The other was "very small and quite round" and is identified on the Bellin map, literally, as "I. Ronde." Both were heavily forested and reported to have excellent soil.[100] Round Island, as it is known today, is roughly circular on Bellin's map, but later sources suggest that the name actually derived from the profile of the elevation dominating its interior.[101]

It was the dramatic form of the third island, "Michillimakinac," that most impressed Father Charlevoix. It appeared "almost round and very high," and could be seen at a distance of twelve leagues. The island possessed special significance. To the Indians, it was the birthplace and former abode of their god, "Michbou," and the place had given its name to the entire region. Unlike well-wooded Round Island and Bois Blanc, however, Charlevoix described Michilimack-

inac as "a barren rock, being scarce so much as covered with moss or herbage."[102] Perhaps it had been partially deforested during years of seasonal use for fishing camps. The island of Michilimackinac had not supported a permanent population since the Jesuit experiment of 1670–71. By the 1690s, however, Cadillac reported that it was "occupied only during the fishing season, when an abundance of fish is caught all round it."[103]

Cartographer Jacques-Nicolas Bellin provided two imaginary additions to his map, one of them being a tiny body of land between St. Martin Island and Little St. Martin. A more obvious addition is "la Grosse Isle," placed just north of the island of Michilimackinac. No such land, in fact, exists, and there is no explanation as to why Bellin included it in his composition. The name "la Grosse Isle" was regularly applied to the island of Michilimackinac.[104] It seems likely that the cartographic curiosity of this additional island crept onto Bellin's map from an assumption that the two names represented different bodies of land. Figure 1.14 is not the only instance in which Bellin added "phantom" islands to the Great Lakes. His *Carte des Lacs du Canada* (Paris, 1744), which also appeared in Charlevoix's book, included at least three in Lake Superior.[105]

The Ottawa appear to have established a village on the south shore of the Straits before the fort of Michilimackinac was built there in 1715. They moved to a new site at L'Arbre Croche on Lake Michigan in 1742 but remained frequent visitors to the French post. An eighteenth-century engraver pictured this Ottawa warrior, adorned with European trade goods. *Mackinac State Historic Parks, MI (1985.105.1).*

Jacques Testard de Montigny (1663–1737) was an officer of colonial troops who served across New France during his long career. He commanded Michilimackinac in 1730–33, when he was in his late sixties. This portrait, by an unidentified artist, shows Montigny about 1715. *Château Ramezay Museum Collection, Montréal (1998.814).*

This fort contains 40 houses all very badly built

Ensign Michel Chartier de Lotbinière

From the time of its reestablishment on the south shore of the Straits in 1715, the post of Michilimackinac depended on a wooden stockade for the security of its inhabitants and garrison. These defenses had never been so important as they were during the summer of 1747. On July 2 an Ottawa named Nequiouamin met secretly with the commandant, Ensign Charles-Joseph de Noyelles, and the missionary, Father Pierre Du Jaunay. Nequiouamin warned that the Huron and other nations of the West, including the Ottawa of Detroit and Michilimackinac, were conspiring with the Iroquois and the British "to destroy the French and drive them to the other side of the sea."[106]

New France was already at war, engaged against the British in the colonial phase of the War of the Austrian Succession that had shaken Europe since 1744. The Native American nations of the upper country had faithfully fulfilled their role as military allies. But the effects of the conflict trickled down to the posts of the West as the war disrupted commerce and the flow of goods. Traders from the British colonies actively solicited the business and the allegiance of tribes in the Ohio country, and the summer of 1747 brought violent uprisings of the Miami of northern Indiana and disaffected Hurons at Detroit.[107] The French had never before faced so widespread a threat to their relations with the Native American nations of the West.

Although the exact chain of events is unclear, it seems that soon after Nequiouamin delivered his warning, a group of young warriors requested a council in the fort and arrived armed with knives. They were confronted by the ringing of an alarm bell and defensive preparations by the garrison of twenty-eight soldiers. The plotters departed and were not allowed thereafter to enter the fort, but they continued their mischief outside its walls. Hostile warriors ran off or killed the horses and cattle of the inhabitants and offered "diverse insults and threats at the fort." The Ottawa of Saginaw Bay killed three traders on their way to Michilimackinac, canoes were attacked on Georgian Bay, and the Ojibwas of La Grosse Isle—the island of Michilimackinac—stabbed a Frenchman there. Alarmed, the commandant called upon passing voyageurs to bolster his garrison and, on July 23, dispatched reports of the unrest to Canada.[108]

French authorities took swift action when news of the uprising reached Québec early in August. The governor sent reinforcements and provisions in a successful effort to "restore tranquility at the post" and "to place it in a proper state of defence against all attacks of the Indians."[109] It was probably this crisis and the temporary increase in the garrison to one hundred men that allowed the fort at Michilimackinac to be repaired and expanded. These changes were illustrated in 1749 by the only plan of the post known to survive from the French period.

Figure 1.15 was the work of Ensign Michel Chartier de Lotbinière, a colonial officer who had been dispatched from Canada to examine the traditional Ottawa River-Lake Nipissing-French River canoe route to Georgian Bay and Michilimackinac and to report on the state of the most important post in the northern lakes. Peace had returned to New France in 1748 with the conclusion of the European war and the pacification of the Indians of Detroit and Michilimackinac. The events of the last few years had been a wake-up call, however, and the governor, the Marquis de La Galissonière, was determined to forestall future troubles. Lotbinière's trip to Michilimackinac was one of three expeditions ordered to the West in 1749 to mark French claims and map the most important posts.[110]

Lotbinière arrived at Michilimackinac on September 22, 1749, and remained until October 7. Although delayed at first by rain and wind, he was able to survey the post and complete the remarkable plan illustrated here. Lotbinière also prepared a detailed *mémoire* or report on Michilimackinac, its environs, and its population. The officer mapped other features of the Straits as well, apparently as part of a larger composition recording his route from Montréal to Michilimackinac. This was incomplete at the time of his return to Canada late in October, and, although the ensign promised a "fair copy" by the end of 1749, no such map is known to survive.[111]

Although Ensign Lotbinière did not identify the relationship of the fort to the water on his plan, his survey was oriented with north and the Straits at the bottom. The fortifications were drawn with particular care, and it is no surprise that Lotbinière's report begins with an assessment of Michilimackinac's defenses. Despite what had been accomplished in the last few years, he thought the place "very badly built." Lotbinière described the cedar stockade as twelve feet high, arranged in a "square or just about, with four bastions, that is to say what they call bastions." A large triangular yard belonging to the missionary and enclosing an icehouse (*glacière*) and an oven (*four*) interrupted the defenses of the western face of the fort. A semi-subterranean powder magazine was located in the southeastern corner of the stockade, enclosed by its own modest security fence.[112]

The 1749 plan shows how the walls of Michilimackinac had been expanded during the 1740s. "Within and around the enclosure, at a distance of 6 or 7 feet," wrote Lotbinière, "stands a palisade that used to be the fort before the war." The space between the old and new stockades had been put into use as a *chemin de ronde,* or sentry walk, and the only elevated firing platforms were located in the bastions. Small sentry boxes at the salients of the southeast and northwest bastions provided sheltered lookouts for the guard.[113] The four small bastions appear to have been retained from the earlier fort.

Thus, when the margins of the enclosure were moved out seven feet to create the *chemin de ronde*, bastion flanks originally fifteen feet in length were shortened to the paltry eight described disparagingly by Lotbinière.

Inside the stockade, the engineer charted the houses of the inhabitants with great care. Modern comparisons with the archaeological master map have demonstrated a remarkable accuracy. The name of each inhabitant or owner is written on the building, and the church and guardhouse are identified. "This fort contains 40 houses," wrote Lotbinière, "all very badly built. . . . Most of the houses are built of upright posts caulked inside and outside with clay. . . . Many are still covered with bark." Only a few of the better structures and the church were made of squared logs and roofed with boards.[114] The church, now named for St. Anne, was one of the newer buildings in the fort. It had been constructed around 1743 after the Jesuit priest moved the mission of St. Ignace to the new Ottawa village at L'Arbre Croche.[115]

The layout of the buildings within the stockade predated the expansion of the 1740s and is believed to be a feature of the previous decade.[116] Orderly rows of houses demonstrate a planned uniformity not found at Detroit during this period.[117] Nearly all the habitations at Michilimackinac were constructed as attached row houses with enclosed yards. These were laid out in two parallel east-west ranges on the south side of the fort and a single east-west line on the north. The open space between was maintained as a square or *place d'armes*, flanked on the east by a north-south row house and on the west by the church and residence of the priest. In the center of the square, spaced between gates in the north and south walls, stood a public *calvaire* or representation of the crucifixion that probably topped a well shown in later plans (see Figs. 2.2 and 2.3).

Beyond the walls of the fortified village Lotbinière shows only the enclosed yard of the Jesuits and a single stable and two ovens (*fours*) a short distance from the south gate. Interestingly, the "stable of M. Langlade" was placed with military necessity in mind—at an angle to the fort so that its sides could be flanked by gunfire from the bastions on the south wall. This would have prevented an enemy from taking shelter behind the building.

Very little information survives regarding changes that might have taken place at Michilimackinac following Lotbinière's departure and during the last twelve years of French control. No plan of the post is known until 1765 (Fig. 2.2), and that shows essentially the same arrangement of houses as on the 1749 map. Other than the removal or addition of a few structures, no significant reorganization of the buildings would take place before the British abandoned the mainland post in the 1780s.

One unintentional change occurred in 1751, when careless smokers set the guardhouse on fire. This is the structure shown by Lotbinière inside and to the left of the north gate (*corps de garde*). The building was soon repaired, with each voyageur then at the post contributing a picket, confirmation that the guardhouse was of the *poteaux en terre* (vertical picket) construction common to most of the houses at Michilimackinac. Since the rest of the fort was in need of repairs, Governor La Jonquière authorized the commandant to have it "enlarged on the Lake side" and to have a new guardhouse constructed.[118]

No documentation has been found to confirm that Fort Michilimackinac was further enlarged after 1751, but by the time it was mapped again in 1765 the outline of the stockade had been significantly expanded and altered into a truncated hexagon by the relocation of the north and south walls. These changes probably occurred late in the French regime and will be discussed with Figure 2.3.

Michel Chartier de Lotbinière (1723–98) had acquired considerable skill as a draftsman by the time he completed his plan of Michilimackinac in 1749. The colonial officer is perhaps best known for supervising the construction of Fort Ticonderoga in 1755. This portrait is a copy, by L. Duroingal, from an eighteenth-century original. *Library and Archives Canada (C-011236).*

Although bitter enemies of the French from 1712 until the 1730s, the Foxes were represented among the sixteen Native American nations that attended Michel Péan's great council at Michilimackinac in August 1754. Jonathan Carver encountered the Foxes in 1766 and included this copperplate engraving of a family group in his *Travels Through the Interior Parts of North America* (London, 1778). *Clements Library, University of Michigan.*

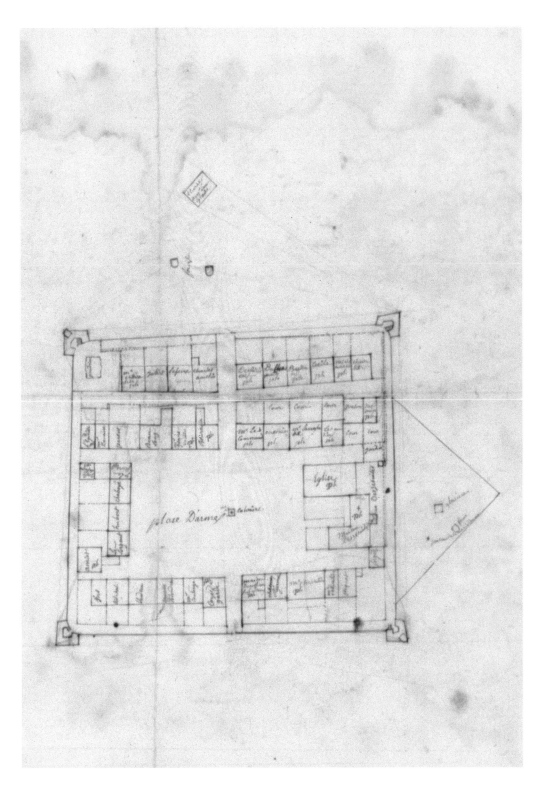

FIGURE 1.15

TITLE: [Plan of Michilimackinac]. [Detail].

AUTHOR: Ensign Michel Chartier de Lotbinière, Troupes de la Marine (1723–98).

DATE DEPICTED: October 1749.

DATE OF WORK: October 1749.

DESCRIPTION: 73 x 53.5 cm. Pen and ink on paper.

PROVENANCE: Drawn by Lotbinière during his time at Michilimackinac between September 22 and October 7, 1749. The map was presented to Governor La Galissonière upon Lotbinière's return to Québec late in October. Transferred to National Map Collection from Division of Manuscripts, October 23, 1974.

COLLECTION: Library and Archives Canada, Ottawa, ON (H2/1250-Michilimackinac-[1749]).

TRANSLATIONS OF SELECTED LABELS (LEFT TO RIGHT FROM TOP):

ecurie a Mr Landglade—Langlade's stable
fours—bake ovens
Mr Le Command—commandant
place D'armes—parade ground
calvaire—crucifix
Eglise—church
Maison des Jesuits—Jesuits' house
Forge—forge or blacksmith shop
glaciere—ice house
poteau de la meridienne—post of the meridian
Corps de garde—guardhouse
Maison des officiers subalterne—junior officers' house

Alexander Henry (1739–1824), as depicted in the frontispiece portrait of his *Travels and Adventures* of 1809. Peter Maverick engraved Henry's likeness from a portrait miniature. *Clements Library, University of Michigan.*

"A post of great consequence in this Upper Country"

1761–1796

Alexander Henry felt his apprehensions rising as his canoe set out from Isle aux Outardes.[1] It was September 1761, and ahead lay ten miles of open water to be traversed in the birch bark vessel. To the northwest was St. Martin Bay with its two low, forested islands. In the distance lay his goal, the island of Michilimackinac, its form resembling "a turtle's back" for which Henry was told it had been named. Soon after, a squall struck the canoe, and the voyageur paddlers were at the point

of throwing their cargo overboard to lighten the boat when the wind subsided as suddenly as it had arisen. The rest of the crossing was without incident.

The threats of nature had been overcome, but they were not the source of Alexander Henry's concern. On the island, he was told, was a "village of Chippeways" with one hundred warriors. Henry was the first Englishman to approach Michilimackinac since the governor of New France had surrendered his colony to British forces at Montréal in September 1760. A year had passed, but British soldiers had yet to occupy the fort at Michilimackinac. The first subject of King George III to enter the Straits of Mackinac was doing so disguised as a Canadian voyageur, his face and hair smeared with dirt and grease to obscure his complexion. Henry was eager to engage in the rich fur trade of the region despite the very real possibility that the Ottawa or Ojibwa would kill him on sight. France had surrendered Canada to Britain, but the Native Americans of the upper Great Lakes had yet to sign a treaty of peace and bury the hatchet of six years of bitter warfare.

Henry and his Canadian companions landed on the island, where the Ojibwas asked for the latest news. They were most interested to know whether "any Englishman was coming to Michilimackinac." Henry experienced a moment of panic as one warrior looked directly at him, laughed, and pointed him out to a friend. The Englishman feared that his disguise had been penetrated, but it proved to be a false alarm, and Henry never learned what had attracted the warrior's attention. The party was permitted to cross the Straits to the fortified French village on the south mainland.[2]

This was only the beginning of years of adventure for Alexander Henry at Michilimackinac and in the fur-trading lands of western Canada. The French residents of the post offered him a cordial welcome, although they were unanimous in advising that he "could not stay at Michilimackinac without the most imminent risk." It was not long before the Ojibwa learned that one of the despised Englishmen had slipped through their fingers. Henry was able to assuage them with presents and diplomacy. Then came word that the Ottawa of L'Arbre Croche would visit. Henry and two other British traders met with them several times over the next few days, spending their nights armed and barricaded in a house in fear for their lives. Finally, at noon on September 28, 1761, their apprehensions ended with the arrival of a large force of British troops from Detroit, who raised the Union flag and officially took possession of the post.[3]

So began thirty-five years of British occupation of the Straits of Mackinac. English-speaking traders like Henry soon joined the red-coated soldiers and came to dominate the operations of the Canadian fur trade. Most abandoned their former headquarters in Albany and adopted Montréal as the natural center of the commerce in pelts. The laborers of the fur trade and the inhabitants of posts such as Michilimackinac and Detroit, however, remained overwhelmingly French throughout the British regime. Guaranteed possession of their property and free practice of their religion by the 1760 articles of capitulation and, later, the Québec Act of 1774, most French-speaking Canadians made the transition with little difficulty. It was a situation with which British authorities were never entirely comfortable. Their soldiers watched over French populations in the forts and towns and large numbers of formerly hostile Native Americans in the surrounding forests. The troops distrusted these potential local enemies as they stood guard against more distant threats such as a resurgent France and Spain, and, eventually, their own American colonists.

Alexander Henry and Lieutenant William Leslye, Fort Michilimackinac's first British commandant, found the post little changed from the way it had been depicted by Ensign Lotbinière in 1749. Henry counted thirty houses within the stockade, "neat in their appearance, and tolerably commodious; and a church, in which mass is celebrated, by a Jesuit missionary." He thought the number of resident families might have been equal to the number of houses, though this was probably something of an exaggeration. The fur trade provided the economic lifeblood of the post. "Michilimackinac is the place of deposit, and point of departure, between the upper countries and the lower," Henry wrote in his recollections. "Here the outfits are prepared for the countries of Lake Michigan and the Missisipi, Lake Superior and the north-west; and here, the returns in furs, are collected, and embarked for Montréal."[4] His summary of the role of Michilimackinac would remain apt throughout its years as a British post and well into the nineteenth century.

Events of the two years following the arrival of Henry and Leslye showed that the extension of British sovereignty into the Great Lakes was a perilous enterprise. From Michilimackinac, small detachments of soldiers occupied tiny forts at Sault Ste. Marie, Green Bay, and St. Joseph near the foot of Lake Michigan. Trade resumed under the new order. But misunderstandings of the culture and the needs of Native Americans by British administrators and traders soon soured relations. By the spring of 1763 the West was ready to explode in a general Indian war. Over the next few months nearly every British post would be attacked, and nine would either fall or be abandoned.[5]

"The Pickets of the Fort were all repaired or New, as well as the Powder Magazine, a very few Years ago; I am Sorry to hear already that they are decayed and Rotten." GENERAL THOMAS GAGE

Michilimackinac's turn came on June 2. Large numbers of Ojibwa and Sacs had gathered at the post, where they daily played baggatiway, a form of lacrosse. Lieutenant Leslye and Captain George Etherington, commandant since the summer of 1762, stood just outside the open gate of the fort to watch the fun. It was all over in a moment. "They came up behind us, seized and carried us into the woods," Etherington rather sheepishly reported. Then the players rushed into the fort "where they found their squaws, whom they had previously planted there, with their hatchets hid under their blankets." Lieutenant John Jamet, nineteen soldiers, and a trader named Tracy died in the assault. Alexander Henry had chosen not to watch the game and was writing letters when he heard "an Indian war-cry and a noise of general confusion." From his window he saw the Ojibwas "furiously cutting down and scalping every Englishman they found." Henry and Ezekiel Solomon, another trader, both sought shelter in the garrets of Michilimackinac's French inhabitants.[6]

During the next few days the efforts of the inhabitants of Michilimackinac, Jesuit missionary Father Du Jaunay, and, ultimately, the Ottawa of L'Arbre Croche saved the lives of most of the British who had survived the initial onslaught. Many were returned to Montréal later that summer along with the garrison of Fort Edward Augustus at Green Bay, which had been abandoned as untenable. Alexander Henry had a more extended adventure with the family of his Ojibwa friend Wawatam, who had personally rescued him from his captors.[7]

It was September 1764 before troops could reoccupy the post at the Straits of Mackinac, which Captain Etherington had entrusted to the care of former French officer Charles Langlade.[8] At Michilimackinac, as at Detroit and the other posts around the Great Lakes, the events of 1763 were long remembered. Special care was taken by British garrisons thereafter to maintain fortifications and exclude

Native Americans at night. Fifteen years after the attack, trader John Long reported a standing order at Michilimackinac that "no Indian should be permitted to enter the fort with fire-arms; nor any squaw or Indian woman, allowed to sleep within the walls of the garrison on any pretence whatever." Sentries were doubled during Indian councils.[9] Similar measures remained in effect at Detroit into the 1790s.[10]

Another legacy of the Indian uprising was an increasing militarization of Michilimackinac. The garrison that returned in 1764 was twice the size of the one surprised by the Ojibwa. Despite later attempts at troop reductions, Michilimackinac and its successor post on Mackinac Island would usually be occupied by at least two companies of British soldiers. After 1764 the army required more space within the fortified village, where houses were at first rented from the inhabitants before a purpose-built barracks separated the troops from the civilian population after 1769.[11] Beginning around 1764–65 many civilians, both French and British, began to relocate to houses in an unfortified suburb east of the fort. This was probably a reaction to the increased demand for space by the military and the restrictions placed on contact with Native Americans.[12]

Peace brought a resumption of trade and more enlightened policies with regard to Native Americans. Although concerned with the security of the posts and the prevention of another uprising, British soldiers were increasingly seen as a police force to curb the excesses of the traders. The commandants of Michilimackinac were active in efforts to keep the peace between Native American nations of the West, where warfare among tribes such as the Ojibwa and Dakota meant an expensive disruption of trade. Peacekeeping, commerce, and exploration sometimes went together, such as during the command of Major Robert Rogers in 1766–67, when he dispatched Jonathan Carver to learn more about the country along the upper Mississippi River.[13] Rogers's interest in finding a "Northwest Passage" across the continent utilized Michilimackinac as its base until he found himself charged with treason and arrested late in 1767.[14]

Throughout the 1760s and 1770s, the commandants of Michilimackinac also fought a constant battle to preserve a sprawling, wooden fort filled with perishable and flammable buildings. The work never seemed to end. Much of the stockade was reconstructed during 1764–65, but only ten years later the rot was so advanced that the powerful winds of the Straits "blew down half a Curtain of Pickets broke short with the surface of the earth."[15] A whole list of garrison improvements was projected late in 1765, but expense and the difficulty of obtaining materials and skilled labor caused progress to be made at a snail's pace. A barracks was finally constructed in 1769–70; the officers' quarters were rebuilt in 1770; the powder magazine was repaired in 1772; and a badly needed provisions storehouse was completed a year later. To General Thomas Gage in New York, deeply concerned about the expenses of his North American command, the demands must have seemed unceasing. His responses to reports of deterioration were often like that expressed to Captain George Turnbull in 1770: "The Pickets of the Fort were all repaired or New, as well as the Powder Magazine, a very few Years ago; I am Sorry to hear already that they are decayed and Rotten."[16]

Captain Arent S. DePeyster was in command of this wretched fortress in the early summer of 1774 when he received word from General Gage that fighting had broken out in the province of Massachusetts between the king's troops and his colonial subjects. Further communication with Gage's headquarters in Boston would be impossible, so DePeyster was directed to take his orders from Governor Guy Carleton at Québec.[17] Michilimackinac was about to resume its earlier wartime role as guardian of trade, diplomatic contact point with Native American allies, and source of warriors for fighting in distant theaters. This time, however, it would be British soldiers guarding the post against the rebels of their own colonies.

This was to be Michilimackinac's role in the American Revolution. Although at first the British restrained their Indian allies, by 1776 post commandants in the West were ordered to solicit their active military assistance. Experienced partisan leaders such as Charles Langlade were called into service once again, and warriors from Michilimackinac participated in John Burgoyne's ill-fated Saratoga campaign in 1777. In 1778 the war took a different turn as a small force of Virginians under George Rogers Clark invaded the Illinois country and, in February 1779, cut off and captured Detroit's lieutenant governor, Henry Hamilton, at Vincennes in Indiana. From that point, Michilimackinac was on the front line of a long-distance wilderness war where enemy raiders might approach either from southern Lake Michigan or by way of a successful operation against British-held Detroit.[18]

The increased possibility of attack drew greater attention to the fortifications and the position of the post at Michilimackinac. Earlier commandants had described the vulnerability of the site and suggested that it should be relocated, but it was not until the arrival of Lieutenant Governor Patrick Sinclair in October 1779 that any action was taken. Sinclair had fought in America during the French and Indian War and then spent several years commanding a military sailing vessel on Lake Huron. He then obtained one of the appointments as a lieutenant governor authorized under the Québec Act of 1774.[19] Just before his arrival at Michilimackinac, Sinclair paused to examine Mackinac Island, a place with which he was probably quite familiar from his previous service. A few days later, he endorsed the concept of relocating the fort and the civilian community there.

The move appears to have already been approved in principle, for progress was amazingly swift. By the summer of 1780 a fort was under construction on the bluff overlooking the harbor at the southeastern end of the island of Michilimackinac. Ste. Anne's Church had been dismantled and moved, and many residents were rebuilding their houses on lots along the beach below Sinclair's new fort. Several of the more substantial garrison buildings were transported from "Old" Michilimackinac during the winter of 1781, and by summer the garrison had occupied the new, though incomplete fortification. The remnants of the mainland fort and town were either burned or allowed to deteriorate in the sandy soil.

Like its predecessor, the fort on the island of Michilimackinac would never quite be finished, for it suffered from many of the same problems. There were never enough laborers or materials, and the harsh climate meant that the building season was limited.[20] And then there was the expense, both for construction and for the large quantities of trade goods that had to be purchased and distributed to keep the Indians friendly to British interests. It was cost control that brought Patrick Sinclair down in September 1782, after an inspection of the post found "great abuses and neglect."[21] Sinclair was relieved and went to Québec to answer for his debts. The new fort of Michilimackinac was patched up to make it defensible.

Within a year the war was over. Much to the astonishment of British officers and traders, not to mention the Native Americans who inhabited the land, the boundary line separating the new United States from British North America was drawn through the Great Lakes, placing the Straits of Mackinac firmly within the territory of the former. Not surprisingly, Governor Frederick Haldimand ordered work to cease on the still incomplete island fort.[22] Captain Daniel Robertson, Sinclair's successor, was further ordered to seek a replacement site, this time on the British side of the new border. He found one at the mouth of the Thessalon River, just east of the St. Marys. His search proved to be premature, however, for only two months later, in August 1784, Robertson received other orders. British officials had decided that the posts on the U.S. side of the boundary would "not be given up as soon as expected, until the Americans manifest a stronger Inclination (than they have hitherto done) to fulfil on their part, the Articles of the Definitive Treaty."[23] The status of the post of Michilimackinac would remain unresolved for the next twelve years, a boon to British traders who continued to operate unimpeded from a base located within the United States. For the garrison, however, the situation meant that the incomplete fort would be maintained only to the extent necessary to provide basic shelter and security.

This uncertain state of affairs existed into the 1790s. Not only were the British unwilling to give up the posts on the American side of the line, but the Native American nations of the Great Lakes and the Ohio country were prepared to continue a war in which they had been neither defeated nor represented in peace negotiations. The small U.S. Army was fully occupied during those years in establishing and defending forts along the Ohio River. Large-scale American military incursions toward Detroit in 1790 and 1791 caused alarm in Canada and at the contested posts, but both efforts ended in defeat.

Events at a distance would finally bring an end to British control of the Straits of Mackinac. In 1793 Britain became involved in a European war with revolutionary France. The distraction of an American conflict was not to be contemplated, and fitful negotiations to end the diplomatic impasse were renewed. These resulted in Jay's Treaty of 1794, which provided solutions for the problems of the 1783 treaty and opened the way for the transfer of the Great Lakes posts.[24] Meanwhile, in August 1794, American forces under Major General Anthony Wayne won a decisive victory over the Indians at Fallen Timbers in northern Ohio. Leaders of the Native American coalition made peace with the Treaty of Greenville the following summer. Although ratification of Jay's Treaty was delayed until the winter of 1796, it did not prevent the transfer of the posts that summer. On September 1, Major Henry Burbeck took possession of the fort of Michilimackinac from its caretaker garrison of British soldiers.

BRITISH COMMANDANTS OF MICHILIMACKINAC, 1761–1796

Captain Henry Balfour, 80th Regiment of Foot, 1761

Lieutenant William Leslye, 1/60th Regiment of Foot, 1761–62

Captain George Etherington, 1/60th Regiment of Foot, 1762–63

Post unoccupied June 1763–September 1764

Captain William Howard, 17th Regiment of Foot, 1764–66

Major Robert Rogers, superintendent, 1766–67

Captain-Lieutenant Frederick Spiesmacher, 2/60th Regiment of Foot, 1767–68

Captain Beamsley Glazier, 2/60th Regiment of Foot, 1768–70

Captain George Turnbull, 2/60th Regiment of Foot, 1770–72

Captain John Vattas, 10th Regiment of Foot, 1772–75

Captain Arent Schuyler DePeyster, 8th Regiment of Foot, 1774–79

Lieutenant Governor Patrick Sinclair, 1/84th Regiment of Foot, 1779–82

Captain Daniel Robertson, 1/84th Regiment of Foot, 1782–87

Captain Thomas Scott, 53rd Regiment of Foot, 1787–88

Captain Alexander Malcolm, 65th Regiment of Foot, 1788–89

Captain John Parr, 2/60th Regiment of Foot, 1789–90

Captain Edward Charlton, 5th Regiment of Foot, 1790–92

Captain William Doyle, 24th Regiment of Foot, 1792–96

Lieutenant Andrew Foster, 24th Regiment of Foot, 1796

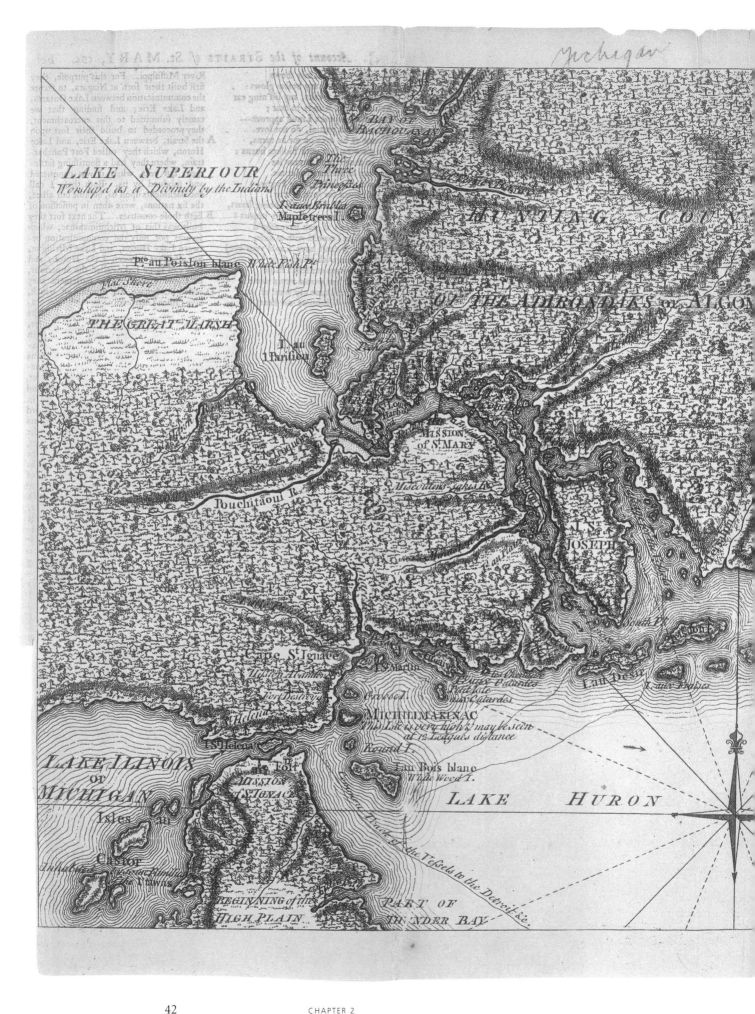

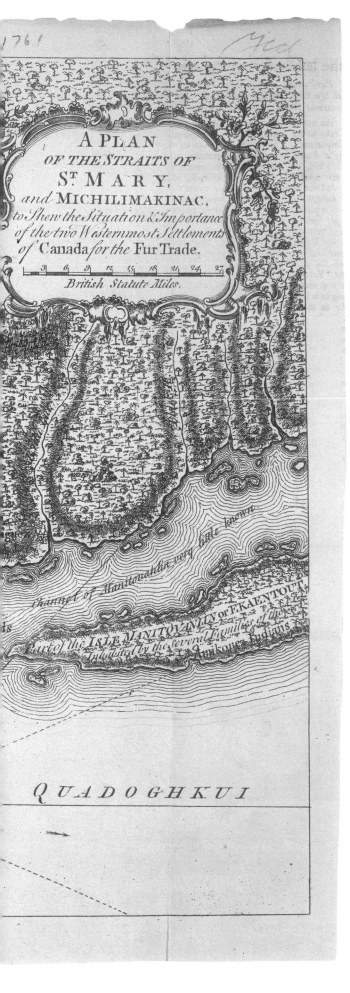

FIGURE 2.1

TITLE: A Plan of the Straits of St. Mary and
Michilimakinac, to Shew the Situation &
Importance of the two Westernmost Settlements
of Canada for the Fur Trade.
AUTHOR: After Jacques-Nicolas Bellin (1703–72).
DATE DEPICTED: 1761 [1716–42].
DATE OF WORK: February 1761.
DESCRIPTION: 24 x 33.1 cm. Copperplate
engraving.
PROVENANCE: Engraved and published in
*The London Magazine: Or, Gentleman's Monthly
Intelligencer* (London: February 1761), facing [64].
COLLECTION: Clements Library, University of
Michigan, Ann Arbor (Range 22, Wheat Box A).

The fort stands on the south side of the strait ... between Lake Huron and Lake Michigan

Alexander Henry

It is just possible that Alexander Henry had seen the February issue of *The London Magazine* by the time he left Montréal for Michilimackinac on August 3, 1761. If so, he might have studied a map that could serve as a guide to his adventures over the next three years. The magazine carried a brief (and incomplete) article titled "A short Account of the Straits of St. Mary, and Michilimakinac," illustrated by the map included here as Figure 2.1.[25]

Canada, including the Michilimackinac region, had been a prize of the British Empire for less than five months by the time this map was printed. No Englishmen had yet had the opportunity to visit the Straits, other than as prisoners of war carried there by Ottawa or Ojibwa warriors. Alexander Henry, a few fellow traders, and the first red-coated soldiers would not arrive until September 1761. Certainly, there had been no opportunity for any sort of British cartographic survey to be undertaken before February of that year. The conquest of New France was a popular topic that winter, however, and the reading public of England and the colonies was hungry for information about Britain's newest American possession.

Drawing on previously published French works could satisfy that demand. The most useful of these was Father Pierre-François-Xavier de Charlevoix's *Histoire et description générale de la Nouvelle France,* which had been in print since 1744. Although an English translation appeared sometime in 1761, probably for the same reasons that motivated the item in *The London Magazine,* the earlier French edition most likely served as the source of the unnamed author's information.[26] The map folded into *The London Magazine* was largely copied from Jacques-Nicolas Bellin's *Carte du Détroit entre le Lac Superieur et le Lac Huron* (Fig. 1.14), which had appeared in the 1744 French editions of Charlevoix's *Histoire.* The 1761 English translation of the Jesuit priest's account of his travels did not include a map of the Straits of Mackinac.

It was probably Figure 2.1 that introduced most contemporary English-speaking readers to the geography of northern Lake Huron and its connections to Lakes Superior and Michigan. A map of the Straits had appeared only once before in an English-language publication, the 1703 translation of Lahontan's *New Voyages to North-America* (Fig. 1.11). It had focused on the immediate vicinity of the French post of Michilimackinac, however, and it lacked the broader context of the 1761 map, which emphasized the relationship of the Straits to the lakes around it and stressed the importance of these water routes to the fur trade. The accompanying article explained that the French had established Fort Michilimackinac for "protecting the communication between the several great Lakes of

Canada, and also their communication between the River St. Laurence, and the River Missisippi."[27]

The London engraver who adapted Bellin's seventeen-year-old cartography made relatively few substantive changes or additions, although the look of the 1761 map is very different than that of its French source. The inclusion of largely imaginary topography and figures of trees representing the thick forests of northern Michigan clutters the composition and makes it more difficult to read than the crisp Bellin map of 1744. There are a few additions, most of which were taken from larger-scale maps of the Great Lakes. Coverage of the Straits extends farther to both the west and the east. The northern part of Lake Michigan is included, along with the Beaver Islands, noted as the home of some of the Ottawas, but their village since 1742 at L'Arbre Croche is not identified. Somewhat more of the south coast of Lake Superior appears, and to the east the map incorporates much of Manitoulin Island.

Details of the Straits come directly from the 1744 Bellin map, including the apocryphal "Grosse I" to the north of the island of Michilimackinac. Round and Bois Blanc islands are shown in relatively accurate proportion to each other, though without any realistic detail. The former mission and fort on the north shore of the Straits are identified, as is the newer post on the south mainland. The second mission of St. Ignace is shown just to the west of Fort Michilimackinac, however, another anachronism since the Ottawa and their church had relocated nearly twenty years earlier.

It was into these troubled waters that Alexander Henry launched his canoe from Isle aux Outardes in September 1761. His first stop was the island of Michilimackinac, where the Ojibwa had a summer village. The island had not been a part of their territory when the French had first come to the Straits. As late as 1736 the Ojibwa—generally known to the French as the Sauteurs—were associated with Sault Ste. Marie and lands to the north. By the summer of 1747, however, these people had a regular, seasonal presence on the island of Michilimackinac.[28] An Ojibwa fishing village would remain a feature of the place until the British purchased it in 1781.

Henry's 1761 visit was very brief, but he returned nearly two years later as a captive and ward of his Ojibwa friend Wawatam. On June 9, having overwhelmed the British garrison a week earlier, the Ojibwas decided to retire to the island of Michilimackinac. As they neared the imposing bluffs, Henry was startled to hear the women in his canoe begin to "utter melancholy and hideous cries," which he soon learned was a traditional lamentation when nearing the burial place of relatives. The large party of Ojibwas landed that evening, and the women quickly erected their lodges. This temporary village soon contained 350 warriors and several times that number of women and children.[29]

After a few days of relative security, Alexander Henry again found his life in jeopardy when the Ojibwas discovered liquor in some captured canoes. Wawatam, concerned about what might happen once intoxication engulfed the village, led his friend into the island, where Henry was the first to describe one of its now-famous rock formations. Climbing up the bluff from the village, he noted that the ground was "thickly covered with wood, and very rocky toward the top." The pair walked for about half a mile and came to "a large rock, at the base of which was an opening, dark within, and appearing to be the entrance of a cave." The cavity was about ten feet wide, and Henry "found the further end to be rounded in its shape, like that of an oven, but with a further aperture, too small, however, to be explored."

This would be his hiding place for the night. In the morning, however, Henry "discovered, with some feelings of horror, that I was lying on nothing less than a heap of human bones and skulls, which covered all the floor!" His second night was spent under a nearby bush. Wawatam appeared the next morning to retrieve his friend. The warrior was unaware of the bones in the cave, so the two explored it together, the first of many tourists to do so. Word of their discovery soon spread through the Ojibwa village and a steady stream of people visited the cave and offered differing theories for the presence of the bones. Henry, influenced by his own recent experiences, chose to believe that the cave was "an ancient receptacle of the bones of prisoners, sacrificed and devoured at war-feasts."[30] The cavern would next be described in 1802 simply as a cave "in the side of the hill," but the publication of Henry's *Travels and Adventures*, in 1809, gave the natural feature an interesting historical context. Henry Schoolcraft was the first to associate the cave with Alexander Henry's adventures when he visited Mackinac Island in 1820, and tourists would seek bones there for many years after.[31]

Alexander Henry visited many of the other places shown on the 1761 *London Magazine* map of the Mackinac region. He spent the winter of 1762 at Fort Michilimackinac and then set out in May to trade at Sault Ste. Marie. Henry found the tiny stockade there "seated on a beautiful plain, of about two miles in circumference, and covered with luxuriant grass." The rapids of the St. Marys River were "beset with rocks of the most dangerous description," but they contained whitefish that were even "more excellent than those of Michilimack- inac."[32] Destruction of the fort there by fire on December 22 sent Henry on a winter's trek back to Michilimackinac, where he witnessed the capture of the post the following June. Although first taken by his captors toward the Beaver (Castor) Islands, Henry and his fellow prisoners were returned to the fort after the intervention of the Ottawas, and from there he went on to his adventure at Skull Cave.

Not long after, Minweweh, "the great chief of the village of Michilimackinac" and architect of the plan to capture the fort, expressed concern for Henry's continued safety. Wawatam's family again disguised him, this time as an Indian, and they set out to fish and hunt on the Bay of Boutchitaouy (St. Martin Bay). His next stop was one of the St. Martin islands, where they fished for sturgeon and enjoyed "a plentiful and excellent supply of food." Late in August, Henry and his adoptive family headed south to winter hunting grounds along the Big Sable River on Lake Michigan. The following spring saw his return to the Straits, the Sault, and eventually down Georgian Bay and overland to Lake Ontario and the British post of Fort Niagara, where he arrived on June 10, 1764.[33] By that time, Alexander Henry had visited nearly every landmark on the 1761 *London Magazine* map of the Straits of Mackinac.

Captain George Etherington (1722 or 1723–1802) commanded Michilimackinac at the time of its capture by the Ojibwa in 1763. He continued his long career in the Royal American Regiment and is shown here in a portrait of about 1787, attributed to John Trotter of Dublin, Ireland. *Regimental Museum, The Royal Green Jackets, Winchester, England.*

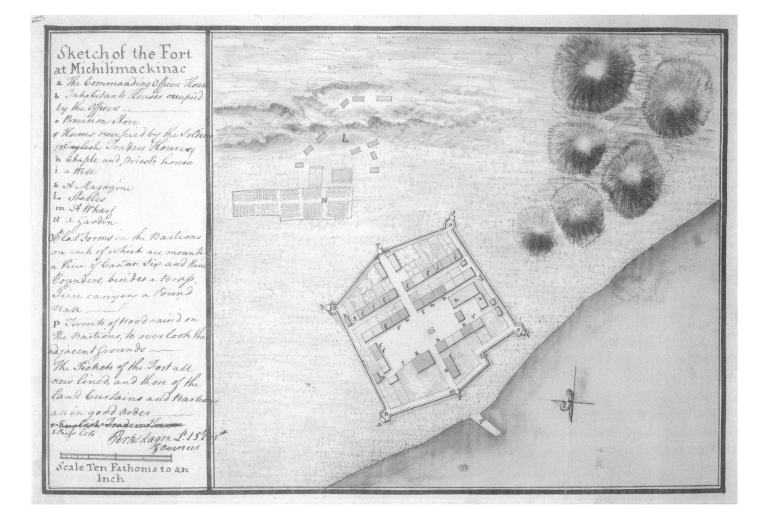

FIGURE 2.2

TITLE: Sketch of the Fort at Michilimackinac.

AUTHOR: Lieutenant Perkins Magra, 15th Regiment of Foot (active 1760–1800; probably d. 1826).

DATE DEPICTED: Summer 1765.

DATE OF WORK: [1765].

DESCRIPTION: 21 x 31.8 cm. Pen and ink with watercolor on paper.

PROVENANCE: Retained in the papers of General Thomas Gage. The papers were purchased by William L. Clements in 1930 and acquired by the Clements Library in 1937.

COLLECTION: Clements Library, University of Michigan, Ann Arbor (Map Division, 6-N-8).

This place is not so bad as represented

Captain William Howard

Alexander Henry returned to Michilimackinac on September 22, 1764, this time openly in the guise of a British trader. He traveled with Captain William Howard and two companies of His Majesty's 17th Regiment of Foot. Perhaps even more impressive to the Indians was the presence of French Canadian volunteers serving as part of this tiny army. They were drawn from the militia of Detroit, and the message was clear. These longtime allies of the Ojibwa and Ottawa would not rise against their British king. The war was over. The Ottawas of L'Arbre Croche were summoned to the fort, and they brought a few Ojibwa chiefs as well, though Henry made no mention of his friend and benefactor, Wawatam. The visitors were ready for peace—Minweweh and the hostile Ojibwas had removed themselves farther west.[34]

Captain Howard had the task of reoccupying Michilimackinac and putting the place "in the best posture of Defence," in as frugal a manner as possible.[35] This would become a familiar admonition to Michilimackinac's commandants as they labored to preserve their wooden defenses against the elements. Howard was pleasantly surprised to find the fort relatively intact. "What part the Indians had destroy'd," he reported, "the Inhabitants had repair'd." The aging stockade was unserviceable in his eyes, however, and the commandant anticipated the need to replace its pickets within the year. Howard set his men to work. Aided by mild weather, the garrison rebuilt some of the bastions and prepared several of the inhabitants' houses for use as quarters, even dismantling three in order to repair them. Although the post had many needs,

particularly decent barracks, the captain optimistically reported, "This place is not so bad as represented."[36]

Howard made numerous demands, of course, for things necessary to accomplish the work at hand. He needed horses to haul pickets, timber, and firewood, additional artillery to bolster the defenses, more men to carry on the work, and barracks to house them properly. With his soldiers quartered in private dwellings, Howard also inquired whether the owners were entitled to rent.[37] His requests were duly forwarded to Major General Thomas Gage, commander of British forces in North America. Gage had questions of his own, and he was most concerned that commandants at Detroit and Michilimackinac should not set the precedent of paying rent for the use of private buildings. In the case of Michilimackinac, the general replied that he had assumed that the place already had a barracks, but that he had "never received any Plan or Report of the Situation of that Post."[38] Gage then requested a plan and carefully specified that he wanted it to show the "Situation, Defence, Barracks, or other Lodgements for the Troops" along with recommendations for whatever else might be necessary for the "Conveniency and Safety" of the garrison.[39]

Gage's order resulted in the plan reproduced here as Figure 2.2, Lieutenant Perkins Magra's "Sketch of the Fort at Michilimackinac." This small but colorful and precisely detailed work was found among the general's papers when William L. Clements purchased them in 1930. Although it was one of the most important visual documents used to support the reconstruction of Fort Michilimackinac in the

Habit of a Woman of the interior parts of North America

After British troops reoccupied Michilimackinac, Native Americans were not allowed within the walls during the hours of darkness. This did not prevent traders from attempting to smuggle female companions past the sentries. In 1779 John Long was caught rolling a barrel containing two Indian women through the gate. Their appearance was probably much like this young woman depicted by a contemporary European engraver. *Mackinac State Historic Parks, MI (1985.102.1).*

late 1950s, the "Magra" plan has always presented historians with a conundrum regarding its creation and purpose. The Magra map has long been assumed to be a different composition than that requested by Gage in 1765 and delivered to him by Captain Harry Gordon late that year. This is because Magra's undated plan was assigned a creation date of 1766, too late to be the one given to Gage the previous autumn. There is, however, no evidence in either Gage's papers or on the plan itself to suggest that it was drawn in 1766, and the date appears to have been assigned by the Clements Library.[40] The plan is signed simply: "Perks Magra Lt. 15th Regt g overseer."

Lieutenant Colonel John Campbell had received Gage's request at Detroit on August 25, 1765, and assured the general that "As soon as I can procure a plan of Michilimakinack I shall transmit it to your Excellency." That could not be done until an engineer was able to make his way to the Straits.[41] Fortunately, Captain Harry Gordon was on the lakes that summer, supervising repairs to Fort Niagara, from which he departed for Detroit on August 27.[42] Once at Detroit, Gordon found himself fully occupied with inspecting the barracks building there and completing a survey and census of the settlement. He seems to have finished his work around September 15 and was back in Albany, by way of Niagara, before October 21.[43] There is no evidence that he visited Michilimackinac or, indeed, that he had had the time to do so. Nonetheless, Colonel Campbell reported to Gage on October 14 that "Capt Gordon has got a Plan of Michilimakinak, with a particular account of its Situation Defences Barracks &c and in what condition everything is at the Post, and what is wanting for the conveniency & safety of the Troops."[44] This has come to be known as the "Gordon" plan, and historians of Michilimackinac have sought it for years.[45]

If Captain Gordon had not personally conducted a survey of Michilimackinac, what was the source of the plan that he had "got"? It seems reasonable to suppose that he got it from Lieutenant Magra, who, as "g[arrison] overseer," was responsible for engineering work at the post. He very likely prepared a plan at Campbell's or Gordon's orders and then sent it to Detroit in time for the engineer to present it to General Gage at New York. The absence of a covering letter with Magra's plan suggests that it had been personally delivered.

Perkins Magra was a young man of promise, probably from the American colonies or the West Indies, who studied at the College and Academy of Philadelphia in 1760–61. Founded by Benjamin Franklin, the school taught the "practical as well as the ornamental," including surveying and drawing.[46] Magra accepted a commission in the 17th Regiment of Foot in October 1761 and probably accompanied Captain Howard to Michilimackinac in the fall of 1764.[47] Ambitious for promotion, he obtained a lieutenancy in the 15th Regiment of Foot in January 1765, accounting for the use of that rank and unit in his signature on the plan.[48] Despite promotion into a regiment then stationed at Québec, Magra remained at Michilimackinac for a time, where he accompanied trader John Porteous on a trip to L'Arbre Croche in August 1765. He probably

drew his plan during August or September. Magra's relief finally arrived on October 15, though it is uncertain whether he departed on the return trip of the vessel four days later.[49] He must have left Michilimackinac before winter set in because, on April 17, 1766, "Lieut. Magra" delivered a letter from Sir William Johnson to General Gage in New York.[50] Perkins Magra could not have been at Michilimackinac during 1766.

Evidence within the plan itself does not dispute a 1765 date. Magra's descriptions of the stockade and its bastions are consistent with their known condition by the late summer of that year. Captain Howard and his men had enthusiastically tackled the repairs needed to their fort, despite their small numbers, and by January 1765 they had rebuilt two bastions and projected completion of work on the other two by sometime in the spring.[51] Comments on Magra's map suggest that the bastions were in good order and that the stockade had been "new lined," that is, smaller pickets had been placed in the gaps between the larger ones to reinforce them and fill in gaps. This is work that could well have been completed with limited means during 1765.

In preparing his map, Lieutenant Magra took great care to differentiate the use of the buildings within the fort. Colonel Campbell reported that the 1765 "Gordon" map provided "a particular account of its Situation Defences Barracks &c." Magra achieved this visually in two ways: by a key and by color. Letters identify buildings used by the garrison or by "English traders." With only one exception, these are colored carmine. Thirteen unidentified structures, presumably still occupied by French inhabitants, are shaded a light pink, while the church and priest's house are gray. This color code would have quickly informed General Gage of the facilities available to the troops.

A "Report of Work wanted to be done at the Fort of Michilimakinac" was sent to Gage from Detroit on November 1, 1765. This, too, supports a 1765 date for the Magra plan. The report proposed building barracks for the officers and men, who are shown scattered in eight and six houses, respectively, on Magra's plan. Although a powder magazine and provisions storehouse existed, the report requested replacement of both as well as construction of an ordnance storehouse and a new and larger guardhouse. A wharf is shown on Magra's plan, and the written request for one probably reflected a needed replacement rather than completely new construction. The Magra plan describes the "land curtains" or walls as being in "good Order," and the fourteen hundred pickets requested in the November 1 report "to compleat the Stockades of the Fort" would have sufficed to repair the lake-side walls.[52]

One final item in the November 1, 1765, report is graphically illustrated on Magra's plan: "Several small Hills near the Fort, that serve as a Cover to an Enemy to be Levelled." The dunes southwest of the walls presented a chronic problem that had been noted by Ensign Lotbinière as early as 1749. Michilimackinac was known for its sandy soil.[53] In 1767 trader John Porteous complained that the "soft small sand" was "intollerably troublesome, both for filling the Shoes & blowing in the Eyes & crevices of houses &c."[54] This was more than an annoyance for the garrison since the shifting hills might allow an enemy to approach the walls without being seen. Every British commandant expressed concern, but the problem could not be solved. "The Drifts from those Hills are like snow Drifts, which we are after every storm obliged to remove," complained Captain Arent S. DePeyster in 1779.[55] The dunes were a factor in the decision to relocate the fort to the island of Michilimackinac later that year. They particularly worried Lieutenant Governor Patrick Sinclair in 1780 when the garrison was at its most vulnerable while making the move. Sinclair even planned, in case American forces suddenly appeared, to construct a defensive work on the commanding dunes to protect the southwestern side of his partially dismantled fort.[56]

Lieutenant Magra's sketch is, in fact, the "Gordon" plan of 1765. As such, it depicts Michilimackinac one year after the return of British troops and before they had begun to replace or construct new garrison buildings.

Captain William Howard would have dressed in similar fashion to this unidentified officer of the 17th Regiment of Foot, depicted about 1764. Howard commanded Michilimackinac from 1764 to 1766. *Courtesy of Bruce Baky.*

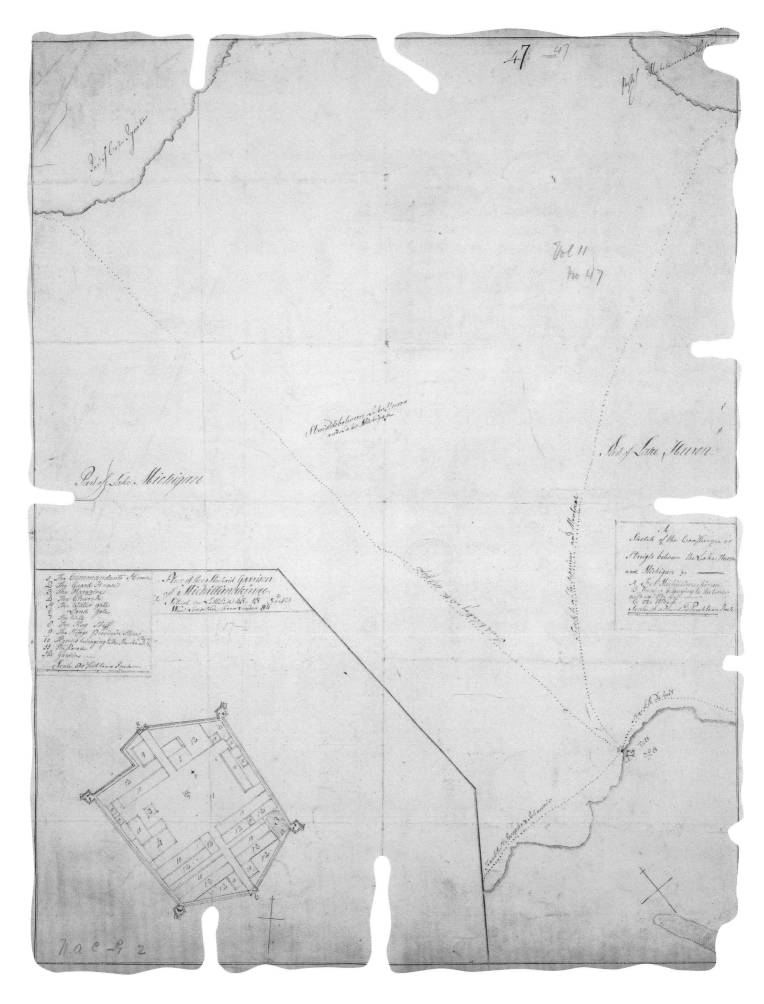

A convenient situation to traffic with the neighbouring Indians

Jonathan Carver

On an early summer's day in 1775 Michilimackinac stirred to news that a flotilla of canoes was approaching from Lake Michigan. This was a common enough occurrence, but it never failed to infuse a sense of excitement into the village. This fleet carried a trader named Peter Pond, who left his account of its arrival in his own colorful orthography. "We all apeard on the Lake about five Miles from Macenac and Approacht in Order," he recalled. "We had flags on the Masts of our Canoes—Eavery Chefe his flock." Pond's vessel sported a large British Union flag, which he hoisted when he was within a mile and a half of the post. The fort raised its colors in turn and "ye Cannon of the Garreson Began to Play Smartley." A crowd gathered on the beach. Their shouts and "hooping" set off a similar reaction in the approaching canoes, and soon "you Could not Hear a Parson Speak." Pond and the Indians came ashore in the midst of this tumult.[57]

Peter Pond was only one of many British traders who followed in the footsteps of Alexander Henry in the decade after the great Indian uprising. Like his fellow traders and thousands of Native Americans, Pond used the waterways of Canada and the Great Lakes to move goods and furs between the lands west and north of

Michilimackinac and the warehouses of Montréal. Canoes, powered by Canadian voyageurs or engagés, provided most of the transport. The routes they traveled had changed little in nearly 150 years.

The importance of the Straits of Mackinac to this movement of furs and goods is neatly expressed in Figure 2.3, which was probably drawn sometime between 1766 and 1769. The map includes a wealth of local detail, including an inset plan of the fort itself at lower left. Most telling, however, is the convergence of four water routes at the post on the south shore of the Straits. Michilimackinac's location made it, in the words of Jonathan Carver, "a convenient situation to traffic with the neighbouring Indians."[58] The major courses to and from Michilimackinac are shown by dotted lines. The "Track to Detroit" followed the Lake Huron coast of Michigan to Niagara and Montréal. The "Track to Lake Superior and Montreal" crossed open water to the island of Michilimackinac before traversing Lake Huron past Isle aux Outardes (Goose Island) to the Detour passage. There, travelers could continue up the St. Marys River into Lake Superior or turn east on the established French River canoe route to Canada. The "Track to St. Josephs and Isleanois" led down Lake Michigan past the Ottawa village at L'Arbre Croche to the Illinois country. The "Track

FIGURE 2.3

TITLE: A Sketch of the Confluance or Streigts between the Lakes Huron and Michigan &c. [Inset:] Plan of the Stockaid Garrison of Michilimakinac. Situate in Lattitude 45 [degrees] 15' North & West Longitude from London 84 [degrees]. [On verso (in areas not covered by the backing):] Sketch of Mitchilmackanack New York N. 9. [and] Scetch of the Straits between Lakes Huron & Michigan.
AUTHOR: Unknown but possibly Lieutenant Diedrich Brehm, 2/60th (Royal American) Regiment of Foot (active 1756–after 1786).
DATE DEPICTED: 1766–69.
DATE OF WORK: [1766–69].
DESCRIPTION: 59 x 46.5 cm. Pen and ink on paper.
PROVENANCE: Unknown other than its association with the records of the Colonial Office.
COLLECTION: National Archives, Kew, London (C.O. 700 North American Colonies General No. 2).

Jonathan Carver (1710–80) was dispatched by Robert Rogers to explore the region north and west of Lake Michigan in the hope of finding evidence of a northwest passage. Carver is seen here in the frontispiece portrait of the 1781 edition of his *Travels Through the Interior Parts of North America*.

Clements Library, University of Michigan.

to LaBay and the Mississipi" braved the width of the Straits to follow the south shore of Michigan's Upper Peninsula to Green Bay and the Fox-Wisconsin river route to the Mississippi.

Canoes regularly traversed all four routes. Alexander Henry arrived in 1761 by crossing from Isle aux Outardes to the island of Michilimackinac and then to the fort. Ten years later, John Porteous described this course in reverse when he "Left Michilac July 12th 1771 at 6 oclock in a small canoe & 4 men to Grosse [Mackinac] Isle so[uth]. end North 65° East 8 Miles."[59] In August 1766 Jonathan Carver carefully recorded his track to Michilimackinac from Detroit and then, on September 3, the commencement of his voyage to Wisconsin. From the fort his boat headed north six miles "over the channel to Cape St. Ignatius" and then four miles west to "Isle St. Helens."[60] Peter Pond's 1775 flotilla reversed Carver's route to approach Michilimackinac from the northwest.

The focal point of the canoe routes on Figure 2.3 is the fort of Michilimackinac. Beyond its walls to the east are two clusters of buildings identified as "Houses belonging to the traders without the fort," the only known depiction of the unfortified "suburb" that developed outside the stockade during the 1760s. The origins of this village are undocumented, but it probably began soon after the reoccupation of Michilimackinac in September 1764.[61] After that

time, the garrison occupied many of the houses within the walls, as shown on the 1765 Magra map (Fig. 2.2). Native American access to the stockade was also severely restricted after 1764, so much so that three years later Indian Department commissary Benjamin Roberts reported that "the Indians grumble very much about being hindered free Entrance to the Fort & have desired me to have My house & the trade outside." In response, General Gage made it clear that security was of paramount importance, that he approved of the exclusion, and that the Indians "Should not, or think they have a right to enter indiscriminately."[62]

Oddly enough, aside from its appearance on this map, there is no reference to the suburb before the late 1770s. Neither Jonathan Carver nor John Porteous mentioned it in their extended descriptions of the post written in 1766 and 1767. By 1778, however, local merchant John Askin reported nearly one hundred structures outside the fort, with steady growth as people continued to build there. Some of the houses were "tolerable good," and Askin was erecting a new one for himself.[63] The post commandant admitted, in the same year, that the suburb had "become a Considerable place," and he even contemplated relocating Ste. Anne's Church from the fort to the new village.[64] The commandant regulated matters of health and safety in the suburb, specifying fire-prevention measures

Robert Rogers (1731–95) was superintendent of Michilimackinac in 1766–67 until he found himself charged with treason and confined at his own post. Rogers was sent to Montréal in 1768, where a court martial found him innocent. This mezzotint was engraved and published in London in 1776 by Thomas Hart. *Clements Library, University of Michigan.*

Few British officers' wives accompanied their husbands to isolated Michilimackinac. Elizabeth Browne Rogers (1741–1812) was a notable exception. She endured a particularly difficult winter following the arrest of her husband in 1767 and left the post with him the following spring. This 1761 oil portrait is by Joseph Blackburn. *Reynolda House Museum of American Art, Winston-Salem, NC (1967.2.5).*

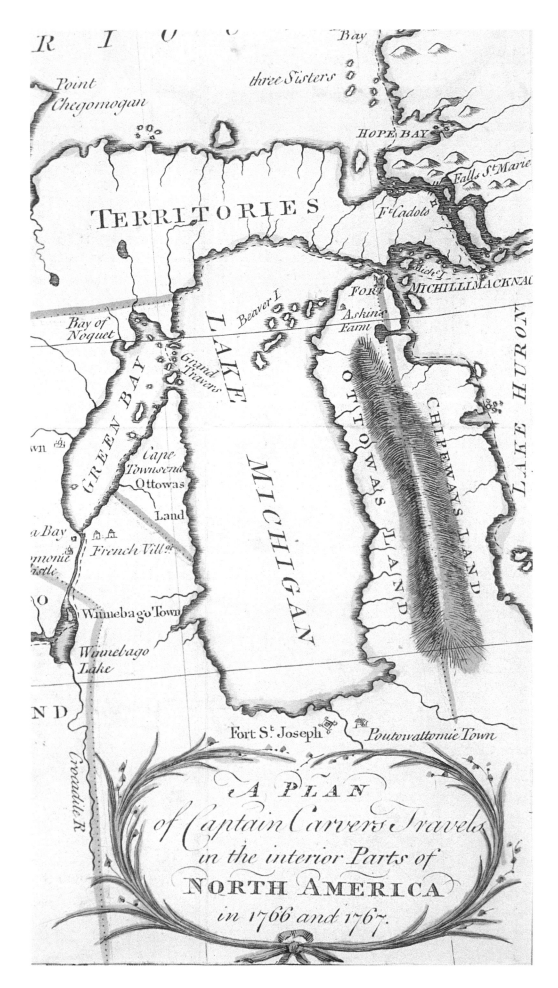

FIGURE 2.4

TITLE: A Plan of Captain Carver's Travels in the interior Parts of North America in 1766 and 1767. [Detail].

AUTHOR: Jonathan Carver (1710–80).

DATE DEPICTED: 1766–68.

DATE OF WORK: 1778.

DESCRIPTION: 27 x 34.5 cm. (whole map). Colored, copperplate engraving.

PROVENANCE: Published in Carver, *Travels Through the Interior Parts of North America, in the Years 1766, 1767, and 1768* (London, 1778 and 1781), 17. The example illustrated is from the 1781 edition.

COLLECTION: Clements Library, University of Michigan, Ann Arbor (Book Division, C-1781-Ca).

and prohibiting the deposit of "sweepings, feathers, or nastiness in the streets." The vulnerability of the traders' houses was a cause for concern, however, and one more argument for relocating the post to the island of Michilimackinac.[65]

The lack of a sheltered harbor at the fort might well have influenced the location of Michilimackinac's suburb. By building farther east, the traders were closer to "a good Cove for Landing," situated about three-quarters of a mile "round the point to the East ward."[66] This feature, known by the 1770s as Chippewa Bay or Chippewa Point, is distinguished on Figure 2.3 by a small indentation on the coast east of the suburb. This was apparently a favored camping place for visiting Indians, and it was convenient enough to the village that John Askin could cart merchandise overland to load a sailing vessel there when the wind was favorable.[67]

Michilimackinac's other satellite location appears on Figure 2.4, a detail of Jonathan Carver's map of the North American interior. "Askin's Farm" stood between the fort and the Ottawa village at L'Arbre Croche (near modern Cross Village). Originally established by the Jesuit missionary after the Ottawas' move from the Straits in 1742, the property passed into Askin's hands after the last missionary departed in 1765. Askin maintained a substantial agricultural operation there and, in 1774, obtained permission from the commandant to develop a second farm only three miles southwest of the fort on what is today known as French Farm Lake.[68]

The center of military activity at Michilimackinac is rendered in considerable detail as an inset on Figure 2.3. Although drawn at least a year later than the Magra plan, the form of the fort and the use of its buildings are similar, but the plan is oriented with north at the top to correspond to its position on the larger map of the Straits. Above the north and south gates stand "two large sentry boxes . . . sufficient for defense against small arms" ("5" and "6"), as described by Jonathan Carver in 1766 and also shown on Magra's composition.[69] The only significant difference from the Magra plan is an expansion of the fenced area around the powder magazine ("3"), which is rendered isometrically, the first piece of Straits of Mackinac architecture to be so shown. Archaeologists have suggested that this dates Figure 2.3 to 1766 or later.[70] It must have been drawn before 1769, when a barracks was finally begun in the middle of the fort.

Only three British-period plans of Michilimackinac exist, and all show the same distinctive outline of the stockade. This raises important questions. When was the roughly square trace illustrated on Lotbinière's 1749 plan (Fig. 1.15) altered to the larger, truncated hexagon first depicted by Magra in 1765? Did this change occur during the last years of the French regime or was it accomplished during the first British occupation of 1761–63 or in the course of Captain Howard's repairs in 1764–65? Were the north and south walls moved at the same time or as part of different projects? Unfortunately, no plans survive to document the transition of the defenses of Fort Michilimackinac, and archaeological evidence is inconclusive, although it has been suggested that the change took place in the 1750s.[71]

In 1751 the French commandant was given permission to expand the stockade in the direction of the lake.[72] Perhaps this created the right-angled jog in the lakeside wall to make room for a large storehouse. The fact that the "King's Provision Store" ("e" on Fig. 2.2 and "9" on Fig. 2.3) was private property and described as an "old shed" in 1770 argues for the lake-side expansion having been made by the French.[73] The more symmetrical expansion on the land side, enclosing a pair of private buildings flanking the south gateway, was probably a French change as well. British sources make no mention of any extension of the walls before the autumn of 1765, and it is highly unlikely that newly created space would have been allotted to private individuals when the military complained so incessantly of a lack of room for the king's buildings.

Although Figure 2.3 can be dated with confidence to 1766–69, there is no firm evidence to suggest who drew it. Unlike the Magra and Nordberg (Fig. 2.5) surveys, this map is not signed. Nor does documentation reveal why or by whom it was prepared. Its survival in the papers of the Colonial Office suggests that the map was sent directly to England rather than to a military officer in North America. Its depiction of canoe routes further implies that it might have been a useful document to illustrate some aspect of the fur trade. Nor is the inset plan of the fort as carefully scaled as the Magra and Nordberg surveys, which were intended to illustrate military defenses and property ownership.

No clue has yet been found to identify the author of Figure 2.3. No engineers are known to have visited Michilimackinac during 1766–69. Jonathan Carver, who was there on two occasions in 1766–68, had the ability to map, but the handwriting does not seem to be his. Lieutenant Diedrich Brehm is a potential candidate. He served as garrison engineer at Detroit from 1762 until May 1767 and visited that post again in 1768.[74] Although he is not known to have visited Michilimackinac, Brehm might have done so or had the resources at Detroit to prepare a map of this sort. The handwriting resembles Brehm's, although the style of the map is different than that of his other known compositions.[75]

It is very extraordinary that no Ground Should belong to the King in his own Fort

Major General Thomas Gage

On the two occasions when British troops arrived to occupy Michilimackinac—in 1761 and again in 1764—the red-coated soldiers did not march into a "fort" in the formal sense. Michilimackinac was unlike purely military facilities such as Niagara or Fort Ontario. Like Detroit, its larger counterpart to the south, Michilimackinac was a village enclosed by a wooden stockade. There was no citadel, where the garrison could be isolated as in fortress towns like Montréal and Québec or most cities in Europe. At Michilimackinac, the few structures owned by King George III were scattered among the privately owned row houses of the inhabitants. This no doubt contributed to the ease with which Michilimackinac fell to the Ojibwa in 1763. Detroit nearly suffered the same fate, and the plot there was foiled only by timely intelligence. A secure barracks area—the "Citadel"—was developed at Detroit in 1764–65.[76]

No such solution was possible at Michilimackinac, with its smaller garrison and fewer resources. When Captain Howard and his troops returned in 1764 there was no choice but to quarter the men in the same manner available to the garrison of 1761–63. There was a house for the commandant, but the other officers and soldiers had to be accommodated in vacant homes. The seasonal nature of the population made that feasible, but Howard considered it only a temporary expedient and requested a barracks to securely house his men.[77] General Thomas Gage allowed that a barracks would be useful, for "If the Garrison was separated from the Inhabitants, it might Answer better, than being mixed with them."[78]

The Magra plan (Fig. 2.2) illustrated the situation as of the summer of 1765. Of thirty-four distinct houses within the stockade, soldiers occupied eight and garrison officers another six. These were in poor condition, some even supported by wooden props.[79] Nor were they suitable for quartering troops in a safe and disciplined manner. Captain Beamsley Glazier described these buildings in detail three years later: "The rooms where the Men are lodged are pickets set in the ground one storrie high, fill'd in with Clay, and the roofs covered with bark, the Chimneys made of clay and wood." These were so dry that they presented a serious fire hazard. Individual rooms were so small that many could not lodge more than seven men, a far cry from the preferred twelve to sixteen.[80]

It is difficult to say why it took five years to provide adequate housing for the troops at Michilimackinac, even though a formal proposal for "A Pile of Soldiers Barracks sufficient to Lodge Two Companys" was submitted in the autumn of 1765.[81] Distance, expense, and other demands were probably factors. It was not until the summer of 1768 that General Gage requested additional information on the state of quarters at Michilimackinac in anticipation of reducing the garrison there to a mere forty men. When Captain Glazier responded, in October, not only did he describe the appalling housing, but he noted casually that "the King has no ground in the Fort" aside from his own quarters and a garden lot that had once been the site of the French commandant's house. Glazier's letter reached Gage in New York on December 17 and clearly touched a nerve. "It is very extraordinary that no Ground Should belong to the King in his own Fort," Gage sputtered. He further demanded a thorough examination of the property claims of the inhabitants and ordered a spot selected for a barracks, even if it meant enlarging the stockade.[82]

Knowing that he could have no response from Michilimackinac before early summer, General Gage forged ahead with plans for a barracks on whatever land Glazier might be able to find. By February 1769 a New York carpenter, Elias Smith, had been engaged to go to Michilimackinac with two assistants. Armed with a plan, probably provided by chief engineer Captain Thomas Sowers, they were to build a four-room barracks for sixty men and repair the commanding officer's house.[83] Captain Glazier received Gage's letter on May 25. Realizing that he had been misunderstood, Glazier attempted to clarify matters. "When I mentioned . . . that the King had no ground but the two Spots," he wrote on June 10, "I ment only the land in the range of Buildings round the Fort, for there is a Square left in the middle . . . which is large enough to erect any publick Buildings His Majesty may have occasion for in this Fort." To illustrate this, he enclosed the plan included here as Figure 2.5.[84]

Captain Glazier assigned Lieutenant John Nordberg to prepare the survey. Like many officers of the Royal American Regiment, Nordberg had some talent for drafting, a skill likely acquired during European military service before he accepted a British commission in 1758. His effort was workmanlike, though not as colorful as Magra's. Nor did he bother to show the stockade in full detail or in entirely accurate proportions. Lieutenant Nordberg's purpose was only to identify the property owned by the King and the Church. Care should also be taken when consulting his directional arrow, which points unconventionally to the south. The lakeshore is thus at the top of the map.

The largest parcel under the control of the army was marked number "2" and represented the commandant's house with a garden behind it. Across the parade ground at "4" was a plot where the French commandant's house had stood until Captain Howard ordered it demolished to make a garden.[85] This building appears on Lotbinière's 1749 plan (Fig. 1.15) with a *corps de garde* (guardhouse) on the site of Glazier's house. Adjacent to the headquarters, at "8,"

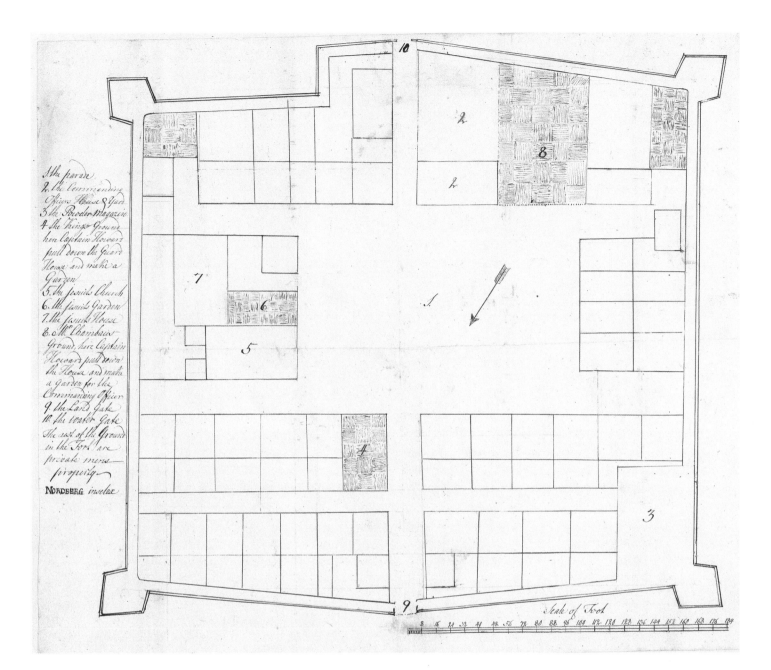

FIGURE 2.5

TITLE: [Draught of the fort of Michilimackinac].

AUTHOR: Lieutenant John Nordberg, 2/60th Regiment of Foot (active 1758–74).

DATE DEPICTED: June 10, 1769.

DATE OF WORK: [June 10, 1769].

DESCRIPTION: 48 x 58.5 cm. Pen and ink on paper.

PROVENANCE: Enclosed in a letter from Captain Beamsley Glazier to Major General Thomas Gage dated June 10, 1769. Retained in Gage's papers. The papers were purchased by William L. Clements in 1930 and acquired by the Clements Library in 1937.

COLLECTION: Clements Library, University of Michigan, Ann Arbor (Map Division, 6-N-9).

is another garden for the commandant, which was on land once occupied by a house claimed by a Monsieur de Chambaud of Montréal but had been appropriated and pulled down by Captain Howard.[86] In the southeast corner of the fort is the powder magazine ("3"), securely fenced and controlled by the military. A pair of unnumbered garden plots in the northwest and northeast corners of the enclosure were presumably intended to represent further patches of Crown land. The provisions storehouse, located in the angle of the stockade by the water gate, is unidentified because it was claimed as private property.[87]

The area of greatest interest to General Gage was undoubtedly the "Parade," identified by the number "1." Here was the land assumed by Captain Glazier to have been reserved for government use, and it was here that Elias Smith would lay out the barracks following his arrival on June 16, 1769. Two of its four rooms were ready for occupancy by December, but it was not until the end of the following July that the building was entirely finished and renovations to the commanding officer's house completed.[88] The new barracks was placed between the numeral "1" and the church complex on Nordberg's map, along the southwest side of and parallel to the street connecting the fort's two gates.

Unfortunately, no plan of Michilimackinac is known to depict the fort with its barracks or the new provisions storehouse completed in 1773 on the site of the old building by the water gate. The three surviving plans of British Michilimackinac are concentrated in the years 1765–69 and so reflect none of the alterations made before or during the years of the American Revolution. Plans were prepared during that time, and they included tantalizing titles such as "Plan of the Fort Michilimakinac on the South main" and "Plan of the Old Fort of Michilimackinac" as recorded on map inventories of the 1780s, but these have been lost.[89]

One final observation might be made based on the three extant maps of Michilimackinac. None clearly shows defensive platforms along the curtains (walls) of the fort. Rather, there appears to have been a fenced *chemin de ronde* at ground level, as in the Lotbinière map of 1749, with platforms only in the bastions, where artillery was mounted and sentry boxes or blockhouses located. Jonathan Carver noted in 1766 that the fort was "defended by four bastions" and that "Each has a platform and mount . . . small cannon."[90] References to repairs made between 1764 and the 1770s refer only to the bastions and their platforms, such as Captain Arent S. DePeyster's report of having "Prop'd the Platforms, made new Stairs leading to them, and from thence to the Block houses."[91] When the defenses were strengthened, in the spring of 1779, the stockade was re-lined with cedar posts "and a banquet [*sic:* banquette or firing step] thrown up so as to fire from a good height Thro' [the] loop holes," a suggestion that the curtains were not defended from elevated platforms.[92]

A barracks for the Michilimackinac garrison was well underway by the time General Gage received Lieutenant Nordberg's plan late in September 1769. The long-awaited building would be moved to Mackinac Island in 1781, where it would shelter troops until 1827.

Native Americans from across the northern Great Lakes came to Michilimackinac each summer. Even the eastern Dakota or Sioux were occasional visitors. This colored engraving of a warrior and his family illustrated Jonathan Carver's *Travels Through the Interior Parts of North America* (London, 1778). Carver encountered the Dakota during his time in the upper Mississippi Valley in 1766–67. *Clements Library, University of Michigan.*

Captain Arent Schuyler DePeyster (1736–1822) commanded Michili-mackinac from 1774 to 1779 before moving on to Detroit and Niagara. His wife, Rebecca Blair (d. 1827), was with him throughout his duty on the Great Lakes. These matching portraits were painted after the couple's return to England in 1785. The original oil paintings are in a private collection. *Photographs courtesy of the Scottish National Portrait Gallery (Negative numbers B-8171 and B-8172).*

The situation is respectable & convenient for a Fort

Lieutenant Governor Patrick Sinclair

Michilimackinac went to war again after rebellious colonists fought the king's soldiers in April 1775.[93] The fighting remained at a distance from Michilimackinac for the next four years, and, with resources needed elsewhere, little was done to improve the post. It remained, in the words of Major Arent S. DePeyster, "a patched picketed fort at best much incumbered with wooden houses & commanded by small arms." The strength of Michilimackinac lay in its importance to the diplomacy and trade that maintained "the good understanding kept up with the Indians."[94]

DePeyster was not complacent, for he realized that "the friendships with the Indians may be depended upon till a greater force appear against us." That force was gathering in the spring of 1779 following the British loss of Vincennes and the possibility that the enemy might strike at Detroit or Michilimackinac from the Illinois country. The post would require defenses stronger than a rotten stockade on an exposed, sandy beach.[95] The deficiencies of Fort Michilimackinac had been apparent for years. It was the "worst situated spot that could be found on all the Coast," lacking any sort of harbor, according to Captain Beamsley Glazier in 1769. The sandy soil drifted into tall dunes that masked the defenses from the southwest. The only sources of firewood were at an inconvenient distance. And the dry, rickety buildings of the fort and suburb were

an invitation to fire. In his analysis of the post, Glazier suggested that the fort be moved eastward to an elevated site near Chippewa Point or, even better, to "the Island called Michilimackinac about 8 Miles North from this Fort, where there is good landing and wood plenty."[96] There was no compelling reason to relocate the post in 1769, so Glazier's suggestion was ignored.

The situation was very different a decade later when Lieutenant Governor Patrick Sinclair arrived to relieve Major DePeyster. He knew all the arguments against the mainland site, and he might well have discussed them with Glazier and others during his own service on Lake Huron in the 1760s.[97] Sinclair arrived with a mandate to find a better location. Before his departure from Québec, General Frederick Haldimand, governor of Canada, had expressed his desire for the removal of the post "to an island more favourable [to agriculture] . . . & more respectable & secure."[98] Haldimand later claimed that he had long been of the opinion that "it would be expedient to remove the Fort, &c. from its present situation to the Island of Michilimackinac."[99] Sinclair stopped to examine the place and found "a very fine Bay well covered by the little White Wood [Round] Island." He reported that "the situation is respectable and convenient for a Fort."[100]

Sinclair arrived at his new command on October 4, 1779, and,

The only known likeness of Patrick Sinclair (1736–1820) is this often-reproduced silhouette showing him as an older man. This copy is from Edwin O. Wood, *Historic Mackinac* (New York, 1918).

Clements Library, University of Michigan.

FIGURE 2.6

TITLE: [On verso:] Plan of the New Fort at the Island of Michilimackinac. [Endorsed on verso:] Plan of the New Fort at the Island of Michilimackinac Enclosed in a letter to Capt. Brehm of the 7th October 1779.

AUTHOR: Lieutenant Governor Patrick Sinclair, 1/84th Regiment of Foot (1736–1820).

DATE DEPICTED: October 7, 1779, proposal.

DATE OF WORK: [October 7, 1779].

DESCRIPTION: 15 x 37 cm. The whole sheet of paper, which includes text and part of Round Island at the bottom, is 45.5 cm. high. Pen and ink on paper.

PROVENANCE: Drawn into the body of a letter from Sinclair to Captain Diedrich Brehm of October 7, 1779. Retained in the papers of General Frederick Haldimand until acquired by the British Library.

COLLECTION: British Library, London (Frederick Haldimand Papers, Add Mss. 21757, f. 267). © British Library Board. All rights reserved.

This Elevated Plain is rich loam mixed wt. Limestone gravel, some of that kind of stone loose, and, in some few places fixed rocks of it

It is a very soft kind of stone when not exposed to the Sun, and when sought for deep is found to be easily crumbled and to resemble Marle

It produces oak, beech, Elm, some Ash & Poplar — on the NW Side there are some Pines but not fit for use — The other woods are good —

In the middle of the Island there is a small Lake, apparently recruited by exhalations and not able to bear any drain from it

There is no stream of water on the Island — Good situations for a Wind Mill

A Vessel can winter here & safely from weather or an Enemy when fortified at the Point marked ✳ thus & on the ridge dotted....

People can fish at all season and with the worst weather without danger from this Island

This is a rising slope of ground on which hay is cut. it yields rich grass — the soil loam and limestone gravel, with more sand than in the upper grounds — cleared to the extent of 40 Acres — The Indians plant no corn here & but little on any part of the Isl.

Haldimand Bay

Low ground yielding Cedar, swamp Laurel, Willow & other aquatics but the soil fit for rich meadow — here is a fine spring of water

This elevation is not rock, but soil easily removed

Scale 200 yards to an inch, to judge of this inaccurate Sketch by

ϟϟϟ The two lines marked are to express the sudden elevation of ground from the ridge which is dotted, and from the plains near the Bay it rises almost perpendicular 36 feet above the ridge

✳ A Fortification here would command the whole bay and over look all the accessible part of the Island from this side, it would seem & the ridge, if any work erected on it and it is not commanded by any ground behind it

N: B I send its appearance from Round Island as I wish You to draw a sketch of the whole, before You shew it to the General, and to urge that so respectable and valuable a situation may be early secured upon — It will give no offence to the Proprietors who wish for it — The Ottawas may be a little jealous at first — that our Fort is to be built on the Chippewa Ground — The present Fort is partly on Ottawa and partly on Chipewa ground which is the only apparent good policy in the first choice of this situation — From this Fort to Haldimand Island is nearly 8 miles, but convenient for St Marys route, Grande River, Huron & Michigan Lakes as this dangerous traverse will be thereby avoided — The Vessels can unload within 6 yards of the Beach, & may be drawn within six feet of the shore in winter at the part of the bay marked ✕, but every where within it is a great depth of water that the bottom is little hard in some places there being a fine sand and a clay marle in this place

It is not improbable that the Fort of Michil. was placed in its present bad situation for the conveniency of the Mission of St Ignace, and the Ottawas, who were found the earliest proselites to Christianity

a Fort or Work at ✳ would protect a Vessel laid up at ✕ in the Bay but never allways being the Enemy two natural approaches from under the banks a & b and therefore wants to be better at c, if afforded equal to check to a Vessel laid up opposite, by commanding their Bank towards c & d. but upon the whole an Engineer should be sent up, as its being impossible to fix the spott for a Fort by a Sketch; as greatly depends upon distances & heights within are better discovered upon the very spott.

A Block house could be sunck at the point ✳ and another at the side of the Ridge c, so as to be covered by the same from one side & a raised rampart from the other, or even sunk into the very ridge itself, the some angular connection with one another, so as to contain all the Traders Stores or houses & to ... it would afford a Better defence than the proposed two half Bastions, as Block houses are the only works which afford a real defence without need of another Work to flank them and at the same time may serve as barracks or Grand Rooms. but nothing I call that can be done without being on the spott, for reasons above mentioned, are mere others

This Island is nearly 2400 Yards distant from the other Island placed here to shew in what manner it shelters Haldimand Bay and leaves it but a very little open to any wind, and that blows over only 3 Leagues of water, it is then only open to about 18 the wind from ENE this Island runs farther to the N. than the paper will admit of

267

three days later, he sent off his arguments for making the move. He had, by that time, dispatched a mason, a carpenter, a brick maker, and "a man acquainted with soil favorable to vegetation" to inspect the island. They spent two days there, and Sinclair joined them to "examine their discoveries." These revealed all the necessary resources—wood, water, clay, stone, and arable soil. Sinclair prepared a sketch map of the south end of the island and a crude topographical view of the same area as seen from across the channel. The map was drawn into his report to Haldimand, and the view was enclosed. These two images (Figs. 2.6 and 2.7) are the first detailed renderings of Mackinac Island.[101]

Patrick Sinclair's map reveals the topography around the harbor. Along the shores of the crescent-shaped bay he depicted a wide swath of gently rising land covered with hay and rich grass. Dramatic bluffs followed the curve of the beach until turning away to the west. Below the turning point, a lower "ridge" paralleled the shore to its southern point. These features are also depicted in the view, which Sinclair said was drawn from "Isle bois blanc," but which appears to have been sketched from Round Island, identified at the lower part of his map as "little White wood or Round Island." The angle of the view is a bit broader than that of the map, spanning the high ground on the southwestern side of Mackinac Island to the point on the eastern bluff known today as Robinson's Folly. Sinclair's sketch also shows, for the first time, the heights in the center of the island.

Over these natural features, Sinclair imposed his plan for a new fortification and village, marking his preferred location for a fort with a confident asterisk. That spot, today the site of Fort Mackinac, dominated everything below. "The point of rising ground overlooks all the accessible beach on that side of the Island," he reported. "In short no situation can be more favourable." No civilian structures would encumber the new fortification. Below Sinclair's asterisk is a proposed stockade, flanked by four blockhouses with a fifth on the commanding ground. This enclosure straddles the lower ridge below the fort site, the area "most convenient for Store Houses, Traders, &ca.," although the new town would actually be laid out along the beach between the lower ridge and the water. Sinclair boldly labeled the harbor "Haldimand Bay" in honor of the man who could approve his plans. It is so called to this day, the earliest place-name applied to any part of Mackinac Island.

The onset of winter delayed Haldimand's response, and final permission for the move was not given until April 1780.[102] That had not kept Sinclair from moving ahead. On October 16 he and Major DePeyster visited the island again, and by October 29 the lieutenant governor had sent a corporal, four soldiers, and a carpenter to begin a wharf in Haldimand Bay and build a blockhouse. By November 5 the first house from the old post had been dismantled and loaded aboard a sailing vessel for the trip to the island.[103] By mid-February 1780 the wharf was well along, and the traders were moving Ste. Anne's Church. It was to be reerected "where the Traders will hereafter be fixed, not in the Fort."[104] With so much committed so soon, Sinclair clearly harbored little doubt about Governor Haldimand's decision.

It was probably late in 1779 when Sinclair sketched a plan for a blockhouse to be built on the island (Fig. 2.8). There is no evidence that the building constructed that winter followed this design. Nor is its exact location known, other than that it was intended to defend

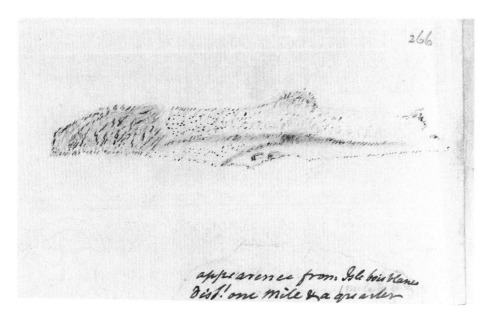

the wharf, which was probably at the foot of today's Fort Street, roughly at the "X" next to the label "Haldimand Bay" on Sinclair's plan of the island.[105] The blockhouse design is today among General Haldimand's papers, cryptically identified on the verso as "Sketch of the Works & Church at Makana." It surely does not depict the church, but the inscription might imply a companion sketch, now lost.

The features shown on Sinclair's blockhouse plan are explained in a separate memorandum. This refers to "Those blockhouses on or near the bank," presumably the five buildings projected to defend the bluff and village. Earth from their foundations was to be thrown down the "bank," along with that from an "officers Barrack" that was to face "the Lake or low ground." The first story of each blockhouse was to be built of stone and used to store provisions. The upper floors were for troops, and the roof was to support a structure "for a Centry to walk on a small gallery at the end of which must be a Centry Box."[106] All of these details are found on Figure 2.8.

Patrick Sinclair was as energetic in obtaining possession of Mackinac Island as he was in designing his post. The island was acknowledged to be the property of the Ojibwa, who had occupied summer camps there since at least the 1740s. Although the fishing season was over by October, Sinclair's map and sketch show "2 Indian Hutts" or bark longhouses on the beach. Governor Haldimand wanted assurances that the Indians would not be offended by Sinclair's activities. He emphasized that a proper agreement should be made and "executed in the fullest & most satisfactory manner, to prevent any after Demands for Purchase Money or claims of the Land."[107] In July 1780 Sinclair reported that he had held a council in the presence of "Chiefs of Eight Different Nations," who welcomed the British presence. The Indians, he wrote, had given up the place, "removed their Houses and formally surrendered it without any Present, as yet." Sinclair assured them that no more of their country would be needed, and that he planned to make cornfields of the whole island. He also announced that they would be excluded from the fort on the upper ground, but that their agent's house and the traders' stores would be accessible in the village. "They expressed much satisfaction with the whole arrangement," Sinclair reported.[108]

Many years later, in 1833, an elderly Indian named Ningwegon recalled going to Mackinac Island with his father and a party of British officers. After dining under some sugar maples near the foot of the bluff, the British asked permission to occupy the island. Ningwegon remembered that consent was immediately given, and the fort was removed to the island the following year.[109] The old man might have remembered the July 1780 council reported by Sinclair. A more formal event on May 12, 1781, resulted in a signed deed and payment of the Ojibwa for their island. One copy of this deed is illustrated as Figure 2.9.

This seminal document of Mackinac Island history would serve as the basis for all future land transactions there. It is one of two originals signed that day by the Ojibwa chiefs, KitchieNegon, Pouanas, Koupé, and Magousseihigan, in the presence of Sinclair, three of his

FIGURE 2.8

TITLE: [Section and roof plan of a blockhouse and redoubt to be built on Mackinac Island]. [Endorsed on verso:] No 52 Sketch of the Works & Church at Makana.
AUTHOR: [Lieutenant Governor Patrick Sinclair, 1/84th Regiment of Foot (1736–1820)].
DATE DEPICTED: 1779 proposal.
DATE OF WORK: [Autumn 1779].
DESCRIPTION: 36 x 45 cm. Pencil on paper.
PROVENANCE: Presumably included in a letter from Sinclair to his superiors at Québec with a brief memo describing the building. Retained in the papers of General Frederick Haldimand until acquired by the British Library.
COLLECTION: British Library, London (Frederick Haldimand Papers, Add Mss. 21758, f. 371). © British Library Board. All rights reserved.

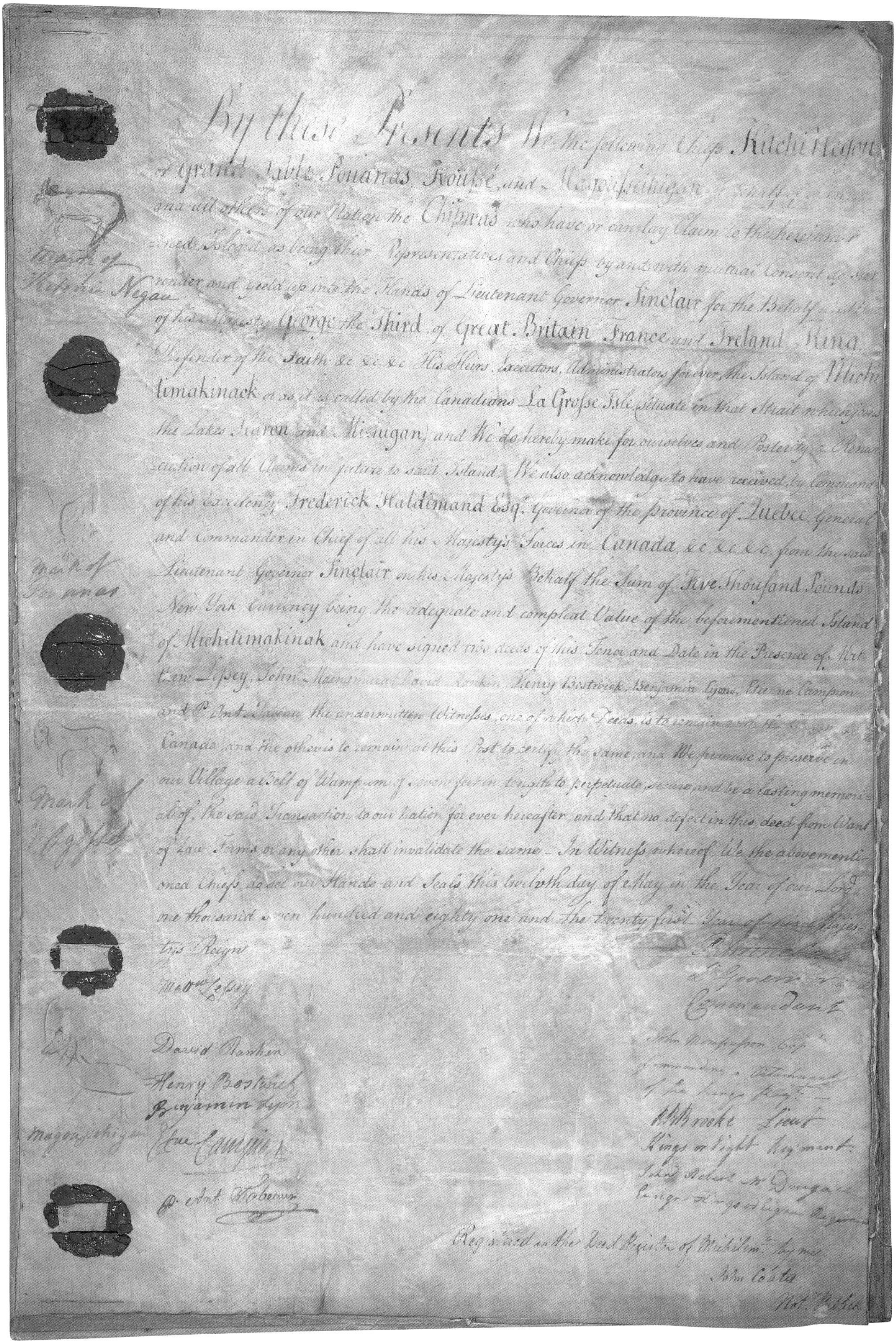

By these Presents We the following Chiefs Kitchi Negon
or grand Sable Pouanas Koupé and Magousseihigen _____ _____
and all others of our Nation the Chipwas who have or can lay Claim to the herein men
tioned Island as being their Representatives and Chiefs by and with mutual Consent do sur
render and yield up into the Hands of Lieutenant Governor Sinclair for the Behalf and Use
of his Majesty George the Third of Great Britain France and Ireland King
Defender of the Faith &c &c &c His Heirs, Executors, Administrators for ever, the Island of Michi
limakinack or as it is called by the Canadians La Grosse Isle situate in that Strait which joins
the Lakes Huron and Michigan, and We do hereby make for ourselves and Posterity a Renun
ciation of all Claims in future to said Island. We also acknowledge to have received by command
of his Excellency Frederick Haldimand Esqr. Governor of the province of Quebec, General
and Commander in Chief of all his Majesty's Forces in Canada, &c &c &c, from the said
Lieutenant Governor Sinclair on his Majesty's Behalf the Sum of Five Thousand Pounds
New York Currency being the adequate and compleat Value of the before mentioned Island
of Michilimakinak and have signed two deeds of this Tenor and Date in the Presence of Mat
thew Lessey John Mac_____ David Rankin Henry Bostwick Benjamin Lyons Etienne Campion
and P. Ant. Tabeau the undermentioned Witnesses, one of which Deeds is to remain with the ____ in
Canada, and the other is to remain at this Post to certify the same, and We promise to preserve in
our Village a Belt of Wampum of seven feet in length to perpetuate, secure and be a lasting memori
al of, the said Transaction to our Nation for ever hereafter, and that no defect in this deed from Want
of Law Forms or any other shall invalidate the same — In Witness whereof We the abovementi
oned Chiefs do set our Hands and Seals this twelfth day of May in the Year of our Lord
one thousand seven hundred and eighty one and the twenty first Year of his Majes
ty's Reign

Mark of
Kitchi Negau

Mark of
Pouanas

Mark of
Koupé

Mark of
Magousseihigen

Matw Lessey

David Rankin
Henry Bostwick
Benjamin Lyon
Etne Campion

P. Ant. Tabeau

P. Sinclair
Lt. Governor and
Commandant

John Macnamara Esq
Commanding a Detachment
of the Kings Regt

A. Brooke Lieut
Kings or Eight Regiment
Iohn Robert Mc Douga__
Ensign Kings or eighty Regiment

Regd. in the Deed Register of Michilim. by me
John Coats
Not. Public

FIGURE 2.9

TITLE: [Deed to Mackinac Island].
AUTHOR: Lieutenant Governor Patrick Sinclair,
1/84th Regiment of Foot (1736–1820) and others.
DATE DEPICTED: May 12, 1781.
DATE OF WORK: May 12, 1781.
DESCRIPTION: 65.5 x 44 cm. Pen and ink,
vermilion, and sealing wax on parchment.
PROVENANCE: Acquired by the Clements
Library from B. T. Batsford in 1957 as a gift from
James Shearer II.
COLLECTION: Clements Library, University of
Michigan, Ann Arbor (Oversize Manuscripts).

officers, and five British and Canadian traders. For a sum of five thousand pounds in New York currency, the Ojibwa leaders gave up their people's claim to the island of Michilimackinac, alternately known to the Canadians as "La Grosse Isle." The participants signed two copies of the deed, one of which was to remain with the governor of Canada and the other at the post. The Chippewa retained a record of the transaction in the form of a seven-foot-long belt of wampum that was to be preserved in their village.[110]

Figure 2.9 is one of the two original, signed deeds, complete with the pictographic signatures of the Ojibwa leaders drawn in vermilion and embellished with red sealing wax. This is presumably the document left at the post, although, if it is, it somehow later made its way into the hands of an English dealer from whom it was purchased for the Clements Library in 1957. The post copy was still at Fort Mackinac in September 1796, when duplicates were made from it for U.S. authorities.[111] In 1895 the Mackinac Island historian John R. Bailey claimed to have once owned "the original parchment deed" to the island that had been among the abandoned papers of the American Fur Company but that it had gone missing.[112] There is no way of knowing if this was the deed now in the Clements Library or simply another manuscript copy. The other signed original is believed to be in the Library and Archives Canada, and a contemporary copy is with General Haldimand's papers.[113]

Captain Thomas Aubrey (1740–1814) led a detachment of the 47th Regiment of Foot to Michilimackinac in 1781 to relieve two companies of the 8th (King's) Regiment after their commander quarreled with Lieutenant Governor Sinclair. Aubrey and his men labored on Fort Mackinac until their departure during the summer of 1782. Nathaniel Hone pictured Aubrey in 1772 as a lieutenant of the 4th (King's Own) Regiment of Foot. *National Museum of Wales (NMW A 101).*

The works injudiciously designed

Captain Gother Mann

Lieutenant Richard Hockings was the first trained engineer to lay eyes on the fort constructed by Patrick Sinclair. Nearly three years had passed since Sinclair had examined Mackinac Island's potential as a new site for the post of Michilimackinac. Now, in September 1782, Lieutenant Hockings had arrived to inspect the results. He had come from Québec with Sir John Johnson and Lieutenant Colonel Henry Hope, who were to conduct their own inquiry into "the cause of the great expenses that had been incurred of late at Michilimackinac." Governor Haldimand charged his inspectors with applying "such temporary remedies to the different abuses that might appear . . . most expedient."[114] These would ultimately include relieving Sinclair of his command and issuing strict new instructions for his successor, Captain Daniel Robertson.[115]

Hockings had five days in which to survey the unfinished fortress and complete a report. His analysis was straightforward, if understated, but it is clear that he did not like what he found. "The Fort is irregular in its construction built of masonry & timber work," he wrote, and no part of it "in a proper state of defence against a surprize." This was a critical consideration since security had been the primary reason for uprooting the established post of Michilimackinac. The new fortification was also very large—too extensive, Hockings felt, to be properly defended by its garrison of slightly more than one hundred men. It was too late for major changes, however. The fort could not be contracted without further exposing its garrison to attack so, the engineer suggested, "It must therefore be secured on its Present Plan."[116]

Wartime expediency thus ensured that Sinclair's imperfect design would survive as the basis for the current Fort Mackinac. The fortified enclosure has remained essentially the same since it was laid out in 1779–81, although changes made by the Americans twenty year later gave it a superficially different look. Lieutenant Hockings drew a plan to illustrate his recommendations for salvaging the work, but this has been lost. It is, nonetheless, possible to trace the process by which Fort Mackinac was designed and constructed prior to his visit by using three plans (Figs. 2.10–12) drawn by Sinclair himself.

Patrick Sinclair was an amateur as a military engineer. Though he grasped many concepts of fortification, he was unable to successfully unify them into an effective design. Sinclair identified the commanding position that dominated the harbor but dismissed higher ground to the north that neutralized its effectiveness. He was forced to compromise between guarding the heights (later the site of Fort Holmes) and covering the town and harbor, something that could not be accomplished from one site.[117] Perhaps a more experienced engineer would have avoided the error. All those who came later would certainly point it out. Sinclair had only halfheartedly requested professional assistance, pleading to his superiors, "for God's sake be careful in the choice of An Engineer & don't send up one of your paper Engineers fond of fine regular Polygons." No one, it turned out, was available, so he was left much to his own devices.[118]

Sinclair initially favored simple fortifications using blockhouses and stockades, both on the high ground and around the town (see Fig. 2.6). As late as May 1780 he reported having gathered materials

Captain Gother Mann (1747–1830) thoroughly inspected Fort Mackinac in 1788. The engineer found the place still unfinished, in poor repair, and barely defensible. This colored lithograph, probably based on a portrait miniature of 1763, was published in Whitworth Porter, *History of the Corps of Royal Engineers* (London, 1889).

University of Michigan Libraries.

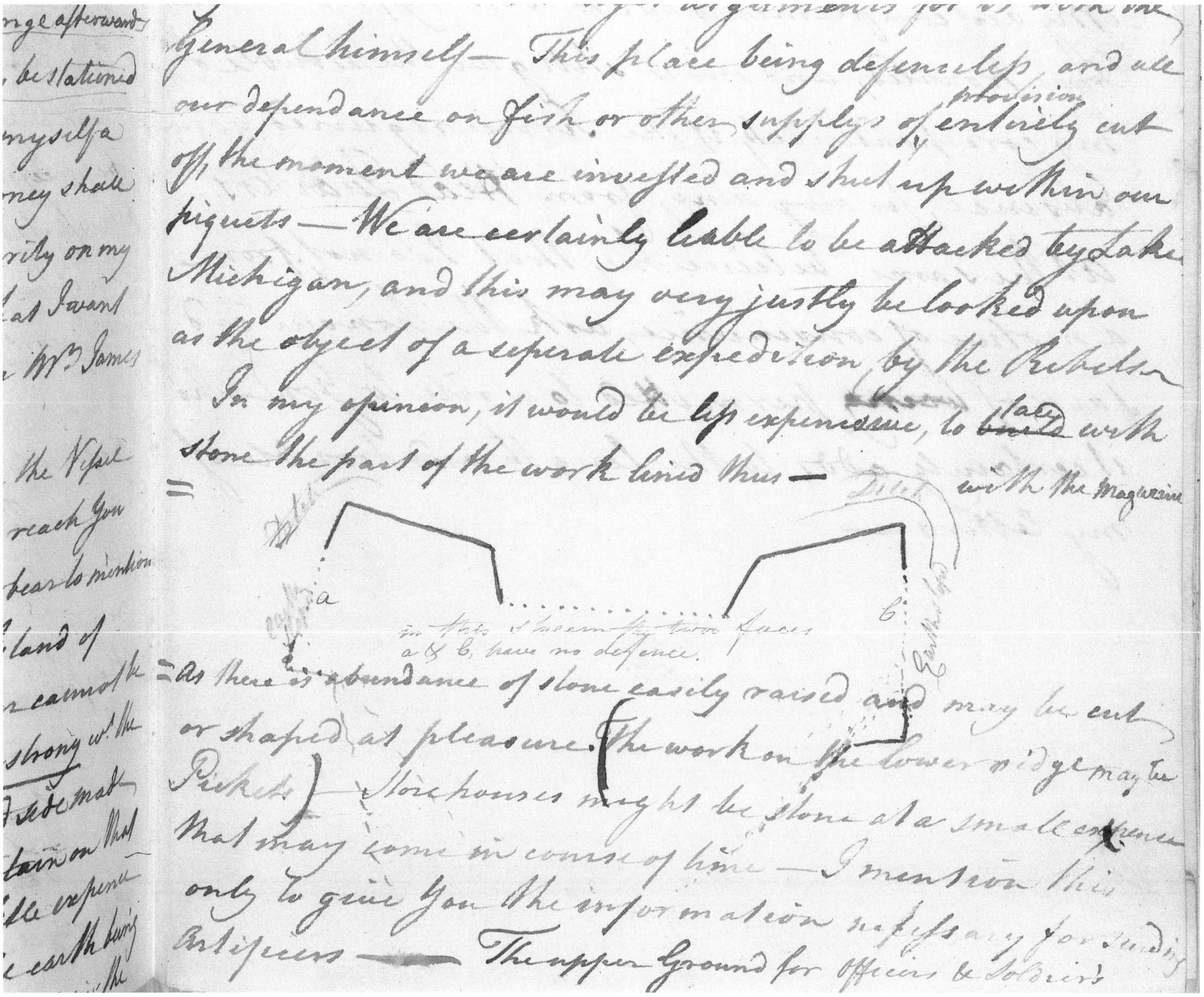

FIGURE 2.10

TITLE: [Rough sketch of a fort proposed to be built on Mackinac Island].

AUTHOR: Lieutenant Governor Patrick Sinclair, 1/84th Regiment of Foot (1736–1820).

DATE DEPICTED: October 15, 1779, proposal.

DATE OF WORK: October 15, 1779.

DESCRIPTION: 9 x 15.5 cm. Pencil, pen, and ink on paper.

PROVENANCE: Drawn into the text of a letter from Sinclair to Captain Diedrich Brehm dated October 15, 1779. Retained in the papers of General Frederick Haldimand until acquired by the British Library.

COLLECTION: British Library, London (Frederick Haldimand Papers, Add Mss. 21757, f. 269). © British Library Board. All rights reserved.

for three blockhouses to be constructed on the "upper ground."[119] This was his last mention of blockhouses for the fort site, and it confused local historians for a century or more by causing the three extant Fort Mackinac blockhouses, all built about 1798, to be identified with Sinclair's proposed buildings.[120] Perhaps the blockhouses were intended for temporary defense. At any rate, within a week of drafting his initial plan, Sinclair sketched the outline of a more elaborate fort into the body of a letter to Captain Diedrich Brehm. It is reproduced here as Figure 2.10.

Sinclair's change of heart might have been influenced by the abundance of limestone on Mackinac Island. On October 15, 1779, he proposed a fort on the bluff protected by two bastions and ditches on its north (land) side. The most exposed parts of the bastions were to be faced with stone, expressed by Sinclair with a solid line. Most of the rest of the enclosure, including the "curtain" or wall connecting the two bastions, was to be constructed of vertical pickets. This fortification would enclose quarters for officers and men, a powder magazine, and the provisions storehouse, while the traders' houses and the buildings of the Indian Department were to be located on the "lower ridge" in an enclosure of pickets.[121]

This crude sketch and Sinclair's earlier map (Fig. 2.6) were given to Captain William Twiss, commanding engineer in Canada, who could not spare an officer from his overworked staff to go to Michilimackinac. Twiss was ordered to prepare plans based on Sinclair's concept, but since the engineer had not seen the ground himself, these were to serve only as a rough guide. "You must endeavour to reconcile his plans to the ground, rather by adhering to the principles he lays down, than by following the Exact figures he proposes," Sinclair was cautioned.[122] This was the best that could be

done at the time, and Sinclair was given carte blanche to proceed.

The lieutenant governor wasted no time. He probably broke ground for his fort sometime in the late spring or summer of 1780, presumably after receiving Twiss's plans. By August 3 Sinclair had proceeded far enough to suggest a name for the new structure— "Fort Haldimand." The governor was unimpressed by such blatant flattery. He responded that he had "never known any advantage result from changing the names of Places long inhabited by the same People" and instructed that the post, "though moved to the Island," was still to be called Michilimackinac, while the fortification was to be known as "Fort Makinac."[123] This is the earliest official use of the abbreviated form of the name that would become common in the nineteenth century.

It would seem from the next extant plan that Captain Twiss modified Sinclair's original concept of two full bastions (that is, each having four sides—two flanks and two faces) to a trace incorporating two "half bastions" (each having only three sides). These were simpler to lay out and construct. A half bastion is depicted on Sinclair's plan of the fort enclosed with a letter of May 12, 1781 (Fig. 2.11). This shows that the first stage of construction concentrated on the western half of the enclosure, and progress was noticeable by February 1781. By May 1 Sinclair reported that he had "one half Bastion and half [a] curtain [made of] Log Work, and the other sides of the New Fort picketted."[124] This describes the form of the fort as sketched in Figure 2.11.

The most substantial part of this construction is labeled "Log Work," a technique that employed parallel, horizontal log walls with the intervening space filled with earth or rubble. This provided protection against artillery and could be constructed quickly using

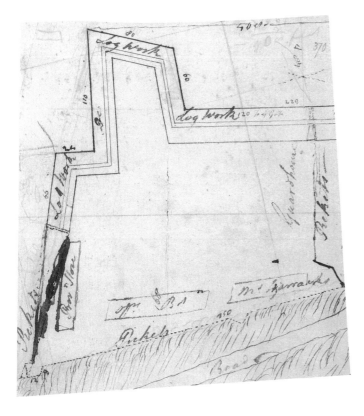

FIGURE 2.11

TITLE: [On verso:] Rough Sketch of the part of the Fort enclosed for temporary security.
AUTHOR: Lieutenant Governor Patrick Sinclair, 1/84th Regiment of Foot (1736–1820).
DATE DEPICTED: May 12, 1781.
DATE OF WORK: [May 12, 1781].
DESCRIPTION: 14.5 x 14 cm. Pencil, pen, and ink on paper.
PROVENANCE: Enclosed in a letter from Sinclair to [General Frederick Haldimand] of May 12, 1781. Retained in the papers of General Frederick Haldimand until acquired by the British Library.
COLLECTION: British Library, London (Frederick Haldimand Papers, Add Mss. 21758, f. 370). © British Library Board. All rights reserved.

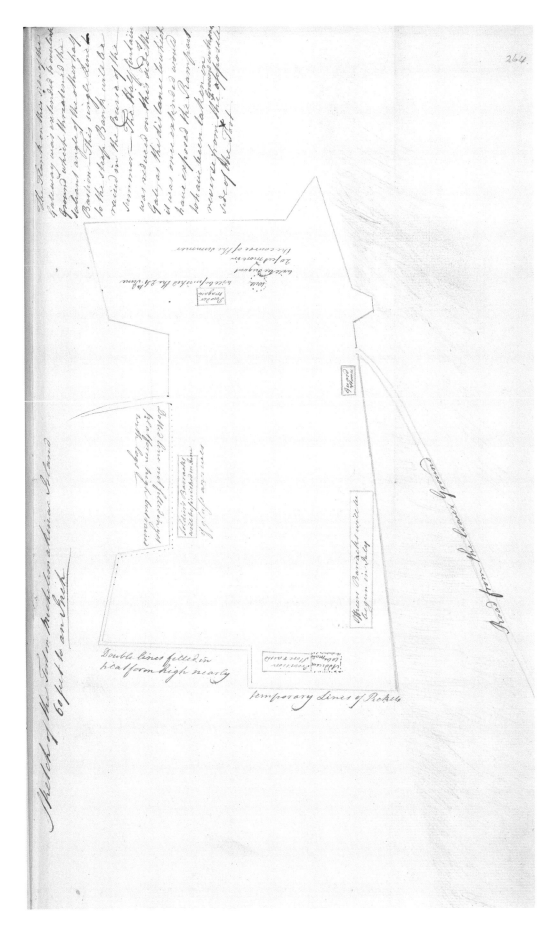

fill from excavation of the ditch and building foundations. Sinclair was particularly interested in security at this point, as he had been unable to move his garrison from the mainland during the summer of 1780 and hoped to do so by late May 1781.[125] The unfinished parts of the defenses were enclosed with pickets. These follow the top of the bluff and close the western end of the fort. Another picket line secured its eastern end. None of Fort Mackinac's distinctive masonry walls had yet been constructed.

Sinclair's plan of May 12 (Fig. 2.11) was the first to project buildings within the fort. These were proposed sites only. Construction had not yet begun on the officers' quarters, and the soldiers' barracks would be placed on the opposite side of the fort behind the log work curtain wall. The barracks had been moved across the ice from the mainland in February, and the provisions storehouse followed soon after.[126] Sinclair's final arrangement of the buildings appears in the plan he drew a month later (Fig. 2.12).

Much had been accomplished by June 15, when Sinclair sent off the last of his drawings. The buildings that had been moved across the ice were being reassembled within the new fort. The provisions storehouse was up by June 6, and Sinclair reported that the barracks was "raising as fast as our scarcity of men, Tools and materials will admit."[127] When he drew his plan, soon after, Sinclair added further details. This time he showed the entire outline of the fort, including both half bastions and two gates. The eastern half of the enclosure was still little more than a trace, however, and only the western walls had been built to any height. A guardhouse, probably relocated from the mainland, was in place near the south sally port. A projected addition to the storehouse had yet to be made. A substantial stone powder magazine was to be finished before month's end, and a well had been begun in the southeastern corner of the fort. Aside from a change in the orientation of the provisions storehouse, the buildings of British Fort Mackinac were in place.

By early July 1781 the barracks had been reassembled, and the stone walls of the powder magazine seem to have been erected. The foundation of an officers' barracks, shown in Figure 2.12, was about to be laid, and work continued on the fortifications. Sinclair had speeded construction by employing Canadian boatmen as laborers, and he hoped to complete the move from the mainland in the fall. In October he promised to do his utmost to finish the fortifications by the end of 1782.[128] Reports cease at that point, and the next was not made until April 1782. Sinclair's only comment was that "the works are getting in forwardness."[129]

This means that a huge amount of limestone masonry was constructed between midsummer 1781 and September 1782, when Lieutenant Hockings described the fort's walls in great detail. The masonry included large portions of the two distinctive gun platforms in the southeastern corner, the south sally port, and the walls that form the land side of Fort Mackinac, pierced by the north sally port. Other sections of masonry had been built to varying heights along the south wall and at the fort's western end. Hockings made it clear, however, that none of this had been completed.[130]

This is where the loss of Lieutenant Hockings's plan is particularly unfortunate, for it was keyed to his report.[131] The engineer also drew sections through the fortifications and appears to have prepared a "Plan of the powder magazine unfinished," a plan of the stone officers' quarters, and probably one of the soldiers' barracks with a report of its condition.[132] These images would greatly illuminate Sinclair's final year of construction on Fort Mackinac. In September 1782 Lieutenant Hockings claimed that with one hundred laborers, two months' time, and "proper exertion," he could put the fortifications "into such a state as to be secure against a surprise."[133] The engineer was left at Mackinac for a time to do just that. The results of his efforts and later repairs or alterations would not appear on a surviving plan until 1796 (Figs. 3.1 and 3.2).

John Johnson (1742–1830) was one of the inspectors sent by Governor Haldimand in 1782 to inquire into Patrick Sinclair's administration of Michilimackinac. Johnson had recently assumed responsibility for Indian affairs, and he paid particular attention to that part of Sinclair's expenses. John Mare painted Johnson's portrait in 1772. *New York State Office of Parks, Recreation and Historic Preservation, Johnson Hall State Historic Site (JH.1971.283).*

A space of land . . . during the pleasure of his Majesty or the Governor

Lieutenant Governor Patrick Sinclair

Relocating the post of Michilimackinac from its site of sixty-five years to an island seven miles across the Straits of Mackinac was an undertaking of considerable proportions. The physical demands of cutting timber, quarrying stone, dismantling and moving buildings and their contents, and then reerecting them at the new site were a heavy burden on the military garrison, and even more so on the civilian community, which provided as much or more of the labor and whose livelihood and daily routine were disrupted for two or three years. Most of the local and seasonal population was engaged in the fur trade, so the effort also entailed financial losses. It meant abandoning or moving houses and diverting employees who would otherwise, in the words of the traders, "be employed in fishing[,] Bringing in our Packs from the different Wintering Posts & Transporting them to Montreal." Despite the inconvenience, most inhabitants agreed that the benefits of Mackinac Island outweighed the hardships of the move, and they cheerfully supported it.[134]

For Patrick Sinclair, there was never any question that the community would follow the garrison. His proposal of October 7, 1779, identified ground below the fort site that would serve as a place for the traders' storehouses and thus preserve Michilimackinac's preeminent role in the fur trade. Indeed, there seems to have been general agreement on the benefits of moving to the island. Within weeks of his arrival, Sinclair reported that "numbers of People established and well lodged have applied for leave to remove their Effects this winter" in the belief that the garrison would be relocated during 1780.[135] Although Sinclair at first suggested that they await Governor Haldimand's orders, his decision to have the traders and their servants move Ste. Anne's Church in February was calculated to ensure that "the Canadians will be drawn to the Island next Year."[136]

The first "house" was taken across the lake in November 1779, although this might have been a government building. By the first week of June 1780, Sinclair could report that the inhabitants were removing their houses.[137] The buildings were dismantled, and the usable wooden components were skidded across the ice in winter or assembled into rafts at Chippewa Point and towed to Haldimand Bay in the warm seasons. This activity continued well into 1781 and probably beyond.[138] Elderly local residents remembered, in the 1830s, that the village had not been completely moved as late as 1783, and that "the transfer from old to new Mackinack seems to have been gradual with the inhabitants."[139]

In order to remove their houses and businesses, the inhabitants of Michilimackinac had to have someplace to go. The site noted for the town on Sinclair's sketch map of October 7, 1779 (Fig. 2.6), straddled the lower ridge in the general vicinity of today's Trinity

Church and Fort Street. When the move began in earnest, however, a more convenient location was adopted that placed the town between the beach and the lower ridge to the south of the fort. A single, long street stretched from the ground below the fort to Lake Huron with lots arranged along both sides of it and others facing the beach. Cross streets allowed access from the beach to the main street. This arrangement is still reflected in the basic layout of the City of Mackinac Island, and its earliest representation appears in a sketch plan drawn about 1790 by Captain David William Smith (Fig. 2.13).

The Smith plan shows the long, main thoroughfare, today known as Market Street. No cross streets appear in the narrow, northern end of the town, but there are several in its broader southern part. These would become, from the top, Hoban Street and French Lane. The third street marks a path inside the stockade that enclosed this fortified colonial village. The defensive picketing is not shown in the Smith plan, but it followed the boundaries of the village on the sides not covered by the fort and the lake. These walls are identified in more detail in a plan of circa 1797 (Fig. 3.3).

Unlike the suburb at Old Michilimackinac, Sinclair intended his new village to be enclosed and protected by two blockhouses and the fort. There is no evidence that the blockhouses were constructed, but the stockade was erected in 1780–81 and remained in place at least until the end of the eighteenth century. Each of Michilimackinac's inhabitants was expected to contribute to the community's security by providing five cedar pickets eighteen feet long and ten inches in diameter. Sinclair reported that they were "cheerfully granted by every white man residing at the post."[140]

The constraints of living within this enclosure caused some complaint from merchants who had become accustomed to the freedom of residing outside the walls of Old Michilimackinac.[141] They had no choice in the matter. The town contained a guardhouse, and a detachment of soldiers was maintained in the village. During the summer of 1784, following a reduction in the number of soldiers, the inhabitants were drawn upon to form a guard of twenty men every night.[142] After the garrison was restored to its usual two companies, the army resumed that duty. The guard had several responsibilities. It provided sentries and security against attack and probably had some police functions as well. The soldiers were also to keep watch for fire.[143]

Establishing a new town meant considering the matter of private land ownership, for the purchase of Mackinac Island from the Ojibwas made the British Crown the landowner. The French inhabitants and later British merchants at Old Michilimackinac all had claims to their lots and houses, although the basis of most holdings was obscure.

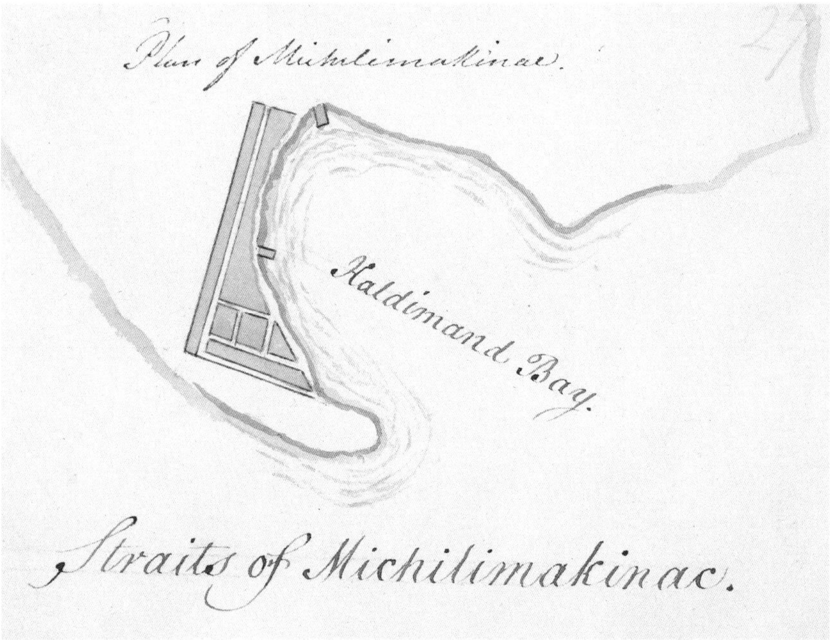

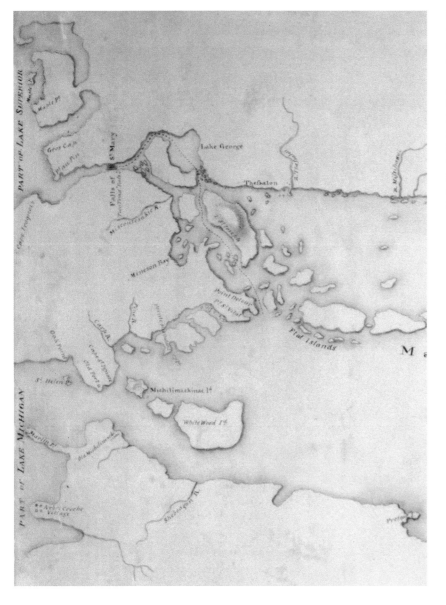

FIGURE 2.13

TITLE: Plan of Michilimakinac.
AUTHOR: Captain David William Smith,
5th Regiment of Foot (1764–1837).
DATE DEPICTED: ca. 1790.
DATE OF WORK: [ca. 1790].
DESCRIPTION: 9.2 x 12.1 cm. Pen and ink
with watercolor on paper.
PROVENANCE: The plan is pasted in a
scrapbook assembled by Smith in the early
1830s. It was retained with his personal papers
until they were acquired by the Toronto Public
Library.
COLLECTION: Special Collections, Genealogy
and Maps Centre, Toronto Public Library
(James Bain Collection, D. W. Smith Notebooks,
Vol. 2, "Views & Plans").

FIGURE 2.14

TITLE: Sketch of Lake Huron 1788,
circumnavigated by Gother Mann, Capt.
commanding Royal Engineers in Canada.
[Detail].
AUTHOR: Captain Gother Mann, Royal
Engineers (1747–1830).
DATE DEPICTED: 1788.
DATE OF WORK: 1788.
DESCRIPTION: 51.3 x 74 cm. Pen and ink
with watercolor on paper.
PROVENANCE: Unknown.
COLLECTION: Library and Archives Canada,
Ottawa, ON (H2/410-Huron-1788).

Governor Haldimand had no doubt as to what the arrangement should be on the island. Michilimackinac was a military post, and wartime expediency must prevail. Any houses or stores at the new site, Sinclair was told, were to be "subject entirely to the direction of the Governor & upon such sufferance as the Kings Interest may require."[144] By the summer of 1780 Sinclair was offering lots to inhabitants as well as to those involved in the Indian trade. The greatest concern of his superiors was that "it will be difficult to make them understand that their Settlements are not their Properties with the Power of Disposal, or making them over to others, the Sole Right of Which must Remain with the King for that Purpose."[145] Deeds granted by Sinclair all specified a "limited Right & Title" to the village lots on which houses and stores were built, and the right to convey, sell, or dispose of these lands only "during the Pleasure of his Majesty, or the Governor & Commander in Chief of the province of Quebec."[146] All deeds were registered with the local notary.

These documents were couched in terms intended to reassure the inhabitants, but the end of the war and the cession of the Straits of Mackinac to the new United States sent a ripple of anxiety through the Michilimackinac community. Concerned that a transfer of sovereignty was imminent, fourteen of the settlement's most prominent members signed a petition in October 1783. In it, they stated their awareness that their grants were conditional and that they might not be recognized by "another Government," from which they could not "reasonably expect the same Indulgence." The signers requested "a confirmation of their Deeds on the Island."[147] No response has been found. Although the transfer to the United States would be delayed until 1796, the question of property ownership remained unresolved. It would fall to administrators of the Northwest and Michigan territories and to the U.S. Congress to settle the matter in coming decades.

The Smith plan includes little detail aside from the street grid. There is no indication of government or public buildings. Ste. Anne's Church is not shown at its new location at the corner of the upper cross street (Hoban). The only additional features are a pair of wharves projecting into Haldimand Bay. Construction of a wharf at which government vessels could be laid up for the winter had been one of Patrick Sinclair's first priorities. He sent workers to the island for that purpose as early as the end of October 1779. By the middle of February, Samuel Robertson, master of one of the vessels, had supervised construction of a T-shaped, stone-filled, timber-crib wharf 150 feet long with twelve feet of water alongside. Robertson eventually prepared several copies of a plan, none of which has survived.[148] This wharf was almost certainly at the site of the structure shown at the curve of the bay on the Smith plan, a spot at the foot of modern Fort Street that has been the location of a "government" wharf ever since.

Haldimand Bay proved to be an unforgiving site for harbor works. About 2:00 AM on December 10, 1780, a forty-foot section of the new wharf was destroyed, probably by wave action. Samuel Robertson attributed the loss to the fact that the cribs had not been properly filled with stones, but he also added that "there is a great swell setts in from the Eastward & perhaps will Require a worke of more time and solidity than Govr. Sinclair was aware of."[149] Sinclair and earlier observers had noted that Round Island provided some shelter for the harbor, but this has never been enough to protect

Lord Edward Fitzgerald (1763–98), an Irish aristocrat and army officer, was one of the first true tourists to visit Mackinac Island. He stopped briefly in 1789 during an adventurous trip through the Great Lakes and down the Mississippi River. This engraving, by T. A. Dean after a painting by William Hamilton, appeared in Thomas Moore, *The Life and Death of Lord Edward Fitzgerald* (London, 1831).
Clements Library, University of Michigan.

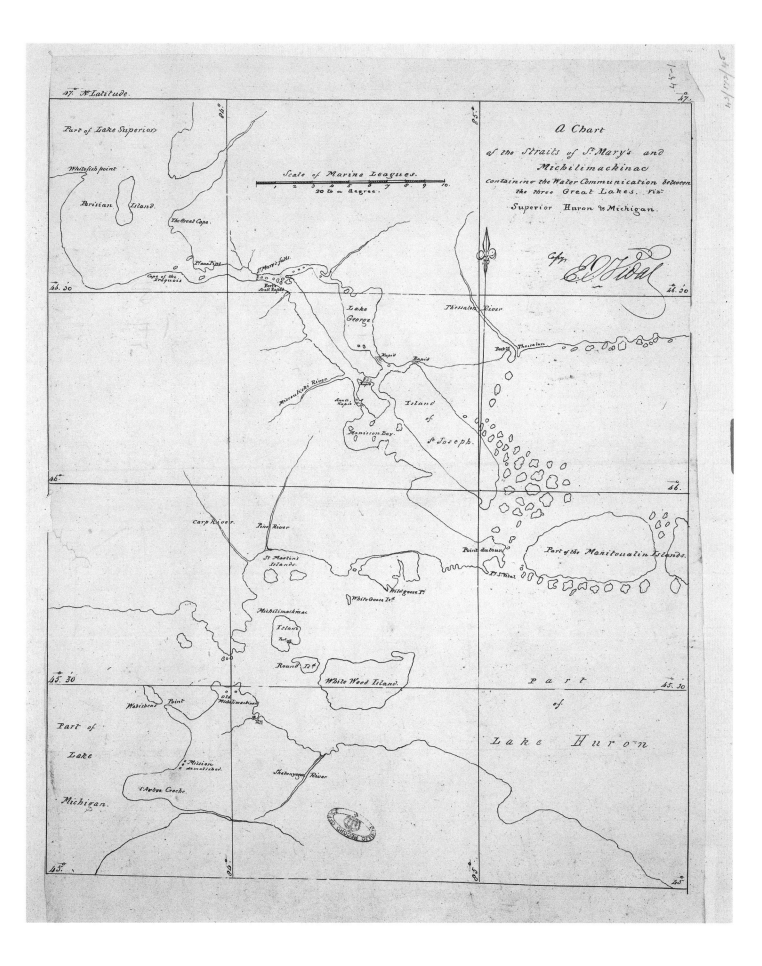

A Chart

of the Straits of St Mary's and
Michilimackinac
Containing the Water Communication between
the three Great Lakes. viz:

Superior Huron & Michigan.

Copy
E O Vidal

vessels from an east wind. The wharf was repaired, but it was "broke to pieces" when the ice went out in the spring of 1784 and damaged again in a September gale.[150] The stubby structure depicted by Smith probably represents a truncated and much-patched version of the original. A second wharf in the middle of the town is not described in any records and was probably a private effort. It does not appear on the town plan of circa 1797 (Fig. 3.3).

Mackinac Island's harbor was its lifeline to the rest the world, and the waterways around it were depicted in a number of maps prepared during the closing days of the British regime. Among the best was a survey of the Lake Huron coast made during a 1788 circumnavigation by engineer Captain Gother Mann (Fig. 2.14). Mann inspected Fort Mackinac during his trip, and he mapped the Straits in some detail. In addition to identifying previous fort sites on the north and south mainlands, Mann included the Ottawa village at L'Arbre Croche and the islands in the Straits, and, for the first time, gave some indication of Lighthouse Point on the north side of Bois Blanc Island. Also named are the Pine and Carp rivers

flowing into St. Martin Bay as well as Mill Creek (unnamed) on the south mainland and the "Sheboagan River" opposite Bois Blanc at the eastern end of the Straits.

Mann's map gives no indication of mainland habitations other than at L'Arbre Croche. The Cheboygan River had earlier been used as a wintering place for British naval vessels. Samuel Robertson laid up the sloop *Welcome* there for two seasons and established "a Dwelling House & Garden by the Edge of the wood," but this practice ended after 1780.[151] A map prepared about the same time as Mann's (Fig. 2.15) and surviving in several versions gives a few additional details, including an indication of buildings at the sites of Old Michili-mackinac and the former Jesuit mission and farm (later Askin's farm) between that place and L'Arbre Croche. The mission is noted as "demolished." Of more importance is a "Saw Mill" shown on the still unnamed Mill Creek. This, the earliest industrial complex in the Straits, had been established by Robert Campbell sometime before 1793, at which time Captain William Doyle contracted for boards from "Campbell's Saw Mill" for repairs at Fort Mackinac.[152]

FIGURE 2.15

TITLE: A Chart of the Straits of St. Mary's and Michilimackinac containing the Water Communication between the three Great Lakes, viz: Superior Huron & Michigan.

AUTHOR: Copy by Emeric Essex Vidal after an unknown cartographer.

DATE DEPICTED: 1785–96.

DATE OF WORK: [1815].

DESCRIPTION: 42 x 35.9 cm. Pen and ink on paper.

PROVENANCE: Removed from CO 42/172/45. The map would have been no. 45 in a volume titled "List of Charts, Plans &c attached to the Report (No 82)." The map is now filed separately.

COLLECTION: National Archives, Kew, London (MPG 1/87).

Two companies of the 5th Regiment of Foot occupied Fort Mackinac in 1790–92. Colored etchings of an officer and soldier were published in London in the latter year, based on drawings by Edward Dayes. *Anne S. K. Brown Military Collection, Brown University Library.*

Henry Burbeck (1754–1848) was the first U.S. commandant of Fort Mackinac. Charles-Balthazar Fevret de St. Memin captured his image in this portrait engraving of 1806.

Reproduced by permission of the Society of the Cincinnati, Washington, DC (L1996 F307).

"A very lonesome place but abounds in high health and excellt. Fish"

1796–1812

Major Henry Burbeck had seen many places while in the service of the United States. His military career had begun in the heady days of 1775, when he and his Massachusetts neighbors took up arms against the British. Burbeck campaigned through the War for Independence and then spent three years as a civilian when Continental forces were disbanded. He returned to service in 1786 after the army was reconstituted to fight the Indians of the Ohio country. Having witnessed the

earliest acts of the American Revolution, it was fitting that this twenty-year veteran should preside at the final curtain. By the late summer of 1796 Michilimackinac was the last of the major Great Lakes posts still in British hands, and its occupation by U.S. troops would constitute the concluding, symbolic event in the struggle for independence.

On September 1 Major Burbeck and the officers and men of his command sailed into Haldimand Bay aboard the sloop *Detroit* to be greeted by the dramatic scene that had attracted Patrick Sinclair. Looming above the harbor was the unfinished Fort Mackinac, "situated on a huge rock of about 150 feet from the water."[1] Straggling along the shore below the fortifications were the log houses of the traders and inhabitants. This was to be Burbeck's new command, a post that Major General Anthony Wayne had warned "was of the first consequence." The new U.S. garrison was in a challenging position. Although American citizens were soon likely to enter the fur trade, British merchants from Montréal dominated the industry, and Michilimackinac was the center of their activities in the northern lakes. The place was also "surrounded by the most numerous and powerful tribes of Indians in the wilderness of the west," people who had been at war with the United States until only a year before.[2] Michilimackinac was the most isolated military outpost of the republic.[3]

The transfer of sovereignty seems to have gone without a hitch. Ratification of Jay's Treaty, late in the winter of 1796, had guaranteed the conveyance of the Great Lakes posts to the United States. On June 1 the British commandants of Fort Ontario, Niagara, Detroit,

and Michilimackinac were ordered to evacuate their fortifications, leaving only caretaker detachments to await the Americans.[4] The British immediately began constructing a new stronghold at St. Joseph Island in the St. Marys River about forty-five miles from Michilimackinac. Lieutenant Andrew Foster and a few men stayed behind to greet Burbeck. The only real ceremony on September 1 seems to have been a joint inspection of the fort and government buildings followed by the signing of a descriptive inventory.[5]

Burbeck and his men were on their own. They found Fort Mackinac to be in ruinous condition, but the American officers went to work making recommendations for its repair (see Figs. 3.1 and 3.2). There were civil arrangements to be made as well. Mackinac Island was now a part of the Northwest Territory of the United States of America, and territorial secretary Winthrop Sargent had accompanied Burbeck for the purpose of integrating the place into that government by appointing public officials. Sargent soon encountered the realities of the seasonal fluctuation in Mackinac's population. He found only twenty resident families, while the summer brought a "great Concourse of persons," numbering from fifteen hundred to two thousand. This required at least three "Conservators of the peace," but Sargent could identify only two "proper Characters" and found it necessary to appoint Major Burbeck to serve as well. He lamented that "very few men of legal Ability or even common Education were to be found in the County." There were political considerations, too. Most of the British residents remained attached to their king, while the majority Francophone Canadian population had been largely excluded from leadership roles. Under such imperfect conditions began American civil government at the Straits of Mackinac.[6]

Documenting land ownership was another priority. The island was now the property of the United States, and Lieutenant Foster surrendered the original 1781 deed that Sinclair had retained at the post.[7] Winthrop Sargent sent a copy to Secretary of State Timothy Pickering and then examined local property records. He found that land transactions at Michilimackinac had sometimes been "extreme loose" and that boundaries were seldom expressed with any precision. However, he believed all claimants could, "by oral testimony, very generally define their lots." Much of the island had been granted away, he reported, and all deeds derived from Lieutenant Governor Patrick Sinclair. In this respect, at least, the records were in better order than those at Detroit.[8] The new American administrator did not suggest that Sinclair's conditional grants be voided, something that must have relieved every proprietor. However, confirmation of most Mackinac land holdings would take another decade and some even longer.

Amid his official duties, Major Burbeck took time to learn something about the island and its community. He counted sixty-four houses in the village. Of the island itself, he ventured, "this place abounds with good health rocks and Fish . . . thats the most I can say of it."[9] Perhaps Burbeck implied that he had found his way to Arch Rock and Sugar Loaf. He had certainly discovered Michilimackinac's reputation for a salubrious climate and tasty trout and whitefish. The sixteen years between the arrival of American troops and the outbreak of the War of 1812 would mark the beginnings of an appreciation for the romantic, natural beauty of the Straits of Mackinac in addition to its military and commercial importance. Just a year after Burbeck's arrival, a fellow officer, Major Caleb Swan, could wax enthusiastic about the "romantic and majestic landscape" of the Straits and the "extensive and sublime view" from the highest point of Mackinac Island. There it was possible, he wrote, to "look into the immensity of Lake Michigan, which looses [sic] itself in the southern hemisphere" and see "the great Lake Huron . . . expanded to the bounds of the horizon."[10] Swan's effusive comments are not isolated examples. In 1800 U.S. senator Uriah Tracy described Mackinac Island as "in itself a natural & great curiosity" that, viewed from the water, looked to him "like Fairyland." In the autumn of 1802, Francis LeBarron, Fort Mackinac's newly arrived surgeon, was the first to describe the island's signature rock formations—Arch Rock, Fairy Arch, Sugar Loaf, and Skull Cave.[11] Other visitors and residents would also soon extol the beauties of the Straits.

Despite such attractions, commerce and security remained the primary concerns for this newest part of the republic. The 1794 treaty with Britain had guaranteed Canadian fur traders access to the lands assigned to the United States, but they remained subject to American import duties. "All the Southern or Mississippi trade, must of necessity pass from Canada by Lake Michigan," General

Anthony Wayne reported to Secretary of the Treasury Oliver Wolcott. Michilimackinac was to be a port of entry. Wayne described it as the "key" but observed that "the door is rather too wide to close without the aid of a Gun or Guard boat" because the fort's position on Mackinac Island could not dominate the water passage. The general suggested a secondary post at Chicago to compensate, but otherwise Michilimackinac was to remain the chief entry point for Lake Michigan and have its own collector of customs.[12]

From a military point of view, few at first questioned the necessity of maintaining a garrison at Michilimackinac. Major Burbeck directed temporary repairs to the fort and its buildings. Then, in 1797, Brigadier General James Wilkinson visited on a tour of inspection. The glaring flaws in the design and position of Fort Mackinac were apparent to the general and his officers. Wilkinson admitted, however, that "this important pass must be secured to the Nation," and he suggested a compromise. Although he believed that a "new Work and different ground" was the only permanent solution, he thought that the existing trace of the post could be "made tenable against small Arms."[13] The former expedient proved impracticable, but Fort Mackinac underwent a major renovation in 1798–99 to render it defensible against Indian attack. This included replacement of the rotting British land defenses with three blockhouses, completion of the unfinished officers' stone quarters, repairs and additions to the masonry walls, and new picketing.[14] The result was to unify the outline of Fort Mackinac into the irregular, near-triangle that it forms today. These improvements were first described when Senator Tracy visited on a fact-finding tour in September 1800.[15]

All this attention to Fort Mackinac and land ownership generated a fair amount of cartography. Little has survived, however, to represent the introduction of U.S. authority and the alterations made to Fort Mackinac. Two plans exist that show the fortifications as the Americans found them in 1796 (Figs. 3.1 and 3.2). Beyond that, the visual record is blank until 1817. General Wilkinson gave Major Burbeck a plan of Fort Mackinac when he visited in August 1797. This showed his proposed demolitions and suggested alterations superimposed on the existing trace, and it probably served as a guide to the renovations accomplished during the next two years. Major John J. U. Rivardi presumably depicted the results in May 1799, when he sent a plan to General Alexander Hamilton from his post at Fort Niagara. Other plans of Fort Mackinac might survive among the papers of Henry Burbeck, although this has proven impossible to confirm.[16] All of these plans relate to Burbeck's command during 1796–99, and there was little or no construction afterward that would have required visual documentation.

Likewise, Mackinac's earliest property maps were probably generated during Henry Burbeck's time. As early as December 1796 Patrick McNiff, a Detroit surveyor, promised to complete a "Plan of Mackina" for General Anthony Wayne, though it is unclear whether this was to be a topographical map, a survey of island property, or a plan of the fortifications. Nor is it known whether McNiff's plan was ever completed, although he possessed cartographic information relevant to Mackinac as late as 1799. Major Burbeck laid out the boundaries of a military reserve on the island during his command, and this almost certainly resulted in some mapping.[17] Any such cartography that survives might be among Burbeck's papers. As it is, the earliest known maps of Mackinac Island and its property divisions were not drawn until 1810 (Figs. 3.6 and 3.7).

Even as the original British design of Fort Mackinac was being altered into a compromise that could be defended against Indian attack, the entire rationale for maintaining a garrison at Michilimackinac was being questioned. In 1798 the United States was drawn into an undeclared naval conflict with France that showed every sign of escalating into a full-scale war. This greatly stressed a small but expanding army that had to guard both coastal and wilderness frontiers. In the spring of 1799 Alexander Hamilton, commanding the northern part of the country during the emergency, expressed his opinion that "the advantages of a Post at Michilimacnac do not compensate for the disadvantages." A garrison there, Hamilton believed, was unlikely to "materially awe" the Indians, while its position in northern Lake Huron was "quite out of the reach of support" in a military emergency. The troops, he believed, would be better deployed to the Detroit garrison.[18]

Although Alexander Hamilton was inclined to abandon Fort Mackinac, he solicited the opinions of General Wilkinson, who had ordered the renovations that were just being completed. Wilkinson argued for the retention of a garrison at Michilimackinac because it was one of those posts that permitted the U.S. government to "exclude all foreign intercourse . . . with our Citizens & our Savages . . . and effectually bar all communication between Canada & Louisiana." Rather than abandon the place, he suggested a new

fortification on the highest ground and a much larger garrison of 250 men.[19] Wilkinson's recommendation was sufficient to sway his superior, in part, but Hamilton remained concerned about economy and was unwilling to relocate the post. He grudgingly agreed to retain a small garrison to guard "one of the portals of our North Western territory & to avoid the appearance to the Indians of an abandonment of that part of the country." In November, Lieutenant Colonel Burbeck was recalled to Detroit with most of his troops, leaving behind Lieutenant Richard Whiley and only thirty-five men.[20]

Within a year, however, this policy would be reconsidered, influenced by the visit of Senator Tracy in September 1800. Tracy found the fort at Michilimackinac to be "the best & much the most important fortress which the United States possesses—on our northern Frontier." He argued for an increase in the garrison from the thirty men he found there.[21] In 1802 the garrison was indeed augmented, and Fort Mackinac held two or more companies of troops until 1805, after which it became a one-company artillery post. The garrison would remain that size until the outbreak of the War of 1812.

Fur remained the business of Michilimackinac, of course. Aside from the imposition of a national boundary between British Canada and the pelt-collecting regions, however, the transfer to an American administration had relatively little impact on day-to-day operations. As most correspondents noted in the decade following the arrival of U.S. troops, British merchants from Montréal continued to dominate the trade. Many were members of joint-stock companies formed during the last decades of the eighteenth century to compensate for the increased operating costs and financial risks created by the American Revolution. Many agents of Canadian companies remained a part of the Mackinac Island community, where they owned property and storehouses.

"There is a great influx of merchants, hired men, and Indians. For three months nothing else is seen but the coming and going of canoes, or Frenchmen and Indians arriving in canoes and as many leaving." FATHER JEAN DILHET

In its basic mechanics, the system for the exchange of European manufactured goods for pelts had changed little from what it had been for a century. Major Caleb Swan carefully inquired into the manner in which Michilimackinac supported the fur trade when he visited in 1797. He agreed with other correspondents that the place was "the only key to the immense, lucrative skin-trade." The primary market for Michilimackinac's traders was the area west of Lake Michigan, from the Illinois River to the upper Mississippi. Brigades of canoes were outfitted annually at Michilimackinac and typically set out for the West in July, returning with furs the following summer. There, they met canoes from Montréal with fresh stocks of goods. These were exchanged for the furs collected during the previous winter, and the cycle began anew.[22]

It was this trade system that helped create the seasonal population fluctuations of Michilimackinac. Most of the houses of the village stood empty during all but the summer months. Then, as Father Jean Dilhet noted in 1804, "There is a great influx of merchants, hired men, and Indians. For three months nothing else is seen but the coming and going of canoes, or Frenchmen and Indians arriving in canoes and as many leaving."[23] The town was bursting at the seams. The Indian storekeeper Thomas Duggan complained, in 1796, that it was easy to rent a house in the winter months, but in summer he had to "seek some other place on account of the Proprietor wanting it for himself and Engagés to live in & store his Goods." In 1802 Dr. LeBarron noted that many of the traders and their employees were forced to live in tents.[24] The busy summer season, with its hundreds of voyageurs and Indians, was a festive and unruly time. Alexander Ross, who traveled from Montréal to Michilimackinac in the summer of 1810, observed tartly that "the Montreal men are expert canoe-men, the Mackina men expert bottle-men." Although he admitted that Canadians drank, sometimes excessively, "to see drunkenness and debauchery, with all their concomitant vices, carried on systematically, it is necessary to see Mackinac."[25]

This rollicking environment was tied to the fortunes of the fur trade. Although these remained generally good for much of the time before the War of 1812, the political tensions created by continuing war in Europe and deteriorating relations between the United States and Great Britain after 1807 had their effects. Embargoes imposed on commerce with Britain seriously affected the fur trade, preventing the importation of British trade goods from the post of St. Joseph and stalling normal operations. In 1808 the United States extended its system of Indian factories to Michilimackinac, further affecting the trade. These government-operated trading houses were intended to provide goods to the Indians at low prices. A factory opened at Michilimackinac late in 1809.[26] By that time LeBarron, who had become involved in commerce in addition to his garrison medical duties, reported, "the Trade of the Country is going to Destruction." A year later Dr. David Mitchell, a holdover from British days, complained that many of the houses of Michilimackinac were in ruins and "the proprietors are entirely removed from the distracted state of Affairs in Europe."[27]

It was during this period of stagnation that the first serious American contender in the fur trade made his presence felt at the Straits of Mackinac. In 1808 New York entrepreneur John Jacob Astor formed the American Fur Company. Three years later he entered into a business agreement with the Canadian North West and Michilimackinac companies by which the South West Company was formed to operate in U.S. territory. The arrangement was limited to a span of only five years, but Astor was in the Great Lakes trade.[28] He sent a nephew, Henry Brevoort, to the Straits to represent his interests in the summer of 1811. Brevoort spent a frustrating month observing the situation and learning about the trade. Astor's goods were of foreign manufacture, so the embargo held them at Fort St. Joseph with no hope of entry. Brevoort could sense the storm rising with the Indians, who did not hide their frustration with the U.S. government. The young businessman condemned "a law which prohibits the admission of European goods into the U States intended to be fairly traded among the Indians, whilst the Am: G[overnmen]t. Are unable (having no stock of Indian goods in the US) to substitute a supply."[29] War would intervene before Astor could make his company's influence felt in the Michilimackinac fur trade.

Two other events of significance marked the years before the War of 1812. The question of land titles had not been forgotten, but the matter was resolved, for the most part, by congressional action and by survey between 1805 and 1810. This generated the first surviving Straits of Mackinac property maps (Figs. 3.5–3.7) and laid the foundation for most private land ownership on Mackinac Island at the beginning of the twenty-first century.[30] The decade before the War of 1812 also saw the first increase in missionary activity since 1765, when the last Jesuit had departed L'Arbre Croche and the church at Michilimackinac. Catholic priests occasionally visited in the years after that time, but Ste. Anne's Church was without a regular pastor.[31] In the aftermath of the arrival of American administration, Father Gabriel Richard spent part of the summer of 1799 on the island and at L'Arbre Croche. His associate, Father Jean Dilhet, did likewise in 1804, but the resources of the parish would not be able to sustain a regular priest until 1830.[32]

It was in this religious vacuum that the first Protestant missionary activities began at Michilimackinac. In the summer of 1802, the Reverend David Bacon, ministering on behalf of the Missionary Society of Connecticut, arrived on Mackinac Island in hopes of establishing a mission among the Ottawa of L'Arbre Croche. He seems to have been encouraged in his endeavor by Senator Tracy, whom Bacon had met at Detroit in 1800, and by other U.S. officials.[33] Although Reverend Bacon was never able to carry out his plans for the mainland mission, he and his wife, Alice, spent two years on Mackinac Island, where they briefly operated a school and attempted to learn the Ottawa language. Disappointed in their efforts to establish themselves at L'Arbre Croche, the Bacons obtained permission to clear land and construct buildings in the interior of Mackinac

Island for a Moravian-style Indian mission village and farm designed to separate Christianized Ottawa from their traditional village. A lack of funds ended their venture in the summer of 1804.[34] The onset of renewed missionary activity—and religious conflict—on Mackinac Island would await the 1820s.

By 1811 Mackinac Island was at an important transition point. War clouds were gathering throughout the West, and commercial change was in the air. In addition, the first stirrings of interest in Mackinac's natural beauty foretold its eventual development as a place of resort. "In this second Eden," Henry Brevoort wrote to his friend Washington Irving in 1811, "I would scramble with you to the summit of a venerable old rock, from whose lofty head you would behold nature's savage face." Brevoort's vision encompassed not only the lakes "studded with innumerable islands and bounded by the most romantic Bays, Inlets, Promontories & Rivers" but also "the seats of future Cities and future Empires."[35] Mackinac had entered the nineteenth century, during which verbal and visual images of its scenery would become known throughout the world.

U.S. COMMANDANTS OF MICHILIMACKINAC, 1796–1812

Major Henry Burbeck, Regiment of Artillerists and Engineers, 1796–99

Lieutenant Richard Whiley, Regiment of Artillerists and Engineers, 1799–1802

Lieutenant Colonel Thomas Hunt, 1st Regiment of Infantry, 1802–4

Lieutenant Colonel Jacob Kingsbury, 1st Regiment of Infantry, 1804–5

Captain Josiah Dunham, Regiment of Artillerists 1805–7

Lieutenant Jonathan Eastman, Regiment of Artillerists, 1807

Lieutenant Presley Neville O'Bannon, Regiment of Artillerists, 1807–8

Lieutenant Porter Hanks, Regiment of Artillerists, 1808

Captain Lewis Howard, Regiment of Artillerists, 1808–11

Lieutenant Porter Hanks, Regiment of Artillerists, 1811–12

The Fort is an irregular work without bastions

Lieutenant Andrew Foster

Henry Burbeck's first impression of the imposing position of Fort Mackinac soon gave way to concerns about how to defend the place. "It is in ruins," he wrote to his friend Captain Moses Porter six days after his arrival, and noted further that "the whole works are in a defenceless state."[36] Burbeck, by that time, had had plenty of opportunity to examine the twenty-five-year-old fortification and its buildings. His evaluation began the day of his arrival, when, in company with Lieutenant Andrew Foster of the former British garrison, Burbeck toured the fort and the government buildings situated in the town below. Foster had prepared a descriptive inventory, which Burbeck was asked to sign at the conclusion of his inspection.[37]

Lieutenant Foster's report was frank and unvarnished, and it provides one of the best accounts of how Fort Mackinac had been roughly finished and maintained in the years following Lieutenant Hockings's 1782 visit. It is possible that Foster was embarrassed by the condition of the fortifications that had been left in his charge. It is likely that he offered some explanation. Soon after Hockings had devised his makeshift plans to complete the defenses, Fort Mackinac had become a victim of international politics. The definitive treaty of peace ending the American War for Independence was signed in 1783, placing Michilimackinac within the United States. By the spring of 1784, however, no arrangements had been made to transfer the Great Lakes posts. Then, in August, came word that the transfer would be delayed indefinitely.[38]

The cessation of hostilities had already brought an end to all work at the post. From the summer of 1783 Robertson and his soldiers had done patchwork, "only keeping the temporary works together, so as to command some Respect for the safety of the Garrison & Traders" from the local Indians.[39] Mackinac's climate had then done its worst. By the summer of 1784 Robertson reported that the picketing, the road up the hill to the fort, and the garrison wharf required "repairing after every shower of Rain, Gust of Wind."[40] Four years later Captain Gother Mann inspected and critiqued the fortifications. He believed they were not worth completing but admitted that "a temporary Business . . . to insure the immediate possession of it, at least to prevent any surprize by Indians or others" was justified. This remained the policy regarding Fort Mackinac for the remainder of the British occupation.[41] Only the most essential work was undertaken, often following the entreaties of commandants such as Captain William Doyle, who pleaded in 1793 for an engineer and workers "to render this Miserable Fortress in some degree tenable."[42]

The transfer of sovereignty finally provided the motivation to repair and complete decrepit Fort Mackinac. Burbeck's garrison included officers with technical skills, who went to work organizing the necessary repairs and alterations. Within ten days of his arrival, Burbeck, assisted by territorial secretary Winthrop Sargent, had taken a "draft of the Garrison," a copy of which was sent to Captain Moses Porter at Detroit by Lieutenant James Sterrett, who seems to have assumed the responsibilities of post engineer. Burbeck allowed that the plan was a "very good one."[43] It seems likely that Figure 3.1 is a copy of that survey, as it is preserved among the papers of Secretary Sargent.

The rudimentary Burbeck-Sargent effort was soon followed by a more precisely drawn plan of Fort Mackinac (Fig. 3.2) that identified the composition of each section of wall and noted the function of each building. Lieutenant Sterrett signed the plan, but Lieutenant Ebenezer Massey, a fellow artillerist, assisted him in his survey. Their field notes survive, in which the officers reveal that they laid down the courses or directions of fortification features with the aid of a pocket compass and measured distances by paces assumed to be of three feet each. Their notes admit that the buildings were added "from memory and not pretended therefore to be by any means accurate." Plan and memorandum were enclosed in a letter from Major Burbeck to General Wayne on October 25.[44]

The two plans include the same general information, though they are quite different in appearance. Figure 3.1 shows the effects of a hurried survey (or careless compass readings), as the angles of the faces and flanks of the two half bastions and their connecting curtain wall are inaccurately drawn in comparison with the same features on Figure 3.2. Nor are there any labels to identify the uses of buildings or the nature or condition of the defenses. This, however, may be because Sargent retained only a simple outline plan, either as a rough copy or perhaps as a template. It seems probable that the version sent on to Captain Porter contained further information.

The Sterrett plan demonstrates a great deal more care in execution and provides additional details as well, particularly when studied with the field notes. Sections of wall marked "No. 1" were constructed of log or rubble-filled log crib work, and these were uniformly rotten and falling down. Lieutenant Foster's inventory indicated as much, and Sterrett's field notes confirm this. The stonework ("No. 2") was generally "firm & good," reflecting either the greater durability of masonry construction or more recent attention and repairs.[45] Both compositions identify a prominent feature—labeled "Ravelin" on the Sterrett plan—which was added after Patrick Sinclair drew his last rendering of the fort in June 1781 (Fig. 2.12). The massive, triangular stone wall, pierced by the north sally port, had been completed by the time of Lieutenant Richard

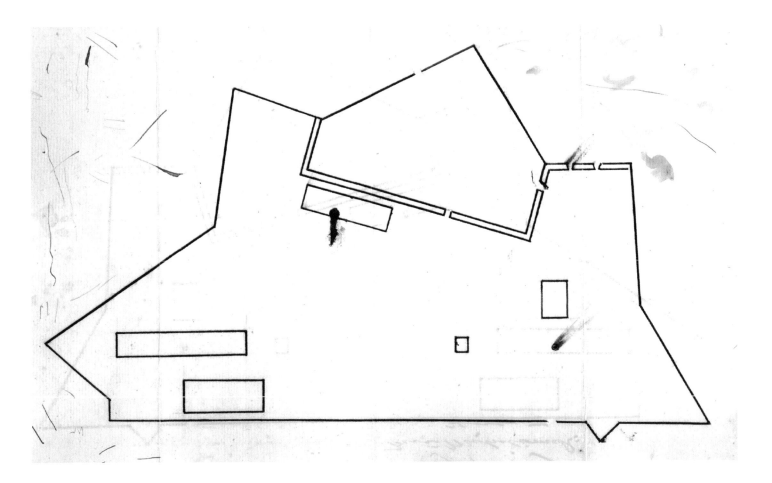

FIGURE 3.1

TITLE: [On verso:] a rough plan of
Fort Michilimakina.
AUTHOR: Probably Territorial
Secretary Winthrop Sargent (1753–1820)
and Major Henry Burbeck, 1st Regiment
of Artillerists and Engineers (1754–1848).
DATE DEPICTED: September 1796.
DATE OF WORK: [September 1796].
DESCRIPTION: 17 x 27.5 cm. Pen and
ink on paper.
PROVENANCE: Retained in the papers
of Winthrop Sargent until deposited
with the Ohio Historical Society.
COLLECTION: Ohio Historical Society,
Columbus (Winthrop Sargent Papers,
Box 3, Folder 11).

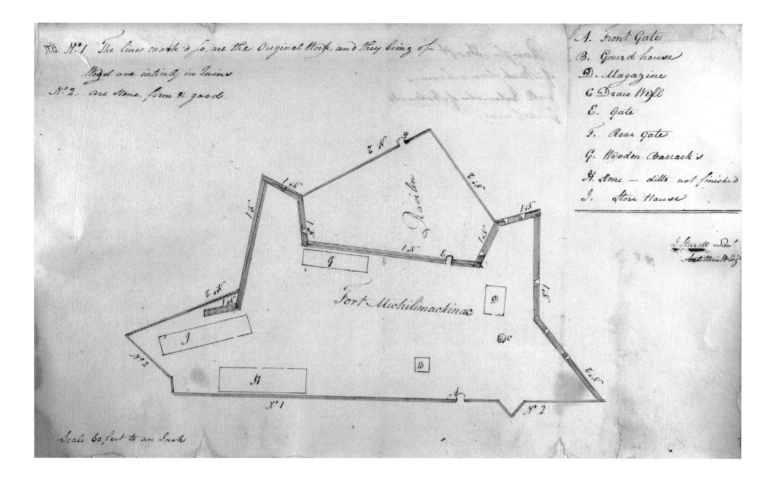

GOVERNOR SARGENT.

U.S. civil authority arrived at Michilimackinac in 1796 in the person of Winthrop Sargent (1753–1820), secretary of the Northwest Territory. This drawing, by Charles-Balthazar Fevret de St. Memin, depicts him in 1802. *Corcoran Gallery of Art, Washington, DC (75.16).*

FIGURE 3.2

TITLE: Fort Michilimackinac. [On verso:] Rough draft of Michilimackinac with estimated materials for repairs.

AUTHOR: Lieutenant James Sterrett, 1st Regiment of Artillerists and Engineers (active 1794–1805), and Lieutenant Ebenezer Massey, 1st Regiment of Artillerists and Engineers (active 1792–d. 1799). Signed: J. Sterrett.

DATE DEPICTED: October 25, 1796.

DATE OF WORK: [October 25, 1796].

DESCRIPTION: 23 x 37.5 cm. Pen and ink on paper.

PROVENANCE: Enclosed in a letter from Major Henry Burbeck to Major General Anthony Wayne of October 25, 1796. Retained in the papers of General Anthony Wayne.

COLLECTION: The Historical Society of Pennsylvania, Philadelphia (Anthony Wayne Papers, Vol. 40, pp. 44, 45).

Hockings's inspection in September 1782, but no plans survive to show it before 1796. It was almost certainly an afterthought by Sinclair, most likely to provide additional protection from artillery on the higher ground north of the fort.

The Sterrett plan also identifies gates and buildings within Fort Mackinac, each of which was described in Lieutenant Foster's inventory. The guardhouse ("B") was a small log house, built to replace its predecessor, which had burned in April 1783.[46] The barracks ("G") and storehouse ("I") were both of log construction and had been moved from the mainland during the winter of 1781. Two stone structures stood within the fort. The powder magazine ("D") was a substantial building protected by an arched stone roof and designed to hold one thousand barrels of gunpowder. On the edge of the bluff stood the sole building of this period to survive in modern Fort Mackinac. The stone barracks ("H"), originally intended for the garrison officers, was begun during the summer of 1781 but remained unfinished and unroofed, its walls erected only as high as the second story and the sleepers and window frames decayed after fifteen years of exposure. In the southeast corner of the fort was a deep well ("C").[47]

Lieutenant Foster's report made no mention of the fatal flaw of Fort Mackinac, which was too far away to appear on plans of the fortifications. Sterrett's field notes are more revealing in this respect. "About NNW of the Fort 600 Yards Distance a hill commanding the same," he added at the very end. This was the elevation that dominates the center of Mackinac Island—the "turtle's back"—and towers some three hundred feet above the surface of Lake Huron and more than one hundred and fifty above Fort Mackinac. Patrick Sinclair had dismissed the significance of these heights when selecting a site for his fort, but its effect had not been lost on engineers like Gother Mann. He recognized that "the Fort is so effectually commanded that it never could resist cannon from hence, as the Garrison would not dare to shew themselves in their works." This was one reason the British had not completed the fort. "I cannot help being of opinion," Mann wrote in 1788, "that as a Military Post, the greater part of the expense bestowed here has been a waste of money. If the Works were intended as a Defence against Musquetry of Indians only, too much was designed, and if against Cannon far too little, and most of that ill judged." Captain Mann at least admitted the dilemma that Sinclair had faced. The town could not be protected from the highest ground, and so the position of Fort Mackinac was an unhappy compromise.[48]

Now an American garrison had to deal with this difficult tactical situation. Burbeck's temporary repairs were followed by the visit of Brigadier General James Wilkinson in August 1797. He admitted that the high ground behind Fort Mackinac "has the most perfect command of it in every quarter," and that "human force and ingenuity could not make it tenable against the attacks of artillery." Therefore, Wilkinson believed, "every expense incurred to this view would be an useless dissipation of labour and treasure."

His compromise solution was to make the place secure against small arms, and he left with the garrison a plan for doing so.[49] This is not known to survive, nor is there much documentation of the project to improve Fort Mackinac, but the work had been completed by the early summer of 1799.[50]

In fact, the first surviving plan to depict the alterations made to Fort Mackinac in 1798–99 would not be drawn until 1817 (Fig. 4.6). When this is compared with the two plans of 1796, Wilkinson's simple solution is apparent. The rotted log-work curtain and half bastions (shown on Fig. 3.2 as "No. 1") were removed and the fill from them redistributed to bolster the defenses. A blockhouse was constructed on the site of each of the two half bastions, with a third perched on the stone wall at the narrow southwestern end of the fort. The officers' stone barracks was completed, and the masonry walls were all repaired. Then, the entire fort was secured with a line of sturdy nine-foot-high pickets in a trace that connected the triangular stone "Ravelin" with the walls on the east and west ends of the fort, giving the roughly triangular shape that Fort Mackinac retains to this day.[51] A careful inspection of the fort will reveal the remnants of the British ditch and the gentle mounds of the two half bastions supporting the north and east blockhouses.

Senator Uriah Tracy was the first to inspect the American makeover of Patrick Sinclair's creation. It was, he reported, "an irregular work, partly built with a strong wall, and partly with Pickets." Among the garrison buildings were "three strong & convenient block houses" and "one stone Barrack for the use of Officers, equal if not superior to any building of the kind in the United States." Tracy made no mention of the commanding ground that would play such a prominent role in the opening drama of the War of 1812. "The post is strong both by nature and art," he optimistically reported, "and the possession of it has great influence with the Indians in favor of the United States."[52]

Around this bason the village is built

Major Caleb Swan

Just as Fort Mackinac was dominated by rising ground, it commanded the village laid out along the shores of Haldimand Bay. "Twenty rods from the rear" of Government House in the town "there is an almost perpendicular ascent of about a hundred feet of rock, upon the top of which stands the fort," Major Caleb Swan wrote following his visit in 1797.[53] Patrick Sinclair had intended his citadel to overlook the harbor and buildings on the lower ground, and this military consideration had dictated the placement of fort and town. The earliest image to depict their relationship is a plan that was probably drawn about 1797 and is illustrated here as Figure 3.3.

The clarity with which this composition illustrates the association of the civilian and military elements of the post of Michilimackinac makes the uncertainty of its origins all the more frustrating. Very little is known about the map titled "Michilmacina," other than it was apparently discovered by the architectural historian Warren L. Rindge in the early 1930s while he was conducting research on Fort Mackinac. Rindge referred to it several times in his 1934 report but gave its location only as "the files of the War Department at Washington."[54] A search of possible record groups and cartographic collections in the National Archives has not revealed the whereabouts of the original. It is reproduced here from a photograph preserved in the collections of Mackinac State Historic Parks.

Nor is anything known about the creation or purpose of this plan. Rindge dated it to 1797 but without further explanation or justification.[55] There is little additional evidence on the map itself. It bears the title "Michilmacina" in the upper left-hand corner, an identification of Haldimand Bay as "The Bason," and the prominent initials "JM," which have usually been assumed to be those of the author. Details within the plan support a date of about 1797, and it must have been drawn before 1798, when the reconstruction of Fort Mackinac was begun. As to authorship, Rindge credited Lieutenant Ebenezer Massey, although his initials do not correspond to those on the map. A lieutenant John Michael did serve in the garrison in 1796–98, but there is no evidence that he created this plan.[56] The only other clue lies in the use of the word "Bason" to describe the harbor, the same term and spelling employed by Major Caleb Swan following his 1797 visit.[57] This, too, may simply be coincidence, but it is not unlikely that a rough sketch map drawn during General Wilkinson's inspection visit might have found its way into the records of the War Department.

If the plan is genuine, which it appears to be despite its uncertain provenance, it gives a fine sense of the manner in which Fort Mackinac was placed to cover and dominate the town. In establishing his fort on the bluff above the harbor and separating the garrison from the civilian community, Sinclair achieved a level of security previously unknown at Michilimackinac. The town itself was enclosed by a stockade, and the "JM" plan is the only image to unmistakably show it intact and in use. Three gates are depicted, one each at the western ends of modern Market and Main streets and another below the fort near the wharf, probably on Main Street, about even with the center of Marquette Park.

The street plan of the town is essentially the same as that shown on the Smith plan of circa 1790 (Fig. 2.13). Major Swan described its appearance with care in 1797. "Around this bason the village is built," he wrote, "having two streets of nearly a quarter of a mile in length, a Roman chapel, and containing eighty-nine houses and stores; some of them spacious and handsome, with white lime plaistering in front, which shews to great advantage from the sea."[58] One of Swan's two streets was presumably the track along the beach, for only Market Street is discernable on the "JM" plan, connected to the shore by at least two cross streets (Astor and Hoban) and possibly a third (French Lane). Smaller stockade fences, shown as dashed lines, define individual lots.

Fort Mackinac perches above all of this, and the military features that allowed it to protect the fortified village may be distinguished even today. The village stockade was covered, or flanked, by gun positions in the southwestern end of the fort. The "lower" gun platform, just above the fort's south sally port and shown as a distinct, black triangle on the "JM" plan, not only flanked the bluff and the road to the garrison but also allowed cannon to fire the length of Market Street. Guns on the platform at the extreme southeastern corner of the fort dominated a short section of village stockade between the bluff and harbor.

A few additional features may be identified outside the bounds of town and fort. At the foot of the East Bluff are three fenced plots that represent the commandant's and subalterns' gardens, described in Lieutenant Foster's 1796 post inventory as measuring 540 by 165 feet and 245 by 173, feet respectively. Both were fenced, and in September 1796 they were filled with vegetables and potatoes left by the departing British garrison. Northwest of the pickets of the village is the "government park," a large pasture for grazing the garrison's cattle and horses.[59] This is distinguished by the sketchy outline of a pond that survives as part of the modern Grand Hotel Golf Course. Directly below the fort is the government wharf, the only one in the harbor at this time. An isolated cluster of four buildings at the eastern end of Haldimand Bay represents the beginnings of sprawl beyond the village stockade. This may be a neighborhood described by Father Jean Dilhet in 1804. "In the suburbs at the fort close to the

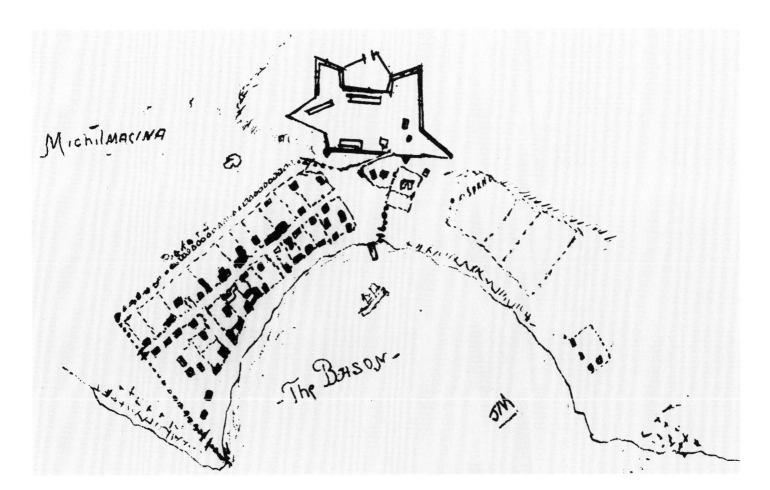

FIGURE 3.3

TITLE: Michilmacina.

AUTHOR: Initials "JM" at lower right are
presumed to be those of the author, possibly
Lieutenant John Michael, 1st Regiment of Infantry
(active 1792–1802). Warren L. Rindge, in his report
of November 1, 1934, attributes this plan to
Lieutenant Ebenezer Massey, 1st Regiment of
Artillerists and Engineers (active 1792–d. 1799).

DATE DEPICTED: 1797?

DATE OF WORK: ca. 1797.

DESCRIPTION: Dimensions unavailable. Drawing
appears to be pen and ink on paper.

PROVENANCE: Unknown, but possibly connected
with the inspection visit of Brigadier General James
Wilkinson in August 1797.

COLLECTION: Unknown, but possibly the
National Archives and Records Administration,
Washington, DC, or another federal collection.
The map is known only from a photograph or
photocopy obtained from an unknown source and
now in the collections of Mackinac State Historic
Parks, Mackinac Island, MI. The photographic
reproduction was apparently obtained by Warren
L. Rindge during research for his report of
November 1, 1934. Rindge cited it several times
as "in the files of the War Department at
Washington."

Fort Mackinac was rebuilt in 1798–99
to a design prepared by Brigadier
General James Wilkinson (1757–1825)
during his inspection tour in August
1797. Wilkinson believed the post
could be secured against Indian
attack but would be helpless against
a force equipped with artillery.
Portrait by Charles Willson Peale.
Independence National Historical Park.

Caleb Swan (1758–1809) was an
army paymaster who accompanied
General Wilkinson to Michilimackinac and wrote a long
description of the post and its
surroundings. He thought the
islands of the Straits formed "a
romantic and majestic landscape
from the sea." Swan is pictured
in a 1799 chalk and wash drawing
by Charles-Balthazar Fevret de
St. Memin. *National Portrait Gallery,
Smithsonian Institution, gift of Mr. and
Mrs. Paul Mellon (S/NPG 74.1).*

town," he wrote, "there are a number of Canadian traders who do considerable trade but not so large as is done by the merchants in the town."[60]

Individual buildings within the village itself are not as readily distinguished, though lots and the figures of houses are shown. The only "public" building was Ste. Anne's Church, which had been moved from the mainland during the winter of 1780 and reassembled near what is today the northeast corner of Hoban and Market streets. The building is on the far side of the church lot on Figure 3.3, set well back from both streets. Several correspondents mentioned the church, and Masses were celebrated there by Father Gabriel Richard in the summer of 1799 and Father Jean Dilhet in 1804. Richard described the building as "very old," but it was constructed of cedar logs and likely, he believed, to last for some time. It measured forty-five by twenty-five feet and was furnished with vestments and basic altar linen. Dilhet also made use of the church furnishings and noted that there was a "presbytery" or house for the priest.[61] Richard repaired the church and rectory during his stay in 1799 as well as the cemetery that filled the rest of the parish lot. Protestant residents contributed half the cost in return for the right of burial there without Roman Catholic ceremony.[62] This was Mackinac Island's earliest public cemetery, and ecumenical use of

the burial ground would continue through much of the 1820s.

The most distinctive complex of buildings outside Fort Mackinac may be found at the eastern edge of the town stockade, directly below the fortifications. This included "Government House," which served a variety of official purposes from the 1780s until a few years after the War of 1812. It was occupied as quarters for the post commandant from at least 1787 until 1805 or even a few years later.[63] The building had probably been used for that purpose since 1781. It is likely that it had its origins in the commandant's house at Old Michilimackinac and had been moved or reconstructed from parts carried over from the mainland.

Government House was large and impressive enough to attract the attention of a number of visitors, who recorded their impressions of it. This was, in part, because of its distinctive, inverted "U" shape, which shows on the "JM" plan. The building was described in Lieutenant Foster's 1796 inventory as 129 feet long and 60 feet wide, the latter dimension including the south-facing wings projecting from the thirty-foot-wide main body of the house. It had brick chimneys and a gallery on the harbor side.[64] Major Swan was impressed enough that he sketched the unique ground plan of Government House into the body of a letter to Captain Frederick Frye, which was later published in the *Medical Repository*. Swan's

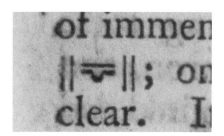

FIGURE 3.4
TITLE: [Outline plan of Government House].
AUTHOR: Major Caleb Swan, paymaster (active 1779–d. 1809).
DATE DEPICTED: August 1797.
DATE OF WORK: 1797.
DESCRIPTION: 5 x 7 cm. Letterpress print on paper.
PROVENANCE: Original sketch drawn into the body of a letter from Swan to Captain Frederick Frye of October 10, 1797. The letter was passed by Frye to Dr. E. H. Smith, editor of the *Medical Repository,* and published in vol. 1, no. 1 (1797): 525–29. The letter and plan were later reprinted in *Magazine of American History* 19 (1888): 74–75.
COLLECTION: Clements Library, University of Michigan, Ann Arbor (Serials 1).

Captain Moses Porter (1756–1822) was transferred from Detroit in 1798 to supervise the reconstruction of Fort Mackinac. This portrait shows him as colonel of the Regiment of Light Artillery circa 1814–21. Although the original painting has been lost, Porter's image survives in a nineteenth-century cabinet card photograph. *Courtesy of Danvers Archival Center, Danvers, MA.*

Father Gabriel Richard (1767–1832) visited Michilimackinac and ministered to the Catholic community at the Straits during the summer of 1799. Richard performed baptisms, blessed marriages, and supervised repairs to Ste. Anne's Church, which had been without a regular pastor since 1765. This portrait is attributed to Detroit artist James Otto Lewis and was probably executed in 1832. *Parish of Ste. Anne de Detroit, Detroit, MI.*

original sketch has been lost, but the magazine's printer replicated it in letterpress type and included it with the text of his letter (Fig. 3.4).

Major Swan described this building as "an elegant government-house, of immense size, and finished with great taste." After inserting his sketch, he further characterized it as "one story high, the rooms fifteen feet and a half in the clear [square]." The complex had a "spacious garden in front, laid out with taste; and extending from the house, on a gentle declivity, to the water's edge." Government House was surrounded by springs and sugar maples, suitable outbuildings, stables, and offices. Best of all, it was "enriched on three sides, with beautiful distant prospects" and the dramatic bluff behind.[65]

Although this was the administrative center of the post of Michilimackinac after 1781, it suffered the same fate as other garrison buildings in that it was seldom in good repair. Senator Tracy commented that it was "large, and very elegant fabric, when viewed from without; but on close inspection I find it out of repair." He thought it not worth maintaining.[66] The building remained in use nonetheless, probably because of the shortage of housing in Fort Mackinac, even after the officers' stone quarters was finally completed in 1798–99, or perhaps because it was more convenient for the commandant to be close to town. Sally Ellis Kingsbury found the house "large and elegant" when she lived there with her family in 1804–5.[67] By 1807 or 1808 the building seems to have been abandoned by the army, and the newly appointed Indian factor was authorized to request its use for the government trading house. Joseph B. Varnum took possession of Government House in November 1809 and, despite its decrepit condition, put it into service as the U.S. factory.[68] It would serve that purpose until the War of 1812.

The mysterious "JM" plan shows the post of Michilimackinac as envisioned by Patrick Sinclair, with the traders' houses safely enclosed in a stockade and tucked below the defenses of Fort Mackinac. It was probably not long after 1797 that the stockade ceased to be maintained and fell into disrepair or was scavenged for firewood and building material. Only property fencing is visible in the next plan of the village, produced in 1817 (Fig. 4.7). The street grid of the eighteenth-century fortified village can still be followed, however, in the downtown heart of the twenty-first-century City of Mackinac Island.

U.S. senator Uriah Tracy (1755–1807) toured the western posts of the United States during the summer of 1800. He was the first to describe the recently renovated Fort Mackinac, and his opinions on the strategic value of the place probably helped prevent it from being abandoned in favor of Detroit. *Collection of the Litchfield Historical Society, Litchfield, CT (CA 1920–1).*

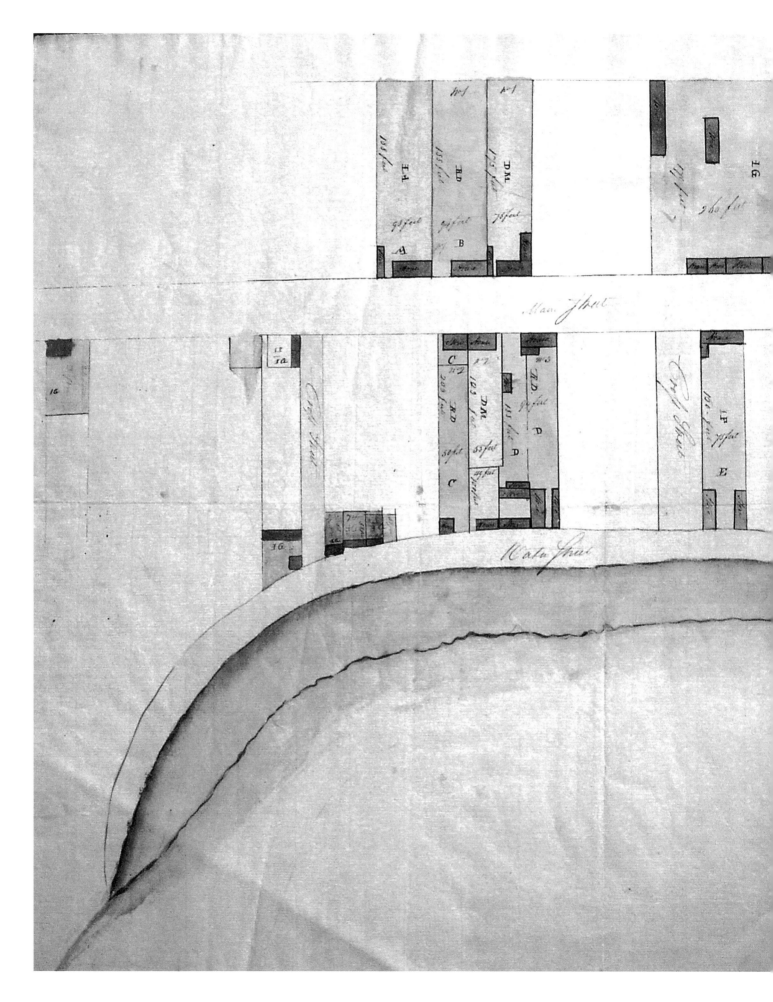

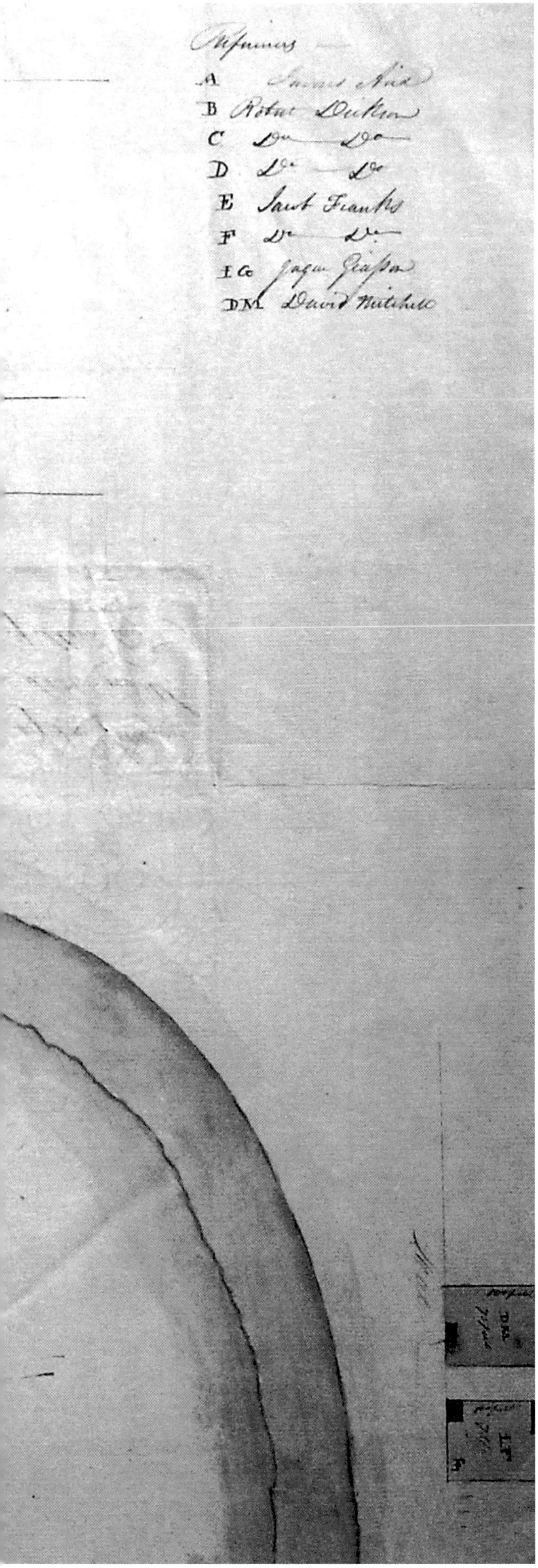

This is the place where infernals rave

Alice Parks Bacon

It seems that everyone who described Michilimackinac in the years around 1800 counted a different number of buildings in the town. Major Burbeck recorded sixty-four houses in 1796. A year later, Caleb Swan saw eighty-nine "houses and stores." Father Richard thought there were "about 50 houses" in 1799, while, three years later, Dr. Francis LeBarron estimated a total of seventy.[69] It is likely that each of these observers had his own standards for what constituted a proper house, and many of the ramshackle, bark-roofed buildings of Michilimackinac might have seemed too insubstantial to enumerate.

Father Jean Dilhet must have counted everything when he ministered at Ste. Anne's in the summer of 1804, for he came up with a total of 150 houses. Typical of most correspondents, Dilhet noted that these were filled to bursting during the summer months, when the population swelled to seven or eight hundred or more. These seasonal residents were merchants and their employees, chiefly of French Canadian origin but also "English, Scotch and Americans." Most departed at the end of the summer, with the merchants leaving "two or three clerks to take care of the houses, do a little business, look after repairs and guard the stores." Laborers, fishermen, woodchoppers, bakers, and a few others remained as well, preparing for the next summer. Mackinac Island even boasted three or four farmers, who were beginning to enjoy success with their plots outside the town.[70] The poorer families eked through the winter by fishing with nets or trout lines on the ice or in the open waters of Lake Huron east of Mackinac Island.[71]

Dilhet had more to say about the village than most. "The town has three important streets regularly laid out," he wrote, "all of them being on the hillside near the lake. The uppermost street is the finest

FIGURE 3.5

TITLE: [On verso:] Sketch of the Situation of certain Lotts in the Village of Michilimc giving dimentions made by actual measurement of the property of Jacob Franks, Robert Dickson and James Aird.
AUTHOR: Possibly Robert Dickson (ca. 1765–1823).
DATE DEPICTED: September 2, 1805.
DATE OF WORK: [September 2, 1805].
DESCRIPTION: 40.7 x 51.3 cm. Pen and ink with watercolor on paper.
PROVENANCE: Enclosed with a letter from Dickson to Solomon Sibley of September 2, 1805, and retained with Sibley's papers. The map has been separated from the papers and filed separately.
COLLECTION: Burton Historical Collection, Detroit Public Library (977.4m16-n.d.-S627).

on account of its width and the number of houses and merchants' shops. The other streets are not so regular or so well lined with houses."[72] Unfortunately, no comprehensive plan survives to show the density of buildings prior to the War of 1812. However, some sense of how the town lots were divided and built on can be obtained from a plan drawn in 1805. It was prepared to support an application by three proprietors for a title to their land and is reproduced here as Figure 3.5.

The advent of U.S. control over its northern frontier, in 1796, emphasized the uncertainties of property documentation in the areas of the Northwest Territory settled under the French and British regimes. Congress began to address the issue in 1804 with the establishment of land boards, including one in Detroit. Persons with developed properties could apply to register their claims in places where Native American title to the land had been properly extinguished. Since the British had formally purchased the island of Michilimackinac, property there qualified for consideration. A second act of March 1805 extended the closing date for applications to November 1 of that year.[73] Figure 3.5 was sent to Detroit on September 2 to meet that deadline.

The village must have seen a flurry of activity in the summer of 1805 as grants from Lieutenant Governor Sinclair were dusted off and sent to Detroit as proof of ownership. Toussaint Pothier was among those going through this exercise. On August 12 he dispatched a letter to Solomon Sibley enclosing his proofs of title. Sibley would argue the validity of Pothier's application and that of two of his friends. Pothier's summary of the history of the lot he occupied suggests how often land had changed hands in the short history of the village of Michilimackinac. Sinclair had granted Pothier's parcel to William Grant in 1781. It was sold to Charles Patterson in 1785, who conveyed the plot in turn to the Montréal firm of McTavish, Frobisher and Company. Pothier purchased it in 1798. The properties owned by his two associates, Michael Dousman and the partnership of Bailly and Rousseau, had already changed hands once and twice, respectively.[74]

Pothier did not see a need to include additional evidence, but Robert Dickson and his associates, James Aird and Jacob Franks, went a step further by enclosing a colorful and informative plan (Fig. 3.5) to support their claims. No authorship is credited, but the handwriting suggests that Dickson could have drafted it. The packet went off to Solomon Sibley on September 2 and included, in addition to the map, original titles to the six properties, an enumeration of the size of each lot, and a list of the number and types of buildings occupying them.[75] For some reason, the map depicted a few additional properties as well—three lots belonging to Dr. David Mitchell and four claimed by Jacques Giasson. Perhaps they had intended to join Dickson, Aird, and Franks in their effort and either withdrew from the group or submitted their titles separately. The paperwork reached Sibley in Detroit, but it would take further congressional action in 1807 and the establishment of a second land board to clear the way for registration of deeds in 1808 and

an official survey of Mackinac Island property in 1810.[76]

While the 1805 effort did not result in the final confirmation of the claims of Dickson and his associates, his plan provides a snapshot of the appearance of lots and buildings in the village of Michilimackinac. Several of the parcels are recognizable today, and at least one of the buildings remains standing. The street plan is familiar as well. Most prominent is the "upper street," so described by Father Dilhet and labeled on the plan as "Main Street." This is today known as Market Street. Two shorter thoroughfares, each marked "Cross Street," represent modern Hoban (left) and Astor (right). Water Street, today known as Main, follows the shoreline. According to Father Dilhet, these lanes were not as regular or built up as the principal street. Since the plan shows only the lots claimed by five individuals, the areas between their properties remain blank.

The author of Figure 3.5 was careful to note the use of most buildings, although these must have been only primary structures. Outhouses, stables, and sheds were surely deleted. Each structure is identified as either a "house" or a "store," with most of the latter being what would today be called a "storehouse" as opposed to a retail establishment. Houses generally parallel the streets, while the gable ends of many of the stores face the roadways. As at Old Michilimackinac, many of the buildings are attached to form row houses. Although most of the properties shown are in the main part of town, two parcels claimed by David Mitchell and Jacob Franks are at the lower right, just to the east of the gardens below Fort Mackinac and probably west of modern Bogan Lane. Two dwellings occupied Franks's lot, and it appears that most of the stores were in the main part of town, as suggested by Father Dilhet.[77] Stockade fences delineated boundaries.

Several of these properties are identifiable two centuries after Figure 3.5 was drawn. The largest of them, colored beige and marked with the initials "IG," was designated claim 293 in 1808 and later became the site of the American Fur Company buildings. To the left of this lot, on the north side of "Main Street," is a pink parcel, claimed by Robert Dickson (claim 279 in 1808). The residence below the letter "B" survives as the Biddle House. Directly opposite, on a green-colored lot claimed by David Mitchell, is his impressive, gambrel-roofed, Georgian residence. Known as the Mitchell house, it was photographed many times before its demolition circa 1897. Ste. Anne's Church and rectory are not shown, but they stood on the "church lot" between Dickson's property to the left of the Mitchell house and the left-hand cross street (Hoban). Most of the other parcels can be associated with private claims of 1808 (Fig. 3.6).

Within the bounds of the yards, houses, and stores depicted on the 1805 plan existed a small but active year-round community. The departure of the summer trading population was followed by the onset of winter and the end of regular communications beyond the Straits. "We are here almost out of the World," Thomas Duggan wrote during the winter of 1796, and then asked for news to be sent with the next of the expresses that occasionally brought mail up the wintry lakes to Michilimackinac. "For God's Sake send me some of the latest papers," he added as a postscript.[78] The community had a lively social life to while away the time, and some, at least in the upper echelon of island society, seem to have enjoyed the experience. "I never spent my time so much in amusements as at this place," Sally Ellis Kingsbury, wife of Fort Mackinac's commandant, wrote following the winter of 1805. She attended "entertainments once or twice a week besides private parties." Sleigh rides on Lake Huron and to maple sugar camps on the mainland and nearby islands also helped pass the time.[79] Sleighs followed marked trails across the ice to Bois Blanc Island, the sawmill at Mill Creek, and St. Ignace.[80]

Alice Bacon, wife of the first Protestant missionary, confirmed the winter gaiety of the place, though with a less favorable twist. She had been attempting to learn the Ottawa language to assist her husband in his duties and had received some "indefinite promises" of assistance from David Mitchell. When the winter of 1803 closed in, however, Mrs. Bacon found Mitchell "constantly taken up with amusements, as is customary in all high life here." The imposing Mitchell house was a natural center for social activities. "Card-clubs . . . two evenings in a week for ladies and gentlemen, balls, dinners, tea-parties, etc., occupy nearly all their time, the Sabbath not excepted," Mrs. Bacon informed a friend."[81] She complained of the absence of "true religion," even among the Protestant military officers and their families. "Perhaps Satan never reigned with less control in any place than he has here," was Mrs. Bacon's appraisal. Other than her husband's efforts, the only evidence of religion was that practiced by some of the French Canadian residents in Ste. Anne's, which had no priest but contained, Mrs. Bacon reported, "a few images which they ignorantly worship."[82]

The lower classes were even rougher in her opinion. "The rude savage and the barberous Frenchmen are the principal inhabitants of this friendless region," she wrote soon after her arrival in 1802. And the language of the street was that of the fur trade and the army. "Could you be transported hither and hear the awful language which I daily hear," Mrs. Bacon wrote her friend Jerusha Bayley, "you would be filled with horror, and imagine that this is the place where infernals rave."[83] Some no doubt raved in the taverns maintained in the village. There was even a house offering a billiard table and "shovelboard," at least during the winter of 1808. It was allegedly operated with soldier labor and government property by the commandant, Lieutenant Presley Neville O'Bannon, a former Marine officer and hero in the war against Tripoli of 1801–5.[84]

Prostitution was present as well, although it is unclear how organized it was. Soon after his arrival, in the fall of 1802, Dr. LeBarron reported that he expected his private practice to be "considerable" because of the numbers of traders. They arrived each year "afflicted with a disease which is fashionable among a certain class of our fair country women, and is a constant companion to the copper colored females of this Western hemisphere."[85] Complaints of rampant prostitution at fur trade and military posts dated to the end of the seventeenth century and had remained a fact of life at Michilimackinac.[86]

Despite seasonal isolation, excesses of social life, irreligion, and vice, Mackinac Island was commended by many as a healthy environment. Dr. LeBarron attributed this to "the uninterrupted current of air which constantly passes over the island . . . and dispels all noxious vapours which arise." "No one dies but from casualties or old age," he wrote, coining a catchphrase that would be repeated often in coming decades as the village of Michilimackinac developed its reputation as a resort.[87]

Lieutenant Colonel Jacob Kingsbury (1756–1837) commanded Michilimackinac in 1804–5. His wife, Sally Ellis, thoroughly enjoyed the island's lively social life during the long, isolated months of winter. Colonel Kingsbury is shown in a portrait miniature of about 1802–4. *Reproduced by permission of the Society of the Cincinnati, Washington, DC (M.1976.1.636).*

Alexander Thompson (1759–1809) was among the early American participants in the Michilimackinac fur trade in 1803–5. The former army captain found the business dominated by Canadians. When he left the Straits in the autumn of 1804, Thompson hired Fort Mackinac post surgeon Francis LeBarron to act as his local agent. This oil-on-board portrait, done about 1796, shows Thompson in military uniform. *Photograph courtesy of Linda Zimmermann. Original in a private collection.*

The proprietors of the Lots in the Village . . . found their claims
upon possession——upon Grants . . . and upon their having improved the same

Toussaint Pothier

It was not until July 29, 1810, that the deputy surveyor of the Michigan Territory set out from Detroit to map private land at the Straits of Mackinac. The Michigan Territory had only been established in 1805, and there was much surveying to be done.[88] Aaron Greeley had come to Michigan in 1806 and was appointed to his post two years later. He was soon occupied in recording the many pieces of property confirmed in 1808 by the Land Board to inhabitants living near Detroit, at the River Raisin settlement, and along the St. Clair River.[89] Most of these parcels were well developed, and their owners had successfully demonstrated that they had held possession of them before the arrival of American authorities in 1796.

Greeley was thus a busy man, and it took some time for him to work his way to isolated Michilimackinac. By November 1809 he had completed surveys of the most concentrated areas of settlement. Winter was approaching by that time, however, and Greeley had yet to solve the problem of connecting the surveys in southeastern Michigan with those at the faraway Straits. The land commissioners at Detroit suggested that the Michilimackinac surveys be postponed until the spring of 1810.[90] There was plenty for Greeley to do during the winter, and Governor William Hull put him to work surveying Indian reservations. By April 1810 only Michilimackinac remained to be mapped. Greeley planned to go north on the first available transport from Detroit.[91]

For some reason, however, the work was deferred once again. Finally, on July 29, Greeley set out in a birch bark canoe in company with Thomas Nuttall, a young English botanist embarked on a two-year expedition to describe the flora of North America. The companions were surveyors of very different sorts, but Greeley probably had much to offer Nuttall from his two years of experience in Michigan. Once at Michilimackinac, by early August, Nuttall and Greeley went their separate ways. The botanist joined an American Fur Company expedition headed overland for the Pacific Northwest. He departed for Green Bay on August 12 and eventually traveled down the Mississippi River to New Orleans, departing for England in December 1811.[92] Aaron Greeley set about his more prosaic task of mapping private property.

The surveyor's Mackinac legacy includes the detailed plan of lots in the village, presented here as Figure 3.6. Greeley also prepared large-scale maps of Mackinac Island and the Straits area showing private claims on the south mainland and Bois Blanc Island. His map of the Straits survives, but it is far too worn and faded to be reproduced.[93] The survey of Mackinac Island property outside the boundaries of the village (Fig. 3.7) ultimately generated

a considerable amount of controversy and will be discussed below.

Aaron Greeley's surveys of Michilimackinac represent the final phase of pre–War of 1812 attempts to document private property in the Michigan Territory. The congressional acts of 1804 and 1805 were followed by further legislation in 1807 with more liberal regulations for confirming ownership of developed, private land. In addition to extending the deadline for filing claims to property occupied prior to July 1, 1796, the 1807 act (as revised on April 28, 1808) permitted individuals to apply for more than one tract. It also included a provision allowing those who had developed their properties since July 1, 1796, to claim them by right of preemption and then purchase the land from the federal government.[94] Multiple claims and preemption of lands were important considerations for a number of Straits-area proprietors.

The survey upon which Figure 3.6 was based was completed during August and early September 1810. Greeley worked from property descriptions that had been presented to the Land Board at Detroit between April and December 1808. Each claim had been assigned a number at the time of its consideration, and they all followed much the same formula. Claimants described their property and brought forward one or more witnesses to attest to their possession and use of the land prior to July 1, 1796.[95] This was critical for those with incomplete documentation, and it answered concerns expressed by landowners since the 1780s. As Toussaint Pothier argued in 1805, "The Proprietors of the Lot[s] in the Village of Michilimackinac found their claims upon possession—upon grants from Patrick Sinclair . . . before the Treaty of Peace—and upon their having improved the same . . . by the erection of Buildings and otherwise for the purpose of Trade."[96]

The first of the Mackinac claims—number 101—is typical of most parcels in the village. On April 7, 1808, the Land Board met in Detroit to consider the application of Toussaint Pothier for a lot of 97 by 176 feet. This was bounded in front by the lake, on the rear by the main street (today Market), on the northeast by the street (today Fort) between the town and the public ground below Fort Mackinac, and on the southwest by a lot formerly owned by Messrs. Rocheblave and Porlier. This last is identified on Greeley's map with Michael Dousman, its owner by 1810. Pothier's property had previously been registered on December 26, 1805, under the land legislation of that year. George Meldrum of Detroit appeared before the board to attest that Pothier had, as of July 1, 1796, been "in possession and occupancy of the premises and has continued so to this day." The commissioners ruled that the claimant was entitled to the property, that he should receive a certificate stating that fact, and that the lot should be surveyed and registered in the land office at Detroit.[97]

Sixty-four claims for parcels at the Straits of Mackinac were similarly presented. All but three were on Mackinac Island. One of these was on Bois Blanc (claim 323), and the other two were on the Lower Peninsula mainland (334 and 335). These will be discussed at later points (Figs. 5.23 and 5.24, and 5.28–5.31). Six requests were rejected for various reasons, including, in one case, the lack of a witness. One of those rejected (Michael Dousman's number 324) was later reconsidered, approved, and then rescinded (see Fig. 3.7). At least eleven proprietors filed multiple petitions, with David Mitchell's eight being the largest number. The commissioners confirmed six of Mitchell's as well as most of the others.

A few of the property descriptions presented to the Land Board provided more information than simply the location and dimensions of the lot and its history of ownership. The higher-numbered claims (697–717) note the buildings on each property. That of the heirs of Adhemar St. Martin (claim 697) had a "dwelling-house and stables." Several others, including George Schindler's number 704, included "a house and store-house." André Sarrere noted, with some pride, that the "dwelling-house" on his property (claim 702) had "always been occupied, winter and summer, to this day."

All of the claim numbers and names of the proprietors were recorded on Aaron Greeley's "Plan of the Town and Harbor of Michilimacinac." By 1810 the village had grown since it had been informally mapped in 1797 (Fig. 3.3). The layout of streets and lots is recognizable today, and the area once enclosed by the stockade seems to have changed little, although the pickets had been removed. Market Street and three cross streets (left to right: French Lane, Hoban, and Astor) define the main part of the town. An additional street (today's Squires) links French Lane and Hoban. The most significant growth is apparent at the eastern end of Haldimand Bay, where the suburb has begun to take on the shape of a neighborhood. Buildings were still few in this area by 1810, and many of the properties included large garden plots, but most of the modern streets had appeared. From left to right may be seen today's Church, Truscott, and Mission streets, all linked by the present McGulpin Street.

Two other distinctive features mark the 1810 plan of the village. The eastern end of Market Street terminates in an unidentified triangular piece of ground that today would be part of Marquette Park. Although there is little information about this plot, it seems to have been intended for a public square.[98] Running parallel to the beach is a dotted line, added to the map in 1848 from Greeley's field notes. This marks the position of today's Main Street. In 1810 all the harbor-side properties extended to the water, and the "street" was merely a track along the beach. Washington Irving later described this as "a kind of public promenade, where were displayed all the vagaries of a seaport on the arrival of a fleet from a long cruize."[99]

According to the land act of 1807, the "general and particular plots of all the land surveyed" in the Michigan Territory were to be transmitted to the register of the land office at Detroit, with copies forwarded to the secretary of the treasury.[100] Aaron Greeley's 1810 survey of the village survives today only in a single example held by the National Archives. The history of this copy of his map is somewhat vague. Multiple copies were made in 1810, and Greeley

English botanist Thomas Nuttall (1786–1859) traveled to Mackinac Island with surveyor Aaron Greeley in August 1810 before continuing west to the Mississippi River. During his time at the Straits, Nuttall described the dwarf lake iris (*Iris lacustris*), today the state wildflower of Michigan. This engraving, believed to have been published in 1825, was reproduced in the journal *Chronica Botanica*.

John Jacob Astor's first representative on Mackinac Island was his nephew, Henry Brevoort (1782–1848). The U.S. embargo kept the American Fur Company's trade goods in Canada in 1811, so Brevoort spent an idle and frustrating summer on Mackinac Island. This portrait, by Rembrandt Peale, was owned by Brevoort's grandson in 1918 and was reproduced in Hellman, *Letters of Henry Brevoort*.

PLAN of the TOWN and HARBOUR of MICHILIMACIN

PUBLIC GARDENS

No. 40 Michigan, Sheet 2,
1810-48. To trace the claims,
see index in K. Corrections in
red ink correspond with the
papers.

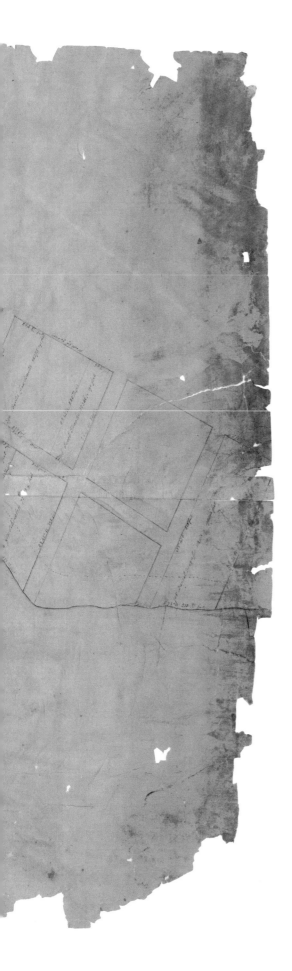

himself carried one to the land office in Cincinnati in the winter of 1811 and then on to Washington.[101] A copy must have been retained at Detroit, but it was lost after the British captured the town in 1812, an event that resulted in the wholesale destruction of Michigan Territory land maps. After the war, Governor Lewis Cass requested replacements from the General Land Office in Washington, and the group of plans sent to Detroit on July 24, 1816, included a "Plan of the Town and Harbour of Michilimacinac with the strait of Michigan, Boisblanc & Macinac Island."[102]

The plan illustrated as Figure 3.6 might be the copy forwarded to Michigan in 1816. A notation at the bottom, written by Surveyor General Lucius Lyon on July 15, 1848, states that this was the only Greeley map of Mackinac that could be found in the Detroit land office at that time. It lacked any courses or distances on the properties, so these were added in blue ink as was the "dotted line representing the position and boundary of a street along the Shore of the Harbor." Greeley's notes were used as the source. The map would then seem to have been returned to the General Land Office in Washington, where it perhaps replaced Greeley's original, which had presumably been lost or worn out by that time.

Aaron Greeley's 1810 effort was the first careful property survey conducted at the Straits of Mackinac. As such, it was the basis for all subsequent mapping of private property. His survey of the village of Michilimackinac and larger parcels outside its bounds serves today as the foundation for much of the private land ownership on Mackinac Island.

FIGURE 3.6
TITLE: Plan of the Town and Harbor of Michilimacinac.
AUTHOR: Aaron Greeley (1773–1820).
DATE DEPICTED: August 1810.
DATE OF WORK: Copy probably made in 1816 with additions in 1848.
DESCRIPTION: 72.5 x 92.8 cm. Pen and ink and colored ink with watercolor outlining on paper.
PROVENANCE: Possibly the plan sent to Governor Lewis Cass at Detroit on July 24, 1816. Returned to the General Land Office in Washington after 1848 and retained in the records of that agency.
COLLECTION: National Archives and Records Administration, College Park, MD (RG 49, Records of the Bureau of Land Management, Old Map File, Michigan 11).

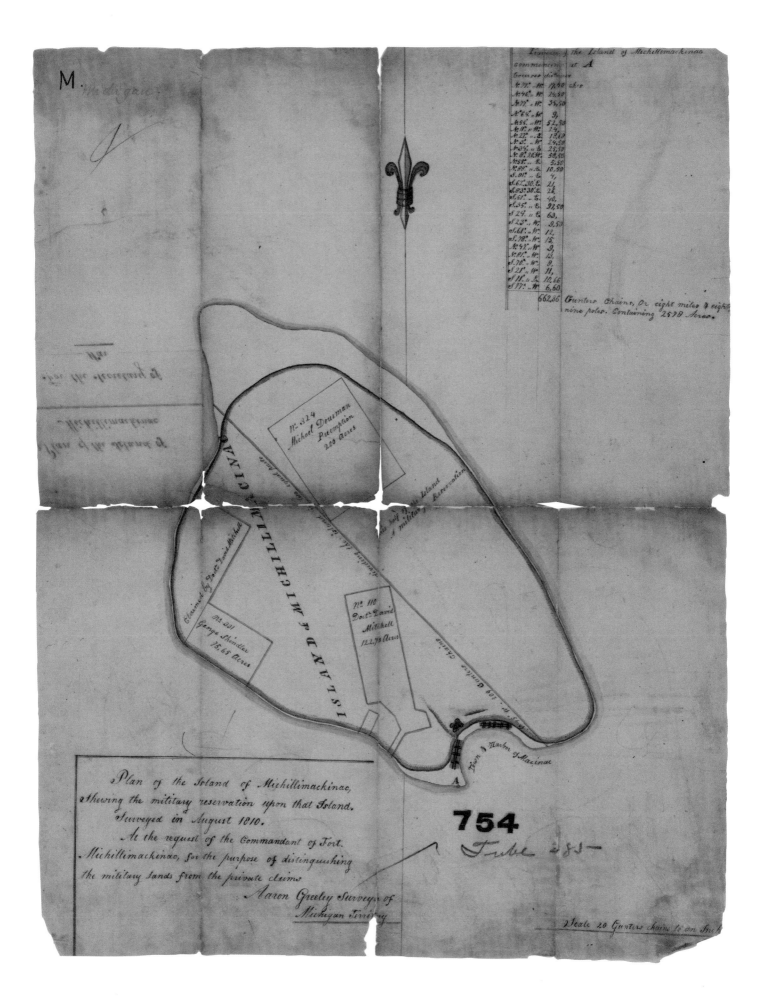

Plan of the Island of Michillimackinac,
shewing the military reservation upon that Island.
Surveyed in August 1810.
At the request of the Commandant of Fort
Michillimackinac, for the purpose of distinguishing
the military lands from the private claims

Aaron Greely Surveyor of
Michigan Territory

754

I have been under the Necessity of requiring that the said survey be suspended

Captain Lewis Howard

By early September 1810 Aaron Greeley was nearing the end of what must have seemed a straightforward and uncomplicated job of surveying. He had platted the village of Michilimackinac (Fig. 3.6), and only the larger parcels in the interior of the island remained to be surveyed. These included four farms and a tract below the bluff along the southwestern shore. Captain Lewis Howard, commandant of Fort Mackinac, had also asked Greeley to survey a line dividing the military reserve from land that had been left for use by the island's inhabitants.

With most of his work completed, Greeley was laying down the boundaries of a two-hundred-acre parcel in the woods at the northwestern end of the island. This was private claim 324, assigned by the Land Board on December 23, 1808, to Michael Dousman by right of preemption. The property included cultivated lands, a house and outbuildings, a road, and even fruit trees. It had all the appearance of a productive farm, something of a rarity among the holdings Greeley had found at the Straits.[103]

It was thus with some surprise that the surveyor found himself confronted by an order from Captain Howard to suspend his survey. When asked his reasons, Howard responded that he thought it encroached "very essentially on the Public Military reserve," and that abandoning the land to private ownership would cause "Great Injury" to the United States. The plot included the best remaining timber on Mackinac Island. Howard suspected that Dousman had ulterior motives. "It is my belief," he wrote to the secretary of war, "that the intention . . . was to get a survey, a final certificate & Deed,

& then sell the wood to the U.S. or let them go some where else for it, off the Island, of course at great cost & inconvenience." The commandant believed that Dousman had filed his claim secretly to avoid a challenge from military authorities.[104] The voracious stoves of Fort Mackinac had deforested much of the island over thirty winters, and the garrison was jealous of its remaining reserves.

Michael Dousman, for his part, was indignant that the army should be meddling in a two-year-old preemption that he considered a done deal. When he submitted his claim, in October 1808, Dousman declared that he had been in possession of the property since 1803, a statement supported by Thomas Cowles. The Land Board postponed its decision until December, when Cowles further testified that, by 1804, there was a house and orchard on the property.[105] Subsequent improvements included "a two story house, a still-house and a mill."[106] The Land Board granted Dousman a right of preemption contingent on receipt of a down payment of one-quarter of the value of the land.

The army and Dousman were squared off for the first of many future conflicts between public and private interests for the limited land and resources of Mackinac Island. Fortunately, despite the interruption, Aaron Greeley completed his survey. It graphically illustrates the clash of interests in a dispute that would linger into the 1820s. The best surviving copy is illustrated here as Figure 3.7. A bold line divides the island. The area to the south and west of this boundary contains the fort, town, and four properties. To the north and east, in the area labeled "This half of the Island a military

FIGURE 3.7
TITLE: Plan of the Island of Michillimackinac, Shewing the military reservation upon that Island. Surveyed in August 1810. At the request of the Commandant of Fort Michillimackinac, for the purpose of distinguishing the military Lands from the private claims. Aaron Greeley Surveyor of Michigan Territory.
AUTHOR: Aaron Greeley (1773–1820).
DATE DEPICTED: August 1810.
DATE OF WORK: [August 1810].
DESCRIPTION: 48.6 x 38.5 cm. Pen and ink with watercolor outline on paper.
PROVENANCE: Probably submitted to the secretary of war. Transferred to the Office of Indian Affairs, probably at the time of the formation of that office in 1824.
COLLECTION: National Archives and Records Administration, College Park, MD (RG 75, Records of the Bureau of Indian Affairs, Map No. 754).

Reservation," is Dousman's claim 324.

Both sides vigorously pursued their arguments through the fall and winter of 1810–11. Captain Howard dashed off letters to Secretary of War William Eustis, to Colonel Jacob Kingsbury at Detroit, and to the members of the Land Board defending his actions and presenting the army's point of view. Orders issued by Colonel Henry Burbeck in February 1808 had instructed Fort Mackinac's commandant to "keep possession of every inch of ground belonging to the public & all the N. & N.E. Sides of the Center of the island belongs to the U. States."[107] To the Land Board, Howard explained that Burbeck had marked the military reserve in the 1790s, and Dousman's preemption included "the most Valuable part of the woodland" within it. His claim also cut off the garrison from the northwestern tip of the island, which could not be reached "except by passing through his land, going by water, or over Hills nearly inaccessible to a Saddle Horse, much more a loaded Team." Dousman could buy the land at two dollars an acre, Howard asserted, and then sell the wood to the army for twenty dollars an acre. He suggested that Dousman relocate to the other side of the line to a plot where he was already growing wheat.[108]

Less information survives to support Michael Dousman's argument. There was, of course, his claim and whatever rights accrued from possession of the land. In September 1811 Dousman again cited the improvements he had made to the property. He dismissed Captain Howard's offer of land on the other side of the boundary as "so situated and of a quality so inferior that I am confident the government would not wish me to accept it."[109] Dousman, with surveyor Greeley in tow, had left Mackinac Island for Detroit on September 12, 1810, to plead his case. Captain Howard must have thought Greeley a creature of Dousman's, because he did not trust the surveyor to deliver his own letters. Instead, he dispatched Lieutenant Archibald Darragh.[110] Following Darragh's return, in November, Howard reported that Dousman and Greeley had been "very free with their tales at Detroit respecting myself & other officers of the Garrison." He was not surprised to hear this about Dousman, to whom "every man not in favor of his interest is of course considered as his enemy." Howard attributed Greeley's attitude to "his natural propensity to live in troubled waters," seeming to imply that the surveyor supported Dousman's position.[111]

Whatever deliberations the Land Board might have had are not recorded. But, on October 17, 1810, Colonel Kingsbury reported that Dousman's preemption had been reconfirmed. Kingsbury had written to the secretary of war, however, and was confident that "it is in his favor to prevent Dousmans receiving a deed." He also solicited the opinion of Colonel Burbeck, who confirmed that the line dividing the island had been respected during his command.[112]

The first Protestant missionary to visit Michilimackinac was the Reverend David Bacon (1771–1817). He and his wife, Alice Parks, resided on Mackinac Island in 1802–4 but were unable to achieve their goal of founding a mission among the Ottawa at L'Arbre Croche. In 1803 they obtained permission to establish a mission village on Mackinac Island, but a lack of funding ended their project the following year. This engraving, from a portrait, appeared in Bacon, *Sketch of the Rev. David Bacon* (Boston, 1876).

Lieutenant Colonel Thomas Hunt (1754–1808) commanded Fort Mackinac in 1802–4. He permitted Reverend Bacon to begin a mission farm on land within the post military reserve. Michael Dousman acquired Bacon's improvements in 1804 and, four years later, claimed one hundred acres by right of preemption, setting off a bitter struggle with the army. This oil-on-tinned iron portrait of Hunt was probably done shortly before his death in 1808.

Collection of James L. Kochan, Frederick, MD.

Lieutenant Presley Neville O'Bannon (1776–1850) ranks among the strangest of Fort Mackinac's commandants. A former Marine lieutenant and the "Hero of Derna" in the war against Tripoli, O'Bannon resigned his Marine Corps commission in 1805 to accept a lieutenancy in the U.S. Army. He commanded Fort Mackinac during the winter of 1807–8. Soon after his departure, island citizens and soldiers accused O'Bannon of numerous malfeasances, but his superiors seem to have taken no action. This likeness is of unknown provenance.

In December the secretary of the treasury told the army that "no individual claim can be successfully opposed to the public right," and on February 28, 1811, Lieutenant Porter Hanks was notified that Dousman's claim 324 had been "set aside."[113] The news came too late for Captain Howard, who had died on January 13 from injuries received in a sleighing accident.[114]

Dousman seems to have taken the news in stride. He appealed to the secretary of war, offering to let the army have the firewood if he could "possess and enjoy quietly the land which has been confirmed to me." No action seems to have been taken before war intervened in 1812.[115] Dousman had already made his down payment, however, and though he attempted to pay the balance in 1816, it was refused. Dousman's money was eventually declared forfeit, though he was still trying to get a refund as late as 1829.[116]

Questions remain concerning Mackinac Island's first major land dispute. How had Dousman carved a farm out of the military reserve? Why was he not confronted before 1810? The answers date back to 1802 and the arrival of the missionary David Bacon, who hoped to minister to the Ottawa at L'Arbre Croche. Bacon never proceeded beyond Mackinac Island, and by May 1803 he reported that he had begun a log house a mile and a half from the village. "We have cleared a little piece of land, and are now fencing and planting our garden," he wrote, adding, "The land is the best on the island."[117] By autumn, Bacon had developed plans to establish a Moravian-style Indian mission village on the land, which he admitted was owned by the government. Relying, perhaps, on his earlier contacts with Senator Uriah Tracy of Connecticut, Bacon was confident that the Missionary Society could obtain a grant of the property from Congress.[118]

Reverend Bacon occupied the land in the first place thanks to the commandant of Fort Mackinac. In an 1810 memo on the dispute with Dousman, Colonel Burbeck remembered that Lieutenant Colonel Thomas Hunt, "(in 1802 or 3) in a pious Godly moment granted liberty to a pretended missionary to make a small settlement on the N. side. this right Mr. Dousman bought and has made his Location as described by C. Howard."[119] With funds running out, Bacon abandoned his plans in the summer of 1804 and left the island. His brother-in-law remained behind and sold the farm improvements to a man "to whom . . . it became ultimately a mine of wealth."[120]

Four years later Michael Dousman filed his claim, stating only that he had been in possession since 1803 and making no mention of Bacon's arrangement. The timing of his claim, in October 1808, might have been intentional. Fort Mackinac had a change in command that August, when Lieutenant Presley N. O'Bannon was relieved. O'Bannon, who had had business dealings with Dousman and others during the winter of 1808, might have looked the other way as Dousman prepared his claim.[121] Thus, when the land controversy exploded in September 1810, Howard was surprised by the "'Secret' Manner" in which he believed the claim had been filed.

This "would never be permitted by the Person Acting for the Government at this Place," he asserted.[122] Perhaps his predecessor had, in fact, abetted the secret.

Aaron Greeley made multiple copies of his survey, one of which survives as Figure 3.7. It went first to the secretary of war but was later transferred to the newly established Office of Indian Affairs. This copy, prepared at the request of Captain Howard, highlights the bounds of the military reserve. Any copies retained in Michigan disappeared during the War of 1812, and a replacement appears to have been among the maps sent to Detroit from Washington in the summer of 1816.[123]

Greeley's map includes other useful details. There is a crude indication of the island's dramatic bluffs. Five large farm claims are shown, two of which were approved—George Schindler's number 331 and David Mitchell's number 110. The latter is today the site of part of the Grand Hotel Golf Course and Harrisonville, or "the village," a residential area. Two other claims were rejected. At the western end of the island is another of Mitchell's, probably number 717, which contained a small house and two or three acres of potatoes and turnips. Below Mitchell's number 110 is an unidentified plot of two acres claimed by Dr. Francis LeBarron as number 596 but also rejected. Perhaps LeBarron remained hopeful of gaining control for, in 1809, he constructed a distillery and horse mill on the property.[124] LeBarron left the island in 1811, but his distillery would have its moment of fame in the opening hours of the British capture of Mackinac Island. The building appears on maps of 1814 and 1817 (Figs. 4.2 and 4.7).

The Dousman controversy generated one further piece of cartography, though it has not survived. On October 1, 1810, Captain Howard reported that Lieutenant John Anderson had run a new survey of the military reserve, a copy of which was to have been forwarded to the secretary of war. Four copies were later requested by his office, one each for the War and Treasury departments, one for the Land Board in Detroit, and one to be retained at Fort Mackinac.[125] Anderson returned to Detroit before winter set in and planned to complete duplicate copies of his survey by spring.[126] Unfortunately, because of "an omission of some Kind," probably because Anderson was preoccupied with plans to retire from the army, these were never sent, and they were lost when the British captured Detroit in 1812. Anderson retained his notes, however, and offered to reconstruct his map in 1816, but this has not survived, if in fact it was ever drawn.[127]

Real fighting would soon eclipse skirmishing over land. Michael Dousman seems to have remained in uninterrupted possession of his farm, but his brush with the U.S. Army might well have influenced his treasonable behavior during the War of 1812 and contributed to a pair of American defeats.

The presence of British forces on Mackinac Island remained undetected until garrison surgeon Sylvester Day (1778–1851) observed the inhabitants fleeing to the distillery. Day warned Lieutenant Porter Hanks and was among the American prisoners paroled to Detroit following the surrender. An unidentified artist painted the doctor in the 1840s. *Courtesy of Vermont Historical Society (VHS A-111).*

"A fortress built by nature for herself"

1812–1820

Early in the morning of July 17, 1812, residents of the village of Michilimackinac awoke to furtive knocking on the doors of their small log houses. The callers proved to be some of their fellow citizens, led by Michael Dousman, captain of the local militia company. Their message was abrupt and clear. British troops, accompanied by Canadian volunteers and nearly six hundred Indian warriors, had landed on the island and were poised to attack Fort Mackinac. Fearing that resistance

by the garrison would make it impossible to control his Native American allies, the British commander had permitted Dousman and his companions to rouse their neighbors and lead them to a place of safety under a guard of his soldiers. The American civilians had, in turn, promised not to give "the least information" to the troops in Fort Mackinac.[1]

A hasty exodus began as women, children, merchants, and voyageurs hurried along Market Street and the other dusty lanes toward the distillery situated several hundred yards west of the village. It was not yet 6:00 AM, and this extraordinary movement of people caught the attention of Dr. Sylvester Day, the post surgeon, as he was passing along the street. The secret was out. Day hurried up the hill to the fort to inform Lieutenant Porter Hanks that the British were on the island. "This, Sir, was the first information I had of the declaration of war," Hanks later wrote to his superior in Detroit.[2]

Although there had been no official warning of the opening of hostilities, recent events had suggested that all was not well in the northern Great Lakes. The local Ottawa and Ojibwa had come to Mackinac Island as usual during the early part of the summer, where they traded at the factory in the old Government House and "professed the greatest friendship for the United States." Then, about the middle of July, Hanks detected a certain "coolness" in their chiefs. On the sixteenth an Indian told him that warriors from many nations were gathering at the British post of Fort St. Joseph. Hanks consulted some of Michilimackinac's American residents and decided to dispatch Michael Dousman as a "confidential person" to determine what was afoot.[3]

It was this circumstance that had made Dousman the messenger

to his neighbors. He had paddled no more than twelve to fifteen miles toward Fort St. Joseph on the evening of the sixteenth before encountering the North West Company's schooner *Caledonia* surrounded by a flotilla of boats and canoes packed with armed men. Dousman was made a prisoner, but either his entreaties or the concerns of Captain Charles Roberts, the British commander, led to the understanding that the American would warn the inhabitants while remaining silent to Lieutenant Hanks.[4] The British vessels continued on their way. About 3:00 AM they rounded the northwestern end of Mackinac Island and arrived off one of the few landing places unobstructed by steep bluffs. There, a rough track led from the beach through Dousman's farm and uphill to the rear of Fort Mackinac. This coincidence of Dousman's simultaneous roles as American scout, British guide, and messenger to the village would, for the rest of his life, cast a shadow of doubt over his loyalty to the United States.

It was an hour before daybreak as the British, Canadians, and Indians splashed ashore with one of the six-pounder cannon they had brought from Fort St. Joseph. John Askin, Jr., noted that this was "dragg'd with velosity thro woods swamps, [and] hills." Captain Roberts credited the "unparalleled exertions of the Canadians" with rowing the boats and hauling the gun "with much difficulty to the heights above the Fort." At 10:00 Roberts drafted a summons demanding unconditional surrender and containing a thinly veiled warning that he wished to "save the effusion of blood, which must of necessity follow the attack of such Troops as I have under my command." The note was entrusted to Toussaint Pothier, who immediately delivered it to Lieutenant Hanks.[5]

The American commandant, by that time, had had four hours in which to consider his predicament. Hanks had ordered his pitifully small garrison of fifty-seven effective soldiers to their posts, distributed ammunition, and prepared the artillery mounted in the blockhouses. The well in Fort Mackinac had long since been abandoned, so the only source of water lay exposed outside the walls. By 9:00 Hanks could see that a cannon had been placed on commanding ground where it was "directed at the most defenceless part of the garrison." A glance at the edge of the woods revealed Indians "in great numbers." Then came Pothier with the surrender demand, accompanied by "Three American Gentlemen," sent to describe the overwhelming enemy force and counsel prudence. Hanks came to the inevitable conclusion that resistance against such force would be futile and would result only in a "general massacre." The lieutenant composed a letter of response, formal articles of capitulation were hastily drafted, and, sometime between 11:00 and noon, Fort Mackinac was placed in British hands as the American colors were lowered.[6] "Not a single person had been injured nor even kill'd," not even "a single fowl belonging to any person whatever," John Askin, Jr., reported, no doubt relieved that so many familiar faces had been spared by Hanks's prompt surrender.[7]

The commencement of hostilities in 1812 was a particularly significant event at the Straits. It marked the beginning of Michili-mackinac's most active military period—a time during which land and naval battles were fought on the island and in nearby waters, new fortifications were constructed or projected, and Fort Mackinac held the largest garrisons of its history. The years between 1812 and 1820 would find Michilimackinac lost and recovered by the United States and then used as a base for the projection of the nation's military and commercial power across the northern lakes and the upper Mississippi Valley. Those eight years would also see the advent of true civil government at a place where, since the last quarter of the seventeenth century, local authority had been largely vested in military officers. More and better maps of the Straits area illustrate these critical years. And, for the first time, significant numbers of surviving sketches, watercolors, and prints preserve realistic views, often inspired by the scenic beauty of the place.

On the afternoon of July 17, 1812, however, Mackinac Island was newly conquered territory. The success of Captain Roberts and his motley force was a signal for the near-complete collapse of American military fortunes in the upper Great Lakes. The garrison of Fort Dearborn, at the mouth of the Chicago River, evacuated its defenses on August 15 and was then attacked by local Indians. A day later, General William Hull surrendered the territorial capital of Detroit and his army of the Northwest, motivated in part by fear that Native American warriors would be turned on the population. "The surrender of Michilimackinac opened the northern hive of Indians," Hull wrote in partial justification for his actions.[8] It would be another ten months before American fortunes began to recover.

The arrival of the British had a very personal and divisive

impact on the population of Mackinac Island. Traders of British citizenship and many Native Americans welcomed the return of royal authority. But, by 1812, the island also had a significant number of American citizens, and they found themselves forced to make a choice. A few days after the surrender, Captain Roberts summoned the community's U.S. citizens to the old Government House. There, he informed them that those who agreed to take an oath of allegiance to King George III could remain on the island. Those who refused would be sent to Detroit with the paroled officers and men of the garrison, where they would face an uncertain exile.[9] Decisions made that afternoon would color island relationships for years to come.

Three prominent American citizens, Ambrose Davenport, John Dousman, and Samuel Abbott, were firm in their convictions. Years later, Davenport recalled that he declared to Captain Roberts, "I was born in America and am determined, at all hazards, to live and die an American citizen." Abbott and Dousman gave similar replies. Samuel Lasley, according to Davenport, "preferred British allegiance."[10] Lasley, a former American soldier, was arrested after the war and sent to Detroit, where he told a much more complicated tale of conflicting loyalties. His decision was made, Lasley claimed, "on the account of my wife and a Large famiely of children mostly all Small and my property being all there."[11] His choice would later cost him a land claim on Mackinac Island and a degree of community respect.

A fifth American, the most controversial of all, was not asked to take the oath. Michael Dousman was allowed to remain on Mackinac Island nonetheless. In 1819 he maintained that he was "claimed as a ci devant [former] British subject, and constrained by their power," but Samuel Lasley (against whom Dousman had leveled charges of wartime treason) bitterly denounced him as a collaborator of the first order. Dousman drew suspicion for his role in warning the villagers, and Lasley claimed that Dousman later did everything from providing supplies to recruiting troops for the British. Soon after the surrender, according to Lasley, Captain Roberts presented Michael Dousman to his Indian allies and declared to the assembled warriors that "this is one of our friends—one that is like ourselves."[12] Although Dousman ultimately became one of Mackinac Island's most influential and wealthy citizens, his wartime activities fueled gossip for the rest of his life. As late as 1854, the year of his death, local rumors persisted that his fortune had its source in treason. "Popular opinion has ever been against him," James J. Strang wrote at that time.[13]

On July 26 the sloop *Salina* and the schooner *Mary* sailed for Detroit with the exiles. Ambrose Davenport, John Dousman, twelve fellow citizens, and the crews of two other captured merchant vessels were aboard the *Salina*. Samuel Abbott, seven more citizens, and three officers and thirty-eight U.S. soldiers sailed on the *Mary*.[14] Lasley and Dousman would remain on the island for the duration of the war.

Continued British successes protected Michilimackinac from an American counterattack for the next two years, allowing the British to consolidate their hold on the northern lakes. Although plagued by shortages of men and supplies, the red-coated garrison was not directly threatened.[15] This long-distance defense crumbled in the autumn of 1813. Naval control of Lake Erie was lost to an American squadron on September 10, followed soon after by the retreat of British and Native American forces from Detroit. The victorious Americans had not forgotten the humiliating loss of Michilimackinac. As early as July 1813, Commodore Oliver Hazard Perry had been ordered to follow up a victory on Lake Erie with a foray into Lake Huron, where he was to "proceed to Michili-Makinac and carry that post." A military force assembled at Detroit in October, but a lack of supplies and deteriorating weather made an assault impossible in 1813.[16] Lake Huron was about to become a theater of the naval war, but the British had no warships to commit to the contest. Michilimackinac would have to depend on its formidable natural defenses and whatever forces could be scraped together.

When news of the military disasters on Lake Erie reached Fort Mackinac, Captain Richard Bullock, the new commandant, consulted with his officers as to what measures to take. Reinforcements were necessary, of course, and Bullock requested gunboats to protect supplies coming from Georgian Bay. His most urgent recommendation was for a blockhouse and stockade on the summit of the hill behind Fort Mackinac. "This height completely commands the Fort," he wrote, "and should an enemy with cannon once get in possession of it, the Fort must consequently fall." Also essential were reliable wells at both the new blockhouse and within Fort Mackinac, where the garrison still depended on a spring outside the walls.[17]

Winter offered time to provide for the needs of Michilimackinac. No ships were constructed, but a reinforcement of regular troops and supplies reached the island on May 18, 1814. Lieutenant Colonel Robert McDouall assumed command and energetically prepared for

"This height completely commands the Fort, and should an enemy with cannon once get in possession of it, the Fort must consequently fall."

CAPTAIN RICHARD BULLOCK

the anticipated assault. Andrew Bulger, one of his lieutenants, later recalled that "all hands were employed in strengthening the defences of the Fort." By July 17 McDouall could confidently report good progress, particularly on "our new works on the Hill overlooking the old Fort." These were nearly complete with a blockhouse in the center.[18] The fortification was probably already known to the troops as Fort George.

When a U.S. naval squadron appeared off Mackinac Island late in July, the defenders of Michilimackinac were alert and prepared. Confusion and indecision in the American command, led by Lieutenant Colonel George Croghan and Commodore Arthur Sinclair, contributed to delays and postponed an assault until August 4. A landing was made on the beach where the British had come ashore in 1812, and the subsequent battle took place in the fields and woods of Michael Dousman's farm. Croghan's force retreated with heavy casualties, and the fleet withdrew in hopes of disrupting the lines of supply to the Michilimackinac garrison. That effort ended in disaster as well, when a British and Indian force captured the blockading schooners *Tigress* and *Scorpion*.[19] "Thus ended the ill-directed and disastrous expedition against Mackinaw," wrote Humphrey Leavitt, an Ohio soldier and participant.[20]

What could not be gained on the battlefield was achieved by negotiation. The Treaty of Ghent, signed on Christmas Eve 1814, ended hostilities and precluded a new campaign in 1815. "Our Negociators as usual have been egregiously duped," growled Lieutenant Colonel McDouall, who was briskly preparing for another attack. "They have shown themselves profoundly ignorant of the concerns of this part of the Empire," he continued, and then drew on Shakespeare to emphasize his disappointment: "I am penetrated with grief at the restoration of this fine Island, a 'Fortress built by Nature for herself.'"[21] The Americans returned on July 18, 1815. Although elaborate preparations had been made for this event, the transfer was completed within thirty minutes, and British troops left Mackinac Island for the last time.[22]

The return of Michilimackinac to the United States marked the beginning of significant changes in military, commercial, and civil affairs at the Straits. Fort Mackinac and the new redoubt on the hill behind it, rechristened Fort Holmes by the Americans, received a substantial garrison—more than three times the number of soldiers assigned before the war. Fort Holmes was strengthened and occupied during the summer months, and military engineers addressed long-term defensive needs during 1816–17 with surveys and projects for new fortifications (Figs. 4.6, 4.7, and 4.10–4.12). During the summer of 1816, Mackinac Island saw even larger numbers of troops as the post served as a staging point for establishing forts at Green Bay and Chicago. Much of this attention was based on the perception that the geographical situation of Michilimackinac was "admirably fixed to intercept all intercourse between Lake Huron and Michigan" and that secure possession of the place was of "immense importance for the future safety of the whole N.W. frontier."[23]

This significance extended to the Native American nations of the upper lakes. Lewis Cass, governor of the Michigan Territory, declared Michilimackinac "the most important point so far as respects the Indians upon the Northwest frontier," partly because it was a regular gathering place for them. Cass recommended an Indian agency there to counteract the efforts of the British, who had established a new post on Drummond Island near the mouth of the St. Marys River. He provisionally appointed a former army officer, William H. Puthuff, to serve as agent.[24] The appointment was confirmed, and Puthuff and his successors would thereafter meet with thousands of Native Americans each year as they visited Mackinac Island to trade or to use it as a way station on their trips to collect presents and annuities from the British.[25]

Commercial change was in the wind as well; it might better be termed a storm. The war had prevented John Jacob Astor from capitalizing on his participation in the South West Company and denied him access to its assets on Mackinac Island. These included furs stored in warehouses and property and buildings that would give Astor's new American Fur Company a foothold in the trade. One of his agents, Ramsay Crooks, even accompanied the American naval expedition in 1814 and then returned later that fall under a flag of truce to recover some of Astor's property.[26] Establishment of the American Fur Company on Mackinac Island had to await the return of U.S. authority. The firm moved into the buildings on the lot (claim 101) confirmed to Toussaint Pothier in 1808 (Fig. 3.6). This had become part of the South West Company's holdings and was purchased by Astor in 1817.[27] There, fronting the beach and bounded by modern Fort and Market streets, the American Fur Company began its efforts to dominate the fur trade within the United States.[28] It would be the end of the decade before the company acquired more spacious property on Market Street and constructed the Stuart House and warehouse that stand there today.

Astor's position was greatly strengthened by the passage of legislation in the winter of 1816 that barred all but American citizens from engaging in the fur trade within the boundaries of the United States. This sea change in the way the trade operated effectively excluded the Canadian competition, but this could not be accomplished overnight. Most of the experienced labor for the fur trade still had to be found in Canada. The legislation ensured busy times for the military officers and the Indian agent at Michilimackinac. During the summer of 1816, four boats from the garrison were constantly "manned and cruising" to intercept traders and examine licenses.[29]

Mackinac Island was taking on a civic personality as well. By a proclamation of March 15, 1817, followed by an act of April 6, the governor and judges of the Territory of Michigan established the Borough of Michilimackinac and specified its duties and privileges.[30] The new local government was to be made up of a warden, two burgesses, a clerk, a treasurer, and a marshal. Its authority covered a wide range of civic concerns—taxation, the maintenance of walks and highways, regulation of nuisances and domestic animals, fire prevention, burial of the dead, wharves and anchorages, and even the planting of shade trees. The first borough meeting took place in July, with an annual meeting to be held each November thereafter.

City government began its work in December 1817 with a comprehensive fire-prevention ordinance. By April 1818 the warden and burgesses had passed acts for the preservation of sheep, dog control, and the cleanliness of the public streets and had prohibited "ston'd horses" (stallions) from running at large. A poll tax and a real property tax were established during the same period.[31] On April 13, 1818, William H. Puthuff, Indian agent and newly elected borough warden, was licensed to extend the first commercial wharf in the harbor at the foot of "a cross street" (today's Astor) leading from Market Street to the shore.[32] Local government was further strengthened in October 1818, when the village was named the "seat of justice" for newly formed Michilimackinac County.[33]

By 1818 the scars of the War of 1812 were healing, and the post of Michilimackinac must have seemed a more sophisticated and settled place thanks to the establishment of local government, a court, and the regional headquarters of a major business operation. Relations with Britain had also improved, so much so that the strategic value of Fort Mackinac was again being questioned. In February 1818, Major General Jacob Brown advocated abandoning the post. He cited many of the same reasons put forth by Alexander Hamilton in 1799. Michilimackinac did not really command any pass since the Straits were too wide to be controlled from the fort. The place was far from support in the event of an emergency, and it had inevitably become "a haunt for idleness & vice." While Brown allowed that "a fortress in the Indian country is never a negative value," he wanted military posts to be placed as far forward as possible. Sault Ste. Marie offered a location where U.S. troops could watch Indians, traders, and the border with British Canada all at the same time.[34]

Brown visited Michilimackinac on a tour of inspection in the summer of 1819, and although Fort Mackinac was ultimately preserved, it was clear that its military value was fading. The size of the garrison was reduced, Fort Holmes was not actively occupied after 1817, and plans to construct new fortifications on its site were abandoned. Mackinac Island was nonetheless growing in stature as a principal outpost of the American Fur Company, and the coming decade would see it become a religious center as well.

BRITISH COMMANDANTS OF MICHILIMACKINAC, 1812–1815

Captain Charles Roberts, 10th Royal Veteran Battalion, 1812–13

Captain Richard Bullock, 41st Regiment of Foot, 1813–14

Lieutenant Colonel Robert McDouall, Glengarry Light Infantry Fencibles, 1814–15

U.S. COMMANDANTS OF FORT MACKINAC, 1815–1820

Colonel Anthony Butler, Regiment of Riflemen, 1815

Major Willoughby Morgan, Regiment of Riflemen, 1815

Major Talbot Chambers, Regiment of Riflemen, 1815–16

Colonel John Miller, 3rd Regiment of Infantry, 1816

Lieutenant Colonel John McNeil, 5th Regiment of Infantry, 1816–17

Captain Benjamin K. Pierce, Corps of Artillery, 1817–19

Lieutenant Colonel William Lawrence, 3rd Regiment of Infantry, 1819–20

Captain Benjamin K. Pierce, Corps of Artillery, 1820–21

WARDENS OF THE BOROUGH OF MICHILIMACKINAC, 1817–1820

William H. Puthuff, 1817–21

The village of Macana lies in a circular form, around the harbor

Josiah Dunham

In September 1812 an unnamed correspondent to *The Washingtonian,* a Windsor, Vermont, newspaper, described the relationship of the village of Michilimackinac to its harbor. The houses facing the bay, he wrote, stood "on an inclined plane reaching from the foot of the rock, on which the fort stands, to the water's edge." The author was probably the paper's editor, Josiah Dunham, a former Fort Mackinac commandant, and his letter was published as news of the military disasters on the Great Lakes was sweeping the United States. The writer's colorful description fleshed out accounts of the loss of Michilimackinac. Of the village itself, he continued, "the streets are narrow, but regular and cleanly—the houses and other buildings are compact, mostly of one story, and built of the lightest materials."[35]

This is only one of a number of written descriptions of the village of Michilimackinac as it was during the era of the War of 1812. In 1813, for the first time, these word pictures were supplemented by a view of the harbor, town, and fort that had been taken by the British in July 1812. The hand-colored aquatint (Fig. 4.1) was published in Montréal under the title *Michilimackinac on Lake Huron,* complete with a celebratory dedication to Sir George Prevost, governor-general of British Canada, under whose command Captain Charles Roberts and his men had wrested the important fur-trading post from the Americans.

Little is known of the artist whose work provided the basis for this revealing image. His name was Richard Dillon, Jr., and he is believed to have served with the volunteer militia of Montréal during the War of 1812. Dillon appears to have made his living primarily as a clerk or accountant. His father, who published the younger man's drawing, is somewhat better documented as an artist, engraver, and, possibly, a hotelier in Montréal.[36] Nor are the circumstances or date of the artist's visit to Michilimackinac recorded. Dillon might have sketched the place after its capture by the British or, possibly, a few years before. Little more is known about the creation of this print, other than that Thomas Hall was its engraver.

Whatever the circumstances, Richard Dillon did justice to the appearance of the village of Michilimackinac as it was at the outbreak of war. He presents a vista along Water Street (today's Main) and a glimpse of the architecture and activity of the lively trading community on Mackinac Island. The picture reveals the typical Canadian-style construction of most of its houses, many roofed with bark and some of the aging structures supported by props. Tall palisade fences enclose lots and divide properties, and there is hardly a tree to be seen in the thirty-year-old village and few on the bluffs beyond. The pebbly beach provides a landing place for canoes and bateaux. Larger vessels, such as the schooner in the distance, which might be the North West Company's *Nancy,* had to anchor close to shore to load or discharge cargo.

Dillon also conveys a sense of the relationship of village and fort to the island's topography, although the bluff to the east of Fort Mackinac inexplicably tapers into insignificant hills. An 1817 description by an American officer, Judge Advocate Samuel A. Storrow, could almost serve as a guide to Dillon's view, which was taken from the southern end of the harbor near the site of today's Iroquois Hotel. "After passing the beach, which is lined with Indian wigwams," he wrote, "you enter a contemptible village of forty or fifty houses, filled with a squalid, mixed race of Indians and Canadians. The ground is level for the space of one hundred and sixty yards, when there rises an abrupt eminence of one hundred and twenty-five feet, which extends irregularly from the east nearly to the west of the island. This elevation is ascended diagonally, and on the summit is planted Fort Mackinac, which seems to impend over the village below."[37]

Michilimackinac was a rather different sort of settlement than the agricultural communities found farther to the south, such as Detroit, Sandwich, Amherstburg, and River Raisin. It was a town for trade, and the harsh climate and seasonal cycle of collecting furs ensured that its population would fluctuate throughout the year, as it had since the days of the French. Houses were often occupied only seasonally, and, as the *Washingtonian* writer observed in 1812, they were built in a manner that he considered flimsy, although it was a style of architecture that had been successfully used at the Straits and across much of the Great Lakes since the seventeenth century.

The building at the extreme left of Dillon's composition is an archetypal example of housing at Michilimackinac. It appears to stand at the corner of one of the cross streets (Hoban) and might be on the property claimed in 1808 by Jean Baptiste Carron (Fig. 3.6, number 699). Carron's tract had been improved with a house and a warehouse.[38] This parcel appears on the 1805 map of selected lots in the village (Fig. 3.5), colored beige and marked with the initials "IG" for Jacques Giasson. The house in that composition faces the beach, and the warehouse or "store" is behind it with its gable end on the cross street.

The building at the left of the Dillon print appears to have some age on it and, like some of its neighbors, is supported by props wedged against the facade. It might well have been a contemporary of a similar house that William Burnett proposed to construct in 1794. The trader laid out detailed specifications: "The House to be thirty foot in front, and twenty-five feet wide. Between the two floors within to be eight foot. The front door to be in the middle, and one on the back right opposite the front door. Two windows to be in the

FIGURE 4.1

TITLE: Michilimackinac on Lake Huron. To His Excellency Sir George Prevost Bart. Governor General and Commander in Chief of all his Majesties Forces in British America. This Print is humbly Inscribed by his Excellency's most obedient humble Servant Richard Dillon Junr.

AUTHOR: Richard Dillon, Jr. (1772–after 1856). Engraved by Thomas Hall.

DATE DEPICTED: 1812.

DATE OF WORK: 1813.

DESCRIPTION: 28 x 31 cm. Colored aquatint.

PROVENANCE: Published in Montréal in 1813 by Richard Dillon, Sr.

COLLECTION: Clements Library, University of Michigan, Ann Arbor (Print Division, E-7).

front, one to be on each side of the door, and two windows to be on the back . . . the same as the front. A window to be on each gable end of the house, to be in each front room." Its roof was to be "covered with bark."[39] Many of the other houses farther down the beach exhibit similar characteristics, and some of the larger structures are probably warehouses.

Richard Dillon's view does not provide a look down the main street, which was behind the houses shown along the beach. This, today's Market Street, was acknowledged by most visitors to be the best thoroughfare in town. Ste. Anne's Church stood where the cross street (Hoban) met Market, and is thus masked by the house at the extreme left. In 1819 Dr. John J. Bigsby described the old church building as "a disgraceful wooden ruin, standing among the neat white habitations of the citizens." According to Father Gabriel Richard, the church was "destroyed" that year, and the congregation hoped to build a replacement.[40]

The only other "public" building visible in the Dillon view may be seen below Fort Mackinac and to the right of the schooner. This is Government House, since 1809 the U.S. Indian factory, where Michilimackinac's American citizens gathered after the surrender to choose between exile and allegiance to King George III.

The structure seems to have survived the War of 1812, and it appears on William Eveleth's detailed map of Mackinac Island of 1817 (Fig. 4.7). By that time, it might have served one final use as the U.S. Indian agency. It seems to have disappeared by 1820, a victim of either fire or accumulated neglect.

William Eveleth's 1817 plan of the village (Fig. 4.7) corresponds very neatly with the scene shown by Dillon. The Eveleth map shows individual properties and buildings as well as the pattern of streets and alleys. It was for this original part of town, described as being "within the limits of the old Pickets" or defensive stockade, that the warden and burgesses of the Borough of Michilimackinac passed their first ordinance on December 4, 1817. It was for the prevention of fire, probably the greatest fear of Michilimackinac's inhabitants. Fifteen articles regulated the maintenance and sweeping of chimneys, the use of stovepipe, the storage of hay and straw, and the quantity of gunpowder that could be kept in town. The ordinance was followed, in April 1818, by an act "for the promotion of health and cleanliness" that suggests some of the olfactory details of life in the village of Michilimackinac. The ordinance required householders to keep the streets in front of their properties "clean shovelled raked or swept." It further specified fines for throwing animal or vegetable matter,

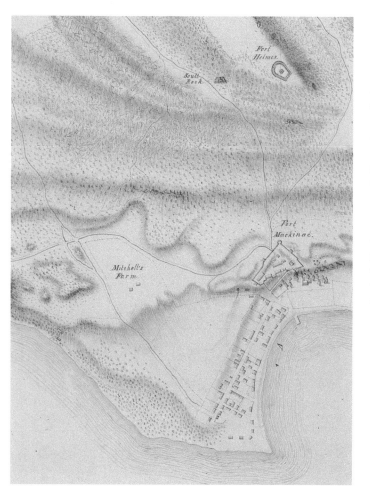

On the morning of July 17, 1812, the citizens of Michilimackinac sought shelter in Francis LeBarron's distillery a few hundred yards west of the village. The building stood by a spring near the site of the modern Grand Hotel swimming pool. This detail, from Lieutenant William S. Eveleth's 1817 map (Fig. 4.7), shows the distillery near the shore at far left.

British troops had no need to haul their six-pounder cannon to the highest point of Mackinac Island to dominate the fort. Longtime residents later recalled that the invaders "planted a gun in the road" on "a little ridge which separates this hollow from the parade ground (and only a few paces from it)." The spot was probably where the road to "Scull Rock" crosses the first rise above Fort Mackinac. *Clements Library, University of Michigan.*

excrement, or soapsuds into the street, particularly the large quantities of fish intestines that were a waste product of Michilimackinac's renowned trout and whitefish.[41]

The fort and town depicted by Richard Dillon provided the stage for Britain's first major success of the War of 1812. Along its narrow streets the townspeople fled to the distillery for safety and later returned to face the victors. Overlooking this village on the morning of July 17, 1812, Lieutenant Porter Hanks decided to surrender his post to protect the inhabitants. Later that afternoon, the picturesque harbor in the foreground was the scene of one final, colorful pageant in the British capture of Michilimackinac. Learning of the American surrender, the Indians who surrounded the fort hastened back to the beach that has been known ever since as "British Landing." Then, according to Indian factor Matthew Irwin, "entering their boats & Canoes, at the bow of each [of which] were British streamers, [they] made for the harbour facing the fort & as they approached it, kept up a very animated discharge of small arms, which was returned very often from the Fort, with ordnance."[42]

Oliver Williams (1774–1834) was caught in the surprise capture of Michilimackinac when his merchant vessel, *Friend's Good Will,* dropped anchor in Haldimand Bay soon after the garrison had capitulated. Williams was paroled to Detroit, but his sloop was a prize of war. She was taken into British service as the *Little Belt,* later fighting for the Royal Navy at the Battle of Lake Erie. *The Detroit Historical Society (91.68.1).*

Dispatches carried to Fort St. Joseph by Canadian fur trader William McKay (1772–1832) encouraged Captain Charles Roberts to organize his surprise attack on Fort Mackinac. In 1814, McKay was appointed to command a company of "Michigan Fencibles" recruited at Michilimackinac. That summer, he led a successful expedition against the American post at Prairie du Chien, Wisconsin. McKay was later appointed to the Indian Department and was portrayed in an officer's uniform by Levi Stevens in 1816. *McCord Museum, Montréal (M-17684). Gift from the estate of Mrs. M. C. Jacques.*

SIR JOS JEBB.

Captain Roberts's bold stroke against Michilimackinac would not have been possible without the military and moral support of Native American warriors. These Ottawa men from Michilimackinac, depicted at Montréal in 1814, had very likely participated in the surprise attack on Fort Mackinac two years earlier. This watercolor is attributed to Sir Joshua Jebb. *© 2007 Peabody Museum, Harvard University, Cambridge, MA (41-72-10/390 T344).*

In truth, no one acquired any military glory in this affair

Humphrey Leavitt

U.S. naval vessels began to gather off Mackinac Island late in July 1814, with the goal of recovering the post that had been lost two years before. Commodore Arthur Sinclair commanded a formidable squadron, made up of the heavily armed brigs *Niagara* and *Lawrence,* the schooners *Caledonia, Tigress,* and *Scorpion,* and three supply ships. Packed aboard the vessels were 750 soldiers led by Lieutenant Colonel George Croghan. The squadron had sailed into Lake Huron on July 14, but then diverted to seek the British supply base on Georgian Bay and then destroy the buildings of Fort St. Joseph and Sault Ste. Marie. The sailors captured the trading schooner *Mink* in the St. Marys River and incorporated her into the squadron. It was not until July 25 that most of this naval force hove within three miles of Mackinac's east shore.[43]

No doubt officers and men alike strained for a view of fabled Michilimackinac. Humphrey Leavitt was aboard the *Caledonia,* serving on the staff of Lieutenant Colonel William Cotgreave's regiment of Ohio volunteers. He could tell that the British garrison was prepared. "With the aid of a glass we could see that the business of strengthening and completing the fortifications was in active progress," he later remembered. From the quarterdeck of the *Niagara* Lieutenant Colonel Croghan observed "that the enemy had strongly foretified the height overlooking the old Fort of Mackinac." The sight seems to have disheartened him, and he later reported that he "at once despair'd of being able, with my Small force, to carry the place by storm."[44]

Croghan's pessimism seems to have set the tone for the whole affair, a striking instance of the psychological effect exerted by the commanding bluffs and heights of Mackinac Island. The fleet contained plenty of competent naval and military officers, but the only one known to have sketched his impression of the scene was Captain Charles Gratiot, the expedition's engineer, who was with Croghan aboard the *Niagara.* Gratiot drew a simple topographical view, which he later inset on an equally rough sketch map of Mackinac Island and its surrounding waters and islands (Fig. 4.2). Captain Gratiot never intended his crude map to be a finished work, and he only sent it to Brigadier General Joseph G. Swift after the war, in February 1816, because he did not have another "correct chart of the island and environs."[45] Gratiot forwarded his little map to illustrate ongoing discussions about how best to fortify the heights behind Fort Mackinac.

Viewed from the water, Michilimackinac looked like a fortress indeed, and Forts Mackinac and George probably hoisted British colors once the American vessels were seen approaching. Captain Gratiot found himself on Mackinac Island on two occasions during the campaign, on August 4 and 5, but he had only limited opportunity to observe details of its topography, and he lacked any prewar cartography to support his observations. His map thus distorts the shape of the island and identifies only details visible from the ships or what could be seen during the heat of battle on August 4. The town and the two forts are identified, as is "Lebarons Still House" below the bluff on the island's southwestern shore. This was the distillery constructed in 1809 by post surgeon Francis LeBarron and used as a refuge for the citizens when the British landed in 1812. The identity of this large, isolated building was probably revealed to Gratiot by Michilimackinac exiles Ambrose Davenport and John Dousman, both of whom had joined Croghan's expedition to provide the benefit of their local knowledge.[46]

Captain Gratiot's map is a far cry from the finely detailed survey completed in 1817 by Lieutenant William S. Eveleth (Figs. 4.7 and 5.13). The island is nearly square in Gratiot's composition, and, perhaps reflecting Croghan's apprehensions, it appears fortlike with formidable bluffs emphasizing its shape. Nearby bodies of land are identified and provide geographical context for Mackinac Island. Their forested shores figured in the early stages of the campaign. Humphrey Leavitt apprehensively perceived "swarms of Indians . . . peeping from the main land and the adjacent islands with the evident design of aiding the British to defend the fort."[47] Figures of houses mark the small settlement at Point St. Ignace. Gratiot's notations record some of the movements of the squadron in the days following its arrival in the Straits.

Navy surgeon Usher Parsons first saw Mackinac Island from the deck of the brig *Lawrence,* and he kept a precise diary throughout the operation. After anchoring southeast of the island, as shown on Gratiot's map, the squadron briefly landed a few troops on Round Island on July 26. The *Lawrence* and the *Tigress* sailed around the northwestern end of Mackinac Island that evening to observe the place from the southwest. It proved difficult to maintain communications between the separate elements of the squadron. American boats passing between Round and Bois Blanc islands were fired on by Indians, so *Tigress* was sent back around Mackinac Island with the information that had been gathered. The schooner *Scorpion* joined the *Lawrence* on July 30, and their "Cruising ground" is shown on Gratiot's map. Lieutenant Colonel Croghan came aboard the *Lawrence* for a council of war on July 31 and left the meeting finally determined to attempt an assault. The fleet had been at Mackinac for six days, and Parsons puzzled over the colonel's "Strange dallying." Ohio volunteer Leavitt considered the "hovering about the island" an unaccountable delay.[48]

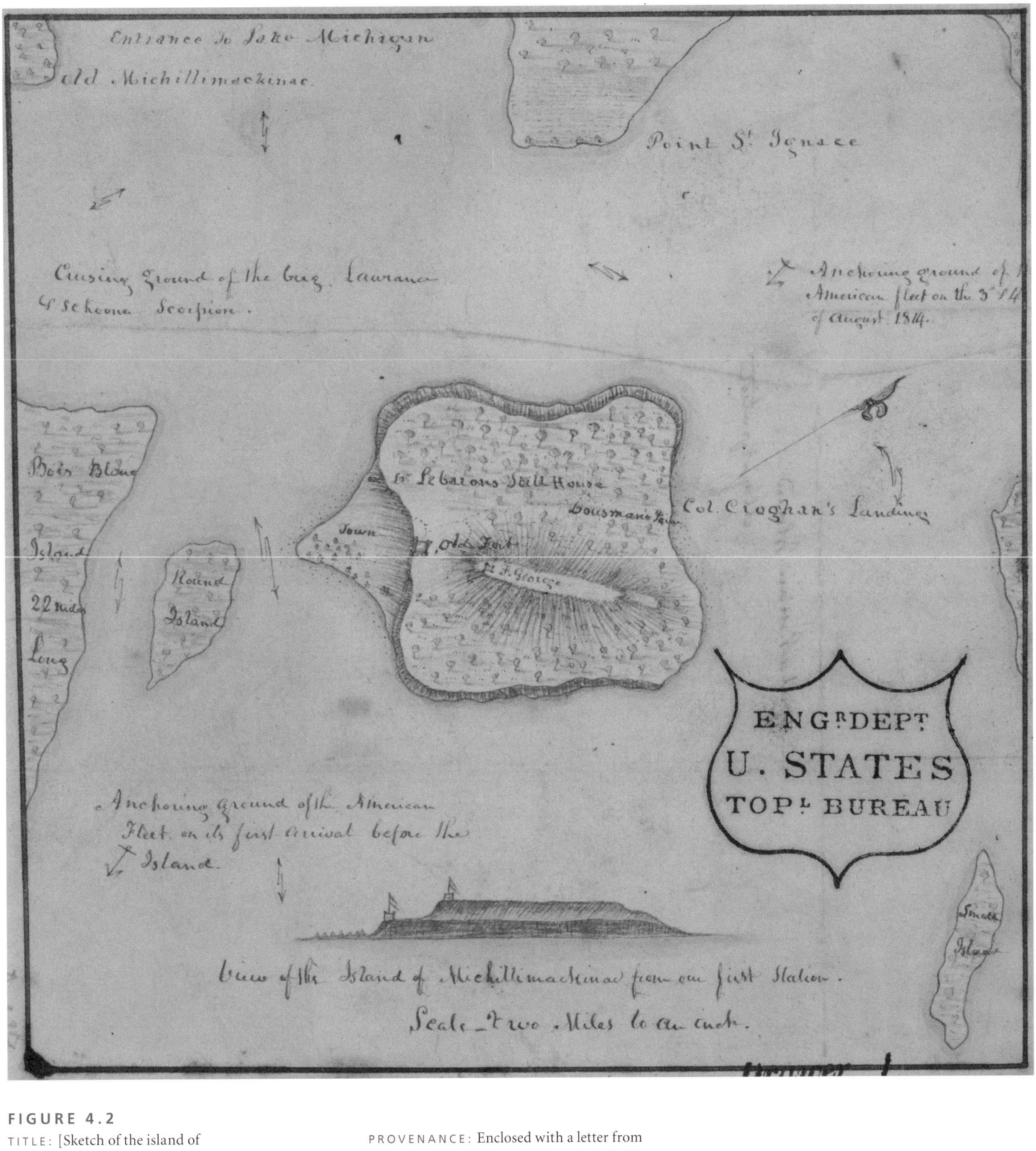

FIGURE 4.2

TITLE: [Sketch of the island of Michilimackinac]. [Inset:] View of the Island of Michillimackinac from our first Station.
AUTHOR: [Captain Charles Gratiot, Corps of Engineers (1788–1855)].
DATE DEPICTED: August 1814.
DATE OF WORK: [1816].
DESCRIPTION: 19.5 x 20 cm. Pencil, pen, and ink on paper.

PROVENANCE: Enclosed with a letter from Gratiot to Brigadier General Joseph G. Swift dated February 10, 1816. Retained in the records of the chief of engineers.
COLLECTION: National Archives and Records Administration, College Park, MD (RG 77, Records of the Chief of Engineers, Fortifications Map File, Drawer 1, Sheet 30).

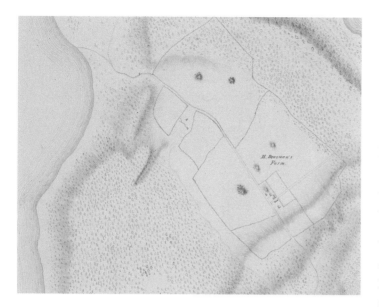

This detail from Lieutenant William S. Eveleth's 1817 topographical map (Fig. 4.7) shows the Dousman farm. Croghan's landing force marched from the beach at the upper left and was opposed by McDouall's troops and Indian warriors positioned behind the elevation at the lower right. Major Holmes and his men were fired upon somewhere near the ridge at bottom center. *Clements Library, University of Michigan.*

It was probably at the meeting on July 31 that Croghan decided to attempt a landing. Concerned about directly assaulting the island's formidable defenses, he opted for the more conservative course of occupying a position from which he could "annoy the enemy by gradual and slow approaches, under cover of my artillery." This, Croghan hoped, would encourage the desertion of the many Indian warriors who had gathered to support the British. Croghan had "learned from individuals, who had lived many years on the island," that the cleared land of Michael Dousman's farm afforded such a position.[49] Davenport and John Dousman were surely his advisors.

Sometime on August 3 the elements of the squadron reunited between Mackinac Island and Point St. Ignace. Action was again delayed until the next day, however. At about 11:00 AM on August 4, Parsons reported, the vessels "came to anchor in line of battle abreast of the N.W. side of Mackinac Island . . . on which the British landed when they took the fort from us."[50] Gratiot identified the beach on his map as "Col. Croghan's Landing." The slow pace of the campaign continued, and it was another two hours before troops began to fill the landing boats. At 2:00 PM Sinclair's warships commenced a devastating bombardment. British Lieutenant Andrew Bulger

Lieutenant Colonel Robert McDouall (1774–1848) conducted a determined and successful defense of Michilimackinac in 1814. When he later commissioned a painting commemorating this achievement, artist William Dashwood included a green-clad figure representing the colonel in the uniform of the Glengarry Light Infantry Fencibles. Detail from Figure 4.3. *Mackinac State Historic Parks, MI.*

recalled it as "a tremendous fire, which completely swept the landing place."[51] By 3:00 the troops had disembarked, formed ranks on the beach, and commenced their march up the road toward Dousman's farm.

The Americans' "strange dallying" that day provided four hours for Lieutenant Colonel McDouall to make his own preparations. Leaving only a few defenders in Forts Mackinac and George, McDouall assembled about 200 British and Canadian soldiers and 350 Indian warriors. These he marched to a low ridge on the southeastern side of the Dousman farm where the slope provided "a natural Breast work" for his men with open fields to the front and tangled forest on either flank. The white troops held the ridge, while the Indians defended the woods.[52]

Captain Gratiot marched up the road with Croghan, having volunteered his services as adjutant. If he sketched the battlefield, the plan has not survived, and his map simply records the location as "Dousman's." Parsons remained aboard *Lawrence*. There, pocket watch in hand, he listened for the sounds of combat. Fifteen minutes after Croghan's troops left the beach Parsons heard the first booming of British field pieces, soon followed by the rattle of musketry. He thereafter recorded intermittent bursts of gunfire as the combatants grappled in the rough and brushy terrain. At about 4:10 Parsons heard firing of "considerable rapidity accompanied with yelling." Major Andrew Hunter Holmes, Croghan's second-in-command, had been ordered to outflank the western end of the British position. His column stumbled into a party of Menominee warriors, led by a chief named Tomah, and it was routed with the deaths of the major and a dozen men. Twenty minutes later, Parsons could tell that Croghan's troops were retiring, and by 5:00 PM firing had ceased, and the landing force was back at the boats.[53]

With troops aboard, the vessels hoisted anchor and moved offshore. Parsons tended wounds throughout the night, including those of Captain Isaac Van Horne, Jr., Lieutenant Hezekiah Jackson, and an unnamed sergeant, all of whom had died by the morning of August 5.[54] The body of Major Holmes had been left on the battlefield. Later that day Croghan sent Captain Gratiot to Fort Mackinac under a flag of truce to request his remains, which were successfully recovered and taken aboard in the evening.[55] Gratiot was no doubt blindfolded as he was taken to Lieutenant Colonel McDouall, so he would have seen little of the British fortifications. It would be two more years before he had the opportunity to examine Fort Mackinac in detail.

Canadian fur traders and voyageurs bolstered the British forces defending Michilimackinac in 1814. John Johnston (1762–1828) led a detachment of militia from Sault Ste. Marie. During the battle of August 4, Colonel McDouall entrusted Fort Mackinac to Johnston with a skeleton force of twenty-five militiamen. Joseph Wilson painted Johnston in Belfast, Ireland, in 1789.

Collection of the Chippewa County Historical Society, Sault Ste. Marie, MI.

Twenty-three-year-old Lieutenant Colonel George Croghan (1791–1849) commanded the 1814 military expedition against Michilimackinac. A hero of the northwestern campaign of 1813, Croghan proved unable to organize an effective assault on the defenders of Mackinac Island. He sat for John Wesley Jarvis in 1816, but the location of that portrait is unknown. John Henry Witt executed this fine, mid-nineteenth-century copy.

Rutherford B. Hayes Presidential Center, Fremont, OH.

Major Andrew Hunter Holmes (ca. 1792–1814) was to have led the troops destined for Michilimackinac but was replaced by Croghan and served thereafter as his second-in-command. Holmes was killed during the battle of August 4 while attempting to outflank the British position. This portrait, of unknown provenance, was first reproduced in Edwin O. Wood, *Historic Mackinac* (New York, 1918).

Clements Library, University of Michigan.

The enemy's vessel was boarded and carried

Lieutenant Andrew Bulger

Commodore Arthur Sinclair put the best possible spin on his report of the events of August 4, 1814. He and Croghan both blamed the repulse of the landing force on "the impenetrable thickness of the woods" that concealed Indian warriors and impeded the movements of American troops.[56] Sinclair believed that Croghan's soldiers could have made no further progress and that "no advantage gained could be profited by." The colonel, he reported, had withdrawn his men in "a masterly manner." Croghan, for his part, announced that he did not think it prudent to make another attempt.[57]

To a naval officer, the British position posed daunting obstacles. "Mackinac is, by nature, a perfect Gibraltar, being a high inaccessible rock on every side, except the west," wrote Sinclair, and that avenue had led to Croghan's defeat. Sinclair would have preferred to make a landing below Fort Mackinac, where the Indians would not have been so effective and the heavy guns of his ships would have out-classed the British artillery. However, after drawing fire from the fort, the commodore was forced to admit, "its site being about 120 feet above the water, I could not when near enough to do him an injury, elevate [cannon] sufficiently to batter it." Fort George, he noted, was even higher.[58] Usher Parsons had witnessed an exchange of fire between Sinclair's *Niagara* and a British gun near a block-house on July 27. This was probably the same incident observed by islander Samuel Lasley, who watched a large brig approach Sinclair's preferred landing place on the shore near "the old Still house." The British directed a heavy gun at the warship, and, when the brig returned fire, Lasley recalled, the twenty-four-pound ball struck "a patch of Potatoes belonning [sic] to me and did considerabal Damage to the potatoes." Curious, the old soldier retrieved the shot from his garden, which was probably on his property on the western end of Market Street, far below Fort Mackinac.[59]

Mackinac's topography had foiled direct assault, but Croghan and Sinclair still held naval control of Lake Huron. Their new strategy was to starve the British into submission. The two officers decided to proceed with part of the fleet and three companies of troops to destroy the base on the Nottawasaga River through which Michilimackinac could be supplied from York (Toronto). The *Lawrence* and the *Caledonia* were dispatched to Detroit with the sick and wounded—nearly one hundred of them.[60] The vessels parted company near Thunder Bay on August 11. Humphrey Leavitt, who had been desperately ill for much of the campaign, slept on the wet deck of *Caledonia* to escape the "groanings and cries of agony" and the "intolerable stench" of the wounded.[61] *Caledonia* had an additional burden for the voyage down Lake Huron. "Have the dead in tow for Detroit," Parsons noted. The remains of Major Holmes,

sealed in a coffin weighted with cannonballs, followed behind the schooner, preserved in the cold lake water for later burial.[62]

Two days later, Sinclair anchored the *Niagara, Tigress,* and *Scorpion* off the mouth of the Nottawasaga River at the southern end of Georgian Bay. A short distance upstream, guarded by a blockhouse, lay the North West Company's schooner *Nancy*. Too old and light for naval service, she could nonetheless transport supplies to the Michilimackinac garrison. The *Nancy* was already laden, defended only by Lieutenant Miller Worsley of the Royal Navy, twenty-one seamen, and a few Indians. It was too late to mount an attack on August 13, but gunfire from the ships and Croghan's troops destroyed the blockhouse the next day. The *Nancy* and her cargo perished too, set afire by Worsley's retreating men.[63]

The next day, as Sinclair prepared to sail for Detroit, he issued orders to Lieutenant Daniel Turner, of the *Scorpion*. Noting that it was "all important to cut the enemy's line of communication from Michilimackinac to York," he instructed Turner to keep up "a rigid blockade" at the mouth of the Nottawasaga until October, "suffering not a boat or canoe to pass in or out of the river." He assigned the *Tigress,* under Sailing Master Stephen Champlin, to assist. There was a second route by which Mackinac could be supplied, so Sinclair allowed Turner, should he "deem it proper," to send the *Tigress* to cruise northern Georgian Bay between the mouth of the French River and St. Joseph Island. "Wishing you a pleasant cruize," Sinclair cheerfully concluded his orders before turning the *Niagara* toward Detroit.[64]

Lieutenant Worsley and his men had not retreated far. About a week after Sinclair sailed away he set out for Michilimackinac in two boats and a large canoe with seventeen sailors and whatever provisions they could carry. The boats arrived on August 31, having passed the American schooners near the Detour Passage. Worsley went immediately to Colonel McDouall and argued that the American vessels "might be attacked with every prospect of success," especially as they had taken up widely separated positions, far from the Nottawasaga River.[65] McDouall, a naturally aggressive leader, agreed. The destruction of *Nancy* had put his garrison perilously close to starvation. He had already cut rations and even butchered a few of the island's horses to supplement fish taken from the lake.[66]

McDouall approved Worsley's plan to break the blockade. Four boats were outfitted, one crewed by the Royal Navy and the others by three officers and fifty-four men of the Royal Newfoundland Regiment under Lieutenant Andrew Bulger. Field pieces were mounted in the bows of two of the boats. The flotilla sailed on the evening of September 1, accompanied by canoes full of Indian

FIGURE 4.3

TITLE: [*Tigress* and *Scorpion* carried into Mackinac].
AUTHOR: William Dashwood (active 1820s) after
Richard Dillon, Jr. (1772–after 1856), George Heriot
(1766–1844), Robert McDouall (1774–1848), and others.
DATE DEPICTED: September 7, 1814.
DATE OF WORK: 1820s.
DESCRIPTION: 40.6 x 55.9 cm. Oil on canvas.
Signed W. Dashwood 182—?
PROVENANCE: Painted by Dashwood for Lieutenant
Colonel Robert McDouall. Purchased in 2000 by
Mackinac State Historic Parks from Kaspar Gallery,
Toronto, Ontario.
COLLECTION: Mackinac State Historic Parks,
Mackinac Island, MI (2000.60.1).

warriors. Near Detour, at sunset on September 2, the raiders spotted the *Tigress.* After hiding for most of the next day, they rowed in the evening with muffled oars across six miles of Lake Huron and were within one hundred yards of the schooner before being challenged and fired on. The *Tigress* was "boarded and carried" in a rush. Champlin went down, his thigh shattered by grapeshot fired from the boats. Lieutenant Bulger reported that "the defence of this vessel did credit to her officers," all of whom were wounded. The American prisoners were sent to Mackinac the next day.[67]

Worsley and Bulger planned to sail in search of the *Scorpion,* but on September 5 she was seen approaching. The British had done nothing to alter the *Tigress,* and her "American pendant was kept flying." Lieutenant Turner was carelessly unaware of the ruse. The schooners lay at anchor, two miles apart, throughout the night. At dawn on September 6, Worsley quietly slipped his moorings and sailed down to the *Scorpion.*[68] American seaman David Bunnell watched her approach with a feeling that "all was not right," but his shipmates laughed off his warning. The *Tigress* slid across the bow of the *Scorpion,* fired a twenty-four-pounder cannon, and dispatched a boarding party of sailors, soldiers, and Indians.[69] Surprise was nearly complete, and in "five minutes her deck was covered with our men and the British flag hoisted over the American," reported Worsley. The two actions had cost ten American and twelve British casualties.[70]

On September 7 Lieutenant Worsley "conducted the blockading force in triumph" into Haldimand Bay.[71] The arrival of the *Tigress* and the *Scorpion* was one of the memorable events of the war at Michilimackinac. It was particularly gratifying for Robert McDouall, and he chose that moment in time to commemorate his successful defense of the island. Sometime in the 1820s the colonel commissioned a little-known artist named William Dashwood to picture the scene as he remembered it. McDouall had returned to his hometown of Stranraer, Scotland, in 1816. There he planned "to embellish [his] retreat" with paintings of his wartime friends.[72] It is likely that McDouall commissioned Dashwood's painting with this idea in mind.

Dashwood based his view of Mackinac Island on Richard Dillon's *Michilimackinac on Lake Huron* (Fig. 4.1), a copy of which was likely provided by McDouall himself. Details of the topography, the town, and fort are largely derived from the print. But Dashwood added further elements that bring greater animation to his composition and give it its own value as a historical source. The captured schooners tack into the harbor, the smaller *Tigress* in the lead, with British ensigns flying above their American colors. The guns of Fort Mackinac roar out a salute. Native Americans cluster on the beach, in a group copied by Dashwood from the published images of George Heriot and other available visual sources.[73] One warrior points to the vessels, no doubt impressed by the military prowess of his British allies.

Commodore Arthur Sinclair (1777–1831) commanded the naval squadron that carried Croghan's soldiers to Michilimackinac. Although his warships were powerfully armed, their heavy guns proved ineffective against the elevated positions of Forts Mackinac and George. This portrait miniature shows Sinclair as a lieutenant. *Collection of James L. Kochan, Frederick, MD.*

Commodore Sinclair ordered Lieutenant Daniel Turner (1794–1850) to blockade Michilimackinac with the schooners *Tigress* and *Scorpion.* After the British captured *Tigress,* they used the vessel, still flying American colors, to surprise and take Turner's *Scorpion* on September 6. A postwar court martial acquitted the lieutenant of charges of negligence. This contemporary portrait, from an unidentified printed source, depicts Turner about 1813. *Courtesy of U.S. Naval Academy Museum.*

The summer's victories were impressive enough that Colonel McDouall may be excused for having himself painted into the left background of the scene, sporting the distinctive green uniform of the Glengarry Light Infantry Fencibles.[74] He, too, points out the captured schooners to a pair of Native Americans, while what may be McDouall's dog dabbles in the surf. The *Tigress* and the *Scorpion* are rendered quite realistically, down to their pivot-mounted twenty-four-pounder guns, a further indication that Dashwood's composition was supervised by his patron. The finished oil painting is the visual equivalent of oral history, and it sheds a remarkable amount of light on an event that had taken place a decade earlier.

The Mackinac garrison had further reason to celebrate the capture of the American schooners. As prizes of war their value would be distributed among the men who had taken them. The vessels and their contents were evaluated by a group of knowledgeable Michilimackinac merchants, who declared their worth to be £16,014 and 11 1/4 pence. This substantial sum would eventually be divided according to a long-established system based on rank. Military forces had been so prominent in the victory that Governor-General George Prevost recommended that the entire Michilimackinac garrison share in the windfall, rather than just those who had been in the boats. The schooners were taken into naval service, appropriately renamed *Confiance* and *Surprise*.[75] Their first duty was to transport the supplies needed to see McDouall's garrison through the winter.

The year ended less happily for American aspirations for the recapture of Michilimackinac. Lieutenant Turner and most of the captured sailors went to Québec as prisoners of war.[76] Sailing Master Champlin and the wounded were paroled, arriving at Erie, Pennsylvania, on November 6 aboard the schooner *Union*.[77] By that time Commodore Sinclair had already been under the "mortifying necessity" of reporting this final failure of the 1814 campaign. He was chagrined by the "little regard" Turner had paid to his detailed orders. The result was that the Michilimackinac garrison had regained the communications "on which their very existence depended."[78] For the time, nothing more could be done but plan for a renewed effort for 1815.

Sailing Master Stephen Champlin (1789–1870) was severely wounded when a British and Indian force surprised his schooner, *Tigress,* on the night of September 2–3, 1814. Champlin suffered from the effects of his injury for the rest of his life. An unidentified artist pictured him late in a long naval career. *Courtesy of U.S. Naval Academy Museum (69.1.18).*

Altogether inadequate for defense

Colonel Anthony Butler

As Colonel Anthony Butler and his detachment of U.S. troops came within sight of Michilimackinac, on August 18, 1815, they could easily distinguish the most significant improvement made to the post's defenses since 1812. Fort Mackinac perched on the bluff overlooking the harbor, but above and beyond it was another fortification dominating the scene from the island's highest point. Veterans of 1814 would have recalled Fort George, the redoubt constructed by the British earlier that year. It had been designed to protect Fort Mackinac against attack from higher ground, a concern expressed repeatedly by military men for more than thirty years. The bitter experiences of 1812 and 1814 now ensured that the commanding hill could no longer be disregarded when planning for the future defense of Michilimackinac.[79]

Butler had come to accept the post from its last British garrison. The formalities were brief. His troops landed at 2:00 in the afternoon, the U.S. flag was hoisted to a salute from the brig *Niagara*, and Colonel McDouall and his men departed soon after.[80] Butler then had time to settle in and inspect his command. The fortifications and buildings reflected heavy use and some improvement during three years of British occupation. "The old fort Michilimackinac is in perfect order," Butler reported on August 6, but "the new fort George on the elevation above the old fort, is in an unfinished state, and as a Military work altogether inadequate for defence."[81] Improvements had been underway when the British learned of the end of the war, and work had ceased, thus accounting for the incomplete state of Fort George.[82] Butler departed soon after, leaving it to his successors to render Michilimackinac's fortifications tenable should war once again visit the Straits.

It is a bit surprising that Colonel Butler used the British name for the little fort and blockhouse on the "turtle's back," called as it was for King George III. This must have irritated the American troops. At some point in August or early September the redoubt was rechristened Fort Holmes in honor of the senior American casualty of Croghan's 1814 assault.[83] Throughout the late summer and fall a detachment guarded this critical fortification until winter ended any possibility of a British attack.[84]

Fort Holmes was immediately incorporated into the defensive plan for Michilimackinac. Major Talbot Chambers, a successor to Butler, also acknowledged that the outpost was incomplete, and he set about making it as strong as possible with the resources at his disposal. These were meager enough, and Chambers could do little except finish some of the gun platforms, mount artillery, and store provisions to withstand a siege. He also developed a plan for defending the island. Chambers fully recognized the importance

of Fort Holmes. In the event of an emergency, he planned to station Captain Benjamin K. Pierce there with most of his artillerymen, supported by a detachment of riflemen. Colonel Chambers had no confidence in Fort Mackinac. In an emergency he would hold it "as long as it may be practicable," but if the enemy pointed artillery at him he planned to retreat with the balance of the garrison to Fort Holmes. There, properly supplied, he did not "fear the best two thousand troops that Britain can send against us, even were they to be headed by a Wellington."[85] Without holding Fort Holmes, wrote one of Chambers's officers, Fort Mackinac was "entirely untenable."[86]

The dominant position of Fort Holmes is graphically illustrated in a watercolor view drawn from Round Island in September 1817 (Fig. 4.4). The artist, Major Francis Smith Belton, is the only person known to have depicted Fort Holmes in active use. His composition reinforces descriptions of Mackinac Island's rugged topography and brushy, second-growth timber. It also shows how Fort Holmes commanded Fort Mackinac, which in turn covered the harbor and village below. Belton probably recorded Fort Holmes during the last months of its active use since the outpost does not seem to have been regularly occupied after the autumn of 1817.[87]

Major Belton's view was also the first to be made from Round Island since Patrick Sinclair scribbled his rough sketch in 1779 (Fig. 2.7). The presence of a steamboat is an anachronism, since the first to navigate the upper Great Lakes, *Walk-in-the-Water*, did not voyage to Detroit until 1818 and to Mackinac Island the following summer. Perhaps Belton was projecting the future, or he might have completed his fair drawing later than September 1817. An unsigned copy of the same scene (Fig. 4.5), perhaps by a different hand, displays similar features, including a steamboat, although the topography of Mackinac Island is somewhat more accurately represented.

With Michilimackinac secured and its fortifications at least temporarily repaired, it was time to consider future improvements. No plan of Fort Mackinac had been prepared since 1799, and Fort Holmes had never been mapped, so careful drawings were needed. These were probably begun during 1816 under the direction of Major Charles Gratiot.[88] The engineer completed his surveys when he returned to Mackinac Island in August and September 1817.[89] By November Gratiot could send plans and sections of both Fort Mackinac and Fort Holmes to Washington with Lieutenant Eveleth's topographical map of the island.[90] The plans of the forts were combined into a single composition (Fig. 4.6) complete with tables of reference and some sense of the adjacent topography.

Gratiot's plan of Fort Mackinac reflects its appearance two years after the end of the war, with the addition of a wooden officers'

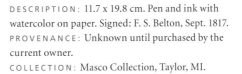

FIGURE 4.4

TITLE: Michillimackinac from Round Island.
AUTHOR: Major Francis Smith Belton, assistant inspector general (ranked as lieutenant in the 4th Regiment of Infantry) (active 1812–d. 1861).
DATE DEPICTED: September 1817.
DATE OF WORK: September 1817.

DESCRIPTION: 11.7 x 19.8 cm. Pen and ink with watercolor on paper. Signed: F. S. Belton, Sept. 1817.
PROVENANCE: Unknown until purchased by the current owner.
COLLECTION: Masco Collection, Taylor, MI.

FIGURE 4.5

TITLE: [In pencil:] Mackina. 1817.
AUTHOR: [Major Francis Smith Belton, assistant inspector general (ranked as lieutenant in the 4th Regiment of Infantry) (active 1812–d. 1861)].
DATE DEPICTED: 1817.
DATE OF WORK: [1817?].
DESCRIPTION: 11.7 x 19.8 cm. Pencil with watercolor on card.
PROVENANCE: Unknown until purchased by Bentley Historical Library.
COLLECTION: Bentley Historical Library, University of Michigan, Ann Arbor (Francis S. Belton Collection, UAs).

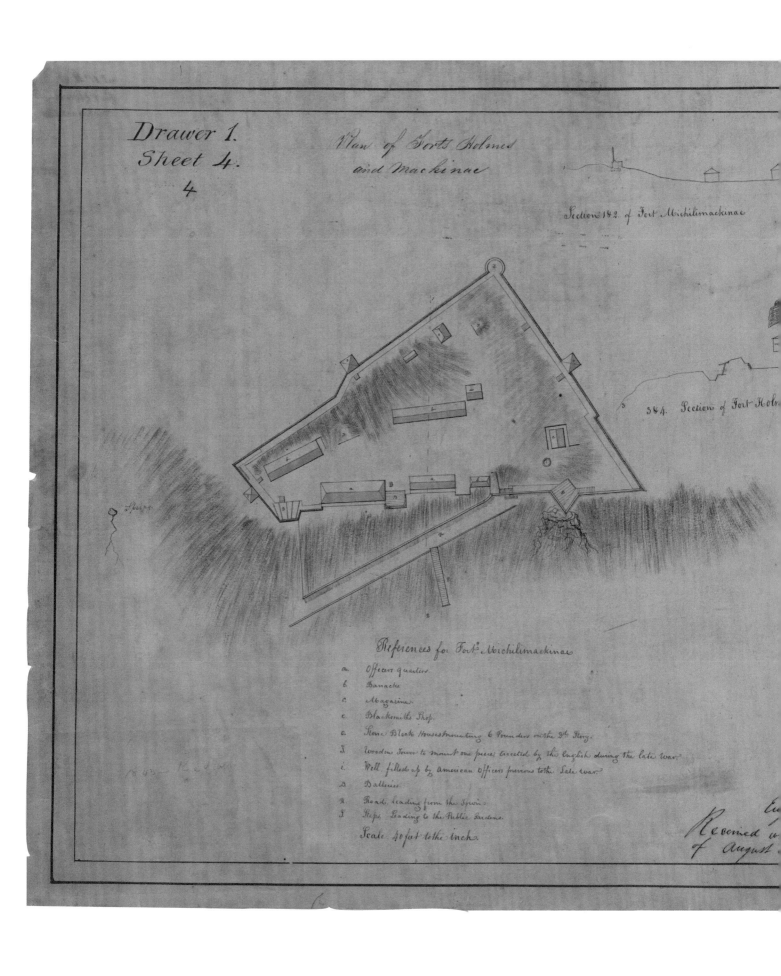

Drawer 1.
Sheet 4.
4

Plan of Forts Holmes
and Mackinac

Section 1 & 2. of Fort Michilimackinac

3 & 4. Section of Fort Holme

References for Fort. Michilimackinac

a.   Officers quarters.
b.   Barracks
c.   Magazine
c.   Blacksmiths Shop.
d.   Stone Block Houses mounting 6 Pounders on the 2d. Story.
f.   Wooden Tower to mount one piece; erected by the English during the late war.
i.   Well filled up by American Officers previous to the late war.
h.   Batteries.
g.   Road, leading from the Town.
j.   Steps, leading to the Public Gardens.

Scale 40 feet to the inch.

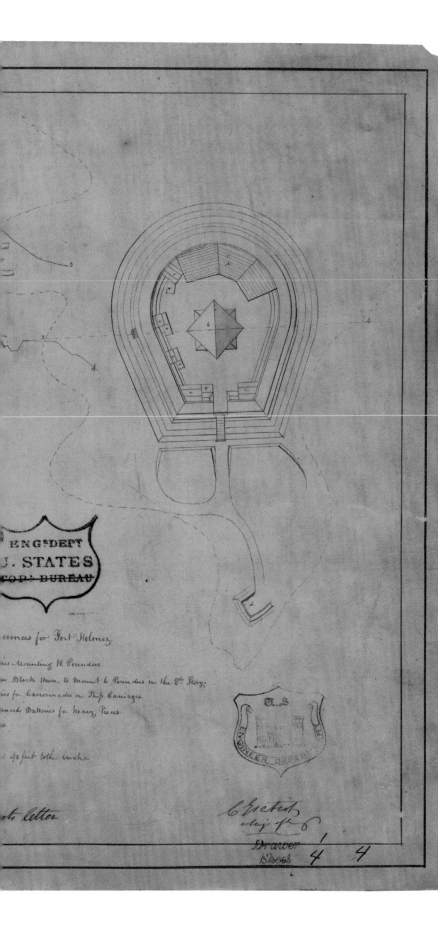

FIGURE 4.6

TITLE: Plan of Forts Holmes and Mackinac.
AUTHOR: Major Charles Gratiot, Corps of
Engineers (1788–1855).
DATE DEPICTED: November 1817.
DATE OF WORK: [November 25, 1817].
DESCRIPTION: 49.5 x 63 cm. Pen and ink on
paper. Endorsed at lower right: C. Gratiot Maj.
PROVENANCE: Enclosed with letter of
November 25, 1817, from Gratiot to Brigadier
General Joseph G. Swift. Retained in the records
of the chief of engineers. A notation on the plan
indicates that the plan was later consulted and
returned with Colonel John J. Abert's letter of
August 5, 1843.
COLLECTION: National Archives and Records
Administration, College Park, MD (RG 77,
Records of the Chief of Engineers, Fortifications
Map File, Drawer 1, Sheet 4-4).

Major Charles Gratiot (1788–1855) first
saw Michilimackinac as a staff officer on
Croghan's 1814 expedition. In the three
years following the conclusion of the
War of 1812, he drew plans of Mackinac
Island's fortifications and prepared
designs for a permanent Fort Holmes.
Thomas Sully painted the engineer's
portrait about 1820. *West Point Museum Art
Collection, United States Military Academy, West Point,
NY (WPM 9053).*

quarters on the edge of the bluff ("a," right) erected during 1816.[91] Most of the other buildings and walls predated the War of 1812. The old fort was poorly regarded. In 1815 Colonel Chambers granted that its position was "completely inaccessible" to attackers and commanded the water. However, the fortification was based on an insubstantial stone wall topped with wooden pickets and defended by three blockhouses ("e"). These Chambers considered cramped and so "illy constructed as to be incapable of enfilading in any direction." He feared that even a heavy field piece "would in a few minutes batter it about the ears of its defenders, without receiving the least annoyance. . . . Were we solely dependent upon the resistance which fort Mackinaw would be enabled to make, our situation would be indeed Deplorable." The fort at least had storehouses and barracks sufficient to support three hundred men.[92]

Unfortunately, Fort Mackinac still lacked a secure source of water. The 1817 plan describes the old well in the fort ("i") as "filled up by American officers previous to the Late War." Exactly when this occurred is not known. Senator Uriah Tracy described "a well of never failing water" in 1800, but the shaft had gone out of use sometime during the following decade, and there had been no water available in the fort when the British appeared in 1812.[93] Future garrisons would wrestle with the inconvenience of obtaining water, often by horse-drawn cart, from springs below the fort or from Lake Huron.

The garrison enjoyed a temporary reprieve when Lieutenant Daniel Curtis devised an ingenious machine to pump water to the fort. The water was moved 140 feet from the spring shown at the extreme left of Figure 4.6 below the west blockhouse. Curtis's "hydraulic machine" was in operation by August 1819, replacing the labor of ten men with that of two. Employing the "common principle of a forcing pump," they could supply the garrison with a day's worth of water in an hour.[94] Captain David B. Douglass described the machine in 1820 as "two forcing pumps combined as in the fire engine and worked by the strength of men applied to a large pendulum."[95] Wear and tear to the wooden pistons compromised its efficiency, but requests for iron components were made in vain.

U.S. troops returned to Michilimackinac in July 1815 aboard the brig *Niagara*, commanded by Lieutenant Samuel Woodhouse (178?-1843). Both the warship and its captain were veterans of the unsuccessful 1814 expedition, at which time Woodhouse was in command of the schooner *Caledonia*. His portrait, from about 1808, is attributed to Rembrandt Peale. *Collection of James L. Kochan, Frederick, MD.*

By the autumn of 1822 the machine had been "suffered to go to decay."[96]

Gratiot's plan shows five buildings that stand today in Fort Mackinac—the two officers' quarters ("a") and three blockhouses ("e"). The outline of the walls has changed little. The most obvious missing element is a circular wooden tower ("f") at the apex of the triangle. This was designed to support a heavy gun on a pivot carriage to fire against Fort George. The British had completed the tower by the end of February 1815, and it remained a feature of Fort Mackinac's defenses as late as October 1829.[97] The deteriorating structure was then "almost in ruins," and it probably disappeared that winter.

Fort Holmes is shown as it was completed and maintained by its U.S. garrison after July 1815. The place was only "a blockhouse surrounded by a circular parapet of earth," little more than a fieldwork of the kind often constructed in Canada during the War of 1812.[98] Timbers supported the earthen wall, which was ringed by a ditch and fraizing—horizontal pickets projecting from the parapet. The gun platforms completed by Chambers's men are at the rounded end of the fort, where cannon could cover the gradual slope from the northwest that was the likeliest avenue of approach by an enemy. Positions for heavier, long-range guns mark the inaccessible bluff facing Fort Mackinac. The cross section shows a substantial log blockhouse with an attached flagpole and a door that probably faced the rounded end of the fort.

The former Fort George remained an active part of Michilimackinac's defenses through the end of 1817.[99] At that time, Major Gratiot submitted plans for a more sophisticated replacement (Figs. 4.10–4.12), but it was never constructed. The blockhouse stood for another few years as the earthen walls began to deteriorate. In 1819 Lieutenant John A. Dix saw "a Block house enclosed in an earthen epaulement & pallisade" but was more impressed by the view, which he considered the "most perfect picture of romance" he had ever seen. The fort was unoccupied but standing when Henry Schoolcraft and Captain David B. Douglass visited the following year.[100] When Lieutenant Henry Bayfield of the Royal Navy stopped at Mackinac Island in 1822, however, he noted that the blockhouse had been removed since his last visit in 1817 and rebuilt as a stable. This was done during the winter of 1821–22, and the stable would be a feature of the garrison gardens below Fort Mackinac until the first decade of the twentieth century.[101]

Almost as an afterthought to his letter discussing the possibilities for Fort Holmes, Major Gratiot noted that he also enclosed a plan and section of Fort Mackinac. He had no suggestions or recommendations for improving or replacing the larger fortification.[102] Its position was hopelessly flawed, and its future utility would be only to accommodate a garrison in relative comfort. The obsolescence of Fort Mackinac accounts for the lack of plans of the place after 1817. None survives from that time until 1845 (Fig. 7.21), although notations on Figure 4.7 suggest that Gratiot's 1817 project was consulted in 1843, probably because of U.S.-Canadian border tensions. No action was taken, however, and Fort Mackinac would receive no attention from an officer of the Corps of Engineers until 1850 (Fig. 8.1).

e from Round Island. F.S.

No scenery can be more sublime

Judge Advocate Samuel A. Storrow

The recovery of Michilimackinac was a satisfying achievement for the United States and a boon to the budding American Fur Company. But, amid the military and commercial activity that marked the postwar years, there was also an upsurge of interest in the scenic features of the Straits of Mackinac. Thoroughly professional soldiers or businessmen were increasingly likely to note the islands and waters for their beauty as well as their utility. "The situation of this island is most beautiful and interesting," wrote an officer in the fall of 1815. "This is the most elevated island on the lakes," he continued, "its highest ground is several hundred feet above the lake."[103] Dramatic topography indeed, as succeeding generations of visitors would discover.

Topography was a critical military concern, of course. Patrick Sinclair had selected Mackinac Island for his post, in large part, because of its commanding elevations. Military engineers had subsequently discussed the strength and the vulnerability of Fort Mackinac, both a result of the island's distinctive topography. The British, first as attackers and then as defenders, had utilized the rugged terrain to their advantage. But it was not until the years immediately following the War of 1812 that the rock formations and other scenic landmarks drew much attention. Visitors found the prospect from the island equally appealing. Its highest point, at Fort Holmes, was the most popular vantage. It afforded, one officer wrote, "a very extensive prospect uninterrupted on the expansive lake in one direction, and enlivened on the other by the main, on the right and left, with beautiful islands scattered around."[104] This was a panorama that, with the island's many picturesque natural sites, would thereafter draw the attention of artists and writers.

The reestablishment of a U.S. garrison generated a flurry of activity by military officers and engineers. The options for fortifying Mackinac Island were studied and debated, but a true understanding of how best to defend the place could not be had until the island's topography was fully understood. Earlier maps had focused on property ownership and the boundaries between public and private land, while little detail of the island's terrain had been recorded. This oversight was corrected in 1817 when Lieutenant William S. Eveleth carefully mapped Mackinac Island.

Military engineering on the upper Great Lakes had, since 1814, been the responsibility of Major Charles Gratiot. He served as Croghan's engineer that year and stopped at Mackinac Island during 1816 on his way to establish Fort Howard at Green Bay.[105] Both visits resulted in some mapping of the Straits (Figs. 4.2 and 4.14), although at larger scales and with relatively little detail. During the summer and early fall of 1817 Gratiot surveyed Forts Mackinac and Holmes

and drew proposals for new fortifications (Figs. 4.6, 4.10–4.12). This left him little time to conduct a topographical survey of the island.

Fortunately, by the summer of 1817, Gratiot's requests that a junior officer or "some Young Gentleman [*sic*] from the academy be furnished me as assistant Engineers" had been answered.[106] Lieutenant William Sanford Eveleth had joined Gratiot at Detroit and was soon off to Michilimackinac. Eveleth was a graduate of the Military Academy at West Point and had been commissioned in the Corps of Engineers in March 1815.[107] It is unclear when he reached the Straits, but on July 2 Eveleth was ordered to serve as a member of a court martial that was to convene at Fort Mackinac on July 21. This was a secondary duty, of course, for his primary assignment was to prepare a topographical map of Mackinac Island to complement Gratiot's surveys of the forts. By November 2 Lieutenant Eveleth had completed his work and was preparing to return to Detroit for the winter.[108]

The fruit of his labors was the first comprehensive topographical map of Mackinac Island. Wonderfully detailed, it shows terrain as well as roads and man-made features. Eveleth drew at least two copies. One was endorsed by Major Gratiot and sent to the chief of engineers on November 25, 1817. Described by Gratiot as "a topographical chart of the vicinity" and titled "Map of the Island of Michilimackinac," this copy bears the stamp of the Topographical Bureau and is today in the collections of the National Archives (Fig. 5.13).[109] The other known copy of Eveleth's survey was probably completed about the same time. Virtually identical, but in better condition, its history is not as well documented. The map was discovered in New York City

FIGURE 4.7

TITLE: Map of the Island of Michilimackinac.
AUTHOR: Lieutenant William Sanford Eveleth, Corps of Engineers (active 1813–d. 1818).
DATE DEPICTED: November 1817.
DATE OF WORK: [November 1817].
DESCRIPTION: 71.2 x 58 cm. Pen and ink on paper. Signed below neat line at right: Drawn by W. S. Eveleth, U.S. Engineers.
PROVENANCE: A copy of the original map now in the National Archives. Discovered in an abandoned building in New York City. Purchased by the Clements Library in 1978.
COLLECTION: Clements Library, University of Michigan, Ann Arbor (Map Division, 6-N-21).

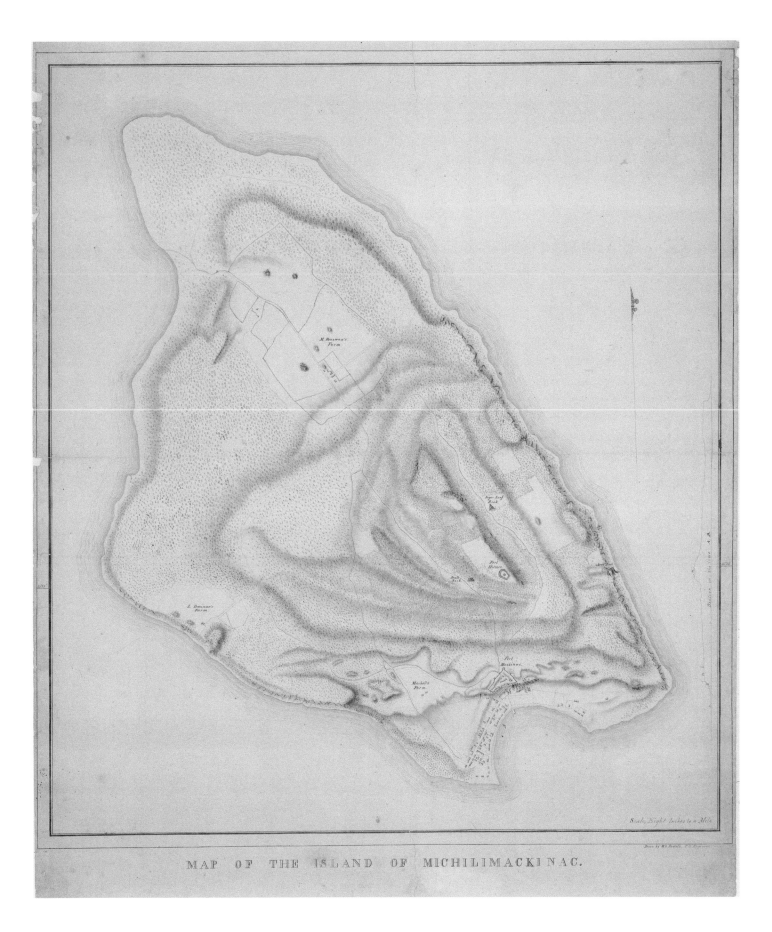

MAP OF THE ISLAND OF MICHILIMACKINAC.

in the 1970s and acquired by the William L. Clements Library. It is illustrated here as Figure 4.7.

Lieutenant Eveleth's careful work reveals more about Mackinac Island than any other image of its time. Although the shape of the island's northwestern end is distorted, the engineer was able to map the topography with a precision that permits many features to be recognized. A cross section at right provides a sense of the overpowering height of the bluffs. Also revealed is the state of the island's vegetation after nearly forty years of occupation. Relatively little land seems to be fully cleared, and what appears to be forest was, for the most part, a scrubby second growth. The lack of larger timber had, by 1817, forced soldiers and civilians alike to obtain their firewood and building material from Bois Blanc Island. Major Talbot Chambers described the foliage of Mackinac Island as "under brush, so thick as to render it almost impenetrable," and one of his officers reported that the ground was "covered with a small growth of wood, impenetrably thick."[110] Samuel Storrow left a more attractive impression of uneven ground "intersected by numerous small winding paths, overshadowed by alders, birch, and pines, which form a natural arbor in every direction."[111]

Many of the paths noted by Storrow are found on the Eveleth map. It is remarkable that so many roads still in use on Mackinac Island were already well established by 1817. In fact, much of the modern road net was present. Garrison and British Landing roads connect Fort Mackinac to the Dousman farm and British Landing. Cadotte Avenue leads from the southwestern end of the village to join Garrison Road near the modern airport. Another thoroughfare goes to Sugar Loaf Rock, while even Scott's Cave Road may be identified as a rough track that had probably been used to remove whatever firewood remained on land still claimed as part of the military reserve.

Other man-made features are rendered in considerable detail, down to the shape of roofs on individual buildings. Forts Mackinac and Holmes correspond with the plans of both fortifications prepared in 1817 (Fig. 4.6). Houses, stores, streets, and fence lines can be picked out in the village, which was still largely confined to the southwestern end of Haldimand Bay. Ste. Anne's Church faces Market Street northeast of the corner of modern Hoban Street, with the priest's house a few yards away on the same lot. The large buildings of the American Fur Company—the warehouse and Stuart House—had not yet been constructed on Market Street by the fall of 1817. What must be part of the old Government House, probably utilized by the Indian agency in 1817, is just below Fort Mackinac. The only wharf is that maintained by the army.

Aside from the forts, little evidence of the War of 1812 is found on Eveleth's map. LeBarron's still house, where the island's citizens

Civilian contractors provided the foodstuffs consumed by U.S. troops at frontier military posts. James Thomas (1780–1842), working from Detroit, held the contract for Fort Mackinac in 1817. Nathaniel Rogers probably painted this miniature portrait in the early 1820s. *Clements Library, University of Michigan.*

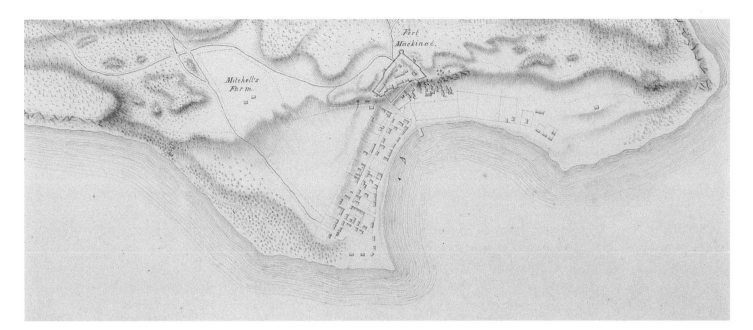

The orientation of this detail of the village and Fort Mackinac, from William S. Eveleth's map (Fig. 4.7), corresponds closely to Richard Dillon's view of a few years earlier (Fig. 4.1). *Clements Library, University of Michigan.*

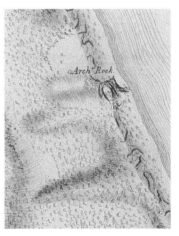

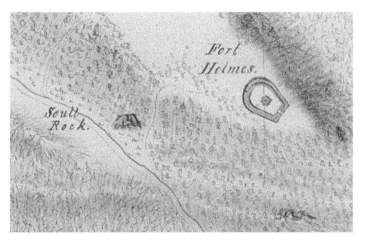

The first known rendering of Sugar Loaf Rock is found on Eveleth's map. Detail of Figure 4.7. *Clements Library, University of Michigan.*

Arch Rock, as depicted on Eveleth's map. The path through the woods suggests that the dramatic geological formation was already a popular attraction by 1817. Detail of Figure 4.7. *Clements Library, University of Michigan.*

The cave in "Scull Rock" had historical associations, known to some early Mackinac visitors from Alexander Henry's *Travels and Adventures in Canada* (New York, 1809). Henry Brevoort was one of the first writers to mention the cavern. In a letter of June 26, 1811, he described "an Indian Catacomb in the side of a Rock filled with bones that have lain there a century since." Souvenir hunters eventually carried off the human remains. The earliest view of Skull Cave is found on Eveleth's map of 1817 (Fig. 4.7). *Clements Library, University of Michigan.*

had retreated in 1812, appears by a spring below the bluff on the southwestern shore. It was in use as "Reaume's distillery" in 1823, but by 1832 the site had become only a landmark—"the place called the Distillery."[112] The fields, fences, buildings, and rocky outcrops of "M. Dousman's Farm" are nicely detailed in the center of the island, and Eveleth's map is useful in reconstructing the events of August 4, 1814, but he did not identify the area of the fighting. American officers often visited the battlefield in the postwar years, including Major General Jacob Brown, who rode around it in 1819.[113]

Eveleth's map also includes the earliest renderings of Mackinac Island's celebrated rock formations. "Arch Rock," "Sugar Loaf Rock," and "Scull Rock" all appear in miniature views. Samuel Storrow was among the first to describe Arch Rock and Sugar Loaf in detail, and he was on the island at the time Eveleth was conducting his survey. On the eastern cliffs Storrow encountered "one of the most interesting natural curiosities I have ever witnessed . . . an immense and perfect arch" towering 140 feet above the lakeshore. Farther inland he found "Sugar Loaf Rock (a conical rock of that name)," which led him to theorize on the geological formation of the island and prehistoric lake levels.[114]

Storrow scrambled down the bluff below Arch Rock by "fastening to the shrubbery and projecting rocks" and made it safely to the beach. Above him, "half hid in trees," Arch Rock seemed "suspended in the air." This was his favorite perspective and, he added, "from the Lake it appears like a work of art." It is very likely that Major Francis Smith Belton accompanied Storrow on his adventure. Belton was an assistant adjutant general who, like Judge Advocate Storrow, was on a tour of inspection in the fall of 1817, ordered to report on the posts of Fort Gratiot, Michilimackinac, Green Bay, and Chicago.[115]

In between his official duties, Belton drew at least one view of Mackinac from Round Island (Figs. 4.4 and 4.5). He also found the time to compose the first artistic impression of Arch Rock and the precipitous bluffs of the island's eastern shore (Fig. 4.8). The major appears to have made his drawing from a small boat bobbing offshore. Apparently awed by the natural spectacle, he exaggerated the span of the arch and the size of the cavity beneath it.

Francis Belton continued a long military career, but the talented Lieutenant Eveleth was not so fortunate. He continued to assist Major Gratiot in Detroit during the winter of 1818. That summer, he accompanied Lieutenant John L. Smith, a fellow engineer, on yet another tour of inspection of military sites along Lakes Huron and Michigan, visiting Mackinac Island again in August before proceeding to Green Bay and up the Fox River. Upon completion of his duties there, Eveleth went by canoe to Chicago.[116] He reached Fort Dearborn safely and sailed for Detroit on October 2 aboard the schooner *Hercules*. On October 3–4, however, the vessel encountered "one of the most dreadful gales of wind within the recollection of the oldest inhabitants" of the region. The *Hercules* was wrecked with all hands lost, and, at first, the only evidence of Eveleth to be recovered was his drafting scale, "an old uniform coat . . . two handkerchiefs, and a part of his flute."[117] A search party found his body a few days later and identified it by the distinctive coat buttons of the Corps of Engineers. The lieutenant was buried in the sand dunes beneath a cluster of pines in what is now Laporte County, Indiana, his grave marked only by a blazed sapling.[118] Lake Michigan had deprived history of a talented and musical topographical engineer, who was the first to clearly define the terrain of Mackinac Island.

Although John Jacob Astor (1763–1848) never saw Mackinac Island, other than through a balance sheet, his American Fur Company dominated the place from the end of the War of 1812 until the mid-1830s. This engraving was made from a painting by Alonzo Chappel, copied from a portrait in the possession of Astor's family. *Clements Library, University of Michigan.*

The energetic Ramsay Crooks (1787–1859) was John Jacob Astor's senior manager of American Fur Company operations. Crooks first went to Michilimackinac in 1814 under a flag of truce in an attempt to recover some of Astor's property. He returned in 1815–16 to establish the company's northern headquarters on the island and was a frequent visitor thereafter. Crooks was a member of the syndicate that purchased the faltering company from Astor in 1834. Jules Emile Saintin portrayed him in 1857. *Wisconsin Historical Society (WHi 2593).*

FIGURE 4.8

TITLE: The Arched rock Michillimackinac.
AUTHOR: Major Francis Smith Belton, assistant
inspector general (ranked as lieutenant in the 4th
Regiment of Infantry) (active 1812–d. 1861).
DATE DEPICTED: September 1817.
DATE OF WORK: September 1817.
DESCRIPTION: 9.7 x 16.5 cm. Pen and ink with
watercolor on paper. Dated at lower left: Sep. 1817.
Signed at lower right: F. S. Belton.
PROVENANCE: Unknown until purchased by the
current owner.
COLLECTION: Masco Collection, Taylor, MI.

The projected work for the defence of the Island of Michilimackinac

Major Charles Gratiot

By the autumn of 1817 Mackinac Island and its forts had been inspected, surveyed, and mapped to the point where work could begin on improvements to its defenses. Given the acknowledged faults inherent in the position of Fort Mackinac, any expenditure of labor and treasure was sure to be made on the commanding heights occupied by Fort Holmes. The avenues open to an attacker were limited, and the great hill—the "turtle's back"—was the key to the defense of Michilimackinac.

Judge Advocate Samuel Storrow provided the best analysis of the defensive situation of Mackinac Island. "The east and a greater part of the west sides, are impracticable of ascent," he wrote to Major General Jacob Brown late in 1817. "The shores of the north are lower, and the only parts where a lodgement could be effected. But even were the foothold gained [by an enemy], the winding paths, abrupt eminences, and tangled under-growth would preclude an advance beyond it." "With such advantages of ground," Storrow continued, "a weak garrison could cripple any assailing force before it could reach Fort Holmes, which position might be the citadel as well as the summit of the island." The heights themselves would be easy to defend. The position, Storrow noted, was "unassailable except on one side, which, being narrow, might be fortified by art."[119] The artist would be Major Charles Gratiot of the Corps of Engineers.

Though no one questioned the importance of fortifying the hill, there was some discussion as to how this might best be accomplished. After examining the position, in July 1815, Colonel Anthony Butler suggested that redoubts "at two points of that ridge must be estab-lished." He promised to include "a detailed report on the subject" in his next communication to the secretary of war, but no map has been found that might have supported his recommendations.[120] The crude sketch included here as Figure 4.9 might illustrate his concept, although it is equally conceivable that Butler was not alone in advocating multiple fortifications to cover the vulnerable rear of Fort Mackinac. Figure 4.9 seems to be associated, in the records of the Corps of Engineers, with a tour of the northern frontier of the United States made in the fall of 1815 by engineer majors Isaac Roberdeau and John Anderson. They went as far west as Detroit, and it is possible that they visited Michilimackinac as well.[121]

Figure 4.9 presents a sketchy rendering of the Straits of Mackinac, centering on Mackinac Island and providing a few details of its topography and man-made features. A square on the "Heights" undoubtedly represents Fort Holmes. Three more to the left of Fort Mackinac could indicate proposed outposts, although none stands on "the ridge" as recommended by Butler. This little map is so similar to Charles Gratiot's sketch of the island as he had seen it

in 1814 (Fig. 4.2) that there must be some relationship. Perhaps Roberdeau and Anderson conferred with Gratiot while they were in Detroit in 1815. Like the Gratiot map, Figure 4.9 identifies "Dousman's," "Le Barrons Distillery," and the site of Croghan's 1814 landing, the last place embellished with a cluster of boats. Of additional interest is the earliest identification on a map of "arch Rock" and a tiny triangle below the word "Heights" that might be intended to represent Sugar Loaf.

Major Gratiot disagreed with Colonel Butler's concept for defending Michilimackinac. "I can see no necessity of having so many detached works, as he proposes for its security," he wrote to the chief of engineers in February 1816. Gratiot did not yet have good surveys of the island to bolster his opinion, so he forwarded his 1814 sketch (Fig. 4.2). This, he believed, would illustrate the logic of having only "a single work on the ridge," which he thought should be placed at its southern extremity with its strongest front facing the gradually sloping ground to the northwest. A detached battery of four or five heavy cannon could cover the lake and Fort Mackinac. Major Gratiot was impressed by the strength of this site against any sort of attack, even one employing siege trenches. "No fear of regular approaches on the ridge need be apprehended," he reported, "as the assailant would have to force his way through a solid bed of rock, and another almost insurmountable obstacle he would have to conquer, is the steep ascent, up which he must bring his artillery, if he intends battering." This, in the major's opinion, was "next to impossible."[122]

Whatever was constructed, Gratiot continued, should be built of stone, an abundant commodity on Mackinac Island. Plentiful too was the lime needed for mortar to bind the masonry together. Labor might also be obtained locally—from the garrison of Fort Mackinac. This would reduce the expenses of hiring and transporting workmen to the Straits, and the soldiers could, Gratiot reasoned, "in the course of two or three Summers, complete all the necessary defences proposed." Gratiot's biggest problem was a shortage of time, for he anticipated establishing new forts at Green Bay and Chicago during 1816 with all the attendant demands on his department. The major requested an assistant engineer and additional staff to handle the workload.[123]

Planning for the reconstruction of Fort Holmes was delayed for a year by the construction of Fort Dearborn and Fort Howard. When Major Gratiot and Lieutenant William S. Eveleth returned to Mackinac Island in the summer of 1817, however, their work proceeded rapidly. Eveleth surveyed the island, and Gratiot's plans of Fort Mackinac and Fort Holmes were probably out of the way by

FIGURE 4.9

TITLE: [Sketch map of Mackinac Island].

AUTHOR: [Major Isaac Roberdeau, Corps of Topographical Engineers (1763–1829)], probably after Major Charles Gratiot (1788–1855).

DATE DEPICTED: Fall 1815.

DATE OF WORK: [1816].

DESCRIPTION: 33 x 19.6 cm. Pencil on paper.

PROVENANCE: The sketch is probably associated with Roberdeau and Anderson's tour of the northern frontier in the summer of 1816. Retained in the records of the chief of engineers.

COLLECTION: National Archives and Records Administration, Washington, DC (RG 77, Records of the Office of the Chief of Engineers, Entry 222, Reports of Fortifications and Topographical Surveys, 1816–1823, Folder 1817–1819).

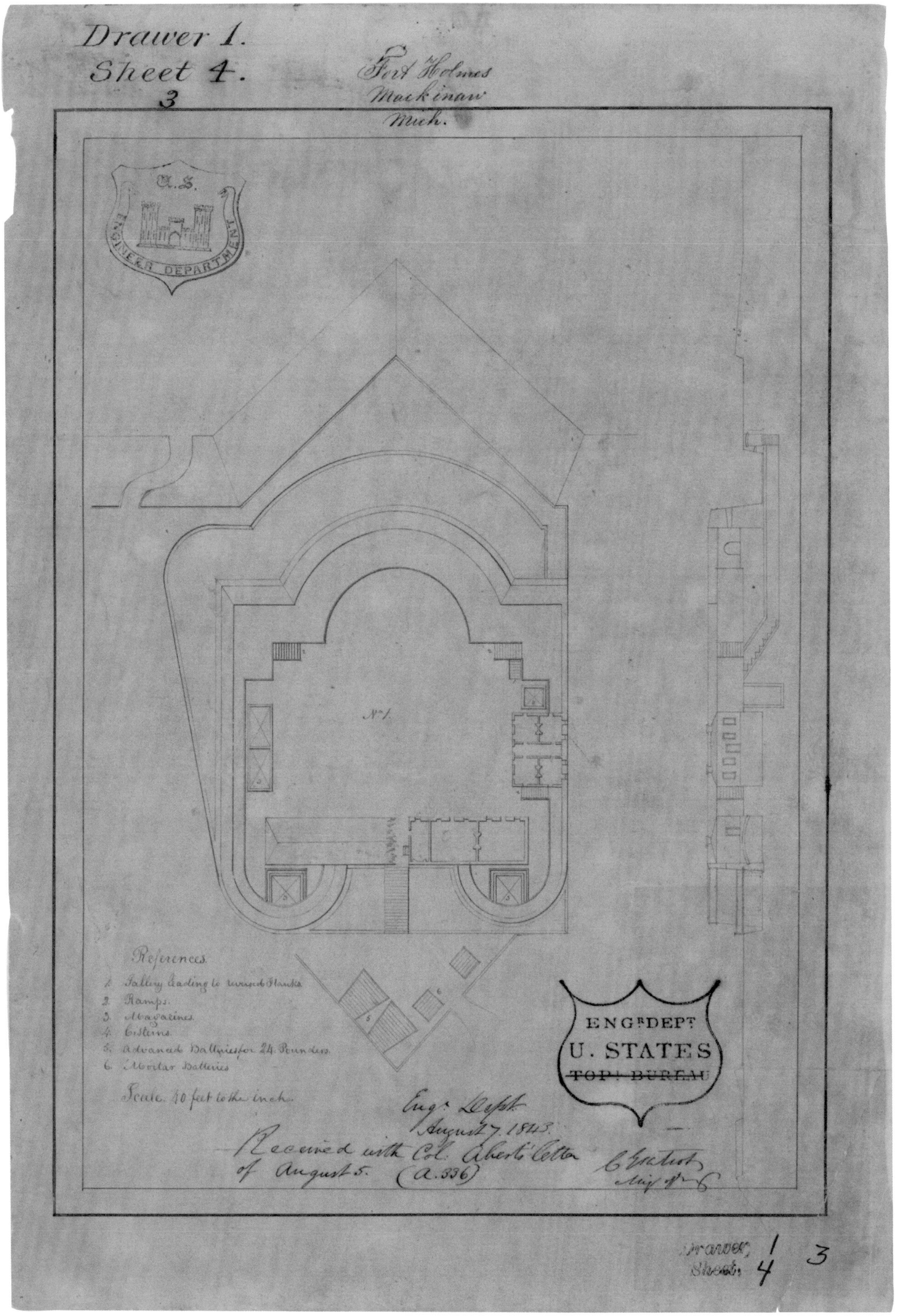

Fort Holmes
Mackinaw
Mich.

References

1 Gallery leading to revised flanks
2 Ramps.
3 Magazines
4 Cisterns
5 Advanced Batteries for 24 Pounders
6 Mortar Batteries

Scale. 40 feet to the inch.

Engr Dept
August 7, 1845.

Received with Col. Abert's Letter
of August 5.   (a. 336)

ENGᴿ DEPT
U. STATES
TOPⁱ BUREAU

C. Gratiot
Maj ᵗⁱ G

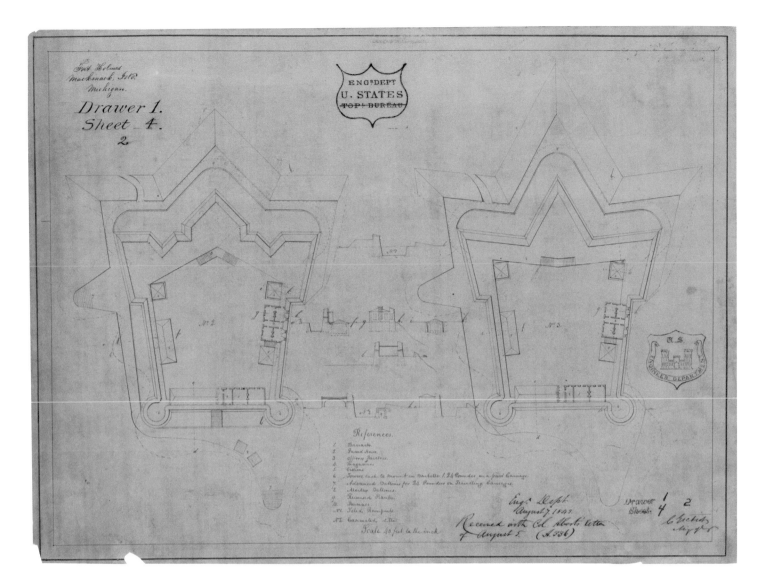

FIGURE 4.10

TITLE: Fort Holmes Mackinaw Mich. No. 1.

AUTHOR: Major Charles Gratiot, Corps of Engineers (1788–1855).

DATE DEPICTED: 1817 proposal.

DATE OF WORK: [November 25, 1817].

DESCRIPTION: 41 x 28.5 cm. Dimensions are for whole sheet as title is outside neat line. Pen and ink on paper. Signed at lower right: C. Gratiot Maj. Engrs.

PROVENANCE: Enclosed with Gratiot's letter to Brigadier General Joseph G. Swift dated November 25, 1817. Retained in the records of the chief of engineers. A notation on the plan indicates that the plan was later consulted and returned to the Engineer's Department on August 7, 1843, with Colonel John J. Abert's letter of August 5.

COLLECTION: National Archives and Records Administration, College Park, MD (RG 77, Records of the Chief of Engineers, Fortifications Map File, Drawer 1, Sheet 4-3).

FIGURE 4.11

TITLE: Fort Holmes Mackinack. Isld. Michigan. [No. 2 and No. 3 on plans].

AUTHOR: Major Charles Gratiot, Corps of Engineers (1788–1855).

DATE DEPICTED: 1817 proposal.

DATE OF WORK: [November 25, 1817].

DESCRIPTION: 37.5 x 51.3 cm. Pen and ink on paper. Signed at lower right: C. Gratiot.

PROVENANCE: Enclosed with Gratiot's letter to Brigadier General Joseph G. Swift dated November 25, 1817. Retained in the records of the chief of engineers. A notation on the plan indicates that it was later consulted and returned to the Engineer's Department on August 7, 1843, with Colonel John J. Abert's letter of August 5.

COLLECTION: National Archives and Records Administration, College Park, MD (RG 77, Records of the Chief of Engineers, Fortifications Map File, Drawer 1, Sheet 4-2).

September. In the course of the summer Gratiot also began to prepare designs to replace the earthen walls and wooden blockhouse at Fort Holmes. These are illustrated here as Figures 4.10–4.12.

Major Gratiot had completed final drafts by November 25, at which time he forwarded his Michilimackinac plans to the chief of engineers. With the Fort Holmes proposals went Eveleth's survey of the island and Gratiot's own drawings of the current state of Forts Mackinac and Holmes. "Estimates of the Projected work" were included as well. In his covering letter, the major justified the need for a new fortification on the heights by arguing that the British had hastily built Fort Holmes during the war. "Its dimensions together with its construction," he wrote, "does not present a sufficient defence to recommend its reconstruction in permanent materials."[124]

His alternative was a small, stone fort, and the "permanent materials" of which it would be built included 1,449 cubic "toises" of stone, 300,000 bricks, 100,000 feet of plank, 100,000 shingles, and 655 large pieces of timber. Nearly 3,000 man-days of labor would be required to excavate ditches in the rock and erect masonry. Carpenters and blacksmiths were needed (2,518 days), not to mention boatmen to move materials to Mackinac Island (6,300 days) and teamsters (2,920 days) to haul them to its highest point. To complicate matters, the major noted, "no laboring men in country—must be obtained from Pennsylvania or Ohio." With civilian workers, the project would cost the United States $98,986.95. Even the alternative of using soldiers put the price at $37,899.85.[125]

Gratiot's surviving plans represent three variations on essentially the same design for a small, modern, self-sufficient fort. Gratiot, an early graduate of the United States Military Academy (1806), was a contemporary of the engineers who would develop the nation's sophisticated new coast-defense forts in the years after the War of 1812. French military engineers, who were themselves exploring new styles of fortification, had influenced their education. Among them was Pierre Charles L'Enfant, who in 1794 had stressed the doctrine that all kinds of forts, even specialized batteries, be capable of self-defense "against a vigorous attack."[126] The Fort Holmes designs were intended to do just that.

Gratiot numbered his proposals 1 through 3, observing that "either will equally answer the Safety of the heights." They vary in details, but each is arranged so that the strongest line of defense faces northwest, the direction from which an enemy would be most likely to approach. Design 1 (Fig. 4.10) is perhaps the most modern for 1817, incorporating "reversed flanks" ("References—1") on the outer side of the ditch. This feature employed an underground gallery, accessible by a tunnel from the fort (shown in a sectional drawing), that allowed defenders to fire back on enemy soldiers who had entered the ditch. Designs 2 and 3 (Fig. 4.11) have more conventional fronts. These are detailed on the third sheet (Fig. 4.12) as either of solid construction or casemated—that is, with firing galleries built into the walls. Gratiot preferred the latter because the "defences

would be increased at a small additional expence" and the casemates provided useful storage space in a small fort.[127]

The gate is on the southeastern front on all three plans, away from the potential threat. That side also shelters a detached battery for cannon and mortars to cover Fort Mackinac and the lake. Round towers support pivot-mounted twenty-four-pounder cannon on the southeastern sides of plans 2 and 3. The general arrangement of the garrison buildings is much the same in each plan, with barracks flanking the gateway and officers' quarters, magazines, and cisterns arranged around the parade ground.

Cisterns were a critical element of all three designs. If Fort Mackinac was plagued by the lack of a secure source of water, Fort Holmes was even more vulnerable. When Fort George was nearly completed, in July 1814, Lieutenant Colonel McDouall reported the position "one of the strongest in Canada" but "its principal defect is the difficulty of finding water near it."[128] The British had not located a spring or dug a successful well by the late winter of 1815, so they constructed underground tanks for four hundred barrels of water.[129] These had to be filled either with rainwater or by hauling barrels to the top of the island. Nor were the Americans able to solve the problem after their return in 1815. In 1820 Henry Schoolcraft found an abandoned but "very deep" well shaft at Fort Holmes a fine place to collect mineral specimens.[130] Gratiot's plans for a new Fort Holmes incorporate capacious cisterns, presumably fed by rainwater collected from roofs.

At the end of 1817 it seemed likely that the hill above Fort Mackinac would soon be crowned by a new fortification. Circumstances dictated otherwise. By the winter of 1818 the resources of the Corps of Engineers were being shifted to coastal defense, and Major Gratiot was soon transferred to work on the forts of Hampton Roads, Virginia.[131] Tensions with Britain had also lessened somewhat as the War of 1812 began to slip into memory. And, by 1818, Major General Jacob Brown and others were questioning the benefits of maintaining a garrison at Michilimackinac.[132] In light of these developments, the considerable cost of rebuilding Fort Holmes seemed an unnecessary expenditure. The project was quietly abandoned.

The Gratiot plans bear additional notations suggesting that they were dusted off and studied as late as 1843. Colonel John J. Abert, head of the Topographical Bureau, consulted all of Gratiot's Mackinac plans before returning them to the chief of engineers on August 5. Abert's covering letter has been lost, so it is unknown whether he studied them for topographical use or reconsidered them for strengthening the defenses of Mackinac Island during a period of border tensions with British Canada.[133] No further action was taken, at any rate. The earthworks of Fort Holmes would remain undisturbed as a picturesque ruin to become one of the most popular scenic attractions for nineteenth-century tourists.

FIGURE 4.12

TITLE: Fort Holmes Mackinaw Mich. No. 2 [and] No. 3.

AUTHOR: Major Charles Gratiot, Corps of Engineers (1788–1855).

DATE DEPICTED: 1817 proposal.

DATE OF WORK: [November 25, 1817].

DESCRIPTION: 32.4 x 74.5 cm. Pen and ink on paper. Signed at lower right: C. Gratiot.

PROVENANCE: Enclosed with Gratiot's letter to Brigadier General Joseph G. Swift dated November 25, 1817. Retained in the records of the chief of engineers. A notation on the plan indicates that it was later consulted and returned to the Engineer's Department on August 7, 1843, with Colonel John J. Abert's letter of August 5.

COLLECTION: National Archives and Records Administration, College Park, MD (RG 77, Records of the Chief of Engineers, Fortifications Map File, Drawer 1, Sheet 4-1).

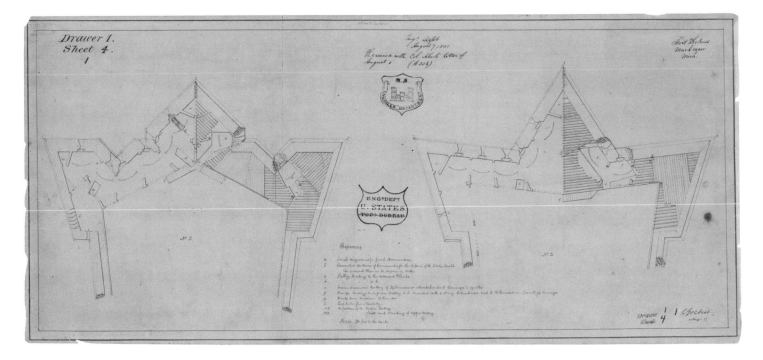

Captain Benjamin Kendrick Pierce (1790–1850) was an officer and sometimes commandant of Fort Mackinac from 1815 to 1821. In 1816 he wed a local woman, Josette, the daughter of Magdelaine La Framboise. About 1820, Pierce constructed an impressive home for his mother-in-law that survives today as part of Harbour View Inn. This portrait, by an unidentified artist, depicts Pierce in the post-1821 uniform of the U.S. artillery. Descendants of the captain owned the painting in the 1970s, but its current location is unknown. *Photograph courtesy of Mackinac State Historic Parks, MI.*

Colonel John McNeil (1784–1850) commanded Fort Mackinac in 1816–17. The officer had made a name for himself during the hard-fought 1814 battle of Lundy's Lane, and he was a brother-in-law of Captain Benjamin K. Pierce. Henry Willard painted Colonel McNeil sometime between 1825 and 1835. *Collections of the State of New Hampshire, Division of Historical Resources.*

Michilimackinac . . . is a long, low cloud on the edge of the horizon

Dr. John J. Bigsby

It was about 9:00 in the morning on Saturday, June 19, 1819, when Indians, soldiers, and residents of the Borough of Michilimackinac looked to Haldimand Bay and beheld a sight never before seen on the waters of the Straits. A steamboat was churning its way into the harbor, the first to navigate the waters of Lake Huron. While many in Mackinac's business and military communities had probably seen such a vessel on Lakes Erie or Ontario or on the Hudson or St. Lawrence River, this was a new experience for most residents and the Native Americans camped on the beach. Some perhaps felt, as Dr. John J. Bigsby put it, that they were witnessing the arrival of some "new monster, its strange entrails, wreathing vapours, and great white wings."[134]

The steamboat was *Walk-in-the-Water,* a name that rather aptly described its motion as the side-wheeler crawled across the channel from Round Island. Onboard were a number of notables, the most important of whom was Major General Jacob Brown, who had come to inspect Fort Mackinac and the other posts in the northwestern lakes. These Great Lakes steamboat pioneers had traveled from Detroit in three days, though not without incident. The vessel's sails were in use for much of the voyage, and on Friday afternoon a contrary wind and heavy seas had slowed progress to a mere one and one-half knots. As the gale increased, the prudent captain anchored in the lee of Bois Blanc Island. By dawn the wind had abated, and the passengers were soon able to enjoy the "beautiful effect on approaching the harbor" with Fort Mackinac overlooking all.[135] Lieutenant John A. Dix, one of Brown's aides, declared Mackinac Island "the most romantic place I ever saw."[136]

Two days later, the owner of *Walk-in-the-Water* treated citizens of Michilimackinac and "several Indians of distinguished families & of friendly tribes" to an excursion into Lake Michigan. The deck was crowded as the steamboat crossed the Straits and circled between Point St. Ignace and the site of Old Michilimackinac. Captain Roger Jones, General Brown's senior aide, found the scene aboard "altogether novel." "On one side of the deck, ladies and gentlemen were gaily leading down country dances," he wrote, "and on the other side, the painted fantastic Indians, decked in all their tinsel and savage costume, were equally happy, whilst they enjoyed their native dance." After a few hours on the Straits, *Walk-in-the-Water* returned to Haldimand Bay.[137]

Shipborne traffic had increased significantly on the upper Great Lakes in the few years since the end of the War of 1812. Sailing vessels had not yet replaced the workhorse of the fur trade, the bark canoe, but larger boats were seen with greater frequency in the Straits. It would likewise be a long while before steam replaced sail,

but the appearance of *Walk-in-the-Water* signaled a revolution in transportation, one in which Mackinac Island would soon figure as a place where steamboats could replenish the cordwood needed to feed their voracious boilers. On the evening following *Walk-in-the-Water*'s brief tour of the Straits, Captain Jones bid farewell to his wife, Mary Ann, who had traveled with him as far as Michilimackinac and was returning to Detroit escorted by Lieutenant Dix. Their parting provided a vivid contrast between the old and new maritime technologies. As *Walk-in-the-Water* moved out of the harbor, Jones followed "in an Indian cannoe, manned with 14 hands." The paddlers "for a little while kept way with the vessel" but then tired, fell behind, and returned to shore.[138]

The Straits of Mackinac had been a highway for waterborne traffic since prehistoric times, and Mackinac Island had always been its most prominent landmark. As the highest land in the area, it was visible to mariners at some distance. "Twenty-five miles off, Michilimackinac (Mackinaw) is a long, low cloud on the edge of the horizon," wrote Dr. Bigsby, who also visited in 1819.[139] He approached the island from the direction of Canada, and his crude sketch of the view (Fig. 4.13) was taken from the open waters of Lake Huron. Bigsby made many drawings during his years in Canada between 1818 and 1827, and some of them illustrate his 1850 account of his travels, *The Shoe and Canoe.* Bigsby's rough view of Mackinac might have been intended for a second edition, but it was never published. The sketch holds few details other than the contrast between canoes in the foreground and a sailing vessel between Mackinac and Round islands.

Given the importance of Michilimackinac to communications with Lakes Michigan and Superior, it was the logical place from which to extend a U.S. military presence farther west to Green Bay and Chicago. The latter had been the site of Fort Dearborn before it was abandoned and destroyed during the war. It controlled the southern portage route to the Mississippi by way of the Illinois River. Green Bay had never had a U.S. post, but it marked the beginning of the Fox-Wisconsin River passage to the Mississippi. Military garrisons and Indian agencies were thought necessary at both places to regain American influence over the Indians, curtail their contacts with the British in Canada, and enforce commercial regulations that, after the winter of 1816, excluded foreigners from the fur trade.[140] With Michilimackinac secured, troops were ordered to establish the other posts in the summer of 1816.[141]

Mackinac Island was crowded with soldiers that summer, to the point that it was necessary to quarter some of the transient units in the village.[142] The demands of the new post at Green Bay also

Michilimackinac 15–20 miles distant.

FIGURE 4.13

TITLE: Michilimackinac 15–20 Miles Distant.
AUTHOR: Dr. John Jeremiah Bigsby (1792–1881).
DATE DEPICTED: 1819 or 1820.
DATE OF WORK: 1819 or 1820 (if original sketch)
or as late as ca. 1850 if a later copy or sketch from
memory.
DESCRIPTION: 11.8 x 19.2 cm. Pen and ink on
paper.
PROVENANCE: Tipped into a unique, grangerized
edition of Bigsby, *The Shoe and Canoe* (London,
1850), 2:145. Acquired by Library and Archives
Canada sometime before 1920. The dealer who sold
the book described it as the author's own copy, and
the volume bears an inscription on its cover: "To Sir
James McGrigor Bart. F.G.S. with the cordial and
grateful Thanks of the Author."
COLLECTION: Library and Archives Canada,
Ottawa, ON (1939-447-88).

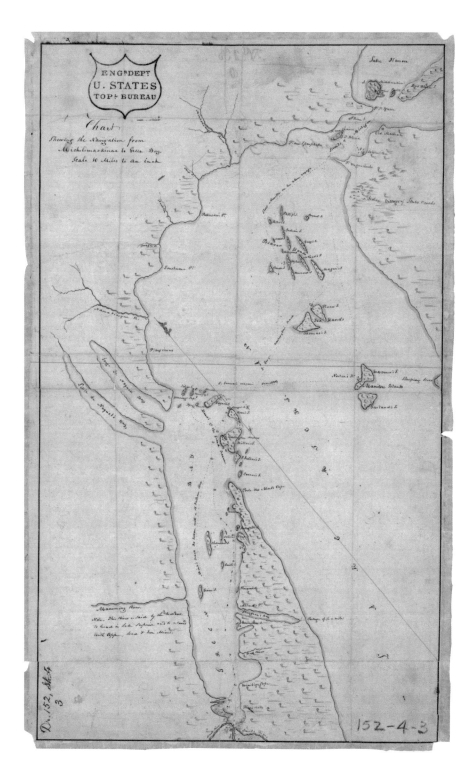

FIGURE 4.14

TITLE: Chart Shewing the Navigation from Michilimackinac to Green Bay.
AUTHOR: [Major Charles Gratiot, Corps of Engineers (1788–1855)].
DATE DEPICTED: August 1816.
DATE OF WORK: [1816].
DESCRIPTION: 49 x 29.3 cm. Pen and ink on paper with gray wash outlining.

PROVENANCE: Retained in the records of the chief of engineers.
COLLECTION: National Archives and Records Administration, College Park, MD (RG 77, Records of the Chief of Engineers, Fortifications Map File, Drawer 152, Sheet 4-3).

The Straits of Mackinac in a detail from Major Gratiot's 1816 map of northern Lake Michigan (Fig. 4.14). This includes the first named rendering of Green Island and several figures representing farms at St. Ignace.

diverted the attention of Major Charles Gratiot from needed work at Michilimackinac, as he was to serve as engineer for the expedition. In July, Colonel John Miller embarked companies of riflemen, infantry, and artillery on chartered merchant vessels and set out for the mouth of the Fox River. Although there had been concern that the local Indians might resist this incursion, the landing proved uneventful, and Major Gratiot was soon at work on a post that was named Fort Howard.[143]

The voyage provided Gratiot with the information needed to produce a most interesting map illustrating the intimate connection between the Straits of Mackinac and Green Bay. It is included here as Figure 4.14 and represents the finished version of his chart.[144] Reminiscent of the unsophisticated style of Gratiot's map of Mackinac Island in 1814 (Fig. 4.2), it provides many details of northern Lake Michigan and the Straits that do not appear on earlier maps. Rough track charts show the progress of Miller's expeditionary force and Gratiot's later explorations. They also reveal the names of four vessels used that summer—*George Washington, General Wayne, Aurilla,* and *Mink. Washington,* which served as Miller's "flagship," was reputed to be the largest vessel on the lakes, and was commanded by Daniel Dobbins, a sailor of some experience during and before the War of 1812.[145] He must have taken particular

satisfaction in this operation—Dobbins had been captain of one of the merchant ships captured by the British at Michilimackinac in 1812.[146]

The Gratiot chart includes most of the islands in the northern part of Lake Michigan. Among them are the Beavers, the Foxes, the Manitous, and most of the islands in Green Bay. Besides mapping these features, Gratiot took it upon himself to name them—most, if not all, after members of the expedition or of the Michilimackinac garrison. These include officers of the Regiment of Riflemen (among them Captain John O'Fallon, Major Talbot Chambers, and Major Willoughby Morgan), the 3rd Regiment of Infantry (Colonel John Miller, Lieutenant Collin McLeod, and at least seven others), and the Corps of Artillery (Captain Benjamin K. Pierce). Sailors are represented as well. A cove and an island are named for Daniel Dobbins and an island in Green Bay for Augustin Grignon, who served as a pilot or guide on *Washington.* The flagship was honored as well in the name of the largest of the islands at the mouth of Green Bay. Only a few of these place-names survive today, notably Washington, Chambers, and Green islands in Green Bay.

The shores of the northern part of Lake Michigan are quite well defined, and a number of rivers are named, but it is apparent that Major Gratiot had more interest in (or a better view of) the islands

Robert Stuart (1785–1848) served as the American Fur Company's resident agent at Mackinac from 1819 to 1835. Stuart was an influential supporter of the Reverend Ferry's Presbyterian mission school and the congregation that constructed Mission Church. The American Fur Company's headquarters, built under his supervision in 1822, is today known as the Stuart House. This portrait was owned by a descendant of Stuart in the 1960s and was reproduced in Helen Marlatt, ed., *Stuart Letters* (New York, 1961).

The visit of Major General Jacob Jennings Brown (1775–1828) was an important event of the summer of 1819 at Mackinac Island. Brown, then commander in chief of the U.S. Army, was studying the defenses of the northern border and considering the fate of Fort Mackinac. He is shown here in a portrait engraving by Asher B. Durand from a James Herring copy of a portrait by John Wesley Jarvis.
Clements Library, University of Michigan.

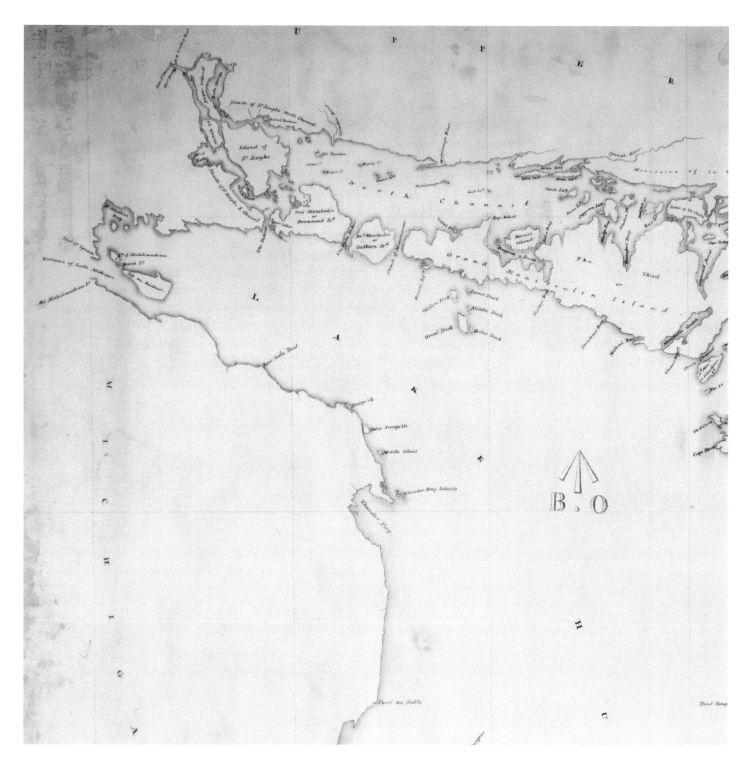

FIGURE 4.15

TITLE: [Map of Lake Huron]. This map was reduced from a Survey made by Lieutenant Bayfield R.N. in the years 1819, 20, 21, and 22. [Detail].

AUTHOR: Lieutenant Henry Wolsey Bayfield, Royal Navy (1795–1885). Copy drawn by Samuel Burt Howlett (1794–1874).

DATE DEPICTED: 1819–22.

DATE OF WORK: January 31, 1825.

DESCRIPTION: 72.5 x 82 cm. Pen and ink with watercolor on paper.

PROVENANCE: Drawn in Inspector General's Office.

COLLECTION: Library and Archives Canada, Ottawa, ON (H2/410-Huron-1822).

in the open lake. Oddly, he did not differentiate the size of Beaver Island from the smaller bodies of land to its north. Gratiot's map also includes what might be the earliest identification of "Sleeping Bear" on the western Michigan shore. The Ottawa village at L'Arbre Croche is shown as well.

Most of the islands of the Straits of Mackinac had well-established names by 1816, so Gratiot was able to place an appellation only on Green Island near Point St. Ignace. It might have been named for Captain John Greene of the 3rd Infantry, but without a complete list of officers on the 1816 expedition, it is difficult to be certain. The moniker stuck, however, and this is its first appearance on a map. Gratiot's attempt to name "Dobbin's Cove" across the Straits from Green Island was less successful. It is today Cecil Bay. Only a few other details mark the Straits of Mackinac. The name "Fort Holmes" appears for the first time on a map of Mackinac Island. And, at St. Ignace, the cartographer sketched three stylized farmhouses and fields to indicate the presence of habitations on the mainland. Similar house symbols appear on Gratiot's plan of 1814 (Fig. 4.2). The site of "Old Mackinau" is marked with the symbol for a fort.

More accurate charts of the Straits would soon be available, thanks to the hydrographic efforts of the Royal Navy. Figure 4.15 is a detail of the Straits from an 1825 copy of a chart of Lake Huron as surveyed by Lieutenant Henry Bayfield in 1819–22. British efforts to map the Great Lakes began immediately after the War of 1812, with work commencing on Lakes Ontario and Erie. Staff for this project was reduced in 1817, and responsibility for continuing the survey into Lake Huron fell to Lieutenant Bayfield. He visited Mackinac Island in 1817 and again in 1822, and it is likely that he charted the eastern half of the Straits in the latter year.[147] The improvement in accuracy from earlier maps and charts is striking. For the first time, Round and Bois Blanc islands are rendered realistically as well as the St. Martin Islands and the Lake Huron coastlines of the Upper and Lower Peninsulas. Bayfield's survey would serve as the basis for charts of the Straits for the next thirty years until the efforts of the U.S. Lake Survey began to produce maps of equal quality.[148]

During his visit in 1819, John Bigsby climbed to the summit of the bluff on the southwestern side of Mackinac Island. From a path winding through the shrubbery, he found the view into Lake Michigan "particularly pleasing." Bigsby could distinguish the tips of Michigan's two peninsulas "at the pretty hamlet of St. Ignatius and its opposite cape." Between them, the water dilated "into a capacious sound with curving woody shores, and sprinkled with islands in the distance." This was the site of the "imaginary line separating Lakes Huron and Michigan," where *Walk-in-the-Water* had demonstrated the coming of the steamboat to Michilimackinac's residents.[149] Towns would soon begin to grow around the military posts at Green Bay and Chicago and at other points on Lake Michigan. Their future commerce would depend on the water passage through the Straits of Mackinac.

Shing-gaa-ba-w'osin led a band of Ojibwa at Sault Ste. Marie and would have visited the new U.S. Indian agency at Mackinac after the War of 1812. Although he was an advocate of peace, some of his people had fought for the British. Shing-gaa-ba-w'osin was pictured by James Otto Lewis at Fond du Lac, Wisconsin, in 1826. Lithograph by Lehman and Duval. *Clements Library, University of Michigan.*

William Beaumont (1785–1853) arrived at Fort Mackinac in June 1820, where he took up his duties as post surgeon and began a private practice in the village. Two years later, the accidental wounding of Alexis St. Martin, a voyageur, presented Beaumont with an unprecedented opportunity to peer into a living human stomach. In experiments, begun in 1825 and conducted over a period of years, Dr. Beaumont deciphered the workings of the digestive system. This portrait miniature has been digitally repaired to remove a pair of cracks. *Courtesy of Wayne County Medical Society of Southeast Michigan.*

In 1821 Deborah Platt Beaumont (1787–1870) traveled to Mackinac Island with her new husband, where they remained until 1825. She and William employed Alexis St. Martin while the doctor coaxed his reluctant patient to submit to his experiments. This portrait miniature, by an unidentified artist, matches that of her husband and might have been painted at the time of their wedding. *Courtesy of Wayne County Medical Society of Southeast Michigan.*

"Mackina owes all its consequence to the fur trade"

1820–1830

Gurdon Saltonstall Hubbard invariably welcomed the end of the busy summer season on Mackinac Island. As a clerk for the American Fur Company, Hubbard spent winters in the field, trading for pelts in the wilderness around Lake Michigan. The coming of spring meant a return to Michilimackinac, his brigade of canoes laden with the winter's harvest. Hubbard and his fellow traders and boatmen swelled the summer population of the village as they delivered their furs,

prepared them for shipment to New York and Europe, and then replenished their stocks of trade goods. Late each summer they departed for yet another winter in the forests.

The young Vermonter was one of the American citizens hired by Ramsay Crooks in the spring of 1818 to put a national stamp on the fur trade as it was carried on within the boundaries of the United States after 1816. He would spend the next six years in the service of John Jacob Astor's American Fur Company and witness the heyday of Mackinac Island as the firm's base of northern operations. Unlike the majority of his coworkers, Hubbard left a detailed reminiscence of his fur-trading days, providing one of the best accounts of the business that dominated Mackinac Island during the 1820s. For Hubbard, each summer meant "a full two months' work, of hard, fatiguing duty." He usually found himself assigned to the warehouse to assist in or direct the reception, inspection, sorting, and packing of furs. In the summer of 1823, Hubbard supervised one hundred voyageurs, working a twelve-hour day that began with roll call at 6:00 AM[1]

As canoes were unloaded, the bundles of furs were carted to the company's fenced yard. There, in the open air, individual pelts were dried, if necessary, and then beaten to remove insects and dirt. Within the hot, dusty confines of the warehouse, Hubbard and his men verified the quantity of furs returned by each brigade and sorted them by type, quality, and color. The skins were then carefully stacked in wooden forms and compacted with a screw press into bales weighing about one hundred pounds each. These were tied, marked, and stored for shipment to Buffalo and, eventually, New York.

As clerk, Hubbard was responsible for keeping accounts of the furs that passed through his hands. The work was completed sometime around the middle of August, and he was then able to find a little recreation before heading to the wilderness once again.[2]

Gurdon Hubbard's labors represented only one part of the beehive of activity at the properties of the American Fur Company and the few remaining independent traders who based themselves on Mackinac Island in the years after the War of 1812. Other employees were busy in blacksmith shops, boatyards, carpentry shops, and storehouses for provisions and trade goods, where preparations were made to replenish the supplies and equipment of the next season's brigades. At first, the American Fur Company's operations centered around the buildings on the lot bounded by Market, Fort, and Main streets (Fig. 3.6, claim 101) that had been acquired from the South West Company in the spring of 1817.[3] In 1818 the lot immediately across Market Street from this property (claim 282) was rented from John Ogilvy. This provided an additional house and store as well as land on which long, bark barracks could be constructed to shelter at least one hundred men of that summer's influx of employees.[4] The property was later purchased, and in 1819 it provided the site for a new retail store, best known today as the Beaumont Museum.[5]

In 1820 the company purchased one of the largest pieces of property in the village, a parcel (claim 293) on Market Street straddling the head of the cross street today known as Astor.[6] This land is still associated with the American Fur Company and is the site of the surviving warehouse (Community Hall) and Stuart House. The lot was conveniently situated. The cross street led

directly to the harbor and terminated at a wharf constructed in 1818 by William H. Puthuff.[7] This was where furs were landed and where, at the first perception of a "boat song" from an approaching canoe, "forty or fifty fur beaters, & as many more Canadian French inhabitants of the village" flocked to welcome the arriving voyageurs. Myra Mason witnessed the scene in 1824, where, amid a "jabbering of French," the arrivals were greeted with a "friendly shake of the hand with a sincerity & warmth of feeling unknown to those who are born in cities."[8]

The summer population of Michilimackinac swelled in other ways during these years. Mrs. Mason observed "people of business & of pleasure" arriving on as many as four boats a week from Buffalo, Erie, and Detroit. Far more numerous, however, were Native American visitors. These people had frequented the Straits as long as there had been fishing and trading opportunities, but the end of the War of 1812 seems to have established a pattern for their summer encampments that would catch the attention of most writers. The presence of a U.S. Indian agency, large numbers of merchants in the village, and the island's convenient location on the way from Lake Michigan to the British post at Drummond Island were all attractive reasons for Indian families to stop.[9] "Their wigwams lined the entire beach two or three rows deep," Gurdon Hubbard noted on his first arrival in 1818.[10] The activities of visiting Native Americans enlivened the summer days. Mary Thompson, an army wife fresh from the East, watched from the piazza of the officers' quarters in Fort Mackinac in July 1822 as some thirty Indians danced on the beach below. "Some entirely naked (*almost*), each took hold of hands—& while one beat on a drum—the others jump up & sing, each dance concludes with one hand laid on the mouth & a loud Yell," she wrote a friend. "This noise has continued all day," she added, with disapproval.[11]

It was well that Michilimackinac remained a center of commerce and transportation and continued to influence the behavior of Native Americans, because the rationale for maintaining a military post there was once again under scrutiny. The abandonment of plans to strengthen the island's fortifications and the subsequent reduction in the size of the garrison from three or more companies to a single one signaled yet another shift in official policy. This was coupled with the deterioration of Fort Mackinac, which, by the spring of 1819, was reported by its commandant to be "in a state of rapid decay." Major General Jacob Brown's inspection visit that summer at least did not result in an immediate call to abandon the fort, and a much-needed commissary storehouse was completed that year.[12] In accord with Brown's interest in a forward strategy for American posts, however, the army constructed Fort Brady at Sault Ste. Marie in the summer of 1822, and an Indian agency was established there to deal with the Native American nations of Lake Superior. When Lieutenant Henry Bayfield visited Mackinac Island that year he was told by several Americans "that they value Michilimackinac much less than Formerly" because of the more advanced posts at Green Bay, Chicago, and Sault Ste. Marie.[13]

Why, then, retain a garrison in Fort Mackinac? When, in the winter of 1825, an evacuation was proposed, territorial governor Lewis Cass came to its defense with a list of reasons. Mackinac Island had the only good harbor available for government use, and it was the long-established transfer point for the fur trade. As such, it attracted large numbers of men who considered the summer gathering "a season of festivity & relaxation from the fatigues & privations of Indian trade." Michilimackinac was also the resort of large numbers of Native Americans. With no local force to police this assemblage, Cass asked, "what is to restrain this temporary discordant population?" "If the Island is left without troops," he argued, "it will not be long before some unfortunate occurrence will demonstrate the impropriety of the evacuation."[14] In January 1826, General Brown admitted that the position must be protected, but added that, in peacetime, the post was "chiefly essential as a measure of police for the Harbour & its neighbouring precincts."[15] Although the army toyed with the idea of establishing a new cantonment on the ground below Fort Mackinac, money was appropriated instead to repair the old

"There appears therefore in the present society of Mackinac the want of a preacher, a school-master, an attorney, and a physician—of merchants there are always too many." HENRY SCHOOLCRAFT

fortifications and replace the most decrepit of its buildings. This was largely accomplished during 1827–29. In 1828 the size of the garrison was even doubled once again to two companies.[16]

The village that was to be protected by this military police force seems to have grown steadily during the 1820s, although there is little mention of the construction of new buildings other than those erected by the American Fur Company. The borough government was active in administering the community. In 1823 it imposed a personal property tax, a tax for relief of the poor, and a real estate tax to pay for a fire engine purchased, in part, by community subscription in 1819. There was a realization of the importance of the island's harbor as well, for ordinances regulating the disposal of wastes in the water and the carrying away of beach gravel were passed in 1824 and 1825.[17] The borough also regularly surveyed and maintained its highways, laying out new roads as needed (see Fig. 5.12).

Mackinac Island was also adapting to a changing clientele of passing travelers and those having business with the American Fur Company. After 1822, high-profile visitors were frequently accommodated in the company's headquarters (the Stuart House), but regular boarding establishments were appearing as well. There had been taverns in the village of Michilimackinac since its earliest days, but, in 1818, William H. Puthuff was the first to advertise space for a "few genteel boarders" in connection with his wharf and commission and storage agency.[18] Captain David Bates Douglass got a "good warm supper and comfortable bed" from Puthuff in June 1820.[19] Albert Ellis stayed with a "Madame Allen" in 1821, and, in 1824, Samuel C. Lasley announced that he had taken over a "large and commodious house" formerly occupied by Captain Arndt, where he offered a tavern and boarding.[20]

Michilimackinac was, otherwise, a place largely devoid of public institutions. There was a courthouse for Michilimackinac County by 1820, but it was apparently the old Indian council house, and the structure seems to have served for borough meetings as well. The town also boasted a "small jail." "There is no regular bred attorney," Henry Schoolcraft noted in that year, though two persons regularly practiced law. "There appears therefore in the present society of Mackinac," he continued, "the want of a preacher, a school-master, an attorney, and a physician—of merchants there are always too many."[21]

The only other public building, the old log church of Ste. Anne, was reportedly "destroyed" in 1819. The parish had been without a regular pastor for many years, although the church council carefully preserved its assets. Priests from Detroit visited occasionally (1799 and 1804), conducting services, baptizing, and blessing marriages. Father Gabriel Richard was on Mackinac Island during the summer of 1821 and again in 1823. Richard's earlier visit probably spurred interest in building a new church, and the parish wardens agreed to circulate a petition asking Congress for a lot at the east end of the village. Influenced, perhaps, by Richard's ongoing project to

construct a substantial new church at Detroit, Michilimackinac's Catholic community hoped to "build the church of stone."[22] Nothing came of this until 1826–27, when, possibly under the direction of Father Francis Badin, a modest log church was constructed on land donated by Madame Magdelaine La Framboise. The building was in place at the eastern end of the village by June 1827.[23] Father Samuel Mazzuchelli later described it as "a little wooden church erected by the piety of the faithful," suggesting that this had been a community effort.[24]

The French population of the Straits had always been at least nominally Catholic. The Protestant British and American merchants and officers had never had a minister to provide religious services, other than during the Reverend David Bacon's time on Mackinac Island in 1802–4. When Jedidiah Morse visited in 1820, he reported that the courthouse served as a place of worship, presumably for the island's Protestants.[25] This religious vacuum was filled in 1822 with the arrival of the Reverend William Ferry and his return the following year with his wife and assistants to found a school for Indian children. After two years of teaching and preaching from rented facilities, Ferry obtained the approval of the American Board of Commissioners for Foreign Missions to construct a substantial dormitory and school for his pupils and staff (see Figs. 5.17–5.19). This was accomplished during 1825, and over the next few years the complex was expanded to include outbuildings, gardens, woodcutting and farming facilities on Bois Blanc Island, and even a farm on the southwestern side of Mackinac Island. Ferry built up a large student body and a robust Protestant congregation that included and received support from many of the prominent American citizens of the island who were associated with the American Fur Company, the Indian agency, and the army.[26]

With this active and growing Mackinac community, it was fortuitous that the U.S. Congress moved, in 1823, to resolve the last remaining uncertainties about land ownership and boundaries at the Straits. This process, begun in 1804–10, had been interrupted by the War of 1812. The 1823 legislation allowed claims for property occupied and developed by individuals as late as July 1, 1812, and thus made some additional parcels eligible for confirmation, particularly those at St. Ignace, where an agricultural community had begun to develop by 1807 or a few years before. The 1823 act also inserted a provision that claimants must have remained loyal to the United States during the War of 1812.[27] A number of Mackinac landowners found themselves on shaky ground in this respect, and the claims process would reveal some lingering community animosities. The army also continued to express concerns that local residents were encroaching on military reserve lands on Mackinac and Bois Blanc islands. Although the surveying process was intended to ease such fears, it proved to be only a skirmish in the continuing battle between local and federal needs.

The new round of land claims required a considerable amount of surveying and the production of maps. Bois Blanc Island was surveyed and platted in 1827, with St. Ignace and the remaining fifteen claims on Mackinac Island undertaken the following year. The resulting property maps (Figs. 5.23–5.28), like their predecessors of 1810, are the foundations of private land ownership for important parts of the Straits. Simplified versions of the surveys of private claims found their way onto maps of Michigan published after the late 1820s (Figs. 5.29–5.31). These familiarized a larger audience of Americans and immigrants with the geography, topography, and property ownership of the Straits of Mackinac.

Yet one more element was injected into the Michilimackinac of the 1820s. The previous decade had witnessed visits by numerous military observers, some of whom recorded their impressions in words, maps, or pictures. Another sort of visitor became the norm during the 1820s. These were men with scientific or bureaucratic purposes, and although many were also soldiers, their interest in the peoples and natural resources of the region tended to have broader purposes—geology, botany, development, education, navigation, anthropology, and even history. The Cass expedition of 1820 brought Henry Schoolcraft and David Bates Douglass to Mackinac. Joseph Delafield and John J. Bigsby were involved in the Anglo-American effort to establish an accurate boundary line between the United States and Canada. Henry Bayfield charted parts of the Straits in 1822. Stephen H. Long paused on the return journey of his second western exploration. Jedidiah Morse and Thomas McKenney were interested in religion and the welfare of the Native Americans.

Many of these scientific tourists, or the members of their expeditions, were capable of recording visual impressions of what they had seen. Their writings often mention completed or proposed drawings, such as Schoolcraft's 1824 request for the return of his "sketches and drawings of scenery" made during the 1820 expedition and loaned to David Bates Douglass.[28] These have not been found, but Douglass's own drawings of Mackinac Island survive (Figs. 5.4–5.9). The journals or accounts of several of these visitors—Schoolcraft, Morse, Bigsby, and McKenney—were published, and drawings made during McKenney's trip (Figs. 5.15 and 5.16) were included as illustrations in his book.

Michilimackinac was not yet a destination for the casual tourist in the 1820s. Military, political, and scientific visitors nonetheless had much to say about the place. Amid their professional discussions of commerce, geology, and Indian affairs one also finds emotional responses to the surroundings. Near the end of his visit in June 1827, as John A. Granger concluded a straightforward description of American Fur Company operations and the village of Michilimack-inac, he let his comments drift toward the romantic and picturesque. "It is said by travellers that 'when you have seen one Lake you have seen all, or viewing one rock, you get an idea of all' but it is not so with Mackinac," he wrote in his journal. "—You must see it, for you can form no idea of it."[29] The decade of the 1830s would welcome literary tourists whose writings would further popularize the beauties of the Straits.

Captain Benjamin K. Pierce, Corps of Artillery, 1820–21

Captain Thomas C. Legate, 2nd Regiment of Artillery, 1821–23

Major William Whistler, 3rd Regiment of Infantry, 1823–25

Captain William Hoffman, 2nd Regiment of Infantry, 1825–26

Major Alexander R. Thompson, 2nd Regiment of Infantry, 1826–28

Major Josiah H. Vose, 5th Regiment of Infantry, 1828–29

Lieutenant Colonel Enos Cutler, 5th Regiment of Infantry, 1829–31

William H. Puthuff, 1817–21
George Boyd, 1822
William H. Puthuff, 1823
Michael Dousman, 1824–25
Jonathan N. Bailey, 1826
Samuel Abbott, 1827–30

The present town of Michilimackinac is pleasantly situated around a small bay

Henry Rowe Schoolcraft

First-time visitors to Mackinac Island, from the late eighteenth century to the present day, have shared one consistent impression—the dramatic vista of the bluffs, forts, and town dominating Haldimand Bay. Forested heights, blue water, and white buildings unfold in a panorama that inspired even the most jaded traveler arriving by canoe, schooner, or steamboat. Charles C. Trowbridge, who stopped in 1820 as part of Governor Lewis Cass's expedition to identify the source of the Mississippi River, wrote that the "town, harbor, and the forts, Mackinac & Holmes, present to the traveller a view at once picturesque and sublime." Perhaps this was the topic of conversation in his canoe, for one of Trowbridge's companions, Captain David Bates Douglass, described the scene in virtually identical terms.[30]

Not surprisingly, the perspective from the harbor or Round Island attracted artists, just as it would photographers of a later time. The visit of Cass's expedition inspired a number of such views. Some survive today, but none has come to symbolize Mackinac Island in the fur-trade era so much as the composition attributed to Captain Seth Eastman of the U.S. Army. His view, showing the town, fort, and harbor from Mission Point at the eastern tip of the island, is best known from a lithograph first published in 1854 and titled simply *Michilimackinack* (Fig. 5.1). Below the scene at left is the straight-forward statement "drawn by Capt. S. Eastman, U.S.A." Eastman's detailed scene was lithographed to illustrate volume 4 of Henry Schoolcraft's *Information Respecting the History, Condition and*

Prospects of the Indian Tribes of the United States (Philadelphia, 1851–57). Schoolcraft knew Michilimackinac intimately. He first visited with Cass in 1820, passing through on numerous other occasions before residing there as Indian agent from 1833 to 1841. Eastman's view was intended to illustrate a place of particular importance in the history of the Native Americans of the Great Lakes.

Despite its much later publication date, the Eastman lithograph has generally been accepted to represent Michilimackinac as it appeared in 1820. The long, low skyline of the village fronting Haldimand Bay shows none of the more substantial construction of the following three decades. There is no sign of the Mackinac County Courthouse (1839) or of the large structures erected on Market Street by the American Fur Company in 1821–22. Nor does the Greek Revival mansion of Samuel Abbott (ca. 1845) appear at the western end of the village. All would have towered at least a full story above the small Canadian-style houses seen along the beach. Two larger buildings on either side of the foot of the ramp to Fort Mackinac can, however, be identified with new construction of 1819—the American Fur Company retail store (left) and the commissary storehouse for the garrison (right). A pair of buildings to the left of the retail store, with their gable ends facing the harbor, then housed American Fur Company operations. The only anachronism for an 1820 date is the tall building at the far right below Fort Mackinac and behind a pair of Native American figures. Its shape and location suggest that it is the Indian Dormitory, built in 1838

Jedidiah Morse (1761–1826) was a prominent clergyman who had made a name for himself as a geographer of the early United States by the time he saw Mackinac in June and July 1820. His visit to the Straits, however, was to examine and report to the secretary of war on the condition of the Indians of the region. Portrait engraving by Waterman L. Ormsby.

Clements Library, University of Michigan.

MICHILIMACKINACK

FIGURE 5.1

TITLE: Michilimackinack.
AUTHOR: Captain Seth Eastman, 1st
Regiment of Infantry (1808–75) after
Captain David Bates Douglass, Corps
of Engineers (1790–1849). Engraved by
John C. McRae (active 1850–80).
DATE DEPICTED: June 1820 with
addition after 1838.
DATE OF WORK: 1854.
DESCRIPTION: 14.4 x 19.8 cm.
Lithograph. Some copies are colored.
PROVENANCE: Published in Henry
Schoolcraft, *Information Respecting the
History, Condition and Prospects of the
Indian Tribes of the United States....*
(1854), 4:188. Reissued in Mary H.
Eastman, *The American Annual* (1855),
79. The copy illustrated here is from
Schoolcraft.
COLLECTION: Clements Library,
University of Michigan, Ann Arbor
(Book Division, Oversize Z Sc).

MACKINAC

FIGURE 5.2

TITLE: Mackinac.
AUTHOR: Captain Seth Eastman, 1st
Regiment of Infantry (1808–75), after
Captain David Bates Douglass, Corps
of Engineers (1790–1849).
DATE DEPICTED: June 1820 with
addition after 1838.
DATE OF WORK: [1853].
DESCRIPTION: 15.5 x 23 cm. Watercolor
on paper. Signed at lower left: S. Eastman
U.S. Army.
PROVENANCE: Unknown until acquired
by the Newberry Library.
COLLECTION: The Newberry Library,
Chicago (Edward E. Ayer Collection).

FIGURE 5.3

TITLE: Mackinac.
AUTHOR: [Captain Seth Eastman, 1st Regiment of Infantry (1808–75)], after Captain David Bates Douglass, Corps of Engineers (1790–1849).
DATE DEPICTED: June 1820.
DATE OF WORK: [1853].
DESCRIPTION: 10.2 x 18.7 cm. Pencil on paper.

PROVENANCE: Collected by David Bushnell and donated by him to the Peabody Museum in 1941.
COLLECTION: © 2007 Peabody Museum, Harvard University, Cambridge, MA (41-72-10/199 T1706).

under the direction of Indian agent Schoolcraft.

Michilimackinack by Seth Eastman presents a most interesting case study of how pre-photographic images could mutate from their original form into something quite different. This usually involved a process of copying from earlier works while making adjustments to give the image more relevance to its time of publication. At least five different versions of the Eastman composition are known, and they demonstrate subtle changes as the original view was made more appropriate to the early 1850s. The scene does, indeed, represent the Michilimackinac of 1820—for the most part—but the original drawing was not the work of the man who signed as the artist of the lithograph of 1854.

During his more than forty-five years as an army officer, Seth Eastman came to be best known for his paintings of American Indian life. Like most of his fellow West Point cadets, Eastman studied drawing during his time at the Military Academy in 1824–29. Upon graduation, he was commissioned a second lieutenant in the 1st Regiment of Infantry. During an active military career, Eastman served around the country, from the upper Mississippi to Texas and

Florida. His years in Wisconsin and at Fort Snelling (1829–32 and 1841–48) and in Texas (1848–49) exposed him to the Native American peoples of those regions and gave him the opportunity to capture their culture in art. Eastman was able to develop his talents well beyond the level of most of his fellow officers. He taught drawing at West Point in 1833–40, honing his skills through lessons, study, and exhibition. From late 1849 to 1855 he was assigned to the Office of Indian Affairs to prepare nearly three hundred plates for the six-volume history of the Indian tribes of the United States, in which his view of Michilimackinac appeared.[31]

All of this provided little opportunity for Seth Eastman to take a firsthand view of Mackinac Island as it was in 1820. He did not even graduate from the Military Academy until nine years later, and his regiment had no service at Fort Mackinac between that time and 1850. Lieutenant Eastman might have passed through in the fall of 1829 on his way to his first posting at Fort Crawford in Prairie du Chien, Wisconsin, but it would have been just as convenient for him to travel by way of the Ohio and Mississippi rivers. There is no evidence that he ever visited Mackinac Island.

FIGURE 5.4

TITLE: [Sketch of Michillimackinac]. [On verso in a different and later hand:] Fort Mackinaw (1820?).
AUTHOR: Captain David Bates Douglass, Corps of Engineers (1790–1849).
DATE DEPICTED: June 7–12, 1820.
DATE OF WORK: [June 7–12, 1820].
DESCRIPTION: 10.3 x 19.3 cm. Watercolor and pencil on paper.

PROVENANCE: This might be the work mentioned in a letter from Lewis Cass to Douglass of September 15, 1826. Cass recalled that Douglass had a sketch of "Michillimackinac" and asked him to give it to Thomas L. McKenney if he had no further use for it. The letter is in Clements Library, David Bates Douglass Papers. The watercolor was retained in the papers of David Bates Douglass.

Donated by Richard Rickard, April 27, 2000.
COLLECTION: Greenslade Special Collections and Archives, Olin Library, Kenyon College, Gambier, OH (99-024)

How then was Eastman able to produce such an accurate view of a place he had never seen? The answer lies in the other surviving copies of the composition. An 1853 watercolor, from which the lithograph appears to have been made, is in the collections of the Newberry Library in Chicago (Fig. 5.2). It is signed "S. Eastman U.S. Army" and contains all of the elements seen in the 1854 lithograph. The same details, except for the Indian Dormitory, appear again in an oil painting titled *Michilimackinac and Fort Mackinac,* thought to have been done about 1854 (not illustrated) and advertised for sale in New York in 1958.[32] The Peabody Museum of Harvard University holds the precursor of all these works (Fig. 5.3). Titled simply "Mackinac," this pencil sketch includes the fort, town, and the prominent tree in the foreground but lacks the canoes and figures of Native Americans that enliven the others. More important, the Indian Dormitory is missing as well. The catalog of Eastman's known works dates the Peabody Museum sketch to 1853.[33]

Figure 5.3 was probably Seth Eastman's study for his oil and watercolor and very likely his copy of whatever view of Michilimackinac had been provided to him as a model. The most

likely source of such an image was Henry Schoolcraft, with whom Eastman worked from late 1849 until 1855 on the plates for Schoolcraft's history of the Indians and in which Figure 5.1 appeared. Schoolcraft had himself made sketches during the 1820 Cass expedition, and some of these were used as models for other plates prepared by Eastman. The list of illustrations for volume 6, for example, describes the Eastman lithograph of the ruins of Old Michilimackinac (Fig. 5.11) as "S. E. tr[aced]. sketch by H. R. Schoolcraft."[34]

Although the model for the Eastman views was likely provided by Schoolcraft, the former Indian agent was not the artist. That distinction belongs to Captain David Bates Douglass, who had traveled with Schoolcraft on the 1820 Cass expedition and who painted the watercolor illustrated here as Figure 5.4. The view is untitled, but it contains all of the elements relevant to 1820 that were included in the Eastman views. Conspicuously absent is the foreground tree, but otherwise the appearance of town, fort, and bluffs remains the same. Written on the verso in a different hand than that seen on other Douglass drawings (Figs. 5.5–5.9) is "Fort

Mackinaw (1820?)," possibly a reflection of later consultation of the drawing.

Captain Douglass was an officer of the Corps of Topographical Engineers in 1820. Following his retirement from the army in 1831 he worked as a civil engineer and later as an educator at Kenyon College in Ohio and Hobart College in New York.[35] Douglass died in the fall of 1849, before the commencement of Eastman's work, but he had corresponded in the 1820s with Schoolcraft about illustrations of scenery and geological specimens collected during the Cass expedition.[36] Governor Cass was also aware of Douglass's drawings, and in September 1826 he wrote to ask him to give his "sketch of Michillimackinac" to Colonel Thomas McKenney, who had just completed a tour of the upper lakes.[37] McKenney probably wanted it to illustrate his own book, which appeared the following year. There is no indication that Douglass complied with Cass's request,

and, if he did, his view was not used. It is likely, however, that Schoolcraft had the opportunity, at some point, to borrow and copy Douglass's view of Mackinac Island. He was then in a position to provide the image to Eastman after 1850. Douglass's original watercolor remained with his papers and is today part of a small collection at Kenyon College.

Seth Eastman copied faithfully, judging by Figure 5.4. But why the sole addition of the Indian Dormitory, which was not constructed until eighteen years after the Cass expedition? The answer can only lie with Schoolcraft's personal pride in a building he had championed and probably designed.[38] It was a crowning achievement of his years as Indian agent at Michilimackinac. As such, Schoolcraft must have considered it to have had an impact on the "condition and prospects" of the Indian tribes of the region and thus to be worth adding to a view of Michilimackinac.

Gurdon Saltonstall Hubbard (1802–86) was a clerk of the American Fur Company when he witnessed the 1822 accident that wounded Alexis St. Martin. Hubbard left a description of the incident in a long and detailed narrative about his years in the fur trade. Late in his life, he acquired land on Mackinac Island, which he eventually developed as a resort-era cottage community known as "Hubbard's Annex." This watercolor on ivory, by Anson Dickinson, was painted about 1828. *Chicago History Museum (1923.56).*

Nothing could be finer subject for the pencil

Captain David Bates Douglass

There can be no doubt that 1820 was a banner year for written descriptions of the Straits of Mackinac. On June 6 the battered bark canoes of Lewis Cass's expedition entered Haldimand Bay in the teeth of strong winds and a heavy swell. The journals of at least four members of that party survive, including one published by Henry Schoolcraft in 1821. Eleven days later, the American geographer Jedidiah Morse arrived to inquire into the condition of the Native Americans resorting to the post of Michilimackinac. His published report had much to say about the place and its people. Then, late in July, Major Joseph Delafield recorded many details when he stopped in the course of his duties to determine the boundary between the United States and Canada. In all, at least seven journals or reports and two later reminiscences preserve a wide range of information about Mackinac Island and its community as it was in 1820.[39]

A few of these visitors were also capable artists, although their visual impressions have not survived as well as their written words. Henry Schoolcraft, Lieutenant Aeneas Mackay, and Captain David Bates Douglass all drew during their time at Mackinac, or they at least attempted to record the scenery before them. On June 12 Schoolcraft and Mackay crossed to Round Island to sketch the town and fort, but their efforts were interrupted by "a fog . . . so dense as to obscure objects at the distance of two hundred yards." It was with difficulty that the pair was able to return to Mackinac Island, where they found that Douglass's attempt to get his own sketch of the town had also been foiled by the mist.[40] It is likely that other visitors made views that summer, although, like any drawings by Schoolcraft and Mackay, these remain to be found.

Fortunately, six sketches by Captain Douglass survive to complement his journal and those of his fellow travelers. Although Douglass was forced to abandon his June 12 view, his composition from Mission Point (Fig. 5.4) captures the appearance of the village and fort from the water. Among his five other surviving works is a unique and revealing image of the village and a rendering of a pair of canoes—little more than well-executed doodles—that depict the vessels used by the Cass expedition (Fig. 5.9). Bark canoes were the workhorses of the American Fur Company as well, and the annual brigades were arriving from the wilderness at the time of Douglass's visit.

Captain Douglass had a number of duties on the Cass expedition. Perhaps the most onerous to him was collecting botanical specimens, each of which had to be carefully gathered, dried, recorded, and preserved.[41] Douglass was far more interested in geology, and his efforts resulted in the first detailed and realistic images of Mackinac Island's signature limestone formations, Sugar Loaf and Arch Rock.

His journal, as well as narratives left by Schoolcraft, Morse, and Delafield, includes some of the earliest scientific descriptions of the geology of Mackinac Island and the nearby St. Martins, which were reputed to have large deposits of gypsum.[42]

The village has always been the first part of the Mackinac Island encountered by visitors. Captain Douglass depicted it from the water (Fig. 5.4), but at some point he also climbed to the crest of the East Bluff and executed a panoramic view looking southwest across the town (Fig. 5.5). The scene is much as described by Jedidiah Morse, who observed it from Fort Mackinac. The military post, Morse reported, was "about seventy or eighty (some say one hundred and fifty) feet above the level below, on which is the village, which surrounds a very safe, commodious, and beautiful circular harbor." Morse counted one hundred buildings, "none of them large or commodious." The island was the summer stopping place for "several thousands of the various tribes of Indians from the south, south west and west" who arrived "with their families, dwellings, furniture and provisions, packed in birch canoes, each of a size suited to the number and wealth of the owner." Most were on their way to the British post at Drummond Island.[43] All the visitors that summer noted the brisk business carried on by the American Fur Company. Henry Schoolcraft observed that "the ware houses, stores, offices, boat yards and other buildings of this establishment, occupy a considerable part of the town plat."[44]

Virtually all of these details may be discerned in Figure 5.5. Canoes are pulled up on the beach, and bark wigwams dot the shore. In the left foreground is a military encampment, probably that of the detachment sent with Governor Cass to project U.S. authority. Three small vessels lie comfortably at anchor in the harbor. There is no sign of a garrison wharf, perhaps reflecting the need for one expressed in 1821.[45] Puthuff's wharf is prominent, however, projecting into Haldimand Bay from the foot of Astor Street. The large building to its left might be his warehouse.

The town of 1820 still occupies its original area, built around two streets, each of about one-quarter mile in length.[46] The houses and stores are primarily the log, Canadian-style buildings seen on earlier renderings. At the end of the village nearest the viewer is the property of the American Fur Company. Two long, narrow buildings, their gable ends facing the harbor, represent the houses and stores acquired by John Jacob Astor from the South West Company (Fig. 3.6, claim 101). These were renovated in 1818, and would serve the firm until new buildings were constructed on Market Street in 1821–22.[47] In later years the left-hand building would become known to travelers as the Northern Hotel and be remembered as late as the 1880s as the

FIGURE 5.5

TITLE: Village of Miche-Mackina.
AUTHOR: Captain David Bates Douglass,
Corps of Engineers (1790–1849).
DATE DEPICTED: June 7–12, 1820.
DATE OF WORK: [June 7–12, 1820].
DESCRIPTION: 10 x 27 cm. Pencil and gray
wash on paper.

PROVENANCE: Retained in the papers of
David Bates Douglass. Donated by Richard
Rickard, April 27, 2000.
COLLECTION: Greenslade Special Collections
and Archives, Olin Library, Kenyon College,
Gambier, OH (99-024).

original Mackinac Island headquarters of the fur-trading giant.[48]

To the right of these two structures, across Market Street, is the company's new retail store, completed in 1819.[49] It was in this building, in June 1822, that a young voyageur named Alexis St. Martin was accidentally shot in his left side at very close range. The blast opened a hole in his stomach. Post surgeon William Beaumont treated St. Martin and then nursed him back to health. When the wound healed without entirely closing, forming a "fistula" that allowed direct access to his patient's stomach, Beaumont seized the opportunity to observe and describe the workings of the human digestive system.[50]

The large building in the trees below Fort Mackinac is the commissary storehouse, built for the garrison in 1819. In this composition, as well as in Douglass's view from Mission Point, it appears as a pair of structures. Perhaps the artist erred in his rendering, or he might have documented the decrepit remnants of the old Government House soon before its demolition, although the location seems too close to town. The garrison gardens dominate the foreground. These were fenced and well developed by 1820. Beaumont described the hospital garden as "handsomely laid out into squares, walks, alleys, etc., with bowers of biennial and perennial plants, fruit trees, etc., besides the germs of other medicinal plants and ornamental flowers."[51] Figure 5.5 suggests this orderly design.

These gardens were contested ground in 1820, not because of civilian encroachment but because of the conflicting needs of the army and the Indian agency. In 1820, with no adequate building from which to conduct his affairs, newly arrived agent George Boyd rented a place in the village. Boyd's requests for a proper agency house identified part of the gardens as a convenient spot. The commandant of Fort Mackinac objected, and Beaumont argued vehemently that Boyd's site would take the entire hospital garden. The matter would not be fully resolved until 1823, when an agency building and supporting structures were built at the extreme northeastern edge of the government land in the right foreground of Figure 5.5.[52]

Captain Douglass and the other members of the Cass expedition explored much of Mackinac Island during their seven days there. Douglass was relieved to see "novel and interesting" topography after weeks of looking at the flat country around Detroit and along Michigan's eastern shore. He visited Fort Mackinac, the abandoned Fort Holmes, Dousman's farm, and even the St. Martin Islands. On June 10, after collecting mineral specimens from the British excavations at Fort Holmes, he climbed down the hill to visit "the Sugar Loaf," which he described as "a singular rock" standing seventy to eighty feet high. Then, joining Governor Cass, Douglass mounted a horse to explore the island. He found the mouth of

Several of the artists and diarists who visited Mackinac Island in June 1820 were members of an expedition to Lake Superior and the source of the Mississippi River led by Michigan Territory governor Lewis Cass (1782–1866). A former soldier and an astute politician, Cass was determined to establish U.S. influence among the Native American nations of the northern Great Lakes. Abraham Tuthill captured his image at Detroit in 1825.
The Detroit Historical Society (63.32.4).

FIGURE 5.6

TITLE: Sugar Loaf Rock—Mackina.

AUTHOR: Captain David Bates Douglass, Corps of Engineers (1790–1849).

DATE DEPICTED: June 12, 1820.

DATE OF WORK: [June 12, 1820].

DESCRIPTION: 12.6 x 19.2 cm. Pencil on paper.

PROVENANCE: Douglass noted in his journal on this date that he had got "good views" of Sugar Loaf. Retained in the papers of David Bates Douglass. Donated by Richard Rickard, April 27, 2000.

COLLECTION: Greenslade Special Collections and Archives, Olin Library, Kenyon College, Gambier, OH (99-024).

FIGURE 5.7

TITLE: [Distant view of Sugar Loaf Rock].

AUTHOR: Captain David Bates Douglass, Corps of Engineers (1790–1849).

DATE DEPICTED: June 12, 1820.

DATE OF WORK: [June 12, 1820].

DESCRIPTION: 13.8 x 23.4 cm. Pencil on paper.

PROVENANCE: Douglass noted in his journal on this date that he had got "good views" of Sugar Loaf. Retained in the papers of David Bates Douglass. Donated by Richard Rickard, April 27, 2000.

COLLECTION: Greenslade Special Collections and Archives, Olin Library, Kenyon College, Gambier, OH (99-024).

FIGURE 5.8

TITLE: [An inside view of Arch Rock].

AUTHOR: Captain David Bates Douglass, Corps of Engineers (1790–1849).

DATE DEPICTED: June 12, 1820.

DATE OF WORK: [June 12, 1820].

DESCRIPTION: 19.8 x 27 cm. Pencil on paper.

PROVENANCE: Douglass noted in his journal on this date that he had got "an inside view of the arch rock." Retained in the papers of David Bates Douglass. Donated by Richard Rickard, April 27, 2000.

COLLECTION: Greenslade Special Collections and Archives, Olin Library, Kenyon College, Gambier, OH (99-024).

FIGURE 5.9

TITLE: [Sketch of two bark canoes].

AUTHOR: Captain David Bates Douglass, Corps of Engineers (1790–1849).

DATE DEPICTED: June 7–12, 1820.

DATE OF WORK: [June 7–12, 1820].

DESCRIPTION: 19.8 x 27 cm. (paper size). Pencil on paper. Drawn on the verso of [An inside view of Arch Rock].

PROVENANCE: Retained in the papers of David Bates Douglass. Donated by Richard Rickard, April 27, 2000.

COLLECTION: Greenslade Special Collections and Archives, Olin Library, Kenyon College, Gambier, OH (99-024).

Skull Cave "strewed with human bones." The party then rode through Croghan's 1814 battlefield, back to Sugar Loaf, and across the plateau to the bluff.[53]

Their destination was Arch Rock. Douglass considered it a "great curiosity" and was impressed by its span and height. He was equally interested to learn that several garrison officers, including Lieutenant Daniel Curtis and the commandant, Captain Benjamin K. Pierce, had dared to walk across it. Even Douglass's late friend and colleague, topographical engineer Lieutenant William Eveleth, had accomplished this feat, which Douglass thought "a rash enterprise."[54] Eveleth must have crossed in 1817. Lieutenant John A. Dix did so two years later, though, he wrote, "not without some little jeopardy to my bones." This daredevil practice was surely as old as the human discovery of Arch Rock. Balancing across would become a popular exploit for nineteenth-century tourists. In 1827, John A. Granger confided to his journal that no one in his party "considered their lives of so little value as to attempt it," but he was told (perhaps as a goad) that at least one woman had already had "the courage or presumption to walk over it."[55]

Captain Douglass must not have carried his sketchbook on his June 10 tour. Two days later, detained on Mackinac Island by adverse winds, he set out to correct the oversight. He "got good views of the Sugar Loaf," he wrote, and later in the day "took an inside view of the arch rock."[56] These sketches survive among his Mackinac drawings. Except for the absence of trees, his view of Sugar Loaf (Fig. 5.6) is easily recognizable today, even to the stunted cedars growing from its crevices. The perspective is from the northwest, with "Keyhole Cave" piercing the great rock. Beaumont noted that Sugar Loaf was "perforated in many places," and reported that the holes, like Skull Cave, were "filled with human bones."[57] Henry Schoolcraft described Sugar Loaf by a common alternate name, "The Natural Pyramid," and opined that it "pleases chiefly by its novelty, so wholly unlike any thing to be found in other parts of the world, and on first approaching it, gives the idea of a work of art."[58] Douglass's second, much rougher sketch of Sugar Loaf (Fig. 5.7) is also from the northwest, though at a greater distance. It is chiefly useful for showing the absence of mature trees on an island that Major Joseph Delafield described, that August, as generally "barren."[59]

Douglass's view of Arch Rock (Fig. 5.8) shows signs of haste, perhaps because he felt a need to return to town, where the expedition's canoes only awaited better weather to proceed to Sault Ste. Marie. Henry Schoolcraft thought the best view of the arch was from the beach, but Douglass approached from Sugar Loaf, atop the island's plateau. Schoolcraft explained the rather narrow angle of Douglass's sketch. "On viewing it from above," he wrote, "you are obliged to approach within ten or twelve feet of the chasm . . . before it is distinctly seen, so that the effect of perspective is lost."[60] Captain Douglass got his sketch and then returned to town. Staring through the "circular cavity" at the beach below, it is unlikely that he reconsidered his decision not to walk across the span.

Captain David Bates Douglass (1790–1849) drew six realistic sketches of Mackinac Island during his visit with the Cass expedition in 1820. Douglass, like Henry Schoolcraft, had a particular interest in geology and the island's rock formations. This engraving, published in Charles Stuart's *Lives and Works of Civil and Military Engineers* (New York, 1871), shows Douglass late in his life. *Clements Library, University of Michigan.*

Like Babylon, Palmyra and Tyre … the glory has departed

Correspondent to the Detroit Gazette

By 1820, forty years had passed since the fortified village and suburb on the south mainland of the Straits of Mackinac had been dismantled and carried across the lake to Mackinac Island. The transfer of the military buildings was well documented, and most of the inhabitants seem to have moved their houses and portable property during 1781–83. There were a few procrastinators. "Some residents lingered a few seasons," Henry Schoolcraft was told in 1834.[61] They were gone by the late 1780s, however, and maps of the Straits area usually identify the mainland location thereafter as "Old Michilimackinac."[62]

Although abandoned in favor of Mackinac Island, the mainland site was not forgotten, and it became a well-known local landmark. Older residents could still recall details of the move as late as the 1830s, and there were visible remains as well. The spot could be seen from passing vessels. Samuel Storrow mentioned "old Mackinac on our left" during his westward voyage to Green Bay in 1817.[63] Boats following the south shore of the Straits often stopped, and there was a general understanding that the former settlement had been the predecessor of the fort and village on Mackinac Island and that it had played a part in the great Indian uprising of 1763. One unnamed gentleman, traveling with Governor Lewis Cass, passed the lonely clearing in June 1825. He mused about its history for the *Detroit Gazette,* convinced that nearly two centuries had elapsed since "the enterprising and adventurous Canadian" had made it a major entrepôt of the fur trade. Old Michilimackinac had no harbor or protection from the lake storms, he stated, so the advantages of Mackinac Island had proven more attractive. The writer compared Old Michilimackinac to long-vanished biblical cities, summing up its fate as "Sic transit gloria Huronae."[64]

The mainland had not been completely abandoned, however. In the mid-1780s Robert Campbell established a sawmill some three miles east of the old fort site, and the property was confirmed to his heirs as private claim 334 in 1808. The 1825 correspondent to the *Detroit Gazette* commented that the location of Old Michilimackinac was also the "site of a small farm."[65] He had probably viewed the place from the water, and he described the establishment of Patrick McGulpin, which was actually west of Old Michilimackinac, fronting part of Cecil Bay. McGulpin's father had occupied that parcel well before 1796. The 640-acre plot, with its "houses, buildings and improvements," passed to the younger McGulpin in 1802 and was confirmed as private claim 335 six years later.[66] The farm buildings, occupied by McGulpin's tenants, were the "three or four houses" described as remaining at Old Michilimackinac when Father Jean Dilhet spent the summer of 1804 at the Straits.[67]

Both Campbell's and McGulpin's claims were carved from an 11,520-acre parcel centered on Old Michilimackinac that had been granted to the U.S. government by the Ojibwa in the 1795 Treaty of Greenville. Reserves of this sort had been allowed around the former British military posts of the Northwest. The treaty negotiators assumed that this was land to which Indian title had been extinguished under the French and British regimes.[68] Although the entire area was technically available for settlement, only Campbell and McGulpin had taken up lands there.

The site of the old fort itself remained unclaimed and unoccupied, although evidence of earlier human activity could easily be discerned. When Major Henry Burbeck visited in September 1796 he found the remains of old picketing almost buried in the drifting sand.[69] The inhabitants had taken what could be transported and reused, and much of what could not be moved had been burned to deny it to the Americans. Features such as chimneys, fences, and foundations were simply abandoned. John Askin, Jr., the son of a prominent trader and commissary at Old Michilimackinac, learned the fate of his father's former home in the summer of 1807 from some of his longtime acquaintances. "One of the Chimneys of the house you built at Old Mackina fell down only last summer," Askin wrote his father, and his garden could be traced by trees that had grown up along the fence lines.[70] Evidence of many other Michilimackinac properties surely remained visible as well.

It was these romantic ruins that inspired Henry Schoolcraft to make a drawing that survives as both a later watercolor and as a lithograph by Captain Seth Eastman (Figs. 5.10 and 5.11). Like Eastman's view of the town and fort on Mackinac Island (Fig. 5.1), the composition illustrated Schoolcraft's history of the Indian tribes of the United States. It did double duty, in fact, being first published in volume 2 (1852) and then again in volume 6 (1857). In between, Mary Eastman used the lithograph in *The American Annual* of 1855. The view of the ruins of Old Michilimackinac was thus produced in considerable numbers and is a well-known image today.

Seth Eastman credited the original artist this time—at least in 1857 when the lithograph was reproduced for the third time—unlike his view of Mackinac Island. Eastman's name appears at lower left on all examples of the print, but only in the list of illustrations for volume 6 of Schoolcraft's history is it credited as being taken from a "sketch by H. R. Schoolcraft." If Schoolcraft's original drawing survives, it remains to be found. The Eastman watercolor, from which the lithograph was made, is signed and dated 1851 and is illustrated as Figure 5.10.[71]

The view of Old Michilimackinac is a strikingly evocative composition that suggests the vanished glories of the site.

FIGURE 5.10
TITLE: Old Fort Mackinac.
AUTHOR: Captain Seth Eastman, 1st Regiment of
Infantry (1808–75), after Henry Rowe Schoolcraft
(1793–1864).
DATE DEPICTED: September 9, 1820.
DATE OF WORK: 1851.
DESCRIPTION: 17 x 24 cm. Watercolor on paper.
Signed: S. Eastman 1851.
PROVENANCE: Unknown before acquired by
Minnesota Historical Society.
COLLECTION: Minnesota Historical Society,
St. Paul (AV 1991.85.9).

RUINS OF OLD FORT MACKANACK, 1763.

PUBLISHED BY LIPPINCOTT, GRAMBO & CO. PHILAD^a

FIGURE 5.11

TITLE: Ruins of Old Fort Mackanack, 1763.

AUTHOR: Captain Seth Eastman, 1st Regiment of Infantry (1808–75) after Henry Rowe Schoolcraft (1793–1864). Engraved by Charles Edward Wagstaff (1808–50) and Joseph Andrews (1806–73).

DATE DEPICTED: September 9, 1820.

DATE OF WORK: 1852.

DESCRIPTION: 15.3 x 20.9 cm. Colored lithograph. Most copies are uncolored.

PROVENANCE: Published in Schoolcraft, *Information Respecting the History, Condition and Prospects of the Indian Tribes of the United States. . . .* (1852), 2:242, and (1857), 6:243. A list of plates added to the latter volume credits authorship to "S.E. [Seth Eastman] tr. sketch by H. R. Schoolcraft." Published also in Mary Eastman, *The American Annual* (1855), 71. The example illustrated here has been removed from a copy of one of these works and colored.

COLLECTION: Clements Library, University of Michigan, Ann Arbor (Print Division, Unmatted Prints).

Its perspective is directly across the Straits, with a rainsquall hanging above Point St. Ignace and the tall bulk of Mackinac Island visible to the right. The sand hills that caused British commandants such concern in the years before the move to Mackinac Island have encroached on the few standing timbers of the old fort, while a pair of visitors ponders the history of the place. When Schoolcraft explored the ground in September 1834, he found that "the town site is now covered with loose sand." There was much to be seen, nonetheless. "The walls of the fort, which are of stone, remain, and the whole site constitutes an interesting ruin," he wrote.[72] By the time the historian Francis Parkman spent an afternoon exploring the site, in the summer of 1845, there was still enough to be seen for his escort, Lieutenant Henry Whiting, to sketch a rough ground plan. The visible remains appear to have been primarily cellar holes or depressions in the ground.[73] Curious visitors had long since begun to dig up and carry away artifacts from the site. In May 1828 Lieutenant Samuel P. Heintzelman found and took home part of a human skull and "an English pewter gill cup with cover."[74]

Dating the view originally captured by Henry Schoolcraft is difficult, primarily because he had so many opportunities to visit the site of Old Michilimackinac during the 1820s and 1830s. The image seems to fit the 1834 description in Schoolcraft's *Personal Memoirs,* but it is more likely that it dates to his first visit in 1820. Returning to Mackinac Island from a circuit of Lake Michigan, Schoolcraft and Douglass camped there on the night of September 8–9. In the morning, they found that a "gale of wind" and heavy swells prevented a safe crossing to the island. Douglass also mentioned "showers of rain" in his journal. Around 11:00 the travelers were able to get their "best voyageurs" to volunteer to make the attempt in a light canoe. "After being tossed upon the billows for several hours," Schoolcraft wrote, the canoe safely reached its destination.[75]

Henry Schoolcraft is known to have made other drawings during his time with the Cass expedition in 1820, so it seems likely that he would have been inclined to include a view of these historic ruins. None of his later accounts of visits to the site of Old Michilimackinac mentions drawings, so he probably felt that he had recorded what was to be seen.

Perhaps the best-known member of Lewis Cass's 1820 expedition was Henry Rowe Schoolcraft (1793–1864). Schoolcraft had a long association with Sault Ste. Marie and the Mackinac region from service as Indian agent at both places. His historical, ethnological, and geological studies earned him an international reputation. Schoolcraft is shown in an 1852 miniature portrait by Maria Louisa Wagner. *Clements Library, University of Michigan.*

Oshawguscodaywayqua (Susan Johnston, ca. 1778–1843) was the wife of Canadian fur trader John Johnston and a daughter of Wabojeeg, an influential Ojibwa leader. Henry Schoolcraft's marriage to the Johnstons' daughter, Jane, in 1823 connected him to many of the sources needed to intimately study the culture and history of the Indians of the northern lakes. Susan's portrait engraving appeared in Thomas McKenney's *Sketches of a Tour to the Lakes* (Baltimore, 1827). *Clements Library, University of Michigan.*

The steamboat *Walk-in-the-Water* carried Dr. William Beaumont and Reverend Jedidiah Morse to Mackinac on its June 1820 voyage into the northern lakes. Among the other passengers were Colonel John E. Wool and Major General Alexander Macomb, who went to inspect the Fort Mackinac garrison. Macomb (1782–1841) was a hero of the War of 1812 and commanded the Fifth Military District from Detroit. Thomas Sully captured his likeness in this 1829 portrait. *West Point Museum Art Collection, United States Military Academy, West Point, NY (WPM 9055). Photograph by René Chartrand.*

Empowered to lay out new highways, streets and public walks

Act of Incorporation

Given the small size of Mackinac Island, one might assume that the regulation of its streets and roads was a low priority of local government. Prevention of fire, order in streets crowded with boisterous Indians and voyageurs, regulation of wharves and vessels, sanitation, trespass, taxation, and the control of domestic animals would all seem of equal or greater concern. Nonetheless, the act of April 6, 1817, incorporating the Borough of Michilimackinac placed all these considerations after roads. In fact, "highways" were addressed in the fourteen lines of Section 6, while all other matters falling under the "Power of wardens and burgesses" were lumped together in the thirty-eight lines of Section 7. Clearly, public thoroughfares were an important concern.

Section 6 begins with the statement that the wardens and burgesses "are hereby empowered to lay out new highways, streets and public walks, for the use of said borough." They were also permitted to "exchange highways for highways, or sell highways for the purpose of purchasing other highways" as regulated by the laws of the Michigan Territory. Highways could be discontinued should they become "unnecessary for public use." Individuals "aggrieved" by road-building activities were given the recourse of the Michilimackinac County Court. The legislation made no distinction between highways on private land and public land.[76]

Official attention to the island's roads predated the formation of the Borough of Michilimackinac. Within months of the organization of the Michigan Territory, in 1805, the island was declared a separate road district (the seventh), and Samuel Abbott was appointed supervisor, responsible for "permanent highways, and temporary and existing roads."[77] Abbott probably continued in this office until he was exiled following the capture of Fort Mackinac in 1812. But even the wartime British garrison needed good roads. Captain Charles Roberts appointed none other than Michael Dousman as "highroad master, or supervisor of highways." Notice of Dousman's authority was posted on the door of Ste. Anne's Church, where it remained until a day or two before the return of American troops in July 1815.[78] Dousman had good reason for this appointment by a foreign power to be quietly forgotten, and by the winter of 1817 William H. Puthuff reported that a supervisor of highways was "much wanted." His recommendation of John C. Potter was accepted and coincided with the establishment of the borough.[79]

The documentation of highways was the motivation for the map drawn by Elijah Warner in the late summer of 1823 and reproduced here as Figure 5.12. It is a road map of the most basic sort, having few points of reference to link it to familiar places in the geography of Mackinac Island. To provide some frame of reference, the National

Archives copy of Lieutenant William S. Eveleth's 1817 "Map of the Island of Michilimackinac" (Fig. 5.13) is reproduced with the Warner survey. Although drafted six years earlier, it includes most of the thoroughfares surveyed in 1823 and is laid out on a similar compass heading. Matching the roads on the two compositions can be done, but it will present something of a puzzle, even for readers intimately familiar with Mackinac Island.

The island was crisscrossed with roads and trails by 1823, and visitors moved with relative ease as they toured natural and historical sites. During his stop in August 1826, Thomas McKenney accompanied post surgeon Richard S. Satterlee on a daylong pony trek. The pair rode from Arch Rock and Robinson's Folly to Sugar Loaf and Skull Cave, then on to Fort Holmes, Croghan's battlefield, and British Landing. Returning to the village along the southwestern shore, McKenney recorded the earliest description of Chimney Rock and Devil's Kitchen (he called it "Manitoulin rock").[80] Much of his route followed established tracks. Figure 5.12 depicts only major roads, but parts of McKenney's course can be traced on it.

The Warner map is probably only one surviving example of an exercise carried out periodically to properly record highways authorized by the borough. Attached to the map—what Warner described as a "protractor plot"—are several sheets giving the courses and distances of six illustrated road segments and a few marginal comments. All of the roads are outside the village, so the street plan along Haldimand Bay is not shown. The descriptive notes of another Warner road survey, conducted in June and July 1827, have also been preserved. Unfortunately, no "protractor plot" survives to illustrate its courses and distances.[81]

Figure 5.12 has only five geographical points of reference. "Lake Huron" is written three times along the left side of the map to identify spots on the southwestern shore of the island. The back of Fort Mackinac is labeled "Fort gate." The "SE Cor. Jno. [John] Laird garden" marks the intersection of Market Street and Cadotte Avenue. A short segment of road between Laird's corner and "Lake Huron" is described in the field notes as "a continuation of Main Street so called" and represents modern Market Street from the foot of Cadotte to its termination at the lakeshore. The longer road tending northwest from Laird's garden is modern Cadotte Avenue with a segment splitting off to cross the future "Borough Lot" (site of today's public school) to the lake. This led to the old LeBarron distillery below today's Grand Hotel swimming pool.

Once past the two shorter road segments, Cadotte Avenue climbs "Grand Hill" to its intersection with Huron and Annex roads. From that point, one long loop turns northeast across David

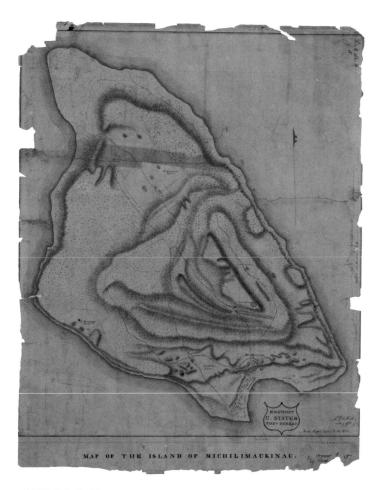

FIGURE 5.12

TITLE: [On verso:] Survey, Report & field Notes of Certain roads on the Island of Michilimackinac.

AUTHOR: Elijah Warner (active 1823–27).

DATE DEPICTED: September 20, 1823.

DATE OF WORK: September 20, 1823.

DESCRIPTION: 62.5 x 40.5 cm. Pen and ink on paper. Signed and certified on field notes by: Elijah Warner surveyor.

PROVENANCE: Filed September 22, 1823, by F. Hinchman, clerk to commissioners.

COLLECTION: City of Mackinac Island, Stuart House Museum, Mackinac Island, MI (Archive, Box E).

FIGURE 5.13

TITLE: Map of the Island of Michilimackinac.

AUTHOR: Lieutenant William Sanford Eveleth, Corps of Engineers (active 1813–d. 1818).

DATE DEPICTED: November 25, 1817.

DATE OF WORK: [November 25, 1817].

DESCRIPTION: 64 x 50.5 cm. Pen and ink with gray wash shading on paper. Signed below neat line: Drawn by W. S. Eveleth. Endorsed at lower right: Charles Gratiot.

PROVENANCE: This map bears a stamp for the Engineer's Department, Topographical Bureau. It is probably the copy submitted to the chief of engineers with a letter from Major Charles Gratiot to Brigadier General Joseph G. Swift of November 25, 1817.

COLLECTION: National Archives and Records Administration, College Park, MD (RG 77, Records of the Office of the Chief of Engineers, Fortifications Map File, Drawer 1, Sheet 4-5).

Mitchell's farm (claim 110) to the gate of Fort Mackinac. It then turns north in a wide arc following the Sugar Loaf Road of recent times past the huge rock, connecting by modern Juniper Trail to today's Scott's Cave Road, and terminating at British Landing, designated by the northernmost "Lake Huron" notation. The only landmark mentioned in the field notes along this route is "the dug way so called," a name that is still applied locally to the place where Scott's Cave Road descends the bluff near its intersection with Tranquil Bluff Trail—"Dugway Hill."

Another road segment begins at British Landing, continues up modern British Landing Road through Michael Dousman's farm, and then inclines southeast along modern Cadotte Avenue through "Harrisonville" back to the intersection of Huron, Cadotte, and Annex. An outer loop to the southwest follows modern Annex and Airport roads past the John Dousman farm to reconnect with Cadotte. A short spur to the southwest cuts through John Dousman's property, descending the steep bluff to the lakeshore by another cut also called "the dugway." This was described, in 1832, as leading to "the fishing ground," probably the spot where Dousman and later owners launched boats to tend their gill nets.[82]

Nearly all of these features, including the Mitchell farm and the two Dousman properties, can be found on the Eveleth map (Fig. 5.13). Modern Garrison Road, leading from Fort Mackinac past Skull Cave to British Landing Road, is not included in Warner's survey. No explanation is given for its absence. Nor is there any indication of a road to the heavily visited site of Fort Holmes. Perhaps these routes, both shown on the Eveleth map, were considered the responsibility of the military garrison.

Upon completion of his survey, on September 20, 1823, Elijah Warner certified its accuracy and filed it with the clerk of the road commission. He followed the same procedures with his survey of 1827. This recorded six additional sections of Mackinac Island's road net in and around the town, including a street from the new Ste. Anne's Church (at modern Main and Church) leading up the east bluff to the back of Fort Mackinac.[83] Most of these "highways" remain in use today.

A different sort of mapping was undertaken a few weeks after Warner completed his road survey. Late in the evening of October 4, the boats carrying Major Stephen H. Long and his companions arrived at Michilimackinac after a "fatiguing days voyage" from St. Joseph Island. Long was on the return leg of an exploration of the sources of the Minnesota River and the Lake Superior boundary of the United States. His party spent the next three days on Mackinac Island, staying at the "mansion of the American Fur Company" as guests of Robert Stuart, Astor's resident agent. While awaiting a vessel to Detroit, Long and his men explored the island, visiting the natural and historic sites like so many others before and since. Finally, on October 7, the major arranged passage on the revenue cutter *A. J. Dallas,* bound for winter quarters in Erie, Pennsylvania.[84]

Although no details are provided in his journal, Major Long apparently spent some of his time preparing a rough map of part of the Straits of Mackinac. His sketch was later copied by Dr. John J. Bigsby, who reduced it to the same scale as his own map of Lake Huron prepared during his service as a British member of the international boundary survey team. Sometime after the publication of Bigsby's reminiscences, *The Shoe and Canoe,* in 1850, his version of Long's sketch was tipped into a copy of the book that was probably intended as a model for a revised edition (Fig. 5.14).

Long's sketch map is unremarkable other than that it defines, with fair accuracy, the circumferences of Mackinac and Round islands. Long also calculated the distances to Mackinac Island from four points on the two mainlands. One of his landmarks is described as "Campbell's," the sawmill on Mill Creek on the south shore of the Straits. Robert Campbell had begun to develop this complex sometime in the mid-1780s, and ownership was confirmed to his heirs as private claim 334. In 1808 it included cultivated lands, "houses, mills, and other improvements" and was known popularly as "Campbell's farm."[85] Although Michael Dousman had purchased the land and improvements in 1819, it would seem from Long's map that local usage continued to refer to the previous owner.[86]

Major Long's visit produced other Mackinac images. Samuel Seymour (active 1796–1825) accompanied his expedition in the capacity of artist. Although Mackinac Island was simply a stopping point on their return trip, Seymour found some of its scenery interesting enough to record. On October 6, Major Long noted in his journal that his artist had done sketches of Sugar Loaf and Arch Rock as well as "an interesting view of the Village and Fort."[87] Seymour was then contracted to complete finished drawings for publication with Long's report. The book appeared in 1824, authored by William Keating and titled *Narrative of an Expedition to the Source of St. Peter's River . . . in the Year 1823.* While it included engravings of some of Seymour's views, the artist was slow to finish another twenty-two illustrations, which were not delivered to Long until April 1825. These included a "Distant view of Mackinac I." and a "View of Sugar Loaf Rock, Mack. I." Although Long admitted that they were "very well executed, and make very handsome pictures," he felt himself under no obligation to accept art that had been completed too late to be used as intended.[88] The disposition of Seymour's Mackinac drawings is unknown, and they have not been located in known collections of his work.

The handwritten sketch/map contains:

sketch made by
Long; reduced to
ale of Dr. Bigsby's
of L. Huron.

Circumf: of
Mackinac Isle $7\frac{60}{100}$ *miles*
Do. of Round Isle $3\frac{92}{100}$ *m.*

Pt. Ignace   Mackina I.
Old Fort / Fort / Town
Pt. La Barke   Bois Blanc I.
Round I.
Old Ft. Mackina
Campbells

Scale —

Courses and Distances —

1.   S 87° W — 3,40 *miles*/100
2. — S 80 W — about 8 1/4 *miles*
3. — S 50 W — about 7 *miles*
4. — S 20 W — 6 85/100 *miles*
5.   S 10 W — 75/100 *m.*
6. ———— 38/100 *m.* ————

FIGURE 5.14

TITLE: Circumf. of Mackinac Isle Do. of Round Isle.

AUTHOR: Dr. John Jeremiah Bigsby (1792–1881) after Major Stephen Harriman Long, Corps of Topographical Engineers (1784–1864).

DATE DEPICTED: October 5–7, 1823.

DATE OF WORK: 1823 to as late as ca. 1850.

DESCRIPTION: 11.8 x 19.2 cm. Pen and ink on paper.

PROVENANCE: Tipped into a unique, grangerized edition of Bigsby, *The Shoe and Canoe* (London, 1850), 2. Acquired by Library and Archives Canada sometime before 1920. The dealer who sold the book described it as the author's own copy, and it bears an inscription on the cover: "To Sir James McGrigor Bart. F.G.S. with the cordial and grateful Thanks of the Author."

COLLECTION: Library and Archives Canada, Ottawa, ON (1939-447-89/90).

An important provision of the Treaty of Ghent, which ended the War of 1812, was that the United States and Great Britain jointly survey and clarify the international boundary line through the Great Lakes. Joseph Delafield (1790–1875), a former army officer, was a member of the U.S. team. He visited the Straits of Mackinac on at least four occasions between 1820 and 1823, recording details in his journal each time. This engraving depicts him late in his life. *Clements Library, University of Michigan.*

Topographical engineer Major Stephen Harriman Long (1784–1864) paused at Mackinac for three days in October 1823 on his return from explorations in northern Minnesota and along Lake Superior. He used some of his time to determine the circumference of Mackinac and Round islands, while his expedition artist, Samuel Seymour (active 1796–1825), made sketches of Mackinac Island. Long was painted from life in 1819 by Charles Willson Peale. *Independence National Historical Park.*

A habitation of Zion's children

Amanda White Ferry

Thomas Loraine McKenney was immensely proud of the huge canoe that had carried him down the St. Marys River and would bear him across Lake Huron to Michilimackinac. Having spent the summer of 1826 with Governor Lewis Cass, traveling and in council with the Indians at Fond du Lac on Lake Superior, McKenney and his companions were on their return voyage to Detroit. At Sault Ste. Marie they boarded a newly painted, thirty-six-foot-long canoe acquired at Fond du Lac. Ten paddlers propelled the five-foot-wide craft, which was equal to the largest of those used in the Lake Superior fur trade.

"The canoe would be an object of interest anywhere, even without paint," McKenney wrote, "but now, ornamented as it is, it is really striking in its effects on all eyes." Around the sides, on a white ground, ran "a festoon of green and red paint," and the "rim" or gunwale was colored in alternating green, red, and white. Each side of the high bow featured "the bust of an Indian chief, smoking, even larger than life." McKenney, Cass, and their fellow passengers sat comfortably beneath an awning also painted in green, red, and white, while the flag of the United States flew from the stern. Emblazoned along both sides of the canoe was "FOND DU LAC," painted in large letters.

At 5:30 on the morning of August 27 this glorious vessel set out from a campsite six miles west of Detour. Two hours later, the island of Michilimackinac appeared on the horizon. The canoe made the traverse to Goose Island before a "fresh breeze" and "over a high and rugged swell." Once at Goose Island, however, McKenney could see that the turbulent waters between it and their destination unsettled the voyageurs. One even refused to proceed, saying that his passengers "knew nothing of the danger." An hour later they agreed to make the attempt, and though the lake was "boisterous beyond what we had expected," McKenney reported, the canoe reached Mackinac Island about 2:30 that afternoon, aided by showers of rain that calmed the waves.[89] Unknowingly, his rough crossing had duplicated that of Alexander Henry sixty-five years before.

McKenney was on the lakes that summer for a number of reasons, not the least of which was the fulfillment of his duties as head of the Office of Indian Affairs, organized two years before under the War Department.[90] Michilimackinac had an Indian agency, but McKenney was most interested in the school for Indian and Métis children founded three years before by the Reverend William Ferry. His travels resulted in a popular book, published in 1827 and containing a pair of images illustrating his visit to Mackinac Island.

Judging by the author's enthusiasm for his canoe, it is likely that he took special pains to include Figure 5.15. It depicts the bark vessel with Mackinac Island in the background. This image was prepared from two sources. McKenney had commissioned an Indian to make a model of a canoe, down to the paddles and awning, which he later presented to Secretary of War James Barbour. Before giving the model to his superior, however, McKenney had Lieutenant John Farley draw a sketch of it, which served as the basis of this lithograph.[91] McKenney's description of the paint scheme seems to have inspired whoever colored the copy illustrated here. The backdrop of Mackinac Island, seen from the northeast, was based on a sketch made by Lieutenant William S. Eveleth in 1817. McKenney probably obtained a copy during his visit to Michilimackinac, and he referred to it twice in his description of the place.[92] Although no finished sketch by Eveleth is known to survive, the land behind the canoe was probably taken from the vertical cross sections included on the right side of both copies of his map (Figs. 4.7 and 5.13).

The source of McKenney's second view of the island (Fig. 5.16) is less certain. It is too crude to have been copied from one by Lieutenant Eveleth. Its only detail is the brilliantly whitewashed bulk of Fort Mackinac. Like most visitors, McKenney was told that "Michilimackinac" meant "Great Turtle." On this point, he wrote, "The figure of the island, its top resembling the shell of a turtle, would confirm the supposition."[93] It seems most likely that Figure 5.16 was derived from a sketch made in August 1826, either by McKenney or by Detroit artist James Otto Lewis, who accompanied the delegation. It is less likely to have been based on a "sketch of Michillimackinac" by Captain David Bates Douglass that Governor Cass attempted to borrow on McKenney's behalf in September 1826.[94]

McKenney and Cass were met at the wharf by Robert Stuart of the American Fur Company, who entertained them with a dinner and a brief visit to Ferry's mission school. Although McKenney often found himself at odds with Astor's company, he and Stuart shared an interest in the goals of evangelical Protestant Christianity. Stuart and his wife were supporters of Ferry's efforts, both at the school and in establishing a Protestant congregation on Mackinac Island. McKenney was eager to learn more of Ferry's activities, but the weather continued nasty on August 28, and the day was spent with the officers of Fort Mackinac. They were occupied in preparations to observe the passing of Thomas Jefferson and John Adams, who had died within hours of each other on July 4, the fiftieth anniversary of the Declaration of Independence. Clear weather on the morning of July 29 was greeted with a salute of thirteen guns from Fort Mackinac followed by "minute guns" fired each half hour as a sign of mourning. The clouds soon returned, however, and lightning and thunder

INDIAN CANOE.

FIGURE 5.15

TITLE: Indian Canoe.

AUTHOR: Lithograph by F. Stewart [or Steward] from a sketch of the canoe by Lieutenant John Farley, 1st Regiment of Artillery (1802 or 1803–1874), and a sketch of Mackinac Island by Lieutenant William Sanford Eveleth, Corps of Topographical Engineers (active 1813–d. 1818).

DATE DEPICTED: August 1826.

DATE OF WORK: 1827.

DESCRIPTION: 9.6 x 16 cm. Lithograph. This example has been colored.

PROVENANCE: Lieutenant Farley sketched the canoe from a model made for Thomas L. McKenney by an elderly Indian. McKenney later presented the model to Secretary of War James Barbour. The background of Mackinac Island from the northeast is based on a sketch by Lieutenant Eveleth. McKenney had a copy in his possession in August 1826. Stewart's lithograph was produced for Pendleton's Lithography in Boston to illustrate McKenney, *Sketches of a Tour to the Lakes* (Baltimore, 1827). The Clements Library has two copies. The colored image reproduced here is pasted to a sheet tipped in before page 285 in copy 2. An uncolored example faces page 200 in copy 1.

COLLECTION: Clements Library, University of Michigan, Ann Arbor (Book Division, C2-1827-Mc, copy 2).

VIEW of MICHILIMACKINAC

FIGURE 5.16

TITLE: View of Michilimackinac.
AUTHOR: Possibly James Otto Lewis (1799–1858)
or Thomas Loraine McKenney (1785–1859).
Lithograph by Moses Swett (active 1826–37).
DATE DEPICTED: August 1826.
DATE OF WORK: 1827.
DESCRIPTION: 9.5 x 15.9 cm. Lithograph.
PROVENANCE: Lithographed by Swett at
Pendleton's Lithography in Boston and included in
McKenney, *Sketches of a Tour to the Lakes* (Baltimore,
1827). The Clements Library has two copies. The
image reproduced here faces page 384 in copy 2.
The example in copy 1 faces page 385.
COLLECTION: Clements Library, University of
Michigan, Ann Arbor (Book Division, C2-1827-Mc,
copy 2).

Thomas Loraine McKenney
(1785–1859) was director of the
two-year-old Department of
Indian Affairs when he stopped
at Mackinac Island in 1826.
McKenney was an advocate of
Indian education, and his trip
resulted in an influential book,
Sketches of a Tour to the Lakes,
published in 1827. While at
Mackinac, McKenney was
particularly interested in
inspecting the Reverend William
Ferry's three-year-old mission
school. McKenney is shown in the
frontispiece of his 1846 book,
Memoirs Official and Personal.

Clements Library, University of Michigan.

THE INDIAN SORCERESS.

Mission Station at Mackinaw.

FIGURE 5.17
TITLE: Mission Station at Mackinaw.
AUTHOR: Unknown.
DATE DEPICTED: 1825–29.
DATE OF WORK: Published ca. 1830.
DESCRIPTION: 5.5 x 7.2 cm. Woodcut.
PROVENANCE: Published in American Tract Society, *Eliza: The Indian Sorceress* (n.p., [1830]), title page.
COLLECTION: Clements Library, University of Michigan, Ann Arbor (Book Division, C2 1830 Am Tract).

echoed the cannon fire, providing a suitably melancholy effect.[95]

Thomas McKenney inspected the mission school later that afternoon, and he described the complex depicted in Figure 5.17. He thought the buildings "admirably adapted" to their purpose. McKenney's details of the largest of them, the "Mission House," appear to have been obtained from Reverend Ferry. Although it was a unified structure, most descriptions treat the Mission House as three separate buildings. "They are composed of a center and two wings," McKenney wrote. The one-and-one-half-story center measured 84 by 21 feet. A pair of two-story wings of 32 by 44 feet flanked the central block. "Every thing in the building is plain," McKenney reported, and the structure has a distinctly New England look, reminiscent of the architecture introduced to Mackinac Island with the American Fur Company buildings constructed in 1819–22.[96]

Figure 5.17 appeared about 1830. The little woodcut depicts Ferry's complex as it was in the late 1820s, before the construction of Mission Church as seen in the similar engraving (Fig. 6.2) first published in 1835. The artist is unknown, but it might have been Amanda Ferry, who drew and who sent a "rough sketch of our situation relative to the village" to a correspondent in August 1825 while the house was under construction.[97] "The prospect is delightful," Sarah Tuttle wrote, "the surrounding shores are a hard beach, covered with bright shining pebbles," and the location "a short distance from the village towards the east," nestled beneath the bluff and Robinson's Folly. By 1826, outbuildings and garden plots filled the gently sloping land around the mission.[98]

Ferry had brought his family to Mackinac Island in 1823, arriving on October 19 and soon renting a house from an "Indian woman," who continued to reside in part of it.[99] She was Magdelaine La Framboise, whom Mrs. Ferry described as the "widow of a Frenchman" and who cared for the children of her deceased daughter and former Fort Mackinac commandant Captain Benjamin K. Pierce.[100] Mrs. Ferry later described their rented lodgings and school as "a small incommodious building." This was the Federal-style residence built by Captain Pierce for his mother-in-law in 1820 (see Fig. 7.17).[101] The house, grand by the standards of Michilimackinac, was small only for the purpose envisioned by the Ferrys.

Early in April 1825 Reverend Ferry received the letter he had been awaiting. The American Board of Commissioners for Foreign Missions authorized him to survey land for a building to accommodate a student body of 150 and the mission "family." Ferry completed his surveys and sailed for Detroit to obtain workmen and materials. Other correspondence arrived during his absence that first, to the consternation of Mrs. Ferry, reversed the decision but then, to her relief, allowed the project to proceed. By early July the framework of the building was ready to be erected.[102] In August the house was dedicated as "sacred for religious institution and for a habitation of Zion's children, and as an asylum as are already or are to hereafter be gathered in from the wilderness."[103] The mission family and students occupied the still-incomplete building in November.[104]

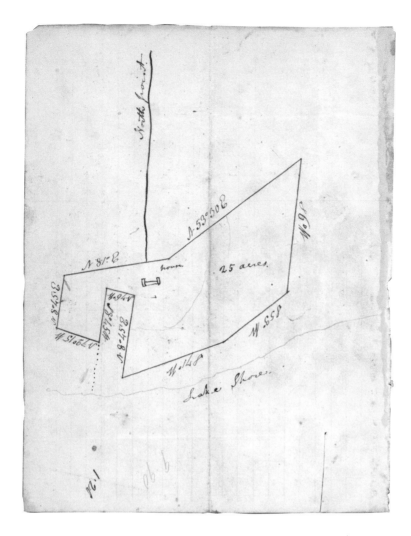

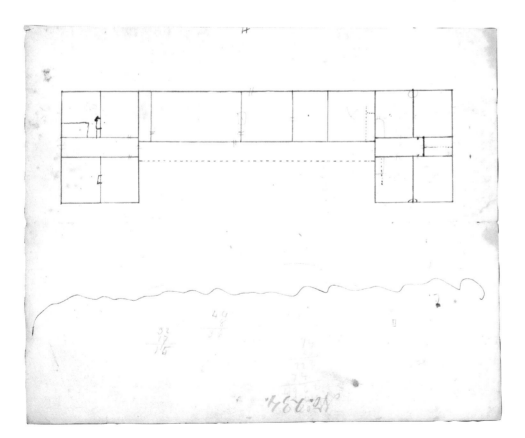

The land for the mission is illustrated in Figure 5.18, a rough survey probably drawn by Ferry himself. The large, irregular parcel was located beyond the village on federal property at Mission Point. Ferry was of the understanding that two-thirds of the cost of constructing his school would be provided by the government, probably because of the perceived benefits to Indian education. The Office of Indian Affairs was willing to allow the use of War Department land. Ferry had requested public ground for his school as early as the winter of 1823, and this was allowed by Congress in March 1826 by a bill "granting the right of occupancy" to the missionary society.[105] The land remained federal property.

The building shown on the survey was detailed in a ground floor plan (Fig. 5.19) sent by Reverend Ferry to a correspondent in September 1827. Although its covering letter identifies individual rooms by numbers, these do not appear on this copy of the plan. However, the neatly drafted sketch suggests how the building was laid out. The ground floor of the west wing (left) included a common sitting room, two family rooms, and a sewing room for girls. Above were bedrooms and hospital rooms for boys and girls. The center had dormitories on the upper level, and the ground floor included (left to right) a passage from the piazza to the backyard, a common dining room, kitchens, and a family room. The ground floor of the east wing had four family rooms and a clothing storeroom. The floor above accommodated four classrooms with removable partitions that allowed the space to be opened up for Sunday worship.

The basement contained provisions storage, carpenters' and shoemakers' shops, and a "dirty boys lodging room."[106]

Thomas McKenney was impressed by what he had seen of the Mackinac mission and could speak of Ferry and his accomplishments only "in terms of unqualified approbation." He departed with just one negative thought, which was that the world was changing for the children who would be taught at Ferry's school. McKenney feared that once they had been educated, "there will be no homes for them to go to; and no theatre for them on which they can turn their acquirements to any profitable account." Lands, farming implements, and agricultural and mechanical training would be necessary, he thought, to assimilate them into the expanding American society. Such assistance would have to come from government, he believed, and then inquired, "what, I will ask, could add more to the glory of our country?"[107]

With his business completed, McKenney toured the sights of Mackinac Island. On the morning of August 30 he again boarded his colorful canoe and headed for Twelve Mile Point (Lighthouse Point) on Bois Blanc Island. There, the wind having freshened once again, the travelers took a "basket of provisions" to the beach for a picnic, joined by the captain of the government revenue cutter that had followed the canoe. After a pleasant hour ashore, McKenney, Governor Cass, and the others rounded the eastern end of Bois Blanc, bid farewell to the Straits of Mackinac, and set their course for Detroit.

Thomas McKenney's 1846 *Memoirs* included this idealized image of a class being taught in an Indian school. Although published two decades after McKenney's Mackinac visit, the scene suggests how the interior of the Mission House might have appeared when Ferry's school was in operation. *Clements Library, University of Michigan.*

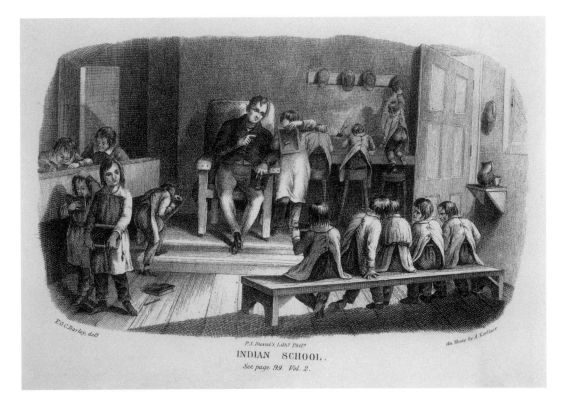

INDIAN SCHOOL.
See page 99 Vol. 2.

The present Fort of Mackinac should be repaired, and not abandoned

Major Alexander Ramsay Thompson

Mary Nexsen Thompson had retired to her berth when she was called to have her first look at Fort Mackinac. It was shortly past midnight on July 5, 1822, and the steamer *Superior* had just entered the calm, moonlit harbor. "Never did I behold a more sublime and picturesque scene," she wrote to a friend. Her attention was drawn to "the high situation of the fort, which stands 160 feet above the level of the water—the walls & buildings of which are white." These stood out from the dark bluff in "the reflection of the moon, which Seemed to Shine this night with increased brightness," giving all "a sublime & majestic appearance."[108]

Mary Thompson was traveling with her husband, Captain Alexander Ramsay Thompson, and she would come to know Fort Mackinac well. The captain was on his way to Sault Ste. Marie to supervise construction of Fort Brady. Four years later, Thompson would take command of Fort Mackinac, and he and his wife would see all the faults behind its romantic, moonlit facade. By 1822 the condition of the fort belied Mrs. Thompson's first impression. "This Fort is very old and going fast to ruin," Lieutenant Henry Bayfield wrote that summer.[109] Details of individual buildings paint an even grimmer picture. By 1825, broken or missing windowpanes were everywhere. The roofs were worn out. The piazzas of the officers' quarters were rotting away. The "company Quarters"—the log barracks from Old Michilimackinac—was "in such a state of decay as to be entirely unfit for Occupancy." The guardhouse required

"considerable repairs," and all three blockhouses had foundation problems. One even had "the appearance of falling."[110]

Worst of all was the post hospital. In 1824, Dr. William Beaumont declared it "wholly unfit even for the most ordinary uses of healthy men." The building was so deteriorated, he reported, "that every Shower in Summer, drenches the walls of the sick wards with rains, every storm in winter fills them with Snow, & the high winds of every season choak them with *Soot, Smoke & ashes*." The building was "nothing but an old Shackling store house" and had, in fact, been constructed for that purpose at Old Michilimackinac in 1773.[111] It probably came into use as a hospital following construction of a new commissary storehouse below the fort in 1819. By 1826 an inspector described the building as "a perfect barn" that leaked so badly that "during a rain the bunks of the patients are moved about from place to place to avoid the wet."[112]

The appalling condition of Fort Mackinac was due to indecision over whether to retain the post, particularly after the establishment of Fort Brady. By the winter of 1826 the matter had finally been resolved in favor of maintaining a garrison on Mackinac Island.[113] What, then, was to be done about a fort that was nearly uninhabitable? Two possibilities presented themselves: it could be repaired or rebuilt at another location. Figures 5.20–5.22 illustrate the two concepts. Relocation seems to have been the option first embraced by the quartermaster general. The fact that planning did not involve the

Major Alexander Ramsay Thompson (1793–1837) commanded Fort Mackinac in 1826–28 and again in 1832–33. Thompson directed the construction of Fort Brady at Sault St. Marie in 1822, and, during his first Fort Mackinac command, he supervised an ambitious program of building and renovations in the aging fort. Portrait by an unknown artist. *Photograph courtesy of Linda Zimmermann. Original in a private collection.*

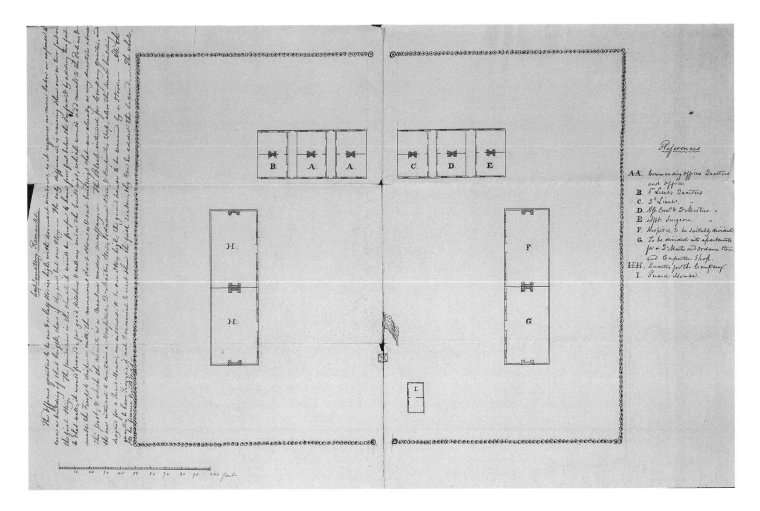

FIGURE 5.20

TITLE: [On verso:] Plan of a Cantonment
for one Company, at Mackinaw.
AUTHOR: [Major Alexander Ramsay
Thompson, 2nd Regiment of Infantry
(1793–1837)].
DATE DEPICTED: November 14, 1826,
proposal.
DATE OF WORK: November 14, 1826.
DESCRIPTION: 24.5 x 39.3 cm. Pen and ink
on paper.

PROVENANCE: Enclosed in letter from
Thompson to Quartermaster General Thomas
Jesup, November 14, 1826. Retained in the
records of the quartermaster general.
COLLECTION: National Archives and Records
Administration, Washington, DC (RG 92,
Records of the Office of the Quartermaster
General, Consolidated Correspondence File,
Fort Mackinac, Michigan. Found in Box 594).

FIGURE 5.21
TITLE: [Sketch of the new hospital in Fort Mackinac].
AUTHOR: [Mary Nexsen Thompson (1790–1858)].
DATE DEPICTED: October 1827.
DATE OF WORK: [October 1827].
DESCRIPTION: 15.5 x 20.5 cm. Pencil, pen, and ink with watercolor on paper.
PROVENANCE: Retained in the Thompson family papers until purchased by the Clements Library in 1998.
COLLECTION: Clements Library, University of Michigan, Ann Arbor (Print Division, G-15).

Office of the Chief of Engineers says much about the reduced military status of Fort Mackinac. It was the quartering of troops that mattered, not the strength of the defenses, which were acknowledged to be obsolete and commanded from Fort Holmes. This explains why no engineer was dispatched and no plans were drawn of Fort Mackinac during the 1820s.

Since defensibility seems not to have been a concern in identifying a new location for the garrison, what possibilities existed? The buildings of the village occupied the land at each end of Haldimand Bay, leaving only the government gardens below Fort Mackinac. This was the site Dr. Beaumont had recommended in 1824 for a new hospital, and the commissary storehouse and stable had already been placed there.[114] Convenience was the principal virtue of the position, since supplies, firewood, and water would not have to be hauled up the bluff. By July 1826 rumors were circulating in the village that a new military establishment would be constructed the following spring in the post gardens.[115]

The concept was approved in August when the adjutant general ordered Alexander Ramsay Thompson, by this time a major, to prepare plans and estimates for quarters for one company of soldiers "below the hill, on the ground occupied for Officers Gardens." The result was the neatly drawn plan illustrated here as Figure 5.20. Thompson followed his orders enthusiastically, noting that the storehouse and barn were already established "in a convenient place for the new buildings," and that there was room left for a woodyard.

He did his best to suggest ways in which the buildings could be "erected in a substantial and handsome manner, at very trifling expense." His troops would provide the labor. Stone for foundations and chimneys could be quarried from the nearby bluff. The soldiers could make shingles, and lime was available from a newly constructed kiln only a mile and a half from the post. Hardware could be salvaged from the old fort. Thompson had found such thrifty measures effective in the construction of Fort Brady in 1822. Only bricks and plank would have to be obtained elsewhere, the former from Green Bay and the latter from a mill at Sault Ste. Marie.[116] For some reason, the commandant chose not to use Michael Dousman's mainland sawmill.

The plan submitted by Major Thompson (Fig. 5.20) accommodated all the needs of a small garrison, aside from defense. Quarters for officers face Haldimand Bay. Barracks, a guardhouse, a hospital, and additional storerooms and shops complete the square. These are surrounded by a rudimentary stockade. Lacking blockhouses or bastions at the corners, or even firing platforms, it is little more than a substantial fence. This cantonment could not be made defensible at any rate, tucked as it was under the bluff and below Fort Mackinac.

The idea for a new post on "the flat" had its detractors. An inspecting officer noted the indefensibility of the location and the potential risk to a garrison.[117] By the beginning of January 1827 even Major Thompson, so enthusiastic about the new site in November, had changed his tune. He now recommended that "the present Fort of Mackinac should be repaired, and not abandoned," a task that could be accomplished with less expense. He had found that the garrison horses could transport wood and water up the hill, and the lower site would be "too much in the Village" with all its temptations.[118] Thompson's argument must have carried weight, for on March 12 the quartermaster general authorized him to repair the old fort and abandon plans for barracks on the lower ground.[119]

The wretched hospital was the first building to receive Thompson's attention. Its condition had become so bad that the surgeon had moved the sick to the officers' wooden quarters, although it was little better.[120] By May the troops were dismantling the old hospital to make room for a proper structure. The new building was enclosed by the end of August, even as repairs were being made to other parts of the fort.[121] The old barracks was also demolished, and the framework for its replacement was up and roofed by October.[122]

Sometime in September or October an artist created the watercolor illustrated here as Figure 5.21, the only image of any sort to depict Major Thompson's hospital of 1827. Although it is unsigned, the drawing was almost certainly the work of the commandant's wife, Mary. It was found among the Thompson family papers, and the style and treatment of architectural details are very like those in an 1819 watercolor of the barracks at Sackets Harbor, New York, identified as having been drawn by Mrs. Thompson.[123]

The watercolor depicts a building virtually identical to the hospital that stands today in Fort Mackinac. The chief difference is that the edifice in the painting is placed at right angles to the existing structure, on the same orientation as the old hospital and utilizing parts of its foundation.[124] As a result, the west blockhouse, which would be visible behind the 1828 hospital, is out of the picture at left. The log structure at right is a remnant of the old hospital, retained as a store for the post sutler.[125] The lack of detail in the windows suggests either that the sashes were not yet in place when Mrs. Thompson made her watercolor or, perhaps, that she simplified her drawing.

It was well that Mary Thompson pictured the new hospital. On the morning of October 31, 1827, when the building was about ten days from completion, it took fire.[126] The lack of water was a serious handicap in fighting the blaze, and the troops carried a "great quantity" up the bluff. Fortunately, it was a windless morning. Otherwise, Amanda Ferry wrote, "the whole village would have been consumed . . . as well as the buildings of the fort." Smoke billowed high above the walls, and sparks from the conflagration drifted to the southeast, setting the roofs of the officers' quarters afire as well as that of the storehouse at the foot of the bluff. The soldiers saved the west blockhouse by covering it with wet blankets, and the isolated blazes were extinguished. For the hospital and sutler Bailey's shop there was no hope, and both burned to the ground.[127]

Major Thompson was calm in the aftermath of the disaster,

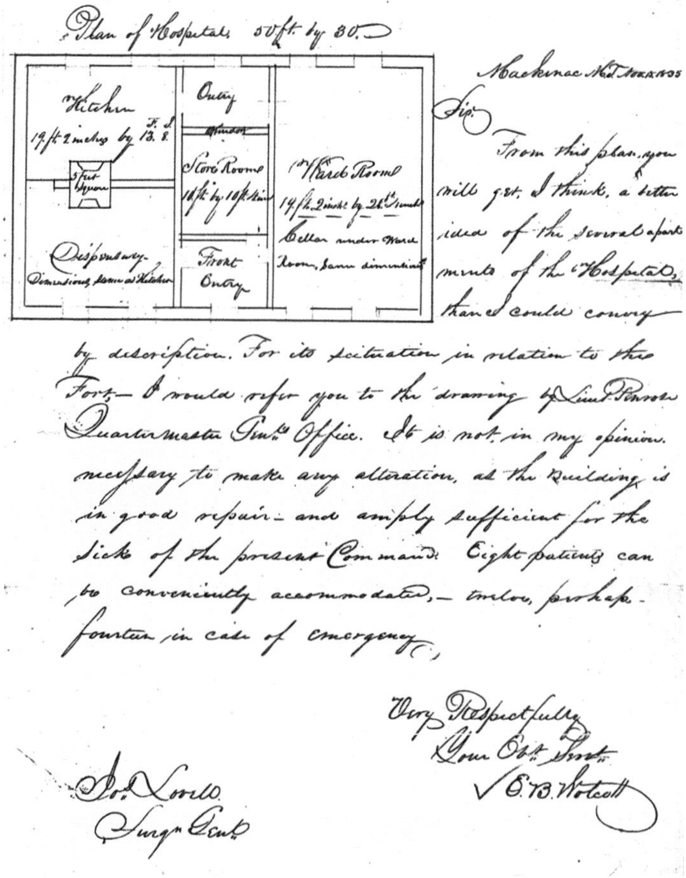

Sir,

From this plan, you will get, I think, a better idea of the several apartments of the Hospital, than I could convey by description. For its situation in relation to the Fort — I would refer you to the drawing of Lieut. Penrose Quartermaster Genl. Office. It is not in my opinion necessary to make any alteration, as the building is in good repair — and amply sufficient for the Sick of the present Command. Eight patients can be conveniently accommodated, — twelve, perhaps fourteen in case of emergency.

Very Respectfully
Your Obt. Servt.
E. B. Wolcott

Jos. Lovell
Surgn Genl.

FIGURE 5.22
TITLE: Plan of Hospital.
AUTHOR: Assistant Surgeon Erastus B. Wolcott (active 1835–39).
DATE DEPICTED: November 15, 1835.
DATE OF WORK: November 15, 1835.
DESCRIPTION: 9.2 x 12.6 cm. Pen and ink on paper.
PROVENANCE: Drawn into a letter from Wolcott to Surgeon General Joseph Lovell, dated at Mackinac, November 15, 1835. Retained in the records of the Office of the Adjutant General.
COLLECTION: National Archives and Records Administration, Washington, DC (RG 94, Records of the Office of the Adjutant General, Quarterly Reports of Sick and Wounded for Michigan Posts)

noting optimistically in his report that "the appropriation is still amply sufficient to complete everything at this post."[128] He forged ahead with his plan to renew Fort Mackinac. By the end of March 1828, materials were being gathered for another hospital, and the troops had occupied the new quarters on the site of the old log barracks.[129] The frame for the hospital had been erected by the end of June, and repairs had been completed to the magazine and blockhouses. Embarrassed by the lack of water to fight the hospital fire, Thompson put his men to work reopening the old British well.[130] This was a challenge, for the shaft was filled with rubbish to the depth of eighty feet. Further progress included repairing the road to the front of the fort.[131]

By September 1828, Major Thompson's time at Fort Mackinac was drawing to a close, and he chose to summarize his achievement, one of the most complete renovations that Fort Mackinac would receive during its years as a military post. "We have now erected and nearly finished seven new buildings, besides repairing the old ones," he informed Quartermaster General Jesup. These included replacement of the barracks, hospital, guardhouse, and blacksmith shop. Three other new structures—a bake house, carpenter shop, and ordnance storehouse—were combined into a long row along the east side of the fort. More remained to be done, but the transformation had been substantial.[132] Inspector General George Croghan (who had led the 1814 expedition against Michilimackinac) was impressed. "This in a short time will be esteemed the most

desireable of our Infantry posts," he wrote, and the new barracks made Fort Mackinac a comfortable billet for two companies.[133] Sadly, Major Thompson's project did not generate any further drawings or plans. Most of the new buildings would not appear on an image until 1845 (Fig. 7.21).

The one exception was the hospital, a plan of which was sketched in 1835 by Assistant Surgeon Erastus B. Wolcott to illustrate his opinions about the building (Fig. 5.22). Although drawn seven years after the completion of Major Thompson's second hospital, Wolcott's sketch probably reveals the original functions of its six rooms. The surgeon reported that it was not necessary to make any further alterations to the building, that it was in good condition, and that its ward capacity of eight patients—twelve in an emergency—was "amply sufficient for the sick of the present command."[134]

Major Thompson's successors completed his projects, and the appropriation for Fort Mackinac had been largely expended by October 1829. Unfortunately, at that time, Lieutenant Colonel Enos Cutler considered the officers' quarters insufficient for his two companies. He requested permission to convert the hospital to housing and to construct yet another building for the sick. As a hospital, he believed, the brand-new building had been "illy constructed and injudiciously located." Cutler's suggestion would require another appropriation of $5,000. This was not forthcoming, and Fort Mackinac would not have new officers' quarters until 1835 or a better hospital until 1860–61 (Fig. 8.41).

Major Thompson was accompanied by his wife, Mary Nexsen (1790–1858), throughout his service on the Great Lakes in the 1820s and 1830s. During her first visit to Mackinac Island, in July 1822, Mary watched from the piazza of the officers' quarters as Native Americans danced on the beach below. They probably appeared much as these Ojibwa warriors, pictured by James Otto Lewis at Prairie du Chien, Wisconsin, in 1825, as they performed the "pipe dance" and the "tomahawk dance." Colored lithograph by Lehman and Duval. *Clements Library, University of Michigan.*

Busily engaged . . . in surveying the Island of Bois-Blanc

Deputy Surveyor Lucius Lyon

For two months during the summer of 1827 Lucius Lyon ran surveys on Bois Blanc, the largest of the islands in the Straits of Mackinac. It was difficult and tedious work, made even more so by high water levels in Lake Huron and the "almost impervious thicket" that covered much of the island.[135] Flatter and swampier than Mackinac and Round islands, Bois Blanc had yet to receive the attention paid to other locations in the Straits. Unlike St. Ignace, Old Michilimackinac, or Mackinac Island, it had never been the site of a settlement. Bois Blanc served primarily as a source of raw materials—timber, firewood, lime, hay, and maple sugar—that were useful to the residents of the Straits.

This is not to say that Bois Blanc had been devoid of human activity. It had been a location for seasonal fishing and spring sugaring since prehistoric times. European occupation began in 1780, just as the post of Michilimackinac was being relocated to Mackinac Island. From that time, the resources of Bois Blanc increased in value as timber was stripped from Mackinac Island. Residents were cutting firewood there before the War of 1812, and Bois Blanc became the primary source of fuel for the army and the American Fur Company after 1815.[136]

The few visitors who recorded their impressions found Bois Blanc an attractive and potentially valuable place. Henry Schoolcraft camped at Point aux Pins on the south shore during his return voyage to Detroit in September 1820. He noted that the lower part of Bois Blanc was "a sandy plain covered with pitch pines," but that the island's soil was generally fertile. A mixed forest of elm, maple, oak, ash, and "white wood" (birch) covered most of it. Birch was the predominant tree and had given the island its name. There was also pasture, where the inhabitants of Michilimackinac grazed cattle and horses in the summer. Bois Blanc, Schoolcraft believed, was "a most valuable appendage" to that community.[137] The tangled thickets encountered by Lucius Lyon in 1827 were very likely in areas where the timber had been cut. Others, like Elizabeth Thérèse Baird, recalled that the woods were "notably clear of underbrush" in the early 1820s.[138]

By 1820 the large island had accumulated more history than was apparent to these visitors. The first non–Native American settler was Charles Gauthier, an interpreter for the commandant of Michilimackinac. In 1780 he established himself on the south shore, in the vicinity of Point aux Pins, by right of purchase from the Indians. Gauthier cleared land, built a house, and moved with his new bride to that isolated setting. He received a deed from Lieutenant Governor Sinclair in 1781, and Major Henry Burbeck reputedly supported the validity of his claim in 1796. By 1807, however, Gauthier had abandoned his farm and let the house go to ruin.[139]

Not long after Charles Gauthier occupied his holdings, Pierre Suissy and a man named Lagarcé or Lagarée were attracted to the western point of the island, probably because of its proximity to Mackinac. Both had cleared and cultivated lands prior to 1796 and constructed houses, stables, and outbuildings. The ubiquitous Michael Dousman purchased Lagarcé's plot in 1804, and he thereafter maintained it as a tenant farm. In 1808 Dousman applied to the Land Board for a deed. The commissioners at first postponed their decision, but, in 1810, after receiving additional evidence, they confirmed 640 acres as claim 323. Aaron Greeley surveyed it during his time at Michilimackinac that fall.[140] Suissy's adjoining property went to Joseph Latard in 1807, and he sold it to Dousman in 1823.[141]

These claims were on territory that had passed into U.S. ownership in 1795. When representatives of the Ojibwa signed the Treaty of Greenville that summer, they confirmed the government's right to Mackinac Island as well as reserves at the old post on the south mainland and at St. Ignace. The Ojibwas then presented Bois Blanc as "an extra and Voluntary gift" and reconfirmed it at a council with Major Burbeck in 1797.[142] Bois Blanc thus became federal property, while Round Island remained Ojibwa land until given up by treaty in 1836.[143] Federal ownership meant that Native American title had been extinguished, so the land was available for use or sale. Dousman thus had a valid right to claim 323 under the provisions of the various land acts of 1804–7.

The only problem was the army's determination to retain control of convenient sources of fuel and timber. Dousman's application was challenged, and although it appeared that claim 323 might be disallowed in the same fashion as his number 324 on Mackinac Island (Fig. 3.7), he was allowed to retain possession.[144] Further legislation in 1823 generated two additional claims on Bois Blanc Island. One, by Dousman, for the parcel recently purchased from Joseph Latard was confirmed. A claim by the "widow and heirs of Charles Gauthier" for the land around Point aux Pins was not. Despite a large volume of testimony in support of Magdaline Gauthier and her family, the commissioners did not consider themselves authorized to confirm her application because "no proof or notice of claim" had been given "within the time limited by law." They recommended instead that the Gauthiers receive a grant of up to 640 acres.[145]

Competition for the island's resources continued to increase. In January 1827 "the inhabitants of the Island of Michilimackinac" forwarded a petition to the General Land Office in Washington observing that "the island of Bois Blanc . . . contains a Considerable body of fine, well-timbered, arable land & that the island is generally susceptible of Cultivation." The surveyor general ordered Bois Blanc

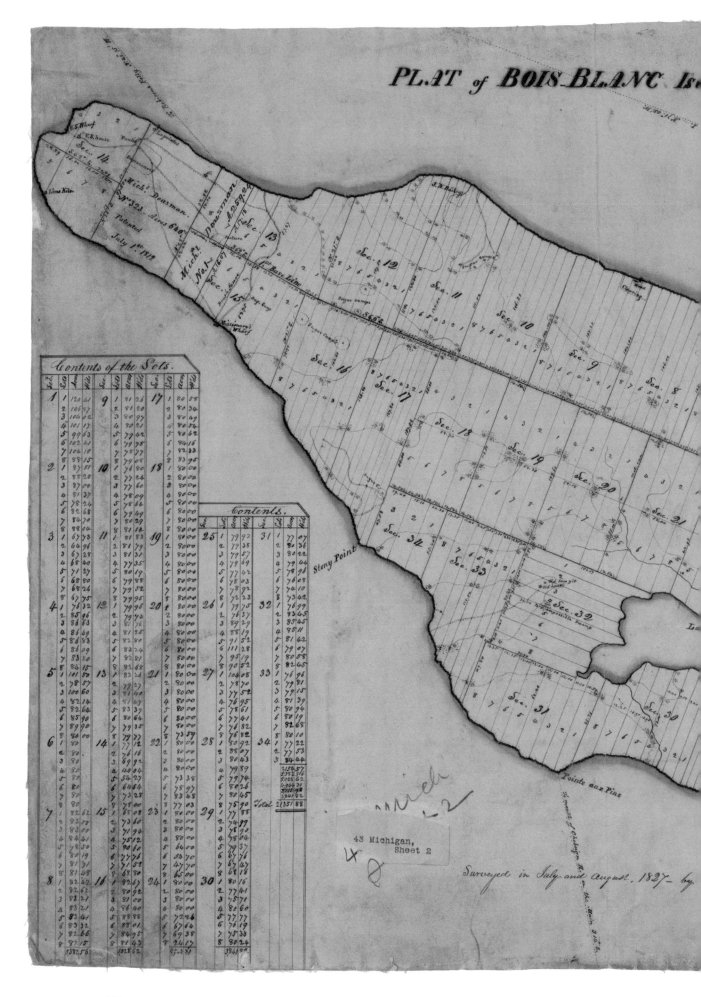

FIGURE 5.23

TITLE: Plat of Bois-Blanc Island, in the Streights of Michilimackinac. Surveyed in July and August 1827—by Lucius Lyon D.S.

AUTHOR: Lucius Lyon (1800–1851).

DATE DEPICTED: August 1827.

DATE OF WORK: [1827 or later].

DESCRIPTION: 44.8 x 57 cm. Pen and ink with watercolor outline on paper.

PROVENANCE: A copy of the original plat filed in the Surveyor General's Office in Chillicothe, Ohio, on October 5, 1827, and later in the General Land Office in Washington. Retained in the Records of the General Land Office.

COLLECTION: National Archives and Records Administration, College Park, MD (RG 49, Records of the Bureau of Land Management, Old Map File, Michigan 18).

surveyed. Well aware of the needs of the Fort Mackinac garrison, however, he instructed the deputy surveyor to consult with the commandant to learn what was "deemed by him necessary to reserve for the Supply of fuel to the U States."[146] Lucius Lyon, a young Vermonter who had moved to Michigan to work on its land surveys, heard a rumor that the island was to be mapped and volunteered for the job.[147] Compensation was set at a rate of three dollars per mile. Later that summer, after his two months of hard work, Lyon would complain that it was not enough and that his survey had been "unprofitable."[148]

Like any such work, Lucius Lyon's survey generated a number of maps, all reproduced from his original field plat. Even the official master map, submitted to the General Land Office with Lyon's field notes in September 1827, was a copy. His original "for the want of better paper at the time, was drawn on paste-board," Lyon admitted.[149] Figure 5.23 is a General Land Office copy of circa 1827. The master map in the General Land Office was traced many times, usually at the request of local authorities or landowners, and many versions no doubt survive in both public and private collections. The collections of the National Archives alone hold at least four, and one is known to be in private hands.

Aaron Greeley had roughly surveyed Bois Blanc in 1810, at least so far as to record Dousman's claim 323. Unfortunately, his field notes could not be found in Washington by 1827. The surveyor general could only forward a copy of part of Greeley's 1810 map showing the relationship of Bois Blanc to Mackinac Island and the mainland.[150] Using this as a starting point, Lyon surveyed the large island into thirty-four irregular sections. Lots within these sections varied in shape and area, but most of those along the coast were laid out in a style similar to the French "long lots" or "ribbon farms" common at Detroit and along the River Raisin. This guaranteed water frontage and access to transportation to prospective owners.

Two concerns of government are reflected on Figure 5.23. As instructed, Lyon consulted with Fort Mackinac's commandant on the matter of a wood reserve and noted the results on his plat. Sections 10–21 and 31–34 were "reserved to supply fuel for the garrison at Michilimackinac." This, with the exception of Dousman's claim 323, amounted to the western half of the island. Lyon deposited a copy of his plat with the garrison, and Major Alexander Ramsay Thompson immediately forwarded a duplicate to the adjutant general.[151] In addition to the reserve, Lyon's survey records some physical features relating to the harvesting of firewood by the army. In section 14, at the western end of the island, is the "U.S. Wharf," a limekiln, and the "U.S. House," a place to shelter work parties. Another pier, the "Missionary Wharf," projects into Lake Huron from section 15. This area was reserved for the garrison, but the missionaries obtained firewood there. The mission also cultivated "one or two fields" on Bois Blanc.[152] It is likely that these were in section 15, accessible from the "Missionary Wharf."

Section 5, encompassing the point on the north side of Bois Blanc, was reserved for a lighthouse. The citizens of Michilimackinac

Lucius Lyon (1800–1851) surveyed Bois Blanc Island during the summer of 1827. Lyon was new to Michigan at the time but later served as U.S. senator. The artist of this oil portrait has not been identified. *Clarke Historical Library, Central Michigan University.*

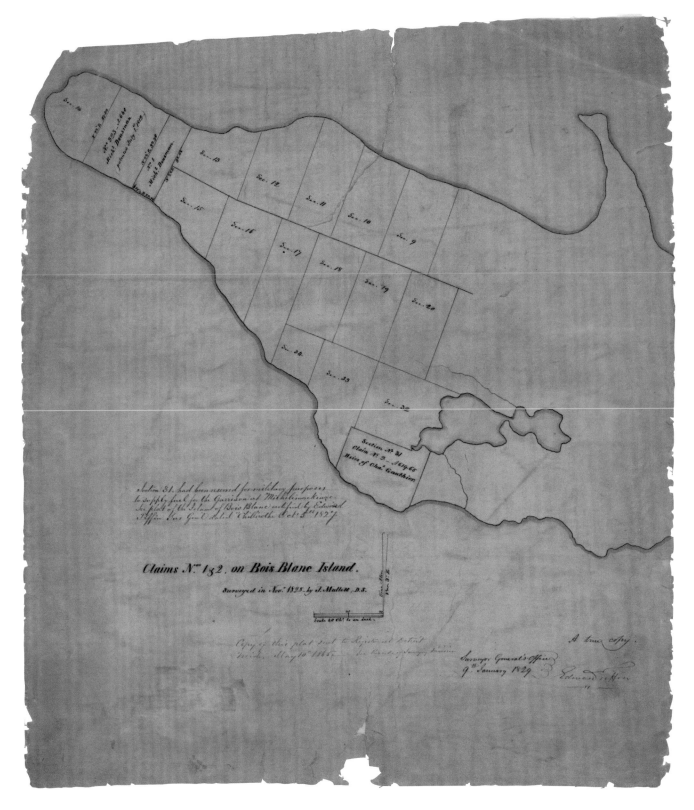

FIGURE 5.24

TITLE: Claims Nos. 1 & 2, on Bois Blanc Island.
Surveyed in Novr. 1828—by J. Mullett, D.S.
AUTHOR: John Mullett (1786–1862).
DATE DEPICTED: November 1828.
DATE OF WORK: January 9, 1829.
DESCRIPTION: 52.8 x 47.5 cm. Pen and ink on paper.

PROVENANCE: Copy presumed to have been sent
to General Land Office on January 9, 1829.
Retained in the records of the General Land Office.
COLLECTION: National Archives and Records
Administration, College Park, MD (RG 49, Records
of the Bureau of Land Management, Old Map File,
Michigan 19).

had petitioned for a beacon in December 1825, recommending that it be placed on "the twelve mile point" to mark dangerous shoals and the low coastline of Bois Blanc.[153] Lyon consulted with Major Thompson and Duncan Stuart, collector of the port of Michilimackinac, on the location and amount of land needed.[154] Both would have been familiar with the Twelve Mile Point site, which, on Lyon's map and thereafter, came to be called Lighthouse Point. A tower and keeper's house was constructed on the tip of the peninsula during the summer of 1829.[155]

Section 31, at Point aux Pins, was surveyed for the widow and heirs of Charles Gauthier. This property is shown in greater detail in Figure 5.24. John Mullett resurveyed these parcels in 1828 when he recorded the additional claims on Mackinac Island and at St. Ignace. The Gauthiers had originally claimed much of the eastern end of Bois Blanc, and Lyon found evidence of their farm in section 32. His map (Fig. 5.23) identifies an "old House" and "old Saw pit." According to Patrick McGulpin, the "remains" of the Gauthier house were still visible in 1823.[156]

Other uses of the island appear on Lyon's map, such as Jonathan N. Bailey's two sites on the north shore in sections 9 and 11. Of greater interest, however, are ten sugar camps in sections 10–12 and 15–17. Each is identified by a circular dotted line with a triangle in the center. Maple sugar making was an annual event in the Straits of Mackinac. "All who were able, possessed a sugar camp," according to Elizabeth Thérèse Baird, whose grandmother, Thérèse Schindler, had

one on Bois Blanc in the early 1820s. Around March 1 "about half" of the inhabitants of Michilimackinac would move to Bois Blanc to begin their preparations. The Schindler camp included a temporary building "made of poles or small trees, enclosed with sheets of cedar bark . . . about thirty feet long by eighteen feet wide." It was "delightfully situated in the midst of a forest of maple, or a maple grove," and the family tapped a thousand or more trees.[157] Lucius Lyon encountered evidence of the larger camps as he surveyed during the summer of 1827, and he noted them on his map.

Residents of Michilimackinac thought nothing of the trip to Bois Blanc, either by boat or by sleigh or dogsled after the lake had frozen. Elizabeth Baird held pleasant childhood memories of going in her "carriole, or dog sledge." "It was handsome in shape, with a high back, and sides sloping gracefully to the front," she remembered. "The outside color was a dark green, the inside a cream color, and the runners black," and it had been named "la Boudeuse" (the pouter), probably after its ten-year-old occupant. The sled was drawn by two dogs, Caribou and Nero, and driven by François Lacroix, a retainer of Elizabeth's grandmother. Years later she recalled the trip across the ice to Bois Blanc as "a delightful one" and the activities at the camp as "varied."[158] In spite of the work of sugar making, it was a harbinger of spring at the Straits and a lively part of Michilimackinac's social life.

INDIAN DOG TRAIN

This lithograph of a Great Lakes "dog train" closely matches Elizabeth Thérèse Baird's description of "La Boudeuse" ("the pouter"), the sled in which she traveled across the frozen Straits to her grandmother's sugar camp on Bois Blanc Island. It appeared in Thomas McKenney's *Sketches of a Tour to the Lakes* (Baltimore, 1827) and is a rare image of winter activities on the northern lakes. *Clements Library, University of Michigan.*

Began at a post on the border of Lake Huron

Deputy Surveyor John Mullett

On the morning of October 13, 1828, John Mullett prepared to survey a considerable portion of Mackinac Island. Acting in his official capacity as deputy surveyor, he was charged with establishing and mapping the boundaries of fifteen parcels claimed as private property under the land act of 1823. Altogether, these made up more than 940 acres, nearly 40 percent of the island. The properties included farms, village lots, and even a cemetery maintained by the parish of Ste. Anne.

The surveyor began by making an observation of the sun's "amplitude" to determine the local magnetic variation that would affect the compass he would use to establish the courses of the boundaries. Mullett found the variation to be two degrees, fifty-eight minutes east and made a record of that fact at the head of his field notes. His other primary tool was at hand—a sixty-six-foot-long, one-hundred-link surveyor's chain that, when stretched tight along an established course by his assistants, allowed him to record consistent distances in full "chains" with fractions expressed by a number of iron links. Now all that was needed was a place from which to begin.

For his base point, Mullett selected "a post on the border of Lake Huron, in the middle of Spring Street, in the village of Mackinaw." It was an appropriate location, standing between the private property of the village and the government ground below Fort Mackinac and near the spot where Patrick Sinclair had built his wharf and begun the development of Mackinac Island a half century before. Mullett's post stood between the modern Chippewa Hotel and State Park Visitor Center at the foot of a thoroughfare that has come to be known as Fort Street.[159] Sighting his compass and sending the chain men forward, Mullett recorded the northeastern boundary of the village—a bearing of north, forty-eight degrees west for a distance of six chains and eighty six links.

From that point the party worked around the perimeter of the village lots surveyed by Aaron Greeley in 1810. Their goal was to establish the outline of the military reserve in the southeastern part of the island. The fifteen claims all lay beyond its bounds. The route took them to Cadotte Avenue and around the eastern boundary of Dr. David Mitchell's claim 110. They followed the upper end of Cadotte (which then extended across today's airport) to British Landing Road and the land claimed by Michael Dousman. Measuring along Dousman's southeastern boundary to the lakeshore, they worked down the coast past "the Arch Rock" and "Folly Rock," through the east end of town, along Haldimand Bay, and finally back to the "place of beginning" in Spring Street.[160]

With the military reserve defined, Mullett began his survey of the parcels claimed as private property in 1823. He began with the largest, that of Michael Dousman, which he designated Private Claim 1. From there, surveying continued down the southwestern side of the island where claims 2 through 7 were carved from the "U.S. Lands" west and south of British Landing Road. The remaining eight properties were in the village. Corners were marked in a variety of ways, many of them perishable—wooden posts, a six-inch-diameter cedar tree, a birch, and so on.

Mullett's 1828 survey provided the information for the map illustrated here as Figure 5.25, a document that records, for the first time, extensive tracts of private property that can still be identified at the beginning of the twenty-first century. These include plots occupied by Grand Hotel (Private Claim 5), the Victorian cottages of Hubbard's Annex (claim 4), the newer developments at Woodbluff, and the Stonecliffe estate (claims 2 and 3). The greater part of Michael Dousman's Private Claim 1 was purchased by the State of Michigan in the 1920s and is preserved as parkland, although a few small pieces had been sold by that time. Mullett completed the process begun by Aaron Greeley in 1810 (Figs. 3.6 and 3.7) and, for the most part, he finalized the distinction between public and private lands on Mackinac Island. On October 22, Lieutenant Samuel P. Heintzelman watched the deputy surveyor finish his job by running the line for the military reservation.[161]

Mullett's finished map was submitted to the General Land Office in Washington as a record of the fifteen claims. Copies were thereafter easily and frequently made for official or private purposes. In 1830, for example, Fort Mackinac commandant Lieutenant Colonel Enos Cutler inquired, "how much of this island, Mackinaw, is actually and indisputably reserved by the United States?" To answer his question, George Graham of the General Land Office sent a copy of the Mullett plat to Secretary of War John H. Eaton.[162] Figure 5.25 is a General Land Office copy made in August 1842 for someone in the Straits area. At least six other nineteenth-century manuscript copies of the Mullett map have been identified in public and private collections, and it is very likely that others survive.[163] Simplified versions of the plat also had wide distribution as insets on John Farmer's popular maps of the surveyed parts of Michigan, first printed in this context in 1830.[164] Figure 5.26 is from the Farmer map of 1836.

John Mullett's survey was the culmination of the federal government's effort to deal with unresolved land claims in the Michigan Territory, some of which had escaped the pre–War of 1812 Land Board and Aaron Greeley's survey of 1810 (Figs. 3.6 and 3.7). Comprehensive surveying of Michigan began after the war. Before the land could be divided into regular, square sections for sale to new arrivals, however, the remaining developed parcels at existing

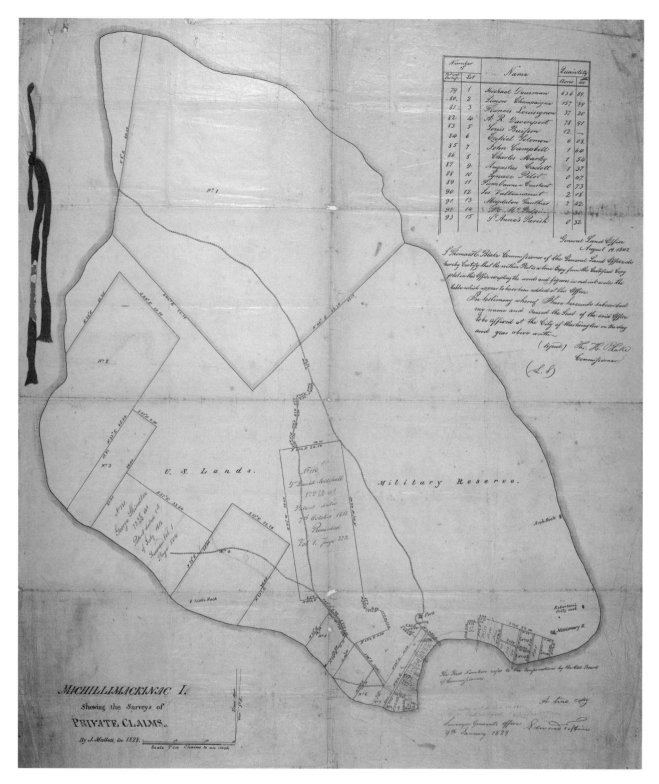

FIGURE 5.25

TITLE: Michillimackinac I. Shewing the Surveys
of Private Claims. By J. Mullett in 1828.
AUTHOR: John Mullett (1786–1862).
DATE DEPICTED: November 1828.
DATE OF WORK: August 19, 1842.
DESCRIPTION: 62.6 x 53.3 cm. Pen and ink
with watercolor on tracing linen.

PROVENANCE: A copy of the Mullett survey,
made in 1842 as per the notation at middle right
and provided to a local person in the Straits area.
Discovered in the Straits of Mackinac area and
donated to the Clements Library by Anna and
Clayton Timmons in 1999.
COLLECTION: Clements Library, University of
Michigan, Ann Arbor (Map Division, 6-O-16).

settlements—Detroit, River Raisin, Sault Ste. Marie, Green Bay, and the Straits of Mackinac—had to be documented and mapped. In 1820 Congress established a new land board to address unfinished business, but it was hamstrung by the loss of local records during the war. A special act of February 21, 1823, provided the solution. Owners who could prove occupancy of properties prior to July 1, 1812, and who had submitted to the authority of the United States during the British occupation of Michigan could claim up to 640 acres. Petitions had to be filed by October 1, 1823.[165]

The extension of an occupancy date from 1796, as specified in the 1807 land act, to 1812 had a significant impact on the remaining Straits of Mackinac land claims. Many of these plots, both on Mackinac Island and at St. Ignace, had been developed since 1796 and thus became eligible for confirmation. There were plenty of witnesses who could attest to the history of these properties. The matter of submission to U.S. authority during the War of 1812 was a touchier matter. Any citizen who had been allowed to remain at Michilimackinac during the war presumably took the British oath of allegiance. Perhaps that is why the land commissioners assumed loyalty on the part of claimants, unless they were challenged, and only six of the seventeen applications for Mackinac Island lands even mentioned the matter.[166] This seems to have been something of an open secret. "It is notorious that these claimants with perhaps a Single Exception were actively Engaged in the Service of the British, as contractors, Agents, or Soldiers during the late War,"

Jonathan N. Bailey complained to the commissioner of the General Land Office in 1827.[167] His protest was ignored, and the land question was soon resolved.

It did not all go smoothly, however, and the neatness and order of the Mullett map belie community tensions and hard feelings remaining from three years of British occupation. Testimony recorded in the application process suggests that wartime behavior was a complicated matter, and charges of collaboration were inevitable. A few claimants were in competition for the same parcels and, as Bailey further asserted, there was some question whether the lands described had, in fact, ever been developed or used as stated.[168]

Bailey's protests notwithstanding, only one island claim was challenged on the grounds of disloyalty before the application deadline. In June 1823 Samuel C. Lasley filed for a piece of land on the southwestern side of the island estimated to contain eight acres. Lasley claimed to have cleared, fenced, and cultivated this plot by May 1810 and to have "continued to submit to the authority of the United States." His application was supported by Augustine Cadotte, himself a claimant for a smaller piece of land (claim 9) near the western end of the village. The depositions were duly forwarded to the land commissioners in Detroit. A week before the October 1 deadline, however, Michael Dousman appeared before the commissioners, swore an oath, and proceeded to knock the pins from under Lasley's claim. "When the British troops took possession of the island of Michilimackinac," Dousman testified, Lasley "declared

Lieutenant Samuel P. Heintzelman (1805–80) watched surveyor John Mullett run the boundary line of the military reserve in the fall of 1828. A junior officer of the Fort Mackinac garrison, Heintzelman kept a detailed diary during his time there. He is shown as a brigadier general during the Civil War in an engraving by John C. Buttre after a photograph by Matthew Brady. *Clements Library, University of Michigan.*

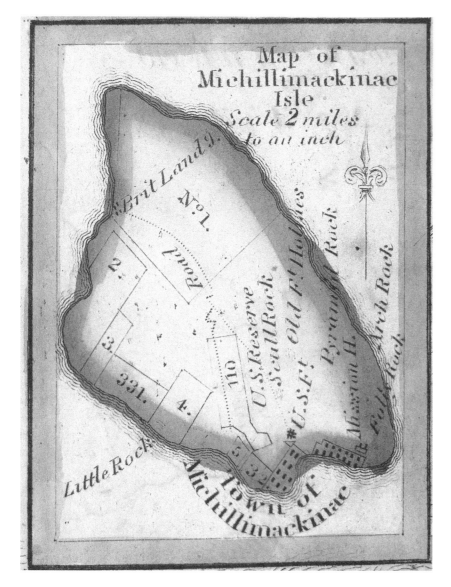

FIGURE 5.26

TITLE: Map of Michillimackinac Isle

AUTHOR: John Farmer (1798–1859) after John Mullett (1786–1862). Engraved by John Farmer.

DATE DEPICTED: November 1828.

DATE OF WORK: Published 1836.

DESCRIPTION: 4.5 x 3.5 cm. Colored copperplate engraving.

PROVENANCE: First appeared as an inset on *An Improved Edition of a Map of the Surveyed Part of the Territory of Michigan by John Farmer 1835* (Detroit, 1835). Repeated on *An Improved Edition of a Map of the Surveyed Part of the Territory of Michigan by John Farmer 1836* (Detroit, 1836). Also on *An Improved Edition of a Map of the Surveyed Part of the Territory of Michigan by John Farmer 1836* (New York, 1836). The detail illustrated here is from the 1836 New York edition.

COLLECTION: Clements Library, University of Michigan, Ann Arbor (Map Division, 6-O-9).

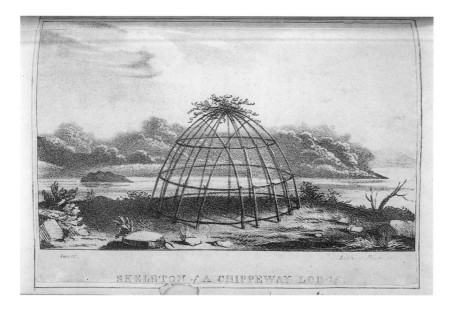

SKELETON OF A CHIPPEWAY LODGE

Thomas L. McKenney's *Sketches of a Tour to the Lakes* included this rendering of the framework of an Ojibwa lodge. Many Mackinac visitors noted the difference between the domed structures used by the Ojibwa and the conical wigwams of the Ottawa. The majority of Mackinac Island views picture the latter. Both types were covered with bark or woven rush mats. One correspondent counted 165 lodges on the beach in June 1821 and estimated that they housed 1,650 men, women, and children.

Clements Library, University of Michigan.

himself a British subject, took an oath of allegiance to the British government, and took arms against the United States during the late war." On October 30 the commissioners rejected Lasley's claim.[169]

Was Samuel Lasley a traitor? In his own defense he admitted to remaining on the island to protect his family and property. The British, he said, allowed him to wear his sword to discourage insults from the Indians. Lasley had served as a U.S. soldier from 1791 until 1808, and he maintained that he had been a loyal American.[170] It did not help Lasley's case that his claim included part of the seventy-eight acres requested by Ambrose Davenport, who had left the island rather than take the British oath.[171] Davenport had supported Dousman's own claim, so perhaps Dousman was returning a favor by accusing Lasley.[172] Ambrose Davenport received his land, which was surveyed as Private Claim 4.

The big winner in Mackinac Island land claims was Lasley's nemesis, Michael Dousman. Having been awarded two hundred acres in 1808, only to see his right of preemption rescinded because of protests by the army (Fig. 3.7), Dousman applied again in 1823. This time he claimed 640 acres, including the area of his original preemption. There was no comment from the army, probably because the usable timber had been removed from the land and the garrison was obtaining its wood from Bois Blanc Island. On October 22, 1823, the commissioners approved the application, which Mullett later surveyed as Private Claim 1.[173] Michael Dousman had acquired more than three times his 1808 plot, and he had done so without having to purchase the land.

No mention was made of Michael Dousman's questionable activities during the War of 1812. A year after the approval of his claim, however, Samuel Lasley sent a blistering deposition to the land office in Detroit. In it, he charged Dousman with any number of disloyal acts, including supplying the enemy, recruiting for them, encouraging the defense of the island against the Americans, and even participating in the capture of Fort Mackinac. John Biddle, register of the Detroit land office, forwarded Lasley's charges to Washington but pointed out that the claims had been settled. He dismissed Lasley's charges as "obviously made as a retaliation" for Dousman's statement that had cost him his own claim.[174] There the matter ended. Dousman received his land, though many of the charges against him seem to have been well-founded.[175] Both men remained members of the island community for many years, Lasley dying in 1844 and Dousman ten years later. It is unclear what part their conflict over land claims played in their later relations, but the ghosts of the War of 1812 clearly lingered on Mackinac Island.

James Otto Lewis's portrait of Jack-o-pa, an Ojibwa chief, depicts the warrior with his bow. Large numbers of Native Americans stopped at Mackinac Island during the 1820s on their way to and from the British posts on Georgian Bay. Lithograph by Lehman and Duval.

Clements Library, University of Michigan.

JACK-O-PA
or the
SIX

A Chippeway Chief

FIGURE 5.27

TITLE: [Plat showing private claims on Point St. Ignace]. [Marked in pencil:] Not Mackinac but west of it 40 N 3 & 4 W.

AUTHOR: [John Mullett (1786–1862)].

DATE DEPICTED: November 1828.

DATE OF WORK: [1828].

DESCRIPTION: 54 x 86.5 cm., which includes an extension at the upper left to show the western parts of claims 11–19. Pencil, pen, and ink on paper.

PROVENANCE: Retained in the records of the General Land Office.

COLLECTION: National Archives and Records Administration, College Park, MD (RG 49, Records of the Bureau of Land Management, Old Map File, Michigan 26).

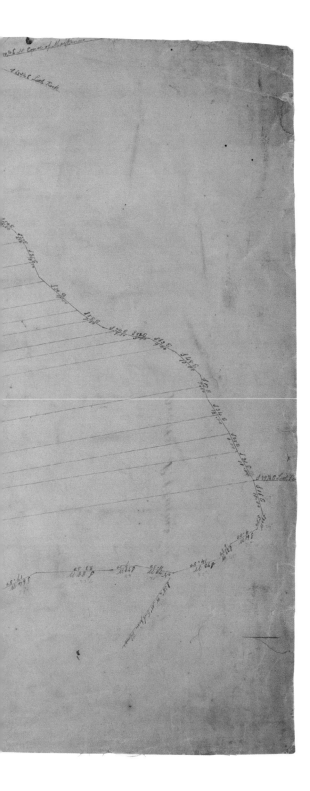

Private Claims at Michillimackinac

Deputy Surveyor John Mullett

By the summer of 1823 Daniel Bourrassa could look over his extensive property on East Moran Bay and feel a certain satisfaction in his accomplishments. He had occupied this land near Point St. Ignace since 1810. During the subsequent thirteen years, Bourrassa had constructed "a dwelling-house, a barn, a stable, and several out-houses" and enclosed "a very considerable field." All this was situated on a long, narrow piece of land nearly five acres in width and eighty in depth.[176] His waterfront faced Mackinac Island, the local market for agricultural commodities such as hay and oats. From the beach, where his buildings were clustered, Bourrassa's land stretched most of the way across the peninsula toward Lake Michigan.

Daniel Bourrassa did not live in isolation on the north shore of the Straits of Mackinac. On either side of his farm were sixteen other occupied parcels of similar size and orientation arranged from the north end of the bay to Point St. Ignace itself, where the shoreline turned west to Pointe La Barbe and Lake Michigan. Clusters of houses and outbuildings marked each property, forming an irregular line of whitewashed structures along the shore. Altogether they made up what Dr. John J. Bigsby described in 1819 as "the pretty hamlet of St. Ignatius."[177]

The members of this St. Ignace community lived in the presence of history, although few if any of them were aware of it. When John Mullett surveyed this land in 1828 he noted the "Ruins of an Ancient Town" along East Moran Bay and "Moran's old Trading Fort" across the peninsula at West Moran Bay. Three years earlier Henry Schoolcraft had camped at St. Ignace before crossing over to Mackinac Island. He "found in the sand the stumps of cedar pickets, forming an antique enclosure." Schoolcraft was familiar enough with the early history of the Great Lakes to speculate that these represented the remains of Father Jacques Marquette's seventeenth-century mission. "Not a lisp of such a ruin had been heard by me previously," he wrote, and none of the locals, either French or Indian, could tell him any more about it.[178]

Perhaps Schoolcraft had encountered the last visible remnants of Fort de Buade or one of the Native American villages associated with the Jesuit mission. The mission buildings had been burned in 1705, and the St. Ignace site was officially abandoned by 1715, replaced by a new fort, church, and village on the south shore of the Straits. It seems unlikely that the place was entirely given up, however. A few squatters appear to have used the oldest of the Michilimackinac sites during the eighteenth century, and the many acres of cleared ground very likely provided one of the sources of hay that are frequently, if imprecisely, mentioned during the early years of the Mackinac Island settlement.[179]

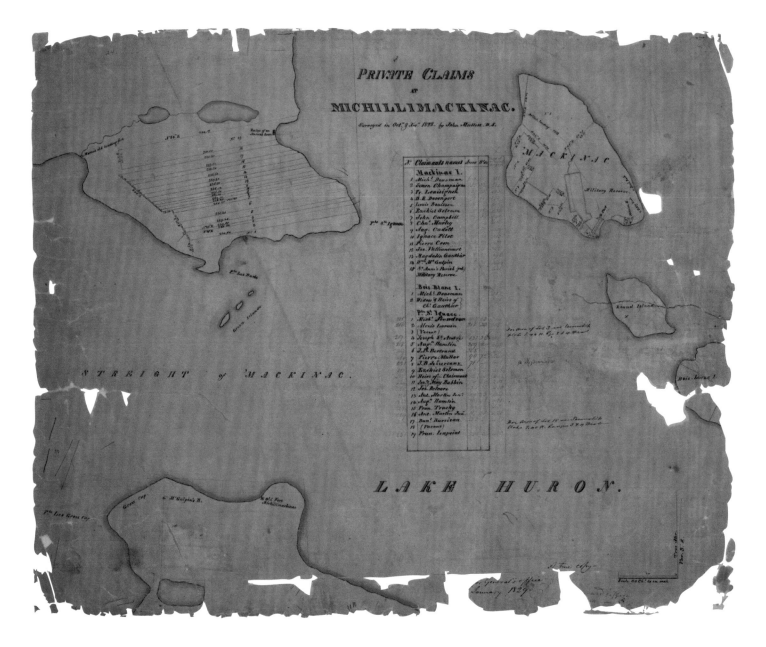

FIGURE 5.28

TITLE: Private Claims at Michillimackinac
Surveyed in Octr. & Nov. 1828 by John Mullett,
D.S.

AUTHOR: John Mullett (1786–1862).

DATE DEPICTED: November 1828.

DATE OF WORK: Copied later, possibly in
January 1829.

DESCRIPTION: 48.5 x 59.5 cm. Pen and ink
on paper with colored outlines of property.

PROVENANCE: This or an earlier version was
sent from the Surveyor General's Office to the
General Land Office in January 1829. Retained
in the records of the General Land Office.

COLLECTION: National Archives and Records
Administration, College Park, MD (RG 49,
Records of the Bureau of Land Management,
Old Map File, Michigan 24).

This circa 1860 study of "The Voyageur,"
by Abby Fuller Abbe, captures the look
of one of the Canadian boatmen who
moved canoes for the American Fur
Company. Many of the first settlers of
St. Ignace were old voyageurs who had
retired to farm and fish. *Minnesota Historical
Society (AV1988.45.264).*

It is unclear when permanent settlement began again at St. Ignace, although it is likely that the attraction was its cleared, arable land, a rare commodity on Mackinac Island. Eliza Chappell, a teacher from the Reverend Ferry's mission school, encountered a "poor hermit," an old "Canadian Frenchman," at St. Ignace in 1833. He claimed to have lived forty years in his hut.[180] If the earliest residents settled at the new St. Ignace as early as 1793, mention of houses and improved property can be traced back only to 1807. Both Michael Jaudron and Alexis Lorain claimed to have settled their tracts on East Moran Bay in that year.[181] Other claimants under the land act of 1823 gave dates for their arrival ranging from 1808 to 1811. When Usher Parsons viewed East Moran Bay from the deck of the brig *Lawrence* in July 1814, he described St. Ignace as "a small settlement of perhaps 5 or 6 families, large fields, &c." St. Ignace even suffered some of the ravages of war that summer. U.S. sailors took fishnets, and two French-speaking residents were interrogated about the size of the British garrison at Fort Mackinac.[182] Tiny representations of houses and fields on Charles Gratiot's maps of the Straits (Figs. 4.2 and 4.14) provide further evidence of organized settlement.

The residents of St. Ignace were among the many undocumented Michigan property owners affected by the land act of 1823. Like their counterparts on Mackinac Island, they were given the opportunity to obtain legal title to property they had occupied and improved before July 1, 1812. The proprietors of nineteen farms did so during the summer of 1823.[183] All but two claims were confirmed, and it was to those properties that John Mullett turned his attention in November 1828 after completing his survey of Mackinac Island. Figure 5.27 represents an early draft of his survey, perhaps his original, and Figure 5.28 connects the "private claims" at St. Ignace and Mackinac Island within the broader context of the Straits area.

None of the claimants had anything to say concerning their reasons for taking up lands at St. Ignace. Nearly all were French, and many were former voyageurs, who had taken the opportunity to leave their occupation to farm and fish.[184] Nor did they suggest a legal basis for their claims. Under the land acts of 1807 and 1823 it was necessary for Indian title to have been properly extinguished before a non–Native American could claim land. The British had not purchased the St. Ignace site. However, at the Treaty of Greenville in 1795, the Indians had granted to the United States "a piece of Land on the Main to the North of the Island, to measure six miles on Lake Huron or the Streight between Lakes Huron & Michigan & to extend three miles back from the water of the Lake or streight."[185] This area was not identified by survey until 1834, when it was shown to be made up of 11,520 acres, including the lands already claimed in St. Ignace, and extending westward well past Gros Cap and almost to Pointe aux Chenes.[186] The St. Ignace properties were thus eligible for confirmation.

When John Mullett set to work at St. Ignace, he found himself surveying on a much different pattern than that on Mackinac Island. The properties would have reminded him of those at the old French settlement of Detroit. Like the farms along the Detroit River, the nineteen properties at St. Ignace were long and narrow, providing each owner with the lake frontage necessary to obtain access to water transportation. It was a pattern inherited at both Detroit and St. Ignace from the St. Lawrence Valley of Canada. Joseph St. Andre's land was typical, "being two acres in width, and extending back from the margin of said lake eighty arpents [French acres]."[187] This took his lot most but not all of the way across the peninsula, leaving unplatted land along the Lake Michigan side. Mullett surveyed all nineteen plots in similar fashion, noting two as vacant.

Modern St. Ignace thus appeared on the cartographic record of Michigan towns. The place would remain a fishing and farming settlement for the next three decades. In September 1827, Elijah Warner recorded a road "laid out of Point St. Ignace" along the lakeshore.[188] In 1833, five years after John Mullett's survey, Eliza Chappell opened a school in a community she reported as having 180 inhabitants. She noted that only "French and Indian languages" were spoken there, and, with a Protestant missionary's eye, declared it a place of "wretchedness and want," dismissing every man in the settlement as "a confirmed drunkard." It did not help that Miss Chappell found nearly all of them to be Catholics.[189] The priest from Mackinac Island tended to their religious needs in a makeshift structure until 1837, when the community had matured sufficiently to erect a proper wooden church, a new St. Ignatius Loyola. The building stands today in St. Ignace. The settlement remained dependent on priests from the island until 1855, when the first resident pastor was assigned to St. Ignatius.[190]

Like his survey of Mackinac Island, Mullett's rendering of St. Ignace became a staple element of Detroit engraver John Farmer's maps depicting the surveyed parts of the Michigan Territory. The St. Ignace properties first appeared on his edition of 1830, inset within a map of the Straits.[191] Mullett's maps of St. Ignace also mark the first cartographic appearance of the name "Pte. La Barbe." Elizabeth Baird remembered the name as meaning "the point where one shaves" and said that it was so called because voyageurs coming from the west all stopped there to groom themselves before proceeding to Mackinac Island.[192] The absence of the name from maps before the late 1820s suggests that it might, in fact, date to the heyday of the American Fur Company and the annual arrival of its canoe brigades from Lake Michigan.

Mullett's general map of private claims at the Straits of Mackinac (Fig. 5.28) was adapted for publication in Farmer's products by combining his cartography with Lucius Lyon's survey of Bois Blanc Island (Fig. 5.23) and even bits of Aaron Greeley's survey of 1810. Three different examples of the Farmer maps of the Straits are reproduced here (Figs. 5.29–5.31). They illustrate how the cartography was altered, either for the convenience of the engraver or, in the case of the third example, to incorporate a change from the traditional name Michilimackinac to the shortened and Anglicized "Mackinaw" after Michigan became a state in 1837. A fine engraving of Mullett's

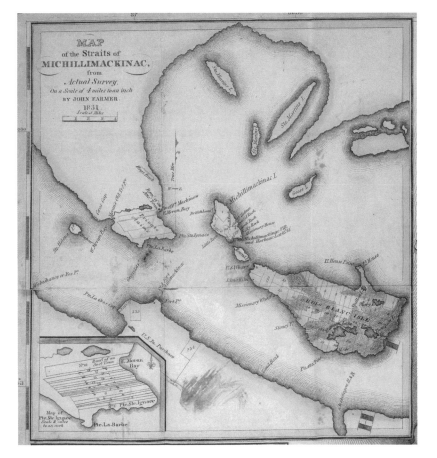

FIGURE 5.29

TITLE: Map of the Straits of Michillimackinac, from Actual Survey. [Inset:] Map of Pte. Ste. Ignace.

AUTHOR: John Farmer (1798–1859) after John Mullett (1786–1862). Engraved by V. Balch and S. Stiles.

DATE DEPICTED: November 1828.

DATE OF WORK: 1831.

DESCRIPTION: 18.5 x 17.4 cm. Colored, copperplate engraving.

PROVENANCE: Inset on *An Improved Map of the Surveyed Part of the Territory of Michigan by John Farmer 1831* (Detroit, 1831).

COLLECTION: Clements Library, University of Michigan, Ann Arbor (Atlas, H-2).

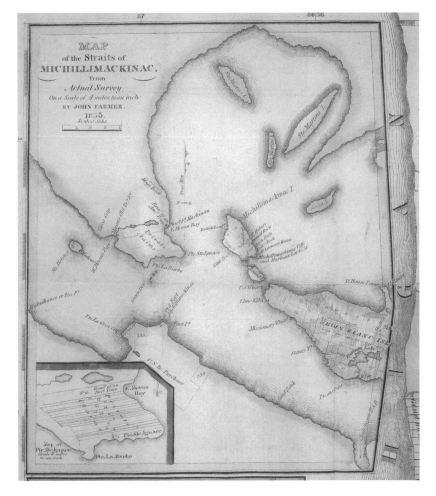

FIGURE 5.30

TITLE: Map of the Straits of Michillimackinac, from Actual Survey. [Inset:] Map of Pte. Ste. Ignace.

AUTHOR: John Farmer (1798–1859) after John Mullett (1786–1862). Engraved by John Farmer.

DATE DEPICTED: November 1828.

DATE OF WORK: 1835.

DESCRIPTION: 18.5 x 15 (irregular) cm. Colored copperplate engraving.

PROVENANCE: Inset on *An Improved Edition of a Map of the Surveyed Part of the Territory of Michigan by John Farmer 1835* (Detroit, 1835). Repeated in the Farmer maps of the same title published in 1836 in Detroit and New York. This version of the map of the Straits is distinguished by a truncated Bois Blanc Island and lower right-hand border.

COLLECTION: Clements Library, University of Michigan, Ann Arbor (Map Division, Atlas, H-2).

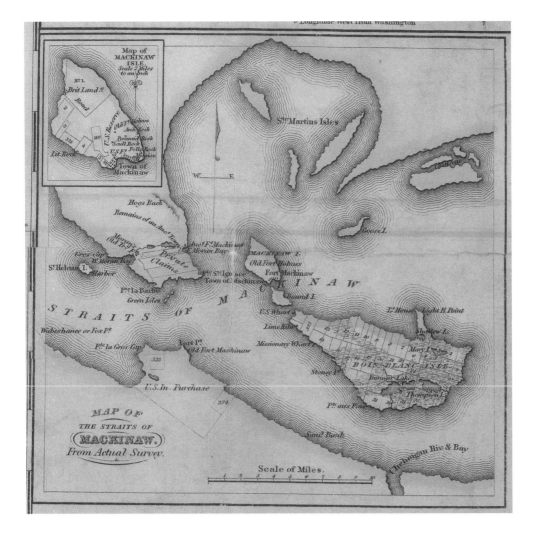

FIGURE 5.31

TITLE: Map of the Straits of Mackinaw from Actual Survey. [Inset:] Map of Mackinaw Isle.

AUTHOR: John Farmer (1798–1859) after John Mullett (1786–1862).

DATE DEPICTED: November 1828.

DATE OF WORK: 1837.

DESCRIPTION: 14.5 x 14.8 cm. Colored copperplate engraving.

PROVENANCE: Inset on *Map of the Surveyed Part of Michigan by John Farmer . . . 1837* (New York, 1837). Repeated on Farmer's map of 1839 and as late as 1855.

COLLECTION: Clements Library, University of Michigan, Ann Arbor (Map Division, 5-M-7)

map of private claims at the Straits was also issued in 1847 with a congressional report on Michigan land claims.[193]

A few observations may be made about all three versions of Farmer's printed maps of the Straits. First, they were intended to show surveyed land. Thus the treatment of St. Martin Bay and its islands, Cheboygan and the south shore, and St. Helena Island are extremely crude, while the areas surveyed between 1810 and 1828 by Greeley, Lyon, and Mullett are accurately rendered. Second, they show nothing of the local topography. The only real detail beyond property boundaries is a rendering of vegetation on Bois Blanc Island, perhaps an attempt to show what parts had been deforested by 1827–28. A misprint also crept in during the process of engraving—the property on Mill Creek (claim 334) is mistakenly labeled "234."

Some additional details appear on these printed maps. The Straits extend westward to St. Helena Island where a "Harbour" is indicated. This records, for the first time, the deep bay on the northeastern side of the island that would later serve a busy fishing village. Although St. Helena was not patented to William Belote

until 1849, fishermen were making use of its harbor by the time these maps were produced.[194] Thomas Nye noted a fishing vessel there when he passed by in November 1837.[195]

The cartography of the eastern end of the Straits is equally vague. A crudely rendered Duncan Bay and the mouth of the Cheboygan River provide the only features along the south shore. Cheboygan had seen occupation by Native Americans and even British sailors in the late 1770s, and a small village of Ottawas was located there in 1816.[196] The area was poorly mapped, however. When James Doty passed in 1820 he described "Sha-baw-e-gun-ing bay" only as an outlet for a river of the same name that drained a lake in the interior.[197] Farmer's published cartography reveals an equal degree of ignorance that would not be addressed until the late 1830s.

Major William Whistler (1783–1863) served on the Great Lakes throughout the 1820s and 1830s and commanded Fort Mackinac in 1833–34. A member of a military family, Whistler was the uncle of artist James Abbott McNeill Whistler. New York artist Grove Gilbert painted Whistler at Fort Niagara in 1831. *Mackinac State Historic Parks, MI (2007.4.1).*

"The wildest and tenderest little piece of beauty that I have yet seen on God's earth"

1830–1840

Godfrey Vigne was puzzled—puzzled as only an Englishman can be when faced with the eccentricities of American language. It was the morning of August 7, 1831, and his steamer was approaching Mackinac Island from Sault Ste. Marie. Like most travelers, Vigne had been informed that "Michilimackinac" was taken to mean "Great Turtle; and so called from its outline bearing a supposed resemblance to that animal when lying upon the water." The Englishman could accept

this, though he admitted being unable to discern "so flattering a likeness." It was not the origin of the island's name that confused him, however. It was the description of its central heights as a "bluff." Vigne found that word "provoking from its absurdity, and constant recurrence in American descriptions of scenery."

"What is a bluff?" Vigne at last asked a fellow traveler as the vessel drew closer to Haldimand Bay. "A bluff, sir! Don't you know what a bluff is?" the American responded. "A bluff, sir, is a piece of rising ground, partly rock, not all of it, with one side steep, but yet not very steep, the other side sloping away, yet not too suddenly; the whole of it except the steep side, covered with wood; in short, sir, a bluff is a bluff!" The Englishman was forced to admit that a bluff towering three hundred feet above Lake Huron dominated the interior of Mackinac Island. He could only console himself that "in the sense in which it is used in America, the word is exclusively their own, and it really would not be fair to call it English."[1]

Godfrey Vigne was among the vanguard of a new class of Mackinac visitor—literary tourists whose observations and opinions would find their way into print in America and Europe and enjoy wide readership on both continents. They popularized and romanticized many familiar elements of Mackinac, particularly its pure and healthy environment, scenic beauty, and increasingly quaint and picturesque village and fort. But they also recorded more serious subjects—the waning days of the fur trade, economic change and religious tensions within the community, and the plight of Native Americans as they grew increasingly dependent for their livelihood on government annuities and the first generation of

affluent sightseers. No fewer than seventeen authors who visited Mackinac between 1830 and 1840 incorporated accounts of their stay into published works about travel in America and on its Great Lakes. The social commentary of some, like Alexis de Tocqueville, Anna Jameson, Harriet Martineau, and Frederick Marryat, are remembered today. Other writers, though less celebrated, were also observant and insightful. A few—Jameson, George Featherstonhaugh, George Catlin, and François de Castelnau—left visual impressions to enliven their narratives. Many others tourists, including Godfrey Vigne, sketched as well. Henry Schoolcraft noted in 1833 that numerous visitors toured the island "with note-book in hand."[2] Their work remains to be rediscovered.

Many of these British, American, French, and even Russian travelers were greeted and guided in their ramblings by Henry Rowe Schoolcraft, Mackinac's first resident literary figure. Although he first came to the Straits in 1820 and stopped often during the next decade, it was Schoolcraft's appointment as Mackinac Indian agent in 1833 that provided him the opportunity to learn about the history of the Straits and expand his studies of regional Native American language and culture. His *Algic Researches* (1839) and *Personal Memoirs* (1851) owe much to his time at Mackinac. Schoolcraft spent all or part of each year on the island from his appointment through 1842, and his *Memoirs* record contact with many visitors, including several who later published travel accounts.

Schoolcraft's role as guide was a diversion but also a chore. Late in August 1835, near the end of a summer marked by a steady stream of visitors, "of some note or distinction, natives or foreigners," who arrived with letters of introduction, he ventured that the Great Lakes could no longer be considered "solitary seas." Instead, as he recorded in his journal two weeks before, "People seem to have suddenly waked up in the East, and are just becoming aware there is a West— to which they hie, in a measure as one hunts for a pleasant land fancied in dreams."[3] The Indian agent was among the first to suggest that the pleasures of Mackinac might attract more than just passing travelers. As early as 1835, he noted, there were those who believed the place would become "a favorite watering place or refuge for the opulent and invalids during the summer." At a time of rampant speculation in Michigan lands, people from Detroit and Chicago were purchasing lots on Mackinac Island.[4] By 1838 the place was becoming known as a summer resort, particularly for those seeking a healthy environment.[5] Visitors were accommodated by two or three rudimentary boardinghouses, the best of which was acknowledged to be that kept by Samuel C. Lasley and his wife, Rachel.[6]

Part of this sudden popularity was a result of steady improvements in transportation through the introduction of larger and more comfortable steamboats. Sitting on the piazza of his substantial agency house facing Round Island, Schoolcraft watched as "the great stream of ships and commerce" passed, bringing visitors of all sorts.[7] Many stopped for only as long as it took their crews to load cords of firewood to feed the boilers for the continuation of the voyage to Detroit, Sault Ste. Marie, Green Bay, or Chicago. In 1836 Harriet Martineau found the island's two small wharves covered with "piles of wood for the steam-boats."[8] Increasing traffic stimulated improvements to the harbor. Samuel C. Lasley erected a new wharf opposite his boardinghouse in 1833, and six years later Michael Dousman extended his own pier, formerly that of the American Fur Company, "for the acomidation of The Large Botes" that were stopping to refuel.[9]

Travel was safer too. The Bois Blanc light had been constructed in 1829 to mark the eastern end of the Straits of Mackinac. In 1832, a light vessel was stationed near Waugoshance Point to illuminate the western approach. Although the Legislative Council of Michigan Territory petitioned Congress in 1835 for a permanent lighthouse at Waugoshance, the floating beacon was not replaced with a permanent structure until 1851. The same petition emphasized the importance of Mackinac Island's harbor to shipping on the upper lakes and requested a survey for improvements to protect it from the heavy swells from Lake Huron.[10] No action was taken, however, and Haldimand Bay would be without protective breakwaters until the twentieth century.

The first view of Mackinac Island from the water invariably impressed even the most experienced traveler. Harriet Martineau took in the scene from the west on the evening of July 4, 1836. "The island looked enchanting as we approached," she wrote, "steeped in the most golden sunshine that ever hallowed lake or shore."[11] Behind the gilded bluffs, however, Mackinac of the 1830s was experiencing change and turmoil that belied its placid appearance from the water.

The town on Haldimand Bay was first and foremost a commercial establishment, its fortunes long tied to the fur trade and the presence of a military garrison. As Henry Schoolcraft put it during a brief stop in 1822, "Apart from its picturesque loveliness, we found it . . . a very flesh and blood and matter-of-fact sort of place."[12]

In 1830 the American Fur Company provided the mainstay of the island's economy. Within five years, however, the industry that had put Michilimackinac on the map in the seventeenth century had virtually disappeared from the local scene. The fur trade was showing signs of stress by the end of the 1820s, beset by changes in the world economy and in fashion. In 1834 John Jacob Astor divested himself of the business that had made him a millionaire and sold his American Fur Company to a group headed by his old lieutenant, Ramsay Crooks. Although the reorganized company diversified into fishing and maintained its properties on Mackinac Island, its northern headquarters were moved farther west. By September 1835 Chandler Robbins Gilman could observe that the "Company have their depot at La Pointe [Wisconsin], and Mackina depends for its existence on its very trifling fisheries, and on the military post."[13] By 1839 the once bustling warehouses, boatyards and Stuart House stood empty.[14] The company staggered on until 1842 when it declared bankruptcy and began to dispose of its assets, including its Mackinac Island properties.[15]

Residents of the Straits found themselves in search of alternative ways of making a living and supporting their communities. As numerous as they might have seemed to Henry Schoolcraft, the first wave of tourists was insufficient to provide substantial economic benefit. Nor was supplying firewood to steamboats a permanent solution. Fort Mackinac and its garrison were a source of some business, but in 1837 the troops were withdrawn and the fortifications remained unoccupied for most of the next three years. The Presbyterian mission school closed the same year. The best news for local merchants was the 1836 Treaty of Washington that provided annuity payments over twenty years to Native American groups that had sold their lands across northern Michigan. The money was paid out each fall on Mackinac Island, with much of it going into local coffers in payment for necessities or for alcohol. Most promising, however, was a developing trade in fish that could be caught and packed at Mackinac and then shipped to markets around the lakes.[16]

The plentiful trout and whitefish of the Straits had provided subsistence for local residents since prehistoric times. Although small quantities were shipped to Detroit and other ports as early as 1824, most was consumed by Mackinac inhabitants or used to support the fur trade. Evidence of fishing was everywhere on Mackinac Island and at St. Ignace. By 1818 the quantity of fish offal was sufficient for its proper disposal to be regulated in one of the earliest ordinances of the Borough of Michilimackinac.[17] In 1835 Enos Goodrich observed that "Not a rod of fence could be found but had a fish net drying upon it," though he still considered fish "the subsistence of the entire population" and not a significant item of

export.[18] George Featherstonhaugh, however, believed that "a profitable fishery" had been established by that time.[19] Although the packing and shipping of fish increased from 1,700 to 4,000 barrels annually between 1835 and 1840, and Mackinac Island had a fish inspector by 1839, this was an infant industry that would not have its full impact until the 1840s.[20]

As Mackinac's economy changed, the presence of a military garrison overlooking the town and harbor from Fort Mackinac remained a reassuring constant, at least for much of the 1830s. The construction and renovation directed by Major Alexander Thompson in 1826–28 had given the post buildings a new lease on life. There were complaints from some of his successors, of course, specifically that the new hospital was badly located and poorly constructed, that quarters for the officers were insufficient, and that the new barracks were too cramped to comfortably accommodate two companies of soldiers.[21] The old British powder magazine was also damp and nearly unserviceable. On a positive note, a new well dug behind the north gate in the fall of 1830 alleviated the fort's chronic water supply problem, at least for the time being.[22]

Despite these concerns, the army was unwilling to expend much more on Fort Mackinac, although the need for additional officers' quarters was compelling enough that a new building was begun in 1834 on the high bank near the flagstaff on the north side of the enclosure. It was completed sometime after August 1835.[23] Popularly known as the "Hill House," the structure marked a significant departure in the design of Fort Mackinac. It was the first undefended building to extend beyond the protective stockade, and it was placed in such a way that it compromised the defenses of the fort by masking the line of fire from the western side of the north blockhouse. Its position was a clear admission that the old fortification was no longer considered defensible.

The new officers' quarters first appeared on a set of three drawings of the post buildings prepared by quartermaster Lieutenant James W. Penrose in February 1835.[24] These were later separated from his written report, however, and are not known to survive. The new building would not be well pictured in a surviving image of Fort Mackinac until at least four years later (Figs. 6.24 and 6.25). That Penrose's drawings—the only official plans of Fort Mackinac known to have been prepared between 1817 and 1850—were made for the Quartermaster General's Department rather than for the chief of engineers further demonstrates that the fortifications were considered obsolete. The post had become little more than a secure barracks complex.

Two years later, even this remnant of Michilimackinac's martial past was gone. In 1837 the garrison was withdrawn for service in the Second Seminole War, the first of five occasions when this would occur before the Civil War. The unaccustomed absence of troops in 1837 "created some uneasiness in the minds of the inhabitants," who remained concerned about the presence of large numbers of Native Americans gathering on Mackinac Island for their annual treaty payments.[25] Such fears proved groundless, even during the period of border tensions created by the meddling of American citizens in the Canadian rebellion of 1837–38. Except for a brief reoccupation during the late summer of 1839, Fort Mackinac would be without a garrison until May 1840.

The 1830s witnessed the demise of yet another Mackinac Island institution when the Protestant mission school closed its doors in 1837. The fortunes of the mission had followed those of its founder, the Reverend William M. Ferry, as well as those of the fur trade, which provided the occupation for many whose children were sent to the school. Ferry had begun his educational ministry on Mackinac Island in 1823, and his mission prospered. The vigorous activities of Protestant evangelicals at Mackinac soon drew a reaction from the island's traditionally Roman Catholic community. Years later, Elizabeth Baird recalled of Ferry's mission, from the Catholic perspective, that "Proselyting [sic] seemed to pervade the atmosphere of the whole establishment" and that the social climate on the island eventually "seemed a religious war."[26]

The controversy tugged at the entire population, to the point where Mrs. Baird was told that "One had to be either a Presbyterian or a Roman Catholic in those days; nothing else for a moment would be tolerated."[27] The tense situation was even reflected in the physical surroundings of Mackinac Island. The Catholics, who had been without a resident priest since 1765 and a church building since 1819, finally obtained the services of a semi-permanent pastor and constructed a new, though modest, log chapel by 1827.[28] The Protestants expanded their congregation under Ferry's energetic leadership and, in the fall of 1829, began to construct their own church.[29] The increasing polarization of the community was even reflected in burial practices. The Presbyterians established their own cemetery at the eastern end of Haldimand Bay, near the new church. By 1833 the practice of burying the dead of both Catholic and Protestant denominations in the old Ste. Anne's cemetery at the corner of Market and Hoban streets had ceased.[30]

This spirit of religious revival and competition was reaching a crescendo by 1829. It culminated in outright confrontation during the winter of 1831. Reverend Ferry preached six weekly sermons at his new church challenging Catholic doctrine. Father Samuel Mazzuchelli, who had arrived on the island in the summer of 1830, answered from the pulpit of Ste. Anne's.[31] When Godfrey Vigne, Alexis de Tocqueville, and Gustave de Beaumont arrived at Mackinac the following summer, it was apparent to them that the "Catholic religion and the Presbyterian communion divide the believers." One of their fellow passengers was Father James Mullon, who had preached his own fiery sermons at Ste. Anne's during the summer of 1829. Mullon was returning to continue the debate, but Reverend Ferry declined his challenge. The two Frenchmen and their English companion went to hear Mullon preach, which he did with "extreme warmth and much talent," though Beaumont found his comments violent and severe with "nothing evangelical about them."[32]

Vigne thought that, without an opponent to debate, the priest felt compelled to explain the whole affair in a "speech more suited to the bar than the pulpit." He, and apparently much of Mullon's audience, found the whole proceeding "exceedingly disgraceful."[33] Islanders, it would seem, were tiring of religious conflict.

The controversy cooled thereafter, but the Catholics had checked rapid Protestant evangelization on Mackinac Island. Father Mazzuchelli claimed victory because Reverend Ferry "had not the consolation of adding to the number of his followers," while he himself made new converts and drew inactive parishioners back to church.[34] The Catholic religion had reasserted its position in the old French community on Mackinac Island, and Ste. Anne's would have a regular pastor from that time on. Within a few years, as the Presbyterian mission teacher Martin Heydenburk complained in 1876, Mackinac's population was "left to the blighting influences of Catholicism."[35]

William Ferry continued to lead his mission school and the Presbyterian congregation until 1834, when he resigned and moved to Grand Haven, Michigan.[36] Henry Schoolcraft attributed his decision to a desire to "provide for a growing family" by entering into secular business.[37] Ferry's departure, however, was dogged with rumors of his inappropriate conduct with a woman that were seized upon by his Catholic opponents and provided grist for island gossip for years. Although prominent local Presbyterians, such as Robert Stuart, believed him blameless, they acknowledged that Ferry's usefulness had come to an end.[38] The American Board of Commissioners for Foreign Missions was unable to find a suitable replacement, and the relocation of American Fur Company headquarters removed many supporters and potential students from the area. In the spring of 1837 the American Board closed the mission, a decision that Schoolcraft thought ill-advised at a time when the Native Americans of the upper Great Lakes were making important land concessions and gravitating to Mackinac Island to collect their annuities.[39] He argued to no avail. By the time Anna Jameson visited in July 1837, Reverend Ferry's impressive Mission House was used largely for storage. William Johnston, an interpreter for the Indian agency, occupied one of its wings.[40] By the end of the year much of the mission's property, aside from the church and house, had been sold.[41]

The fur trade, the mission school, and much of Mackinac's military importance had departed. The coming decade would see the rise of fishing and the beginnings of a resort economy. In 1837 Anna Jameson foresaw a role for the island as a "sort of watering-place for the Michigan and Wisconsin fashionables . . . the 'Rockaway of the west.'" The forlorn Mission House, she suggested prophetically, "will probably be converted into a fashionable hotel."[42]

U.S. COMMANDANTS OF FORT MACKINAC, 1830–1840

Lieutenant Colonel Enos Cutler, 5th Regiment of Infantry, 1829–31

Captain Robert A. McCabe, 5th Regiment of Infantry, 1831–32

Major Alexander R. Thompson, 2nd Regiment of Infantry, 1832–33

Major William Whistler, 2nd Regiment of Infantry, 1833–34

Captain John Clitz, 2nd Regiment of Infantry, 1834–36

Lieutenant James W. Anderson, 2nd Regiment of Infantry, 1836–37

Post unoccupied June 1837–August 1839

Captain Samuel MacKenzie, 2nd Regiment of Artillery, 1839

Post unoccupied September 1839–May 1840

PRESIDENTS OF THE BOROUGH OF MICHILIMACKINAC, 1830–1840

Samuel Abbott, 1830

Edward Biddle, 1831

Samuel Abbott, 1832–43

The harbor forms an exact crescent

Calvin Colton

Calvin Colton had a fine view of Mackinac Island on the morning of Sunday, August 8, 1830. Like Godfrey Vigne, Colton had traveled from Sault Ste. Marie. As his vessel slowed in the transparent waters of Haldimand Bay, he observed his surroundings. "The harbour forms an exact crescent," he wrote, "the tips of its horns being about one mile asunder. The town . . . for the most part, lies immediately on the crescent, near the water's edge, and under the towering rock, which sustains the fort above." Colton thought that the post looked "with open and cheerful aspect towards the Huron waters . . . inviting or frowning according as they are approached by friend or foe."[43] By 1830 the fort's old enemies were far away, and its aspect was most likely to be welcoming.

Colton's word picture describes a Mackinac Island that had reached the zenith of its importance to the Great Lakes fur trade. It could have been written as a guide to Hannah White's colorful image of the harbor, town, and fort reproduced here as Figure 6.1. Miss White, a sister of Amanda Ferry, drew her oil-on-velvet painting at some point between 1830 and 1834 when she visited and then taught at the mission school. Architectural details suggest that it was composed closer to the later date. Despite its naive style and apparent distortions, White's painting presents a fine view of the island and illustrates, for the first time, several prominent buildings that had been constructed during the 1820s.

Although Hannah White's picture is undated, it must have been done before the Ferrys left Mackinac Island in 1834. Mission Church appears at the lower right, so it cannot have been painted before 1830. To the left of Mission Church is Ste. Anne's Church, displaying the addition made in 1831. Most telling of all are the wharves that punctuate the shoreline. The missionary's dock is at right, near the church. Immediately below Fort Mackinac is the L-shaped government wharf that served the military post. To the left is an unidentified wharf and, at the foot of Astor Street, that owned by the American Fur Company. Farthest to the left, flanked by two overturned canoes on the beach, is the wharf constructed during 1833 by Samuel C. Lasley.[44] Hannah White taught children at the mission school as late as 1833–34, so it seems most likely that she painted her picture about that time.[45]

Careful study of White's painting will reward the viewer with much information and recognition of structures that can still be found on Mackinac Island. Dominating all, of course, is Fort Mackinac. The army lavished whitewash on every surface, and the impression of observers, such as Calvin Colton, was that of "the snow-white fort upon its rocky summit." James McCall was aboard the same vessel as Colton. "The Buildings in the fort are one story & a half high," he wrote, "and all white washed; with all, the walls,

parapets and pickets makes an elegant appearance and may be seen at the distance of 30 miles in clear weather."[46] Below the fort are its gardens, storehouse, and stables. Immediately to the right is the Indian Agency House, dating to 1823–24.

The left of the painting depicts the jumbled architecture of the town, which Colton estimated to hold a population of six to seven hundred.[47] Alexis de Tocqueville counted only fifty houses there in 1831, surely a low estimate, but he thought "several of them rather pretty."[48] Among the best were the buildings of the American Fur Company, constructed on Market Street in 1821–22. White shows many of the houses coated with whitewash. One of these, at the head of the left-hand wharf, is probably Lasley's boardinghouse, which had opened for business in 1824. A visitor of 1834 described it as "of one story, with many antiquated additions."[49] On the eastern edge of town, at the corner of Main and Fort streets, is the surviving building of the original American Fur Company complex, whitewashed and with its gable end facing the lake. By about 1840 this Canadian-style house had a square, false front. It was operated as the Northern Hotel by the late 1850s.[50]

Hannah White was particularly familiar with the mission area at the extreme right of her painting. To the right of the post gardens and Indian Agency House stands the whitewashed home of Magdelaine La Framboise, which survives today, its crisp Federal-style design engulfed by modern additions. The house had been built about 1820 by her son-in-law, Captain Benjamin K. Pierce. With the older Mitchell house on Market Street, it was the finest private dwelling on the island.[51] Across Church Street is Ste. Anne's Church and, farther to the right, Mission Church and Mission House. The beach in front of them, and indeed for the length of the harbor, is sprinkled with the wigwams and overturned canoes of visiting Native Americans.

Figure 6.1 also gives a sense of the topography of the south end of Mackinac Island. Robinson's Folly frowns over the scene at far right. Roads climb the steep bluffs to the left of Fort Mackinac (Spring Street and "Turkey Hill") and behind Mission Church ("Mission Hill"). The island is largely deforested, with only clumps of trees beginning to reappear along the top of the bluffs, "forests of slender growth" as Calvin Colton described them in 1830.[52]

Hannah White's little painting reveals the Borough of Michilimackinac during "the palmy days" of the fur trade.[53] Figure 6.2 is an image of about the same time that focuses on the mission complex at the height of its development. The engraving first appeared under the title "Mission House at Mackinaw" in March 1835. The woodblock was later reused with the title "Mackinac Bluffs" in publications of

FIGURE 6.1

TITLE: [Mackinac Island].

AUTHOR: Hannah White (active 1825–34).

DATE DEPICTED: 1833–34.

DATE OF WORK: [1833–34].

DESCRIPTION: 31.5 x 48.5 cm. Oil-on-velvet theorem painting with outlines stenciled and filled in with oil paint.

PROVENANCE: Painted during Hannah White's time on Mackinac Island between 1830 and 1834. Later given to Mrs. Amanda Ferry Hall (niece of the artist) and donated by Mrs. Hall to the trustees of Mission Church in 1911 with instructions that the picture be "loaned" to the Michigan Historical Society should the church ever disband. The trustees voted to have the painting framed and hung in the church's vestibule. It was among the items found in Mission Church when the building and its contents were transferred to the Mackinac Island State Park Commission in 1954–55.

COLLECTION: Mackinac State Historic Parks, Mackinac Island, MI (1997.00.27).

Mackinac Bluffs

FIGURE 6.2

TITLE: Mackinac Bluffs.

AUTHOR: Unknown.

DATE DEPICTED: ca. 1830.

DATE OF WORK: Published 1847 and 1848.

DESCRIPTION: 9.2 x 15.3 cm. Woodcut.

PROVENANCE: Originally published with the title "Mission House at Mackinaw," in *Quarterly Paper of the American Board of Commissioners for Foreign Missions, No. XX* (March 1835): 77. The block was either reused or recut with the title "Mackinac Bluffs" for Robert Sears, *New Pictorial Family Magazine* 4 (1847): 501. It appeared again in Sears, *A New and Popular Pictorial Description of the United States. . . .* (New York, 1848), 521. The image used here is taken from the 1848 work.

COLLECTION: University of Michigan Libraries, Ann Arbor.

the late 1840s, and it has become one of the best-known views of early nineteenth-century Mackinac. Like Hannah White's painting, it shows the missionary establishment after the completion of Mission Church.

The engraving provides no clue to the identity of the artist, although it is not inconceivable that it was Hannah White or her sister. The composition is similar to an earlier view of the mission grounds (Fig. 5.17) that appeared in print about 1830. Figure 6.2 broadens the perspective to include Mission Church and fencing around the adjacent gardens. These contained potatoes and garden vegetables, which, the accompanying article noted, were grown "in great perfection."[54] Scrubby, second-growth forest tops the bluff in both engravings, although it appears thicker than in the White painting.

The presence of Mission Church dates Figure 6.2 to sometime after the spring of 1830. The new meetinghouse was funded by subscriptions from members of the Presbyterian congregation and other islanders. By November 1829 pledges totaled $1,000, and construction could proceed.[55] The work was directed by Martin Heydenburk, who later reminisced about the project, although he confused the dates and some events with his earlier efforts on the Mission House. Logs for timber and board were cut on the Lower

FIGURE 6.3

TITLE: 7 Michillimackinac lac huron 11 aout.

AUTHOR: Gustave de Beaumont (1802–66).

DATE DEPICTED: August 7, 1831.

DATE OF WORK: August 11, 1831.

DESCRIPTION: Dimensions unavailable. Pen and ink on paper.

PROVENANCE: Completed following Beaumont's first stop at Mackinac Island and included in his book of finished sketches. This sketchbook is usually referred to as the Romanet Album.

COLLECTION: Current location unknown. Privately owned in France by the Romanet family as of 1938. Reproduced in George W. Pierson, *Tocqueville and Beaumont in America* (New York, 1938), 304.

FIGURE 6.4

TITLE: [lac huron Michillimackinac 7 aout 1831].

AUTHOR: Gustave de Beaumont (1802–66).

DATE DEPICTED: August 7, 1831.

DATE OF WORK: ca. August 11, 1831.

DESCRIPTION: Dimensions unavailable. Pen and ink on paper.

PROVENANCE: Probably completed following Beaumont's first visit to Mackinac Island and included in his book of finished sketches. This sketchbook is usually referred to as the Romanet Album.

COLLECTION: Current location unknown. Privately owned in France by the Romanet family as of 1938. Reproduced in George W. Pierson, *Tocqueville and Beaumont in America* (New York, 1938), 300.

FIGURE 6.5

TITLE: Michillimackinac 16 Aôut 1831.

AUTHOR: Gustave de Beaumont (1802–66).

DATE DEPICTED: August 7, 1831.

DATE OF WORK: August 16, 1831.

DESCRIPTION: Dimensions unavailable. Pen and ink on paper.

PROVENANCE: Completed following Beaumont's two visits to Mackinac Island and included in his book of finished sketches. This sketchbook is usually referred to as the Romanet Album.

COLLECTION: Current location unknown. Privately owned in France by the Romanet family as of 1938. Reproduced in George W. Pierson, *Tocqueville and Beaumont in America* (New York, 1938), 306

Peninsula mainland and processed at Dousman's sawmill on Mill Creek. The materials were then sledded across the ice to Mackinac Island.[56] Construction was rapid, and the church was dedicated in March 1830. One of Reverend Ferry's students described it later that summer as "a neat & handsome little building" that included schoolrooms in its raised basement level.[57] The building was painted white with green shutters.[58] When Calvin Colton visited that August, he took note of the new landmark, "a Christian church lifting up its steeple" on the edge of town.[59]

Farther west along the beach stood the yellow-painted church of Reverend Ferry's nemesis, Father Samuel Mazzuchelli.[60] It appears on Hannah White's panorama of the island as well as in two views made by Gustave de Beaumont in 1831. As Figures 6.3 and 6.4 demonstrate, Beaumont was less of an artist than was White, and he was more selective in what he included in his drawings. Like many travelers, Beaumont made preliminary sketches of scenes that interested him and later drafted more polished compositions. Both his rough and finished sketchbooks were held in private French collections in the 1930s, although their whereabouts today have not been determined. Fortunately, one of his rough Mackinac drawings and three finished views were reproduced as illustrations in George Wilson Pierson's *Tocqueville and Beaumont in America.*

Figure 6.3 is Beaumont's impression of Fort Mackinac from the harbor, probably based on a sketch made upon his arrival on August 7.

A fellow passenger on the steamer *Superior* wrote a Detroit newspaper that "Nothing but the pencil can give an adequate idea of the picture" that spread before them. "One of the French gentlemen on board had his sketch book out at once," the American continued, "his eye in fine phrenzy rolling from beach to precipice, apparently taking every beauty into his mind, whatever may have been his success in transferring them to his paper."[61] Beaumont depicted what he thought most important. Fort Mackinac is quite accurately rendered, but the town is hastily drawn with many elements omitted. Mission House appears at far right, but the steepled building on the shore is more likely Ste. Anne's Church than Mission Church.

Once ashore, Beaumont hiked along the beach to take a view back toward Fort Mackinac. He dated his preliminary sketch August 7 and later made a finished rendering, included here as Figure 6.4. The fort is more roughly drawn, and Beaumont's impression of the town is, once again, virtually worthless. The *Superior* lies at anchor in Haldimand Bay, and wigwams stand on the beach, although the artist was disappointed that few Indians were to be seen.[62] The significance of this sketch is in its view of Ste. Anne's. The new Catholic church had been constructed on a lot donated by Madame La Framboise and was in place at the corner of Main and Church streets by June 1827. Ste. Anne's was enlarged in 1831 in the aftermath of Father Mazzuchelli's debates with Reverend Ferry. By the time of Beaumont's visit the building had been lengthened by the

Gustave de Beaumont (1802–66) was the traveling companion of Alexis de Tocqueville on his journey through the Great Lakes. An amateur artist, Beaumont drew several views of Mackinac Island. This portrait sketch was in family hands in 1938 and was reproduced in George W. Pierson, *Tocqueville and Beaumont in America* (New York, 1938). *University of Michigan Libraries.*

construction of a new sanctuary and sacristy. A rectory had also been built.[63] Ste. Anne's would be pictured again in 1844 (Fig. 7.17), and the church would remain in essentially this form until it was demolished in 1873 to clear the site for the existing building.

Beaumont and his companions spent little time in the town before striking off to view the natural wonders of Mackinac Island. He, Tocqueville, and two companions climbed from the beach to the top of Arch Rock, where their local guide was overcome by "the vertigo" and had to slide back down the bluff. The visitors continued to Sugar Loaf, where Beaumont discovered a few human bones in its small caves. He carried away a piece of one as a souvenir.[64]

Beaumont got a more graphic memento of Mackinac's natural wonders in the drawing he later made of Arch Rock, illustrated here as Figure 6.5. From Sugar Loaf the party visited Skull Cave and then returned to town about 5:00 in the afternoon. While Tocqueville walked through the village, Beaumont and Godfrey Vigne obtained a small boat and went to sketch the arch from the water. Each made a drawing, although only Beaumont's is known to survive.[65] He made his finished sketch on August 16, while returning to Buffalo on the steamboat. Visible within the arch are two human figures, seemingly unaffected by the "dizziness" that had sent Beaumont's guide scrambling back to the beach.

This religious painting of St. Anne teaching the young Virgin Mary is attributed to Mathaus Langus and is believed to have hung over the altar in Ste. Anne's Church during the 1830s. Lieutenant John W. Phelps probably saw it when he visited the building in 1840. In his journal, Phelps criticized the "tawdry finery" of the decorations, adding, "To what school of painting the pictures belonged, I could not even guess—but no good one tho'." *Parish of Ste. Anne, Mackinac Island, MI. Photograph by Jeffrey Dupre.*

Father Samuel Charles Mazzuchelli (1806–64) was pastor of Ste. Anne's Church in 1830–33. During his time at Mackinac, Mazzuchelli engaged in a spirited theological debate with the Reverend William Ferry and worked to counter the effects of Protestant proselytizing among the island's Roman Catholics. This portrait, showing Mazzuchelli in the early 1820s, was in the Dominican convent of Santa Sabina in Rome at the time it was reproduced in the 1915 edition of Mazzuchelli's memoirs. *University of Michigan Libraries.*

This is a bijou of an island

Anna Brownell Jameson

A little after 3:00 on the afternoon of July 26, 1837, Henry Schoolcraft watched a small wooden bateau push off from the shore in front of his agency house. For the first mile or so the five voyageurs of its crew rowed their little vessel. Once beyond the confines of Haldimand Bay the wind was fair for Sault Ste. Marie. The men hoisted a small, square sail and set out across Lake Huron. Their craft skimmed "merrily over the blue waves" and was soon lost from sight.[66]

The Indian agent had come to the beach to see off his wife, Jane Johnston, and their children, who were going to the Sault to visit Mrs. Schoolcraft's mother. They shared the bateau with another passenger, an Englishwoman named Anna Brownell Jameson. For the past five days she had been a guest of the Schoolcrafts and had become very attached to Jané. Anna Jameson had proved herself "a most intelligent and agreeable inmate" of the Indian Agency House.[67] Indeed, she must have seemed unique amid the stream of visitors who sought out Schoolcraft with letters of introduction, each interested in experiencing Mackinac Island with its increasingly well-known scenery and colorful Native Americans. Mrs. Jameson was different than most of Schoolcraft's guests from the east. She was a published author and a married woman traveling unescorted on an adventurous tour around the margins of Lake Huron.

Anna Jameson would write about her experiences, including her five days on Mackinac Island. She was an artist as well. Schoolcraft found her to be "an eminent landscape painter, or rather sketcher in crayon," who kept a portfolio with her as she viewed the attractions of the island. Schoolcraft was impressed by the "freedom from restraint in her motions," which he found "an agreeable trait in a person of her literary tastes and abilities." Mrs. Jameson had also proven herself keenly interested in the Indians, both from a cultural point of view and "as a fine subject of artistic observation."[68]

Jameson was forty-three and well traveled by the time she visited Mackinac Island. The daughter of an Irish miniature painter, whose fortunes had never been very prosperous, she had earned a living as a governess before marrying Robert Jameson in what soon proved an unhappy match. The couple often lived apart, but in the winter of 1837 she joined him in Toronto, where he was serving in a government post. The reunion and a winter in Canada confirmed her unhappiness, and in June she set out on a tour to Niagara, Detroit, and ultimately Mackinac and the Sault.[69] Jameson sketched wherever she visited, and a mounted portfolio of her finished works, probably a selection of what she considered her best drawings, survives today. Her four Mackinac scenes and two portrait sketches focus on the Indians, and, though she visited the usual points of interest, places such as Arch Rock and Sugar Loaf are not represented among her surviving works.

Scattered through Jameson's own narrative is evidence that she made more than just four views while on Mackinac Island. She learned of the opportunity to travel to Sault Ste. Marie with Mrs. Schoolcraft while "sketching and dreaming" in the shade of a schooner moored to one of the wharves. A few days before she bemoaned the fact that she had been so taken by the spectacle of an Indian council in Schoolcraft's office that she neglected to make a single sketch of the participants. "There was not a figure among them that was not a study for a painter," she lamented. Like many of Schoolcraft's visitors, she was driven over much of the island by her host and must have recorded what she saw.[70]

Anna Jameson had her first look at Mackinac Island early on the morning of July 21, 1837, when she came on the deck of her steamer to see the harbor, fort, and town cast in the "softest shades of rose-colour" by the rising sun. The first of her sketches (Fig. 6.6) duplicates that initial view. "Immediately in front rose the abrupt and picturesque heights . . . robed in richest foliage, and crowned by the lines of the little fortress, snow-white, and gleaming in the morning light," she wrote. The waters of the harbor enhanced the scene and "reflected every form as in a mirror," particularly the Indian encampment that lined the beach.[71] At the base of the bluff she would have noticed Schoolcraft's agency house, the sloping ground in front of it "laid out in a garden, with an avenue of fruit trees, the gate at the end opening on the very edge of the lake."[72] The building and its setting impressed most who saw it. Two years earlier George Featherstonhaugh had described it as a "very comfortable house" and thought that it made "a conspicuous figure, being well situated at the foot of the hill, with a good garden in front."[73] Jameson's sketch captures all of these elements, including a derelict chimney and a house to the east of the government property.

The imminent departure of her steamer forced Anna Jameson to hastily disembark so as to remain on the island. She had arrived at Mackinac without a letter of introduction but in the hope that Mrs. Schoolcraft's sister and brother-in-law would have informed them of her coming. The hour was too early, however, to present herself at their door. She was conducted from the pier to a "little inn," where she enjoyed a hearty breakfast of "white-fish, eggs, tea and coffee," but even then it was only a little past six o'clock in the morning. To occupy herself until a decent calling hour, she took her sketchbook and "sauntered forth alone to the beach," observing the Indian families and their lodges. Before she knew it, she had "strayed and loitered" for three hours.[74]

Figure 6.7, dated July 21, is a product of Anna Jameson's walk on the beach. It appears to have been drawn near the southwestern end

Anna Brownell Jameson (1794–1860) was an astute observer who recorded her 1837 visit to Mackinac Island in words and pictures. Jameson took a particular interest in the Indians and was a guest of Henry and Jane Schoolcraft during her five-day stay. Jameson's book appeared in 1839. This watercolor portrait was probably based on an early photograph. *Toronto Public Library (John Ross Robertson Collection).*

FIGURE 6.6
TITLE: [On mount:] Island of Mackinaw—Lake Huron. Indians' Village.
AUTHOR: Anna Brownell Jameson (1794–1860).
DATE DEPICTED: July 21–26, 1837.
DATE OF WORK: July 21–26, 1837.
DESCRIPTION: 13.5 x 23 cm. Pencil and watercolor on paper.
PROVENANCE: Apparently retained by the artist. Sketches placed in the care of the Toronto Public Library by Mrs. J. Watson Bain and donated in 1966.
COLLECTION: Special Collections, Genealogy and Maps Centre, Toronto Public Library (Anna Jameson Sketchbook, No. 22, 966-6L-22).

FIGURE 6.7

TITLE: [On drawing:] Wigwams on the beach at Mackinac—July 21. [On mount:] Wigwams on the Beach at Mackinaw.

AUTHOR: Anna Brownell Jameson (1794–1860).

DATE DEPICTED: July 21, 1837.

DATE OF WORK: July 21, 1837.

DESCRIPTION: 12.3 x 17 cm. Pencil on paper.

PROVENANCE: Apparently retained by the artist. Sketches placed in the care of the Toronto Public Library by Mrs. J. Watson Bain and donated in 1966.

COLLECTION: Special Collections, Genealogy and Maps Centre, Toronto Public Library (Anna Jameson Sketchbook, No. 24, 966-6L-24).

FIGURE 6.8

TITLE: [On drawing:] Mackinac July 25. [On mount:] The Beach at Mackinaw from the Missionary Church door.

AUTHOR: Anna Brownell Jameson (1794–1860).

DATE DEPICTED: July 25, 1837.

DATE OF WORK: July 25, 1837.

DESCRIPTION: 12.3 x 17 cm. Pencil on paper.

PROVENANCE: Apparently retained by the artist. Sketches placed in the care of the Toronto Public Library by Mrs. J. Watson Bain and donated in 1966.

COLLECTION: Special Collections, Genealogy and Maps Centre, Toronto Public Library (Anna Jameson Sketchbook, No. 25, 966-6L-25).

FIGURE 6.9

TITLE: [On drawing:] Machillimackinac. [On mount:] The Beach at Mackinaw.

AUTHOR: Anna Brownell Jameson (1794–1860).

DATE DEPICTED: July 23, 1837.

DATE OF WORK: July 23, 1837.

DESCRIPTION: 12.3 x 17 cm. Pencil on paper.

PROVENANCE: Apparently retained by the artist. Sketches placed in the care of the Toronto Public Library by Mrs. J. Watson Bain and donated in 1966.

COLLECTION: Special Collections, Genealogy and Maps Centre, Toronto Public Library (Anna Jameson Sketchbook, No. 22, 966-6L-26).

FORT MICHILIMACKINAC.

FIGURE 6.10

TITLE: Fort Michilimackinac.
AUTHOR: George William Featherstonhaugh
(1780–1866). Engraved by George S. Measom
(active 1845–62).
DATE DEPICTED: August 17, 1835.
DATE OF WORK: Published 1847.
DESCRIPTION: 6 x 8 cm. Woodcut.
PROVENANCE: Published in Featherstonhaugh,
A Canoe Voyage up the Minnay Sotor.... (London,
1847), 1:148.
COLLECTION: Clements Library, University of
Michigan, Ann Arbor (Book Division, C2-1847-Fe).

of Haldimand Bay with the point of Round Island visible in the background. The Native American visitors and their lodges fascinated the artist. During July most of them were traveling to Georgian Bay to collect their annual presents from the British government.[75] Jameson's careful study of their wigwams is apparent. They were constructed, she noted, of eight to twelve long poles stuck in the ground and arranged in a circle. This framework was then covered or "thatched in some sort with mats, or large pieces of birch bark, beginning at the bottom and leaving an opening at the top for the emission of smoke." Each doorway was covered with a blanket or piece of animal skin. She was later told that the pointed wigwam was the style favored by the Ottawa and Potawatomi, both of whom she encountered on Mackinac Island, while an oblong or domed form was used by the Ojibwa.[76]

Also of interest were the canoes in which the Native American travelers had arrived on the island. All were constructed of birch bark, and they were "exceedingly light, flat-bottomed, and most elegant in shape, varying in size from eighteen to thirty-six feet in length, and from a foot and a half to four feet in width." The pieces of each wigwam, members of the family, all their goods, and even their dogs could be packed into their vessel.[77] Canoes figure prominently in Jameson's sketch of July 21 as well as two later views of Indian

encampments. Figure 6.8 was sketched on July 25 on the beach in front of Mission Church with Round Island clearly visible in the background. Figure 6.9 was completed two days before. It, too, depicts wigwams and an overturned canoe on Mission Point with the town visible in the background across Haldimand Bay.

Anna Jameson found that word of her coming had reached the Schoolcrafts, and they were prepared to welcome her. She lived with them throughout her stay and spent much of her time observing the Indians, their dress, and activities. She witnessed councils and dances, peeked into wigwams to see how they lived, and was clearly fascinated. Like Henry Schoolcraft and many others, however, she could tell that their world was changing. Rapid settlement, the end of the fur trade and the mission, and the influx of visitors and even resorters foretold a very different future for Mackinac. Jameson recognized the attraction of the place as a resort, but admitted that she was glad that the transformation was not yet complete and that she had "beheld this lovely Island in all its wild beauty."[78]

Two other visitors of the mid-1830s also left visual impressions of Mackinac Island, though from a greater distance than did Anna Jameson. George Featherstonhaugh spent five days there in August 1835 on his way to the Mississippi River on a geological investigation. He found lodgings in one of the boardinghouses where, like Mrs.

FIGURE 6.11

TITLE: [Mackinaw from the East].

AUTHOR: George Catlin (1796–1872). Engraved by Myers and Company.

DATE DEPICTED: 1836.

DATE OF WORK: Published 1841.

DESCRIPTION: 9 x 12.2 cm. Engraving.

PROVENANCE: Published in Catlin, *Letters and Notes on the Manners, Customs, and Condition of the North American Indians* (London, 1841), 2:161 (plate 264).

COLLECTION: Clements Library, University of Michigan, Ann Arbor (Book Division, C2-1841-Ca).

Several women were among the literary visitors to Mackinac in the 1830s. English writer Harriet Martineau (1802–76) spent two days on the island in July 1836, which she described in a widely read account of her travels. Martineau emphasized the scenic beauty of Mackinac and likened the view from Fort Holmes to "what Noah might have seen." This portrait engraving, showing her in 1850, is tipped into a copy of James Boyle, *Miss Martineau on America, Reviewed* (1837).

Clements Library, University of Michigan.

Jameson, he was introduced to the renowned fish of the Straits at breakfast. Entering the dining room, he found himself confronted with "a most magnificent salmon trout, weighing at least 30 lb!" that was to be shared by the four guests then in the house. He spent an hour grazing on the giant fish before "retiring from it with regret."[79]

Although Featherstonhaugh did not stay with Henry Schoolcraft, their mutual interests in geology and the Indians drew the attention of the agent, who invited Featherstonhaugh to view his collections and accompanied him on a boat trip around Mackinac and across the channel to Round Island.[80] Featherstonhaugh sketched all along the way, and on Round Island the group indulged their curiosity by disturbing several Indian graves. The geologist admitted that this constituted "absurd and irrational" behavior on his part, but he carried off a few souvenirs nonetheless.[81]

George Featherstonhaugh explored much of Mackinac Island, sketching scenery and examining its geology and flora as he went. The only one of his images known to survive, however, is an engraving in his book, published in 1847 and included here as Figure 6.10. The sketch on which it was based was made as he left the island on August 17, 1835. It shows the island from the west, with its vertical features greatly exaggerated. As the steamer moved through the Straits the artist was "struck with the great beauty of the scene" and tried to capture "the lofty island, the old French fort [Holmes] conspicuous in the distance, [and] the American fort, of dazzling whiteness, just above the town."[82]

An artist of greater renown visited in 1836, though he apparently did not seek out Schoolcraft and did not feel it necessary to comment on "Mackinaw," which he thought had already been "an hundred times described."[83] George Catlin is best known today for his paintings of the Indians of the upper Mississippi and eastern Plains. He saw Mackinac on his way from Sault Ste. Marie to Green Bay. Catlin's view shows Mackinac Island from the east with an impression of the town, the outline of Fort Mackinac, and, far to the right, the bulk of Arch Rock projecting from the bluff. The higher levels of the island display thicker foliage by 1836, but the bluffs themselves are still largely devoid of trees and brush. Catlin's original sketch survives in the National Archives, and Figure 6.11 is an engraving reproduced in his *Letters and Notes* of 1841.

Harriet Martineau, another writer and 1836 visitor, last gazed on Mackinac from the same perspective as Catlin's view as she regretfully departed on July 5. "We watched the island as it rapidly receded," she wrote as her boat moved along Bois Blanc Island. "Its flag first vanished; then its green terraces and slopes, its white barracks, and dark promontories faded, till the whole disappeared behind a headland and lighthouse on the Michigan shore." Martineau's brief visit had convinced her that Mackinac was "the wildest and tenderest little piece of beauty that I have yet seen on God's earth."[84]

Although most of Anna Jameson's surviving Mackinac Island drawings depict scenes around the harbor, she preserved her sketches of a pair of Native Americans named Mokomaunish (left) and Kee-me-wun. Jameson described the latter, whose name translated as "Rain," as "one of the noblest figures I ever beheld, above six feet high, erect as a forest pine." She then lamented watching him, at first, resist an invitation to join other Native Americans in a drunken revel and then succumb to the "fatal temptation." *Toronto Public Library (966–6L-58).*

A younger, brightly painted Kee-me-wun was portrayed at Fond du Lac, Wisconsin, in 1826 by James Otto Lewis. The artist described him as an Ojibwa chief and translated his name as "Rain." He was almost certainly the same man that Anna Jameson thought to be an Ottawa when she sketched him at Mackinac Island in 1837. Lithograph by Lehman and Duval. *Clements Library, University of Michigan.*

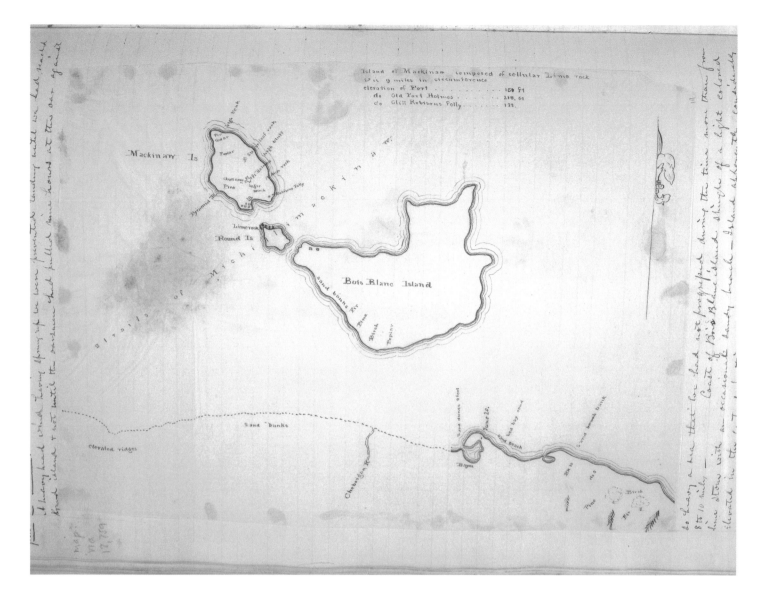

FIGURE 6.12

TITLE: [Mackinac, Round, and Bois Blanc islands].

AUTHOR: Douglass Houghton (1809–45).

DATE DEPICTED: June 21, 1838.

DATE OF WORK: June 21, 1838.

DESCRIPTION: 12 x 17 cm. Pen and ink on paper.

PROVENANCE: Pasted to a page of Houghton's field notes for 1837–41.

COLLECTION: Bentley Historical Library, University of Michigan, Ann Arbor (Douglass Houghton Papers, Field Notes and Observations, 1837–1841).

Douglass Houghton (1809–45) visited the Straits of Mackinac in 1838 and 1839 during his geological survey of the new state of Michigan. Houghton characterized the distinctive "Mackinac limestone," and his field notes say much about prominent natural features on the island and on the Upper Peninsula mainland. Alvah Bradish painted Houghton's portrait sometime between 1835 and Houghton's death ten years later.

Bentley Historical Library, University of Michigan.

This beautifully situated spot commands nearly the whole island

Douglass Houghton

Henry Schoolcraft seems never to have tired of the beauties and wonders of Mackinac Island or the scenic vistas that opened from its promontories and bluffs. In June 1839 he found himself reflecting on Harriet Martineau's published comments about the loveliness of the place. He agreed with her that "it is indeed a spot of rare attractiveness." Schoolcraft's thoughts then turned to what might have been one of his favorite locations, the island's highest point and site of Fort Holmes. Still largely cleared of trees, the summit of the "turtle's back" offered a panorama of islands and blue waters. "The view embraces to the north the head waters of the Huron and the far-off isles of St. Martin, to the west Green Island and the Straits of Mackinaw, and to the east and south Bois Blanc and the Great Lake," Schoolcraft wrote in his journal.[85]

This view had been appreciated long before Schoolcraft's time, and the heights behind Fort Mackinac had demonstrated their strategic value during and after the War of 1812. Fort Holmes had been abandoned for twenty years by the time Schoolcraft recorded his thoughts, but many details could still be picked out from its ruins. Chandler Gilman was guided around the site in the summer of 1835. He found it easy enough to trace the outline of the earthworks. "The sodded walls have lost but little of their height," he wrote, and it was possible to discern "the embrasures where the cannon were placed, the reservoir for water, and the bakehouse."[86] The fort's military days were past, however, and the general consensus was that they would not return.[87] Tourists frequently visited, but it was the splendor of the scenery that encouraged them to scale the heights.

The commanding view from Fort Holmes possessed more than scenic or military value, however. The panoramic vista from the highest spot in the Straits of Mackinac was also attractive to surveyors and mapmakers. Military engineers had climbed the hill on several occasions to calculate its elevation above Lake Huron. Captain David Bates Douglass did so on June 11, 1820, when he estimated the summit to be 270 feet above the lake. Captain Benjamin Pierce of the Fort Mackinac garrison had previously (and more accurately) measured its elevation at 300 feet, and this had become accepted local wisdom.[88] Regardless of such details, Fort Holmes offered the most practical station from which to observe the surrounding lands and waters.

Figures 6.12–6.15, produced during 1838 and 1840, emphasize the importance of Mackinac Island's highest point to the ongoing mapping of the Straits. Surveyors Aaron Greeley and John Mullett had probably visited the spot when they conducted their work in 1810 and 1828. "Old Ft. Holmes" consistently appears as a landmark on the published versions of Mullett's maps of the island and Straits as engraved by John Farmer after 1829 (Figs. 5.26 and 5.29–5.31).

When Douglass Houghton and Bela Hubbard stopped in June 1838 while surveying the coast of Michigan's Lower Peninsula from Detroit to Chicago, Fort Holmes offered a convenient observation point from which to determine the relative bearings of locations along the south shore of the Straits.

Douglass Houghton drew Figure 6.12, which is pasted below his field notes for June 21, 1838. At 5:00 that morning, he and Hubbard had embarked with their crews in an open boat to make the traverse from the Lower Peninsula mainland to Bois Blanc Island. The Michigan shoreline is confidently drawn on Houghton's map to the point where his party set out from Duncan Bay east of modern Cheboygan. To the west of that spot, Houghton rendered the south coast only as a dotted line, with the mouth of the Cheboygan River sketched in. The two geologists had a difficult crossing, and their rowers fought a northwest headwind for nine hours before finding shelter in the lee of Round Island and reaching their Mackinac Island campsite below Robinson's Folly later in the afternoon.[89] Houghton's map carefully depicts the south shore of Bois Blanc, but its north coast is surprisingly inaccurate, especially considering the wide distribution, by 1838, of John Mullett's maps of the Straits and its islands. Mackinac itself seems to have been based on the Mullett-Farmer maps, and "Ft. Holmes" is its most prominent feature.

For the next six days the team examined the geology, topography, and flora of Mackinac, Round, and the St. Martin islands. On June 23, Hubbard set out to determine the elevation of Fort Holmes. He found the highest part of the old earthworks to be 318.530 feet above Lake Huron. Fort Mackinac, visible below, was 151 feet above the water.[90] Four days later, after Hubbard and Houghton had returned to the south mainland to continue their voyage into Lake Michigan, the former completed a sketch of the Straits incorporating what they had observed during the past week. Fort Holmes looks like the hub of a wheel in Figure 6.13, with compass bearings radiating from it like spokes. Some details of the mainland—the "Elevated Ridges" to the south, for example—could best have been observed from the island's heights. As with Houghton's map, a stretch of the south coast is drawn in dotted line and labeled "Not traversed."

A trip around Mackinac Island in a small boat on June 23 and subsequent explorations on foot provided the information used by Hubbard to prepare Figure 6.14. Sketched into his field notes, this rough outline map identifies the principal geological features that had become Mackinac Island's standard attractions—Arch Rock, Sugar Loaf, Robinson's Folly, Skull Cave—as well as the two forts. Lover's Leap appears as well, although Hubbard mislabeled it "Pyramid rock," the name attached to Sugar Loaf on the Mullett-

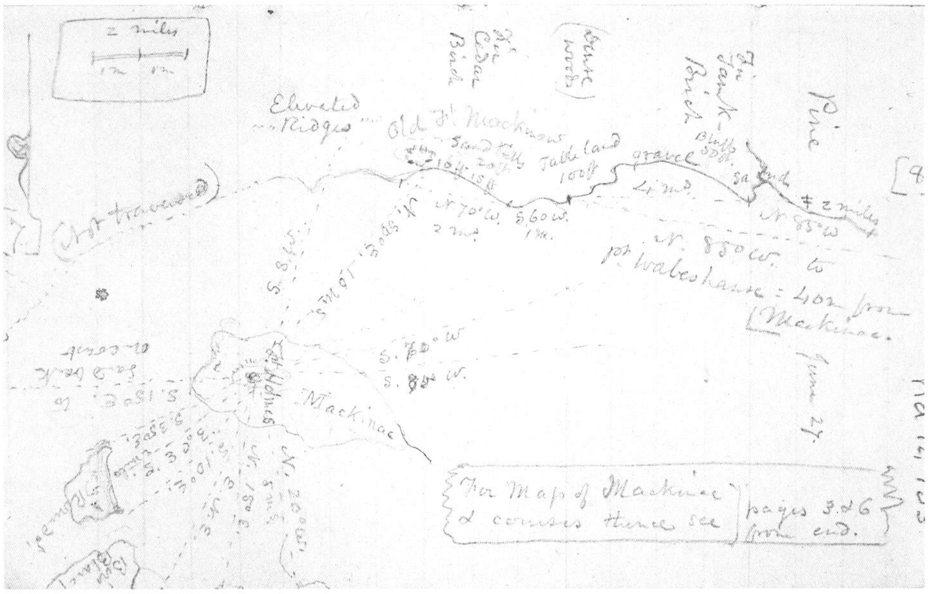

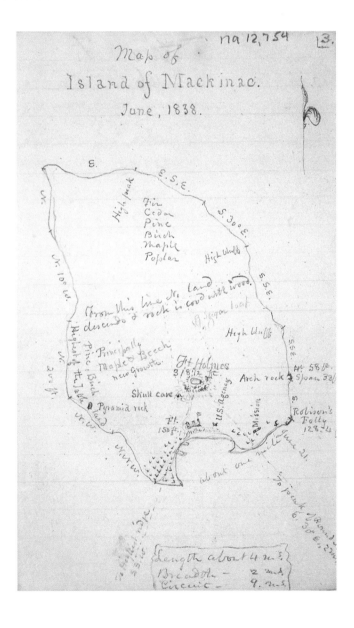

FIGURE 6.13

TITLE: [Map of the Straits of Mackinac].
AUTHOR: Bela Hubbard (1814–96).
DATE DEPICTED: June 1838.
DATE OF WORK: June 1838.
DESCRIPTION: 9.5 x 16 cm. Pencil on paper.
PROVENANCE: Drawn into field notebook for May 19–July 24, 1838, during his survey of the Lower Peninsula coast.
COLLECTION: Bentley Historical Library, University of Michigan, Ann Arbor (Bela Hubbard Papers, 851637, AcAa 2, Box 1, Vol. 2, p. 8).

FIGURE 6.14

TITLE: Map of Island of Mackinac June 1838.
AUTHOR: Bela Hubbard (1814–96).
DATE DEPICTED: June 1838.
DATE OF WORK: June 1838.
DESCRIPTION: 16 x 9.5 cm. Pencil on paper in notebook.
PROVENANCE: Drawn into field notebook for May 19–July 24, 1838, during his survey of the Lower Peninsula coast.
COLLECTION: Bentley Historical Library, University of Michigan, Ann Arbor (Bela Hubbard Papers, 851637, AcAa 2, Box 1, Vol. 2, p. 3).

Farmer maps. Lover's Leap is shown on Mullett's maps (Figs. 5.25 and 5.26) as "Little Rock." Elevations of the principal points are noted on the sketch.

Not identified on Figure 6.14 was another prominent feature between Robinson's Folly and Arch Rock; Hubbard had never heard it spoken of before he viewed it in 1838. He described it as a mass of rock projecting from the bluff, the bottom of which had been hollowed out to resemble a fireplace. "It deserves a name amongst curiosities of the island," he opined. The formation would later become known as Fairy Arch and would be numbered among Mackinac's attractions until it was dynamited in 1953.[91]

Bela Hubbard took the time to add some general notes on topography and the varieties of trees that he had observed on the island. By the late 1830s the forests of Mackinac Island were beginning to recover, at least in areas away from the town and farms. Calvin Colton had noted "forests of slender growth" in 1830, which, five years later, were described by another writer as made up of "small trees and shrubs." In June 1835 Enos Goodrich found "dwarfed timber," which was largely fir and "Mackinaw or white birch." Later that summer Chandler Gilman wrote of "scrubby oak and dwarf maple" and stated that "there are no large trees on Mackina."[92] Most of these species are noted on Hubbard's sketch, although neither he nor Houghton had much to say about vegetation in their field journals, focusing instead on the island's geology.

Hubbard returned to Mackinac Island in 1840, at which time he took the opportunity to sketch a few of the sites he had visited two years before. His view from Fort Holmes (Fig. 6.15) is the earliest image known to have captured that scene. Drawn from the top of the old earthworks, his perspective is toward the Lower Peninsula mainland with Round Island and Bois Blanc to the left, the tips of the mainlands to the right, and Fort Mackinac spread out below. Although roughly sketched, the shapes of the post's walls, blockhouses, and flagpole may be discerned. A fenced enclosure near the fort is the garrison woodyard, completed in 1836.[93]

Although the artist only revealed the vista to the south, Chandler Gilman described the rest of the panorama from Fort Holmes in 1835. Below and to the west he could see "an expanse of well-wooded land" punctuated by a few hills and valleys. Behind and to his right the hill sloped more gradually away from the ruins, forming the narrow plateau on which Fort Holmes had been built. Turning to the north, Gilman could see the northeast shore of Mackinac Island, the St. Martin Islands, and the Upper Peninsula mainland stretching eastward until it was lost in the distance in a "blue line" mingling with "blue clouds or bluer waters" in Lake Huron. The "horns of Bois Blanc, and the woody summit of Round Island" completed "the magnificent circle of view."[94] Hubbard's little

FIGURE 6.15
TITLE: View from Ft. Holmes, Island of Michilimackinac.
AUTHOR: Bela Hubbard (1814–96).
DATE DEPICTED: May 23, 1840.
DATE OF WORK: May 23, 1840.
DESCRIPTION: 10 x 16 cm. Pencil on paper.
PROVENANCE: Drawn into Hubbard's notebook journal for March 26–July 13, 1840.
COLLECTION: Bentley Historical Library, University of Michigan, Ann Arbor (Bela Hubbard Papers, 851637, Box 1, Vol. 7, No. 6117).

FIGURE 6.16

TITLE: Arch rock, as seen from above.

AUTHOR: Bela Hubbard (1814–96).

DATE DEPICTED: May 23, 1840.

DATE OF WORK: May 23, 1840.

DESCRIPTION: 16 x 10 cm. Pencil on paper.

PROVENANCE: Drawn into Hubbard's notebook journal for March 26–July 13, 1840.

COLLECTION: Bentley Historical Library, University of Michigan, Ann Arbor (Bela Hubbard Papers, 851637, Box 1, Vol. 7, No. 6119).

FIGURE 6.17

TITLE: Pyramid Rock. Mackinac. As seen from the plain.

AUTHOR: Bela Hubbard (1814–96).

DATE DEPICTED: May 23, 1840.

DATE OF WORK: May 23, 1840.

DESCRIPTION: 16 x 10 cm. Pencil on paper.

PROVENANCE: Drawn into Hubbard's notebook journal for March 26–July 13, 1840.

COLLECTION: Bentley Historical Library, University of Michigan, Ann Arbor (Bela Hubbard Papers, 851637, Box 1, Vol. 7, No. 6118).

drawing clearly shows the feature that had given the smaller island its name. Known to the French as Isle Ronde, Gilman described it as "round in shape as in name," not for its outline on the map but because the viewer saw "a perfect arch upon the sky, so regularly does the land rise from every side towards the centre."[95]

Bela Hubbard drew his view from Fort Holmes as he rambled about the island on May 23, 1840. Judging by the journal of one of his companions, Charles W. Penny, their walk took them first from Robinson's Folly to Arch Rock, then on to Sugar Loaf, Fort Holmes, and Skull Cave.[96] Hubbard hastily drew Arch Rock and Sugar Loaf (Figs. 6.16 and 6.17) as they visited. The latter he identified as "Pyramid Rock," correcting the error on his 1838 map and employing a popular alternate name of the 1820s and 1830s.

The artist depicted Arch Rock as seen from above. This was the island's premier attraction, described by Hubbard in 1838 as "a narrow band of rock . . . springing into a beautiful & perfect arch." It spanned a chasm opening to the lakeshore about 130 feet below. The rocky arch, Hubbard estimated, was about thirty-three feet long and no more than two feet wide in some parts with a vertical depth of about six feet. He was told that pieces of the rock were constantly breaking away and, like many other observers of his time, speculated that "this beautiful great natl curiosity does not promise to be [of] many years duration."[97] When Hubbard sketched the arch in 1840,

his companion, Charles Penny, expressed the same concern and was certain it would collapse in less than a century.[98]

Hubbard's view of "Pyramid Rock" is more boldly drawn. The perspective is similar to that sketched by Captain David Bates Douglass in 1820 (Fig. 5.6). The artist pictured the huge mass of rock as seen from the north, with "Keyhole Cave" visible and stunted cedars clinging to its summit. A comparison of the Douglass and Hubbard views provides a sense of how the forests were reestablishing themselves. The 1820 sketch shows the ground nearly bare around the rock, while trees and bushes have grown to a height of about fifteen feet in the Hubbard sketch made twenty years later.

Like Arch Rock, Sugar Loaf attracted its share of daredevils, even in 1838. The missionary Peter Dougherty climbed to the top in July of that year, exploring the shallow caverns that pocked the stone. From his perch one hundred feet above the ground Dougherty thought the pinnacle seemed "like some old fortress that had resisted the assault of the foe for ages."[99] Others were less impressed. "Rocks piled upon rocks do not excite so much enthusiasm as some persons affect to feel in their presence," Enos Goodrich recalled of his 1835 visit. He did not "try to push over the sugar loaf rock" as did some of his fellow tourists.[100] For most visitors, however, Arch Rock and Sugar Loaf were firmly established as the principal "natural curiosities" of Mackinac Island.

Bela Hubbard (1814–96) accompanied Douglass Houghton during his 1838 Mackinac visit and stopped again two years later on his way to Lake Superior. Hubbard made rough sketches in his 1840 fieldbook, including small portraits of himself and his companions. Hubbard's self-portrait gives an idea of the effect of travel in an open boat on one's personal appearance.
Bentley Historical Library, University of Michigan.

Bela Hubbard and his friends adopted Native American names during their 1840 trip to Lake Superior. Charles W. Penny (1812–92), shown here in another of Hubbard's pencil sketches, was identified as "Muckwa" or "bear." While at Mackinac, Penny confided to his journal, he ate so many whitefish "that my tail wiggles as I go along the street."
Bentley Historical Library, University of Michigan.

I was impressed with his suavity of manners, and the interest he manifested in natural history

Henry Rowe Schoolcraft

Among Henry Schoolcraft's many eastern visitors during the summer of 1838 was one who was something of a kindred spirit, sharing many of his interests in science and ethnology. "I was impressed with his suavity of manners, and the interest he manifested in natural history," Schoolcraft wrote of François, comte de Castelnau, who called at the Indian Agency House on September 21. His guest arrived at what was probably the busiest time of Schoolcraft's year. The beach in front of the house was crowded with wigwams, and as many as four thousand Native Americans were encamped on Mackinac Island to receive their annuities from the U.S. government. The Indian agent took the time, nonetheless, to chat and presented Castelnau with "some . . . characteristic northern specimens in mineralogy."[101]

The Frenchman, for his part, was delighted to meet the well-known American savant, whom he knew from Schoolcraft's published account of the 1820 Cass expedition to identify the source of the Mississippi River. Schoolcraft greeted Castelnau with "noble and moving" hospitality, and the two conversed for some time on a variety of topics, an exchange Schoolcraft characterized as "familiar." The Frenchman was interested in Schoolcraft's work with the Indians, their languages and traditions, and the fact that he was married to a woman of Native American background. The Indian agent, for his part, recalled that Castelnau mentioned that he was descended from a survivor of the St. Bartholomew's Day massacre during the French religious wars of the sixteenth century. Although he was too polite to ask, Schoolcraft thus assumed that his visitor was "of Protestant parentage," something that was not the case with most of his French-speaking Mackinac neighbors. The meeting was a high point of Castelnau's tour, and he went away with lasting memories of the courtesy with which he had been received.[102]

Castelnau was "a French gentleman on his travels in America," and his voyage produced a book and a series of lithographs. The latter were presumably based on his own drawings, recording what he saw during an extended visit to the Great Lakes in the summer and fall of 1838. This took Castelnau three times to Mackinac Island, a place he recognized for its importance to lake travel as a port of entry, refueling stop, and point of natural interest. Although it is impossible to say during which visits Castelnau drew the scenes published in his *Vues et Souvenirs de l'Amérique du Nord,* details in his text afford a few suggestions and complement his revealing if somewhat naive images.

The Frenchman's first view of the Straits of Mackinac came late in the day on August 28, 1838, as his steamer churned toward a fueling stop at the island. Figure 6.18 preserves the scene spread before him as the vessel passed along the north shore of Bois Blanc Island. Castelnau doubtless asked questions of fellow travelers, and he was somewhat amused to learn that the Americans had corrupted the name of the largest island in the Straits to "Boblaie." Beyond lay "la petite île Ronde," which, he was told, was named for its shape. In the distance was Mackinac Island, where the steamer stopped for firewood. This provided an opportunity for a brief look at the town before the vessel continued into Lake Michigan.[103]

Although embellished with a large and probably imaginary sailing vessel, Castelnau's view of the three islands captures the scene with fair accuracy. The harbor, town, and fort of Mackinac Island are visible at right, with a suggestion of the huge encampment of wigwams that lined the beach. The picture is most useful, however, for its depiction of Bois Blanc Island and a pair of structures on Lighthouse Point. Although the artist seems to have been unaware of what he drew, the house and stubby tower provide a rare look at the site of one of the most dramatic lighthouse stories of the Great Lakes.

Acting on a petition of the residents of Michilimackinac, the United States had constructed a tower and keeper's quarters on Bois Blanc in 1829. Eber Ward was appointed keeper, a position he would hold for fifteen years.[104] Bois Blanc Island proved a difficult place to build and maintain a stone light tower, however, and the quality of construction was not the best. By the spring of 1833 Ward was complaining of deterioration and lack of maintenance.[105] No real action was taken, and the problems were only aggravated by rising water levels in Lake Huron. By September 1837 Ward was warning that the tower might collapse. The lake bank had been eroded to within about five feet of its foundation, and the cellar of the residence was full of water, which rose and fell "in the same proportion as the Lake."[106]

The crisis came less than three months later. Ward had crossed to Mackinac Island, leaving his daughter Emily and a young friend, Bolivar Brooks, to tend the light. When a "perfect gale" blew through the Straits on December 9, Emily kept the light burning "until the last possible moment." By 5:00 in the afternoon water was sweeping around the foundation, and she decided to save the lamp apparatus. Making five trips up and down the 150 steps to the top of the tower, Emily removed it piece by piece before retreating with Bolivar to the keeper's house. The rain passed, and in the bright moonlight the pair watched the waves beat against the tower. Suddenly, they saw a "long zigzag line" run from its base to its top. The tower tottered. "Come Bolivar," Emily ordered, and as they fled to the woods "the huge pile of masonry" came down with a crash. Three days later Eber Ward salvaged what he could and reported the disaster.[107]

Pl. 21.

Lith. par Aumont.

Lith. Ligny. r. Salle au Comte, 10.

Ile de Michilimakimac
(Lac Huron.)

FIGURE 6.18

TITLE: Ile de Michilimakimac (Lac Huron).

AUTHOR: François, comte de Castelnau (1812–80).
Lithograph by Aumont.

DATE DEPICTED: August 1838.

DATE OF WORK: 1842.

DESCRIPTION: 17.4 x 22.2 cm. Lithograph.

PROVENANCE: Published in Castelnau, *Vues et Souvenirs
de l'Amérique du Nord* (Paris, 1842), plate 27.

COLLECTION: Clements Library, University of Michigan,
Ann Arbor (Print Division, G-7).

Fort Américain,
dans l'Ile de Michilimakimac.

FIGURE 6.19

TITLE: Fort Américain dans l'Ile de Michilimakimac.

AUTHOR: François, comte de Castelnau (1812–80). Lithograph by Jacques Prat.

DATE DEPICTED: September 1838.

DATE OF WORK: 1842.

DESCRIPTION: 17.4 x 22.2 cm. Lithograph. This example has been colored.

PROVENANCE: Published in Castelnau, *Vues et Souvenirs de l'Amérique du Nord* (Paris, 1842), plate 26.

COLLECTION: Clements Library, University of Michigan, Ann Arbor (Print Division, G-7).

Village Ottowa
Ile de Michilimakimac.

FIGURE 6.20

TITLE: Village Ottowa Ile de Michilimakimac.

AUTHOR: François, comte de Castlenau (1812–80). Lithograph by Jacques Prat.

DATE DEPICTED: September 1838.

DATE OF WORK: 1842.

DESCRIPTION: 17 x 21.7 cm. Lithograph.

PROVENANCE: Published in Castelnau, *Vues et Souvenirs de l'Amérique du Nord* (Paris, 1842), plate 25.

COLLECTION: Special Collections Library, University of Michigan, Ann Arbor.

Lith. par Prat.

Roche Folie de Robinson

Lith Ligny et C.ie r. Salle-au-Comte, 10

FIGURE 6.21

TITLE: Roche Folie de Robinson. Ile de Michilimakimac.
AUTHOR: François, comte de Castlenau (1812–80). Lithograph by Jacques Prat.
DATE DEPICTED: September 1838.
DATE OF WORK: 1842.
DESCRIPTION: 17 x 21.7 cm. Lithograph.
PROVENANCE: Published in Castelnau, *Vues et Souvenirs de l'Amérique du Nord* (Paris, 1842), plate 21.
COLLECTION: Clements Library, University of Michigan, Ann Arbor (Print Division, G-7).

The tremendous southeast gale caused damage across the Straits area. The government and American Fur Company wharves at Mackinac Island were badly damaged, and the U.S. wharf on Bois Blanc was "totally destroyed." Three large sections of stockade were blown down at Fort Mackinac.[108] The fort was then unoccupied, but the Bois Blanc lighthouse was too important to be left in ruins, so the tower was rebuilt during 1838.[109] Castelnau's image captures the new light under construction, just to the left of the keeper's house.

If Fort Mackinac still displayed any ravages of the gale by the time of Castelnau's visit, they do not appear on his view from the heights to the west of the post (Fig. 6.19). This image was probably made late in September or early in October 1838 when he stopped at Mackinac for his third visit and found the time to examine the place more thoroughly. Although the fort had no garrison, its caretaker, Ordnance Sergeant R. J. Dunn, flew the national colors daily. He also excluded visitors from the fort, as one disappointed traveler discovered in July 1838.[110] To draw his picture, Castelnau stationed himself atop the road, probably Spring Street ("Turkey Hill"), leading up the bluff. There, the town was laid out at his feet, though he rendered it

so naively that it is difficult to distinguish individual structures. At the foot of the road is a large building behind the former American Fur Company retail store, and the grassy field is the government pasture, though several fences suggest the encroachments on public land that so vexed successive fort commandants.

Castelnau seems to have indulged his particular interest in Native Americans during his second visit to the island on September 20–21. It was on the latter date that he described in detail his examination of the extended, temporary village of Ottawas and Ojibwas that crowded the beach. Like other observers, Castelnau distinguished between the conical, bark-covered lodges of the Ottawa, shown in his scene, and the rounded houses of the Ojibwas that used woven mats to keep out the weather.[111] Castelnau's view of the Ottawa encampment (Fig. 6.20) is the most animated of his Mackinac scenes. It includes several figures, children playing among the canoes, and a few of the ubiquitous dogs found in Indian encampments. Anna Jameson had been struck, the previous summer, by the fact that around each lodge "lurked several ill-looking, half-starved yelping dogs."[112] A few years later, in 1845, Canadian artist

FIGURE 6.22

TITLE: La Roche arquée Ile de Michilimakimac.

AUTHOR: François, comte de Castlenau (1812–80). Lithograph by Jacques Prat.

DATE DEPICTED: September 1838.

DATE OF WORK: 1842.

DESCRIPTION: 17 x 21.7 cm. Lithograph.

PROVENANCE: Published in Castelnau, *Vues et Souvenirs de l'Amérique du Nord* (Paris, 1842), plate 24.

COLLECTION: Special Collections Library, University of Michigan, Ann Arbor.

FIGURE 6.23

TITLE: Roche dit le Pain de Sucre Ile de Michilimakimac.

AUTHOR: François, comte de Castlenau (1812–80). Lithograph by Jacques Prat.

DATE DEPICTED: September 1838.

DATE OF WORK: 1842.

DESCRIPTION: 17 x 21.7 cm. Lithograph.

PROVENANCE: Published in Castelnau, *Vues et Souvenirs de l'Amérique du Nord* (Paris, 1842), plate 23.

COLLECTION: Special Collections Library, University of Michigan, Ann Arbor.

Paul Kane was amazed when one of these "audacious brutes" dashed into his tent and "bolted off" with a lighted tallow candle.[113]

Castelnau's three remaining compositions (Figs. 6.21–6.23) were products of his third visit in late September or early October. They picture a trio of increasingly popular natural curiosities, most significantly Robinson's Folly, depicted in detail for the first time. The cliff at the southeastern corner of the island's bluffs had, during the 1830s, joined the more established attractions of Arch Rock and Sugar Loaf as a mandatory point of interest. This landmark had caught the attention of visitors since at least 1820, when Henry Schoolcraft and James Doty were the first to mention it in their writings. Robinson's Folly was already a well-known place, but the popular tales of the origin of its name were not recorded until the 1830s. In 1836 Chandler Robbins Gilman published an account of his 1835 visit to Mackinac Island under the title *Life on the Lakes*. In it, he first attributed the name to "a former commandant of Mackina" who used the spot "as the scene of his revels." Later in his book, Gilman spun an elaborate and floridly romantic tale of how "Robinson," his Native American lover, and her jealous Indian suitor were dashed to pieces after a desperate struggle on the cliff.[114]

Gilman's Robinson's Folly story would gain its greatest popularity later in the nineteenth century and into the twentieth. Most early visitors, Castelnau among them, heard a more conservative account of how Robinson (actually Captain Daniel Robertson, who commanded Fort Mackinac in 1782–87) built a pleasure house or "folly" at the scenic spot. Years later, the rocky outcrop collapsed, taking the remains of his house with it to the

beach below.[115] Although Gilman was the first to tell the tale, its elements were a part of local lore well before 1835. Thomas McKenney wrote of the "ruins of Robertson's Folly" in 1826, and "Folly Rock" appears on John Mullett's 1828 survey (Fig. 5.24). In July 1838 Samuel Lasley told geologist Bela Hubbard that he remembered a "huge overhanging ledge" that had crashed to the ground below the cliff at some point during his forty years on the island.[116] Figure 6.21 is a detailed and realistic view of Robinson's Folly including shattered pieces of rock beneath the precipice.

Castelnau chose to depict Arch Rock from above, and he does not appear, from his narrative, to have descended to the beach (Fig. 6.22).[117] The attraction was most accessible from the top of the bluff, and it was often the first stop on a walk that would continue to Sugar Loaf, Fort Holmes, and Skull Cave. His composition of the arch is not as realistic as that of Robinson's Folly, but it captures the yawning chasm opening to a view of Lake Huron.

A further suggestion that François de Castelnau followed a set path to tour Mackinac's natural curiosities is his view of Sugar Loaf (Fig. 6.23). His perspective, like that of David B. Douglass in 1820 (Fig. 5.6) and Bela Hubbard in 1840 (Fig. 6.17), is from the north, where there was a substantial clearing in the growing woods. The height of the trees, as in Hubbard's sketch, indicates a steady recovery of the island's forest. Castelnau found two little caverns in the rock but did not include them in his view.[118]

François de Castelnau's text and pictures further popularized Mackinac and its natural wonders to an international audience. It was, he suggested, a place that "merits the attention of the traveler."[119]

Besides drawing views of scenery, François, comte de Castelnau, tried his hand at a few portraits of the Native Americans he encountered on the northern lakes. Wissegong, an Ojibwa man, was among them. Lithograph by Jacques Prat, published in Castelnau's *Vues et Souvenirs de l'Amérique du Nord* (Paris, 1842). *Special Collections Library, University of Michigan.*

Castelnau sketched Piniswaneket, an Ojibwa woman, either at Saginaw Bay or Mackinac Island, where he spent some time exploring the Indian camps in September 1838. His visit came during the annual assemblage of Native Americans to collect their treaty payments. Lithograph by Jacques Prat, in *Vues et Souvenirs*. *Special Collections Library, University of Michigan.*

Fort and Island of Mackinaw.

C. F. Davis, Del. 1839.

FIGURE 6.24

TITLE: Fort and Island of Mackinaw.
AUTHOR: Caleb F. Davis (1810–70).
DATE DEPICTED: August 1839.
DATE OF WORK: August 1839.
DESCRIPTION: 21 x 25.5 cm. Pen and ink on paper. Signed at lower right: C. F. Davis, Del. 1839.
PROVENANCE: Retained in the Davis family. It was exhibited in the Gallery of Fine Arts, Fireman's Hall, Detroit, in 1852 where it was described by the title: "Port [sic] and Island of Mackinac." Donated to the Mackinac Island State Park Commission in April 1969 by Mrs. Fred Dickson of Detroit, great-granddaughter of the artist.
COLLECTION: Mackinac State Historic Parks, Mackinac Island, MI (1985.14.1).

These moss covered relics … contrast singularly with the adjoining white houses, stores &c

George Fuller

George Fuller tried to take in everything as the sailors moored his steamer to the wharf in Haldimand Bay on a July afternoon in 1837. A boisterous crowd had gathered on the pier to greet the newcomers. This "motley assemblage" included "French & Indians, sailors & soldiers," who "presented a sight more picturesque & attractive than any we had ever seen," he later recalled. Fuller's voyage through the Straits from Lake Michigan had included the usual colorful sightings of Indian canoes, a glimpse of Old Michilimackinac, the dramatic bluffs and white fort of Mackinac Island, and rows of wigwams lining its beach. The last hour or so had been further enlivened by Captain Thomas Holdup Stevens, a naval officer and veteran of Croghan and Sinclair's 1814 campaign, who amused the party "in describing the little engagement in which he figured off this island."

As the vessel was being secured, Fuller had time to contemplate the "remarkable transparency" of the water in the harbor, a phenomenon described by many contemporary visitors. "We could easily distinguish the many colored pebbles at the depth of 50 feet while fish of no mean size were sporting carelessly around our stern," he wrote. Above him towered Fort Mackinac with "the stars and stripes of our country waving in the summer breeze." Nearer at hand was "the neat village, with its ancient and modern buildings."[120] Fuller's recollections correspond closely to the scene depicted in August 1839 by the Detroit artist Caleb F. Davis. His pen-and-ink drawing is reproduced here as Figure 6.24.

By the end of the 1830s the Borough of Michilimackinac was displaying a growing contrast between the old and the new. In spite of the relocation of American Fur Company operations and the demise of the mission, newer, American-style architecture was gradually replacing the old, Canadian-style log houses. Some of these buildings had appeared during the 1820s, but construction, particularly of new stores, continued during the period of Michigan land speculation in the mid-1830s. When Bela Hubbard stopped on his surveying mission in 1838, he recognized that "some few new houses" had appeared since his last visit two years before, particularly in the eastern part of the village. Harriet Martineau noted in 1836 that the "better houses" stood along the beach terrace where they were most noticeable from the water. Those of the "old French village," by contrast, were "shabby-looking, dusky, and roofed with bark." To Hubbard, this "old part" of the town seemed "rapidly verging into the antique."[121]

The "antique" appearance of the village interested many visitors and added to the other picturesque qualities of Mackinac. The simple street plan reminded François de Castelnau of villages in his country, and George Fuller speculated that the houses were facsimiles of "domiciles of the same grade in the sunnier land of France."[122] Although their design owed something to French architecture, the colder climate of Québec and New France had exerted a greater influence on Michilimackinac's small log houses.

Particularly intriguing to visitors was the construction of these "moss covered relics." Many had been built like the houses of Old Michilimackinac, "by setting rows of cedar posts in the ground, the chinks well corked with moss, and the roofs of cedar bark."[123] Chandler Gilman noted that they were constructed "as they make fences here," although other houses were of more substantial materials, "some of unbarked, others of squared logs, others again coated with cedar bark, as they lay on shingles with us."[124] Increasingly, by Gilman's time, these were the homes of Mackinac's poorer citizens, "French and Indian fishermen" as Enos Goodrich described them in 1835. Many of the older houses were in poor repair, displaying holes in their roofs, hanging shutters, and broken-down doors.[125]

Caleb Davis's view does not reveal much of these ruder dwellings, perhaps because most stood on the western and back margins of the town, and the more substantial buildings along Water Street masked their presence. Davis probably also had an interest in showing the Borough of Michilimackinac at its best. He was a professional artist who had established himself in Detroit in 1832, offering to paint anything from signs to military standards. Among his advertised services was drawing public buildings with "neatness and despatch." A Davis view of the growing city of Detroit had been published as a lithograph in 1833 or 1834.[126] It is possible that he visited Mackinac with the intention of producing a marketable image. If so, the project went no further, though the artist later exhibited his Mackinac scene at Fireman's Hall in Detroit in 1852 and allowed Benson J. Lossing to copy and reproduce it in his *Pictorial Field Book of the War of 1812* of 1869.[127]

Architecture and the appearance of the town seem to have been the artist's priorities, as he rendered the topography of Mackinac Island in rough and exaggerated fashion. The bluffs are too high, the turtle's back is not high enough, and Robinson's Folly projects like a ski jump, bearing little resemblance to Castelnau's more precise view of the year before. The buildings are much more carefully drawn than is the island, and Fort Mackinac is shown in considerable detail. On the high bank beneath the flagpole may be seen the earliest depiction of the new officers' quarters, the "Hill House" completed in 1835.

The buildings of the borough are neatly depicted as well, although the neighborhood east of the Indian Agency House has been unaccountably compressed so that Ste. Anne's Church and

Mission Church appear to stand next door to each other. The La Framboise house may be seen to the left of Ste. Anne's. The main part of town is more carefully drawn, although the sails of a fast-moving schooner obscure its westernmost end, the site of the growing shantytown of fishermen's shacks. A half dozen substantial, American-style buildings dominate Main Street, while the cupola of the new courthouse may be seen on Market Street. The American Fur Company warehouse and the Stuart House are immediately to the right of the courthouse. The company's former retail store is visible near the base of the ramp to Fort Mackinac, while the last two waterfront buildings on the right are the original South West Fur Company buildings of circa 1810 that had been taken over by Astor's firm in 1817. One of these would later become the Northern Hotel. The artist chose not to show any of the wharves that projected into the harbor.

The newest structure in Caleb Davis's view is the Michili-mackinac County Courthouse, which had only just been completed by the time of his visit. The Borough of Michilimackinac had been the judicial seat of the county since its formation in October 1818, but in 1820 the court was accommodated in the old Indian council house.[128] The county's financial circumstances did not allow the erection of a proper public building for some years, but in February 1838 the residents of Michilimackinac requested a remission of state taxes for a term of years in order to fund a courthouse.[129] The effort was successful, and the handsome building was completed in 1839. It was often used for other purposes when court was not in session. In May 1840 Charles Penny attended Presbyterian services in the "new courthouse," and in November an itinerant actor proposed to "spout Shakespeare" there. His performance was perhaps too successful, for the enterprising thespian was seen drunk in the street the next day.[130]

Another recent and conspicuous addition to the architecture of Michilimackinac is visible below and to the right of Fort Mackinac. This large and handsome two-story building is the Indian Dormitory, constructed in 1838. It was a result of the 1836 Treaty of Washington, by which the Ottawa and Ojibwa relinquished most of northern Michigan in return for twenty years of annuity payments to be made at Mackinac Island. Article 7 of the treaty promised that the U.S. government would maintain blacksmith and gunsmith facilities at Mackinac and "build a dormitory for the Indians visiting the post, and appoint a person to keep it, and supply it with firewood." The structure was the brainchild of Indian agent Henry Schoolcraft.[131]

Getting the building in place proved to be somewhat more difficult than expected. Objections to the expense were raised in Congress and in the War Department, and Schoolcraft and his superiors explored several possibilities for fulfilling the treaty

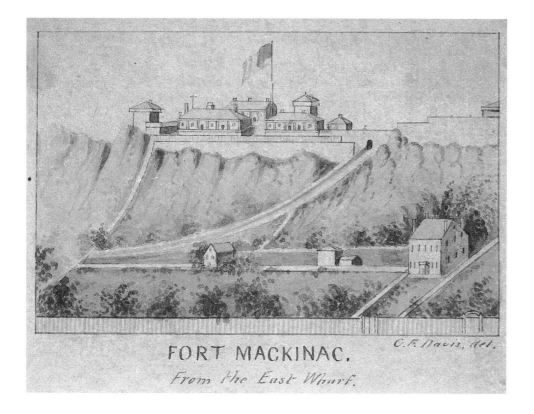

FORT MACKINAC.
From the East Wharf.

FIGURE 6.25
TITLE: Fort Mackinac. From the East Wharf.
AUTHOR: Caleb F. Davis (1810–70).
DATE DEPICTED: August 1839.
DATE OF WORK: [1839–45].
DESCRIPTION: 8.3 x 11.6 cm. Pen and ink with gray wash on card. Signed at lower right: C. F. Davis, del.
PROVENANCE: Owned by the wife of Captain Martin Scott, commandant of Fort Mackinac from 1842 to 1845. Found among Mrs. Scott's possessions after her death on the steamer *Arctic* in 1854, apparently by her cousin, Marietta (Mrs. A. J.) Langworthy of Milwaukee, Wisconsin. Acquired by the Clements Library before 1968.
COLLECTION: Clements Library, University of Michigan, Ann Arbor (Print Division, H-1)

obligation. Early in 1837 Schoolcraft first suggested that the Indian Agency House be altered for use as a dormitory when necessary but then, in the spring, proposed to purchase the recently closed Mission House. The building was occupied for this purpose during the summer of 1837, at which time Mrs. Jameson noted that the Indian interpreter lived there. This idea also met official disapproval, however, and in August 1837 Schoolcraft submitted his own design for a purpose-built dormitory. This was accepted, and the agent advertised for a contractor. All of this activity generated a number of plans, most prepared by Schoolcraft, but none has yet been located.[132]

Henry Schoolcraft designed a two-story building with a ground plan measuring 36 by 40 feet. It was to contain kitchen and storage facilities in the high stone basement, quarters for the keeper and staff, an office, and accommodations on the top floor. Although the dormitory was to have been completed by July 1, 1838, it was not ready until September, when Schoolcraft accepted it on behalf of his department. The land around the dormitory was fenced later in the fall, and by the summer of 1839 it appeared as depicted by Caleb F. Davis.[133]

The Indian Dormitory may be seen on two other Davis views of Mackinac. Both depict the identical scene, focusing on Fort Mackinac, the government grounds below, and the Indian Dormitory. The view is from the "East Wharf," probably the pier that formerly served Reverend Ferry's school on Mission Point. The smaller of the two drawings is illustrated here as Figure 6.25. The other (not illustrated) is in the collections of the Detroit Historical Museum. It shows, in addition, the blacksmith and gunsmith's workshops that stood at the foot of the bluff behind the dormitory.

Figure 6.25 might date to Davis's 1839 visit, and there is nothing in the composition to suggest otherwise. Given his occupation, it is likely that he produced views on demand, and he no doubt retained sketches of popular subjects to allow him to do so. The artist might also have visited again at some point over the next several summers. Whatever the case, the provenance of Figure 6.25 suggests that he made the tiny drawing somewhat later than 1839. It belonged to Lavinia McCracken Scott, the wife of Fort Mackinac's commandant during 1842–45, and was probably produced closer to that time. A distinctive weather vane at the western end of the officers' stone quarters supports this reasoning, as it appears in a bird's-eye view of Fort Mackinac drawn for Captain Scott in 1845 (Fig. 7.21). The weather vane is not shown in either of the other Davis views, and it is possible that it was added to Figure 6.25 at the request of the Scotts.

The Indian Dormitory was the brainchild of Henry Rowe Schoolcraft (1793–1864), who also appears to have designed the building. He was Indian agent at Mackinac from 1833 to 1842. A bearded Schoolcraft was pictured in 1855 in *The Knickerbocker Gallery*. *Clements Library, University of Michigan.*

Wa-em-boesh-kaa, pictured with his pipe by James Otto Lewis at the treaty of Fond du Lac in 1826, was an Ojibwa chief, the kind of prominent Native American for whom the Indian Dormitory was to provide accommodations. The building was little used for that purpose, as most Indians preferred to camp on the beach. Lithograph by Lehman and Duval. *Clements Library, University of Michigan.*

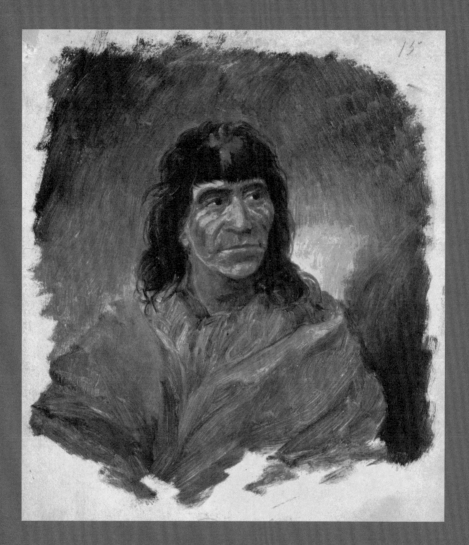

Now-on-dhu-go was an Ottawa
chief from the villages on Lake
Michigan. Paul Kane captured his
likeness in this striking, oil-on-
paper portrait of 20.2 x 24.3 cm.,
done on Mackinac Island in 1845.
Stark Museum of Art, Orange, TX (31.78/190,
EOP 27).

"One of the busiest little places in the world"

1840–1850

Twilight was just coming on as a group of fashionable gentlemen lounged on the porch of the Mission House on a July evening in 1847. Horace Greeley and his friend, Lewis Gaylord Clark, were enjoying the timeless view of the "deep, *deep* blue waters" of Lake Huron when their attention was drawn to an object not far from shore. The pair first watched in fascination and then studied the phenomenon more closely through a spyglass. They agreed that they could only be observing

"an enormous sea-serpent, elevating its head, undulating its humps, and 'floating many a rood' upon the translucent Strait." The hotel's proprietor concurred, marveling that he had never seen anything like it in his ten years at Mackinac.

Hoping for a closer look at this mysterious creature, Greeley and "Old Knick," as Clark styled himself, rushed to the beach with enormous "kangaroo bounds," only to find that they had been deceived by the Straits of Mackinac. Their "sea-serpent" proved to be nothing more than "the dark side of a long undulating, unbroken wave, brought into clear relief by the level western light" as the sun set over Lake Michigan.[1] Perhaps it was the natural intoxication of Mackinac's healthy air that had affected the imaginations of two distinguished editors and sent them cavorting down the marshy beach. Greeley made it clear that he had not sampled any of the liquors dispensed to patrons of the Mission House, which, by the summer of 1847, had a reputation as "the best hotel on the island."[2]

The wave that had assumed the guise of a lake monster had very likely been caused by one of the growing numbers of vessels coming and going in Haldimand Bay. "Mackinaw, during the season of navigation, is one of the busiest little places in the world," Charles Lanman wrote after his 1846 visit.[3] The island had become an obligatory stop for vessels transiting the increasingly busy Straits of Mackinac as well as a port for the working craft of the northern fisheries. "All the upper lake steamers and sail craft stop at the wharf for an hour or two to wood," Robert Sears reported to the *Democratic Free Press* in July 1847. This gave their passengers time to stroll through the village and even as far afield as Fort Holmes to enjoy the

view. As many as four passenger steamers arrived daily, sending up to one thousand travelers or immigrants to empty merchants' shelves of "Indian curiosities," purchase fresh fish, or buy rolls and biscuits from the island's four bakeries. "Thus 'curiosity' is gratified and the stomach filled," Sears observed, and Mackinac businessmen found a useful supplement to trade.[4]

Some of these visitors arrived on handsome steamers such as the *Empire,* 270 feet long with a saloon extending much of that length. The vessel boasted fine furniture, a barbershop, and staterooms fitted up with "white dimity, ensuring either cleanliness or a quick detection of the contrary."[5] Such comfort was in increasing demand by those who could afford it, although less affluent travelers made do with much less. Many of these were recent immigrants from northern Europe bound for new lives in Michigan, Wisconsin, and even farther west. Some went only as far as Mackinac Island or St. Ignace. During the 1840s a steady influx of Irish, largely from counties Mayo and Galway, found the fishing good at Mackinac and remained to put their own stamp on the communities at the Straits.[6]

The majority of Mackinac's boat traffic did not carry passengers. Fish was the cargo, and the emerging industry of the 1830s had, by the middle of the following decade, come to dominate the commercial life of the Straits. Although a few small operators still brought furs to the harbor, fish had replaced beaver. The highly desirable trout and whitefish of northern Lake Huron and Lake Michigan were caught as far away as Grand Traverse Bay and taken to Mackinac Island to be processed, packed, and shipped. In 1840 four thousand barrels of fish were exported to more southerly ports. That number had increased fivefold by 1846, when sixteen thousand barrels of whitefish and four thousand of trout were loaded at Mackinac's wharves. Much of it was salted, but fish was also iced and shipped in wheeled "cars" as far as Buffalo, New York. A traveler observed in 1848 that at Mackinac's wharves one would be sure to see "two or three large boxes on wheels, hauled on the deck by tough-looking fishermen of the genuine French breed."[7]

This trade generated a demand for ice, which was harvested and stored at Mackinac during the winter, and for salt, which had to be imported. The construction of barrels reportedly employed as many as four hundred workers in 1847. By that time Mackinac's merchants, "all of them more or less," were involved in the industry, not so much in catching fish as in supplying nets, barrels, and salt to fishermen or purchasing and shipping their catch. When Robert Sears arrived at Mackinac on July 23, 1847, he encountered some familiar names from fur-trading days—Edward Biddle, Michael Dousman, Ambrose Davenport, and Jonathan P. King. Now they were on the wharf "giving directions for shipping fish."[8]

Fish and tourists both required improvements to the infrastructure of Mackinac Island. Coopers' shops and warehouses sprang up in and around the town. In 1839 Michael Dousman extended his wharf at the foot of Astor Street to better accommodate the increasing size and number of arriving boats.[9] Earlier that year, John Orr and Company and the partnership of Edward Biddle and John Drew each received permission to build wharves. Between 1846 and 1849 the borough or village government permitted construction of four more, while the older Dousman and Lasley piers were lengthened.[10] When bylaws were drawn up for the newly incorporated Village of Mackinac in June 1848, the first four of its seven sections addressed concerns relating to the harbor or fishing. The position of harbormaster was created, and the disposal of fish offal was further regulated. It was thereafter to be dumped on the "vacant lot" along Cadotte Avenue to the west of the village.[11] This parcel, usually known as the "Borough Lot," had been granted about 1832 to the local government by the War Department for "Public purposes."[12]

Further improvements were underway on shore, although the growing number of fishermen's huts and cooper's shops probably seemed too insubstantial to be identified as new construction by most travelers. In 1842 James K. Paulding could only note "few houses which appear to have been recently built, and fewer still building."[13] Most continued to describe the "antique" appearance of the village, a feature that was attractive to many. Sarah Fuller, tired of the "raw, crude, staring assemblage of houses" she found in most of her American travels, was charmed to find at Mackinac "an old French town, mellow in its coloring, and with the harmonious effect of a slow growth, which assimilates, naturally, with objects around it." She did not detect, in 1843, the "hard press of business as in American towns elsewhere."[14]

But business there was, and aside from fishing and tourism much of it still revolved around the Native Americans who passed through each season on their way to the British posts on Georgian Bay and then returned to Mackinac Island for their U.S. annuity payments in September and October. These cash disbursements attracted a flock of merchants, "all endeavoring to entice the government stipend from the poor Indian, with their merchandize."[15] Some of these goods arrived in the form of alcohol. The artist Paul Kane was only one of many who witnessed the effect of the prohibited but clandestine and virtually unpreventable sale of liquor during annuity payment time. "Many an Indian who travels thither from a long distance returns to his wigwam poorer than when he left it," he wrote, "his sole satisfaction being that he and his family have enjoyed a glorious bout of intoxication."[16]

This annual assemblage strained the accommodations available on Mackinac Island. While Native American visitors erected their wigwams along the beach, traders and travelers who wished to remain longer than a fueling stop had to seek space in the few available public houses. Many found them full. Reverend John H. Pitezel eventually got lodgings with a local family in September 1843.[17] When another clergyman, James Beaven, stopped in August of the following year, public accommodation was unavailable because of the numbers of Indian traders and men bound for the copper country of Lake Superior or young fellows "travelling west for pleasure and recreation."[18]

In fact, few lodgings were available. In 1842 Daniel Drake maintained that Mackinac had "three plain but comfortable houses of entertainment for strangers" but neglected to name them.[19] Best known was the Lasley House, which had been the island's premier "hotel" since 1824. Although the place received a few bad reviews, Mrs. Lasley's cooking won over most guests, and the "public house" was described in 1834 as "neat & well carpeted."[20] The building itself was unimpressive. Joseph Le Conte described it in 1844 as "a mere tumble-down shanty of rough unpainted boards, apparently in the last stages of dilapidation." To his surprise, he found his room "scrupulously clean and tidy."[21] Another visitor of 1844 remarked on the casual atmosphere of the place and its average of three beds to a room.[22] Otherwise, the chief attraction of the Lasley House seems to have been tame bears that were kept chained near the front door.[23] Its aging proprietor, Samuel Lasley, could recall Mackinac back to the 1790s, but he possessed minimal hospitality skills. Joseph Le Conte found him a "huge, fat, tumble-down looking person" who greeted his guests "indifferently." As to promoting Mackinac Island tourism, when Le Conte attempted to discuss the wonders of Arch Rock and Sugar Loaf, Lasley replied, "Yes, people talk of them as worth seeing; but for my part, I'd much rather see a dog-fight."[24]

More and better hotels were needed. Daniel Drake suggested that "a summer boarding house" might be constructed on the East Bluff. A more practical solution appeared in the fall of 1844, when Reverend Beaven was told of plans to convert the old Mission House, little used since 1837, into a "lodging house."[25] The American Board of Commissioners for Foreign Missions owned the building, although it stood on public land.[26] The board was nonetheless in a position to rent the property, and it opened for business in 1845 as the Mission House.[27] William Cullen Bryant stayed there in August 1846, but he found that the addition of this larger hotel had done little to reduce the crowding.[28] By 1848 "two principal lodging-houses" vied for island business: the Lasley House and the Mission House.[29] The O'Malley House, a large, purpose-built hotel, would join them the following summer. It remains in operation today as the Island House.[30]

The 1840s were a time of change for local government as well. Islanders had lived under the authority of the Borough of Michili-mackinac since 1817. In March 1847, however, the Michigan legislature repealed its charter and dissolved the borough, vesting authority and assets in the Township of Holmes.[31] Municipal government was reestablished a year later when the legislature passed an act to incorporate the Village of Mackinac. The new body was given essentially the same powers and responsibilities that had been granted the old borough, although under the abbreviated name that was being used with increasing frequency.[32] The Village of Mackinac began to function in June 1848 when its officials drafted a brief set of bylaws focusing on harbor regulation, sanitation, and the ever-present concern about fire.[33]

The island's oldest local institution received a new lease on life when soldiers reoccupied Fort Mackinac on May 18, 1840. The national colors were hoisted and, in the words of Lieutenant John Wolcott Phelps, "the old walls again resounded to the rumbling drum."[34] A pattern had been established, however, by the evacuation of the garrison during times of crisis elsewhere. Regular troops would be replaced with Michigan volunteers in 1847 during the war with Mexico, and the post was evacuated for five months in 1848. It was not until November of that year that a permanent regular garrison was once again in place.

The army's willingness to move Fort Mackinac's soldiers reflected uncertainty about the usefulness of a small garrison in an obsolete and isolated fortification. No such doubts existed, however, in the minds of visitors and writers about the future of the beautiful island. "The manifest fate of Mackinac . . . is to be a watering-place," William Cullen Bryant wrote confidently after his stay in 1846.[35] Bryant no doubt had in mind visitors of all sorts, but he and others referred particularly to those who would come for the type of extended stay that was popular in the spas of Europe and the eastern United States. Mackinac Island had been projected as a promising resort as early as the 1830s, and travelers' writings of the following decade drove the point home. In *The Northern Lakes* of 1842, Daniel Drake identified Mackinac as "the most important summer residence to which we can direct the attention of the infirm and of the fashionable."[36] They were already coming during the 1840s and would arrive in greater numbers still in the next decade.

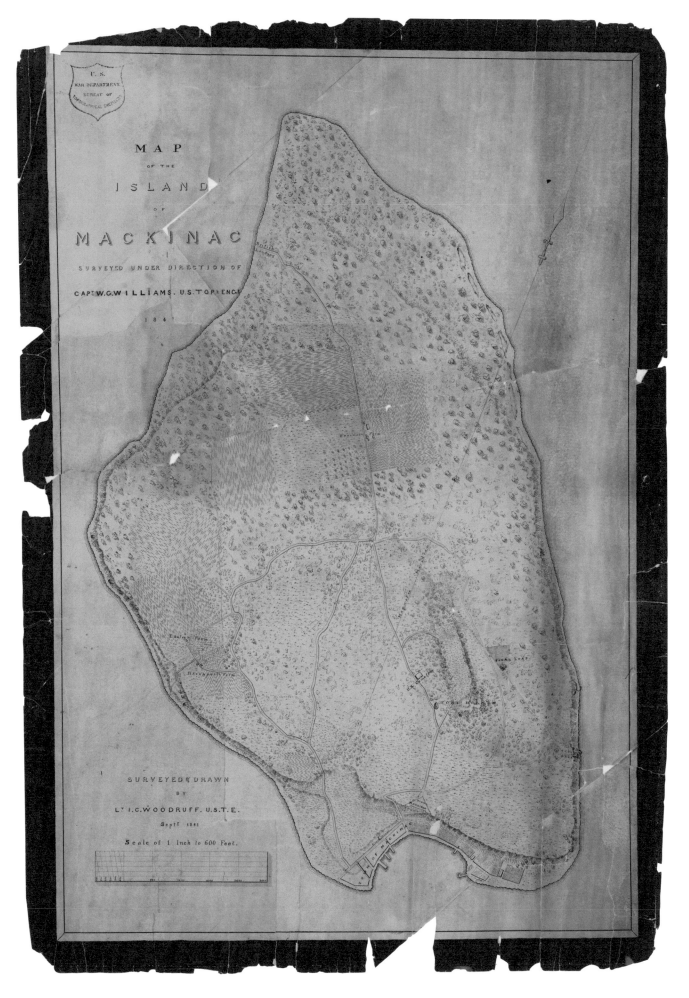

MAP
OF THE
ISLAND
OF
MACKINAC
SURVEYED UNDER DIRECTION OF
CAPT. W.G. WILLIAMS. U.S. TOP. ENG.
1841

SURVEYED & DRAWN
BY
LT I.C. WOODRUFF. U.S.T.E.
Sept 1841

Scale of 1 Inch to 600 Feet.

Michilimackinac, whose formidable name has been most judiciously softened into Mackinac

James K. Paulding

Horse-drawn carriages were no novelty on the island of Mackinac by the summer of 1846. When William Cullen Bryant stopped in August, he enjoyed being "driven out in the roads that wind through its woods" as he took in the points of interest. Although most visitors toured on foot, those with time to explore farther afield appreciated the convenience of a vehicle. Horses and carriages traversed the forested hills on roads that had served Mackinac Island since before the War of 1812. Bryant was impressed that these were "paved by nature with limestone pebbles, a sort of natural macadamization" that was a by-product of the rocky terrain.[37]

Mackinac's roads had been surveyed long before William Cullen Bryant's visit, and local officials carefully plotted their courses (see Fig. 5.12). These were only rough schematic plans, however, and, prior to 1841, only one map had recorded both the topography and road system of Mackinac Island in any detail. Despite some distortions in the shape of the island, William S. Eveleth's 1817 effort (Figs. 4.7 and 5.13) showed both major routes and smaller paths as they were at that time. Figure 7.1 demonstrates how little the streets and roads had changed by 1841.

Lieutenant Israel Carle Woodruff's "Map of the Island of Mackinac" was not intended to show roads, although the main thoroughfares, village streets, and a few individual buildings and farms provide useful addenda to his composition. Nor are property boundaries represented. Woodruff's map was drawn as a topographical survey, although it was hastily done and records only the most prominent of the island's terrain features. Its most important contribution was to accurately render the shape of Mackinac Island,

and, as such, it figures in efforts by the U.S. government to more precisely map the coastlines of the Great Lakes, an initiative that would develop into the U.S. Lake Survey.

The 1841 map of Mackinac Island had its origins in a project suggested by Captain William G. Williams, an officer of the Corps of Topographical Engineers and Woodruff's superior. Williams had been appointed superintendent of harbor improvements for Lake Erie in the fall of 1838, an assignment he undertook with vigor. The engineer soon completed a detailed trigonometric survey of the vicinity of Buffalo, New York, employing triangulation, a technique that allowed the accurate computation of bearings and distances using a chain of imaginary triangles projected from known points. Williams suggested that this method might be used to survey the rest of the Great Lakes, thereby producing far more accurate maps and charts. His recommendation resulted in an appropriation by Congress in the late winter of 1841 to begin a survey of the northwestern lakes, commencing at Green Bay and including part of the Straits of Mackinac.

Williams, assisted by a staff of junior officers, began work in the summer of 1841. In addition to preparations made at Green Bay, a detachment, apparently under the command of Lieutenant Woodruff, established triangulation stations on Mackinac Island, the St. Martin Islands, and the mainland. One of these, perhaps the most important of all, was located at Fort Holmes, a spot visible from most of the Straits. Topographical surveys were then undertaken at Mackinac, Round, and Bois Blanc islands and at St. Ignace.[38] Only Woodruff's map of Mackinac Island has been found. It is included here as Figure 7.1.

Although Lieutenant Woodruff's survey contains a great amount of information, it cannot be considered comprehensive, and it lacks the level of detail of the 1817 Eveleth map. Woodruff indistinctly rendered many features or, in a few cases, omitted them entirely. Lacking further documentation about his intentions, however, it is difficult to determine his rationale for including or ignoring elements of the island's topography and architecture. Since Woodruff's primary assignment was to accurately determine the outline of Mackinac Island, it is likely that he was under no obligation to depict all of its details. His map is, nonetheless, a good snapshot of its physical characteristics in 1841.

Lieutenant Woodruff went to some trouble to represent the vegetation of the island, ranging from farm plots to areas of brush and growing forest. Mackinac's timber had continued to recover, although one 1841 visitor still described only "dwarf pines, and some resinous shrubs, and natural woods of stunted growth."[39]

FIGURE 7.1

TITLE: Map of the Island of Mackinac Surveyed Under the Direction of Capt. W. G. Williams. U.S. Topl Eng. 1841; Surveyed & Drawn by Lt. I. C. Woodruff U.S.T.E. Septr. 1841.
AUTHOR: Second Lieutenant Israel Carle Woodruff, Corps of Topographical Engineers (active 1832–d. 1878).
DATE DEPICTED: September 1841.
DATE OF WORK: September 1841.
DESCRIPTION: 75.8 x 52 cm. Pen and ink on paper.
PROVENANCE: Prepared during early Lake Survey work. Retained in the records of the chief of engineers.
COLLECTION: National Archives and Records Administration, College Park, MD (RG 77, Records of the Office of the Chief of Engineers, Civil Works Map File, O91).

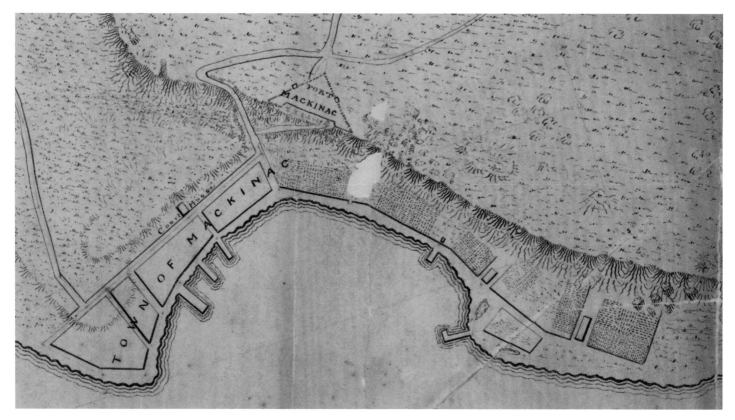

This detail of the village, from Lieutenant Israel C. Woodruff's 1841 map (Fig. 7.1), includes wharves, the street plan, the new courthouse of 1839, and the Catholic and Protestant churches. The Indian Dormitory was shown below Fort Mackinac where a hole now mars the plan.

Three farms are identified by name—Dousman's, Davenport's, and Lasley's—distinguished by farm buildings and stylized fields. Michael Dousman's property, site of the 1814 battle, includes orderly ranks of fruit trees representing his orchard. For some reason, Woodruff chose not to identify the old Mitchell farm (claim 110) located along Cadotte Avenue north and west of the town. This, one of the island's earliest farms, passed to Edward Biddle before the 1850s and is today the site of part of the Grand Hotel Golf Course and the residential area known as Harrisonville. Buildings stood on the Mitchell property as late as 1842 (see Fig. 7.4), but they do not appear on Woodruff's survey.

The roads recorded by Lieutenant Woodruff largely conform to those shown by Lieutenant Eveleth in 1817, although the street leading from the upper end of Cadotte Avenue to the rear of Fort Mackinac has been omitted. Some of Eveleth's paths seem to have been converted into more substantial thoroughfares by 1841, notably those leading to the plateau of Fort Holmes and one branching off the Fort Mackinac-Sugar Loaf road to lead curious tourists to Arch Rock. Additional tracks are also seen in the area of the Davenport and Lasley farms. The latter property was originally owned by George Schindler (claim 331) and had more recently been Reverend Ferry's mission farm. Samuel Lasley had acquired it by 1838, after the demise of the mission the previous year, and it would pass to

William Scott following Lasley's death in October 1844.

The plan of the Borough of Michilimackinac had changed little since it was last mapped in 1817, with the exception of the extension of Market Street to the lakeshore and further development at the eastern end of Haldimand Bay. Although they are imprecisely rendered, it is possible to pick out a few individual buildings— Ste. Anne's Church, Mission Church, and the Mission House. Fort Mackinac and the Michilimackinac County Courthouse are identified. The label "Town of Mackinac" anticipates the name of the new municipality of 1848, for the village recorded by Woodruff was still officially the Borough of Michilimackinac.

The most significant additions to the village are its new or lengthened wharves. Three large piers extend from shore. That on the right (at the foot of Astor Street) is Dousman's, formerly owned by the American Fur Company and originally built by William H. Puthuff in 1818. The widest wharf, farthest to the left, is probably the one constructed by Samuel Lasley in 1833.[40] Between Dousman and Lasley's is the newest of the three, although it is uncertain whether it represents John Orr and Company's structure or that of Biddle and Drew, both approved in 1839.[41] It is probably the latter. At the eastern end of the harbor is the old L-shaped missionary wharf and another much smaller pier.

A short distance north and west of the village, tucked between

Michilimackinack.-

FIGURE 7.2
TITLE: Michilimackinack.
AUTHOR: Lieutenant William Fairholme,
71st Regiment of Foot (1819–68).
DATE DEPICTED: August 9, 1840.
DATE OF WORK: ca. 1843.
DESCRIPTION: 13 x 21 cm. Pencil with wash.
PROVENANCE: Included in a copy of Fairholme's
journal of an expedition to the prairies of Missouri
in 1840. Fairholme presented this copy of his
journal to Caroline Fairholme, probably his
mother, in 1843. Retained in the family until
acquired by the Huntington Library in 1977.
COLLECTION: The Huntington Library, San
Marino, CA (HM 40696).

Cadotte Avenue and Lake Huron, is the former federal parcel that had passed to the borough about 1832 and eventually became known as the "Borough Lot." A road was surveyed across this property in 1832 to the site of the old LeBarron distillery, although it does not appear in Woodruff's plot.[42] This area was made the dumping ground for the wastes of the fishing business in 1848, although a small schoolhouse also occupied a portion of the lot in 1848.[43] The land is today once again the location of the local school.

Deeper in the island, Lieutenant Woodruff depicted the well-known rock formations, although Skull Cave is shown only as an unlabeled drawing. He also included, for the first time, the "U.S. Cemetery." It is likely that the plot on Garrison Road near Skull Cave had been used as a military burying ground as early as the 1820s, although it was not described until 1835. Chandler Gilman passed by that summer and noted a dozen graves protected by a picket fence that had been erected by a former fort commandant. Only two of the graves had wooden headboards, with "inscriptions painted in black letters on them." One marked the remains of a soldier who had drowned as recently as the summer of 1834.[44]

William Cullen Bryant was perhaps the first Mackinac visitor to recount in detail a typical carriage excursion, and his route may be traced on Lieutenant Woodruff's map. On August 19, 1846, Bryant and his companions hired a man to take them on "a drive to the western shore." It would be many years before a road was constructed around Mackinac Island, so their trip began behind Fort Mackinac and followed Garrison and British Landing roads. Much of the way was forested, and the track "twined through a wood of over-arching beeches and maples, interspersed with white-cedar and fir." Their first stop was Skull Cave, "a cliff sprouting with beeches and cedars, with a small cavity at its foot," which their guide said was remarkable for the bones that had once been found in it. A short distance farther on was the garrison burial ground. "There are few buried here," observed one of the party, "the soldiers who come to Mackinac sick get well soon."

As the carriage descended British Landing Road the group passed Dousman's farm, "surrounded with beautiful groves" with a "luxuriant" beech tree, said to be a monument to Major Andrew Hunter Holmes, who had died in the battle there. British Landing was the last stop of the tour, and Bryant and his friends strolled along the beach with its transparent water and "pebbles so clean that they would no more soil a lady's white muslin gown than if they had been of newly polished alabaster." Looking across the lake they could see a "church with its spire" and the roofs of farmhouses in St. Ignace. Farther to the north a friend pointed out the mouth of the Carp River, which by 1846 already had a reputation for good sport fishing.

The driver broke their idyll. "Your boat is coming," he told them, pointing out the steamer *St. Louis* "making rapidly for the

Island with a train of black smoke hanging in the air behind her." The carriage retraced its route to Fort Mackinac and town, and within an hour and a half Bryant was in his stateroom. "The world has not so many islands so beautiful as Mackinac" was his parting comment.[45]

From the deck of the *St. Louis* the passengers looked on the village with its fort perched high above, much as shown in the hasty sketch made in August 1840 by British lieutenant William Fairholme (Fig. 7.2). The artist rendered the fort well, including the officers' quarters completed in 1835. His view of the town, however, like Lieutenant Woodruff's map, omits many details, although it emphasizes the palisade fences so common to Mackinac.

Lieutenant Fairholme kept a diary as well, and he was ambivalent about the name of the place he visited, calling the locale "Michilimackinac" and the fort "Mackinaw."[46] When Eliza Steele wrote of the island in her 1841 book, she felt it necessary to explain the place as "Michilimackinac, or Mackinaw, or Mackinac as it is commonly spelt and pronounced."[47] In 1841 Lieutenant Woodruff consistently used "Mackinac" to describe the island, town, and fort on his map, and in 1848 the Michigan legislature adopted that spelling for the newly created village. The name reflected the increasing popularity of the shortened form in use today although it would be many more years before "Michilimackinac" came to specifically describe the old mainland post of the eighteenth century.

James Silk Buckingham (1786–1855) was an Englishman who published an extensive description of Mackinac Island following his visit in July 1840. He took an interest in the fact that Edward Biddle, "an opulent white trader," had a Native American wife. Their daughters,

Buckingham recorded, were "handsome, though dark," and had been well educated at boarding schools in the East. Buckingham's portrait is from the frontispiece of his *America, Historical, Statistic and Descriptive* (London, 1841).

Clements Library, University of Michigan.

John C. Pemberton (1814–81), shown as a Confederate general during the Civil War, was a lieutenant of the Fort Mackinac garrison in 1840–41. Island tradition has long suggested a romantic attachment between the young officer and Sophia, one of Edward Biddle's daughters.

Mackinaw, painted against the clear blue sky

Eliza Steele

By the autumn of 1842 Captain Henry Francis Ainslie had seen a great deal of Canada and the Great Lakes. His regiment, Her Majesty's 83rd of Foot, had served in British North America since the spring of 1834. During that time, its companies had been stationed from Halifax to the banks of the Detroit River. In 1837–38, the 83rd confronted rebellious Canadians and fought organized groups of American "Hunters" or "Patriots" when they crossed the border into Upper Canada in an attempt to separate the colony from its connection to Great Britain.[48]

Captain Ainslie had held his rank in the regiment since 1831, and he had been with it through most of its Canadian service. Most recently, the captain had been stationed in London, Canada West (Ontario), and, since July 1842, in Toronto. With the border tensions of the last few years largely relaxed, Ainslie was finally in a position to treat himself to a pleasure journey on the American lakes. By September he had reached Sault Ste. Marie and the Straits of Mackinac, where he stopped to tour Mackinac Island. Like so many other travelers, his steamer then took him into Lake Michigan to visit the towns growing up along its Wisconsin and Illinois shores. Ainslie passed through the Straits once more in October, returning to his post in Toronto aboard the *De Witt Clinton*. He had seen at least a bit of the United States.

When the 83rd embarked for England in June 1843, Captain Ainslie took with him much more than just memories of his service in the Canadian colonies. He also carried an impressive visual record in the form of finely rendered watercolor drawings of the places he had seen. Like so many military and naval officers of his day, Henry Francis Ainslie had been trained to draw, and he seems to have possessed talent beyond the norm for his profession. Many of Ainslie's watercolors survive today, including fifty-two in the collections of Library and Archives Canada showing places from Québec City to Gros Cap on Lake Superior. The Chicago Historical Society holds another group of eleven paintings, most made during 1842 to document the artist's Great Lakes tour.[49] These include five depicting the Straits of Mackinac (Figs. 7.3–7.7).

The Straits area was at its most colorful at the time of Captain Ainslie's visits in September and October 1842. "The scenery of the island is remarkably fine," wrote C. Donald MacLeod in the latter month. "This autumn time had clad the forests with a thousand hues," he continued, and "between the crisom-leafed [*sic*] maple, the purple and gold ivy and beach [*sic*], and the green eternal cedar . . . the naked rocks start out."[50] Although Ainslie's colors are more subdued than those described by MacLeod, his views of Mackinac Island and the site of Old Michilimackinac give a sense of seasonal change as well as of the rugged, rocky bluffs. Early autumn was colorful in

other ways, for that was the time of the greatest assemblage of Native Americans on Mackinac Island. The artist encountered them both coming and going.

It was on his return voyage in October that Ainslie captured the full length of Mackinac Island as seem from the passage between the Michigan peninsulas (Fig. 7.3). This is perhaps the island's most handsome profile, and its distinct levels are very clearly defined with several important landmarks visible. Most of the island's upper elevations display new-growth forest, which the Reverend John H. Pitezel described in 1843 as primarily maple, birch, poplar, cedar, and balsam, a mix "giving to the landscape richness and variety."[51] Most of the steep bluffs and farmed areas are still denuded of trees, however, and in the middle of the view, atop the western bluffs, Ainslie included the buildings of the Lasley and Davenport farms. To the right are the shining, whitewashed walls of Fort Mackinac, marked by U.S. colors, with the village below.

As the *De Witt Clinton* neared the island, Ainslie attempted a second view focusing on its inhabited southern end and, in the water nearby, a flotilla of canoes (Fig. 7.4). The small bark craft are jammed with Ojibwa passengers, their lodge poles, and personal belongings. When Daniel Drake visited Mackinac in the summer of 1842, he likened the groups of canoes coming to and going from the island to a "fleet of Lilliputian barques" or, with their sails raised to catch a fair wind, "a scattered flock of gigantic swans, gracefully moving through the azure waters."[52] Captain Ainslie's watercolor reveals their destination, an encampment of wigwams on the island's southwestern shore on the "vacant lot" owned by the Borough of Michilimackinac.

Ainslie rendered other details with military precision. A mast on the earthworks of Fort Holmes is probably the triangulation tower raised by Lieutenant Woodruff in 1841 to survey Mackinac and adjacent islands. The dominance of its position over Fort Mackinac is readily apparent, although the larger fort looks impressive enough with its whitewashed walls and huge garrison flag. Eliza Steele thought Fort Mackinac a "very beautiful, and conspicuous object" when she visited in 1840. From her perspective the post presented "the appearance of a long white line of buildings inserted into the top of the island high above the town." Steele noted "picturesque blockhouses and the pretty balconied residences of the officers . . . having the banner of the 'stripes and stars' waving over them."[53] Captain Ainslie visually recorded much the same impression.

Directly below Fort Holmes may be seen the cleared land of the old Mitchell farm, distinguished by its farmhouse and fencing. The land was used to raise hay and grow the renowned "Mackinac potatoes" as well as oats and some corn, all typical island crops.

FIGURE 7.3

TITLE: [On original mount:] United States, Island of Mackinaw, October 1842. [On verso:] Fort & Island of Macinaw October 1842.

AUTHOR: Captain Henry Francis Ainslie, 83rd Regiment of Foot (1803–79).

DATE DEPICTED: October 1842.

DATE OF WORK: October 1842.

DESCRIPTION: 36 x 26 cm. Pen and ink with watercolor on paper.

PROVENANCE: From an album of eleven watercolors titled "Sketches in Canada and the States of Illinois & Michigan. 1841, 42, 43. H. F. Ainslie." Apparently retained in the artist's family. Photographic copies at the Library of Congress indicate that a previous owner, Major J. P. Kempthorne of New Zealand, had once loaned the sketchbook to that institution for an exhibit. Purchased by the Chicago Historical Society in 1963.

COLLECTION: Chicago History Museum (1963.762f).

FIGURE 7.4

TITLE: [On original mount:] United States, Mackinaw Island & Fort, Chippeway Indians travelling, taken from the steamer *De Witt Clinton*. [On verso:] Fort & Island of Mackinaw from the steamer *De Witt Clinton*, October 1842.

AUTHOR: Captain Henry Francis Ainslie, 83rd Regiment of Foot (1803–79).

DATE DEPICTED: October 1842.

DATE OF WORK: October 1842.

DESCRIPTION: 36 x 26 cm. Pen and ink with watercolor on paper.

PROVENANCE: From an album of eleven watercolors titled "Sketches in Canada and the States of Illinois & Michigan. 1841, 42, 43. H. F. Ainslie." Apparently retained in the artist's family. Photographic copies at the Library of Congress indicate that a previous owner, Major J. P. Kempthorne of New Zealand, had once loaned the sketchbook to that institution for an exhibit. Purchased by the Chicago Historical Society in 1963.

COLLECTION: Chicago History Museum (1963.762e).

C. Donald MacLeod (1821–65) visited Mackinac Island in October 1842. He found the scenery "remarkably fine," especially with the autumn forest "clad . . . with a thousand hues." His portrait engraving appeared in *The Knickerbocker Gallery* in 1855. *Clements Library, University of Michigan.*

The Native American encampments on Mackinac Island were filled with women and children as whole families came from across the northern lakes to collect their annuities. James Otto Lewis painted this Ojibwa woman and child at Fond du Lac, Wisconsin, in 1826, but they would have been an equally familiar sight on the beach at Mackinac in 1842. Lithograph by Lehman and Duval. *Clements Library, University of Michigan.*

FIGURE 7.5

TITLE: [On original mount:] United States, Fort & village of Michilimackinac, State of Michigan. Chippeway Indians encamped to receive their Annual presents Sept. 1842. [On verso:] Fort and village of Mackinaw, with the Indian encampment Sept. 1842.

AUTHOR: Captain Henry Francis Ainslie, 83rd Regiment of Foot (1803–79).

DATE DEPICTED: September 1842.

DATE OF WORK: September 1842.

DESCRIPTION: 26 x 36 cm. Pen and ink with watercolor on paper.

PROVENANCE: From an album of eleven watercolors titled "Sketches in Canada and the States of Illinois & Michigan. 1841, 42, 43. H. F. Ainslie." Apparently retained in the artist's family. Photographic copies at the Library of Congress indicate that a previous owner, Major J. P. Kempthorne of New Zealand, had once loaned the sketchbook to that institution for an exhibit. Purchased by the Chicago Historical Society in 1963.

COLLECTION: Chicago History Museum (1963.762c).

FIGURE 7.6

TITLE: [On original mount:] United States,
Natural Arch of Mackinaw Island Septr. 1842.
[On verso:] Natural Arched rock on Mackinaw
Island Lake Huron September 1842.
AUTHOR: Captain Henry Francis Ainslie,
83rd Regiment of Foot (1803–79).
DATE DEPICTED: September 1842.
DATE OF WORK: September 1842.
DESCRIPTION: 36 x 26 cm. Pen and ink with
watercolor on paper.
PROVENANCE: From an album of eleven
watercolors titled "Sketches in Canada and the
States of Illinois & Michigan. 1841, 42, 43. H. F.
Ainslie." Apparently retained in the artist's family.
Photographic copies at the Library of Congress
indicate that a previous owner, Major J. P.
Kempthorne of New Zealand, had once loaned
the sketchbook to that institution for an exhibit.
Purchased by the Chicago Historical Society
in 1963.
COLLECTION: Chicago History Museum
(1963.762b).

Elizabeth Baird remembered the farmhouse. It was "comfortable-looking, one story in height, painted white with green blinds," and was located, as Ainslie shows it, "in about the center of the farm, far back from the road" in what is today the upper part of the Grand Hotel Golf Course.[54]

Below Fort Mackinac lies the town, its appearance foreshortened by the view so that the vacant Mission House and Mission Church are prominent in the background. Captain Ainslie provides a good impression of the clustered buildings at the western end of the village. These were mostly "of one or two stories; built of boards and in many instances roofed with cedar bark."[55] A few roofs even sag in their picturesque antiquity. Canoes are drawn up along the beach, and Robinson's Folly overlooks the scene from the distance.

Captain Ainslie's earlier stop, in September, allowed time for some sightseeing. He indulged himself by climbing to the top of the bluff west of Fort Mackinac and visiting Arch Rock. From the heights above town he sketched a view (Fig. 7.5) very similar to that made by François de Castelnau in 1838 (Fig. 6.19), though considerably more accomplished. The spot offered a popular vista for artists, and Ainslie took full advantage of it to show Fort Mackinac (with a rather imaginative flag) and details of the Mission Point area. The artist's choice of a view from outside the walls suggests that he did not attempt a professional courtesy call on Captain Martin Scott, the current U.S. commandant.

Tucked below the fort one can distinguish the end of the Indian Dormitory and, farther down the street, the La Framboise house, the low roof and steeple of Ste. Anne's, and the much more prominent Mission Church. With the season of annuity payments in full swing, the shoreline is packed with wigwams. "A hundred conical lodges, on the beach in front of the village, with as many birch canoes drawn out of the water, may be seen at a single stroke of the eye," Daniel Drake observed at about the same time as Ainslie's visit.[56] A wharf and fishing boats punctuate the Indian encampment.

It is likely that Captain Ainslie sketched other Mackinac attractions, but the only one to survive as a finished watercolor is his view of Arch Rock, seen from above and illustrated here as Figure 7.6. It is one of the most accurate and colorful of the pre-photographic period. Perhaps Ainslie noticed the initials that fellow tourists had, for years, carved into its limestone. If so, he might have discovered those of two of his prominent fellow British subjects, Harriet Martineau and Frederick Marryat, which were identified by another traveler in October 1842.[57]

FIGURE 7.7

TITLE: [On original mount:] United States, Site of Old Fort Mackinaw, State of Michigan, Oct. 1842, where in 1763, 3 officers & 60 British soldiers were treacherously massacred by the Indians. [On verso:] OLD Mackinaw, with the French Fort where the Massacre of British troops took place by the French & Indians 1763. taken October 1842.

AUTHOR: Captain Henry Francis Ainslie, 83rd Regiment of Foot (1803–79).

DATE DEPICTED: October 1842.

DATE OF WORK: October 1842.

DESCRIPTION: 36 x 26 cm. Pen and ink with watercolor on paper.

PROVENANCE: From an album of eleven watercolors titled "Sketches in Canada and the States of Illinois & Michigan. 1841, 42, 43. H. F. Ainslie." Apparently retained in the artist's family. Photographic copies at the Library of Congress indicate that a previous owner, Major J. P. Kempthorne of New Zealand, had once loaned the sketchbook to that institution for an exhibit. Purchased by the Chicago Historical Society in 1963.

COLLECTION: Chicago History Museum (1963.762d).

One final Straits of Mackinac landmark caught the attention of Captain Ainslie's pencil and brush. On his return from Lake Michigan in October, about the time he sketched Mackinac Island from a distance, the artist rendered the tip of the Lower Peninsula mainland. The place had particular associations for Ainslie, a British soldier who had spent years in the wilds of North America. His label for Figure 7.7 identifies the subject as the "Site of Old Fort Mackinaw . . . where in 1763, 3 officers & 60 British soldiers were treacherously massacred by the Indians." Perhaps the captain was disappointed, because little could be seen from the middle of the channel. Ainslie created a pleasant landscape nonetheless. Apparently the only visible evidence of the old fort was the clearing to the left of center, seemingly marked by some Indian lodges. When the historian Francis Parkman visited the site in August 1845, he explored the ground and picnicked there, but the sketch map of the ruins drawn by his companion, Lieutenant Henry Whiting, shows little that can be associated with plans of the fortified village drawn during its active days.[58]

"The view on approaching Michilimackinac is one of the loveliest I ever saw," wrote another British officer, Lieutenant William Fairholme, in 1840.[59] From the quality of his watercolors, it is difficult to believe that Captain Henry Francis Ainslie did not share his sentiment.

The island abounds in picturesque views

"Morleigh"

Henry Francis Ainslie's sophisticated watercolors open colorful windows to the Mackinac of 1842. For the most part, however, they provide rather distant views that convey a fine sense of the topography of Mackinac Island and the site of Old Michilimackinac but do not invite the viewer into the streets of the town or the parade ground of the fort. Such detailed compositions are rare in the pre-photographic era, but they do exist. Thus, the five pen-and-ink sketches (Figs. 7.8–7.11 and 7.22) attributed to one Francis Melick Cayley are of particular value in picturing Mackinac as it was during the early 1840s.

These drawings are titled but unsigned, and the attribution of Cayley as the artist is based on a notation that accompanied the images when the current owner purchased them from a dealer. From this and other sources it is known that Francis Melick Cayley was born in Russia of an English family. He moved to Canada in 1836, settling in Toronto, where he held some provincial appointments in the 1840s and 1850s. Cayley has been described as an amateur artist who decorated the walls of his home with scenes from *Faust*.[60] Nothing is known of the circumstances that took him to Mackinac.

The dates of Cayley's time in Canada are consistent with details in his five Mackinac drawings. This is important because the sketches are not dated, and so elements within them must serve to establish the period of time they represent. The presence of the Michilimackinac County Courthouse in Figure 7.10 is firm evidence that the images could not have been created before 1839. Likewise, the old South West Company warehouse (the Northern Hotel) displays its later square, false front in Figures 7.8 and 7.10, and its companion building has been removed. Neither of these changes had yet occurred when Caleb F. Davis pictured the town in August 1839 (Fig. 6.24).

It is not so easy to establish a terminal date for Cayley's drawings. Few of the buildings constructed in the Borough of Michilimackinac during the 1840s are either well documented or readily identifiable. Matthew Geary is thought to have erected his substantial house at the eastern end of Market Street about 1842, but it is not to be seen in Figure 7.10. Nor does the prominent, Greek Revival–style home of Samuel Abbott appear at the opposite end of the village. It was constructed sometime before 1851. Three of Cayley's views of Fort Mackinac (Figs. 7.8–7.10) display the distinctive fish-shaped weather vane on the western end of the officers' stone quarters, known to have been in place by 1845 and perhaps installed during the command of Captain Martin Scott (1842–45). The only other clues are to the season of the year. Mackinac's trees are in full foliage, but no wigwams are to be seen on the beach, suggesting early summer before Native Americans began to gather for their annuity payments. With the information available, it seems safe to assume that Cayley's

drawings date to the period 1840–43, roughly contemporary with Captain Ainslie's visits.

Another consideration in studying the Cayley drawings is the manner in which they were produced. All are so well proportioned as to be almost photographic. A comparison of Cayley's image of the west blockhouse of Fort Mackinac (Fig. 7.9) and Captain Ainslie's nearly identical scene (Fig. 7.5) with a photograph will show that Cayley's is much more precise in its rendering of architecture and topography. Likewise, Cayley's view of the town and fort from the harbor (Fig. 7.8) accomplishes the difficult task of accurately representing the height of the bluff. It thus seems possible that the artist employed artificial means to prepare his sketches. This he could have done with a portable "camera obscura" or a "camera lucida," devices that permitted the projection of a scene so that it could be traced or drawn on a piece of paper with a high degree of realism.

Whatever his technique, Francis Melick Cayley's sketches allow a modern audience to follow him on a virtual tour of parts of Mackinac Island, particularly the town. This begins with Figure 7.8, a scene from one of the wharves or, more likely because of its higher angle, from the deck of the steamer that brought the artist to Mackinac Island. Laid out before the viewer is Michael Dousman's wharf, located on the site of the modern "Coal Dock." Behind its barrels of fish and stacks of cordwood is the eastern end of the village from Astor Street on the left to Fort Street on the right. No buildings yet encroach on the beach side of Main Street. Overlooking all is Fort Mackinac with the garrison gardens, provisions storehouse, and stable at the foot of the bluff.

Dousman's wharf is one of the most revealing parts of the composition, for this is the only pre-photographic image of Mackinac that shows substantial details of the shipping of barreled fish and the provisioning of cordwood to steamboats. James S. Buckingham, who saw Mackinac in 1840, noted that not less than three thousand barrels of whitefish and trout were then shipped annually at a value of twelve dollars and fifteen to twenty dollars per barrel, respectively.[61] At the same time, the need for firewood made it necessary for nearly every passing steamer to pause at Mackinac Island to refuel. The wood was cut on Bois Blanc Island or on the mainland, transported in small vessels like the schooner moored to the wharf, and stacked for ready access. The sailors, often assisted by the less affluent passengers, loaded the wood aboard their steamboat. Gustav Unonius, a Swedish immigrant bound for Wisconsin, was put to this task before he could briefly tour the island in October 1841.[62]

Once this work had been done, Unonius and his companions could visit the fort and town. The boldly painted sign "Injun

Curiosities" on the front of the store opposite the wharf in Figure 7.8 was intended to attract their custom. J. Elliot Cabot described this message in 1848 as "posted up in large letters to attract the steamboat passengers during their brief stop."[63] Unonius and other travelers noted that Indians brought in the goods to trade with local merchants when they visited the island. The "curiosities" consisted of a variety of furs as well as "maple sugar and wild rice; and of articles made by the squaws, such as moccasins, small bags, baskets, and various kinds of toys devised from birch bark." Everything was "fashioned very neatly and sometimes quite tastefully ornamented with beads and fine porcupine quills."[64] This was a commerce that could be traced back to fur-trading days, and as early as 1820 Henry Schoolcraft described similar items made by the Indians that were "generally in demand as articles of curiosity."[65] Native American products remained standard Mackinac souvenirs well into the twentieth century.

To the right of the curiosities store is a line of buildings along modern Main Street representing the mixed architecture of Mackinac Island at the beginning of the 1840s. Steep-roofed Canadian-style houses are interspersed between newer and boxier American buildings, some of which were or would later become hotels. False fronts had begun to appear on the gable ends of some of the older Canadian-style buildings as well, such as that second from the right, the former storehouse of the South West and American Fur companies that would later become the Northern Hotel.

It is likely that Francis Cayley explored the village and then climbed the road leading to the bluff west of Fort Mackinac. There he set up on roughly the same spot that Castelnau and Ainslie had to capture a view that includes part of the fort and the Mission Point area of town (Fig. 7.9). Most of the details are the same as in Ainslie's 1842 view, although no wigwams are in evidence. Madame La Framboise's house is particularly well shown just above the Indian Dormitory, and a pair of fishing schooners may be seen at the wharf opposite it. Fort Mackinac appears in exact proportion, the roof of the officers' stone quarters sporting its fish-shaped weather vane and part of the "Hill House" visible at the extreme left.

Like Ainslie, Cayley seems not to have entered Fort Mackinac. Rather, he made his way to the rising ground to the north of the post and sketched a view of the back of the fort that will be illustrated later as Figure 7.22. From that point, the artist followed paths or a rough road to the East Bluff where he set up to make a view of the village (Fig. 7.10). The streets and buildings were neatly laid out before the artist, from the Indian Agency House and Indian Dormitory in the foreground to the increasingly built-up western end. On Market Street, from right to left, one can distinguish the old American Fur Company retail store and then the cluster of four large buildings making up the American Fur Company clerk's quarters, Stuart House, and warehouse and the Michilimackinac County Courthouse, inexplicably shown without its distinctive steeple. Along the waterfront may be seen the same mixed block of buildings depicted in Figure 7.8 although there is no false front on the "Injun Curiosities" building. At least three wharves extend into the harbor, the nearest being Dousman's and the farthest probably Lasley's. The wharf between them is probably the one constructed in 1839 by Biddle and Drew. Behind the town rises the low ridge that marked the stockade line of Patrick Sinclair's original settlement, still largely cleared of trees. A few bushes have begun to encroach on the slope of the East Bluff.

At some point in his wanderings the artist climbed to Fort Holmes to take in the view. Then, continuing in a northwesterly direction along the upper plateau, he came to a steep bluff from which he had a view of a "curious lump of stone" in the forest below (Fig. 7.11). Most pre-photographic images of Sugar Loaf were drawn from ground level, usually from the north. Cayley, however, stood high above at what today is known as Point Lookout. The spot had likely been a popular vista since the plateau was cleared of trees to open a field of fire around Fort Holmes, but the Reverend Jackson Kemper was the first to mention it in July 1834.[66] In 1835 Chandler Robbins Gilman described looking at Sugar Loaf from "a rocky bluff more than two hundred feet high, and so nearly perpendicular that the least spring would have cleared it." Below, Gilman saw "an expanse of thickly-wooded land, perhaps half a mile wide" interrupted only by the dramatic mass of rock.[67] By the time Sarah Fuller visited in August 1843 the adventurous could descend from the eminence to Sugar Loaf by "a long and steep path" that is today marked by a stairway.[68]

Francis Melick Cayley's wonderfully detailed drawings appear to have once been part of an artist's sketchbook or portfolio. He probably made other Mackinac views. If so, these have been lost, but the five that survive present the most precise images of Mackinac Island that would be seen before the introduction of photography.

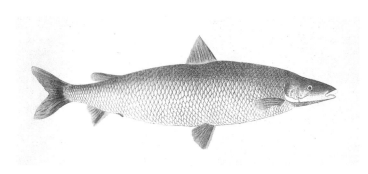

Whitefish was king on Mackinac Island during by the 1840s. This fine example was engraved for Thomas L. McKenney's *Sketches of a Tour to the Lakes* (Baltimore, 1827). *Clements Library, University of Michigan.*

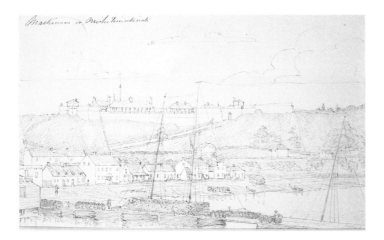

FIGURE 7.8

TITLE: Mackinaw or Michilimackinak.
AUTHOR: [Francis Melick Cayley (1809–90)].
DATE DEPICTED: ca. 1840–43.
DATE OF WORK: ca. 1840–43.
DESCRIPTION: 14.4 x 23.5 cm. Pen and ink on paper.
PROVENANCE: Originally part of a sketchbook, with the individual leaf later separated and pasted to another sheet of paper. In pencil on the back of one sheet is written: "Francis Melick Cayley / Toronto / 1809–1874 / 3rd Son of John Harriet Cayley / of St. Petersburg." Retained in the artist's family. Purchased from a dealer in 1993.
COLLECTION: Masco Collection, Taylor, MI.

FIGURE 7.9

TITLE: Mackinaw.
AUTHOR: [Francis Melick Cayley (1809–90)].
DATE DEPICTED: ca. 1840–43.
DATE OF WORK: ca. 1840–43.
DESCRIPTION: 14.4 x 23.5 cm. Pen and ink on paper.
PROVENANCE: Originally part of a sketchbook, with the individual leaf later separated and pasted to another sheet of paper. In pencil on the back of one sheet is written: "Francis Melick Cayley / Toronto / 1809–1874 / 3rd Son of John Harriet Cayley / of St. Petersburg." Retained in the artist's family. Purchased from a dealer in 1993.
COLLECTION: Masco Collection, Taylor, MI.

FIGURE 7.10

TITLE: Mackinaw.
AUTHOR: [Francis Melick Cayley (1809–90)].
DATE DEPICTED: ca. 1840–43.
DATE OF WORK: ca. 1840–43.
DESCRIPTION: 14.4 x 23.5 cm. Pen and ink on paper.
PROVENANCE: Originally part of a sketchbook, with the individual leaf later separated and pasted to another sheet of paper. In pencil on the back of one sheet is written: "Francis Melick Cayley / Toronto / 1809–1874 / 3rd Son of John Harriet Cayley / of St. Petersburg." Retained in the artist's family. Purchased from a dealer in 1993.
COLLECTION: Masco Collection, Taylor, MI.

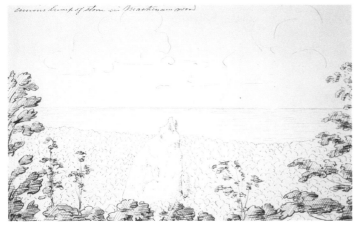

FIGURE 7.11

TITLE: curious lump of stone in Mackinaw wood.
AUTHOR: [Francis Melick Cayley (1809–90)].
DATE DEPICTED: ca. 1840–43.
DATE OF WORK: ca. 1840–43.
DESCRIPTION: 14.4 x 23.5 cm. Pen and ink on paper.
PROVENANCE: Originally part of a sketchbook, with the individual leaf later separated and pasted to another sheet of paper. In pencil on the back of one sheet is written: "Francis Melick Cayley / Toronto / 1809–1874 / 3rd Son of John Harriet Cayley / of St. Petersburg." Retained in the artist's family. Purchased from a dealer in 1993.
COLLECTION: Masco Collection, Taylor, MI.

The greatest "lion" of the island is the Arch Rock

C. Donald MacLeod

Sarah Margaret Fuller was much taken with the beauty of Mackinac Island when she visited in August and September 1843. A particular attraction of the place was its size, a microcosm of the beaches, woods, scenery, and people she had encountered during a summer's tour of the Great Lakes and Midwest. Fuller had already seen Niagara Falls, Detroit, Chicago, the prairies of Illinois, and the growing town of Milwaukee on Lake Michigan. Now it was time for a more intimate setting. "It is charming to be on an island so small that you can sail round it in an afternoon, yet large enough to admit of long secluded walks through its gentle groves," she later wrote. Like so many others, Fuller particularly enjoyed the bluffs and rock formations, "lofty walls of stone, richly wooded, which rise . . . in various architectural forms.[69]

Sarah Fuller, whose book, *Summer on the Lakes,* appeared in 1844, was an observer in the style of the intelligent, inquisitive, and independent women travelers of the 1830s whose writings had helped introduce Mackinac to the reading public. An avowed feminist, Transcendentalist, and already a successful author and editor, she numbered Ralph Waldo Emerson among her close friends and had written for his literary journal, *The Dial,* in 1840–42. Sarah Fuller found herself traveling the lakes in the summer of 1843 at the invitation of another friend, James Freeman Clarke, and his sister, Sara Ann. While Sarah Fuller recorded their journey in words, Sara Clarke preserved three visual impressions of Mackinac Island.

"My companion carried about her sketch-book with her," Fuller wrote of the three days in September that the pair spent together on Mackinac Island.[70] Clarke's views of Arch Rock and Robinson's Folly survive in the special illustrated edition of Fuller's book (Figs. 7.12, 7.13, and 7.15).

Sarah Fuller's introduction to Mackinac Island was a bit more colorful than that of most modern-day visitors. Late in the evening of August 20, as her steamer slipped into Haldimand Bay, the captain announced their arrival by firing off a barrage of rockets. It was the beginning of annuity time, and the shoreline was packed with the wigwams of visiting Native Americans. The colorful, bursting rockets "greatly excited the Indians, and their yells and wild cries resounded along the shore." Fuller had temporarily parted company with the Clarkes, not to be reunited until her second visit to Mackinac Island in September, so she accompanied a group of passengers to a "strange hotel," probably the Lasley House. Their walk took them through the noisy throng of Ojibwa and Ottawa visitors as "the pants and snorts of the departing steamer" reminded her that she was now isolated until the appearance of another vessel.[71]

Arriving at the hotel, Sarah was disappointed in her hopes of obtaining private accommodations. It was annuity time, after all, and there were no rooms to be had. The sophisticated Massachusetts woman spent the night in "the common parlor and eating-room," which guaranteed that she would rise early the next morning to

Sarah Margaret Fuller (1810–50) spent nine lonely days on Mackinac Island in August 1843. She returned with her traveling companions in September, during which time Sara Clarke drew views of the premier rock formations that were later engraved and published in Fuller's 1844 book. This oil-on-canvas portrait, by an unidentified artist, is believed to depict Fuller sometime between 1835 and 1845. *Collection of the Litchfield Historical Society, Litchfield, CT (X1922–1).*

ARCHED ROCK AT MACKINAW

FIGURE 7.12

TITLE: Arched Rock at Mackinaw.

AUTHOR: Sara Ann Clarke (1808–after 1888).

DATE DEPICTED: September 1843.

DATE OF WORK: 1844.

DESCRIPTION: 14.3 x 7.9 cm. Engraving.

PROVENANCE: Published in Margaret Fuller, *Summer on the Lakes, in 1843* (Boston, 1844), frontispiece of illustrated edition.

COLLECTION: Clements Library, University of Michigan, Ann Arbor (Book Division, C2-1844-Os, copy 2).

ARCHED ROCK FROM THE WATER

FIGURE 7.13
TITLE: Arched Rock from the Water.
AUTHOR: Sara Ann Clarke (1808–after 1888).
DATE DEPICTED: September 1843.
DATE OF WORK: 1844.
DESCRIPTION: 8 x 15.3 cm. Engraving.
PROVENANCE: Published in Margaret Fuller, *Summer on the Lakes, in 1843* (Boston, 1844), 171 of illustrated edition.
COLLECTION: Clements Library, University of Michigan, Ann Arbor (Book Division, C2-1844-Os, copy 2).

FIGURE 7.14
TITLE: The Natural Bridge at Mackinac.
AUTHOR: Paul Kane (1810–71).
DATE DEPICTED: July 1845.
DATE OF WORK: [July 1845].
DESCRIPTION: 29.2 x 24.4 cm. Oil on paper.
PROVENANCE: Unknown.
COLLECTION: Stark Museum of Art, Orange, TX (31.78/183, EOP 20).

FIGURE 7.15
TITLE: Mackinaw Beach.
AUTHOR: Sara Ann Clarke (1808–after 1888).
DATE DEPICTED: September 1843.
DATE OF WORK: 1844.
DESCRIPTION: 8 x 14.8 cm. Engraving.
PROVENANCE: Published in Margaret Fuller, *Summer on the Lakes, in 1843* (Boston, 1844), 249 of illustrated edition.
COLLECTION: Clements Library, University of Michigan, Ann Arbor (Book Division, C2-1844-Os, copy 2).

MACKINAW BEACH

begin her explorations. Her hotel was filled with traders come to deal with the Indians, and although Fuller found many of them "half wild and wholly rude," she admitted that they were also "good-humored, observing, and with a store of knowledge to impart, of the kind proper to their place."[72]

Her next nine days were spent learning about Mackinac Island and awaiting a boat bound for Sault Ste. Marie. Fuller later remembered this time as "the 'lonesome' nine," because her companions were absent. After a brief visit to Sault Ste. Marie, where she was reunited with the Clarkes, Fuller and her friends returned to Mackinac Island for three September days spent "walking or boating, or sitting at the window to see the Indians go" as their annuities were received and spent.[73] It was during this time that Sara Clarke made the sketches for the prints illustrated here.

Not surprisingly, Sara Clarke chose Arch Rock as the subject for two of her views. By 1843 it had become, indisputably, "the greatest 'lion' of the island," whose other standard attractions included Sugar Loaf, Skull Cave, Fort Holmes, Lover's Leap, and several smaller geological formations.[74] Sarah Fuller had read extensively in preparation for her trip, including books by Henry Schoolcraft, Anna Jameson, and Thomas McKenney, so she had seen their descriptions of Arch Rock. She was nonetheless surprised by the "perfection" of the arch. Sara Clarke captured its delicate span in Figure 7.12. The women did not walk across it, although the natural bridge regularly tempted daredevils. Reverend John Pitezel, who also visited in August 1843, revealed the trick to crossing the narrow passage—he and his companions removed their boots and went in their stocking feet. Pitezel was only concerned when he came to the narrowest part, only a foot wide and marked by "some small twigs of cedar" that appear in Clarke's view.[75]

Sarah Fuller considered the arch perfectly formed, whether seen from above while looking into the "transparent waters" of

Lake Huron or viewed from the shore below. She and Clarke did both, scrambling up and down a rough path used for decades by tourists. Figure 7.13 was drawn from a point much farther offshore, however, during a canoe excursion. The women prevailed on some traders to hire two Indians who, Fuller wrote, "would not only take us out, but be sure to bring us back." Thinking it amusing to be thus ferrying two white women, the paddlers braved the swells of the lake, splashed water into the canoe, and crossed in front of a departing steamer.[76] Once in the lee of the island, Clarke had her opportunity to sketch Arch Rock, set off by "Michibou's Rock" on the beach below and Fairy Arch, visible in the trees to the left.

Robinson's Folly was the subject of Sara Clarke's third view (Fig. 7.15). The artist carefully depicted the rocky outcropping, still largely bare of vegetation in September 1843. Along the beach below is part of the extensive Native American encampment that had proved so fascinating to Sarah Fuller during her "lonesome" nine days at Mackinac in August. Like so many other tourists, she had been attracted by the colorful prospect presented by the camp. The wigwams were covered by "amber brown matting," while their occupants were scattered along the beach, "the women preparing food . . . over the many small fires; the children half-naked, wild as little goblins, were playing both in and out of the water." Fuller found this "a scene of ideal loveliness, and these wild forms adorned it, as looking so at home in it."[77] Robinson's Folly is not identified in the title of Clarke's view, but it provides a dramatic backdrop for the peaceful scene of Native Americans and their scattered wigwams.

Like Anna Jameson before her, however, Sarah Fuller was also interested in the lives of Mackinac's Native Americans, particularly those of the women. She wrestled with the varying perceptions of these people as expressed by many of the authors she had read prior to her visit. "Why will people look only on one side?" she wondered. "They either exalt the Red man into a Demigod or degrade him into a beast." Her narrative then discusses at length the observations of earlier writers about the status of women and marriage among Native Americans.[78]

Like most other writers Fuller recognized and criticized the sale of alcohol to the Native Americans who visited Mackinac each summer and fall. She even attributed the peaceful scene in the village she described to the fact that it was a Sunday, the shops were closed, and the Indians "had no firewater to madden them."[79] When the Canadian artist Paul Kane traveled to Mackinac Island in July 1845 he had much the same impression. Apparently the annuities were paid earlier that year, for he found the beach crowded with the lodges of an estimated 2,600 Indians. This assemblage had attracted the usual throng of traders who filled the island's hotels and boarding-houses and brought "large quantities of spirituous liquors" to be sold clandestinely.[80] Most contemporary writers consistently described the results, "scenes of woe and wretchedness" as Reverend Pitezel put it in 1843. Although Indian Agent Robert Stuart had taken particularly firm measures to control the sale of alcohol that summer,

they were still insufficient to prevent the "ravages of this destroyer." Pitezel witnessed raving and fighting, drunken singing and dancing, and lodges filled with intoxicated occupants.[81]

Paul Kane traveled to Mackinac from Sault Ste. Marie in 1845 for a firsthand look at Mackinac's huge gathering of Native Americans. His intention was to "sketch their most remarkable personages," so he pitched his own tent among the wigwams, a decision he soon regretted when their "famishing dogs" managed to steal most of his provisions. Kane spent three weeks on the island, taking the likenesses of a number of Native Americans but also making drawings of "picturesque spots" and even artifacts such as wampum belts presented by the British during the War of 1812.[82] Kane's finished view of Arch Rock (Fig. 7.14) is probably the finest and best proportioned rendering of the feature he described as "a natural bridge, which all strangers visit." His painting of Robinson's Folly (Fig. 7.16) is of the same quality. Like Sara Clarke's likeness, it includes the ubiquitous wigwams and canoes that marked the height of each Mackinac summer during the 1840s.

Mani-tow-wa-bay, or "He-Devil," was a veteran Ojibwa warrior, painted at Mackinac by Paul Kane in 1845. Kane heard that he had taken nine scalps in battle but, when under the influence of liquor, became "one of the most violent and unmanageable" of his people. Kane, like many other writers, was appalled by the quantity of alcohol available clandestinely to the Indians during annuity payment time at Mackinac. *Collection of Glenbow Museum, Calgary, Canada (63.72).*

Sarah M. Fuller had read extensively about the Indians prior to her visit to Mackinac Island. She took a particular interest in the women and "held much communication by signs" with them. Fuller was impressed by the "parental love" she witnessed in the camps on the beach. James Otto Lewis depicted these Ojibwa women and their children at Fond du Lac in 1826. Lithograph by Lehman and Duval. *Clements Library, University of Michigan.*

FIGURE 7.16

TITLE: [Robinson's Folly].
AUTHOR: Paul Kane (1810–71).
DATE DEPICTED: July 1845.
DATE OF WORK: [1846].
DESCRIPTION: 31.1 x 24.4 cm. Oil on paper.

PROVENANCE: Signed "Lake Superior 1846." This is presumably an error as Kane had little time to complete finished pieces at Mackinac during his brief return visit that year. The Stark Museum identifies this by the title "Rocky Headland with Wigwams in Foreground."
COLLECTION: Stark Museum of Art, Orange, TX (31.78/192, EOP 29).

There was here a Catholic mission and a priest

Reverend John H. Pitezel

Mackinac Island presented several distinctive landmarks to passengers aboard vessels passing through the Straits. First to be seen from a distance was the high and "peculiar" shape of the island itself that, most observers admitted, resembled the turtle for which it had been named. The brilliantly whitewashed walls of Fort Mackinac appeared next, visible for miles across the lake. Only a few prominent architectural details stood out as travelers entered the harbor. Returning from Chicago in October 1840, Lieutenant John Wolcott Phelps pointed these out to a lady friend—the Mission House, the Indian Dormitory and Agency House, and three spires marking the courthouse and a pair of churches.[83]

Perhaps it was a sign that evangelical fervor had cooled since the 1820s and 1830s that relatively few writers of the 1840s discussed the churches in their descriptions of Mackinac Island. The buildings and their steeples were certainly prominent enough, as the drawings of Henry Ainslie and Francis Cayley demonstrate. Most who wrote about Mission Church and Ste. Anne's Church seem to have been clergymen, however, and lay visitors generally had little to say. Fortunately, a pair of artistic clerics visually documented the Catholic and Protestant church buildings as they appeared in 1844 (Figs. 7.17 and 7.18).

While most writers focused their attention on natural and historic sites and the Indians, a few touched on religion at Mackinac. Much had changed since the sectarian conflict of 1829–31 sparked formal and heated exchanges between Reverend Ferry and Fathers Mullon and Mazzuchelli. Ferry had departed in 1834, and no permanent minister had been found to replace him. His mission and school closed three years later. The Presbyterian congregation continued, after a fashion, its meetings, often led by Indian agent Henry Schoolcraft.[84] When Peter Dougherty arrived in the summer of 1838, intent on establishing a new Protestant Indian mission at L'Arbre Croche, he noted that the Presbyterian church was "a very good building with a steeple and bell." Unfortunately, he lamented, "there is no voice of the living teacher heard to proclaim the glad tidings in it on the Sabbath from its altar." Not surprisingly, the congregation asked Dougherty to preach while he was on the island.[85]

Mission Church was thereafter used for Presbyterian services whenever a minister was available. Dougherty presided in the building from time to time, and on one Sunday in August 1843 he addressed a group of Indians there through his interpreter. Later that afternoon John H. Pitezel, a visiting Methodist minister, spoke to the white congregation, and his associate, "Brother Brown," preached to the Indians in the evening.[86] Mission Church remained in usable condition, despite the absence of a full-time minister, although

Presbyterian meetings were sometimes held at the Michilimackinac County Courthouse. In May 1840 Charles Penny noted that attendance at the service there was "very small" but proportionally as large as that on a normal Sunday in one of the churches at Detroit.[87]

While the island's regular Protestant congregation had withered, the Catholic parish of Ste. Anne maintained most of its vigor. Protestant correspondents deplored this fact, considering Catholicism "an influence which is deadly against the spread of a pure Christianity," especially among the Indians. Reverend Pitezel noted that most of the island's inhabitants were Catholics and that they had the benefit of "a priest on the spot." "They wear the cross and count their beads," he continued, "but are kept in ignorance of the Bible."[88] Ste. Anne's had enjoyed a permanent pastor since the late 1820s, and the priest also served the new church in St. Ignace.[89]

The pastor of Ste. Anne's in the summer of 1844 was Father Otto Skolla, a Franciscan priest who had arrived in New York from Austria late in 1841. Skolla was first sent to Detroit to minister to the growing population of German immigrants in that city. His aspirations were to serve as a missionary to the Indians, however, and, in June 1843, he was assigned to Mackinac. There he remained until September 1845 when his continued requests to be sent to an Indian mission were granted, and he moved to La Pointe on Lake Superior. Skolla was popular with the congregation of Ste. Anne's, where he also attracted many of the Irish Catholic soldiers from the Fort Mackinac garrison with "short" sermons given in his limited English.[90]

Father Skolla possessed a talent for more than brief homilies. He also liked to draw. Skolla occasionally painted religious pictures for his churches, and by 1849 he had made drawings of all his missions and sent them to his Franciscan brothers in Europe. These included Ste. Anne's and probably the church at St. Ignace as well.[91] Father Skolla, in fact, made at least two paintings of Mackinac. The larger of these showed "the whole island of Mackinac with the church, presbytery, some houses and wigwams of Indians." In the background could also be seen the church of St. Ignatius on the mainland. The size of this painting was such that Father Skolla feared it would not safely reach his brother, Francis, so he did not send it to Europe. Instead, he forwarded a smaller composition showing only "the church of Mackinac." By July 1845 Father Skolla had received confirmation that this painting had reached Francis, so it is likely the scene was prepared sometime during 1844.[92]

That painting was probably the image engraved and published in 1906 in Antoine Rezek's history of the diocese of Sault Ste. Marie and Marquette. The original work had been discovered in the Franciscan monastery of Tersat, near Fiume, Hungary (today Rijecka,

FIGURE 7.17

TITLE: [The church of Mackinac].
AUTHOR: Father Otto Skolla (1805–79).
DATE DEPICTED: 1844.
DATE OF WORK: 1906.
DESCRIPTION: 7.8 x 10.4. Engraving.
PROVENANCE: Engraved from a painting executed by Skolla and discovered in the Franciscan monastery at Tersat, near Fiume, Hungary (today Rijeka, Croatia), where Father Skolla had died. First reproduced in Antoine Rezek, *History of the Diocese of Sault Ste. Marie* (Houghton, 1906), 2:66. It was again reproduced in Edwin O. Wood, *Historic Mackinac* (New York, 1918), 1:388.
COLLECTION: University of Michigan Libraries, Ann Arbor.

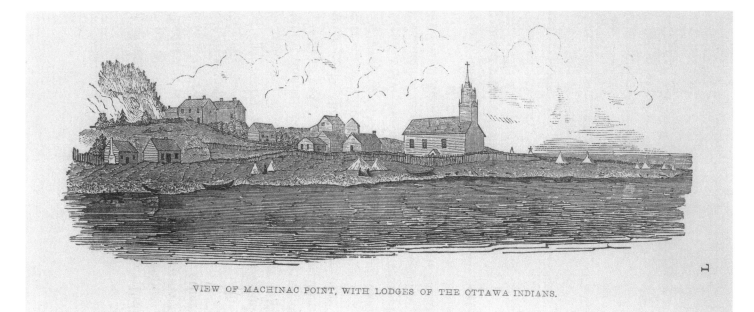

VIEW OF MACHINAC POINT, WITH LODGES OF THE OTTAWA INDIANS.

FIGURE 7.18

TITLE: View of Machinac Point, with Lodges of the Ottawa Indians.
AUTHOR: Reverend James Beaven (1801–75).
DATE DEPICTED: August 1844.
DATE OF WORK: 1846.
DESCRIPTION: 6 x 14 cm. Woodcut.

PROVENANCE: Published in Beaven, *Recreations of a Long Vacation; or a Visit to Indian Missions in Upper Canada* (London and Toronto, 1846), 109.
COLLECTION: University of Michigan Libraries, Ann Arbor.

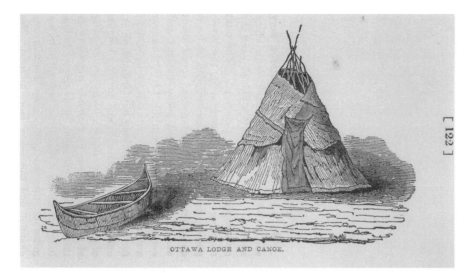

OTTAWA LODGE AND CANOE.

FIGURE 7.19

TITLE: Ottawa Lodge and Canoe.

AUTHOR: Reverend James Beaven (1801–75).

DATE DEPICTED: August 1844.

DATE OF WORK: 1846.

DESCRIPTION: 7 x 11.5 cm. Woodcut.

PROVENANCE: Published in Beaven, *Recreations of a Long Vacation; or a Visit to Indian Missions in Upper Canada* (London and Toronto, 1846), 122.

COLLECTION: University of Michigan Libraries, Ann Arbor.

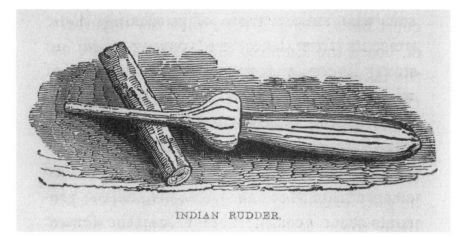

INDIAN RUDDER.

FIGURE 7.20

TITLE: Indian Rudder.

AUTHOR: Reverend James Beaven (1801–75).

DATE DEPICTED: August 1844.

DATE OF WORK: 1846.

DESCRIPTION: 3 x 8 cm. Engraving.

PROVENANCE: Published in Beaven, *Recreations of a Long Vacation; or a Visit to Indian Missions in Upper Canada* (London and Toronto, 1846), 138.

COLLECTION: University of Michigan Libraries, Ann Arbor.

Croatia), where Father Skolla had retired and died in 1879.[93] The current whereabouts of the painting is unknown, but the engraving appears to preserve most of its details. The published image became much more familiar after it was again reproduced in Edwin O. Wood's *Historic Mackinac* of 1918.

Ste. Anne's Church is at the center of Father Skolla's composition, and the Canadian-style row house to its right is the rectory. Both buildings appear much as they did following the enlargement of the church and construction of the house in 1831.[94] The facade and steeple of Ste. Anne's conform to sketches made by Gustave de Beaumont in August of that year (Figs. 6.3 and 6.4). Lieutenant John Wolcott Phelps, who attended Mass in the building in October 1840, described a simple sanctuary with church furniture "in humble imitation of the splendor of the parent church."[95] This unassuming log building would serve the parish until 1873.[96]

To the left of the church, Father Skolla depicted the stately home of Madame Magdelaine La Framboise. Captain Benjamin K. Pierce, her son-in-law, built this Mackinac Island landmark before the death of his wife, Josette, in November 1820.[97] It stands on the western side of the lane that is today Church Street on property granted to the La Framboise family in 1808 (claim 710). Magdelaine La Framboise was

the chief benefactor of the Catholic parish for many years. The small log church shown by Father Skolla had been constructed by June 1827 on another of her family's properties (claim 711) that she granted to the parish in October of that year. Madame La Framboise had buried her daughter and infant grandson on that lot in 1820, and she would be interred with them beneath the church following her own death in 1846.[98]

Two streets to the east of Ste. Anne's stood Mission Church, and it was also captured in an image in August 1844. The artist was a priest of the Church of England, James Beaven, who left his post in Toronto that summer to inspect a mission at Sault Ste. Marie. He stopped at Mackinac Island on his way to and from that place. Reverend Beaven published an account of his trip two years later and enlivened his narrative with "a few sketches, by an untaught and hitherto unpractised hand, supposing that they would add life and interest" to the book. Beaven admitted that they were all "unartist-like pictures."[99] Those that can be associated with his time at Mackinac include a workmanlike view of Mission Point and its buildings, a wigwam and canoe, and an "Indian rudder" (Figs. 7.18– 7.20) as well as a pair of crude sketches of Indians observed at Mackinac. Beaven's style is indeed unsophisticated, although no more so than Father Skolla's.

Reverend Beaven's "View of Machinac Point" (Fig. 7.18) is the most revealing of his compositions and provides an interesting comparison to Father Skolla's painting. Although drawn seven years after the closing of Reverend Ferry's school, it shows the Mission House, Mission Church, and their outbuildings in some detail and from a different angle than that depicted in an earlier engraving of about 1830 (Fig. 6.2). A few of the smaller private houses at the eastern end of town appear as well, and the wigwams punctuating the beach reflect Beaven's visit at annuity payment time. The large Mission House stands at the foot of the bluff, empty and forlorn. Although the artist regretted the demise of the mission school, he was told that plans were afoot to open the building as a "lodging house," an event that would occur the following year and give the Mission House an entirely new and long lease on life.[100]

Skolla and Beaven's views depict Mackinac Island's two traditional church buildings as they were in the 1840s. The Michili-mackinac County Courthouse, visible in one of Francis Cayley's compositions (Fig. 7.10), often provided a third location for religious services, although that building was more regularly the site of legal proceedings, borough meetings, and even theatrical performances. Mackinac Island also had a fourth place of worship in 1844. And, unlike Mission Church, it had a resident pastor. Chaplain John O'Brien had regularly conducted Episcopalian services in the barracks of Fort Mackinac since his appointment to the post in 1842. He would remain a fixture of garrison and community religious life until 1861.[101] Reverend Beaven attended O'Brien's services in this unlikely venue and preached there himself at the chaplain's invitation.[102]

James Beaven discovered many details in which O'Brien's Episcopalian ceremony differed from those of the Church of England. These "irregularities" appeared in O'Brien's services in the Fort Mackinac barracks as well as in those conducted by the chaplain in the courthouse later each Sunday. The latter attracted "all classes of people," many of whom were voluntary attendees and not members of a church. Reverend Beaven explained the differences by the fact that O'Brien was a "clergyman in the reformed church in the States."[103] It must have been apparent to him, nonetheless, that religion was practiced regularly and in many different ways at Mackinac.

REV. OTTON SKOLLA, O.S.F.

The Franciscan priest Otto Skolla was pastor of Ste. Anne's in 1843–45. As a hobby, he executed both religious paintings and views of his churches, including those on Mackinac Island and at St. Ignace. The origin of this image of Father Skolla is unknown, but it might have been based on a self-portrait. It was engraved for Antoine Rezek's *History of the Diocese of Sault Ste. Marie and Marquette* (Houghton, 1906–7). *University of Michigan Libraries.*

OTTAWA INDIAN CHIEF.

Reverend James Beaven was an amateur artist who had no pretensions about his abilities. He captured several scenes at Mackinac in 1844, including this seated Ottawa chief, and included them as illustrations in his 1846 book, *Recreations of a Long Vacation. University of Michigan Libraries.*

Like his sketch of an Ottawa chief, Beaven's drawing of an unidentified, seated Indian shows the man clothed in fabric garments obtained from Mackinac's merchants. From Beaven, *Recreations of a Long Vacation. University of Michigan Libraries.*

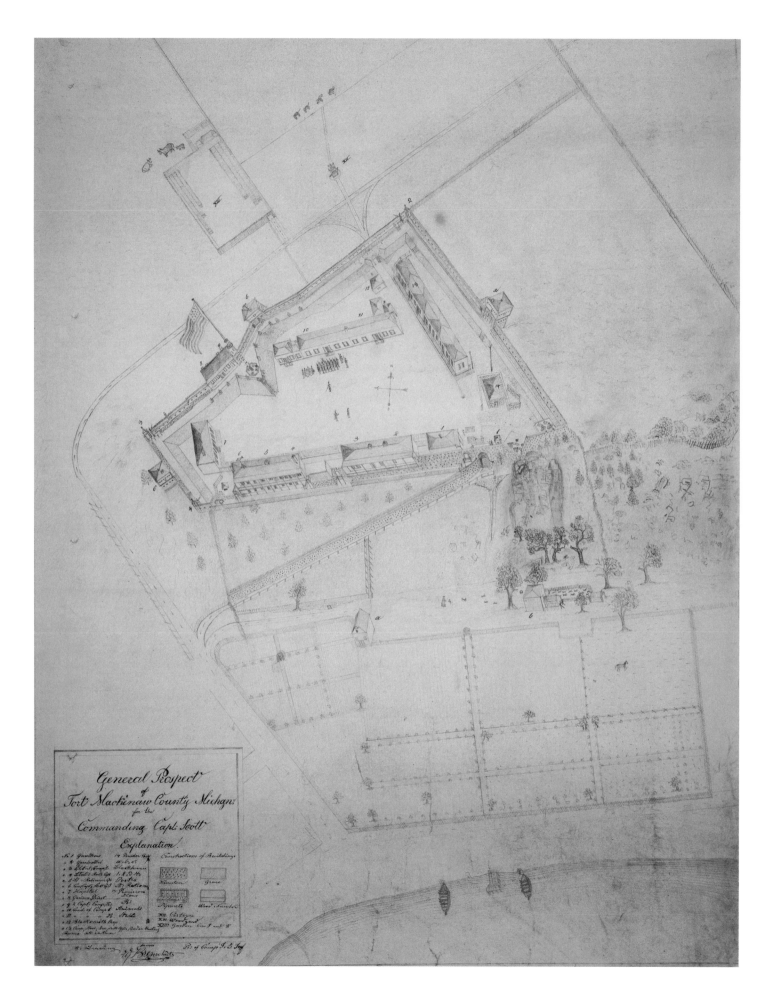

It is kept with extraordinary neatness

Reverend James Beaven

On a late August day in 1844 the Reverend James Beaven toiled up the long, steeply sloping road to Fort Mackinac. Like so many visitors, before and since, he intended to explore the fortifications and perhaps enjoy a panorama of the Straits. To his left, a retaining wall followed the walkway to the summit of the bluff. On his right, the hill dropped away abruptly, giving a progressively more dramatic view of the town and harbor as he climbed toward the fort. The road beneath his feet was surfaced with "a kind of concrete" made of the island's abundant limestone. At the top of the track Beaven came to an arched stone gateway, "the ordinary entrance" to Fort Mackinac.[104]

Once past the sentry, Reverend Beaven found himself by the guardhouse. There he could see the length of the fort with its immaculately graveled parade ground surrounded by tidy, whitewashed buildings. "It is kept with extraordinary neatness," Beaven noted. Captain Martin Scott had been in charge of Fort Mackinac for the past two years, and he had a reputation as an officer who liked things just so. Among other improvements, Scott had ordered "spitting boxes" placed all around the enclosure to keep his men from soiling the white gravel with tobacco juice. And, Reverend Beaven observed, "if a carriage passes through the yard, the tracks of its wheels are effaced by boughs (which answer the purpose of brooms) as soon as it is gone."[105] A Fort Mackinac visitor

in 1843 found it difficult to imagine "how any thing could be kept in a more neat and orderly manner."[106]

Captain Scott's obsession with order and cleanliness was perhaps a reaction to the condition into which Fort Mackinac had fallen by 1840. Its buildings had stood empty for much of the time from 1837 to 1840, guarded by a lone sergeant who could do little but report the ravages of wind and weather as they occurred.[107] When a new garrison arrived, in May 1840, Lieutenant John Wolcott Phelps was impressed by the appearance of Fort Mackinac from the harbor, but on closer inspection he found it "a very Turkish City, as ruinous and dilapidated as it had been at first imposing." The troops were put to work mounting cannon and repairing breaches in the pickets, some of which probably dated to the great storm of December 1837.[108]

Regular maintenance and buckets of whitewash soon returned Fort Mackinac to a more imposing appearance, but it was the arrival of Captain Scott in 1842 that accelerated the pace of repairs. The post had undergone its last major renovation fifteen years earlier, and there was much to be done. By September 1844 Scott's troops had repaired large sections of the masonry walls, replaced most of the fort's picketing, and installed new roofs and flooring where needed. They had fenced the drill field north of the fort, graveled the parade ground, resurfaced the ramp leading up the face of the bluff, and

---

FIGURE 7.21

TITLE: General Prospect of Fort Mackinaw County Michgn: for the Commanding Capt: Scott.
AUTHOR: Private William G. Brenschutz, 5th Regiment of Infantry (active 1844–45).
DATE DEPICTED: 1845.
DATE OF WORK: [1845].
DESCRIPTION: 59 x 46 cm. Pencil on paper mounted on board.
PROVENANCE: Drawn for Captain Martin Scott (1788–1847). His wife, Lavinia McCracken Scott (d. 1854), kept the drawing after his death. It later passed to her first cousin, Mariette McCracken Langworthy, and then to her daughter, Mary Langworthy Temple, and her daughter Eleanor Temple. Ms. Temple, then of Muskegon, Michigan, presented it to the Clements Library on May 13, 1941.
COLLECTION: Clements Library, University of Michigan, Ann Arbor (Map Division, 6-O-15).

KEY TO MAP ADAPTED FROM BRENSCHUTZ'S "EXPLANATION"
1—Guardhouse
2—Surgeon's Quarters
3—Lieutenant, Company I
4—Lieutenant, Company K
5—Lieutenant, Company K
6—Captain Scott's Quarters
7—Hospital
8—Chaplain's Quarters
9—Captain, Company K
10—Soldiers' Quarters, Company K
11—Soldiers' Quarters, Company I
12—Blacksmith Shop
13—Carpenters, School, Laundry (?),
Commandant's Office, Quartermaster Stores
14—Powder Magazine
a b c—Blockhouses
1–4—Sentry Posts
a—Provisions Storehouse
b—Stable
XII—Well
XIII—Woodyard
XIIII—Post Garden (below fort and unnumbered)

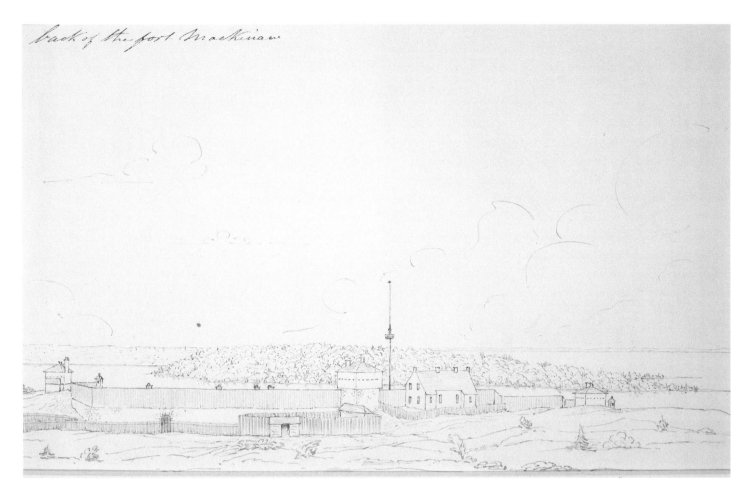

FIGURE 7.22
TITLE: back of the fort Mackinaw.
AUTHOR: [Francis Melick Cayley (1809–90)].
DATE DEPICTED: ca. 1840–43.
DATE OF WORK: ca. 1840–43.
DESCRIPTION: 14.4 x 23.5 cm. Pen and ink on paper.
PROVENANCE: Originally part of a sketchbook, with the individual leaf later separated and pasted to another sheet of paper. In pencil on the back of one sheet is written: "Francis Melick Cayley / Toronto / 1809–1874 / 3rd Son of John Harriet Cayley / of St. Petersburg." Retained in the artist's family. Purchased from a dealer in 1993.
COLLECTION: Masco Collection, Taylor, MI.

FIGURE 7.23
TITLE: [In pencil at upper left in another hand:] Michillimackinack.
AUTHOR: Paul Kane (1810–71).
DATE DEPICTED: July 1845.
DATE OF WORK: [July 1845].
DESCRIPTION: 18 x 25 cm. Pencil on card.
PROVENANCE: Gift of Raymond A. Willis, in 1946. The Royal Ontario Museum catalog describes this work as "[Fort and Indian Village, Michilimackinac, Mich.]."
COLLECTION: With the permission of the Royal Ontario Museum, Toronto (946.15.255). © Royal Ontario Museum.

even cut a new road from the rear of the garrison to the town. All this had cost the Quartermaster General's Department the paltry sum of $35.48 thanks to Scott's frugal use of soldier labor and the availability of stone, lime, timber, charcoal, and shingles from government land on the islands of Mackinac and Bois Blanc. Only a few more roofs and floors required attention, work that could be completed, it was estimated, for twenty-five dollars or so.[109]

Captain Scott must have been justly proud of the transformation he and his men had wrought at Fort Mackinac. What better way to preserve a record of this achievement than by having a detailed drawing made of the old post looking its best? The fortuitous arrival of a talented amateur artist provided the commandant an opportunity to commemorate the renaissance of his post in the remarkable bird's-eye view illustrated here as Figure 7.21.

The artist had an unlikely background. Twenty-five-year-old William Brenschutz was a native of Berlin, who enlisted in the U.S. Army at Philadelphia on August 1, 1844. Brenschutz told the recruiting officer that he had been a barber in civilian life. The new soldier was assigned to Company I of the 5th Infantry Regiment, Martin Scott's command. Brenschutz joined it at Fort Mackinac on October 25, 1844.[110] The timing was perfect. Scott's renovations had largely been completed, and winter was approaching. The season of cold and isolation would allow plenty of time for the newly minted Private Brenschutz to compose and execute a "General Prospect of Fort Mackinaw."

If William Brenschutz had indeed been a barber then he had somehow learned a great deal about proportion and drawing, for his skills seem more appropriate to a painter, engraver, or lithographer. Captain Scott learned of his talents, and the soldier-artist was soon at work measuring and sketching the fort. It is possible that Brenschutz had access to a garrison copy of Major Gratiot's 1817 survey or Lieutenant Penrose's 1835 plan of the fort's buildings, but it is more likely that he gathered fresh data to compose his drawing. Not only was it necessary to accurately position the architectural features of the fort, but the artist also had to project the view from an imagined point several hundred feet in the air. It is a task that he achieved admirably, and no finer image of Fort Mackinac exists from either before or after the introduction of photography.

The title of Private Brenschutz's "General Prospect" makes it very clear that it was prepared for Captain Scott. Ironically, this piece of personal art is the only known plan to depict Fort Mackinac in detail between the years 1817 and 1863.[111] It is the earliest image to record the buildings constructed in 1828–29 and the only one to document the facade of the 1828 soldiers' barracks ("10–11" by Brenschutz's key) and the row of shops and offices that parallels the road between the two gateways ("13"). Both buildings burned in the 1850s. The other structures are also rendered in exquisite detail, including the old British powder magazine ("14"), complete with its lightning rod. This robust structure was demolished in 1878 to make way for a new commissary storehouse. Fish-shaped weather

Paul Kane (1810–71) was perhaps the most competent artist to visit Mackinac, which he did in 1845 and again briefly the following summer. Kane left a considerable number of sketches and paintings of Mackinac scenery and took a particular interest in the Native Americans he found there. This oil-on-paper self-portrait of 20.6 x 17.0 cm. was executed in 1848. *Stark Museum of Art, Orange, TX (31.78/197, WOP 27).*

vanes are shown on the north blockhouse and officers' stone quarters although, inexplicably, they point opposite the breeze that ripples the garrison flag. Brenschutz depicted all of the improvements made under Captain Scott's direction, from picketing to stairways and the four sentry posts ("1–4"). A visual key at lower left identifies the manner in which different building materials (masonry, pickets, wood, and even grass) are rendered.

The detail is equally fine for features located on government property outside the walls. To the north may be seen the newly fenced drill ground marked by a pair of field guns and limbers with some of the garrison cattle nearby. The woodyard ("XIII") was first enclosed for security in 1836. The well ("XII") was dug in 1830, although it would have been of little service in the event of a siege. Some of these details also appear in Figure 7.22, the fifth of Francis Melick Cayley's fine Mackinac views of circa 1840–43, included here for comparison. Cayley shows the back sides of several buildings depicted in the Brenschutz plan, although there is no sign of the well with its elaborate cover.

Several roads meet at the north sally port of Fort Mackinac on Figure 7.21. The one on the left plunges down the bluff to join modern Fort Street between the gardens (today Marquette Park) and the village. The list of improvements made to the garrison between

October 1843 and September 1844 includes a new road "from the rear of the Fort to the Lake," and Brenschutz appears to have been the first to depict the steep and dangerous track usually called "Fort Hill."[112] Below the bluff are the gardens (Brenschutz neglected to draw the Roman numeral "XIIII" that connects them with his key), provisions storehouse, and stable. A puny government wharf may be seen at the shore, and a single, faintly drawn house to its left is the only evidence of town. Much of the area below the fort may be seen from a different perspective in a contemporary sketch made by Paul Kane from the East Bluff during his visit in July 1845, included here as Figure 7.23.

A careful study of Private Brenschutz's drawing of Fort Mackinac will reveal many other human details, several of which may be personally connected to Captain Scott. The garrison musicians and a detachment of troops are mustered in front of the barracks, and it is very likely that the left-hand officer of the pair facing the men from across the parade ground is Scott himself. The captain's residence was in the western end of the stone quarters ("6"). The decor of its rooms reflected Scott's prowess as a hunter and marksman. "The walls were decorated with every conceivable form of weapons of war and of chase," Joseph Le Conte recalled of his visit in 1844. Trophies hung on every side, "elk horns, buffalo

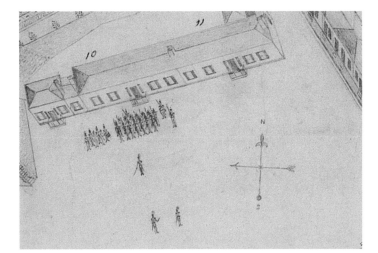

heads, bear-skin rugs, and snarling heads of panthers."[113]

Two details below the fort might also be personal references. Captain Scott was known for his fine horses and pack of hunting dogs, which he kept at his various postings. A large horse pastured in the garrison field could be his "splendid black," Dandy.[114] The enclosure attached to the stable ("b") is clearly a kennel occupied by a dozen dogs. To the left, another five canines rush toward a lone figure. Is this Lavinia McCracken Scott, the captain's wife? She was reportedly a crack shot and seems to have shared her husband's interest in hunting.[115]

Rich in detail, Private Brenschutz's bird's-eye view of Fort Mackinac provides a snapshot of the post as it appeared no later than the early summer of 1845. The artist did not date his work, but his actions provide a time by which he must have completed the "General Prospect" for Captain Scott. Soldiering apparently did not agree with Private Brenschutz—or he got wind that his company would soon be transferred to Texas. On July 22 he deserted and melted into the civilian population once again, leaving behind his drawing and debts to Fort Mackinac's sutler (33.07¢) and laundresses ($.01).[116]

The Scotts left soon after. War clouds were gathering on the Texas-Mexico border, and the 5th Infantry was sent there. On September 6, 1845, Captain Martin Scott gave up the command of Fort Mackinac. He and his men boarded a steamer for the first stage of a journey that would take them to Corpus Christi and, eventually, Mexico City. The officers and soldiers were parted from their wives for the journey. John Harris Forster witnessed "affecting" scenes on the wharf that day. One middle-aged Irish woman bid farewell to her husband and two sons serving as drummer boys.[117] Lavinia Scott was certainly there to bid farewell to her Martin. He never returned, as he was killed in action at Molino del Rey, Mexico, on September 8, 1847.[118]

Captain Scott was remembered at Mackinac for some time, both for his skill as a marksman and for his care of the fort. Two years after his departure a visitor commented that during Scott's command, he had made it "a pattern fort, for neatness" and that his successors still seemed "to vie with each other in adding their mite to it" through the regular application of whitewash.[119] By the 1850s the captain's memory had been perpetuated in the name of a cave that became a popular tourist destination (Fig. 8.12). Lavinia McCracken Scott took good care of Private Brenschutz's drawing, a souvenir of three years spent with her husband at Fort Mackinac. After her death in the sinking of the steamer *Arctic* in 1854, the "General Prospect" passed to her cousin and then through her family until it was presented to the William L. Clements Library in 1941.

DEATH OF COLONEL MARTIN SCOTT, AT THE BATTLE OF MOLINO DEL REA.

Captain Martin Scott (1788–1847) was known as the best marksman in the U.S. Army and as an avid hunter. He commanded Fort Mackinac from 1842–45 and supervised extensive repairs to the post. No portrait of Scott is known, but his heroic death at the Battle of Molino del Rey, Mexico, in 1847, was colorfully portrayed in this woodcut published in the *Rough & Ready Almanac* of 1849. *Courtesy of Thomas G. Shaw.*

When Martin Scott led his men of the 5th Infantry to Texas in September 1845, they were relieved at Fort Mackinac by soldiers of the 2nd Infantry under Captain Silas Casey (1807–82). Like many officers of this period, Casey later served in the Civil War and was depicted in the 1860s by an unidentified artist. *Chicago History Museum (1920.566).*

Evidences of erosive and undermining action are everywhere visible

John Wells Foster

John Wells Foster was perfectly capable of appreciating the romantic beauty of Mackinac Island. Its "precipitous cliffs, occasionally crowned with clumps of foliage," drew the attention of all the passengers as his steamer approached from Lake Huron. The island's dramatic topography came as a welcome relief to Foster after the flat and heavily forested eastern shore of the Lower Peninsula that he had found so "low and void of scenic interest." Once in the harbor, he could take in the colorful old town on its "gently curving bay" dominated by limestone bluffs. Foster, however, had come to look at Mackinac Island from a much different perspective than his fellow travelers. He was a geologist who perceived "a narrow, alluvial plain" with "detrital deposits" and "terraces" where the others noted only a slope rising gently to the foot of the bluffs and a beach sprinkled with wigwams. "This island . . . is as interesting in a geological, as in a picturesque point of view," he concluded.[120]

The geology of the Straits of Mackinac had been examined on earlier occasions, though usually from an immediately practical point of view. Patrick Sinclair was interested in Mackinac Island's limestone as a source of building material and its steeply rising land for defensive positions. Army engineers had mapped the different levels of the island for military purposes. Tourists appreciated the vistas created by its bluffs and the fantastic rock formations with their romantic associations. Only a few earlier visitors, such as Henry Schoolcraft and David Bates Douglass in 1820 and Douglass Houghton and Bela Hubbard in 1838–40, had taken the time to carefully examine and describe what they could determine of the geology of the island and surrounding area. They searched for fossils on Mackinac Island and described the composition and layering of the local limestone and soils, noting a number of geological features that were "peculiar to it."[121]

These earlier investigations were necessarily cursory and restricted by the limited time available to explore the island and other prominent features at nearby Point St. Ignace and Gros Cap. A more systematic study of the geology of the Straits had to await the arrival of John Wells Foster and his associate, Josiah Dwight Whitney, in June 1849. Even then, Mackinac was a diversion for the two geologists, whose primary purpose was to complete a survey of mineral lands in Michigan's Upper Peninsula. Foster and Whitney had been working on this project since 1847.[122] Their official report was published in two parts in 1850 and 1851, and Figures 7.24–7.32 illustrated their discussion of the geology of the Straits area and of Mackinac Island in particular.

By 1849 Foster and Whitney could describe the geology of the Straits region using comparisons with similar deposits of limestone that had been recorded in Canada West (Ontario) and New York State. They discovered evidence of what was known as the "Onondaga salt group," a New York formation of which the Straits of Mackinac seemed to mark the western limit. There were also plentiful examples of the "Mackinac limestone" previously described and named by Douglass Houghton.[123] Like the geologists who had preceded them, Foster and Whitney found that Mackinac Island and the St. Ignace peninsula abounded in examples of brecciated or broken and re-cemented limestone, a phenomenon most obviously manifested in the famous rock formations. The harder breccia was devoid of any evidence of fossils, which were common in the softer, intact limestone strata. Most striking, however, were indications that the local topography had been greatly influenced by the movement of water. "Evidences of erosive and undermining action are everywhere visible along the cliffs of the island," their analysis concluded.[124]

Foster and Whitney's report was accompanied by a number of small illustrations and three attractive plates showing Arch Rock, Sugar Loaf, and Gros Cap. Figure 7.24, titled simply "Mackinac," was intended to set the scene by depicting the island from the east, emphasizing its elevation, and identifying its primary landmarks, from the "signal" mast at the site of Fort Holmes to the fort and village below. The simplicity of this view made it a popular and much-copied illustration that would reappear in several publications over the next two decades.[125]

The "white and weather-beaten" limestone cliffs suggested in Foster's view of the island introduced one of the primary discoveries made by the two geologists in 1849. An alert observer, they suggested, would soon realize that what appeared to be bluffs of solid rock were, in part, terraces of limestone gravel and pebbles. This feature was so different from other deposits found along the lower elevations of the shores of the upper lakes that curiosity was sure to be aroused. These loose materials were heaped against the solid cliff and appeared at several different elevations on the island. "It is evident to the observer that deposits so essentially different cannot belong to the same [geological] period," they suggested. Moving westward along the harbor and shore of the island, Foster and Whitney began to distinguish series of gravel terraces, which they illustrated in a rough topographical sketch and a pair of sections (Figs. 7.25–7.27).[126]

The terraces, clustered close together where the land rose most abruptly near Lover's Leap (section "a-b") and farther apart where the slope was more gradual to the west of Fort Mackinac (section "c-d"), appeared like "a giant stair-case." The geologists had no difficulty tracing the different levels, and the gravel deposits that

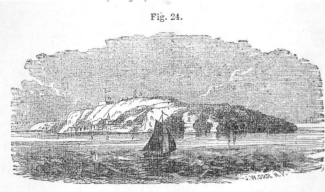

Fig. 24.

Mackinac.

1. Lover's Leap.　2. Harbor.　3. Village.　4. Fort.　5. Signal.
6. Sugar Loaf.　7. Mission.　8. Robinson's Folly.

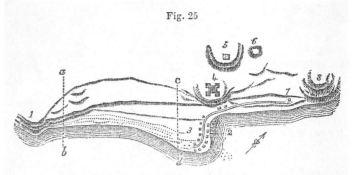

Fig. 25

Topographical Sketch of Mackinac.

1. Lover's Leap,　2. Harbor,　3. Village,　4. Fort,　5. Signal,
6. Sugar Loaf,　7. Mission,　8. Robinson's Folly.

FIGURE 7.24

TITLE: Mackinac.
AUTHOR: [John Wells Foster (1815–73)]. Engraved by John William Orr (1815–87).
DATE DEPICTED: 1849.
DATE OF WORK: 1851.
DESCRIPTION: 6.5 x 9.6 cm. Engraving.
PROVENANCE: Published as Figure 24 in Foster and Whitney, *Report on the Geology and Topography of a Portion of the Lake Superior Land District* (Washington, DC, 1850–51), 2:249.
COLLECTION: University of Michigan Libraries, Ann Arbor.

FIGURE 7.25

TITLE: Topographical Sketch of Mackinac.
AUTHOR: [John Wells Foster (1815–73)].
DATE DEPICTED: 1849.
DATE OF WORK: 1851.
DESCRIPTION: 6 x 9.2 cm. Engraving.
PROVENANCE: Published as Figure 25 in Foster and Whitney, *Report on the Geology and Topography of a Portion of the Lake Superior Land District* (Washington, DC, 1850–51), 2:249.
COLLECTION: University of Michigan Libraries, Ann Arbor.

Fig. 26.　　　　Fig. 27.

Fig. 26. Section along the line *a b*, in Fig. 25.
Fig. 27. Section along the line *c d*, in Fig. 25.

The first section was taken immediately east of the Lover's Leap, where the terraces are in close proximity. Starting from the beach, which, at the time of the measurement (June 22, 1849,) was five feet above the lake-level, we found the following order of succession:

No.			Width.	Height.
1. A terrace			10 feet.	9.5
2. "	"		10 "	22.
3. "	"	more distinct	50 "	42.
4. "	"	with a slope of 50°	55 "	105.
5. Summit of a limestone ridge				147.

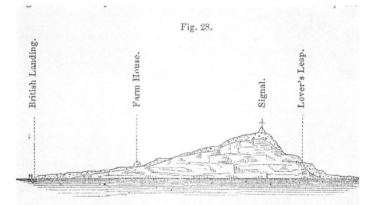

Fig. 28.

British Landing.　Farm House.　Signal.　Lover's Leap.

Section of the Island of Mackinac.

FIGURES 7.26 AND 7.27

TITLE: Section along the line a b, in Fig. 25; Section along the line c d, in Fig. 25.
AUTHOR: [John Wells Foster (1815–73)].
DATE DEPICTED: 1849.
DATE OF WORK: 1851.
DESCRIPTION: 2.8 x 10.3 cm. Engraving.
PROVENANCE: Published as Figures 26 and 27, respectively, in Foster and Whitney, *Report on the Geology and Topography of a Portion of the Lake Superior Land District* (Washington, DC: 1850–51), 2:250.
COLLECTION: University of Michigan Libraries, Ann Arbor.

FIGURE 7.28

TITLE: Section of the Island of Mackinac.
AUTHOR: [John Wells Foster (1815–73)].
DATE DEPICTED: 1849.
DATE OF WORK: 1851.
DESCRIPTION: 6 x 11.2 cm. Engraving.
PROVENANCE: Published as Figure 28 in Foster and Whitney, *Report on the Geology and Topography of a Portion of the Lake Superior Land District* (Washington, DC, 1850–51), 2:251.
COLLECTION: University of Michigan Libraries, Ann Arbor.

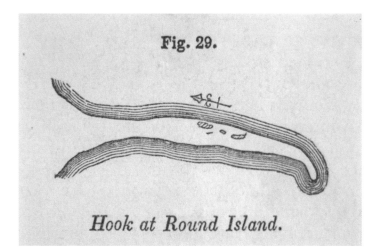

Fig. 29.

Hook at Round Island.

FIGURE 7.29
TITLE: Hook at Round Island.
AUTHOR: [John Wells Foster (1815–73)].
DATE DEPICTED: 1849.
DATE OF WORK: 1851.
DESCRIPTION: 3.5 x 5 cm. Engraving.
PROVENANCE: Published as Figure 29 in Foster and Whitney, *Report on the Geology and Topography of a Portion of the Lake Superior Land District* (Washington, DC, 1850–51), 2:259.
COLLECTION: University of Michigan Libraries, Ann Arbor.

overlaid the native limestone had all the signs of having been formed by a current or wave action. Indeed, some of them had double slopes and looked for all the world like beaches.[127]

As the team proceeded around the southwestern and northeastern shores of the island, they found no indication of terraces along the steep bluffs on those sides. But, where the topography moderated toward the northwestern point, they encountered a series of ancient beaches that had many of the characteristics of the terraces on the island's southeastern end, although they were much wider. As the geologists followed the road from British Landing toward Fort Mackinac, they climbed successive beaches until, near the Dousman farmhouse, they reached a "remarkable ridge" that, they believed, corresponded with the highest terrace on the island's southeastern end. This was the elevation that had served as the British defensive position during the 1814 Battle of Mackinac Island. Figure 7.28 provides a rough comparison of land levels at both ends of the island and contrasts the terraces near town with the gentler beaches on the northwestern end. Dousman's "Farm House" may be seen at the foot of the ridge known to later geologists as "Battlefield Beach."[128]

Although they did not entirely understand the process, Foster and Whitney had hit upon evidence of the fluctuations in prehistoric lake levels that had helped sculpt the distinctive shape of Mackinac Island and the higher topography of other parts of the Straits. They also identified water-formed terraces on Round Island and on the Upper Peninsula mainland at the foot of Rabbit's Back, Point St. Ignace, and Gros Cap. The geologists suggested that uplifting of the land had accounted for the relative changes in the height of the lake waters and that there had been time "for the formation of beaches at each change of level." The terraces occurred at too great a height, they believed, to have been caused by "mere fluctuations of the lake level."[129]

Later scientists would determine that the geological history of the Straits region was far more complex and involved both postglacial uplifting of the land and dramatic changes in lake levels over a span of ten thousand years. The geological formations examined by Foster and Whitney had been created by the action of two major glacial lakes with many intervening stages. Lake Algonquin had covered all but the highest point of Mackinac Island, and the much later Lake Nipissing had washed its shores about fifty feet above the modern lake level. As Foster and Whitney suggested, there had been plenty of time between these stages for the formation of beaches at different levels.[130]

During their visit to Mackinac, the two geologists also recorded evidence of more recent shaping of the land by water action. Among their interests was the formation of "Hooks, or Spits" that occurred where loose materials, such as sand and gravel, extended into the lakes beyond the native rock to form barren peninsulas. They found examples at several locations on Lake Superior, but one of the best was visible from Mackinac Island. Figure 7.29 illustrates the hook found at the extremity of Round Island.[131] Standing directly opposite Haldimand Bay, Round Island's barren tip had provided a favorite vantage for artists since Patrick Sinclair's day (see Fig. 2.7). It is today best known for the historic lighthouse that has occupied the spot since 1895.

No survey of the geology of Mackinac Island would have been complete without the inclusion of its most famous natural formations, Arch Rock and Sugar Loaf. Foster and Whitney's report included well-composed lithographs of both, which are reproduced here as Figures 7.30 and 7.31. Arch Rock is dramatically pictured from below, towering over the beach and the giant boulder, "Michabou's Rock," that still rests at the edge of the shore. The geologists recognized the similarity between the arch and formations along the Lake Superior shoreline at the Pictured Rocks. It was evident that the "denuding action" of water that had carved the natural bridge could only have occurred when the original limestone cliff had been near the level of a large body of water. Arch Rock was, in fact, sculpted by the action of glacial Lake Nipissing. Recognizing the popular appeal of this formation, the authors acknowledged that it was worth a visit, though they were certain that continued action of weather would soon destroy the famous landmark.[132]

FIGURE 7.30
TITLE: Arched Rock—Mackinac.
AUTHOR: [John Wells Foster (1815–73)].
DATE DEPICTED: 1849.
DATE OF WORK: 1851.
DESCRIPTION: 19.9 x 11.6 cm. Tinted lithograph.
PROVENANCE: Published in Foster and Whitney, *Report on the Geology and Topography of a Portion of the Lake Superior Land District* (Washington, DC, 1850–51), 2:plate XVIII.
COLLECTION: University of Michigan Libraries, Ann Arbor.

FIGURE 7.31
TITLE: Sugar-Loaf, Mackinac.
AUTHOR: [John Wells Foster (1815–73)].
Lithograph by Ackerman Lithography, New York.
DATE DEPICTED: 1849.
DATE OF WORK: 1851.
DESCRIPTION: 19.9 x 11.5 cm. Tinted lithograph.
PROVENANCE: Published in Foster and Whitney, *Report on the Geology and Topography of a Portion of the Lake Superior Land District* (Washington, DC, 1850–51), 2:plate XIX.
COLLECTION: University of Michigan Libraries, Ann Arbor.

FIGURE 7.32

TITLE: Gros Cap of Lake Michigan.
AUTHOR: [John Wells Foster (1815–73)]. Lithograph by
Ackerman Lithography, New York.
DATE DEPICTED: 1849.
DATE OF WORK: 1851.
DESCRIPTION: 11.5 x 20.1 cm. Tinted lithograph.
PROVENANCE: Published in Foster and Whitney, *Report on
the Geology and Topography of a Portion of the Lake Superior
Land District* (Washington, DC, 1850–51), 2:plate XVII.
COLLECTION: University of Michigan Libraries, Ann Arbor.

Sugar Loaf was correctly identified as having once formed a part of the mass of the great hill that makes up the highest level of the island. The geologists dismissed the possibility that the huge rock, towering above the surrounding forest, could have been moved to its location by the action of water.[133] Sugar Loaf had, in fact, been separated from the larger body of limestone by Lake Algonquin as the softer connecting material was worn away, leaving the tall breccia spire to stand on its own. As in earlier views of Sugar Loaf, Foster's scene provides a measure of Mackinac Island's growing forest.

At Gros Cap west of St. Ignace the geologists observed yet another "isolated tower" of brecciated limestone and preserved its appearance in Figure 7.32. They recognized the "tower-like mass near the extremity of the point" as an outlier of the main body of rock visible on the right side of the sketch. Douglass Houghton had examined this feature in 1839 and described it as a "naked point of *Mackinaw* limestone standing 150 feet high" similar to the formations seen on the island. A Frenchman had begun clearing land for a farm by the time of Houghton's visit to Gros Cap, and the buildings in Foster's view represent his establishment ten years later. Foster and Whitney believed that, like Arch Rock, the great tower would not long survive. It was, they predicted, "ultimately destined to be undermined and destroyed" by the action of Lake Michigan.[134] Like Arch Rock and Sugar Loaf, however, it proved to be more durable than expected.

Louis Agassiz, James Cabot (1821–1903), and their companions left Mackinac Island for Sault Ste. Marie on June 24, 1848, in a Mackinaw boat, which Cabot described as a "cross between a dory and a mud-scow." Even at this late date, many travelers found themselves using an open boat when a steamer was not available. This title-page illustration, from Agassiz and Cabot's book, *Lake Superior* (Boston, 1850), shows the party traveling either by canoe or in early Mackinaw boats. *Clements Library, University of Michigan.*

Charles Lanman (1819–95) was an author and artist who visited the Straits of Mackinac in August 1846. Although he toured Mackinac Island with his sketchbook at hand, none of his drawings are known to survive. Lanman is shown here, in traveling clothes, in the frontis-piece portrait of his *Adventures of an Angler in Canada* (London, 1848).

Clements Library, University of Michigan.

Naturalist Louis Agassiz (1807–73) stopped at Mackinac Island in 1848 on his way to Lake Superior. The professor turned a fishing expedition into a lesson for the members of his party who were new to ichthyology. He dissected their catch and then commenced "a discussion of the classification" of each fish. Agassiz is shown a few years later in this steel engraving. *Clements Library, University of Michigan.*

The manifest fate of Mackinac . . . is to be a watering-place

William Cullen Bryant

Even as geologists Foster and Whitney were clambering over the bluffs and prehistoric beaches of Mackinac Island, others were examining those rugged and picturesque heights with an entirely different purpose in mind. William B. Ogden was thinking of ways by which he might escape the oppressive summer heat of Chicago and retreat for a time to a place of comfort and tranquility. He knew Mackinac Island from previous excursions, and he had walked the road from the Mission House to Fort Mackinac. This took him up what would become known as Mission Hill and then along the bare crest of the East Bluff to the fence marking the edge of the drill field behind the military post.[135]

Along the way, Ogden enjoyed a fine view of the Straits and Haldimand Bay with the Village of Mackinac laid out at his feet and the fort looming farther along the bluff. This vista had attracted artists such as David Bates Douglass, Francis Cayley, and Paul Kane (see Figs. 5.5, 7.10, and 7.23), and Kane had sketched the road itself as it rose toward Fort Mackinac. Near the highest point of the bluff the track turned away from the crest to avoid a rocky elevation, thus creating a triangular piece of secluded, forested ground. By August

1849 Ogden had paced out its boundaries and given considerable thought to how he might construct a "summer Lodge" there that would enable him to spend the "hotter portions" of the season at Mackinac.[136]

Predictions that the cool and healthy climate would make Mackinac Island a summer resort had increased steadily since the 1830s, and by the middle of the following decade writers such as William Cullen Bryant, Daniel Drake, and others considered this an inevitable development. Indeed, their writings actively promoted the idea.[137] Horace Greeley suggested that the optimum time to reside at Mackinac was from mid-June to mid-September, when the region's "nine months' winters are divided from each other by three months' cold weather."[138] A few people from more southerly locales had apparently purchased properties in the town by 1849, but most early resorters were dependent on the island's rooming houses and hotels. By the summer of 1848, however, the village could boast only two major establishments, the Mission House and Lasley House, and these were frequently fi:lled to overflowing.[139] Charles O'Malley recognized the need for more accommodations and, in July 1849, completed and opened a "large and commodious Hotel." At first touted as the "O'Malley House," it was called the "Huron House" in the early 1850s before finally becoming known as the "Island House." It operates under that name today as Mackinac Island's oldest hostelry.[140]

Even with such improvements, the crowded hotels lacked the privacy, convenience, and comfort desired by more affluent families. In the days before advance reservations, arriving visitors often found all the rooms taken. The solution was obvious, and it had been suggested long before 1849. Following his visit in 1840, the English author James S. Buckingham pointed out that Mackinac Island was sufficiently large to accommodate "many villas and summer residences."[141] What more charming spot than the summit of the prominent eastern bluff, a place that, in 1842, Daniel Drake suggested would make one of the most attractive places in the United States for a "summer boarding house."[142]

The East Bluff, extending from Fort Mackinac to Robinson's Folly, stands out in most views of the island. Figure 7.33 is typical. This romantically framed scene was engraved from a drawing made about 1846 by another Chicago visitor, Francis Howe. A boating excursion to Round Island apparently provided the opportunity to picture Mackinac Island from the opposite side of the channel.

William Butler Ogden was one Chicagoan who had experienced the "meagre" public accommodations of Mackinac Island and was determined to have a place suitable for an extended stay with his

Horace Greeley (1811–72) was another influential American writer who described his brief visits to the Straits in 1847. Greeley declared that "a stroll at Mackinac is worth a day in any man's life," and allowed that the place would be "an inviting summer residence for invalids." This oil portrait of Greeley is by an unknown artist. *Clements Library, University of Michigan.*

New York editor Lewis Gaylord Clark (1808–73) accompanied Horace Greeley on his 1847 Great Lakes trip. They stayed at the Mission House, which Greeley declared "the best hotel on the island." While relaxing on its piazza, the pair became convinced that they had sighted a lake serpent. Closer inspection proved it to be an undulating wave backlit by the setting sun. Clark is shown in an engraving from *The Knicker-bocker Gallery* (New York, 1855). *Clements Library, University of Michigan.*

The Isle, Mackinaw.

FIGURE 7.33

TITLE: The Isle, Mackinaw. Engraved from a drawing by the late Francis Howe, of Chicago, taken about the year 1846.
AUTHOR: Francis Howe (1811–50).
DATE DEPICTED: ca. 1846.
DATE OF WORK: 1861 and 1867.
DESCRIPTION: 7 x 10.1 cm. Engraving.
PROVENANCE: Published in Barber and Howe, *Our Whole Country....* (Cincinnati, 1861), and again in Barber and Hall, *All the Western States and Territories....* (Cincinnati, 1867), 284. The example illustrated is from 1867 publication.
COLLECTION: Clements Library, University of Michigan, Ann Arbor (Book Division, C2-1867-Ba).

William Cullen Bryant (1794–1878) seems to have thoroughly enjoyed his time at the Straits in 1846. He wrote glowingly of the experience, concluding, "the world has not many islands so beautiful as Mackinac." Bryant is depicted here in an engraving published in *The Knickerbocker Gallery* of 1855. *Clements Library, University of Michigan.*

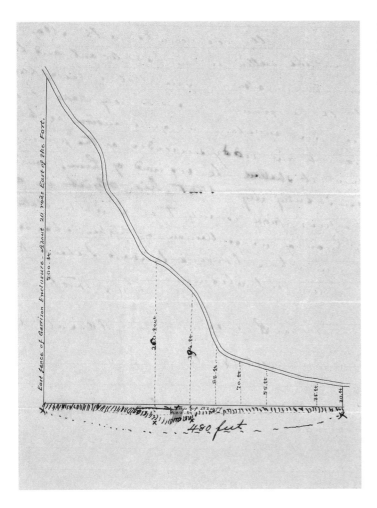

FIGURE 7.34

TITLE: [Diagram of the premises which
William B. Ogden desires permission to occupy].

AUTHOR: William Butler Ogden (1805–77).

DATE DEPICTED: August 8, 1849.

DATE OF WORK: August 8, 1849.

DESCRIPTION: 25 x 20 cm. Pen and ink on paper.

PROVENANCE: Enclosed with letter of August 8, 1849,
from Ogden to Major Charles H. Larnard. Forwarded
by Larnard with his letter of August 23 to Major General
Thomas S. Jesup. Retained in the records of the Office
of the Quartermaster General.

COLLECTION: National Archives and Records
Administration, Washington, DC (RG 92, Records of
the Office of the Quartermaster General, Consolidated
Correspondence File, Fort Mackinac, Michigan).
Found in Box 594.

family. Ogden possessed the means to do so, both financially and politically. A successful land developer and businessman, he was elected Chicago's first mayor in 1837 and later served as a city councilman. Ogden soon became involved in the construction of railways, and by 1849 he was president of the nearly completed Galena and Chicago Union Railroad. In later years he would serve as the first president of the Union Pacific and participate in a wide variety of Chicago civic organizations.[143] In order to achieve his goal at Mackinac, however, he would have to wrestle with the fact that the spot he had selected for his "summer Lodge" was part of the military reserve.

On August 8, 1849, amid the steamy heat of Chicago, William Ogden carefully framed his request in a letter to Major Charles H. Larnard, commandant of Fort Mackinac. Ogden began by expressing his concern over the poor quality of public accommodations on the island and his desire to find a place for a summer home. The difficulty, he pointed out, was that the largest part of the island was government land and "the most desirable situations for building" along the "front and East side" were included in the military reservation. He had selected a site, he pointed out, based on its convenience to "the Hotel under the bluff" and the fact that the land appeared to have no particular utility to the operations of the military post. To illustrate his description of the parcel, Ogden included his own carefully drawn sketch of a triangular plot with its base extending along the bluff for 480 feet east of the fence that enclosed the army's drill field. The road to the Mission House delineated the third side of the property. Ogden's little map is illustrated here as Figure 7.34.

This ground had never been occupied or improved by the army, Ogden argued, and it had nothing of value to be removed or destroyed. The land was, in fact, "in a very rough state" and his efforts could only improve it. Should he be allowed to build there, he assured Major Larnard, he would be willing to remove himself and return use of the land to the army whenever it might be required for military purposes. Not only did Ogden suggest building his house there, but he also hoped to construct a stairway down the bluff to the hotel below, the newly opened O'Malley House.[144] This would have allowed his family to take their meals there.

William Ogden had made his preparations with care. He had probably been on Mackinac Island earlier in the summer to walk out and draw the parcel described in his letter. Ogden had also solicited a personal recommendation from William L. Marcy, who had served as U.S. secretary of war from 1845 until March 1849. Marcy assured Quartermaster General Thomas S. Jesup that he knew of no gentleman of higher character. Marcy's undated comments were written on the back of Ogden's letter and appear to have been added after it reached Washington.[145] It also seems likely that Ogden had spent some time with Major Larnard in order to couch his request in terms that emphasized the uselessness of the land to the garrison.

The letter then began its trek through army channels. On August 23 Major Larnard forwarded Ogden's request to Major

General Jesup. Larnard verified the accuracy of the sketch map and confirmed that the government had never used the land in question. Nor was it likely to be needed in the future. Larnard was also able to express "personal knowledge" of the "high character and standing" of Mr. Ogden. He was certain that, should the property ever be needed, it would be surrendered as promised.[146]

Quartermaster General Jesup took some time to consider the application. Army buildings and lands were his responsibility. He had dealt with property concerns on Mackinac Island on a number of occasions, primarily as they related to encroachments on the reserve or the permitted use of government property for the Reverend Ferry's mission school. It was not until January 2, 1850, that he sent his recommendation to the secretary of war. Jesup had no objections based on military necessity. Should Ogden's request be granted, he believed that the prompt surrender of the land, if needed, was critical and that measures "to preserve the cedar and other trees on the ground" were essential. But then came the caveat. If permission were granted, Jesup wrote, "numerous requests will no doubt be made by others which it would be difficult to refuse without subjecting the War Department to the charge of favoritism."[147] This was an argument that carried weight with George Washington Crawford, who had succeeded William Marcy as secretary of war. Three days after receiving the quartermaster general's comments, he decided to "disallow said application."[148]

William Ogden would not build his cottage on the East Bluff. He was ahead of his time by thirty-five years. The leasing of public lands for the construction of summer homes would not occur until after the military reserve had been designated a national park and the officers of the Fort Mackinac garrison found themselves doing extra duty as park administrators. The East Bluff would not see its first cottages until 1885, eight years after the death of William Butler Ogden.[149]

William Butler Ogden (1805–77) was one of the first to request the use of land for construction of a summerhouse on one of Mackinac Island's dramatic bluffs. Despite considerable influence and sterling references, army officials rejected his 1849 application for fear it would result in requests from others. This oil portrait of Ogden, by George Alexander Healy, was painted in 1855–56.

Chicago History Museum (1901.1.DUP4).

GEO. G. MEADE.
MAJ. GENL U.S.A.
COMMANDER OF THE POTOMAC ARMY.

Permanent marking of the boundaries of public lands on Mackinac Island was accomplished in 1857 under the direction of Captain George Gordon Meade (1815–72). Six years later, the former topographical engineer would command a huge federal army at the Battle of Gettysburg. Ehrgott, Forbriger and Company of Cincinnati produced this equestrian lithograph of the general during the Civil War. *Clements Library, University of Michigan.*

"Mackinaw is now in a transition state"

1850–1860

"Mackinac is certainly one of the most delightful spots in the whole North," Delancey Floyd-Jones wrote his father and sister from Sault Ste. Marie in July 1849. The young New Yorker had only just arrived there after spending a few days on Mackinac Island and was belatedly fulfilling a promise to describe what he had seen. He had been most favorably impressed and could think of no other place that combined so many "health improving qualities." It was these that had kept him from

writing—"circumstances unforseen" as he put it—activities such as hunting and fishing excursions, walks, and "rides innumerable." At least, the young man assured his relatives, he could not be accused of having passed his time in bed.[1]

Although Floyd-Jones was a lieutenant in the U.S. Army, his letters have nothing to say of Fort Mackinac, even though it was then occupied by a detachment of his own regiment.[2] His time had been spent as an enthusiastic visitor. Like so many other Great Lakes tourists of his era, the lieutenant found himself traveling and socializing with a group of people who shared his itinerary on the steamboats plying the western waters. While Floyd-Jones might well have been going to Sault Ste. Marie on army business, many of his acquaintances were embarked on pleasure voyages. Among his circle were a Colonel Wells and his daughter, who, upon their arrival at Mackinac Island, had taken rooms at the Mission House. Floyd-Jones and "his party" lodged elsewhere, probably at the new O'Malley House, where he described "opulent quarters" and expressed a desire to spend the rest of the summer. Colonel and Miss Wells were equally pleased with their accommodations, and even more so with the island. "With Mackinac they may [be] said to be properly crazy," the lieutenant reported.[3]

Delancey Floyd-Jones could give several reasons for his friends becoming "Mackinac crazy," as he put it in another of his letters. Most prominent among them was the relief provided by the island's northern climate during the worst of the Midwest summer's heat. Thermometers at Mackinac did not need to be graduated above eighty-five degrees, he boasted, a welcome change from the "steaming and fuming" of July in his post at Detroit or on his native Long Island.

And the air was fresh, occasioned by the cooling effect of the winds that constantly circulated over Lakes Michigan and Huron.[4] Mackinac Island had a well-established reputation for natural beauty and quaint sights by the 1850s, but the benefit that seems to have outweighed everything else for visitors was its salubrious climate.

As predicted since the 1830s, this feature had made the island something of a haven for invalids. Dr. Daniel Drake, who had begun to promote Mackinac as a health resort in 1842, described it in an 1850 publication as a "delightful hot-weather asylum to all invalids" who would benefit from escaping "crowded cities, paludal exhalations, sultry climates, and officious medication."[5] The prominent American educator Horace Mann spent part of the summers of 1856 and 1857 there, "in search of the fugitive, health." He at least found relief from the summer's heat in the island's "paradisiacal weather" that, he declared, was "just warm enough not to be cold, and just cold enough not to be warm."[6] Aaron Bellangee took his wife, Margaret, to Mackinac in July 1854 in an attempt to improve her rapidly declining health, a hope that proved to be in vain when she died and was buried on the island two weeks later. Bellangee noted that many of their fellow resorters had come in search of fresh air and other "restoratives" to health.[7] The island was particularly popular with people from the southern states.[8]

Mackinac's continued growth as a health and pleasure resort seemed assured, and the decade of the 1850s saw further promotion of this role. The appearance of illustrated newspapers provided a national vehicle to describe and exhibit the benefits and wonders of the Straits. Well-illustrated articles appeared in *Harper's New Monthly Magazine* in 1853, *Ballou's Pictorial Drawing-Room Companion* in

1855, and *Frank Leslie's Illustrated Newspaper* the following year. Gazetteers and guides to the Great Lakes, such as those produced by John Disturnell (1857), described and pictured the Straits area and its attractions, and a continuing stream of travel books and articles included accounts of visits to the island. Soon after the end of the decade, Mackinac was even making its first tentative appearances in American literature. Edward Everett Hale's classic short story, "The Man Without a Country" (1863), begins with the narrator impatiently awaiting a steamboat at the Mission House.[9] The first of Constance Fenimore Woolson's Mackinac stories, based in part on her summers spent on the island in the 1850s and 1860s, was published in the July 1870 issue of *Putnam's Monthly Magazine*.[10]

The growth of a summer resort community further stimulated the improvement of amenities for its care. During the 1850s new hotels joined the old Lasley House, the Mission House, and the commodious O'Malley House of 1849. The Lake Superior House was in operation before 1854, and the Lake View opened its doors in 1858. As if to emphasize that the fur trade was truly a thing of the past, the American Fur Company's old headquarters (the Stuart House) was converted to a hotel. Known as the "Grove House" or sometimes the "Dousman House," it was welcoming guests by 1852 or 1853.[11] By about 1854–56 the former South West Company/American Fur Company warehouse on Main Street was operating as the Northern Hotel, its name emblazoned on a false front facing the harbor (see Fig. 8.30). Other, smaller establishments and stores sprang up as well, though most have gone unrecorded. By 1859 Mackinac Island had a newspaper, the *Mackinac Herald,* that combined news with longer, souvenir articles on Mackinac lore for tourists.[12] There was even some renewed pressure on the army to release land in the military reserve to construct private residences.[13] By 1854 no one would doubt, as Aaron Bellangee observed, that the people of Mackinac Island made their living from "taking Boarders" and from fishing.[14]

It was the latter activity that occupied Joseph Austrian in 1851. He worked that summer for his relatives, who ran a dry goods store and were also involved in the fish business. Like many other Mackinac merchants, they supplied nets and equipment to fishermen and then took their catch for shipment elsewhere. Austrian was put to work in a warehouse crammed with hundreds of barrels of fish. His job was to repack their contents in preparation for loading the containers aboard outbound steamers. "I did not find the occupation enticing or agreeable," he later wrote, complaining that the salt brine ruined his clothing.[15] The fish, most caught at a distance from Mackinac, were salted, weighed, and repacked in barrels or half barrels made of white pine by the island's many coopers. These were "duly marked with the weight and the name of the packer." Robert Clarke, who visited in July 1852, noted that commercial fishing was Mackinac Island's principal industry and constituted a trade of "great, and it is believed increasing, magnitude."[16]

The importance of Mackinac Island to the northern fisheries reached its zenith during the 1850s. Fishing schooners vied for space in the harbor with arriving and departing passenger and cargo steamers. Four new wharves were approved during the decade, including a large one near the foot of Fort Street run by William Wendell that was in use as early as 1852.[17] Older piers were improved or extended. However, although fishing would remain an important part of the local economy well into the 1870s, it was already becoming apparent that the prosperity it provided could not last forever.[18] Evidence of over fishing had begun to appear as early as 1852.[19] Even more noticeable was competition from other ports. In 1854, James J. Strang, the Mormon "king" of Beaver Island, asserted that the fish trade at Mackinac "must soon cease." Much of it, he claimed, had already been diverted to places such as Washington Harbor in Wisconsin, Duncan (Cheboygan), Detour, St. Helena Island, and his own capital of Saint James on Beaver Island.[20]

"King" Strang was hardly an objective forecaster of the future of Mackinac Island, although he accurately pointed out that its importance as a port was declining as new northern towns developed. His further prediction that efforts to turn the island into a "fashionable resort" would fail proved farther from the mark.[21]

"Heretofore it has been the Indian's congregating place, but its aboriginal glory is rapidly departing, and it will soon be a fashionable resort of summer travellers." CHARLES LANMAN

Strang and his Mormon followers had begun to settle on Beaver Island in 1849, where they established farms and fished in northern Lake Michigan. Economic and political competition between the two island communities, coupled with an aversion to Mormonism and Strang's personal behavior by the established French and Irish populations of the Straits, soon set the stage for conflict. This was played out on the fishing grounds and in the courts. Matters reached a climax soon after disaffected members of Strang's own community mortally wounded him on June 16, 1856. The Beaver Island Mormons were left leaderless, and the issue was resolved with further violence.[22]

The 1856 "war" between Mackinac and Beaver Island quickly entered the realm of local folklore, and details of the climactic event are fuzzy. By 1870 Constance Fenimore Woolson could write romantically about a "brilliant naval battle" and compare the ragtag squadron of boats that embarked from Mackinac Island to "the primitive flotillas of Homer's day." This "conquering fleet returned in triumph to Mackinac," she concluded, having scattered the Mormons to other parts.[23] The actual details were much more sordid, although the results were essentially as Woolson described. Early in July 1856, a few days before Strang died in Wisconsin, the Michilimackinac County sheriff led a mob to Saint James, where they destroyed and looted property and drove most of the Mormons from the island.[24] Brayton Saltonstall later remembered Mackinac Island's "company of volunteers" returning victorious with "a drove of horses" from which his father selected a pony for the boy and his siblings.[25]

Mackinac had fought its last war, and it is well that this conflict had not required the defenses of the aging and increasingly decrepit fort that overlooked the town. Despite the wholesale repairs undertaken in the mid-1840s and the coats of whitewash that allowed it to project a military appearance, Fort Mackinac had long since reached the end of its usefulness as a fortification. The War of 1812 had proved that it was hopelessly commanded from the site of old Fort Holmes, and the 1850s brought new threats in the event of another conflict with Britain. Steam power made for more versatile warships that could bombard land positions much more effectively. Even Constance Woolson understood that "one gunboat could easily level Fort Mackinac to its limestone foundations."[26] By 1856 it was possible to transport heavy siege artillery by railroad from Toronto to Collingwood, Ontario, on Lake Huron and from there by steamer to Mackinac. Only "earthen & enlarged works of strong profile" would stand a chance against a modern attacker, Fort Mackinac's commandant counseled in the spring of 1856.[27]

Such a project was impracticable by that time, and the garrison was forced to make do with what was already in place. Commandants remained uncertain whether the post would even be "kept up" as an active station.[28] The old masonry walls continued to deteriorate in Michigan's fierce climate. They were surveyed for possible repair in 1850 (Fig. 8.1), but little was done thereafter beyond what the garrison could accomplish. In June 1853 Major Thomas Williams described his post as "in a state of reproachful dilapidation, looking much like an abandoned ruin." The repairs he suggested were intended to do no more than satisfy "*appearances*."[29] Although drawn images of the period project the impression of a neat and orderly fortification, closer examination of the earliest photographs reveals the poor condition of its walls.

Although the army had given up on Fort Mackinac as a defensible position, it remained an active garrison until the outbreak of the Civil War. The post was unoccupied for two winters during the 1850s, but otherwise its buildings were maintained and even improved. Devastating fires swept the fort in 1855 and 1858, the first destroying the company barracks and the second its replacement as well as the blacksmith shop and a long row of storehouses and offices. The quarters were rebuilt each time, however, and a new office for the commandant, a bake house, a quartermaster storehouse, and a hospital were constructed in 1859–61. Plans were even considered for the renovation and enlargement of the old stone and wooden officers' quarters, although nothing came of the proposal (see Figs. 8.21, 8.22, 8.24, and 8.42). The Engineer's Department might have given up on the fortifications, but the Quartermaster General's Department clearly anticipated that a garrison would still require adequate shelter and services.

With its strategic military role a thing of the past, Fort Mackinac was viewed increasingly as a curiosity and an artifact of earlier times. It had long been among the list of Mackinac attractions, if only for the view it provided, and most visitors of the 1850s included the fort in their walks about the island. Juliette Starr Dana "went through it" in July 1852. When Robert Cummins visited, three summers later, he was fortunate that his companion was an acquaintance of Major Williams, who gave them a personal tour of "the beautiful grounds of the Fort."[30] Williams, who commanded from 1852 to 1856, was a proponent of repairing and improving Fort Mackinac. He also seems to have been perfectly comfortable to have his post considered a local attraction. Williams and his troops contributed martial pomp to island summers with military drills and by daily conducting artillery target practice in Lake Huron.[31] Fort Mackinac and its garrison were beginning to take on some of the functions of historical attraction and guardian of scenic public lands that would become institutionalized in the establishment of Mackinac National Park in 1875. A careful survey of government property in 1855 and the permanent marking of its boundaries two years later were intended to prevent further encroachment and preserve these lands for public use (see Figs. 8.25 and 8.26).

Even as Mackinac's popularity among tourists continued to increase during the 1850s, one of its most picturesque and longtime annual events was fading away. The 1836 Treaty of Washington had provided for annuity payments to be made to Native Americans over the course of twenty years, and the end was drawing near. For years, late summer and autumn at Mackinac had been enlivened by the arrival of thousands of Indians. They crowded the beach with their canoes and wigwams and collected their money from the Indian agent, only to be enticed by traders seeking to relieve them of it as soon as possible. Payments were disbursed at the old Indian Agency House, even after the Indian superintendent's office was moved to Detroit in 1851 and the agent returned only at annuity time.

Major Thomas Williams witnessed one of the last such gatherings in November 1854. The agent, Henry C. Gilbert, was late in arriving that year and had been anxiously awaited by the Indians encamped along the shore in front of the fort gardens. The money was distributed on the afternoon of November 20, and then it was the merchants' turn. "This is their harvest," Williams wrote his wife. The town was a riot of activity with goods displayed everywhere. "Red & green & blue & yellow shawls, blankets & kerchiefs, are displayed from the doors & windows & suspended from ropes stretched from one roof or projection to another," he continued, adding with disapproval that "rum" was freely offered "to put them in trading humor." The "harvest" of 1854 must have been a good one. "The natives [merchants] are rejoicing with fire crackers & signal rockets this evening," Williams reported.[32] Native Americans would travel to Mackinac Island and camp on the beach for decades to come, but after the end of treaty payments there were fewer of them and they came primarily to sell curios for the tourist trade.

Even before the last treaty payments, the Indian agency buildings were falling into disuse. The Indian Agency House was rented out after 1851, although Major Williams tried to have it turned over to the army for use as a storehouse.[33] The Indian Dormitory, never much utilized for the accommodation of Native American visitors, was occupied as an office for U.S. Lake Survey personnel in 1852 and then as a customs house after 1858.[34] In 1867, after the customs office was moved to Sault Ste. Marie, the building was made available for the island's school, a function it would serve for the next century.[35]

"Mackinaw is now in a transition state," Charles Lanman had concluded in his 1847 book, *A Summer in the Wilderness.* "Heretofore it has been the Indian's congregating place, but its aboriginal glory is rapidly departing, and it will soon be a fashionable resort of summer travellers."[36] By 1860 the Indian agency and the fur trade were gone, fishing was passing its prime, Fort Mackinac was an obsolete curiosity, new and more viable towns were appearing at mainland locations, and the way forward lay with the tourist and resort trade. Blessed with a "peculiar location, picturesque scenery, and the tonic character of its climate," Mackinac was destined to become "one of the most attractive watering places in the country."[37] The final transition would be interrupted by civil war, but the end of that conflict would set the stage for an economy based almost entirely on the summer visitor.

When the men were not drilling they were propping up the fort

Constance Fenimore Woolson

The November winds were just beginning to herald the approach of winter when Major Charles H. Larnard arrived at Mackinac Island with his command of the 4th United States Infantry. The major and his men had soldiered through the recent war with Mexico. Now, as 1848 drew to a close, they found themselves reassigned halfway across the continent to one of the northernmost posts of the United States. Larnard's company was the first regular army unit to occupy Fort Mackinac since the summer of 1847. Michigan volunteers had guarded the walls for much of the time since, but the old fort had stood empty once again following their departure in the spring of 1848.

Like any new commandant, one of Major Larnard's first duties was to inspect the condition of his post. He was clearly disturbed by what he found. It came as no surprise to him that the buildings were old and once again in need of repair, but the condition of the stone walls that kept Fort Mackinac from sliding down the steep bluff was cause for immediate concern, if not alarm. "The walls of the Fort are cracked in many places, so as to require propping," he reported to his superiors in the Department of the East, "and it is to be feared that they will give way at these points in the Spring."[38] It had been only three years since Private William Brenschutz depicted a neat and structurally sound Fort Mackinac (Fig. 7.21). Captain Scott's repairs had obviously not corrected the faults of aging masonry walls that had been exposed to Mackinac's climate for nearly seventy years.

Winter was no time to attempt repairs, and Larnard's garrison lacked the means to do so in any case. As the season progressed, the major and his officers became increasingly worried about the stability of the "enclosing and sustaining walls," predicting in March 1849 that they were likely to fall in the spring if not promptly repaired.[39] The crisis came in May when thirty feet of the retaining wall below the south sally port gave way, endangering the main entrance to Fort Mackinac and the towering section of stone wall above the gate and between the guardhouse and lower gun platform. To make matters worse, twenty feet of retaining wall along the ramp leading to the fort also collapsed. "If not soon checked this dilapidation must destroy the whole front on that side of the work," Larnard warned the quartermaster general.[40]

The problem facing Major Larnard's garrison was nothing new. Since the days of the British, Fort Mackinac's commandants had wrestled with the instability of the bluff. The geologists who visited Mackinac Island in 1849 could have pointed out that the walls were not all built on solid limestone and that much of the face of the hill was composed of fragmented materials that were particularly susceptible to the effects of moisture, frost, and erosion. A few new retaining walls had been constructed since 1817 (see Fig. 4.6), and

the general layout of the walls as they were in 1848–49 may be seen on Private Brenschutz's 1845 bird's-eye view (Fig. 7.21). Visible among these was the recently collapsed masonry below the south sally port, located at an especially vulnerable point where runoff from the parade ground was channeled over the bluff.

Larnard and his men were apparently able to stem the immediate damage, but a more permanent solution was required. The commandant corresponded with the quartermaster general on matters relating to his post, and he was persuasive enough that Major General Thomas Jesup requested the assistance of the Engineer's Department. The latter office was responsible for fortifications, while Jesup and his staff supervised quarters for the troops. Fort Mackinac had received no attention from an engineer since Major Charles Gratiot's work in 1817, and Jesup had to convince his engineering counterpart, Brigadier General Joseph Totten, that the old post could still be considered a fortification rather than merely a barracks complex. It was not until May 1850 that Totten informed Jesup that the secretary of war had given permission for him to assign an engineer to report on the state of the walls of Fort Mackinac.[41] On the same day, Totten wrote to Lieutenant John Newton at Detroit, ordering him to proceed to Mackinac Island to examine the situation.[42]

Newton set off soon after June 1, and by June 20 he had returned to Detroit, prepared his report, and submitted a rough plan of what he had found (Fig. 8.1). This was the first engineer's draft of Fort Mackinac to have been drawn since 1817, and its focus on the fortifications is evident. Only five of the post's buildings are shown, and these only because they in some way affected the defense of the perimeter. To the right of Newton's plan may be seen four cross sections through the retaining walls at different points and a framing plan for new wooden decking to support cannon in the lower gun platform that overlooked the town and the south sally port. Notations explain the meaning of the numbers shown on the plan and the engineer's use of red lines to indicate "the necessity of immediate repair" or proposals for new construction. Lieutenant Newton apologized that, because he went to Mackinac specifically to examine the condition of the walls, he had not taken all the instruments necessary for making a complete survey. As a result, he admitted, the angles of the walls had not been drawn with complete accuracy.[43]

Newton's findings were much as expected. He discovered that along the lakefront, nearly all sections were "very defective and show the necessity of ultimate replacement." He used numbers to prioritize the urgency of repair for all sections, but even the best parts, he

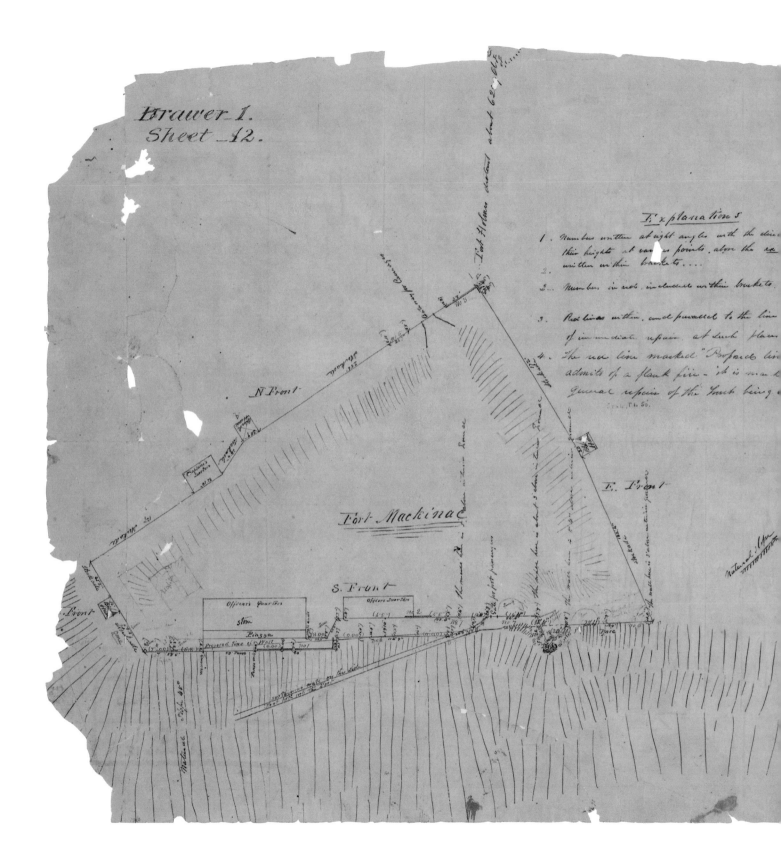

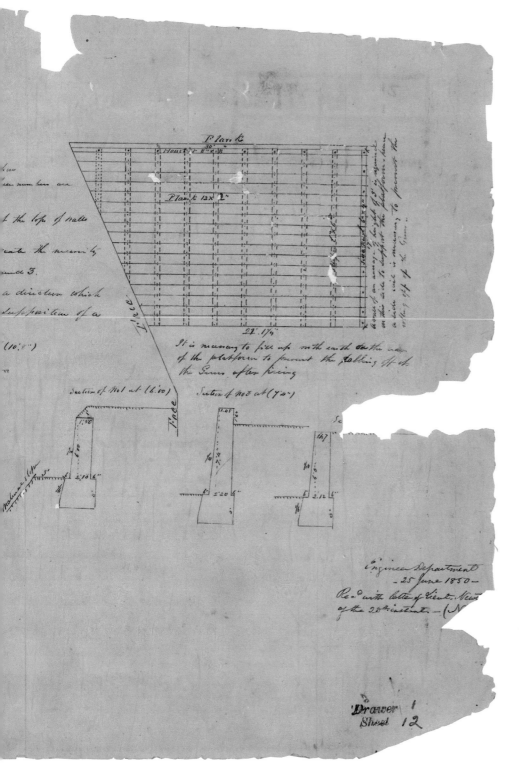

FIGURE 8.1

TITLE: Fort Mackinac.

AUTHOR: Second Lieutenant John Newton, Corps of Engineers (1823–95).

DATE DEPICTED: June 1850.

DATE OF WORK: [June 20, 1850].

DESCRIPTION: 38.3 x 67.5 cm. (irregular). Pen and ink on paper with red line highlighting details.

PROVENANCE: Received in Engineer's Department, June 25, 1850, with Newton's letter of June 20. Retained in the records of the chief of engineers.

COLLECTION: National Archives and Records Administration, College Park, MD (RG 77, Records of the Office of Chief of Engineers, Fortifications Map File, Drawer 1, Sheet 12).

reported, would require reconstruction within a few seasons. The stone walls on the three land faces were topped with a defensive stockade, but the masonry was "so imperfectly constructed, both in the character of the stone wall, and of the mortar," that it was likely that sections would topple each spring while new defects developed elsewhere. "It is apparent, therefore," he summarized, "that the Fort Mackinac requires total rebuilding."

But was it worth the expense? Lieutenant Newton did not venture an opinion on the strategic value of the old post, but he admitted to "going beyond the literal instructions" of his orders to comment at length on the defensive strength of its position. The "steepness of the natural slope" on the south edge of the fort was its strongest attribute, and that side could be made "unassailable." However, for the fort to be effective, that front would have to be rebuilt to support heavy, seacoast-style guns that would be effective against warships in the lake. An attacker could easily approach the land fronts, and the site of Fort Holmes, 620 yards away by Newton's estimate, completely dominated Fort Mackinac. Other elements of the defenses did nothing to compensate. The loopholes of the stockade built under Captain Scott's direction in 1844 had been cut at the wrong height, and Newton doubted that the three antiquated blockhouses could withstand the shock of firing the small cannon mounted in them. To make matters worse, the north wall was compromised by "an entire interruption of the defensive line by the interpolation of a frame building marked in the drawing 'Chaplains Quarters'"—the "Hill House" of 1835.

Then came the crux of the matter. Fort Mackinac, Newton proposed, would require either extensive repairs or complete reconstruction. "If repairs be undertaken for a *military* purpose," he added, a much more complete and extensive survey would be necessary. On the other hand, he continued, "if all intentions of converting this old work to any useful military purpose be not entertained . . . all repairs would apply simply to the convenience and preservation of the Quarters—or to forming an enclosure around the buildings." That being the case, then responsibility for the work "belong[ed] not of right to the Engineer Department." Newton then presented his estimates: $773.00 to make immediately required repairs and $2,719.50 for future work on the walls. More extensive changes would "require a special estimate."[44]

What would be the purpose of such expensive work? Lieutenant Newton and other officers agreed that earthen fortifications armed with heavy, seacoast-style artillery would be required to substantially improve the defense of Fort Mackinac.[45] But what would those guns control? "A popular delusion is prevalent that this fort commands the straits," wrote a correspondent to a New York newspaper in July 1860. "It would, in fact," he suggested, "interpose very feeble opposition to the passage of an armed vessel from Buffalo to Chicago." The light field guns and single mortar then in Fort Mackinac were useful primarily for "garrison exercise."[46] These or even larger guns would have "no Command of the Straits," William Johnston wrote

in 1857.[47] The U.S. Army was not about to pour large sums of money into a fortress that could not defend the waterway. By the late 1850s, informal suggestions had even been put forward that the site of Old Michilimackinac offered a better location for a new fort than Mackinac Island.[48] Lieutenant Newton's report effectively allowed the Engineer's Department to wash its hands of the question, and the responsibility for maintaining both the buildings and the walls that supported them would thereafter lie with the Quartermaster General's Department.

The Newton report seems to have had little or no effect on the upkeep of Fort Mackinac. Major Larnard and his successors continued to watch their walls deteriorate as they responded to each new crisis with patchwork repairs. In April 1851, twenty or thirty feet of wall in front of the officers' stone quarters tumbled down the bluff and had to be replaced. The spot had been labeled "No. 1" on Newton's plan. The garrison quartermaster again appealed for "complete and thorough repairing throughout."[49] In May 1852 another breach "of many square yards" opened up on the lake side of the fort. At the same time, more than sixty feet of wall by the north sally port was reported to be eighteen to twenty-four inches out of plumb ("No. 3" on Newton's plan), and the walls required extensive repairs in general.[50] Four years later, a "considerable portion" of the south front was again on the verge of collapse. "Our walls are crumbling," Major Thomas Williams wrote the quartermaster general, noting that even the wooden pickets were rotten and had to propped from the outside. Each event, he reported, "is best met with immediate repairs:—as the replacing of a score of stones or pickets, deferred, may easily involve the falling of an entire flank or face [of the walls]." Williams admitted what the army had decided years before—doing more would be a "useless expenditure" because Fort Mackinac, as it existed, could no longer compete in a modern war for control of Lake Huron.[51]

Lieutenant John Newton's plan of Fort Mackinac bears evidence of having been further consulted, probably about 1859–60. Lightly penciled half circles on the gun platforms in the southeastern corner of the enclosure suggest sites for mounting seacoast artillery, and the ground plan of a new "Hospital" is sketched into the opposite end of the parade ground. That building was designed in the summer of 1859 (Fig. 8.42), but, when it was constructed, it was placed outside and to the east of the fort. Serious repairs to the walls themselves would have to await post–Civil War days. Photographs of Fort Mackinac through the 1860s reveal open mortar joints, areas of masonry loss, emergency wooden revetments, and a general disarray of the old stone walls.

Then visit ye lovers of pleasure and sight-seeing

Daniel S. Curtiss

Fort Mackinac might have been in decline by the summer of 1850, but its reputation—and that of the island and its vicinity—as a healthy place was surely on the upswing. Army officers had realized, since the 1790s, that Michilimackinac was a post where disease tended to be far less prevalent than at most installations, whether they protected the cities of the Atlantic and Gulf coasts or the expanding western frontier. "Than this post, there is not a more healthful one in the United States," wrote Surgeon General Thomas Lawson in 1840. Hospital records for the period from 1829 to 1838 support his claim.[52] The military certainly contributed to spreading the good word. In 1836 Captain John Clitz shared a popular local cliché with Harriet Martineau. "The island is so healthy," he told her, that "people who want to die must go somewhere else."[53] Frederick Marryat heard the same story from another islander the following summer. "We have good air, good water, and what we eat agrees with us," he added by way of explanation.[54]

Dr. Daniel Drake began to tout Mackinac as a healthy resort with his small book, *The Northern Lakes,* published in 1842. Eight years later, he produced a much longer and more professional treatise on the principal diseases of the interior parts of North America, a work that devoted three and one-half closely set pages of text to promoting Mackinac as "a delightful hot-weather asylum," particularly for the sick. Figure 8.2 illustrated that book and provided a frame of reference for Drake's glowing account of the virtues and beauties of the developing resort. "Mackinac," he began, "is at once the name of an island, a strait, a village, and a fort."[55] All of these features appear on the map, which was drawn by Charles A. Fuller, a former army officer who then worked for the Corps of Engineers. His cartography appears to have been derived from representations of the Straits that had appeared as insets on maps of Michigan since the late 1820s (Figs. 5.29–5.31).

Drake's arguments for the health benefits of Mackinac ran the gamut from the quantifiable—the fitness of the military garrison as demonstrated by army records—to the intangible—the "serenade of the waters" as waves lapped the beach or "the heavens illuminated with an aurora borealis." From a more practical standpoint he believed that latitude, geology, topography, air circulation, and water temperature all contributed to preventing and even remitting illnesses, especially fevers. Drake dubbed Mackinac "Queen of the Isles" and enthusiastically described the view from its summit. "Green and blue are the governing hues," he wrote, "but they flow into each other with such facility and frequency that . . . it seems, as if by magic transformed into another." To the west could be seen the "indented shores" of the Upper Peninsula; to the south was the

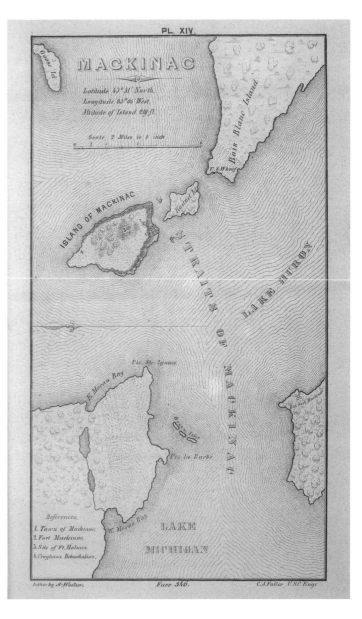

FIGURE 8.2

TITLE: Mackinac.
AUTHOR: Charles Alexander Fuller (active 1830–d. 1890). Lithograph by A. Wocher.
DATE DEPICTED: 1850.
DATE OF WORK: 1850.
DESCRIPTION: 11.5 x 20.7 cm. Lithograph.
PROVENANCE: Published in Daniel Drake, *A Systematic Treatise, Historical, Etiological, and Practical on the Principal Diseases of the Interior Valley of North America* (Cincinnati, 1850), 346.
COLLECTION: Clements Library, University of Michigan, Ann Arbor (Book Division, C2-1850-Dr).

STRAITS OF MACKINAW.

FIGURE 8.3

TITLE: Straits of Mackinaw.
AUTHOR: [Robert E. Clarke].
DATE DEPICTED: July 1852.
DATE OF WORK: March 1853.
DESCRIPTION: 3 x 11.5 cm. Engraving.
PROVENANCE: Published in Clarke, "Notes from the Copper Region," *Harper's New Monthly Magazine* 6, no. 34 (March 1853): 434. The view, under the same title, appeared again in the upper right corner of a map, *Johnson's Michigan & Wisconsin* (New York, 1861).
COLLECTION: Clements Library, University of Michigan, Ann Arbor (Serials 1).

"distant and smoky line of elevated table-land" of the Lower. Round Island formed "a beautiful foreground," while Bois Blanc stretched away to the east and the St. Martin Islands and Les Cheneaux to the north "complete the archipelago."[56] Who could resist such a description when read in the hot, dusty, and smoky environment of a Cincinnati, St. Louis, or Chicago summer.

Fuller's map neatly complements Drake's description, incorporating only a few errors, such as placing the site of Croghan's 1814 landing on the wrong side of Mackinac Island and "Old Fort Mackinac" (Old Michilimackinac) at some distance from its actual location. The orientation of the map, with east at the top, corresponds to the view perceived by travelers approaching the Straits from Chicago or Milwaukee. Robert E. Clarke came from that direction in July 1852 on his way to Lake Superior. He was the first to produce an article on Mackinac for one of the new illustrated magazines and newspapers that were gaining popularity by 1850. Clarke's view of the "Straits of Mackinac" (Fig. 8.3) is from the west, and it introduced his readers to the appearance of the three islands that dominate the eastern end of the waterway.

Clarke's essay includes three additional Mackinac scenes (Figs. 8.4– 8.6). Not surprisingly, these depict the island's signature geological formations, Arch Rock and Sugar Loaf. Clarke was probably the artist, and it is very likely that he made other views during a stay of at least three days. If so, they were not reproduced with his story. His surviving images appeared in the March 1853 issue of *Harper's New Monthly Magazine* but were also reproduced in other publications as late as 1870. The pictures are enlightening, but Robert Clarke's text is even more useful for what it reveals about the activities of a tourist of the 1850s.

Modern Mackinac Island visitors are accustomed to tightly scheduled ferry arrivals, but the erratic movements of contemporary steamboats governed Robert Clarke's itinerary. His vessel from Chicago moored at Mackinac Island at 2:00 in the morning. Despite the late hour, the "accommodating proprietor" of the Mission House was on the wharf with an omnibus and baggage wagon to see his guests to the "elevated and commanding, yet retired situation" of his hotel. The arrival of new patrons in the middle of the night caused quite a disturbance, but it seems to have been a typical occurrence.[57] Juliette Starr Dana, who stayed at the Mission House on two occasions in July and August 1852, complained of her first evening there that "the house was in an uproar all night with people coming & going in two boats from some places on Lake Michigan."[58] Clarke thought the hotel comfortable, although crowding clearly remained a problem during the height of Mackinac's season. Mrs. Dana found the Mission House full when she arrived on July 28, and she could obtain only "rather inferior" quarters overlooking the kitchen yard where any view was blocked by the steep bluff behind the building. She was more fortunate on her second visit on August 17, when she got "three nice rooms."[59]

Robert Clarke was intent on seeing whatever was "curious and interesting," so he began the day following his arrival by climbing the bluff from his hotel and walking through the woods for a view of Arch Rock from above. It appeared to him as "a soaring arch suspended in mid-air, which shuts out the horizon." Below he could see the waters of the lake "dancing in the sun-beams," and he made a sketch (Fig. 8.4) before cautiously descending the bluff to look up at it from below. The top of Arch Rock, Clarke noted, appeared to have been "well-trodden," and he was later told that three of the "ladies of Mackinaw" had actually walked across the span. From the beach below the natural bridge, Clarke explored the smaller opening known in more recent times as Sanilac Arch.

Climbing back up the steep path, Clarke then continued through the woods to Sugar Loaf, where he speculated on what had separated the gigantic rock from the nearby hill and made a drawing of the scene (Fig. 8.5). His perspective differs from most in that it is from the road between Sugar Loaf and the hill and does not reveal "Keyhole Cave" on the side to the viewer's left. The rock was dotted with a "wild growth of vines and stunted cedars." Clarke obtained yet another look at Sugar Loaf by climbing to the top of the adjacent bluff—Point Lookout—before returning to the Mission House.[60]

The weather was "clear and fine" on the morning of the second day of Clarke's visit, so he made an early start and climbed again to the site of Fort Holmes. There he took in the scenery from the top of the "Observatory," which had been built as a triangulation tower by engineers of the Lake Survey. The view was well worth the ascent, revealing everything from the Lower Peninsula and St. Ignace around to British Landing and the islands to the north and east. It was Sunday, so his next stop was Fort Mackinac and the Episcopalian service conducted there by Chaplain John O'Brien. Although attendance was large, most of the members of the congregation were "strangers," and there were few soldiers in evidence, even though the service was held in a barracks room. This Clarke attributed to the fact that the peacetime army was "chiefly foreign and of the Catholic religion." Services completed, the traveler returned to his hotel for a dinner of speckled trout.

Later in the afternoon, Clarke and some companions took a tour of Mackinac Island of a type that seems to have been particularly popular in the 1840s and 1850s. The group hired "a little sloop" and a local crew to sail around the island. These trips usually followed a

THE ARCH ROCK.

FIGURE 8.4
TITLE: The Arch Rock.
AUTHOR: [Robert E. Clarke].
DATE DEPICTED: July 1852.
DATE OF WORK: March 1853.
DESCRIPTION: 10 x 6 cm. Engraving.
PROVENANCE: Published in Clarke, "Notes from the Copper Region," *Harper's New Monthly Magazine* 6, no. 34 (March 1853): 434. The image was reused with the title "Arch Rocks. Lake Superior" in the right-hand margin of *Colton's New Railroad Map of the States of Ohio, Michigan, Illinois. . . .* (New York, 1865), in Alexander Winchell, *Sketches of Creation* (New York, 1870), and in James A. Van Fleet, *Old and New Mackinac* (Ann Arbor, 1870 and later), 138.
COLLECTION: Clements Library, University of Michigan, Ann Arbor (Serials 1).

Dr. Daniel Drake (1785–1852) became an enthusiastic advocate of Mackinac as a health resort after his visit to the island in 1842. He found the place "exempt" from "autumnal fevers" with many other benefits to well-being. Drake spread the word with books published in 1842 and 1850, proclaiming Mackinac "Queen of the Isles." Charles A. Meurer painted the doctor's portrait sometime in the 1840s. *Cincinnati Museum Center– Cincinnati Historical Society Library.*

counterclockwise route, and although a stiff east wind was blowing, the boat easily rounded Mission Point and followed the northeast shore past Arch Rock. From the water the bluffs reminded Clarke of the coasts of Italy and the arch itself of "the remains of some Roman structure." The scene was worth a picture (Fig. 8.6). Otherwise, he found the shoreline of no particular interest other than for the balsam firs, which had grown to a height of thirty to fifty feet and now dominated the forest.

Rounding the northwestern end of the island, the water calmed, and the boat passed, in succession, British Landing, St. Ignace, Lover's Leap, and the cleared farmland on the southwestern bluffs. As the vessel neared Haldimand Bay, it got among a large field of gill nets, but the crew deftly tacked around them and into the harbor to conclude an excursion of an hour and one-half. Along the way, the sailors had regaled their passengers with tales of the "massacre" at "Old Mackinaw" and other local stories. One of the men even admitted that he had once crossed Arch Rock, but only by sitting down and working his way across with his hands.[61]

Robert Clarke's time on Mackinac was punctuated with visits to the town, carriage rides, and shopping for Indian curiosities. He observed the fishing trade and described excursions across St. Martin Bay for sport angling at the Carp River. The latter activity had grown in popularity in the 1840s, and in 1848 the steamer *St. Louis* even carried a group of "inveterate anglers" there to fish for trout. Pigeon hunting was popular as well.[62] Other diversions included "ten-pins," but Clarke regretted that Mackinac lacked any provisions for "bathing" other than in the frigid lake. He compared a swim in Lake Huron to Alexander the Great "bathing in the cold river Cydnus."[63]

Complementing the sights and outdoor activities of a visit to Mackinac was the food, dominated of course by the ever present but nonetheless delicious trout and whitefish for which the place was now famous. Robert Clarke found that fish, "fried, baked, and boiled, or broiled," formed a part of every meal at the Mission House, although there were also "beefsteaks of matchless tenderness," and the dishes made from "flour and meal" were equally as good. Native whortleberries provided a Mackinac dessert staple. They were eaten in pastries or by themselves, and were "so delicious of flavor as scarcely to crave the aid of sugar," although pitchers of cream from the island's farms added to the treat.[64] Nearly every visitor of the time also mentioned the local potatoes, "celebrated in this whole region for their size and mealiness," as one visitor explained in 1848.[65] Mrs. Dana also agreed that the table at the Mission House was "very good."[66]

Robert Clarke was pleased with what he had seen of Mackinac Island. A visitor of "quiet and reposeful disposition," he declared, could pass a fortnight "very satisfactorily," and even those "more restless and impetuous" would find plenty to do. Then, having arrived in the middle of the night, he departed on the Ward Line's *London* "past midnight" on August 2 to continue his journey to Sault Ste. Marie and the Lake Superior copper country.[67]

THE SUGAR LOAF ROCK.

ARCH ROCK—DISTANT VIEW.

FIGURE 8.5

TITLE: The Sugar Loaf Rock.
AUTHOR: [Robert E. Clarke].
DATE DEPICTED: July 1852.
DATE OF WORK: March 1853.
DESCRIPTION: 6 x 5 cm. Engraving.
PROVENANCE: Published in Clarke, "Notes from the Copper Region," *Harper's New Monthly Magazine* 6, no. 34 (March 1853): 435. The image was reused in Alexander Winchell, *Sketches of Creation* (New York, 1870), and in James A. Van Fleet, *Old and New Mackinac* (Ann Arbor, 1870 and later), 140.
COLLECTION: Clements Library, University of Michigan, Ann Arbor (Serials 1).

FIGURE 8.6

TITLE: Arch Rock—Distant View.
AUTHOR: [Robert E. Clarke].
DATE DEPICTED: July 1852.
DATE OF WORK: March 1853.
DESCRIPTION: 6 x 5.5 cm. Engraving.
PROVENANCE: Published in Clarke, "Notes from the Copper Region," *Harper's New Monthly Magazine* 6, no. 34 (March 1853): 436.
COLLECTION: Clements Library, University of Michigan, Ann Arbor (Serials 1).

The walks on this island are delightful

Juliette Hanna Starr Dana

While the Mackinac drawings of Robert E. Clarke appeared in print during the winter of 1853, a fascinating group of sketches made later that year and the next by a much more talented illustrator was never engraved or published. Alfred Rodolph Waud, their creator, later rose to considerable prominence amid the chaos of the Civil War by providing a steady stream of accurate, detailed, and action-packed images to illustrated newspapers. Although he at first drew for the *New York Illustrated News,* Waud's Civil War work is best known from the pages of *Harper's Weekly,* which hired him away in 1862. As *Harper's* "special artist" at the front, Waud documented the activities of the Army of the Potomac in battle and in camp for the rest of the war. His association with the publications of the Harper Brothers would continue until 1890.[68]

Alfred R. Waud's visits to Mackinac are documented only by ten of his sketches that survive as part of a larger archive of his work in the Historic New Orleans Collection. Unfortunately, relatively little is known of the artist's career before he went to the *New York Illustrated News* in 1860. He had been in the United States for ten years by that time, having arrived in New York City from England in 1850 with hopes of finding work as a scene painter in a theater then under construction on Broadway. This employment was not yet available, so Waud pursued whatever artistic labor he could obtain, including freelance jobs for illustrated publications. The artist soon gravitated to drawing views of places and activities. His earliest known sketches are dated 1851 and were made around Boston, other parts of New England, New York, and Washington. By 1853 Waud

had a studio on Broadway, and he appears in the 1854–55 New York City directory located on Fulton Street.[69]

Despite his settled addresses, Waud was willing to travel on assignment or on speculation to obtain salable images. This is presumably what took him to Mackinac Island in the fall of 1853 and again in 1854, based on dates scrawled on four of his drawings. Mackinac Island was a regular stop on the steamship route to Milwaukee and Chicago, so two visits were not out of the question, even if Waud was still a struggling artist. If he was on assignment, none of his Mackinac sketches was published. But Waud might have been working on speculation, for he typically retained a large reserve of material for future use. There is circumstantial evidence that three Mackinac Island views published in *Frank Leslie's Illustrated Newspaper* in September 1856 were based on his work (see Figs. 8.29, 8.31, and 8.32). Since *Leslie's* did not begin publication until late in 1855, however, the artist was probably working independently at Mackinac. Other drawings in the Historic New Orleans Collection show that he visited Detroit on the same trips.[70]

Whatever their provenance, Alfred Waud's renderings of scenes and scenery on Mackinac Island are gems of detail. Eight of the ten were done in pencil, and many bear notations about color or other details that would have allowed more finished compositions to be completed at a later time. The other two are more polished, incorporating simple washes or pigments for emphasis. Waud's Mackinac Island sketches provide crisp glimpses of the place in the early 1850s, and several are unique images of subjects not otherwise

The realistic sketches of Alfred R. Waud (1828–91) captured the appearance of the Mackinac community in the early 1850s. Most of his drawings were probably intended for use in illustrated newspapers. This 1849 pencil sketch, by Arthur Allum, was drawn before Waud's arrival in the United States. It was reproduced in Ray, *"Our Special Artist,"* and credited to the Malcolm F. J. Burns Collection.

FIGURE 8.7

TITLE: Mackinaw 1854.
AUTHOR: Alfred R. Waud (1828–91).
DATE DEPICTED: 1854.
DATE OF WORK: 1854.
DESCRIPTION: 10.5 x 29.8 cm. Pencil on paper.
Signed at lower right: ARW.

PROVENANCE: Part of a Waud sketchbook or portfolio. Acquired by Historic New Orleans Collection in 1977.
COLLECTION: Historic New Orleans Collection (1977.137.38.10).

FIGURE 8.8

TITLE: Fort Holmes Mackinaw [at top left:] highest point used for triangulation.
AUTHOR: Alfred R. Waud (1828–91).
DATE DEPICTED: 1853–54.
DATE OF WORK: [1853–54].
DESCRIPTION: 7.9 x 22.6 cm. Pencil on paper.

PROVENANCE: Part of a Waud sketchbook or portfolio. Acquired by Historic New Orleans Collection in 1977.
COLLECTION: Historic New Orleans Collection (1977.137.38.9).

FIGURE 8.9
TITLE: Sugarloaf rock Mackinaw.
AUTHOR: Alfred R. Waud (1828–91).
DATE DEPICTED: 1853–54.
DATE OF WORK: [1853–54].
DESCRIPTION: 10.8 x 12.1 cm. Pencil on paper.
PROVENANCE: Part of a Waud sketchbook or portfolio. Acquired by Historic New Orleans Collection in 1977.
COLLECTION: Historic New Orleans Collection (1977.137.38.11).

documented in the period. They may be arranged in a logical order that presents another "tour" of the sights of Mackinac Island. Eight are included here, while one appears later as Figure 8.20 and another is too unfinished to reveal much detail.[71]

The first of Alfred Waud's drawings (Fig. 8.7), dated 1854, was made from the beach along the eastern end of Haldimand Bay, not far from Ste. Anne's Church. The view is toward the town, which is shown in considerable detail, with William Wendell's new wharf at left. Fort Mackinac overlooks the scene, and in the foreground are coopers' shops or fishermen's houses. The two large buildings at right center are the Indian Dormitory (left) and the Island House Hotel. The latter, depicted here for the first time, went through several name changes in its early years. Upon completion, in 1849, it was called the O'Malley House, although most early accounts refer to the hotel without a name.[72] Emblazoned on its facade in the 1854 Waud view is what Historic New Orleans Collection curators have interpreted as "Hurt [?] House," but which is almost certainly "Huron House," the hotel where Aaron Bellangee and his wife rented a room for two weeks in July 1854.[73] It was known as the "Island House" by 1859, but it is possible that the name was not in use much before that time.[74]

Moving into the island, the artist climbed to old Fort Holmes and made two sketches along the ridge (Figs. 8.8 and 8.9). The first shows the triangulation tower constructed on the ruins of Fort Holmes. Some sort of platform was in place there early on, certainly by 1841, and a mast appears at Fort Holmes in views of the island from 1842 and later. The structure shown by Waud was probably of somewhat more recent origin, however. Its shape is of the type built by officers of the U.S. Lake Survey. It combines two frameworks, with the three central posts designed to support a theodolite, a very precise transit, and the outer, four-post structure providing a platform for the surveyor. The separate foundations prevented movement that would have disturbed the instrument.[75] Although built for official use, this tower soon became a popular lookout for tourists. Robert Clarke and Juliette Starr Dana both climbed it in July 1852, and by 1855 many visitors were unaware of its original purpose.[76] By 1860, guidebooks recommended the "triangular station" for the premier view of the Straits.[77]

Continuing northwest along the bluff, Waud drew a pencil sketch of Sugar Loaf from Point Lookout, complete with notations about vegetation and color. Robert Clarke found the appearance of the great rock from above to be "grand and imposing. . . . its isolated position, with its bold form breaking the outline of the island" striking the beholder with "wonder and delight."[78] Waud added a smaller sketch from ground level at the bottom of his composition.

From the southwestern side of the central hill, Waud apparently went by road to British Landing. Or did he land from a small boat while circumnavigating the island? The artist made at least one and possibly two sketches at that point, one dated October 1853 and both having Indian encampments as their subject (Figs. 8.10 and 8.11).

FIGURE 8.10

TITLE: Indian encampment near the British Landing Id of Mackinaw.
AUTHOR: Alfred R. Waud (1828–91).
DATE DEPICTED: October 1853.
DATE OF WORK: October 1853.
DESCRIPTION: 13.7 x 23.5 cm. Pencil, ink, and Chinese white on paper. Signed at lower left: AR Waud.

PROVENANCE: Part of a Waud sketchbook or portfolio. Acquired by Historic New Orleans Collection in 1977.
COLLECTION: Historic New Orleans Collection (1977.137.38.7).

FIGURE 8.11

TITLE: Wigwam of bark and mats—Mackinaw.
AUTHOR: Alfred R. Waud (1828–91).
DATE DEPICTED: 1853–54.
DATE OF WORK: [1853–54].
DESCRIPTION: 9 x 27 cm. Pencil on paper. Signed at lower right: AR Waud.
PROVENANCE: Part of a Waud sketchbook or portfolio. Acquired by Historic New Orleans Collection in 1977.
COLLECTION: Historic New Orleans Collection (1977.137.38.15).

FIGURE 8.12
TITLE: Scotts Cave Mackinaw.
AUTHOR: Alfred R. Waud (1828–91).
DATE DEPICTED: 1853–54.
DATE OF WORK: [1853–54].
DESCRIPTION: 15.4 x 21.4 cm. Pencil on paper.
PROVENANCE: Part of a Waud sketchbook or portfolio.
Acquired by Historic New Orleans Collection in 1977.
COLLECTION: Historic New Orleans Collection
(1977.137.38.17i).

It was a relatively easy walk from British Landing to Scott's Cave
(Fig. 8.12), although early guidebooks cautioned that this was an
"unfrequented trail" that should not be followed without a guide.[79]
Waud not only found the cavern but also made one of the few
existing images of it, either drawn or photographic. Scott's Cave
was a relatively new attraction, first described, though without a
name, in 1840. Bela Hubbard explored it that August as "a new object
of interest" on the island near Dousman's farm. The entrance was
low, much like that of Skull Cave, but once inside the roof rose to
a height of about eight feet and, Hubbard wrote, "by our torches of
birch bark we discovered ourselves to be in a circular cavern of about
10 ft. diam." There were no stalactites, he added.[80] James Van Fleet
identified the site on the map in his *Old and New Mackinac* of 1870,
recommending that adventurers prepare for a visit by providing
themselves with "a lamp or candle" as little sunlight penetrated the
opening. The entrance was low, he added, but once inside, "the giant
Goliath might stand erect."[81] Unfortunately, like Fairy Arch, Scott's
Cave was blown up in 1953, presumably as a safety measure.[82]
The feature is today remembered in the name of a road that passes
beneath a bare section of bluff, below which the cavern was once
located.

But what was the origin of the name? It does not appear in
sources before the time of Waud's sketch, and guidebooks of the
1860s and 1870s refer to it alternately as "Scott's or Flinn's Cave."[83]
No individual named "Flinn" has yet been identified in relation to
Mackinac Island or the cavern, but "Scott" has usually been assumed
to be Captain Martin Scott, who commanded Fort Mackinac in
1842–45 and was killed in Mexico in 1847.

Although the cave was probably named for the captain, even
this attribution is tenuous. Martin Scott was well-known as a
marksman and hunter and might well have explored all the nooks
and crannies of Mackinac Island, including the isolated cave. In the
summer of 1846 William Cullen Bryant drove to British Landing
on a road "cut through the woods by Captain Scott."[84] This might
have been British Landing Road, but it is also possible that the
commandant had had his men reopen the old track along the route
of Scott's Cave Road (Figs. 4.7, 5.12, and 5.13) to make the "new"
geological attraction more accessible. It was not until 1855 that an
island landmark was specifically associated with Martin Scott. This
was described as "Scott's Peak," however, and its exact location was
not revealed. Did the name refer to the bluff above the cave or to a
point on the southwestern side of the island at the farm that, by the
1850s, was owned by island businessman William Scott?

Features of William Scott's farm are depicted in two of Waud's
sketches (Figs. 8.13 and 8.14). For what reason is difficult to fathom.
The larger farm of Michael Dousman was far better known, both for
agriculture and as the site of the 1814 battle. Scott's farm was located
atop the steep bluffs on the southwestern side of the island, and it
had been farmed by a succession of owners. Originally confirmed to
George Schindler in 1808 as claim 331, it had passed to John Dousman
and then, in 1827, to the Reverend Ferry as a farm for his mission
school. With the closing of the mission in 1837, it went to Samuel
Lasley (see Fig. 7.1) and then, probably soon after his death in 1844,
to William Scott. It was easily accessible by road from town and from
British Landing, and, by 1855, locals knew the prominent bulge on
the southwestern side of the island as Scott's Point.[85]

One of Waud's sketches of Scott's farm, dated 1853 (Fig. 8.13),
depicts a modest house, probably the residence of the owner's tenant,
and a log outbuilding. The house stood on the modern Hedgecliff
property (formerly the Scott farm) until its surviving wooden
elements were salvaged and stored by Mackinac State Historic Parks
in the winter and spring of 1983. This is believed to have been John
Dousman's farmhouse, although it might just as well have been a
feature of the original Schindler farm.[86]

The second Waud sketch (Fig. 8.14) depicts cleared and fenced
land, a substantial barn, and, in the background, structures that
might be those shown in Figure 8.13 but from the opposite direction.
Figure 8.14 corresponds in many details to an early stereo
photograph of the old "Schindler" farm and its rocky fields.[87]

Although many questions surround the Alfred Waud drawings
of Mackinac Island, they provide some of the best images of their
time and illustrate several features that would otherwise have gone
entirely undocumented.

FIGURE 8.13

TITLE: Scotts Farm—Mackinaw.

AUTHOR: Alfred R. Waud (1828–91).

DATE DEPICTED: 1853.

DATE OF WORK: 1853.

DESCRIPTION: 5.9 x 16.1 cm. Pencil on paper.

PROVENANCE: Part of a Waud sketchbook or portfolio.
Acquired by Historic New Orleans Collection in 1977.

COLLECTION: Historic New Orleans Collection (1977.137.38.16).

FIGURE 8.14

TITLE: Scotts Farm—Mackinaw.

AUTHOR: Alfred R. Waud (1828–91).

DATE DEPICTED: 1853.

DATE OF WORK: [1853].

DESCRIPTION: 8.6 x 20.7 cm. Pencil on paper.

PROVENANCE: Part of a Waud sketchbook or portfolio.
Acquired by Historic New Orleans Collection in 1977.

COLLECTION: Historic New Orleans Collection (1977.137.38.8).

Mackinaw and Its Scenery

Ballou's Pictorial Drawing-Room Companion

As Mackinac's reputation grew, so did the interest of the American popular press in what was becoming the most fashionable resort of the Great Lakes. The island and surrounding area possessed natural beauty, geological wonders, a colorful history, visiting Native Americans, opportunities for boating, hunting, and fishing, good food, and romantic settings, all within a healthy environment that was increasingly attractive to city dwellers of the rapidly industrializing United States. Just as Mackinac frequently appears in glossy travel publications of the early twenty-first century, so too was it a likely subject for the illustrated newspapers and magazines that were reshaping Americans' views of the world in the 1850s.

The advent of weekly publications filled with images of events, people, and places brought an information revolution to mid-nineteenth-century America. More efficient techniques for converting artists' drawings to mass-produced illustrations put a whole new face on the delivery of news and information. The process of lithography greatly reduced the costs and time involved in producing pictures to accompany printed text. People could now read of news—everything from disasters to political developments—and at the same time see an artist's rendering of the subject and its participants. In many cases, the events depicted had occurred within the week since the last edition of the paper. The medium was also appropriate for less time-sensitive subjects. By the early 1850s one could learn about distant and exotic places through images as well as text.

Such publications depended on a steady flow of drawings from artists in the field, and editors were on the lookout for appropriate visual material. It was no doubt the pursuit of marketable images that had taken Alfred R. Waud to Mackinac Island in 1853 and 1854. Staff and freelance illustrators regularly submitted drawings from around the country and the world. Pictures were obtained from amateur artists as well. Such appears to have been the case with four views of Mackinac Island (Figs. 8.15–8.18) that appeared in the May 5, 1855, issue of *Ballou's Pictorial Drawing-Room Companion*, a Boston paper that was in the forefront of the new medium. They illustrate a long article titled "Mackinaw and Its Scenery." Given the date of publication and the nature of the seasons on the Great Lakes, the drawings on which these views were based must have been made sometime during 1854 or before.

While the editor of *Ballou's* did not reveal the name of the artist, it was important that his readers be assured of the authenticity of the pictures. To this end he noted, by way of introduction, that "an officer of the U.S. Army" had drawn them "upon the spot," expressly for the paper. "Their fidelity will be immediately acknowledged by those who have the good fortune to examine the wild and romantic scenery his pencil has delineated," the editor confidently asserted.[88] Since many officers of the U.S. Army had been taught drawing as a part of their studies at the Military Academy, any number of possibilities present themselves as to the identity of the artist. The most likely prospect is Major Thomas Williams of the 4th Regiment of Artillery, who had taken command of Fort Mackinac in 1852.

Thomas Williams hailed from Detroit, and he had graduated twelfth in his class at West Point in 1837, later seeing extensive service in Florida and Mexico.[89] Williams demonstrated fair skill as a draftsman (see Figs. 8.19, 8.21, 8.22, and 8.24), and he occasionally illustrated letters to his wife with rough sketches (see Fig. 8.23). It is possible that Williams, who was interested in Mackinac Island and had married a local woman, also provided all or part of the text that supports the four images. The article identifies the 4th Artillery as the unit occupying Fort Mackinac and describes the earlier services and death of the "celebrated" Captain Martin Scott. Both passages suggest that a military man provided the text as well as the pictures.

Although not the best views of Mackinac Island to be produced during the 1850s, the engravings that appeared in *Ballou's* add to the body of pre-photographic visual information about the place, and the text provides details specific to the pictures themselves. The first (Fig. 8.15) depicts the "quaint old French town, with its overhanging fortress." A comparison with the same scene captured by Francis Cayley in the early 1840s (Fig. 7.8) will show that the *Ballou's* artist greatly simplified and distorted his composition. Fort Mackinac is rendered with fair accuracy. The town is another matter entirely, and little reliance may be placed on this representation of its appearance. The most useful information from the text is that the small house at extreme left—"a little out of place," the writer admitted—was said to have been moved from Old Michilimackinac. "It was built originally of small logs or poles, and subsequently covered with clapboards," he noted, adding that the building was "almost a ruin."[90] This edifice, described by James J. Strang as a "rotten old building," was pointed out to visitors as "the first house erected on the island." It was occupied in 1854 as "a tippling shop."[91]

The wharf that juts prominently into the foreground is also significant. Although its appearance has no doubt been simplified (Mackinac's docks were never free of fish barrels, firewood, or freight), this is the pier constructed by William Wendell as early as 1852. It is seen here before the owner was allowed to extend the structure in 1856.[92] A house that stood at the foot of this dock for many years has not yet been constructed—or the artist omitted it. A cluster of wigwams is visible on the spot where, Major Williams told his wife in November 1854, the Indians had erected their "rude,

VIEW OF THE TOWN OF MACKINAW.

Bayard Taylor (1825–78) visited Mackinac Island early in the season of 1855. His published remarks provide a rare glimpse of the place in the springtime, and Taylor was the first to describe trillium blossoming in the woods. His portrait is from *The Knickerbocker Gallery* and was published in the year of his visit to Mackinac. *Clements Library, University of Michigan.*

FIGURE 8.15

TITLE: View of the Town of Mackinaw.

AUTHOR: An officer of the U.S. Army, probably Major Thomas Williams, 4th Regiment of Artillery (1815–62).

DATE DEPICTED: 1854?

DATE OF WORK: May 5, 1855.

DESCRIPTION: 16 x 24 cm. Lithograph.

PROVENANCE: Based on a sketch made "upon the spot" by an unnamed U.S. officer. Published in the May 5, 1855, issue of *Ballou's Pictorial Drawing-Room Companion*, 280, with an article titled "Mackinaw and Its Scenery." Later copied for use in Benson J. Lossing, *The Pictorial Field Book of the War of 1812* (New York, 1869), 269.

COLLECTION: Clements Library, University of Michigan, Ann Arbor.

FIGURE 8.16

TITLE: Arch Rock, Mackinaw.

AUTHOR: An officer of the U.S. Army, probably Major Thomas Williams, 4th Regiment of Artillery (1815–62).

DATE DEPICTED: 1854?

DATE OF WORK: May 5, 1855.

DESCRIPTION: 18.5 x 15 cm. Lithograph.

PROVENANCE: Based on a sketch made "upon the spot" by an unnamed U.S. officer. Published in the May 5, 1855, issue of *Ballou's Pictorial Drawing-Room Companion*, 280, with an article titled "Mackinaw and Its Scenery." Later copied for use in Benson J. Lossing, *The Pictorial Field Book of the War of 1812* (New York, 1869), 268.

COLLECTION: Clements Library, University of Michigan, Ann Arbor.

FIGURE 8.17

TITLE: Arch Rock.—Second View.

AUTHOR: An officer of the U.S. Army, probably Major Thomas Williams, 4th Regiment of Artillery (1815–62).

DATE DEPICTED: 1854?

DATE OF WORK: May 5, 1855.

DESCRIPTION: 17 x 13.5 cm. Lithograph.

PROVENANCE: Based on a sketch made "upon the spot" by an unnamed U.S. officer. Published in the May 5, 1855, issue of *Ballou's Pictorial Drawing-Room Companion*, 281, with an article titled "Mackinaw and Its Scenery."

COLLECTION: Clements Library, University of Michigan, Ann Arbor.

THE SUGAR LOAF, OR PYRAMID ROCK.

FIGURE 8.18

TITLE: The Sugar Loaf, or Pyramid Rock.
AUTHOR: An officer of the U.S. Army, probably Major Thomas Williams, 4th Regiment of Artillery (1815–62).
DATE DEPICTED: 1854?
DATE OF WORK: May 5, 1855.
DESCRIPTION: 17 x 13.5 cm. Lithograph.
PROVENANCE: Based on a sketch made "upon the spot" by an unnamed U.S. officer. Published in the May 5, 1855, issue of *Ballou's Pictorial Drawing-Room Companion*, 281, with an article titled "Mackinaw and Its Scenery."
COLLECTION: Clements Library, University of Michigan, Ann Arbor.

open, mat tents, in a row along the beach from the wharf at Wendell's, in front of our Garden, to beyond Mrs. Abott's."[93]

Figure 8.16 presents a respectable view of Arch Rock as seen from above, enlivened by one of the many daredevils who regularly crossed the narrow span. Three other figures make their way down the perilous trail to the water's edge, while a small sloop passes by, possibly bearing tourists hoping to get a look from the lake. The author of the article asserted that Arch Rock was "second only to the Natural Bridge in Virginia" and towered one hundred feet above the

water, buttressed by the native rock on each side. The top of the arch was about forty feet above the steep slope directly below.[94] Bayard Taylor agreed with this estimate of the height of the "rude natural portal." He attempted a crossing in the spring of 1855 but could get only as far as the "keystone" before the "loose and disintegrating" condition of the stone caused him to reconsider his actions and beat a hasty retreat.[95]

"The view from the water is quite as curious and more novel than that from the land," the author of the *Ballou's* article continued. The second impression of Arch Rock is from that perspective (Fig. 8.17) and is much more romanticized than the one from the top of the bluff. Perhaps this was because of the difficulty of obtaining a view through the arch because of the surrounding rock falls and tumbled trees, exaggerated in the view. "It is necessary to draw your boat very nigh to the shore in order to see the light of the sky beyond and beneath the arch," the author offered by way of explanation. The artist must have done just that in order to complete his sketch.

The depiction of Sugar Loaf (Fig. 8.18) is the most amateurish of the series, featuring an out-of-proportion couple gazing at the craggy rock with a few stunted cedars growing from its crevasses. They stand directly below Keyhole Cave, one of the "tall, shallow caves, resembling niches" that occur on that side of the rock. These openings, speculated the author, might once have been "receptacles for sacrifices and offerings," perhaps recalling local stories that human bones had once been found in the caves of Sugar Loaf as they were at Skull Cave. The *Ballou's* author, however, debunked the belief that the "little green mounds" seen in the foreground were the graves of slaughtered war captives. These were found all over the island, he reported, and a few other visitors mention them. They were dismissed as "nothing more than the inequalities often noticed on the surface of limestone countries."[96] Usually known today as "tip-overs," the hummocks are created by the uprooting of trees and the subsequent decomposition of stumps and trunks.

The presence of tip-overs suggests that the forests of Mackinac Island had, by 1854, finally regenerated to the point where they were more than just low scrub. The *Ballou's* author reported that "here, there, and everywhere, tower the tufted crowns of spruce trees," while Bayard Taylor described birch and cedar with trilliums and anemones blooming on the springtime forest floor. The woods were "filled with flirtation walks and lover's lanes," and, the *Ballou's* correspondent wrote, "the shady paths of Mackinaw are not to be ignorantly sneered at." Many other sights were to be seen. "This island indeed is invested with interest," he added, listing rock formations such as Lover's Leap, "Devil's Chimney" (Chimney Rock), Devil's Kitchen ("a Plutonic cave"), and the "Giant's Causeway" (Giant's Stairway near Arch Rock). Mackinac had arrived as a true place of resort. "It sits upon the green waters as a gem," the writer concluded, "reflecting the brightest light in the history of the Northwest."[97]

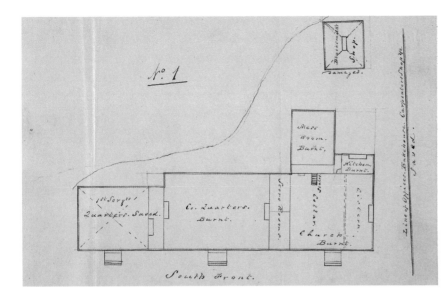

FIGURE 8.19
TITLE: No. 1 [Buildings destroyed by fire on January 3].
AUTHOR: Major Thomas Williams, 4th Regiment of Artillery (1815–62).
DATE DEPICTED: January 3, 1855.
DATE OF WORK: January 29, 1855.
DESCRIPTION: 12.5 x 19.5 cm. Pen and ink on paper.
PROVENANCE: Enclosed with letter of this date from Williams to Major General Thomas S. Jesup. Retained in the records of the Office of the Quartermaster General.
COLLECTION: National Archives and Records Administration, Washington, DC (RG 92, Records of the Office of the Quartermaster General, Consolidated Correspondence File, Fort Mackinac, Michigan, 1819–90). Found in Box 594.

FIGURE 8.20
TITLE: Gateway to Ft. Mackinaw 1854.
AUTHOR: Alfred R. Waud (1828–91).
DATE DEPICTED: 1854.
DATE OF WORK: 1854.
DESCRIPTION: 21.2 x 15 cm. Pencil and ink wash on paper.
PROVENANCE: Part of a Waud sketchbook or portfolio. Acquired by the Historic New Orleans Collection in 1977.
COLLECTION: Historic New Orleans Collection (1977.137.38.12).

There's fire in the garrison, Major!

Sergeant David R. Morrison

Major Thomas Williams was fast asleep in the early hours of January 3, 1855. At first, he only dimly perceived "loud knocking" on the door to his apartment in the officers' stone quarters. It was 3:30 as he stumbled from his bed and into the chilly corridor leading to the front of the building. There stood David Morrison, sergeant of the guard. "There's fire in the garrison, Major!" Morrison blurted out as soon as the captain opened the door. "Where?" Williams asked. "In the chapel," the sergeant replied. The major dressed hastily and then crossed the snow-covered parade ground to the one-story wooden barracks on its opposite side. There he found the room used as a chapel "filled with a dense smoke, blinding & stifling" from a fire raging in the cellar beneath his feet.

Fire was the worst peacetime nightmare for anyone in Fort Mackinac because fighting a blaze required large quantities of water, a commodity that was always hard to come by atop the bluff, particularly in winter. Fortunately, the garrison was better prepared than it had ever been, thanks to a system of cisterns and water catchments installed in the larger buildings in 1853.[98] The post had a fire engine as well, and this was quickly rigged as a bucket brigade of soldiers formed to fill its tanks. Flames and smoke barred the way to the water beneath the chapel, but the men had access to the cistern below the noncommissioned officers' quarters in the opposite end of the building. When that had been emptied, the line re-formed to move water from the cisterns in the officers' stone quarters and then, in succession, from those in the hospital and the "Hill House" overlooking the parade ground. The well outside the north sally port was still functional, and it was tapped in desperation, while the garrison horses, "assisted by all the drays & wagons to be had in town," hauled water up the steep road from the lake below.

For awhile the prospect of controlling the blaze was "flattering." Then hope faded, only to be regained. For six hours soldiers and citizen volunteers fought the fire "with alternate hope & despair" until, at 9:30, "the flames burst thro' the roof of the chapel & men's quarters in many places at once, & thro' the clapboards of the east end of the building." Half an hour later, the entire structure, aside from an extension on its western end used as quarters for a married sergeant and his family, had burned to the ground. The firefighters had at least saved part of the building and also, through great exertion, the nearby blacksmith shop, a row of shops and offices to the east of the barracks, and, most important, the powder magazine. Indeed, Williams had feared at one point that the whole fort would burn, stockades and all. He was proud that his troops had "worked like old firemen; no hurry, no panic," and that the townspeople had turned out to help. By 3:00 in the afternoon the major could pause to

write his wife. "We all rejoice at our escape & are delighted our misfortune was not greater," he told her. From the windows of his quarters, Williams could see "the naked foundations & the four huge chimneys standing alone like so many wizard sentinels guarding the solitude & desolation around them."[99]

The major was hardly in despair, and he had already taken the steps necessary to deal with the disaster. Even as he wrote, his tired soldiers were cleaning up the ruins, and Williams cheerfully told his wife that "in a few days we shall look pretty decent again." The men would be quartered for the winter in four unused rooms and offices. Williams had already ordered a board of garrison officers to investigate the cause of the fire. It met later that day, and, on January 4, the commandant enclosed its findings with his own report to Quartermaster General Jesup. As Williams had already speculated to his wife, the board found spontaneous combustion to be the cause. Vegetables had been stored in the cellar below the chapel, protected by straw previously used to bed down the post horses.[100] A few of the vegetables were recovered, most of them well cooked. The roasted potatoes were distributed to the indigent of the town who had helped fight the fire.[101]

Over the next three weeks Major Williams prepared floor plans and drawings to illustrate what had been lost and how he proposed to provide replacement quarters for his men.[102] The old barracks had been constructed in 1828 as part of Major Alexander Thompson's renovation of Fort Mackinac. Williams drew a floor plan of the building (Fig. 8.19), thus preserving a record of how it had been utilized by his garrison. The plan corresponds closely to the appearance of the barracks in Private Brenschutz's bird's-eye view of 1845 (Fig. 7.21, 10–11). The structure had enclosed two large rooms, each intended to accommodate a company of soldiers, as well as additions for the first sergeant's quarters, a kitchen, and a mess room for the men. Also shown in this plan is the nearby blacksmith shop, which was damaged, and the west wall of the line of shops and offices depicted in the Brenschutz view. Alfred R. Waud had captured an image of the blacksmith shop and nearby north sally port the year before the fire in an exceedingly rare view made within the walls of Fort Mackinac (Fig. 8.20).

One detail that stands out on Williams's floor plan is the identification of the east barracks room as a "Church." The space had been used for that purpose ever since Reverend John O'Brien's appointment as garrison chaplain in 1842.[103] Both army and civilian personnel were accommodated in this makeshift chapel each Sunday by moving the bunks aside, and many Mackinac visitors described the experience. Reverend James Beaven, himself an Episcopalian

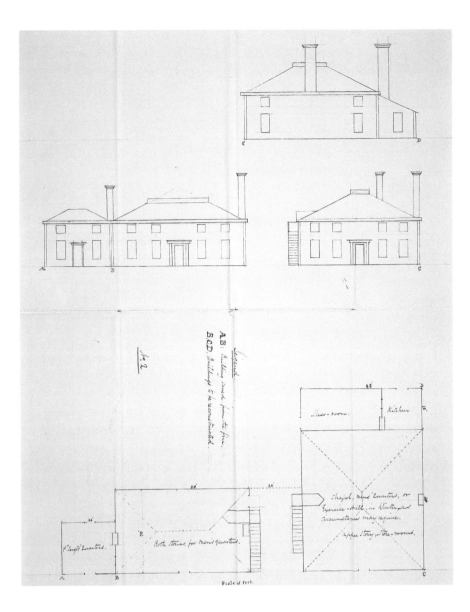

FIGURE 8.21

TITLE: No. 2 [Plan for the construction of public buildings at Fort Mackinac].

AUTHOR: Major Thomas Williams, 4th Regiment of Artillery (1815–62).

DATE DEPICTED: January 29, 1855, proposal.

DATE OF WORK: January 29, 1855.

DESCRIPTION: 39.8 x 31.5 cm. Pen and ink on paper.

PROVENANCE: Enclosed with letter of this date from Williams to Major General Thomas S. Jesup. Retained in the records of the Office of the Quartermaster General.

COLLECTION: National Archives and Records Administration, Washington, DC (RG 92, Records of the Office of the Quartermaster General, Consolidated Correspondence File, Fort Mackinac, Michigan, 1819–90). Found in Box 594.

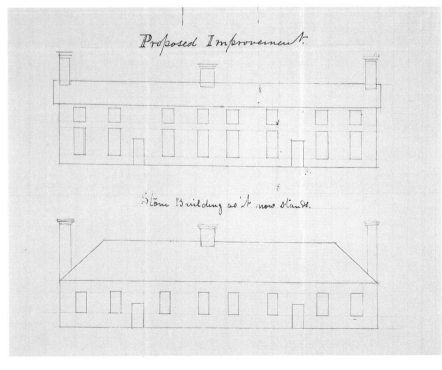

FIGURE 8.22

TITLE: Proposed Improvements. Stone Building as it now stands.

AUTHOR: Major Thomas Williams, 4th Regiment of Artillery (1815–62).

DATE DEPICTED: July 1855.

DATE OF WORK: July 1855.

DESCRIPTION: 19.6 x 25 cm. Pen and ink on paper, with buildings drawn in red ink.

PROVENANCE: Drawn into the text of "Report of the Condition of public quarters at Fort Mackinac, Mich: and of Repairs and additions for the same," July 1855, by T. Williams, Capt. 4th Artillery Commanding, Fort Mackinac. Retained in the records of the Office of the Quartermaster General.

COLLECTION: National Archives and Records Administration, Washington, DC (RG 92, Records of the Office of the Quartermaster General, Consolidated Correspondence File, Fort Mackinac, Michigan, 1819–90). Found in Box 594.

priest, participated in one of O'Brien's services in August 1844. He noted that it was conducted in "one of the large wards occupied by the men," and he thought it odd to be in a church with soldiers' "beds all rolled up along one side, and their accoutrements suspended all along the other side of the apartment."[104] Ten years later, Quaker Aaron Bellangee found it disconcerting to attend a religious service in such martial surroundings.[105]

Along with the floor plan of the lost building, Williams forwarded his proposal for its replacement (Fig. 8.21). Here the visual documentation becomes problematic, for it is not known how closely this design was followed when the men's quarters were rebuilt during the summer of 1855. Williams proposed a pair of two-story buildings, probably for the purpose of separating the two companies of troops that were sometimes assigned to Fort Mackinac. The left-hand structure utilizes much of the footprint of the burned barracks, incorporating the surviving sergeants' quarters but raising its roof to match the new construction. The right-hand building is substantially deeper than its predecessor, but it includes a replacement "Chapel," which could also serve as quarters and as a drill hall for the troops during the winter. Both of the new barracks incorporate exterior stairways allowing access to rooms on the second floor.

Were the new quarters constructed in this manner? It does not appear that they were, although the style of roof and facade might have been much as designed by Major Williams. A report of July 1855 implies that only a single building was then under construction, and it was to be a story and one-half in height.[106] Following the destruction of this new barracks, in 1858, it was described as having been "a large wooden building about 100 feet long and two stories high."[107] A report from May 1857 adds only that it had been "badly planned and poorly

constructed."[108] A fifteen-thousand-gallon cistern was installed on the hill behind it to improve fire protection and provide water to the soldiers' kitchen and washrooms through a system of pipes.[109] Little more is known, for the new barracks was not pictured before it burned.

By the summer of 1855, with work underway on new barracks, Major Williams was in a mood to suggest further improvements, this time to the elderly officers' quarters of Fort Mackinac. Three buildings were then used for that purpose. The newest (the "Hill House") had been constructed in 1835 and required only a few repairs. The stone and wooden quarters overlooking the town were much older, however, dating to 1798 and 1816, respectively. Both were in poor condition, and the latter building was "very much out of repair" and generally worn out. Williams, who seems to have had a liking for half stories, suggested that the walls of the two officers' quarters could be raised to provide additional space and, with new roofs and other repairs, would be much more comfortable for their occupants. To illustrate his proposal, he sketched existing and proposed facades for each building and floor plans for the wooden quarters showing its room arrangement "as it is now" and as he proposed to alter it (Figs. 8.22 and 8.24).[110]

Major Williams had his own apartment in the stone quarters, where he occupied the eastern half of the building. He had commanded Fort Mackinac since 1852, and since arriving on the island had met and wed Mary Neosho Bailey, the daughter of an island businessman. In the autumn of 1854 Williams escorted his pregnant wife, whose pet name was "Maddie," to Fort Hamilton, New York, where she could await the birth of their first child in more comfortable surroundings. Williams then returned to Fort Mackinac, where he wrote to Maddie almost daily through the winter. One letter,

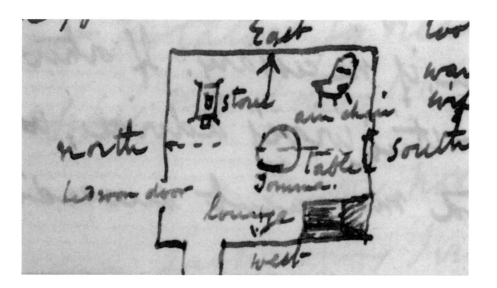

FIGURE 8.23
TITLE: [Plan of Major Williams's quarters].
AUTHOR: Major Thomas Williams, 4th Regiment of Artillery (1815–62).
DATE DEPICTED: November 22, 1854.
DATE OF WORK: November 22, 1854.
DESCRIPTION: 2.8 x 3.5 cm. Pen and ink on paper.
PROVENANCE: Drawn into body of letter from Williams to his wife, Mary Williams, dated November 22, 1854. Retained with the Williams Family Papers.
COLLECTION: Burton Historical Collection, Detroit Public Library (Williams Family Papers).

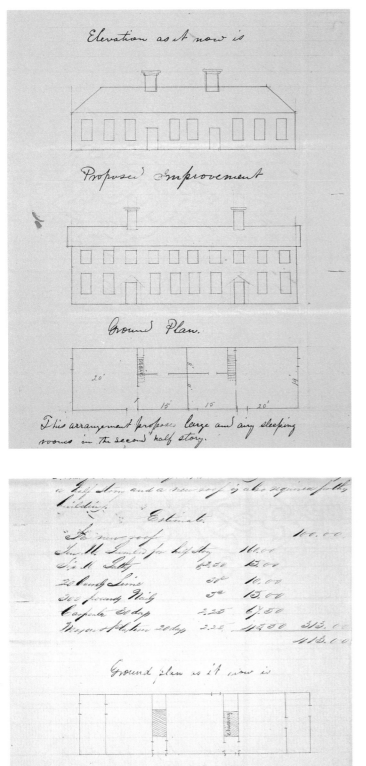

FIGURE 8.24

TITLE: Ground plan as it now is. Elevation as it now is. Proposed Improvement. Ground Plan.

AUTHOR: Major Thomas Williams, 4th Regiment of Artillery (1815–62).

DATE DEPICTED: July 1855.

DATE OF WORK: July 1855.

DESCRIPTION: Ground plan as it is: 7 x 19.5 cm.; other three together: 25 x 19.5 cm. Pen and ink on paper, with buildings drawn in red ink.

PROVENANCE: Drawn into the text of "Report of the Condition of public quarters at Fort Mackinac, Mich: and of Repairs and additions for the same," July 1855, by T. Williams, Capt. 4th Artillery Commanding, Fort Mackinac. Retained in the records of the Office of the Quartermaster General.

COLLECTION: National Archives and Records Administration, Washington, DC (RG 92, Records of the Office of the Quartermaster General, Consolidated Correspondence File, Fort Mackinac, Michigan, 1819–90). Found in Box 594.

drafted on November 22, included a tiny sketch (Fig. 8.23) in which the lonesome major showed how he had rearranged the southeast chamber of their quarters to provide his own Spartan dressing room. It included only a stove, a table, a lounge, and a large chair that had belonged to Williams's recently deceased father. The south window, he told her, opened toward Round Island, and from the table he could look to the east "towards his Maddie."[111] The stove, he later told her, had been moved from the hall and its efficiency had been greatly improved by shortening the length of pipe connecting it to the chimney. "The water hasn't frozen once in my dressing room," he wrote in February. "I wash there in comfort."[112] His crude little sketch is the only pre-photographic depiction of an officer's room in Fort Mackinac.

The alterations proposed to the stone and wooden officers' quarters by Major Williams were quietly ignored by the Quartermaster General's Department. Like the crumbling walls of Fort Mackinac, the buildings would be maintained only to the degree necessary to accommodate a garrison in relative comfort. Williams and his men of the 4th Artillery moved to a new posting in October 1856, and the fort would stand empty through the winter.[113] Fresh garrisons would arrive thereafter, and new buildings would be constructed as needed, but the historic early officers' quarters escaped attempts to modernize them and survived in much their original form until the U.S. Army was finally done with Fort Mackinac in 1895.

The Public lands . . . had never been clearly defined

Captain George G. Meade

Fort Mackinac's commandants had myriad responsibilities. Chief among them, of course, was the defense of the post. As the War of 1812 faded into memory and the fort into obsolescence, however, concerns of a more mundane nature increasingly dominated their attention. The garrison had to be provided with food, water, and fuel; crumbling walls and buildings had to be maintained and repaired; soldiers had to be exercised and disciplined; relations had to be kept up with local residents and Native Americans; prominent visitors had to be entertained and treated with courtesy; and paperwork of all sorts was required by army departments. Of all these tasks, however, probably none proved so onerous as keeping watch over the "public lands" appertaining to Fort Mackinac.

The limited area of Mackinac Island was, and remains today, the primary cause of contention between public and private interests. When U.S. forces occupied Fort Mackinac in 1796, the government inherited boundaries laid down during fifteen years of British occupation. These included a military reserve, generally accepted to include the north and east half of the island, and large parcels on the southwestern half that had not yet been granted for private use (Fig. 3.7). Additional land was confirmed to private ownership in the 1820s (Fig. 5.25). Aaron Greeley mapped these boundaries in 1810 and John Mullett in 1828. Nearby Bois Blanc Island was also largely federal land, sprinkled with a few private claims. It was mapped by Lucius Lyon in 1827, with roughly half its area set aside as a firewood reserve for the Fort Mackinac garrison (Fig. 5.23).

These surveys, and the maps that documented them, would seem to have defined the public land in the Straits area. In fact, it was not that easy, and exceptions, both official and unofficial, clouded the situation. Reverend William Ferry was allowed the use of public land for his mission school (Fig. 5.18), and the buildings were leased to private individuals after his establishment closed in 1837. The federal government granted land near the village on the south shore of the island to the Borough of Michilimackinac about 1832 for "public purposes." This "vacant lot" (today usually known as the "Borough Lot") later became a dumping ground for fish offal and the site of a squatters' village.[114] And then there were the constant, niggling requests from citizens for the use of public land and outright encroachments by those who did not bother to ask. In the spring of 1830 Lieutenant Colonel Enos Cutler informed the adjutant general that he had refused all requests for the use of government land but that John A. Drew was about to enclose a "large field" of it. Cutler wished to stop him, but, he pointed out, the War Department had already overlooked similar encroachments. If the commanding officer was not authorized to prevent trespasses, Cutler warned, "the

Government will soon find itself without a foot of land on this Island beyond the limits of the Fort."[115] In response, Washington officials cited the 1828 Mullett survey as defining the boundaries between public and private lands.[116]

Copies of surveys had been deposited at Fort Mackinac, but the transient nature of garrison administrations ensured that such documentation was easily misplaced. In May 1843 Lieutenant Henry Whiting feared losing four fields of government land, cultivated for "several years by citizens." He lacked the evidence needed to expel the trespassers, however. "No plot of the Military reservation . . . is at this post," Whiting wrote in frustration.[117] Eight years later, Major Charles Larnard inquired whether the military reserve included all the publicly owned land on the island or if it had defined limits. "There is nothing to find on record here by which any limit or boundary is fixed," he complained.[118] "The Public lands on the island of Mackinac . . . had never been clearly defined in their limits," explained Captain George G. Meade six years later.[119]

The frequency of disputes only increased as the island became more "settled and covered with private claimants." Continued appeals to the War Department finally resulted in action. In 1855 the Bureau of Topographical Engineers was charged with surveying and marking the public lands on Mackinac Island.[120] The talent to undertake this work was readily available, as engineers of the U.S. Lake Survey had been at work at the Straits of Mackinac since 1849, with offices in the Indian Dormitory during at least part of that time. By 1855 they had completed topographical maps of Mackinac Island, Round Island, and the adjacent mainland.[121] In May 1855 the Topographical Bureau assigned the Mackinac survey to Captain John Navarre Macomb, then commanding the Lake Survey crew at the Straits.[122] Figure 8.25 illustrates the results of his work.

Macomb had plenty of current topographical data on Mackinac Island. To assist him in defining boundaries, the General Land Office in Washington provided "copies of the record of the original survey"— John Mullett's 1828 work (Fig. 5.25). The Lake Survey crew ran the necessary lines, apparently in the fall of 1855, and "connected" the boundaries to their own detailed topographical work. The season ended, however, before Macomb could arrange to have permanent markers manufactured and installed.[123] A finished plan was completed during the winter and submitted to the Topographical Bureau on April 3, 1856.[124] This map and at least three other manuscript copies are preserved today in the National Archives and are described in appendix A. Figure 8.25 is the earliest duplicate of the original, completed on June 18, 1857. It has been used here because its color is more sharply defined than that of the original.

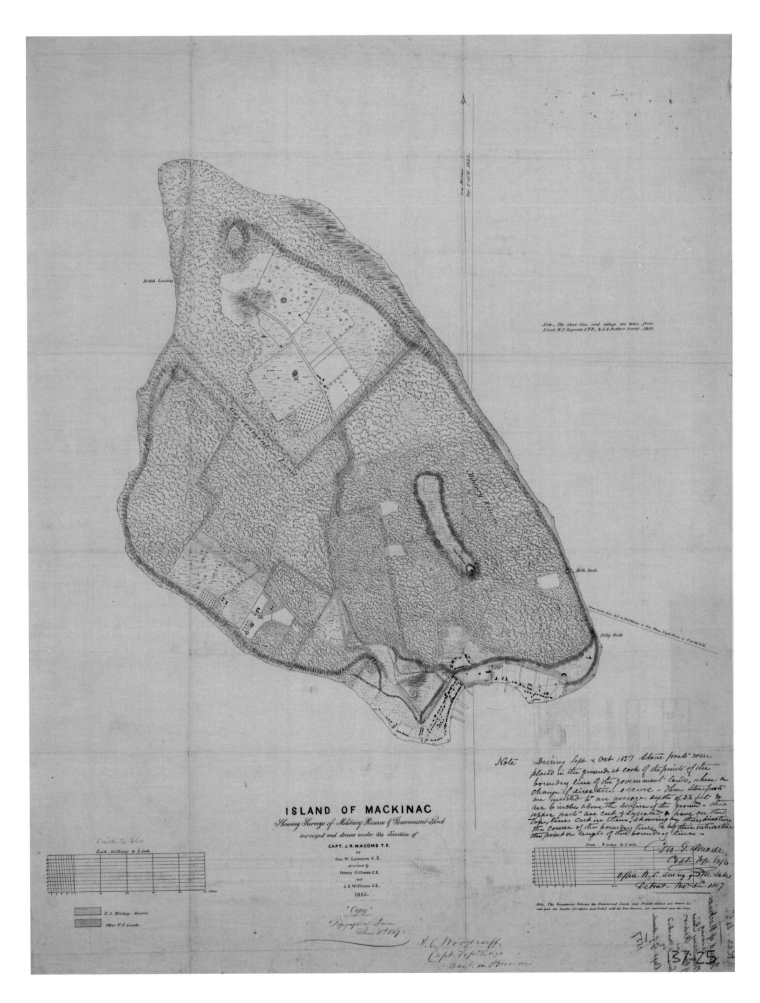

ISLAND OF MACKINAC

Showing Surveys of Military Reserve & Government Land

surveyed and drawn under the direction of

CAPT. J. N. MACOMB T.E.

BY

Geo. W. Lamson C.E.

Assisted by

Henry Gillman C.E.

and

J. B. Williams C.E.

1855.

"Copy"

Captain John Navarre Macomb's careful survey of Mackinac Island was done with such precision that individual buildings can be identified. This detail of the town, from Figure 8.25, also shows the wharves and uses crosses to mark the old Catholic cemetery at the corner of Hoban and Market streets and the still active Protestant cemetery near Mission Church.

The Macomb map identifies government lands by color, with the "military reserve" (northeast of Garrison Road) outlined in orange to distinguish it from the "other lands," which are shown in green. Ultimately, both areas would be consolidated in 1875 to form Mackinac National Park. The land around the Mission House is shown as federal property, but the "Borough Lot" is not. Topography, vegetation, roads, and buildings, including five substantial wharves, are rendered in sparkling detail based on surveys conducted in 1852.[125] The major buildings of town can be easily identified, and Fort Mackinac appears as it did before the January 1855 fire. While the land side of Main Street is built up, no structures yet encroach on the beach aside from one or two at the foots of the wharves. William Wendell's new pier is shown below Fort Mackinac. It appears to have been completed as early as 1852.

The public lands having been surveyed, it only remained to mark them. This could not be accomplished in 1855, but in June 1856 the adjutant general ordered Major Thomas Williams to organize the project. A letter from Captain Macomb a month later provided specifications for stone markers, which, Macomb believed, could be made in Detroit at a cost of one dollar each. These were to be three-foot-long, six-inch-square limestone posts, six inches of which were to project above ground level. Their flat tops were to be inscribed with the directions of the boundary lines, and one of the lateral faces was to be emblazoned with the initials "U.S." Williams dashed off a letter with a rough sketch to enlighten the adjutant general. It is illustrated here as Figure 8.26.[126]

Alas, the task was to prove more complicated than expected. On July 29 Major Williams sent another sketch to S. P. Brady of Detroit requesting an estimate for the delivery of forty-two posts and delivery if they could be provided for one dollar each. Brady replied with the disappointing news that the cost would far exceed

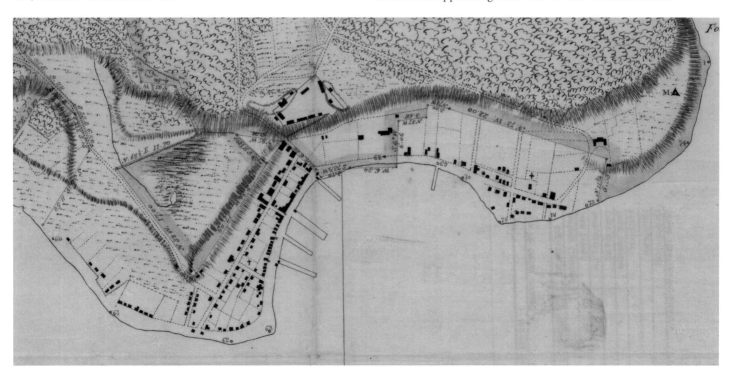

Macomb's estimate. Since only one hundred dollars had been budgeted, Williams decided that a contract would "have to wait" further authorization.[127] The matter had not been resolved by the time Williams evacuated Fort Mackinac in October, and the post stood empty that winter. When Captain Arnold Elzey arrived with a new garrison in May 1857, he was at first occupied with repairs to Fort Mackinac. Then, in July, he received the unwelcome news that he was also expected to install the boundary markers.[128] Elzey made it clear that he could not undertake this task without neglecting his other duties, that the cost would be much more than estimated, and that he did not feel capable of locating the temporary wooden pins placed by the surveyors in 1855. He requested relief from this assignment, and, the next day, threw the responsibility back on the Topographical Bureau.[129]

Elzey's argument was accepted, and, in August, Captain George G. Meade was given funds to obtain and install the monuments. Meade detached George W. Lamson to supervise the work, which he accomplished by October 15, 1857. Lamson had worked on the original survey under Macomb and easily found the points at which the stone markers were to be set. He prepared a final report and a map, which were submitted to the Topographical Bureau.[130] Meade added a handwritten notation to Figure 8.25 describing the markers and reporting their installation in September and October 1857.[131]

Amid the rich detail shown on the Macomb map are the four cemeteries in use on Mackinac Island in the 1850s. Each is identified by the simple figure of a cross, with a headstone further distinguishing the new Catholic cemetery on Garrison Road. The original Ste. Anne's graveyard may be seen at the junction of Market and Hoban streets near the southwestern end of the town. It was ordered closed in December 1851 and was soon replaced by the current burying ground opposite the Fort Mackinac Post Cemetery, not far from Skull Cave.[132] In August 1852 Juliette Starr Dana visited this "new" cemetery, and noted that few burials had yet been made there. She could see only one stone in the nearby military burying ground.[133] When the remains of Charlotte O'Brien, wife of Fort Mackinac's chaplain, were interred in the post cemetery in March 1855, her coffin bore a silver memorial plate. Captain Thomas Williams sketched it in a letter to his wife (Fig. 8.27).[134]

Mackinac's fourth cemetery may be found near Mission Church at the northeastern end of town. The Presbyterian congregation had established this graveyard, probably in the late 1820s as tensions increased between the Protestant and Catholic communities. It was still in use in 1855 but was ordered closed as a public nuisance in October 1856.[135] The current Protestant cemetery on Garrison Road was established soon after.

The Macomb map provides a fine sense of the dramatic topography of Mackinac Island, a feature also captured in a watercolor by British traveler Sir Daniel Wilson in July 1855 (Fig. 8.28). The island's heights, viewed from the east, are delicately outlined by the light of a setting sun. A flag marks Fort Mackinac, with, as Bayard Taylor wrote in the spring of the same year, "the wooded centre of the Island rising in the rear and the precipitous cliffs of gray rock flanking it on both sides." "The appearance of the place," he assured his readers, "is very picturesque."[136]

FIGURE 8.26
TITLE: [Sketch of a boundary marker for the Military Reserve].
AUTHOR: Major Thomas Williams, 4th Regiment of Artillery (1815–62).
DATE DEPICTED: 1856 proposal.
DATE OF WORK: July 28, 1856.
DESCRIPTION: 3 x 1.5 cm. Pen and ink on paper.
PROVENANCE: Drawn into text of letter from Williams to Colonel Samuel Cooper, July 28, 1856. Letter retained in post letterbook of 1855–66. This was eventually acquired by the Bentley Historical Library.
COLLECTION: Bentley Historical Library, University of Michigan, Ann Arbor (Fort Mackinac Letterbook, 1855–66, 851251 CA.5c, p. 21).

FIGURE 8.27
TITLE: [Sketch of a silver plate affixed to the coffin of Charlotte O'Brien].
AUTHOR: Major Thomas Williams, 4th Regiment of Artillery (1815–62).
DATE DEPICTED: March 19, 1855.
DATE OF WORK: March 19, 1855.
DESCRIPTION: 4.8 x 5.5 cm. Pen and ink on paper.
PROVENANCE: Drawn into body of a letter from Williams to his wife, Mary Williams, dated March 19, 1855. Retained with the Williams Family Papers.
COLLECTION: Burton Historical Collection, Detroit Public Library (Williams Family Papers).

FIGURE 8.28

TITLE: Island of Mackinaw, Lake Huron, July 25th, 1855.
AUTHOR: Sir Daniel Wilson (1816–92).
DATE DEPICTED: July 25, 1855.
DATE OF WORK: July 25, 1855.
DESCRIPTION: 15.7 x 23.3 cm. Watercolor over pencil on paper.
PROVENANCE: Retained in the Wilson family. Acquired by Library and Archives Canada as part of a collection of 185 watercolors from Wilson's descendants in Perthshire, Scotland, through the niece of the creator.
COLLECTION: Library and Archives Canada, Ottawa, ON, Eaton Foundation Collection (1995-213-2).

The village of Mackinaw is a clean place, consisting nearly altogether of white frame houses

Dr. Robert H. Cummins

When Robert H. Cummins awoke before 6:00 on the morning of August 26, 1855, he found that his steamer had arrived at Mackinac Island. After dressing, Cummins went on deck for a look around the harbor. "The first object that greets the sight is the battlements of the Fort above us," he wrote. This was a satisfying discovery for someone who had been looking forward to visiting a place "so famed in the annals of war." Around him was the bustle of the wharves, surrounded by steamers, fishing boats, and canoes. On shore he could see the town, "consisting nearly altogether of white frame houses." Otherwise, Cummins found "nothing remarkable about it." His few hours on the island were spent in the usual rush of sightseeing, from the observatory at Fort Holmes to Arch Rock, Sugar Loaf, and the fort. Then, like so many day tourists of the mid-nineteenth century, Cummins boarded his vessel for the voyage to Detroit.[137]

Something of Cummins's impression of the village may be shared by studying a detailed group of lithographs that appeared in the September 20, 1856, issue of *Frank Leslie's Illustrated Newspaper.* Included here as Figures 8.29, 8.31, and 8.32, these show the built-up area around Haldimand Bay with a realism that was rare until photography became common during the next decade. These images document the Village of Mackinac as it was in the 1850s. They also correspond with three of the drawings made by Francis Melick Cayley ten years earlier (Figs. 7.8–7.10), inviting a comparison of how the town had changed since that time. The *Leslie's* views, based on sketches made by a talented illustrator, are complemented by a watercolor by Edwin Whitefield, a professional artist of the time (Fig. 8.30). Figures 8.29–8.32, like Cayley's work, have been arranged to provide a "walk" around the village to experience it from different perspectives.

Before embarking on a stroll, however, two questions must be addressed. When were these views made, and who were their creators? The latter question may be answered with assurance for Figure 8.30 because the artist, Edwin Whitefield, signed his work at the lower left. Although the picture is undated, it contains hints as to when it was drawn. Most useful is the name "Lake Superior House" painted on the facade of the left-hand hotel on Main Street. In May 1859, P. A. Smith announced the opening of the American House, "Formerly known as the Lake Superior House," which he had "thoroughly and comfortably fitted up."[138] Whitefield's watercolor is thus unlikely to have been painted later than the summer of 1858 or much before 1854, by which time the Lake Superior House was in operation. The artist is known to have sailed from Detroit to Chicago in July 1856, and his steamer almost certainly touched at Mackinac Island to refuel. This would have provided an opportunity to draw Figure 8.30. A trip

to Sault Ste. Marie in June 1855 is another possible source of the image.[139] Coloring notations at the upper right suggest that the artist intended the painting for future commercial use.

The *Leslie's* views are more problematic, and they lack obvious clues as to the date of their creation. They could not have been drawn later than the summer of 1856, although they might well have been done several years before that time. The engravings were published with only three paragraphs of text describing Mackinac Island in the most general terms. The absence of a more substantial article suggests that the pictures were filler and might have been engraved from older art. Architectural features in town or in the fort provide little help. The presence of Wendell's wharf in two of the scenes points to a date after 1852, but the small size of the house on it shows that it predates Whitefield's watercolor.

Nor did *Leslie's* credit the illustrator. He was talented in rendering city scenes, but so were many of the staff and freelance artists whose work appeared in the paper. The only hint is found on the starboard paddle box of the steamer depicted in Figure 8.29. In the spot where the vessel's name would have been painted is what appears to be the word "Waud." Does this suggest that Alfred R. Waud drew the scenes when he visited Mackinac Island in 1853 and 1854? Their style is consistent with the sketches he made during those trips (Figs. 8.7–8.14), although *Leslie's* was not in publication by that time. Did he later submit drawings retained in his personal archive? Or is the presence of the name on the paddle box simply an engraver's error or a coincidence? The "Ward" Line operated many of the passenger steamers that called at Mackinac during this time. Perhaps Waud was indeed the artist and succumbed to the temptation to credit himself by subtly altering the name on a Ward Line steamer. For the time being, the artist's identity remains speculative.

Whatever their origins, the three engravings and one watercolor show Mackinac during the mid-1850s. Figure 8.29 represents the scene described by Cummins on his arrival in August 1855. An Indian canoe and a trio of fishing boats dominate the foreground, while the "Waud" or "Ward" steamer is moored to one of the wharves, probably Biddle's or Dousman's. Wendell's newer pier is in the distance with another steamboat on its far side. Larger buildings have appeared on the wharves, along with heaps of a new fuel—coal. Gone is the cordwood that had once been a staple of the Mackinac economy. When Bayard Taylor's vessel stopped for five hours in the spring of 1855 it was to "take on some coal" transported to Mackinac aboard a pair of schooners.[140]

Fort Mackinac dominates the scene, of course, and the buildings of the eastern end of Main Street are visible behind the coal piles.

TOWN OF MACKINAC, ON LAKE HURON, STATE OF MICHIGAN.

FIGURE 8.29

TITLE: Town of Mackinac, on Lake Huron, State of Michigan.

AUTHOR: Unknown, but possibly Alfred R. Waud (1828–91).

DATE DEPICTED: 1853?

DATE OF WORK: September 20, 1856.

DESCRIPTION: 26.5 x 37.5 cm. Lithograph.

PROVENANCE: Published in *Frank Leslie's Illustrated Newspaper* 2 (September 20, 1856): 232. One of a group of three images accompanied by three paragraphs of commentary titled "Mackinac."

COLLECTION: Mackinac State Historic Parks, Mackinac Island, MI (1977.102.1).

Fort at Mackinaw. *Walls & road a dull white limestone sometimes approaching pale ochre*

FIGURE 8.30

TITLE: Fort at Mackinaw.

AUTHOR: Edwin Whitefield (1816–92).

DATE DEPICTED: ca. 1856.

DATE OF WORK: ca. 1856.

DESCRIPTION: 23.5 x 33.5 cm. Watercolor over pencil on paper with notations in pencil. Signed at lower left: E. Whitefield.

PROVENANCE: Purchased from Mrs. Flora Ramsay in 1953.

COLLECTION: With permission of the Royal Ontario Museum, Toronto (953.125.4a). © Royal Ontario Museum.

Edwin Whitefield's watercolor (Fig. 8.30) presents a closer view, with Wendell's wharf prominent on the right. The proprietor's name is painted on his expanded building, which stands on the site of the Chippewa Hotel. Two of the hotels along Main Street, the Northern and the Lake Superior House, are identified on their facades. On Market Street, behind and to the right of the Lake Superior House, stand the Matthew Geary House and the former American Fur Company retail store, by this time sporting three dormers and a square "widow's walk."

A "View from the Fortifications" (Fig. 8.31) utilizes the popular outlook from the summit of Fort Hill. Not only did this spot give a dramatic prospect of Fort Mackinac, but it also provided an unobstructed look at the eastern end of Haldimand Bay. Prominent buildings there include the Island House Hotel, Ste. Anne's Church, and Mission Church. The Island House, built as the O'Malley House and known as the "Huron House" by 1854, is the darkly shaded structure below Fort Mackinac. Of the two churches, noted a newspaper correspondent of July 1860, one had been built by the Presbyterians, but "ministers of all protestant denominations" were "permitted to occupy its pulpit." Nearby was Ste. Anne's, "the little chapel of the old mother church."[141] Mission Point, which

VIEW FROM THE FORTIFICATIONS, MACKINAC, MICHIGAN.

FIGURE 8.31

TITLE: View from the Fortifications, Mackinac, Michigan.
AUTHOR: Unknown, but possibly Alfred R. Waud (1828–91).
DATE DEPICTED: 1853?
DATE OF WORK: September 20, 1856.
DESCRIPTION: 12 x 26.5 cm. Lithograph.
PROVENANCE: Published in *Frank Leslie's Illustrated Newspaper* 2 (September 20, 1856): 236. One of a group of three images accompanied by three paragraphs of general comment titled "Mackinac."
COLLECTION: Mackinac State Historic Parks, Mackinac Island, MI (1977.101.1).

TOWN AND HARBOR OF MACKINAC, MICHIGAN.

FIGURE 8.32

TITLE: Town and Harbor of Mackinac, Michigan.
AUTHOR: Unknown, but possibly Alfred R. Waud (1828–91).
DATE DEPICTED: 1853?
DATE OF WORK: September 20, 1856.
DESCRIPTION: 12 x 26.5 cm. Lithograph.
PROVENANCE: Published in *Frank Leslie's Illustrated Newspaper* 2 (September 20, 1856): 237. One of a group of three images accompanied by three paragraphs of general comment titled "Mackinac."
COLLECTION: Mackinac State Historic Parks, Mackinac Island, MI (1977.100.1).

Henry F. Ainslie had shown covered with wigwams in 1842 (Fig. 7.5), is now packed with coopers' shops and small houses. Of this change the 1860 correspondent wrote that "Indians—the remnants of a perishing race—frequent the vicinity," but their much-diminished trade was in "curiosities."[142] By 1854 most camped on the beach from the fort gardens to the dock visible in Figure 8.31.[143]

The foreground of Figure 8.31 includes a view of Fort Hill, the roadway up the bluff to the rear of Fort Mackinac. It was used by tourists who did not care to climb the ramp to the south sally port and by the army to haul supplies and ammunition to the fort. It was also the route taken by water wagons as needed, particularly to fight the January 1855 barracks fire. Island children found it a "grand sledding place" in the winter. "Flying so fast that the rider was fairly dizzy," determined youngsters could make it all the way to the frozen harbor if they could successfully avoid traffic on Main Street.[144]

The last of the *Leslie's* scenes, Figure 8.32, is perhaps the most enlightening, showing the town as seen from the East Bluff above the Island House Hotel, visible in the center foreground. The wharves correspond with the arrangement shown on the 1855 Macomb map (Fig. 8.25), but no coal piles are evident. A solid line of hotels and stores borders Main Street, and all intervening spaces have been occupied in what has now become the principal business district. The Michilimackinac County Courthouse and the buildings formerly owned by the American Fur Company are easily distinguished on Market Street. The Stuart House, in the center of the group, was by this time in operation as a hotel, usually called the Grove House.[145] In the distance and well beyond the village is a further sign of expansion. Buildings along the crest of the hill before Lake Huron mark a new neighborhood, including the squatters' houses that had sprung up on the "Borough Lot."

Other intriguing details may be coaxed from the *Leslie's* engravings. One is a large artillery piece on the beach below Fort Mackinac in Figure 8.32. It is probably the cannon used for daily exercise and target practice in the lake by Major Thomas Williams's gunners between 1852 and 1856. Williams even applied for army funds to build a floating target and requested the use of the old Indian Agency House as a storeroom for implements and munitions so his troops would not have to carry them up and down the hill from the fort. The old building, out of sight to the right of the cannon, was "easily accessible to the battery," Williams reported.[146]

Another feature of interest is the large Greek Revival–style house at the far end of Market Street, distinguished by its classical portico. It appears in the left foreground of Reinhard Wernigk's first Mackinac photograph of July 1856. The home was built, probably in the mid-1840s, by Samuel Abbott, one of Mackinac's most prominent citizens.[147] Constance Saltonstall Patton recalled it as "large and spreading" with a wing on each side. "These wings were lower than the central building, which ran up two stories and an attic" with "Grecian columns" to support the roof. Even its site was impressive. It stood on a "terrace which gradually ascended" at the head of Hoban Street, where it was visible from the harbor.[148] By the time of Abbott's death in April 1851, his house was the best on the island. It was valued, with its lot, at $3,000 with an annual tax bill of $89.59. Following Samuel's death, the property went to his brothers, and in 1852 Abbott's widow moved to another house near the Island House Hotel, probably the Greek Revival building (still extant) shown in the left foreground of Figure 8.32.[149]

Abbott's brothers resided in southern Michigan, so the house was rented thereafter. William Saltonstall and his family were the tenants in 1856 and 1857.[150] It was in this house that Mackinac's first photographer briefly lived in 1856 and the Saltonstall children enjoyed two fondly remembered summers of their childhood.[151] On the morning of July 2, 1857, however, the house "took fire and was totally consumed." The blaze began near or in a chimney, and

within a few minutes the structure was enveloped in flames. A bucket brigade from the lake at the foot of Hoban Street had little effect, and the house burned so rapidly that much of Saltonstall's furniture was destroyed. The building was a total loss. Abbott's property was not insured, and a sale of salvaged material three weeks after the fire recovered only $25.21 for the unfortunate owner.[152] The Saltonstall family was able to relocate to Mrs. Abbott's other home, "near the Island House." Such was the assistance offered by their island neighbors that, Constance later recalled, "we dined in our new house before the sun set."[153]

This pipe smoker was captured taking his ease on a piazza, probably that of the Island House Hotel, in 1859. His formal dress is typical of the tourists who came to Mackinac by steamboat in the years just before the Civil War. *Detroit Institute of Arts, Founders Society Purchase, Gibbs-Williams Fund (55.237.77). Photograph © 2005, The Detroit Institute of Arts.*

An anonymous but artistic tourist of 1859 sketched this exceedingly rare image of a working woman from Mackinac's first resort era. The artist described her as "Our Pretty Waiting Maid, Island house–Mackinau, July 1859." *Detroit Institute of Arts, Founders Society Purchase, Gibbs-Williams Fund (55.237.80). Photograph © 2005, The Detroit Institute of Arts.*

A site for a great central city in the lake region

Jacob Ferris

James J. Strang was no booster of Mackinac Island, and he bore little love for its inhabitants, many of whom were in competition over fishing grounds with his own Mormon followers on Beaver Island. By 1854 Strang was convinced that his rival community's days as an important commercial location were numbered and that the "decay of Mackinac" had begun. "Extraneous circumstances, and not natural advantages, made Mackinac," he declared. There was much truth to his argument, which Strang bolstered with a litany of setbacks suffered by the only organized municipality in the Straits area. The island lacked land for agriculture, firewood, or timber. The fur trade and the Protestant mission school had come and gone. Mackinac's fishing industry was threatened, Indian treaty payments were nearly done, and the military establishment was a shadow of its former self. The island's retail trade slowed this "progress of decay," but even that was only supported by the "convenience of docks and storehouses." Strang scoffed at efforts to turn the place into a resort and was certain that the opening of a canal at Sault Ste. Marie would divert leisure traffic to Lake Superior.[154]

The development that would bring about the final downfall of Mackinac Island, Strang predicted, was competition from new communities on the mainland. Indian land claims in northern Michigan had been extinguished in 1836, the Lower Peninsula was largely surveyed, and settlement was creeping northward. Any lingering threat from the British and Indians had disappeared. So, Strang suggested, it was more logical for new arrivals to settle at other points in the vicinity "where better land bears a less price, and the facilities of commerce are greater," and where opportunities presented themselves for "agriculture and manufactures." "There are better harbors on both shores of the Straits," Strang maintained, and he claimed that Mackinac Island had already lost its position as the sole stopping point for passing steamers.[155]

Strang's predictions of the demise of Mackinac Island were premature, but, by 1854, settlement had begun to spread across the Straits area for many of the reasons he cited. The earliest search for better agricultural and timberland had led to Bois Blanc Island and St. Ignace. Bois Blanc remained little more than a giant wood reserve, but St. Ignace was an active agricultural community by the time of the War of 1812 (Fig. 5.27). By 1838 state gazetteers recognized "Pointe St. Ignace" as a village with a church and a population of two hundred. Douglass Houghton found a small dock there in 1839 and a community of fifty families, most of them former voyageurs who farmed and fished.[156] St. Ignace received its share of Irish immigration in the 1840s, and its church, houses, and fields were landmarks noted by many Mackinac visitors.[157] By 1860, however, the place was still

considered a "mixed Canadian and Indian settlement," most notable for its farms.[158] Serious commercial growth would await the post–Civil War years and the eventual arrival of the railroad.[159]

It was a site on the Lower Peninsula mainland that would be the first to experience real industrial development, and that was already underway by the time James J. Strang published his predictions. The mouth of the Cheboygan River had long been a landmark at the southeastern extremity of the Straits of Mackinac, but it attracted little attention before the 1840s. The southern coast of the Straits offered opportunities for water-powered industry first exploited in the 1780s by Robert Campbell. He established his saw- and gristmills farther west at Mill Creek on land that was part of the military reserve of Old Michilimackinac. It was confirmed to his heirs in 1808 as Private Claim 334. The mills, owned by Michael Dousman after 1819, serviced the Mackinac Island community until at least 1839.[160] Indian title to the lands around the Cheboygan River was not extinguished until the treaty of 1836. Eight years later, in the fall of 1844, Jacob Sammons built a house at Cheboygan and was joined by other settlers the following year. Sammons was a cooper, and although fishing was an attraction, the mainland offered seemingly inexhaustible stands of timber, and the Cheboygan River provided sites for water-powered industry.[161]

The place grew in rapid, if disorganized, fashion. A water-powered sawmill was established in the winter of 1845–46 followed by a steam mill two years later. Small-scale shipbuilding commenced in 1847. By the early 1850s the place had a school and a hotel and other trappings of a growing frontier town. A post office was established in 1846 under the name "Duncan," which came to refer to the settlement on the east side of the Cheboygan River and at Duncan Bay, while "Cheboygan" was usually applied to the town on the west side of the river. In 1854 James J. Strang identified "Duncan" as one of the places that was drawing off Mackinac Island's fish trade.[162] Wood processing provided the heart of a new industry, however, and the construction of docks on Duncan Bay in 1850 and a mill complex there in 1851–53 circumvented some of the disadvantages to navigation caused by the narrow and shallow Cheboygan River. The village would be organized under the name "Cheboygan" in 1871.[163]

As St. Ignace slumbered and Cheboygan was being cut from the forest, plans were afoot for the most ambitious scheme for urban development in the area. This was to be a planned effort at the narrowest part of the Straits of Mackinac. Its location, at the tip of the Lower Peninsula, was well-known to visitors for its historical importance as the site of Old Michilimackinac, the military and fur-trading post of French and British days. In 1853 a Cincinnati

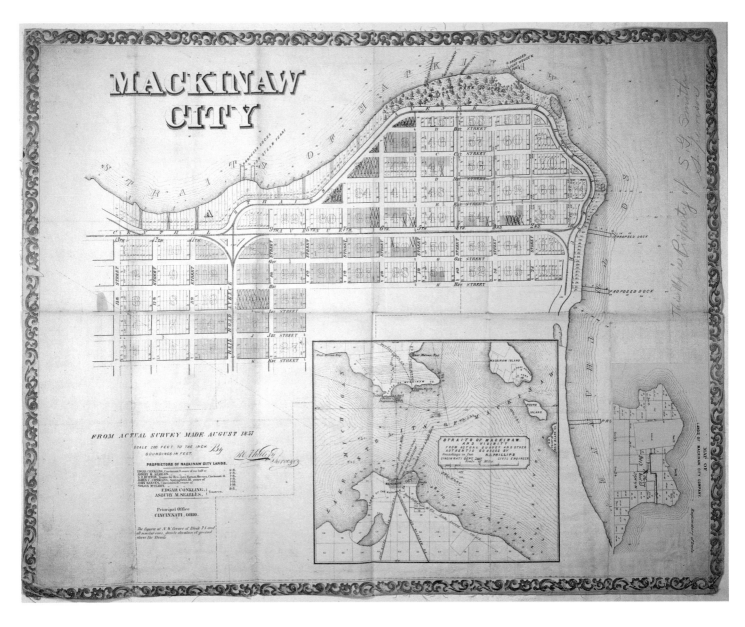

FIGURE 8.33

TITLE: Mackinaw City from Actual Survey Made August 1857.
[Inset:] Straits of Mackinac and Vicinity from actual survey
and other authentic sources by R. C. Phillips, Civil Engineer,
Cincinnati Sept. 1857. [Inset later pasted on at lower right:]
Map of Lands of Mackinaw City Company.
AUTHOR: Robert C. Phillips (active 1857–65).
Lithograph by Middleton, Wallace and Company.
DATE DEPICTED: August 1857.
DATE OF WORK: 1857.
DESCRIPTION: 54 x 68.7 cm. Lithograph on paper with
later coloring.
PROVENANCE: Issued in Edward Deering Mansfield,
Exposition of the Natural Position of Mackinaw City. . . .
(Cincinnati, 1857). The name of the lithographer has
been covered on the copy illustrated.
COLLECTION: Mackinac State Historic Parks,
Mackinac Island, MI (2006.00.58).

businessman, Edgar Conkling, assembled a small group of investors to
purchase about 1,800 acres of land where a city could be laid out and
constructed.[164] The Mackinaw City Company had the site surveyed
and laid out in lots during the summer of 1857. Later that year it
offered a prospectus with the map illustrated here as Figure 8.33.

The prospectus set forth, in glowing but businesslike terms,
the advantages of investing in the scheme to found a commercial
metropolis at the Straits of Mackinac. "If one were to point out, on
the map of North America, a site for a great central city in the lake
region," Jacob Ferris had written in 1856, "it would be in the
immediate vicinity of the Straits of Mackinaw." A city there "would
have the command of the mineral trade, the fisheries, the furs, and
the lumber of the entire North," he claimed. "It might become the
metropolis of a great commercial empire. It would be the Venice of
the Lakes."[165] This theme was expanded by Edward Deering Mansfield
in the forty-eight-page prospectus of the Mackinaw City Company
under the grand title *Exposition of the Natural Position of Mackinaw*

City and the Climate, Soil, and Commercial Elements of the Surrounding Country. The offering included a notice "To the Public" signed by Edgar Conkling and Asbury M. Searles as "trustees" of the project.[166]

Mansfield's pamphlet included a finely produced map of a survey made in August 1857 by Robert C. Phillips, an Ohio surveyor. It illustrated the offering and put forth a vision of the city that was projected to rise on the site. Phillips added his own written evaluation to the prospectus, which followed Conkling and Searles's statement.[167] "Mackinaw City" was to be a "city of the first class" with broad, tree-lined avenues of 100 to 150 feet in width and streets 80 feet wide. These would serve town lots of 50 by 150 feet "affording ample room for permanent, convenient and ornamental improvements." Surveyor Phillips, in his report, addressed practical matters such as elevation and drainage. And, he added, Mackinaw City would be a good place to live. "The health of the locality, like that of the surrounding islands, is proverbial," he wrote, due in large part to the "invigorating and pleasant breezes" that already attracted thousands of visitors to the Straits each summer.

Then there were the advantages that would guarantee the commercial success of a city. Phillips noted "ample and safe harbors" adjoining the land on the east, north, and west. The "eastern bay," he added, was "well known to navigators" and offered a refuge in the event of storms. Phillips claimed to have seen as many as twenty vessels sheltering there at one time. This was Chippewa Bay, from which goods and houses had been dispatched to Mackinac Island in the early 1780s. The promoters promised "the erection of docks at the most important places" and the establishment of ferries across the Straits. Proposed sites for these services are shown on Phillips's survey. An inset plan of the Straits projects the future railroads and connecting ferries that would literally put Mackinaw City on the map.

The most far-sighted element of the plan for Mackinaw City may be seen in the wooded area at the very northern tip of the proposed town. This was to be a twenty-acre public park including the grounds of the old fort "sacred in the history of the country." The area was described as being in its "natural condition" in 1857, but "the skillful hand of the horticulturalist" could soon beautify it with paths, lawns, and avenues. Conkling and Searles offered a site for a lighthouse as well, not to mention one for fortifications should the government have any future need of them.

The pamphlet and Phillips's plan must have enjoyed wide circulation because numerous examples survive today. The copy of the map illustrated here as Figure 8.33 was altered by later use when it was in the hands of S. G. Smith, a local supervisor. Lots have been colored or marked off, and a small printed map showing the lands of the Mackinaw City Company and the boundaries of the town projected by Phillips has been pasted on at lower right. Altogether, it is a good example of the sort of city-builder's promotional plan that enjoyed wide popularity in the growing western regions of the United States during the nineteenth century. The names of the proprietors and their trustees are proudly displayed, along with their shares of ownership, below the title imprint.

Despite this smooth presentation, the project was ahead of its time. By 1860 Conkling had become the sole proprietor.[168] William P. Strickland produced his *Old Mackinaw; or, the Fortress of the Lakes* that year. His history of the region was heavily laced with a description and further promotion of Conkling's scheme. Such efforts were largely to no avail, however, and "financial revulsion" in the late 1850s and the eruption of civil war in 1861 provided further impediments to success.[169] A few of the investors suffered. One of the two copies of Mansfield's pamphlet in the Bentley Historical Library in Ann Arbor includes sarcastic notations by a detractor of the project. One reads: "Edward [Mansfield], Please tell us how much the mackinaw city company pays for the lies you tell in this Exposition." To further drive home his point, the unknown writer altered the title page to read: "An Exposition of a splendid chance of being cheated out of your money" by "Eloquent land Hucksters" promoting a country riddled with "Fever & Ague."[170]

Edgar Conkling survived his business setbacks, and he renewed efforts to develop his metropolis following the Civil War.[171] In 1869 he had a dock constructed at Mackinaw City, and the first settler arrived from Cheboygan in the winter of 1870. But, as with other mainland locations, Conkling's "great central city" would have to await the coming of the railroad, an event that occurred soon after his death in December 1881.[172]

Edgar Conkling (1813–81) of Cincinnati, Ohio, had a vision of a "great central city" at the tip of Michigan's Lower Peninsula. Although he had the site platted in 1857, economic conditions delayed execution of his plans until the 1870s and early 1880s. David Broderick Walcutt painted this oil portrait of Conkling in July 1849.

Courtesy of Ken Teysen, Teysen's Historical Museum/Mackinaw Area Historical Society, Mackinaw City, MI.

It is one of Nature's beauty spots

New York Tribune

"There is one of a cluster of islands in the Straits of Michilimackinac—a conspicuous and brilliant diadem upon the brow of the transparent waters of the Northwestern Lakes," a correspondent to the *New York Tribune* wrote effusively in 1859. "It is one of Nature's beauty spots," he continued, the site of some of the "most thrilling and interesting historical incidents" as well as distinctive "natural monuments." That island was Mackinac, and by 1859 it had become one of the country's most attractive "watering places." It was firmly established as a popular destination for those seeking "mental and physical relaxation from the labors and anxieties of an active business life, or a cool retreat from a Southern sun."[173]

Perhaps that was the purpose for a visit, in July and August 1859, by a talented but anonymous artist whose sketchbook preserves thirty-six pages of pencil drawings documenting at least eight days in the Straits of Mackinac and Les Cheneaux area. The sketches are of a quality that suggests a professional creator or a very talented and well-trained amateur. The subjects of most of the scenes are easily identifiable, and many include notes or titles as confirmation. Quite a few are dated, and these help reconstruct the movements of the artist during what was probably a fairly typical resort vacation on Mackinac Island in 1859. Seven of these drawings are reproduced here as Figures 8.34–8.40, while a view of Fort Mackinac appears later as Figure 8.41. A list of the sketches made on Mackinac Island may be found in appendix A.

Although the bound sketchbook, embossed on the cover only with the work "Album," provides little to identify the artist, a few conclusions may be drawn from the bits of written and visual information found in the individual sketches. Our traveler began his journey in Chicago and dated a drawing there on July 22, 1859. The first Mackinac picture was made four days later. His last Mackinac sketch is dated August 3, and the intervening time seems to have been spent on the island, interrupted only by a visit to Les Cheneaux Islands on July 28. The artist traveled by steamboat with at least one companion, who appears in a number of his sketches. This was a fellow named "Pomeroy," and his presence suggests that the artist was a man and not one traveling with a family. There are some hints that the sketcher might have been an Englishman or at least an easterner. His party stayed at the Island House Hotel, where he drew a "pretty waiting maid." A variety of images of fellow passengers or hotel guests and Indian women punctuate his views of scenery. Taken together, the pictures in the anonymous artist's "Album" leave us with the impressions of a Mackinac visitor during one of the last resort summers before the Civil War.

It seems likely that the artist arrived at Mackinac Island on July 25, possibly late in the night as seems to have been the experience of so many travelers of that time. Much of the next day was probably spent exploring the town and, perhaps, the fort. At some point during the day, however, he made his way to British Landing and took a view of the beach and the mainland at St. Ignace (Fig. 8.34). British Landing was then one of the most popular historical sites on Mackinac Island, and the artist probably made his way there in a horse-drawn vehicle down the road from Fort Mackinac. A correspondent to the *New York Tribune* that year suggested that this was likely to have been "a jolting horse cart," one the many two-wheeled, Canadian-style drays found on the island. The driver, the correspondent complained, was usually a Métis islander, "a mixed-breed . . . who neither speaks nor understands the King's English."[174]

The following day, July 27, was somewhat better documented, and the drawings reveal visits to Arch Rock and Lover's Leap. Perhaps it was after clambering down to the beach below Arch Rock that the artist captured his companion, Pomeroy, gazing meditatively from atop a large limestone boulder (Fig. 8.35). He also made a fine view of Arch Rock from below (not illustrated) before crossing to the opposite side of the island to visit points of interest along the high bluff there. Figure 8.36 offers a unique, pre-photographic perspective of the village from the west, preserving the view over the town and harbor toward Round Island. It appears to have been drawn from the rocky summit of Lover's Leap, seen in the foreground. The artist depicted the back of the town, including the fishermen's huts bordering the "Borough Lot." That piece of ground is the clear space along the beach between the town and the trees.

Figure 8.37 was probably sketched soon after, showing Lover's Leap from the foot of the bluff. This is the earliest-known surviving view of that natural feature. Lover's Leap had been a popular attraction since the 1820s, when it appeared on John Mullett's survey map (Fig. 5.25) identified as "Little Rock." The limestone stack was associated with a popular, romantic tale of a bereaved Indian maiden, but one anonymous traveler in 1848 was more impressed by the beautiful view toward the mainland and the far-off Manitou Islands in Lake Michigan.[175] In 1844 the Reverend James Beaven reported that the great rock afforded a "good look-out" in all directions because of the absence of timber on its summit.[176]

Our artist left Mackinac Island on July 28 for a trip to Les Cheneaux Islands, where he made a number of drawings. These include Indian lodges, the bark-covered house of a chief that he described as "Shawbwaway's Palace," and the log house of Father A. D. J. Piret, who was then pastor of the church in St. Ignace but also served as a missionary to the Indians.[177] The trip was almost

FIGURE 8.34

TITLE: British Landing Mackinac July 26, 1859.

AUTHOR: Anonymous American.

DATE DEPICTED: July 26, 1859.

DATE OF WORK: July 26, 1859.

DESCRIPTION: 11.7 x 18.8 cm. Pencil on paper in sketchbook.

PROVENANCE: Purchased 1955.

COLLECTION: Detroit Institute of Arts. Accession number 55.237.15. Founders Society Purchase, Gibbs-Williams Fund. Photograph © 2005 The Detroit Institute of Arts.

FIGURE 8.35

TITLE: Mackinac—July 1859. Pomeroy Ruminans.

AUTHOR: Anonymous American.

DATE DEPICTED: July 1859.

DATE OF WORK: July 1859.

DESCRIPTION: 11.7 x 18.8 cm. Pencil on paper in sketchbook.

PROVENANCE: Purchased 1955.

COLLECTION: Detroit Institute of Arts. Accession number 55.237.13. Founders Society Purchase, Gibbs-Williams Fund. Photograph © 2005 The Detroit Institute of Arts.

FIGURE 8.36

TITLE: Mackinac July 27 1859.
AUTHOR: Anonymous American.
DATE DEPICTED: July 27, 1859.
DATE OF WORK: July 27, 1859.
DESCRIPTION: 11.7 x 18.8 cm. Pencil on paper in sketchbook.
PROVENANCE: Purchased 1955.
COLLECTION: Detroit Institute of Arts. Accession number
55.237.17. Founders Society Purchase, Gibbs-Williams Fund.
Photograph © 2005 The Detroit Institute of Arts.

certainly made in a Mackinaw boat. According to the *New York Tribune* correspondent, a hired vessel with two local crewmen could sail from Mackinac Island to the Carp River in two hours, so the artist might well have been able to visit Les Cheneaux in one-day's time.[178] He was back on Mackinac Island on July 29, where he sketched a view of Sugar Loaf (not illustrated).

The Mackinac Island scenes drawn after July 29 are studies done on the beach or in the harbor or sketches of fellow guests at the Island House. The three illustrated here (Figs. 8.38–8.40) depict Mackinaw boats of the type that had probably carried the artist on his excursion to Les Cheneaux Islands (Fig. 8.38). By the end of the 1850s these swift craft had become the workhorses of local fishing, largely replacing the canoe among the inhabitants of Mackinac Island. William Cullen Bryant reported, in 1846, that the "Mackinac navigators have also given their name to a boat of peculiar form, sharp at both ends, swelled at the sides, and flat-bottomed, an excellent sea-boat it is said, as it must be to live in the wild storms that surprise the mariner on Lake Superior."[179] According to Constance Fenimore Woolson, these craft were at their best "with a gale behind them" when, with "their great white sails tilting far to one side, they skim the white caps."[180] When not ferrying tourists to the Carp River or around Mackinac Island, these working vessels were used for tending fields of gill nets, set in up to fifty fathoms of water.

FIGURE 8.37
TITLE: Lover's Leap. Mackinac July 27, 1859.
AUTHOR: Anonymous American.
DATE DEPICTED: July 27, 1859.
DATE OF WORK: July 27, 1859.
DESCRIPTION: 11.7 x 18.8 cm. Pencil on paper in sketchbook.
PROVENANCE: Purchased 1955.
COLLECTION: Detroit Institute of Arts. Accession number 55.237.21. Founders Society Purchase, Gibbs-Williams Fund. Photograph © 2005 The Detroit Institute of Arts.

By 1859 it was still common for the crew of a single boat to haul in twenty to thirty trout of from six to sixty pounds and up to one hundred whitefish weighing from two to six pounds.[181]

Perhaps the artist spent one of his early August days on Lake Huron with some of the fishermen he captured sitting by their boats on the beaches of Mackinac Island. They are studies in relaxation, although evidence of work is all around them. Two of the men in Figure 8.39 rest on wheelbarrows that were probably used to move fish from the beach to the packinghouses. Beyond them, a Mackinaw boat departs Haldimand Bay, its "great white sails" tilting to one side. A meal is being prepared over a fire beside the boat in Figure 8.40, much as had been done since prehistoric days on the beaches of the Straits of Mackinac. Fishnets are casually draped over the gunwale of the boat while Round and Bois Blanc islands form a scenic backdrop.

Further sketches depict a variety of types of people the artist encountered on his voyage or in the hotel. They display a certain whimsy that suggests he was studying those around him and commenting on their manners, dress, or appearance. Steamboating on the Great Lakes was still quite an adventure and not for the faint of heart, particularly those used to finer behavior in eastern or European cities. "Cannot say I think much of western manners," New Yorker Juliette Starr Dana wrote in her diary while at Mackinac in July 1852. "There is a coarseness & want of refinement about all that I have seen yet, & they appear so *new*."[182] Whatever his itinerary during his last few days on Mackinac Island, our artist drew his final Mackinac studies on August 3 and probably set out soon after for Chicago, Detroit, or Sault Ste. Marie.

FIGURE 8.38

TITLE: Mackinac Aug. 3 1859.
AUTHOR: Anonymous American
DATE DEPICTED: August 3, 1859.
DATE OF WORK: August 3, 1859.
DESCRIPTION: 11.7 x 18.8 cm. Pencil on paper in sketchbook.
PROVENANCE: Purchased 1955.
COLLECTION: Detroit Institute of Arts. Accession number 55.237.45. Founders Society Purchase, Gibbs-Williams Fund. Photograph © 2005 The Detroit Institute of Arts.

FIGURE 8.39

TITLE: Mackinac Aug 1, 1859.
AUTHOR: Anonymous American.
DATE DEPICTED: August 1, 1859.
DATE OF WORK: August 1, 1859.
DESCRIPTION: 11.7 x 18.8 cm. Pencil on paper in sketchbook.
PROVENANCE: Purchased 1955.
COLLECTION: Detroit Institute of Arts. Accession number 55.237.37. Founders Society Purchase, Gibbs-Williams Fund. Photograph © 2005 The Detroit Institute of Arts.

FIGURE 8.40

TITLE: Aug 2, 1859.
AUTHOR: Anonymous American.
DATE DEPICTED: August 2, 1859.
DATE OF WORK: August 2, 1859.
DESCRIPTION: 11.7 x 18.8 cm. Pencil on paper in sketchbook.
PROVENANCE: Purchased 1955.
COLLECTION: Detroit Institute of Arts. Accession number 55.237.41. Founders Society Purchase, Gibbs-Williams Fund. Photograph © 2005 The Detroit Institute of Arts.

The 1859 sketchbook of an anonymous Mackinac visitor includes a composition titled "Young America. My Opposite Neighbor at Table, Mackinac, July 30, 1859." The artist recorded an additional bit of dinnertime chatter from the boy: "Guess your legs are pretty long, or else your shoes be." The meal was probably taken at the Island House Hotel. *Detroit Institute of Arts, Founders Society Purchase, Gibbs-Williams Fund (55.237.70). Photograph © 2005, The Detroit Institute of Arts.*

In a military point of view this Fort is worthless

William M. Johnston

Fort Mackinac stood empty once again. It was August 1857, and, for the fifth time in twenty years, a departing garrison had carefully locked up the buildings, turned over the keys to a lone ordnance sergeant, and marched down the bluff to board a waiting steamboat. Captain Arnold Elzey and his men of the 2nd Artillery had spent just sixteen months at Fort Mackinac, and the winter of 1857–58 would be the second time in only three years that no sentinels watched over the Straits and the town. No one in the village below could have believed that the old limestone fortress stood very high on the U.S. Army's list of military posts.

At least one Mackinac Islander was prepared to question the army's reasons for holding on to the aging walls and buildings. "In a military point of view this Fort is worthless," William M. Johnston wrote bluntly to Secretary of War John B. Floyd a short time after the troops departed. Its guns could not bar the Straits of Mackinac to hostile forces, and it had no command over the Indians who remained in the region. The old fort was, Johnston claimed, "merely a *Wonder* to scientific strangers." He could not understand why the War Department kept it up, at great expense, instead of establishing new fortifications at the more commanding location on the mainland at "Old Mackinac," soon to be known as Mackinaw City. Johnston proposed that since the post had been evacuated, its quarters could be leased for use as a school. If Indians were still a concern to the community, then he, a former interpreter of the Indian agency, pledged to protect the citizens himself should a garrison no longer occupy Fort Mackinac.[183]

William Johnston's suggestion was not accepted, and it would be another ten years before Mackinac Island got a government building for its school—the former Indian Dormitory. Johnston's request, however, emphasized the generally acknowledged obsolescence of Fort Mackinac and the uncertainty of its future. There was no hope that the fortifications could resist modern ships and artillery, and there was no likelihood that they would be rebuilt to be able to do so. The healthiness of the post had become its chief advantage. "The fortress is reduced from an important military position to a mere hospital to recruit the health of soldiers long employed in sickly climates," James J. Strang asserted in 1854.[184] It would have been difficult to find anyone to dispute his statement.

Troops returned, nonetheless, in May 1858, and Fort Mackinac would remain in service until the spring of 1861 when the crisis of civil war called for every available unit of the tiny regular army. Captain Henry C. Pratt and his men arrived in 1858 to find the same sort of dilapidation encountered by most new commandants over the past half century. The last report on the garrison's buildings had

been made late in May 1857, and it is unlikely that the previous garrison had found the time to correct very much before their departure less than three months later. The litany of dilapidation was all too familiar. Many parts of the stone walls were "crumbled and tumbled." Garrison fences were "rotten and fallen down in many places." The quarters for officers and men were out of order, and the barracks, less than two years old, was poorly constructed and had problems with its roof and chimneys. The hospital was old, and its roof leaked. The new cisterns, designed by Major Thomas Williams, were declared "entirely out of order and . . . of *no service* as they now stand."[185]

Captain Pratt had little time to digest this information before disaster relieved him of the responsibility for repairing three of the post buildings. The wind was blowing from the east on the afternoon of June 9, 1858, when a sentry noticed smoke coming from the roof of the bake house in the long, one-story row building on the east side of the fort (Fig. 7.21, "13"). This old, tinder-dry, wooden structure had narrowly escaped the conflagration of January 1855, but this time it stood no chance. Worse, the wind directed the flames toward the new barracks and the blacksmith shop by the north sally port. Both were soon afire. There were seven cisterns in Fort Mackinac awaiting just such an emergency, but they would no longer hold water and were found to be "utterly worthless." The soldiers pumped what they could from the well outside the north gate and hauled more from the lake below, but the row house, barracks, and blacksmith shop were soon given up for lost. As they burned, the troops focused on saving the north blockhouse, officers' quarters ("Hill House"), and hospital. This was accomplished, with great effort, by covering them with wet blankets.[186] Mercifully, the east wind pushed the fire away from the powder magazine.

This fire was followed by the required investigation by a board of officers, who determined that it had originated in the bake house. They also decided that, with sufficient water in the cisterns and a good hose and force pump, the blaze could have been contained. Moreover, they were of the opinion that potentially hazardous buildings, such as the bake house and blacksmith shop, should not have been located within such a confined fort.[187] In the future, they should be outside the walls. As for barracks, Captain Pratt crowded his men into the old officers' wooden quarters and drew up a plan and estimates for a permanent replacement, the fourth such building to stand inside Fort Mackinac.[188] His plan has not been found, so it is not known whether the existing barracks in Fort Mackinac was built to his specifications or the Quartermaster General's Department provided the design.

Captain Pratt urged rapid action to complete the replacement

building before winter, and by the first week of August he was expecting delivery of the necessary lumber on the beach below Fort Mackinac.[189] The quartermaster general finally authorized the rebuilding of "the barracks &c" in an order of July 28, but work had to cease at the beginning of December because of the cold. Construction recommenced in the spring, and the job was "nearly completed by the end of June 1859."[190] Figure 8.41 is the first image known to show any part of the handsome, two-story, frame building that still dominates the parade ground of Fort Mackinac. A tiny bit of its roof and a chimney appear between the officers' wooden quarters and guardhouse in this pencil sketch made in August 1859 by an anonymous visitor.

Although the barracks was, by far, the largest building erected in the aftermath of the 1858 fire, other structures were also needed. Reports of the work accomplished during 1858–59 consistently refer to "the barracks & c" or "the buildings erected during the past year" without providing more specific details.[191] The post was in need of a new blacksmith shop, bake house, quartermaster storehouse, and headquarters to replace those that had burned. A plan of Fort Mackinac, drawn by Walter Griswold in June 1863, clearly shows that five buildings in addition to the barracks were constructed between 1858 and the evacuation of the post in the spring of 1861. These include a bakery outside the northeast wall and an unidentified building on the site of the old blacksmith shop just inside the north sally port.

FIGURE 8.41
TITLE: [Fort Mackinac from the harbor].
AUTHOR: Anonymous American.
DATE DEPICTED: August 1859.
DATE OF WORK: August 1859.
DESCRIPTION: 11.7 x 18.8 cm. Pencil on paper in sketchbook.
PROVENANCE: Purchased 1955.
COLLECTION: Detroit Institute of Arts. Accession number 55.237.51. Founders Society Purchase, Gibbs-Williams Fund. Photograph © 2005 The Detroit Institute of Arts.

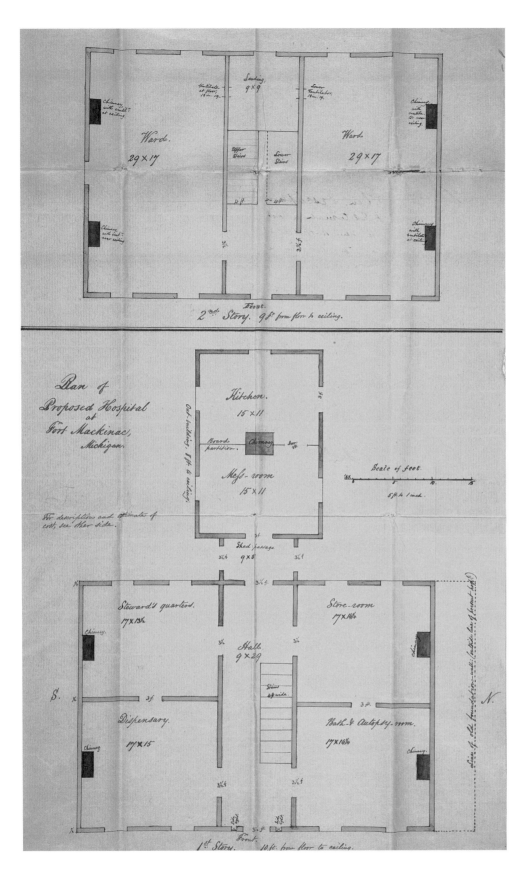

FIGURE 8.42

TITLE: Plan of Proposed Hospital at Fort Mackinac, Michigan.

AUTHOR: [Assistant Surgeon John Frazier Head, active 1846–85].

DATE DEPICTED: July 15, 1859, proposal.

DATE OF WORK: [July 15, 1859].

DESCRIPTION: 51 x 31 cm. Pen and ink on yellow paper with gray and blue highlights on architectural features.

PROVENANCE: Enclosed with Captain Henry C. Pratt's "Report of the annual inspection of the public buildings at Fort Mackinac Mich.," dated July 27, 1859, and sent to Quartermaster General Thomas S. Jesup. Retained with the Records of the Office of Quartermaster General.

COLLECTION: National Archives and Records Administration, Washington, DC (RG 92, Records of the Office of the Quartermaster General, Consolidated Correspondence File, Fort Mackinac, Michigan, 1819–90). Found in Box 595.

Both were removed later in the nineteenth century, but two other new structures shown on the Griswold plan survive today. Although labeled "Quarters" on the 1863 plan, they appear to be the existing post headquarters and quartermaster storehouse that occupy the southern end of the old row house site.[192]

While the headquarters and storehouse have traditionally been assigned construction dates of 1853 and 1867, respectively, they would seem to have actually been a part of the 1858–59 program. A single chimney peeping above the wall over the south sally port in Figure 8.41 probably marks the headquarters building. That structure also appears in at least one early Civil War–period photograph showing both it and the barracks recently completed and not yet painted.

Figure 8.41 is a fine study of the fort as it appeared on the eve of the Civil War. As with all views from the harbor, only the structures along the bluff may be seen, and the interior, aside from what is revealed of the new barracks, is masked from view. With the exception of the buildings outside the walls, however, the appearance of the fort today has changed little since 1859. Visible below the bluff are the commissary storehouse of 1819 (left) and the old Fort Holmes blockhouse that was moved and converted to a stable during the winter of 1821–22. A carriage and a pair of tourists pass along the street below the fort, a sight that would not be out of place in the early twenty-first century.

The right margin of Figure 8.41 ends at the eastern edge of the walls and therefore does not show the site of the last post building to be constructed before the outbreak of the Civil War. This was the hospital that today dominates the top of the bluff and houses the offices of Mackinac State Historic Parks. Post commandants had complained of Major Thompson's 1828 hospital almost from the day that officer relinquished command, but Captain Pratt was the first to get results. On July 15, 1859, his post surgeon, J. Frazier Head, carefully detailed the deficiencies of the old building's design, roof, foundations, and condition. Pratt's annual inspection report, forwarded to the quartermaster general on July 27, enclosed Head's evaluation and a plan for a new hospital, illustrated here as Figure 8.42.[193]

Head probably drafted the neatly drawn and colored floor plan himself. It depicts a "substantial frame building" of two stories with a semi-detached outbuilding behind to serve as a mess room and kitchen and to lessen the possibility of fire in the main structure. The whole was to be sided with clapboards. Head estimated its cost at $2,302.00.[194] The interior arrangement of his proposed building bears a strong resemblance to the "new" post hospital as it exists today, although Head's plan does not show a piazza along the facade. It is also clear that he intended his hospital to stand within Fort Mackinac on the site of the 1828 building. It was to be of the same width but slightly shorter. Head's ground floor plan reflects this by a dotted line labeled "Line of old foundation wall: (outside line of present hospl.)." A penciled addition to Lieutenant John Newton's survey of June 1850 (Fig. 8.1) also marks a building of roughly the

Captain Arnold Elzey briefly commanded Fort Mackinac after his arrival with a company of the 2nd Artillery in May 1857. Elzey successfully argued that the task of placing government boundary markers on Mackinac Island properly belonged to the engineers who had conducted the survey. The captain and his men evacuated the fort at the end of the summer. This portrait, by Christian F. Schwerdt, was painted following Elzey's service in the Civil War. *Chicago History Museum (1920.576).*

same shape as Head's design within the western end of the fort walls. It is labeled simply "Hospital."

Captain Pratt's request for a new hospital received favorable consideration, and funds were appropriated for it in 1859 or 1860. The money had not been released as late as the beginning of July 1860, however, and construction does not appear to have commenced before the end of that summer.[195] The new hospital was probably erected in the fall and winter, but it is unlikely to have been completely finished by the time Pratt's troops evacuated Fort Mackinac in April 1861. Nor was it constructed on the site originally suggested, thus sparing the 1828 hospital. The old building was converted for use as a commissary storehouse and other such purposes, while the new hospital rose on the high bluff just beyond the gun platform at the southeastern corner of the fort.[196] The site inside the walls had long been criticized for its lack of fresh breezes and light, and a later inspector noted that the new hospital had intentionally been erected on a "high, airy site."[197] Its brilliantly white, two-story piazza is still an impressive sight when seen from the harbor below.

David V. Tinder Collection, Clements
Library, University of Michigan.

THE ARCHED ROCK AT MACKINAW.

"It is about ninety feet in height, and is crowned with an arch of near sixty feet sweep. From its great elevation, the view through the arch, upon the wide expanse of water is of singular beauty and grandeur."—Page 41.

5

This engraving, titled "The Arched Rock at Mackinaw," appeared as an illustration in Henry Howe, *The Great West* (New York, 1851). It is one of many instances of the reuse of a published image in a later book. In this case, the scene was copied from Sara Clarke's "Arched Rock at Mackinaw" (Fig. 7.12) that first appeared in the illustrated edition of Sarah M. Fuller's *Summer on the Lakes, in 1843* (Boston, 1844). Author's collection.

"Remarkably dull times we are having"

Civil war burst upon the United States in the spring of 1861, just as Mackinac merchants and hoteliers were preparing for the annual throng of resort visitors and steamboat passengers. The *Mackinac Herald* anticipated the effect this was likely to have on the usual summer traffic, particularly travelers from the steamy southern states. "Remarkably dull times we are having," the paper's editor noted in the May 18 issue. But there was always hope. "Cheer up," he added, forecasting that 1861 was still likely to be a good tourist year and recommending that the island's hotels continue to advertise in his paper. "It would also be good policy," he suggested, "to reduce the usual prices for board—and thus *bring* visitors here."[1]

Four years of bitter civil war would, in fact, bring an end to the Straits of Mackinac's first resort era, just as it would usher in the age of photography. The island's normal rhythm changed in the spring of 1861, and it would not resume until the fighting had ended. In April, Captain Henry C. Pratt led Fort Mackinac's garrison to Washington to protect the capital. Even the old fort's cannon were called to service when orders arrived to send them to Chicago for use as needed.[2] The fishing, lumbering, and shipping industries of the Straits had a role to play in the war effort, of course, and local men would serve in Michigan regiments throughout the conflict. Nor was Fort Mackinac entirely forgotten. A company of Michigan volunteers arrived in 1862 to guard three prominent Confederate political prisoners, but the fort's only wartime garrison departed in the fall. The post would not be reoccupied until 1865.[3]

Tourism gradually revived after the war, and by 1870 Mackinac was again increasing in stature as a resort. New development followed as shops, hotels, cottages, and churches were constructed, particularly after the establishment of Mackinac National Park in 1875. The Victorian resort era had dawned, and it would be visually documented through photography with comprehensiveness undreamed of before 1861. This new realism is reflected in a stereo photograph of the 1860s that closely corresponds to one of the views published in *Frank Leslie's Illustrated Newspaper* in 1856 (Fig. 8.32).

Mackinac scenes were every bit as picturesque following the introduction of photography, but they would be recorded thereafter with unblinking, black and white objectivity. Visual documents of the pre-photographic era—drawn and printed images—were far more subjective, as a comparison of the stereo photograph and Figure 8.32 will demonstrate. Artists and engravers had the power to simplify, beautify, or "improve" that which they depicted or to omit details if they were not considered relevant or interesting. Derelict outbuildings, broken windows, laundry, or unsightly plumes of smoke need not mar an otherwise pleasant scene as they would in a photograph. The subjectivity of drawn or printed images must be considered when using them as historical documents.

The pre-photographic, visual record is also incomplete in a number of important areas. It is significant that few Mackinac artists depicted people in much detail. Most probably lacked the skill to do so. Paul Kane and a few others made portraits of prominent or interesting Native Americans, but most Mackinac images focus on architecture, scenery, or topography. With a few exceptions, human beings are not pictured at work in the fishing grounds, warehouses, fields, shops, or fort. There are few sketches of visitors or Indians wandering the streets of the town. Nor are people depicted at play unless, like the occasional worker, they appear as part of a larger composition. Interior spaces were also largely overlooked, so their appearance must be reconstructed from written descriptions or floor plans. Even more striking is the total absence of pictures depicting scenery or activities during Mackinac's dramatic winters. Surviving, pre-photographic images, in fact, convey very little sense of the seasons. Perhaps this is because most artists visited during the warmer months and thus missed the transformations of fall, winter, and spring.

Despite these shortcomings, drawn and printed images provide our best windows on life at Mackinac prior to photography. The maps and pictures illustrated or described here represent all that are known to survive. Others, surely, remain to be found, and each new discovery will add a bit more information to the historical record. "A stroll at Mackinac is worth a day in any man's life," Horace Greeley wrote in 1847. While it is no longer possible to enjoy the Mackinac of Greeley's time and before, historical images and the written accounts that complement them can at least help us re-create something of the experience.

Catalog of Mackinac Maps, Plans, and Views to 1860

The images illustrated in this study represent, at best, a fraction of the maps, plans, and drawings of the Straits of Mackinac area produced before 1861. The best or most significant of those known to survive have been reproduced in the preceding pages. Others have been omitted, usually because they are simply duplications of the same composition or because they are in such poor condition that they would not convey any useful information. Many more maps and drawings are described in written documents but have either succumbed to the ravages of time or have not been located in the course of assembling this iconography.

The descriptive list presented below includes all surviving, described, or presumed nonphotographic Mackinac images from the years prior to the Civil War. It is comprehensive only in the sense that it represents the images or descriptions of images that have been uncovered to date. Many others undoubtedly survive in private or public collections, where they remain unidentified, misidentified, or hidden away in the pages of journals, sketchbooks, or official reports. It is hoped that these will eventually be revealed and become available to students of the history and iconography of the Straits of Mackinac.

The list ranks all known Mackinac images in chronological order and gives the current locations of those that have been examined in the course of this study. Dates in bold type identify existing items, while those with dates in plain type are known only from descriptions in documents and are not believed to survive. Bibliographic citations and abbreviations are as in the notes to the main text.

1615—[Le Canada faict par le Sr de Champlain]—by Samuel de Champlain. Manuscript map on which the 1616 engraving was based.

1615 (proof copy printed ca. 1650 from 1616 plate)—[Le Canada] faict par le Sr de Champlain 1616—by Samuel de Champlain. Unique proof copy of copperplate engraving. John Carter Brown Library. [**Not illustrated**]. This includes the cartographic information shown on the later Duval imprints of 1653–77 but with no name given to Lake Erie and much less information on the native nations of Canada.

1615 (published 1653–77)—Le Canada faict par le Sr de Champlain—by Samuel de Champlain. Printed from the 1616 plate as altered by Pierre Duval. Clements Library (4-A-12). [**Figure 1.1**]. Several states of this map were produced as late as 1677.

1629 [Carte de la nouuelle france. . . .]—by Samuel de Champlain. Manuscript map on which the 1632 engraving was based.

1629 (published 1632)—Carte de la nouuelle france. . . .—by Samuel de Champlain. Published in Champlain, *Les voyages de la Nouvelle France, occidentale, dicte Canada. . . .* (Paris, 1632). Clements Library (C-1632-Ch). [**Figure 1.2**].

1640s (published 1656)—Le Canada, ou Nouvelle France, &c. . . .—by Nicolas d'Abbeville Sanson. Clements Library (Atlas, W-1-D). [**Figure 1.3**]. Shows the Great Lakes region as it was known in the 1640s, including a fully formed Straits of Mackinac.

1670 Carte du Lac Ontario et des habitations qui l'environnent Ensemble le pays que M. M. Dollier et Galiné, missionaires du Seminaire St. Suplice ont parcouru. 1670—by René Bréhant de Galinée. Original manuscript map, which had been lost by 1870. Included cartographic details of northern Lake Huron and Georgian Bay.

1670 (copied 1854 and published 1895)—Carte du Lac Ontario et des habitations qui l'environnent Ensemble le pays que M.M. Dollier et Galiné, missionaires du Seminaire St. Suplice ont parcouru. 1670—by René Bréhant de Galinée. Later copy of the original map reproduced in Gravier, *Carte des Grandes Lacs*, Clements Library (Map Div. Gr). [**Figure 1.4**].

March 16, 1671—[Figure of a parhelion observed at Sault Ste. Marie]—by [unknown]. Original "painting" on which the 1672 engraving was based.

March 16, 1671 (published 1672)—[Figure of a parhelion observed at Sault Ste. Marie]—by [unknown]. Printed in *Relation . . . 1670 & 1671*, opp. 155. Clements Library (C-RJ-1672-Da). [**Figure 1.6**].

1671—[Lac Superieur et autres lieux ou sont les missions des Peres de la Compagnie de Iesus comprises sous le nom d'Outaouacs]—by [Fr. Claude Allouez and Fr. Claude Dablon]. Manuscript map on which the 1672 engraving was based.

1671 (published 1672)—Lac Svperievr et avtres lievx ou sont les missions des Peres de la Compagnie de Iesus comprises sovs le nom d'Ovtaovacs—by [Fr. Claude Allouez and Fr. Claude Dablon]. From *Relation . . . 1670 & 1671.* Clements Library (6-L-5). [**Figure 1.5**]. Popularly known as the "Jesuit Map."

1671 (copied 1672 or later)—Lac Tracy ou Superieur avec les dependances de la Mission du Saint Esprit—by [Fr. Claude Allouez and Fr. Claude Dablon]. Service historique de la Marine (old 4044B-73). [**Not illustrated**]. Manuscript copy of the "Jesuit map" showing most of the same details.

1671 (copied 1672 or later)—Lac Superieur et autres lieux ou sont les missions des peres de la Compagnie de jesus Comprises Sous le nom D'outaoüacs—[Fr. Claude Allouez and Fr. Claude Dablon]. Service historique de la Marine (old 4044B-74). [**Not illustrated**]. Manuscript copy of the "Jesuit map" showing most of the same details.

ca. 1675—Lac Hvron ou Karegnondi ou Mer Dovce des Hvrons—by [Louis Jolliet]. Service historique de la Marine (Receuil 67, Carte 48). [**Figure 1.7**].

1679 (published 1704)—[Construction of the *Griffon*]—by [Fr. Louis Hennepin]. In Hennepin, *Aenmerkelyke Voyagie,* Clements Library (C-1704-He). [**Figure 1.8**].

1679 (published 1896 from original of 1684)— Carte de la Louisiane ou des Voyages du Sr. de La Salle & des pays qu'il a découverte depuis la Nouvelle France jusqu'au Golfe Mexique, les années 1679, 80, 81 & 82—by Jean Baptiste Louis Franquelin. Facsimile from manuscript copy of original that had been lost by 1896. Engraved for Thwaites, *Jesuit Relations,* vol. 63. Clements Library (2-H-10). [**Not illustrated**]. Shows some population details for Indian villages at the Straits of Mackinac.

August 20, 1682—[Plan of a fort for the Hurons at Michilimackinac]—by [unknown]. Presented to the Hurons of Michilimackinac by Governor Frontenac at the conclusion of a council held at Montréal. *DRCHSNY,* 9:183.

August 20, 1682—[Plan of a fort for the Kiskakon Ottawas at Michilimackinac]—by [unknown]. Presented to the Kiskakon Ottawas of Michili-mackinac by Governor Frontenac at the

conclusion of a council held at Montréal. *DRCHSNY,* 9:183.

1688 (published 1703)—Carte Generale de Canada Dediée au Roy de Danemark Par son tres humble et tres obeissant et tres fidele serviteur Lahontan—by Captain Louis-Armand de Lom d'Arce de Lahontan. In Lahontan, *Nouveaux voyages,* 2:1. Clements Library (C-1703-La). [**Figure 1.9**].

1688—[Michilimackinac]—by Captain Louis-Armand de Lom d'Arce de Lahontan. Manuscript map on which the engravings of 1703 and later were based.

1688 (published 1703)—[Michilimackinac]— by Captain Louis-Armand de Lom d'Arce de Lahontan. In Lahontan, *Nouveaux voyages,* 1:116. Clements Library (C-1703-La). [**Figure 1.10**]. Original edition, with map legends in French.

1688 (published 1703)—[Michilimackinac]— by Captain Louis-Armand de Lom d'Arce de Lahontan. In Lahontan, *New Voyages to North America,* 1:89. Clements Library (C-1703-La). [**Figure 1.11**]. Map legends in English.

1688 (published 1703)—[Michilimackinac]— by Captain Louis-Armand de Lom d'Arce de Lahontan. In Lahontan, *Nouveaux voyages,* 1:116. Clements Library (C-1703-La). [**Figure 1.12**]. Pirated, reversed version of the map with legends in French.

ca. 1716 (drawn ca. 1717)—Plan de Missilimakinak avec la description de la route du Missisipi—by [after Captain Louis-Armand de Lom d'Arce de Lahontan]. Updated details by an unknown hand. The Newberry Library, Edward E. Ayer Collection (Map 30, Sheet 109). [**Figure 1.13**].

1716–42—[Carte du Détroit Entre le Lac Superieur et le Lac Huron, avec le Sault Sainte Marie et le post de Michillimakinac]—by [unknown]. Manuscript maps on which the Bellin title of 1744 was based.

1716–42 (published 1744)—Carte du Détroit Entre le Lac Superieur et le Lac Huron, avec le Sault Sainte Marie et le Post de Michillimakinac, Dressé sur les Manuscrits du Dépôt des Cartes et Plans de la Marine 1744—by Jacques-Nicolas Bellin. In Charlevoix, *Histoire et description générale de la Nouvelle France,* 3:280. Clements Library (C2-1744-Ch). [**Figure 1.14**].

ca. August–September 1731—[Plan for a machicolated redoubt at Michilimackinac]— by Capt. Gaspard-Joseph Chaussegros de Léry. Mentioned in letter of April 8, 1732, from Maurepas to Beaharnois and Hocquart, at which time the project was declined. Quoted in Roy, *Hommes et choses du Fort Saint-Frédéric.*

October 1749—[Plan of Michilimackinac]—by Ensign Michel Chartier de Lotbinière. Library and Archives Canada (H2/1250-Michilimack-inac-[1749]). [**Figure 1.15**].

October 1749—[Map of the environs of Michilimackinac]—by Ensign Michel Chartier de Lotbinière. In the relation accompanying his 1749 plan of Michilimackinac, Lotbinière says that he made a "plan of this fort and surrounding area." He later noted that "The map showing these sites [the Straits and its islands] as well as the entire route [from Canada], a fair copy of which I had no time to make [I] will give [you] this year." Gérin-Lajoie, "Fort Michilimackinac in 1749," 4, 8.

1761 [1716–42] (published February 1761)—A Plan of the Straits of St. Mary and Michilimakinac, to Shew the Situation & Importance of the two Westernmost Settlements of Canada for the Fur Trade—by [after Jacques-Nicolas Bellin]. Published in *The London Magazine* (London: February 1761), facing [64]. Clements Library (Range 22, Wheat Box A). [**Figure 2.1**].

1762—A Tour from Fort Cumberland North Westward round part of the Lakes Erie, Huron and Michigan, including part of the Rivers St. Joseph, the Wabash and Miamis, with a Sketch of the Roads from thence by the Lower Shawanoe Town to Fort Pitt. 1762—by Ensign Thomas Hutchins. The Huntington Library (HM 1091). [**Not illustrated**]. The map accurately defines the Lower Peninsula of Michigan, shows the islands in the Straits, and identifies the site of Fort Michilimackinac.

Summer 1765—Sketch of the Fort at Michilimackinac—by Lieutenant Perkins Magra. Clements Library (6-N-8). [**Figure 2.2**].

1766–69—A Sketch of the Confluance or Streigts between the Lakes Huron and Michigan &c.— by [unknown but possibly Lieutenant Diedrich Brehm]. National Archives (C.O. 700 North American Colonies General No. 2). [**Figure 2.3**]. Inset on it is "Plan of the Stockaid Garrison. . . ."

1766–69—Plan of the Stockaid Garrison of Michilimakinac—by [unknown but possibly Lieutenant Diedrich Brehm]. National Archives (C.O. 700 North American Colonies General No. 2). [**Figure 2.3**]. Inset on "A Sketch of the Confluance. . . ."

1766–68 (published 1778 and 1781)—A Plan of Captain Carver's Travels in the interior Parts of North America in 1766 and 1767—by Jonathan Carver. Published in Carver, *Travels,* Clements Library (C-1778-Ca and C-1781-Ca). [**Figure 2.4**]. Identifies John Askin's farm between L'Arbre Croche and Michilimackinac.

March 17, 1769—[Plan for a barracks at Michilimackinac]—by [Captain Thomas Sowers?]. Mentioned in letter of this date from General Gage to Captain Glazier enclosing a contract for construction of the building. Thomas Gage Papers, vol. 84, CL.

June 10, 1769—[Draught of the fort of Michilimackinac]—by Lieutenant John Nordberg. Clements Library (6-N-9). [**Figure 2.5**].

October 7, 1779—[On verso:] Plan of the New Fort at the Island of Michilimackinac—by Lieutenant Governor Patrick Sinclair. British Library (Frederick Haldimand Papers, Add Mss. 21757, f. 267). [**Figure 2.6**].

October 7, 1779—[Sketch of the Island of Michilimackinac] appearance from Isle bois blanc Dist. one Mile & a quarter—by Lieutenant Governor Patrick Sinclair. British Library (Frederick Haldimand Papers, Add. Mss 21757, f. 266). [**Figure 2.7**]. Pasted over one corner of "Plan of the New Fort. . . ." of this date.

October 15, 1779—[Rough sketch of a fort proposed to be built on Mackinac Island]—by Lieutenant Governor Patrick Sinclair. British Library (Frederick Haldimand Papers, Add Mss. 21757, f. 269). [**Figure 2.10**].

Autumn 1779?—[Section and roof plan of a blockhouse and redoubt to be built on Mackinac Island]. [On verso:] No 52 Sketch of the Works & Church at Makana—by [Lieutenant Governor Patrick Sinclair]. British Library (Frederick Haldimand Papers, Add Mss. 21758, f. 371). [**Figure 2.8**].

Autumn 1779?—[Sketch of the church at Mackinac]—by [Lieutenant Governor Patrick Sinclair]. The existence of this plan is suggested from the endorsement on the section and plan of a blockhouse proposed to be built on Mackinac Island. British Library (Frederick Haldimand Papers, Add Mss. 21758, f. 371).

Autumn 1779?—Plan of a Block House proposed for the new Fort at Michilimakinac Island—by [Lieutenant Governor Patrick Sinclair?]. No. 28 on list of plans in the Surveyor General's Office at Quebec, ca. 1790. *MPHC,* 24:43.

Autumn 1779?—Plan of Do [blockhouse] with alterations—by [Lieutenant Governor Patrick Sinclair?]. No. 29 on list of plans in the Surveyor General's Office at Quebec, ca. 1790. *MPHC,* 24:44.

Autumn 1779?—Section of the same [blockhouse]—by [Lieutenant Governor Patrick Sinclair?]. No. 30 on list of plans in the Surveyor General's Office at Quebec, ca. 1790. *MPHC,* 24:44.

ca. 1779—Sketch of the Island of Michilimakinac at the Northwest end of Lake Huron—by [unknown]. No. 20 on list of plans in the Surveyor General's Office at Quebec, ca. 1790. *MPHC,* 24:43.

ca. 1779—Plan of the Fort Michilimakinac on the South main—by [unknown]. No. 21 on list of plans in the Surveyor General's Office at Quebec, ca. 1790. *MPHC,* 24:43.

ca. 1779—Brovillon [rough sketch] of Do [Fort Michilimakinac on the South main] with remarks—by [unknown]. No. 22 on list of plans in the Surveyor General's Office at Quebec, ca. 1790. *MPHC,* 24:43.

ca. 1779—Plan of the Old Fort of Michilimackinac—by [unknown]. Included on a "List of Plans," ca. 1784. British Library (Frederick Haldimand Papers, Add Mss. 21886). This might be one of the two ca. 1779 plans listed above.

February 15, 1780—[Plan of the wharf under construction at Mackinac Island]—by [Lieutenant Governor Patrick Sinclair or Samuel Robertson. Enclosed in a letter from Sinclair to Brehm of this date. *MPHC,* 9:538.

April 1780—Plan and section of a Fort proposed for the Island of Michilimakinac &c April 1780—by [Captain William Twiss?]. No. 23 on list of plans in the Surveyor General's Office at Quebec, ca. 1790. *MPHC,* 24:43. The attribution of Twiss as the author of this and the other proposals listed below is suggested in Brehm to Sinclair, Apr. 17, 1780, *MPHC,* 9:534.

April 1780?—Plan of the Interior Line of the Parapet to Do [fort proposed for Island] being 1,546 feet in circuit—by [Captain William Twiss?]. No. 24 on list of plans in the Surveyor General's Office at Quebec, ca. 1790. *MPHC,* 24:43.

April 1780?—Plan and Section of a Fort proposed for the Island of Michilimakinac being Second Project, the interior 1,689 feet in circuit—by [Captain William Twiss?]. No. 25 on list of plans in the Surveyor General's Office at Quebec, ca. 1790. *MPHC,* 24:43.

April 1780?—Ditto a third project [for a fort on the Island] 951 feet ditto [in circuit]—by [Captain William Twiss?]. No. 26 on list of plans in the Surveyor General's Office at Quebec, ca. 1790. *MPHC,* 24:43.

April 1780?—Section to above plans [3 plans for a fort on the Island]—by [Captain William Twiss?]. No. 27 on list of plans in the Surveyor General's Office at Quebec, ca. 1790. *MPHC,* 24:43.

April 26, 1781—[Plan of the Island and Wharf at Michilimakinac]—by Samuel Robertson. Enclosed with letter of this date from Robertson

to Schank, *MPHC,* 9:642. This is probably a variation of one of the wharf plans listed below. Robertson noted that it was made from memory as he had turned in all original plans before leaving Michilimackinac.

April 1781?—Rough sketch of the wharf of Michilimakinac—by [Samuel Robertson?]. No. 31 on list of plans in the Surveyor General's Office at Quebec, ca. 1790. *MPHC,* 24:44.

April 1781?—Fair copy of do. [wharf]—by [Samuel Robertson?]. No. 32 on list of plans in the Surveyor General's Office at Quebec, ca. 1790. *MPHC,* 24:44. This might also be the plan enclosed in Sinclair to Brehm of Feb. 15, 1780, *MPHC,* 9:538.

April 26, 1781—[Plan of Lakes Huron and Michigan]—by Samuel Robertson. Enclosed with letter of this date from Robertson to Captain John Schank, *MPHC,* 9:642.

May 12, 1781—[Deed to Mackinac Island]—by Patrick Sinclair and others. Clements Library (Oversize Manuscripts). [**Figure 2.9**].

May 12, 1781—Rough sketch of the part of the Fort enclosed for temporary security—by Lieutenant Governor Patrick Sinclair. British Library (Frederick Haldimand Papers, Add Mss. 21758, f. 370). [**Figure 2.11**].

June 15, 1781—Sketch of the Fort on Michilimakinac Island—by Lieutenant Governor Patrick Sinclair. British Library (Frederick Haldimand Papers, Add. Mss. 21757, f. 264). [**Figure 2.12**].

September 20, 1782—Plan of Fort Michilimakinac shewing its present state with a project for securing it against surprise before the winter sets in by Lt. Hockings Sept. 20th 1782—by Lieutenant Richard Hockings. No. 34 on list of plans in the Surveyor General's Office at Quebec, ca. 1790. *MPHC,* 24:44. Hockings's report survives.

September 20, 1782—Sections of the same [Hockings plan]—by Lieutenant Richard Hockings. No. 35 on list of plans in the Surveyor General's Office at Quebec, ca. 1790. *MPHC,* 24:44.

September 1782?—Plan of the powder magazine unfinished at Michilimakinac—by [Lt. Richard Hockings?]. No. 36 on list of plans in the Surveyor General's Office at Quebec, ca. 1790. *MPHC,* 24:44.

September 1782?—Plan of the officers Barracks at Do [Michilimakinac]—by [Lieutenant Richard Hockings?]. No. 37 on list of plans in the Surveyor General's Office at Quebec, ca. 1790. *MPHC,* 24:44.

1782—Plan of Barracks & Report thereon 1782—by [Lieutenant Richard Hockings?]. Included on a "List of Plans," ca. 1784. British Library (Frederick Haldimand Papers, Add Mss. 21886).

1782?—Plan of the Fort & Village at Michilimack-inac—by [unknown but possibly Lieutenant Richard Hockings]. Included on a "List of Plans," ca. 1784. British Library (Frederick Haldimand Papers, Add Mss. 21886). It is also possible that this is a plan of the mainland post by an unknown author.

1782?—Plan of the Fort & sections of Do.—by [unknown but possibly Lieutenant Richard Hockings]. Included on a "List of Plans," ca. 1784. British Library (Frederick Haldimand Papers, Add Mss. 21886). This might be one of the Hockings plans of September 1782.

1785–96—A Chart of the Straights of St. Mary's and Michilimackinac containing the Water Communication between the three Great Lakes vizt. Superior, Huron and Michigan—by [unknown]. Library and Archives Canada (V30/410-St. Marys River-1815). [Not illustrated]. This map has been illustrated a number of times (see Armour and Widder, *At the Crossroads,* 181) and is associated with Library and Archives Canada microfiche number 44767. Their catalog describes it as an 1815 copy by Emeric Essex Vidal after a map by Capt. W. F. W. Owen. Details of the map clearly place it in the period 1785–96, however, and it has an earlier look to it, so there may be some confusion in the catalog record.

1785–96 (copied [1815])—A Chart of the Straits of St. Mary's and Michilimackinac containing the Water Communication between the three Great Lakes, viz: Superior, Huron & Michigan—by Emeric Essex Vidal after an unknown cartographer. National Archives (MPG 1/87). [Figure 2.15].

Autumn 1788—Sketch of Lake Huron 1788, circumnavigated by Gother Mann, Capt. commanding Royal Engineers in Canada—by Captain Gother Mann. Library and Archives Canada (H2/410-Huron-1788). [Figure 2.14]. Insets show Falls of St. Mary and Matchedash Bay.

Autumn 1788—Sketch of Lake Huron 1788, circumnavigated by Gother Mann, Capt. commanding Royal Engineers in Canada—by Captain Gother Mann. Library and Archives Canada (H2/410-Huron-1788, copy 2). [Not illustrated]. A second, contemporary manuscript copy of the Mann map of Lake Huron. Insets show Falls of St. Mary and Matchedash Bay.

December 6, 1788—[Lake Huron, 1788]—by Captain Gother Mann. National Archives (C.O. 700 Canada No. 38E). [Not illustrated]. Sent with Mann's report of this date (No. 38F)

reporting on defenses of the military posts of the upper lakes. Insets show Falls of St. Mary and Matchedash Bay.

December 6, 1788 (copied later)—[Lake Huron, 1788]—by Captain Gother Mann. National Archives (MPG 272). [Not illustrated]. Insets show Falls of St. Mary and Matchedash Bay.

ca. 1790—[Lake Huron and Straits of Mackinac]—by Captain David William Smith. The North-umberland Estates, Alnwick, Northumberland (D. W. Smith's "History of the 5th Regiment," vol. 4, 187A/208). [Not illustrated]. A very rough plan of Lake Huron and the Straits of Mackinac identifying important places in the area.

ca. 1790—Plan of Michilimakinac—by Captain David William Smith. Toronto Public Library (James Bain Collection, D. W. Smith Note-books, vol. 2, "Views & Plans"). [Figure 2.13].

September 11, 1796—[Draft of the garrison of Michilimackinac]—by Winthrop Sargent and Major Henry Burbeck. Mentioned in letter of this date from Burbeck to Captain Moses Porter. Sent to Porter by Lieutenant James Sterrett. Burton Historical Collection (Moses Porter Papers). This was probably very similar to the plan in the Winthrop Sargent Papers, Ohio Historical Society.

September 1796—[On verso:] a rough plan of Fort Michilimakina—by [Winthrop Sargent and Major Moses Porter]. Ohio Historical Society (Winthrop Sargent Papers, Box 3, Folder 11). [Figure 3.1].

October 25, 1796—Fort Michilimackinac—by Lieutenant James Sterrett and Lieutenant Ebenezer Massey. Historical Society of Pennsylvania (Anthony Wayne Papers, vol. 40, pp. 44 and 45). [Figure 3.2].

December 19, 1796—[Plan of Mackina]—by Patrick McNiff. The author promised this map in a letter of this date to Major General Anthony Wayne. Clements Library (Wayne Family Papers).

1796?—Sketch of the Streights of St. Mary between Lake Huron and Lake Superior with part of the Coast of Lake Huron and Michilimacinac—by [unknown]. Enclosed in letter of Dorchester to Portland. National Archives (MPG 34). [Not illustrated]. Includes inset plan of the Falls of St. Mary. This might be related to the Mann maps or to the 1785–96 maps.

1796?—Sketch of the Streights of St. Mary between Lake Huron and Lake Superior with part of the Coast of Lake Huron and Michilimacinac—by [unknown]. Enclosed in letter of Dorchester to Portland. National Archives (MPG 40). [Not illustrated]. Another copy of the above but lacking the inset plan of the falls of St. Mary.

1796–99—[Survey of military reserve at Michili-mackinac]—by [Major Henry Burbeck or his officers?]. Burbeck had a military reserve laid out during his time at Mackinac Island. Mentioned in Howard to Secretary of War, Oct. 1, 1810, *TP,* 10:333.

1796–99—[Maps, plans, and drawings of Fort Mackinac and Mackinac Island]—by [garrison officers]. A number of maps and plans believed to be associated with Major Henry Burbeck's command at Michilimackinac (1796–99) are said to survive in the "Oscar Barck Collection" at Fraunces Tavern, New York, New York. This collection was unprocessed and inaccessible as of February 2006, and it has not been possible to identify or describe individual maps and plans relating to the Straits of Mackinac.

May 2, 1797—[A description of the harbour of Michilimackinac]—by [unknown]. Received on "a paper" by Thomas Duggan at Fort St. Joseph and mentioned by him in his journal on this date. Clements Library (Thomas Duggan Journal).

August 19, 1797—[Plan of the present works showing demolitions and proposed improvements to Fort Mackinac]—by Brigadier General James Wilkinson. Enclosed with a letter from Wilkinson to Burbeck of this date. West Point Museum (Fort Mackinac Orderly Book, 6).

August 1797—[Outline plan of Government House]—by Major Caleb Swan. Sketch drawn into the body of his letter to Captain Frederick Frye of Oct. 10, 1797.

August 1797 (published 1797)—[Outline plan of Government House]—by Major Caleb Swan. Drawn into letter from Swan to Captain Frederick Frye dated Oct. 10, 1797, as printed in the *Medical Repository* 1, no. 1 (1797): 527. [Figure 3.4].

1797?—Michilimacina—by JM [Lieutenant John Michael?]. Location of original unknown. Photographic copy held by Mackinac State Historic Parks. [Figure 3.3].

May 2, 1799—[Plan of Michilimackinac]—by [Major John J. U. Rivardi]. Enclosed with a letter from Rivardi to Alexander Hamilton of this date. Library of Congress (Alexander Henry Papers). A summary of the letter is in *AHP,* 23:92.

September 2, 1805—[On verso:] Sketch of the Situation of certain Lotts in the Village of Michilimc giving dimentions made by actual measurement of the property of Jacob Franks, Robert Dickson and James Aird—by [possibly Robert Dickson]. Burton Historical Collection (977.4m16-n.d.-S627). [Figure 3.5].

June 1810—[View of Fort Mackinac]—by George Washington Whistler. Described in letter from Captain John Whistler to Colonel Jacob Kingsbury of Jan. 5, 1813. Burton Historical Collection (Jacob Kingsbury Papers, L5:1812–13, vol. 20). The Whistlers left Chicago on June 26 and were in Detroit by July 5. George W. Whistler was then ten years old.

August–September 1810 (drawn September 1810 or later)—Survey of the Island of Michilli-mackinac in August 1810 . . . Survey of the Island of Bois Blanc performed September 10th 11th & 12th 1810 . . . Survey of a tract on the main including the old Fort at Michill. . . . —by Aaron Greeley. National Archives and Records Administration (RG 49, Old Map File, Michigan 10). [**Not illustrated**]. Possibly Greeley's original. It is very badly worn and faded.

August 1810 (traced ca. 1900–1915)—Survey of the Island of Michillimackinac in August 1810. . . . —after Aaron Greeley. National Archives and Records Administration (RG 49, Special Published Maps, Michigan 1). [**Not illustrated**]. Blueprint of a tracing of Mackinac Island from Greeley's larger map of surveys in the Straits.

August 1810 (traced 1915)—Survey of the Island of Michillimackinac in August 1810. . . . —after Aaron Greeley. State Archives of Michigan. [**Not illustrated**]. Made from the tracing in National Archives and Records Administration.

August 1810—Plan of the Island of Michilli-mackinac, Shewing the military reservation upon that Island. Surveyed in August 1810. At the request of the Commandant of Fort Michillimackinac, for the purpose of distinguishing the military Lands from the private claims—by Aaron Greeley. National Archives and Records Administration (RG 75, Records of the Bureau of Indian Affairs, Map No. 754). [**Figure 3.7**].

August 1810—[Plan of the town and harbor of Michilimacinac]—by Aaron Greeley. Manuscript survey map on which later copies were based.

August 1810 (probably copied in 1816 with additions in 1848)—Plan of the Town and Harbor of Michilimacinac—by Aaron Greeley. National Archives and Records Administration (RG 49, Old Map File, Michigan 11). [**Figure 3.6**].

August 1810 (copied 1816)—[Continuation of the strait of Michigan exhibiting the Islands of Michilimacinac with the strait of Michigan, Boisblanc & Macinac Island]—by [Aaron Greeley]. Copy of original survey sent to Detroit from Washington with a letter from Meigs to Audrain, July 24, 1816, *TP*, 10:660–61.

August 1810 (copied 1827)—[Islands of Bois Blanc and Michilimackinac]—by Aaron Greeley. A copy of part of Greeley's map of the Straits sent from the General Land Office with letter of Graham to Tiffin, May 17, 1827, *TP*, 11:1079.

September 1810—[Survey of the island of Michili-mackinac]—by Lieutenant John Anderson. Mentioned in a letter from Anderson to Eustis, Feb. 2, 1811, with promised completion of duplicates by May 1, 1811. *TP*, 10:339. The survey was undertaken in September 1810. See Howard to Eustis, Oct. 1, 1810, *TP*, 10:333. The map was not sent to Washington and was destroyed by the British after their capture of Detroit. See Anderson and Roberdeau to Swift, Jan. 15, 1816, RG 77, Buell Collection, National Archives and Records Administration.

1812—[Michilimackinac on Lake Huron]—by Richard Dillon, Jr. Original drawing on which the 1813 engraving was based.

1812 (published 1813)—Michilimackinac on Lake Huron—by Richard Dillon, Jr. Published in Montréal by Richard Dillon, Sr., 1813. Clements Library (Print Division, E-7). [**Figure 4.1**].

August 1814 (drawn 1816)—[Sketch of the island of Michilimackinac]. [Inset:] View of the Island of Michillimackinac from our first Station—by [Captain Charles Gratiot]. National Archives and Records Administration (RG 77, Fortifications Map File, Drawer 1, Sheet 30). [**Figure 4.2**].

September 7, 1814 (painted 182[—])—[*Tigress* and *Scorpion* carried into Mackinac]—by William Dashwood. Mackinac State Historic Parks (2000.60.1). [**Figure 4.3**].

Fall 1815—[Sketch map of Mackinac Island]—by [Major Isaac Roberdeau]. National Archives and Records Administration (RG 77, Entry 222, Reports of Fortifications and Topographical Surveys, 1816–1823, Folder 1817–1819). [**Figure 4.9**].

August 31, 1816—Chart of the Courses and distances from Michilimackinack to Green Bay taken and protracted by Major Charles Gratiot of the Engineers—August 31st 1816—by Major Charles Gratiot. National Archives and Records Administration (RG 77, Fortifications Map File, Drawer 152, Sheet 4-1). [**Not illustrated**].

August 31, 1816—Chart Shewing the Navigation from Michilimackinac to Green Bay—by [Major Charles Gratiot]. National Archives and Records Administration (RG 77, Fortifications Map File, Drawer 152, Sheet 4-3). [**Figure 4.14**]. Contemporary, fair copy.

September 1817—Michillimackinac from Round Island—by Major Francis Smith Belton. Masco Collection. [**Figure 4.4**].

September 1817—Mackina. 1817—by [or after Major Francis S. Belton]. Bentley Historical Library (Francis S. Belton Collection, UAs). [**Figure 4.5**].

September 1817—The Arched rock Michillimack-inac—by Major Francis Smith Belton. Masco Collection. [**Figure 4.8**].

November 25, 1817—Plan of Forts Holmes and Mackinac—by Major Charles Gratiot. National Archives and Records Administration (RG 77, Fortifications Map File, Drawer 1, Sheet 4-4). [**Figure 4.6**].

November 25, 1817—Fort Holmes Mackinaw Mich. No. 1—by Major Charles Gratiot. National Archives and Records Administration (RG 77, Fortifications Map File, Drawer 1, Sheet 4-3). [**Figure 4.10**].

November 25, 1817—Fort Holmes Mackinack. Isld. Michigan. [No. 2 and No. 3 on plans]—by Major Charles Gratiot. National Archives and Records Administration (RG 77, Fortifications Map File, Drawer 1, Sheet 4-2). [**Figure 4.11**].

November 25, 1817—Fort Holmes Mackinaw Mich. No. 2 [and] No. 3—by Major Charles Gratiot. National Archives and Records Administration (RG 77, Fortifications Map File, Drawer 1, Sheet 4-1). [**Figure 4.12**]. Two designs for fortified fronts.

November 25, 1817—Map of the Island of Michilimackinac—by Lieutenant William Sanford Eveleth. National Archives and Records Administration (RG 77, Fortifications Map File, Drawer 1, Sheet 4-5). [**Figure 5.13**].

November 25, 1817—Map of the Island of Michilimackinac—by Lieutenant William Sanford Eveleth. Clements Library (6-N-21). [**Figure 4.7**]. A contemporary copy of the map that is in the National Archives.

1817—[Sketch of the Island of Michilimackinac]—by Lieutenant William Sanford Eveleth. Described by Thomas L. McKenney in 1827 as showing the island "as it is approached from the south-east and is an excellent representation of it." McKenney, *Sketches of a Tour to the Lakes*, 385. The description might actually refer to the vertical section of Mackinac Island found on the left side of Eveleth's 1817 map.

1817 (copied August 1826)—[Sketch of the Island of Michilimackinac]—by Lieutenant William Sanford Eveleth. Reduced and copied by Thomas L. McKenney and enclosed with his letter from Mackinac of Aug. 28, 1826. McKenney, *Sketches of a Tour to the Lakes*, 385.

1819 or 1820—Michilimackinac 15–20 Miles Distant—by Dr. John J. Bigsby. In a unique, grangerized edition of Bigsby, *The Shoe and Canoe*, 2:145. Library and Archives Canada (1939-447-88). [**Figure 4.13**].

1819–22 (**drawn ca. 1822**)—Survey of Lake Huron by Lieut. Henry Wolsey Bayfield, R.N. assisted by Mr. Philip Ed. Collins. Mid. in the Years 1819, 20, 21 & 22—by Lieutenant Henry W. Bayfield and Midshipman Philip E. Collins. Library and Archives Canada. [**Not illustrated**]. Copy in Mackinac State Historic Parks library.

1819–22 (**copied 1825**)—[Map of Lake Huron]. This map was reduced from a Survey made by Lieutenant Bayfield R.N. in the years 1819, 20, 21, and 22—by Lieutenant Henry Wolsey Bayfield. Library and Archives Canada (H2/410-Huron-1822). [**Figure 4.15**].

1819–22 (**published 1848**)—Lake Huron Sheet 1—by Lieutenant Henry Wolsey Bayfield. Library and Archives Canada (V12.13a/410-Huron-1848). [**Not illustrated**]. Typical published version of Bayfield's surveys including later additions of lighthouse at Bois Blanc and settlement at St. Ignace.

June 7–12, 1820—[Sketch of Michillimackinac]—by Captain David Bates Douglass. Olin Library, Kenyon College (99-024). [**Figure 5.4**].

June 7–12, 1820—[Sketch of two bark canoes]—by Captain David Bates Douglass. Olin Library, Kenyon College (99-024). [**Figure 5.9**]. Drawn on verso of Arch Rock view.

June 7–12, 1820—Village of Miche-Mackina—by Captain David Bates Douglass. Olin Library, Kenyon College (99-024). [**Figure 5.5**].

June 12, 1820—Sugar Loaf Rock—Mackina—by Captain David Bates Douglass. Olin Library, Kenyon College (99-024). [**Figure 5.6**].

June 12, 1820—[Distant view of Sugar Loaf Rock]—by Captain David Bates Douglass. Olin Library, Kenyon College (99-024). [**Figure 5.7**].

June 12, 1820—[An inside view of the Arch Rock]—by Captain David Bates Douglass. Olin Library, Kenyon College (99-024). [**Figure 5.8**].

June 12, 1820—[View of the town of Michilimackinac]—by Captain David Bates Douglass. Douglass noted in his journal on this date that he was prevented from taking a view of the town by "a very thick fog coming on." Jackman and Freeman, *American Voyageur*, 32.

June 12, 1820—[View of the fort and town of Michilimackinac]—by Henry R. Schoolcraft. He began this sketch from Round Island but was unable to finish it because of a sudden fog. Schoolcraft, *Narrative Journal*, 124.

June 12, 1820—[View of the fort and town of Michilimackinac]—by Lieutenant Aeneas Mackay. Mackay escorted Schoolcraft to Round Island where he began this sketch but was unable to finish it because of a sudden fog. Schoolcraft, *Narrative Journal*, 124.

June 1820 (**drawn 1853**)—Mackinac—by [Captain Seth Eastman] after Captain David Bates Douglass. Peabody Museum, Harvard University, Cambridge, MA (41-72-10/199 T1706). [**Figure 5.3**].

June 1820 (**drawn 1853**)—Mackinac—by Captain Seth Eastman after Captain David Bates Douglass. The Newberry Library, Edward E. Ayer Collection. [**Figure 5.2**].

June 1820 (**painted ca. 1854**)—Machilimackinack and Fort Mackinac—by [Captain Seth Eastman] after Captain David Bates Douglass. Current location unknown. Described in McDermott, *Seth Eastman*, #67, as appearing in 1954 catalog, No. 146, *American Paintings Historical, Genre, Western* (New York: Edward Eberstadt and Sons). [**Not illustrated**]. Oil on canvas.

June 1820 (**published 1854 and 1855**)—Michili-mackinack—by Captain Seth Eastman after Captain David Bates Douglass. Engraved by John C. McRae. In Schoolcraft, *Information*, 6:188, and Eastman, *The American Annual*, 79. Clements Library (Oversize Z Sc). [**Figure 5.1**].

June 1820—[Sketches of "rock scenery"]—by [Henry Schoolcraft?]. In a letter to David B. Douglass of December 16, 1824, Schoolcraft requested the return of eighteen sketches of rock scenery loaned to Douglass. Schoolcraft acknowledged receipt of the drawings in a letter of December 30. Clements Library (David Bates Douglass Papers). His diary records receipt of "a portfolio of sketches and drawings of scenery" on December 25, 1824. Schoolcraft, *Personal Memoirs*, 203. Some of these might have depicted geological formations on Mackinac Island.

September 9, 1820—[Old Fort Mackinac]—by Henry R. Schoolcraft. Original sketch of Old Michilimackinac on which the Eastman watercolor was based.

September 9, 1820 (**drawn 1851**)—Old Fort Mackinac—by Captain Seth Eastman after Henry Rowe Schoolcraft. Minnesota Historical Society (AV 1991.85.9). [**Figure 5.10**].

September 9, 1820 (**published 1852**)—Ruins of Old Fort Mackanack, 1763—by Captain Seth Eastman after Henry Rowe Schoolcraft. Engraved by Charles Edward Wagstaff and Joseph Andrews. In Schoolcraft, *Information*, 2:242, 6:243, and Eastman, *The American Annual*, 71. Illustrated example is in Clements Library (Print Division, Unmatted Prints). [**Figure 5.11**].

September 9, 1820 (**published 1861 and 1867**)—Ruins of Old Fort Mackinaw—by Captain Seth Eastman after Henry Rowe Schoolcraft.

Published in Barber and Howe, *Our Whole Country*, and again in Barber and Howe, *All the Western States and Territories*, 286. [**Not illustrated**].

August 19, 1822—[Sketch of the country in the vicinity of Mackinac]—by "an intelligent man perfectly well acquainted with it." Enclosed in a letter from Lewis Cass to David Bates Douglass of this date. Cass noted that it showed the Cheboygan River. Clements Library (David Bates Douglass Papers).

September 20, 1823—[On verso:] Survey, Report & field Notes of Certain roads on the Island of Michilimackinac—by Elijah Warner. Stuart House Museum (Archive, Box E). [**Figure 5.12**].

October 5–7, 1823—[Circumf. of Mackinac Isle do. of Round Isle]—by Major Stephen H. Long. Sketch from which Bigsby's map of this date was copied.

October 5–7, 1823 (**copied 1823 or later**)—Circumf. of Mackinac Isle Do. of Round Isle—by Dr. John Jeremiah Bigsby after Major Stephen Harriman Long. In unique, grangerized edition of Bigsby, *The Shoe and Canoe*, 2:2. Library and Archives Canada (1939-447-89/90). [**Figure 5.14**].

October 5–7, 1823 (**completed 1825**)—Distant View of Mackinac I.—by Samuel Seymour. Listed among finished drawings completed by Seymour in Long to Macomb of April 23, 1825. Kane, Holmquist, and Gilman, *The Northern Expeditions of Stephen H. Long*, 392.

October 6, 1823—[View of Sugar Loaf Rock]—by Samuel Seymour. Mentioned in Stephen H. Long's journal of this date. Kane, Holmquist, and Gilman, *The Northern Expeditions of Stephen H. Long*, 247.

October 6, 1823 (**completed 1825**)—View of Sugar Loaf Rock, Mack. I.—by Samuel Seymour. Listed among the finished drawings completed by Seymour in Long to Macomb of April 23, 1825. Probably a fair copy of the scene noted above. Kane, Holmquist, and Gilman, *The Northern Expeditions of Stephen H. Long*, 392.

October 6, 1823—[View of Arch Rock]—by Samuel Seymour. Mentioned in Stephen H. Long's journal of this date. Kane, Holmquist, and Gilman, *The Northern Expeditions of Stephen H. Long*, 247.

October 6, 1823—[View of the village and fort of Mackinac]—by Samuel Seymour. Mentioned in Stephen H. Long's journal of this date. Kane, Holmquist, and Gilman, *The Northern Expeditions of Stephen H. Long*, 247.

[Spring] 1825—[Surveys of the Mission property]—by [Rev. William M. Ferry]. Mentioned in letter of July 8, 1825, from Amanda Ferry to Hannah White. Anderson, "Frontier Mackinac Island," 210.

August 13, 1825—[Sketch of the mission buildings]—by Amanda W. Ferry. Enclosed with her letter of this date to Hannah White. Anderson, "Frontier Mackinac Island," 208.

August 13, 1825—[Sketch of the situation of the mission buildings relative to the village, lake, etc.]—by Amanda W. Ferry. Enclosed with her letter of this date to Hannah White. Anderson, "Frontier Mackinac Island," 208.

August 13, 1825—[Charts and maps]—by Amanda W. Ferry. In a letter to Hannah White of this date Ferry mentions "Several of my charts, maps, etc.," which she had "designed" as keepsakes for her brothers. Anderson, "Frontier Mackinac Island," 210.

1825–30—[Mission Station at Mackinaw]—by [unknown]. Original sketch on which the engraving was based.

1825–29 (published ca. 1830)—Mission Station at Mackinaw—by [unknown]. Published in American Tract Society, *Eliza: The Indian Sorceress.* Clements Library (C2 1830 Am Tract). [**Figure. 5.17**].

August 1826—[View of Michilimackinac]—by [James Otto Lewis? or Thomas Loraine McKenney?]. Original sketch on which the Swett lithograph was based.

August 1826 (published 1827)—View of Michilimackinac—by [James Otto Lewis? or Thomas Loraine McKenney?]. Lithograph by Moses Swett. In McKenney, *Sketches of a Tour to the Lakes,* 385. Clements Library (C2-l827-Mc). [**Figure 5.16**].

August 1826—[Indian Canoe]—by Lieutenant John Farley with background details by Lieutenant William Sanford Eveleth. Original drawings on which the Stewart lithograph was based.

August 1826 (published 1827)—Indian Canoe—Lithograph by F. Stewart [or Steward] after Lieutenant John Farley and Lieutenant William Sanford Eveleth. Lithograph by Pendleton's Lithography. In McKenney, *Sketches of a Tour to the Lakes,* 200 (copy 1) and 285 (copy 2). Clements Library (C2-1827-Mc). [**Figure 5.15**].

November 14, 1826—[On verso:] Plan of a Cantonment for one Company, at Mackinaw—by [Major Alexander Ramsay Thompson]. RG 92, Consolidated Correspondence File, National Archives and Records Administration. [**Figure 5.20**].

June 20, 1827—Sugar Loaf Rock, on the island of Mackinac—by John A. Granger. Drawn into in his journal on this date. Current location of original unknown.

June 20, 1827 (copied 1940)—Sugar Loaf Rock, on the island of Mackinac—after John A. Granger. Copy pencil sketch in typescript of Granger diary. Bentley Historical Library (851327 Aa1). [**Not illustrated**].

June 20, 1827—Rough sketch of "The Arched Rock," on the Island of Mackinac—by John A. Granger. Drawn into his journal on this date. Current location of original unknown.

June 20, 1827 (copied 1940)—Rough sketch of "The Arched Rock," on the Island of Mackinac—after John A. Granger. Copy pencil sketch in typescript of Granger diary. Bentley Historical Library (851327 Aa1). [**Not illustrated**].

August 1827—[Plat of the island of Bois Blanc in the Streights of Michillimackinac surveyed in June, July & August 1827]—by Lucius Lyon. Manuscript plat map drawn on pasteboard. Described in Lyon to Tiffin, Sept. 8, 1827, *TP,* 11:1117–18.

August 1827 (copied August 1827)—[Plat of the island of Bois Blanc in the Streights of Michillimackinac surveyed in June, July & August 1827]—by Lucius Lyon. Copy deposited with commandant of Fort Mackinac and mentioned in letter of Thompson to Jones, Sept. 11, 1827, RG 49, National Archives and Records Administration. Copy in Mackinac State Historic Parks library.

August 1827—[Plat of the island of Bois Blanc in the Streights of Michillimackinac surveyed in June, July & August 1827]—by Lucius Lyon. Copied from original plat and submitted with Lyon to Tiffin, Sept. 8, 1827, *TP,* 11:1117–18.

August 1827 (copied September 11, 1827)—[Plat of the island of Bois Blanc in the Streights of Michillimackinac surveyed in June, July & August 1827]—by Lucius Lyon. Copied from the copy deposited with commandant of Fort Mackinac and enclosed in Thompson to Jones, Sept. 11, 1827, RG 49, National Archives and Records Administration. Copy in Mackinac State Historic Parks library.

August 1827 (copied October 5, 1827)—Plat of the Island of Bois Blanc, in the Streights of Michillimackinac. Surveyed in June, July & August 1827—by Lucius Lyon. [Inset added later at left:] M. Dousmans private Claims and Public Surveys adjacent, on Bois Blanc I. In Lake Huron. National Archives and Records Administration (RG 49, Old Map File, Michigan 16). [**Not illustrated**].

August 1827 (copied 1827 or later)—Plat of Bois-Blanc Island, in the Streights of Michilimackinac. Surveyed in July and August 1827—by Lucius Lyon. National Archives and Records Administration (RG 49, Old Map File, Michigan 18). [**Figure 5.23**].

August 1827 (copied later)—Plat Bois Blanc Island, Michigan—by [Lucius Lyon]. National Archives and Records Administration (RG 49, Old Map File, Michigan 20). Appears to be a copy of a later date. [**Not illustrated**].

August 1827 (copied later)—Copy of a Plat of the Island of Bois-Blanc near Michilimackinac Surveyed in the Summer of 1827—by Lucius Lyon. Martin Jahn Collection. [**Not illustrated**]. A copy of later date.

August 1827 (published 1853)—Public Surveys on Isle Bois Blanc in the Straits of Mackinaw—by [Lucius Lyon]. Inset on John Farmer, *Map of the States of Michigan and Wisconsin. . . .* (Detroit, 1853). Bentley Historical Library (M4110 1853. F3). [**Not illustrated**].

August 1827 (lithographed later—1860s?)—Plat of the Island of Bois Blanc, in the Streights of Michillimackinac . . . Surveyed in June, July & August 1827—by Lucius Lyon. National Archives and Records Administration (RG 49, Old Map File, Michigan 17). [**Not illustrated**].

September 5, 1827—[On verso:] Plan of the Mission Premises at Mackinaw—by William Montague Ferry. Enclosed in Ferry to Evarts of this date. Houghton Library, Harvard University (ABC: 18.4.8, Vol. 1, No. 189). [**Figure 5.19**].

September 5, 1827—[On verso:] Plot & Notes of the Point—by William Montague Ferry. Enclosed in Ferry to Evarts of this date. Houghton Library, Harvard University (ABC: 18.4.8, Vol. 1, No. 234). [**Figure 5.18**].

September 5, 1827—[Plot of the point]—by William Montague Ferry. Enclosed in Ferry to Evarts of this date. Houghton Library, Harvard University (ABC: 18.4.8, Vol. 1, No. 234). [**Not illustrated**]. A very rough plat, showing only the basic outline of the mission property.

October 1827—[Sketch of the new hospital in Fort Mackinac]—by [Mary Nexsen Thompson]. Clements Library (Print Division, G-15). [**Figure 5.21**].

November 1828 (copied January 9, 1829)—Claims Nos. 1 & 2, on Bois Blanc Island. Surveyed in Novr. 1828—by John Mullett. National Archives and Records Administration (RG 49, Old Map File, Michigan 19). [**Figure 5.24**].

November 1828 (copied January 9, 1829)—[Mi]chillimackinac I. Shewing the Surveys of [Pri]vate Claims [by John] Mullett in 1828—by

John Mullett. National Archives and Records Administration (RG 49, Old Map File, Michigan 21). [**Not illustrated**].

November 1828 (copied later)—Map of the Island of Michillimackinac. Surveyed A.D. 1828—by John Mullett. National Archives and Records Administration (RG 49, Old Map File, Michigan 22). [**Not illustrated**].

November 1828 (copied 1830)—[Map of the island of Michillimackinac]—by John Mullett. Copy made in General Land Office and forwarded to secretary of war for reference with letter of Graham to Eaton, June 15, 1830, *TP*, 12:179.

November 1828 (published 1830)—Map of Michilli-mackinac Isle—by John Farmer after John Mullett. Inset on *An Improved Map of the Surveyed Part of the Territory of Michigan by John Farmer 1830* (Detroit, 1830). Scale of 4 miles to an inch. See Karpinski, *Bibliography,* 247. [**Not illustrated**].

November 1828 (published 1831)—Map of Michillimackinac Isle—by John Farmer after John Mullett. Inset on *An Improved Map of the Surveyed Part of the Territory of Michigan by John Farmer 1831* (Detroit, 1831). Clements Library (Atlas, H-2). Scale changed to 2 miles to an inch. [**Not illustrated**].

November 1828 (published 1835 and 1836)—Map of Michillimackinac Isle—by John Farmer after John Mullett. Inset on *An Improved Edition of a Map of the Surveyed Part of the Territory of Michigan by John Farmer 1835* (Detroit, 1835). Clements Library (Atlas, H-2). Repeated in the Farmer map of the same title with date of 1836 published in Detroit in 1836, Clements Library (Atlas, Box G), and same title with date of 1836 published in New York by Colton in 1836. Clements Library (6-O-9). [**Figure 5.26**].

November 1828 (published 1837 and 1839)—Map of Mackinaw Isle—by John Farmer after John Mullett. Inset on *Map of the Straits of Mackinaw,* which is inset on John Farmer, *Map of the Surveyed Part of Michigan* (New York, 1837). Clements Library (5-M-7). This is repeated on John Farmer, *Map of the Surveyed Part of Michigan* (New York, 1839). Clements Library (5-M-8). [**Inset on Figure 5.31**].

November 1828 (copied August 19, 1842)—Michilli-mackinac I. Shewing the Surveys of Private Claims. By J. Mullett 1828—by John Mullett. Clements Library (6-O-16). [**Figure 5.25**].

November 1828 (probably copied November 1845)—Michillimackinac I. Shewing the Surveys of Private Claims. By J. Mullett in 1828—by John Mullett. Mackinac State Historic Parks (1986.69). A land office copy. [**Not illustrated**].

November 1828 (copied later)—Michillimackinac I. Shewing the Surveys of Private Claims. By J. Mullett 1828—by John Mullett. A later nineteenth-century copy, badly damaged and in poor condition and in the hands of a private owner. Examined at the Clements Library in 2000. Current location unknown. [**Not illustrated**].

November 1828—[Plat showing private claims on Point St. Ignace]—by [John Mullett]. National Archives and Records Administration (RG 49, Old Map File, Michigan 26). [**Figure 5.27**].

November 1828 (published 1853)—Connections of the Private Claims with the Public Surveys at Pte. Ste. Ignace—by John Farmer after John Mullett. Inset on John Farmer, *Map of the States of Michigan and Wisconsin. . . .* (Detroit, 1853). Bentley Historical Library (M4110 1853 .F3). [**Not illustrated**].

November 1828 (copied later)—Map of the Private Land Claims at Michillimackinac Surveyed AD 1828—by John Mullett. National Archives and Records Administration (RG 49, Old Map File, Michigan 23). [**Not illustrated**].

November 1828 (copied later—possibly January 1829)—Private Claims at Michillimackinac Surveyed in Octr. & Nov. 1828—by John Mullett. National Archives and Records Administration (RG 49, Old Map File, Michigan 24). [**Figure 5.28**]. Marked "A true copy."

November 1828 (published 1829)—Map of the Straits of Michillimackinac, from Actual Survey—by John Farmer after John Mullett. Inset on *An Improved Map of the Surveyed Part of the Territory of Michigan . . . by John Farmer, 1829* (Detroit, 1829). Karpinski, *Bibliography,* 247. [**Not illustrated**].

November 1828 (published 1830)—Map of the Straits of Michillimackinac, from Actual Survey. [Inset:] Map of Pte. Ste. Ignace—by John Farmer after John Mullett. Inset on *An Improved Map of the Surveyed Part of the Territory of Michigan . . . by John Farmer 1830* (Detroit, 1830). Karpinski, *Bibliography,* 247. [**Not illustrated**]. Inset of St. Ignace shown at scale of 4 miles to an inch.

November 1828 (published 1831)—Map of the Straits of Michillimackinac, from Actual Survey. [Inset:] Map of Pte. Ste. Ignace—by John Farmer after John Mullett. Inset on *An Improved Map of the Surveyed Part of the Territory of Michigan by John Farmer 1831* (Detroit, 1831). Clements Library (Atlas, H-2). [**Figure 5.29**]. Scale of St. Ignace inset changed to 2 miles to an inch.

November 1828 (published 1835 and 1836)—Map of the Straits of Michillimackinac, from Actual

Survey. [Inset:] Map of Pte. Ste. Ignace—by John Farmer after John Mullett. Inset on *An Improved Edition of a Map of the Surveyed Part of the Territory of Michigan by John Farmer 1835* (Detroit, 1835). Clements Library (Atlas, H-2). Repeated in the Farmer map of the same title with date of 1836 published in Detroit in 1836, Clements Library (Atlas, Box G), and same title with date of 1836 published in New York by Colton in 1836, Clements Library (6-O-9). [**Figure 5.30**]. Distinguished by truncated Bois Blanc Island.

November 1828 (published 1837, 1839, and later)—Map of the Straits of Mackinaw from Actual Survey. [Inset]: Map of Mackinaw Isle—by John Farmer after John Mullett. Inset on *Map of the Surveyed Part of Michigan by John Farmer . . . 1837* (New York, 1837). Clements Library (5-M-7). Repeated on the Farmer map of the same title in 1839. Clements Library (5-M-8). [**Figure 5.31**]. Repeated in maps of 1840, 1844, 1847, 1850, 1854, and 1855. See Karpinski, *Bibliography,* 258–59.

November 1828 (published 1847)—Private Claims at Michillimackinac Surveyed in Octr. & Novr. 1828—by John Mullett. From U.S. General Land Office, *Report on Michigan Land Claims* (Sen. Doc. 221, 29th Cong. 2nd Sess.), 1847. Clements Library (E-0-B). [**Not illustrated**].

ca. 1830—[View of Mission Church and the Mission House]—by [unknown]. Original sketch on which the engraving was based. Note the similarity to the view of 1825–30.

ca. 1830 (published 1835)—Mission House at Mackinaw—by [unknown]. Published in *Quarterly Paper of the American Board of Commissioners for Foreign Missions, No. XX* (1835): 77. Bentley Historical Library. [**Not illustrated**].

ca. 1830 (published 1847 and 1848)—Mackinac Bluffs—by [unknown]. A retitled printing of "Mission House at Mackinaw," published in 1835. In Sears, *New Pictorial Family Magazine* 4 (1847): 501, and in Sears, *A New and Popular Pictorial Description of the United States,* 521. [**Figure 6.2**].

August 7, 1831—[Michillimackinac]—by Gustave de Beaumont. Preliminary sketch of view of Fort Mackinac from the harbor.

August 7, 1831—7 Michillimackinac lac huron 11 aout—by Gustave de Beaumont. In the "Romanet Album" owned as of 1938 by the Romanet family. Current location unknown. Reproduced in Pierson, *Tocqueville and Beaumont in America,* 304. [**Figure 6.3**]. Finished sketch of Fort Mackinac from the harbor.

August 7, 1831—23 lac huron Michillimackinac 7 aout 1831—by Gustave de Beaumont. Owned as of 1938 by the Beaumont family. Current location unknown. Reproduced in Pierson, *Tocqueville and Beaumont in America*, 300. [**Not illustrated**]. Preliminary sketch of Ste. Anne's Church.

August 7, 1831—[lac huron Michillimackinac 7 aout 1831]—by Gustave de Beaumont. In the "Romanet Album" owned as of 1938 by the Romanet family. Current location unknown. Reproduced in Pierson, *Tocqueville and Beaumont in America*, 300. Finished version of sketch of Ste. Anne's Church. [**Figure 6.4**].

August 7, 1831—[Sketch of the perforated grotto]—by Gustave de Beaumont. Mentioned in his journal for this date. Pierson, *Tocqueville and Beaumont in America*, 302. Preliminary sketch for finished view of Arch Rock.

August 7, 1831—Michillimackinac 16 Aôut 1831—by Gustave de Beaumont. In the "Romanet Album" owned as of 1938 by the Romanet family. Current location unknown. Reproduced in Pierson, *Tocqueville and Beaumont in America*, 306. [**Figure 6.5**]. Finished sketch of Arch Rock from the water.

August 7, 1831—[Sketch of Arch Rock from the water]—by Godfrey T. Vigne. Drawn when the artist accompanied Gustave de Beaumont and they each made a sketch. Mentioned in Beaumont's letters. Pierson, *Tocqueville and Beaumont in America*, 302.

January 23, 1832—[Map of road from the N.W. part of Sylvester's lot to the lake]—by Captain Robert A. McCabe. Drawn into letter of this date from McCabe to Colonel Enos Cutler. National Archives and Records Administration (RG 94, Fort Mackinac Letters Sent, 1829–1836, 106). [**Not illustrated**]. A very rough sketch of the road across the "Vacant Lot" ("Borough Lot").

January 1832—[Survey of the road to the distillery through the vacant lot]—by Michael Dousman. Dousman was authorized to make this survey by a vote of the borough council on January 18. Township Record Book, 62, CHL.

September 20, 1832—[Lot of land granted to John A. Drew]—by [unknown]. Drawn into conveyance of permission of this date signed by Brigadier General George M. Brooke. National Archives and Records Administration (RG 94, Fort Mackinac Letters Sent, 1829–36, 119). Rough sketch of the property in question. [**Not illustrated**].

1833–34—[Mackinac Island]—by Hannah White. Mackinac State Historic Parks (1997.00.27). [**Figure 6.1**].

August 1834—[Point Mackinaw and surrounding area]. Surveyed August 1834 by A. G. Ellis—by A. G. Ellis. Library of Congress (Henry Schoolcraft Papers). [**Not illustrated**]. Photostat in Mackinac State Historic Parks library. A survey of 11,520 acres around Old Michilimackinac ceded to federal government by the 1795 Treaty of Greenville.

August 1834—[Point St. Ignace and surrounding area]. Surveyed August 1834 by A. G. Ellis—by A. G. Ellis. Library of Congress (Henry Schoolcraft Papers). [**Not illustrated**]. Photostat in Mackinac State Historic Parks library. A survey of 11,520 acres around St. Ignace ceded to federal government by the 1795 Treaty of Greenville.

February 2, 1835—[Three drawings of the barracks &c at this post]—by [Lieutenant James W. Penrose]. Enclosed with and described in his letter of this date to Jesup. This was apparently a ground plan showing all the quarters and kitchens in Fort Mackinac. RG 92, Consolidated Correspondence File, National Archives and Records Administration.

August 13, 1835—[Sketches along the shore of Mackinac Island]—by George William Featherstonhaugh. The author describes a boat trip around the island "taking sketches on the way." Featherstonhaugh, *A Canoe Voyage*, 1:141. He made a number of other sketches during his time on Mackinac Island from August 12–17.

August 17, 1835—[Fort Michilimackinac]—by George William Featherstonhaugh. Original sketch on which the engraving was based.

August 17, 1835 (published 1847)—Fort Michilimackinac—by George William Featherstonhaugh. Engraved by George S. Measom. In Featherstonhaugh, *A Canoe Voyage* 1:148. Clements Library (C2-1847-Fe). [**Figure 6.10**].

September 30, 1835—[Survey of a Road Route from Saginaw to Mackinac M.T.]—by Lieutenant Benjamin Poole. Manuscript map transmitted to Major Henry Whiting on this date and forwarded to Quartermaster General's Department. Mentioned in *Report from the Secretary of War*, 2–4. The map includes "Dousman's Saw Mill" on the south shore of the Straits of Mackinac.

September 30, 1835 (published 1838)—Survey of a Road Route from Saginaw to Mackinac M.T.—by Lt. Benjamin Poole. In *Report from the Secretary of War*, Clements Library (D C 1838 2–26). [**Not illustrated**]. Shows Dousman's mill and nearby topography on the south shore of the Straits of Mackinac.

November 15, 1835—Plan of Hospital—by Assistant Surgeon Erastus B. Wolcott. Drawn into letter from Wolcott to Surgeon General Joseph Lovell of this date. National Archives and Records Administration (RG 94, Quarterly Reports of Sick and Wounded for Michigan Posts). [**Figure 5.22**].

1836—[Mackinaw from the East]—by George Catlin. Probably National Archives and Records Administration. U.S. Army Signal Corps photo in Mackinac State Historic Parks photo files. [**Not illustrated**]. Drawing of Mackinac Island from the east and the basis for the 1841 engraving below.

1836 (published 1841)—[Mackinaw from the East]—by George Catlin. Engraved by Myers Company. Published in Catlin, *Letters and Notes,* 2:161 (plate 264). Clements Library (C2-1841-Ca). [**Figure 6.11**].

November 1836—[Plans to alter Indian Agency House to a dormitory for Indians]—by [Henry R. Schoolcraft]. Schoolcraft proposed submitting this in a letter to Harris. May, "The Indian Dormitory," 7.

March 1837—[Plan for a dormitory for Indians]—by [Henry R. Schoolcraft]. Plan on which bids for construction were solicited. Mentioned in communication from Schoolcraft to Harris. May, "The Indian Dormitory," 8.

June 1837—[Plan for converting the Mission House into a dormitory for Indians]—by [Henry R. Schoolcraft]. Sent in letter from Schoolcraft to Harris of about this time. May, "The Indian Dormitory," 9.

July 21–26, 1837—[Sketches of Mackinac Island]—by Anna Brownell Jameson. Henry Schoolcraft described her as an "eminent landscape painter, or rather sketcher in crayon, and had her portfolio ever in hand. She did not hesitate freely to walk out to prominent points . . . to complete her sketches." Schoolcraft, *Personal Memoirs,* 561. Jameson took a particular interest in the Indians. Five examples of her work are known to survive and are listed below. She is presumed to have made additional drawings.

July 21–26, 1837—[On mount:] Island of Mackinaw—Lake Huron. Indians' Village—by Anna Brownell Jameson. Special Collections, Genealogy and Maps Centre, Toronto Public Library (966-6L-22). [**Figure 6.6**].

July 21–26, 1837—[On drawing:] Mokomaunish. Kee me wun. [On mount, in error:] The Widow Jones's Stockbridge where Harriet Martineau lodged—by Anna B. Jameson. Special Collections, Genealogy and Maps Centre, Toronto Public Library (966-6L-58).

[Illustrated without number]. Portrait heads of two Indians, one of whom (Kee me wun) is discussed in the artist's book. Jameson, *Winter Studies,* 2:137–38.

July 21, 1837—[On drawing:] Wigwams on the beach at Mackinac—July 21. [On mount:] Wigwams on the Beach at Mackinaw—by Anna Brownell Jameson. Special Collections, Genealogy and Maps Centre, Toronto Public Library (966-6L-24). [**Figure 6.7**].

July 21, 1837 (**drawn later**)—Indian Lodges on the Beach of the Island of Mackinac—by Anna Brownell Jameson. Special Collections, Genealogy and Maps Centre, Toronto Public Library (JRR 213). [**Not illustrated**]. A later copy of the sketch of this date.

July 23, 1837—[On drawing:] Machillimackinac. [On mount:] The Beach at Mackinaw—by Anna Brownell Jameson. Special Collections, Genealogy and Maps Centre, Toronto Public Library (966-6L-26). [**Figure 6.9**].

July 25, 1837—[On drawing:] Mackinac July 25. [On mount:] The Beach at Mackinaw from the Missionary Church door—by Anna Brownell Jameson. Special Collections, Genealogy and Maps Centre, Toronto Public Library (966-6L-25). [**Figure 6.8**].

August 1837—[Plan for a dormitory for Indians]—by [Henry R. Schoolcraft]. Submitted by Schoolcraft to Harris at this time. May, "The Indian Dormitory," 11, 17.

[November 1837]—[Plan for a dormitory for Indians]—[by Henry R. Schoolcraft]. Plan advertised in the *Detroit Free Press* as available for viewing by potential contractors, probably in November. Mentioned in Clark to Schoolcraft, Dec. 2, 1837, William F. Lawler Papers, Burton Historical Collection.

January 30, 1838—[Plan for building a dormitory at Mackinac]—by Henry R. Schoolcraft. Schoolcraft mentioned in his journal that he sent a plan to Washington on this date. Schoolcraft, *Personal Memoirs,* 586.

June 21, 1838—[Mackinac, Round, and Bois Blanc islands]—by Douglass Houghton. Pasted into his field notes and observations under this date. Bentley Historical Library (Douglass Houghton Papers). [**Figure 6.12**].

June 1838—Map of Island of Mackinac June 1838—by Bela Hubbard. Drawn into a notebook recording surveys of the coast of the Lower Peninsula. Bentley Historical Library (Bela Hubbard Papers, 851637, AcAa 2, Box 1, Vol. 2, p. 3). [**Figure 6.14**].

June 1838—[Map of the Straits of Mackinac]—by Bela Hubbard. Drawn into a notebook recording surveys of the coast of the Lower Peninsula. Bentley Historical Library (Bela Hubbard Papers, 851637, AcAa 2, Box 1, Vol. 2, p. 8). [**Figure 6.13**].

July 7, 1838—[Sketch of Lover's Leap from below]—by [Alvah] Bradish. Mentioned in Peter Dougherty journal on this date. Anderson, "Diaries of Peter Dougherty," 103.

August 1838—[Ile de Michilimackimac]—by François, comte de Castelnau. Original drawing on which the lithograph was based.

August 1838 (**published 1842**)—Ile de Michilimackimac (Lac Huron)—by François, comte de Castelnau. Lithograph by Aumont. From Castelnau, *Vues et Souvenirs de l'Amérique du Nord,* plate 27. Clements Library (Print Division, G-7). [**Figure 6.18**].

September 1838—[Fort Américain dans l'Ile de Michilimakinac]—by François, comte de Castelnau. Original drawing on which the lithograph was based.

September 1838 (**published 1842**)—Fort Américain dans l'Ile de Michilimakinac—by François, comte de Castelnau. Lithograph by Jacques Prat. From Castelnau, *Vues et Souvenirs de l'Amérique du Nord,* plate 26. Clements Library (Print Division, G-7). [**Figure 6.19**]. This example has been colored.

September 1838—[Village Ottawa Ile de Michilimakinac]—by François, comte de Castelnau. Original drawing on which the lithograph was based.

September 1838 (**published 1842**)—Village Ottawa Ile de Michilimakimac—by François, comte de Castelnau. Lithograph by Jacques Prat. In Castelnau, *Vues et Souvenirs de l'Amérique du Nord,* plate 25. Special Collections Library, University of Michigan. [**Figure 6.20**].

September 1838—[Roche Folie de Robinson]—by François, comte de Castelnau. Original drawing on which the lithograph was based.

September 1838 (**published 1842**)—Roche Folie de Robinson. Ile de Michilimakimac—by François, comte de Castelnau. Lithograph by Jacques Prat. From Castelnau, *Vues et Souvenirs de l'Amérique du Nord,* plate 21. Clements Library (Print Division, G-7). [**Figure 6.21**].

September 1838—[La Roche Arquée]—by François, comte de Castelnau. Original drawing on which the lithograph was based.

September 1838 (**published 1842**)—La Roche arquée Ile de Michilimakimac—by François, comte de Castelnau. Lithograph by Jacques Prat. From Castelnau, *Vues et Souvenirs de l'Amérique*

du Nord, plate 24. Special Collections Library, University of Michigan. [**Figure 6.22**].

September 1838—[Roche dit le Pain de Sucre]—by François, comte de Castelnau. Original drawing on which the lithograph was based.

September 1838 (**published 1842**)—Roche dit le Pain de Sucre Ile de Michilimakimac—by François, comte de Castelnau. Lithograph by Jacques Prat. From Castelnau, *Vues et Souvenirs de l'Amérique du Nord,* plate 23. Special Collections Library, University of Michigan. [**Figure 6.23**].

August 1839—Fort and Island of Mackinaw—by Caleb F. Davis. Mackinac State Historic Parks (1985.14.1). [**Figure 6.24**].

August 1839—Fort Mackinac. from the East Wharf—by Caleb F. Davis. Detroit Historical Museum. [**Not illustrated**]. A larger version of the drawing illustrated as Figure 6.25.

August 1839 (**drawn 1839–45**)—Fort Mackinac. From the East Wharf—by Caleb F. Davis. Clements Library (Print Division, H-1). [**Figure 6.25**].

September [?] 1839—Mackanaw. Outawa, Lake Huron—by Lieutenant Richard George Augustus Levinge. Royal Ontario Museum (969.120.1d). [**Not illustrated**]. Sketch of an Indian and child beside a wigwam. Enclosed in a cartouche with his sketch of a canoe.

September [?] 1839—Chippway canoe—by Lieutenant Richard George Augustus Levinge. Royal Ontario Museum (969.120.1d). [**Not illustrated**]. Thought to have been drawn on Mackinac Island. Enclosed in the same cartouche as his drawing of a wigwam.

May 23, 1840—View from Ft. Holmes, Island of Michilimackinac—by Bela Hubbard. Bentley Historical Library (Bela Hubbard Papers, 851637, Box 1, Vol. 7, No. 6117). [**Figure 6.15**].

May 23, 1840—Pyramid Rock. Mackinac. As seen from the plain—by Bela Hubbard. Bentley Historical Library (Bela Hubbard Papers, 851637, Box 1, Vol. 7, No. 6118). [**Figure 6.17**].

May 23, 1840—Arch rock, as seen from above—by Bela Hubbard. Bentley Historical Library (Bela Hubbard Papers, 851637, Box 1, Vol. 7, No. 6119). [**Figure 6.16**].

August 9, 1840—[Michilimackinack]—by Lieutenant William Fairholme. Original field drawing on which the 1843 presentation copy was based.

August 9, 1840 (**copied ca. 1843**)—Michilimackinack—by Lieutenant William Fairholme. Drawn into a presentation copy of the artist's journal. The Huntington Library (HM 40696). [**Figure 7.2**].

ca. 1840–43—Mackinaw or Michilimackinak—by [Francis Melick Cayley]. Masco Collection. [**Figure 7.8**]. Fort and town as seen from the harbor.

ca. 1840–43—Mackinaw—by [Francis Melick Cayley]. Masco Collection. [**Figure 7.9**]. Fort and east end as seen from summit of Fort Hill.

ca. 1840–43—back of the fort Mackinaw—by [Francis Melick Cayley]. Masco Collection. [**Figure 7.22**].

ca. 1840–43—Mackinaw—by [Francis Melick Cayley]. Masco Collection. [**Figure 7.10**]. Town as seen from the East Bluff.

ca. 1840–43—curious lump of stone in Mackinaw wood—by [Francis Melick Cayley]. Masco Collection. [**Figure 7.11**]. Sugar Loaf as seen from Point Lookout.

May 16, 1841—[Diagram of a parhelion viewed from Mackinac Island]—by Lieutenant John Wolcott Phelps. New York Public Library (John Wolcott Phelps Papers, Diaries #2). [**Not illustrated**]. A sketch of this natural phenomenon.

July 19, 1841—[A map of part of our village]—by [Michael Dousman?]. Burton Historical Collection (William Woodbridge Papers, LMS). [**Not illustrated**]. Rough plat map of properties between Main and Market and Hoban and Astor streets.

September 1841—Map of the Island of Mackinac Surveyed Under Direction of Capt. W. G. Williams. U.S. Topl Eng. 1841—by Lieutenant Israel Carle Woodruff. National Archives and Records Administration (RG 77, Civil Works Map File, O 91). [**Figure 7.1**].

September 1841—[Topographical survey of St. Ignace]—Captain William G. Williams et al. Described in Larson, *Essayons*, 37.

September 1841—[Topographical survey of Round Island and Bois Blanc Islands]—Captain William G. Williams et al. Described in Larson, *Essayons, 37.*

Summer 1842—[Topographical map of Mackinac Island]—by Daniel Drake. Drawn during his travels on the upper part of the lakes in the summer of 1842 and noted in Voss, *A History of Floristics*, 29.

September 1842—United States, Fort & village of Michilimackinac, State of Michigan. Chippeway Indians encamped to receive their Annual presents Sept 1842—by Captain Henry Francis Ainslie. Chicago History Museum (1963.762c). [**Figure 7.5**].

September 1842—United States, Natural Arch of Mackinaw Island Septr. 1842—by Captain Henry Francis Ainslie. Chicago History Museum (1963.762b). [**Figure 7.6**].

October 1842—United States, Mackinaw Island & Fort, Chippeway Indians traveling. taken from the steamer Clinton De Witt—by Captain Henry Francis Ainslie. Chicago History Museum (1963.762e). [**Figure 7.4**].

October 1842—United States, Island of Mackinaw, October 1842—by Captain Henry Francis Ainslie. Chicago History Museum (1963.762f). [**Figure 7.3**].

October 1842—United States, Site of Old Fort Mackinaw, State of Michigan, Oct. 1842, where in 1763, 3 officers & 60 British soldiers were treacherously massacred by the Indians—by Captain Henry Francis Ainslie. Chicago History Museum (1963.762d). [**Figure 7.7**].

September 1843—[Sketches of Mackinac]—by Sara Ann Clarke. Sarah M. Fuller says that Clarke carried her sketchbook with her, and she undoubtedly did more drawings than the three published with Fuller's book. Fuller, *Summer on the Lakes*, 250–51.

September 1843—[Arched Rock at Mackinaw]—by Sara Ann Clarke. Original sketch on which engraving was based.

September 1843 (published 1844)—Arched Rock at Mackinaw—by Sara Ann Clarke. Published in illustrated edition of Fuller, *Summer on the Lakes,* frontispiece. Clements Library (C2-1844-Os, copy 2). [**Figure 7.12**].

September 1843 (published 1851)—The Arched Rock at Mackinaw—by [after Sara Ann Clarke]. Published in Howe, *The Great West*, 37. [**Not illustrated**].

September 1843 (published 1861 and 1867)—The Arched Rock, On the Isle of Mackinaw—by [after Sara Ann Clarke]. Published in Barber and Howe, *Our Whole Country*, and in Barber and Howe, *All the Western States and Territories.* [**Not illustrated**].

September 1843—[Arched Rock from the Water]—by Sara Ann Clarke. Original sketch on which the engraving was based.

September 1843 (published 1844)—Arched Rock from the Water—by Sara Ann Clarke. Published in illustrated edition of Fuller, *Summer on the Lakes,* 171. Clements Library (C2-1844-Os, copy 2). [**Figure 7.13**].

September 1843—[Mackinaw Beach]—by Sara Ann Clarke. Original sketch on which the engraving was based.

September 1843 (published 1844)—Mackinaw Beach—by Sara Ann Clarke. Published in illustrated edition of Fuller, *Summer on the Lakes,* 249. Clements Library (C2-1844-Os, copy 2). [**Figure 7.15**].

August 1844—[View of Machinac Point, with lodges of the Ottawa Indians]—by Reverend James Beaven. Sketch on which the engraving was based.

August 1844 (published 1846)—View of Machinac Point, with Lodges of the Ottawa Indians—by Reverend James Beaven. In Beaven, *Recreations of a Long Vacation,* 109. University of Michigan Libraries. [**Figure 7.18**].

August 1844—[Ottawa lodge and canoe]—by Reverend James Beaven. Sketch on which the engraving was based.

August 1844 (published 1846)—Ottawa Lodge and Canoe—by Reverend James Beaven. In Beaven, *Recreations of a Long Vacation,* 122. University of Michigan Libraries. [**Figure 7.19**].

August 1844—[Ottawa Indian chief]—by Reverend James Beaven. Sketch on which the engraving was based.

August 1844 (published 1846)—Ottawa Indian Chief—by Reverend James Beaven. In Beaven, *Recreations of a Long Vacation,* 132. University of Michigan Libraries. [**Illustrated without number**].

August 1844—[Indian rudder]—by Reverend James Beaven. Sketch on which the engraving was based.

August 1844 (published 1846)—Indian Rudder—by Reverend James Beaven. In Beaven, *Recreations of a Long Vacation,* 138. University of Michigan Libraries. [**Figure 7.20**].

August 1844—[Seated Indian at Mackinac]—by Reverend James Beaven. Sketch on which the engraving was based.

August 1844 (published 1846)—[Seated Indian at Mackinac]—by Reverend James Beaven. In Beaven, *Recreations of a Long Vacation,* 145. University of Michigan Libraries. [**Illustrated without number**].

1844—[The island of Mackinac]—by Father Otto Skolla. Described in a letter from Skolla to his brother, July 17, 1845. This composition apparently included the town and a view of St. Ignace. Rezek, *History of the Diocese of Sault Ste. Marie,* 1:363.

1844—[The church of Mackinac]—by Father Otto Skolla. Painting on which the 1906 engraving was based. Mentioned in Skolla to his brother, July 17, 1845. The painting was found in Hungary (Croatia) sometime before 1906. Rezek, *History of the Diocese of Sault Ste. Marie,* 1:363.

1844 (published 1906)—[The church of Mackinac]—by Father Otto Skolla. Published in Rezek, *History of the Diocese of Sault Ste. Marie,* 2:66, and later in Wood, *Historic Mackinac,* 1:388. University of Michigan Libraries. [**Figure 7.17**].

1845 (before July)—General Prospect of Fort Mackinaw County Michgn: for the Commanding Capt: Scott. A drewing from W. Brenschütz pr: of Comp I 5 Inf.—by Private William G. Brenschütz. Clements Library (6-O-15). [**Figure 7.21**].

July 1845—[Sketches of Indians]—by Paul Kane. Kane's *Wanderings* describes a trip to Mackinac in June–July 1845 and the sketching of Indians there. The catalog in Harper, *Paul Kane's Frontier*, lists thirteen studies that might have been done at Mackinac (III-91-94, 97–105). Most are in the Stark Museum of Art.

July 1845—Michillimackinack—by Paul Kane. © Royal Ontario Museum (946.15.255). [**Figure 7.23**]. Town and fort seen from East Bluff.

July 1845—[A Natural Bridge. Mackinac Island]—by Paul Kane. Royal Ontario Museum (946.15.20). Harper, *Paul Kane's Frontier*, III-79. [**Not illustrated**]. A pencil sketch of Arch Rock.

July 1845—[The natural bridge at Mackinac]—by Paul Kane. Stark Museum of Art (A4–13). Harper, *Paul Kane's Frontier*, III-80. [**Not illustrated**]. A pencil sketch of Arch Rock.

July 1845—[The natural bridge at Mackinac]—by Paul Kane. Stark Museum of Art (A4–14). Harper, *Paul Kane's Frontier*, III-81. [**Not illustrated**]. A sketch of Arch Rock.

July 1845—The Natural Bridge at Mackinac—by Paul Kane. Stark Museum of Art (31.789/183, EOP20). [**Figure 7.14**].

July 1845—[The natural bridge at Mackinac]—by Paul Kane. Stark Museum of Art (EOP31). Harper, *Paul Kane's Frontier*, III-83. [**Not illustrated**]. An oil on paper view of Arch Rock.

July 1845—[Robinson's Folly]—by Paul Kane. Stark Museum of Art (31.78/192, EOP29). [**Figure 7.16**]. The museum identifies this as "Rocky Headland with Wigwams in Foreground."

July 1845—[Wooded shoreline. Possibly Mackinac Island]—by Paul Kane. Stark Museum of Art (A4–12). Harper, *Paul Kane's Frontier*, III-85. [**Not illustrated**]. A pencil sketch.

July 1845—[Sugar Loaf Rock]—by Paul Kane. Private collection. Harper, *Paul Kane's Frontier*, III-86. [**Not illustrated**]. A pencil sketch.

July 1845—[Portrait of Indian with landscape with high bluff]—by Paul Kane. Royal Ontario Museum (946.15.41). Thought to be on Mackinac Island. Harper, *Paul Kane's Frontier*, III-87. [**Not illustrated**].

July 1845—[Mani-tow-wah bay or "He-Devil, an Ojibwa chief"]—by Paul Kane. Glenbow Museum. Harper, *Paul Kane's Frontier*, III-88. [**Illustrated without number**].

July 1845—[Now-on-dhu-go, an Ottawa chief]—by Paul Kane. Stark Museum of Art (EOP27). Harper, *Paul Kane's Frontier*, III-89. [**Illustrated without number**].

July 1845—[Birch bark box with quill work]—by Paul Kane. Royal Ontario Museum (946.15.42). Part of a page of studies. Harper, *Paul Kane's Frontier*, III-90. [**Not illustrated**].

July 1845—[Head of Indian wearing a medal]—by Paul Kane. Royal Ontario Museum (946.15.42). Part of a page of studies. Harper, *Paul Kane's Frontier*, III-90. [**Not illustrated**].

July 1845—[Landscape of high bluff and trees or Rocky headland]—by Paul Kane. Royal Ontario Museum (946.15.42). Thought to be on Mackinac Island. Part of a page of studies. Harper, *Paul Kane's Frontier*, III-90. [**Not illustrated**].

July 1845—[Sketches of four wampum belts]—by Paul Kane. Stark Museum of Art (A4–43). Harper, *Paul Kane's Frontier*, III-95. [**Not illustrated**]. Pencil sketches, including a belt with the name of Lieutenant Colonel Robert McDouall from the War of 1812.

July 1845—[Sketches of three wampum belts]—by Paul Kane. Private collection. Harper, *Paul Kane's Frontier*, III-96. [**Not illustrated**]. These sketches appear to be a second version of Harper, III–95.

July–August 1845—Old Fort Mackinaw plan taken by Lieut. Whiting—by Lieutenant Henry Whiting. Original in Francis Parkman's Journal for 1844–1845, Massachusetts Historical Society. Facsimile in Wade, *The Journals of Francis Parkman*, 1:307. [**Not illustrated**]. A very rough ground plan of the visible ruins at Old Michilimackinac.

August 1846—[Sketches of interesting points on Mackinac Island]—by Charles Lanman. Lanman wrote that "at one point" during his stay, "I took my sketch-book for the purpose of portraying some interesting point upon the island." He gave several sketches to ladies who admired his work. Lanman, *A Summer in the Wilderness*, 164.

ca. 1846—[The isle, Mackinaw]—Francis Howe. Original drawing on which the engraving was based.

ca. 1846 (published 1861 and 1867)—The Isle, Mackinaw—by Francis Howe. In Barber and Howe, *Our Whole Country*, and Barber and Howe, *All the Western States and Territories*, 284. Clements Library (C2-1867-Ba) [**Figure 7.33**].

ca. 1846–47—[Mackinaw]—by [Jesse Olney]. Original sketch on which the engraving was based.

ca. 1846–47—Mackinaw—by [Jesse Olney]. Published in Olney, *A Practical System of Modern Geography . . .* , 144. [**Not illustrated**].

June 1849—[Geological section of Mackinac Island]—by [John W. Foster]. Manuscript sketch on which the engraving was based.

June 1849 (published 1850)—[Geological section of Mackinac Island]—by [John W. Foster]. Figure 54 in part 1 of Foster and Whitney, *Report on the Geology and Topography of a Portion of the Lake Superior Land District*, 1:213. [**Not illustrated**]. A cross section through the "turtle's back" to the harbor showing alluvial, drift, and limestone soils.

June 1849—[Mackinac]—by [J. W. Foster]. Original sketch on which the engraving was based.

June 1849 (published 1851)—Mackinac—by [John Wells Foster]. Engraved by John William Orr. Figure 24 in Foster and Whitney, *Report on the Geology and Topography of a Portion of the Lake Superior Land District*, 2:249. [**Figure 7.24**].

June 1849 (published 1857, 1863, and 1871)—Island of Mackinac—by [John Disturnell after John Wells Foster]. In Disturnell, *A Trip Through the Lakes of North America*, 111. Repeated in Disturnell, *The Great Lakes*, (1863), 89, and Disturnell, *The Great Lakes* (1871). [**Not illustrated**].

June 1849 (published 1860)—Mackinac Island—by [after John Wells Foster]. Published in Strickland, *Old Mackinaw*, 76. [**Not illustrated**].

June 1849—[Topographical sketch of Mackinac]—by [John Wells Foster]. Manuscript map on which the engraving was based.

June 1849 (published 1851)—Topographical Sketch of Mackinac—by [John Wells Foster]. Figure 25 in Foster and Whitney, *Report on the Geology and Topography of a Portion of the Lake Superior Land District*, 2:249. [**Figure 7.25**].

June 1849—[Sections through the bluffs of Mackinac]—by [John Wells Foster]. Original sketches on which the engravings were based.

June 1849 (published 1851)—Section along the line a b, in Fig. 25—by [John Wells Foster]. Figure 26 in Foster and Whitney, *Report on the Geology and Topography of a Portion of the Lake Superior Land District*, 2:250. [**Figure 7.26**].

June 1849 (published 1851)—Section along the line c d, in Fig. 25—by [John Wells Foster]. Figure 27 in Foster and Whitney, *Report on the Geology and Topography of a Portion of the Lake Superior Land District*, 2:250. [**Figure 7.27**].

June 1849—[Section of the island of Mackinac]—by [John Wells Foster]. Original sketch on which the engraving was based.

June 1849 (published 1851)—Section of the Island of Mackinac—by [John Wells Foster]. Figure 28 in Foster and Whitney, *Report on the Geology and Topography of a Portion of the Lake Superior Land District,* 2:251. [**Figure 7.28**].

June 1849—[Hook at Round Island]—by [John Wells Foster]. Manuscript map on which the engraving was based.

June 1849 (published 1851)—Hook at Round Island—by [John Wells Foster]. Figure 29 in Foster and Whitney, *Report on the Geology and Topography of a Portion of the Lake Superior Land District,* 2:259. [**Figure 7.29**].

June 1849—[Arch Rock—Mackinac Island]—by [John Wells Foster]. Original sketch on which the lithograph was based.

June 1849 (published 1851)—Arched Rock—Mackinac—by [John Wells Foster]. In Foster and Whitney, *Report on the Geology and Topography of a Portion of the Lake Superior Land District,* 2:plate XVIII. [**Figure 7.30**].

June 1849 (published 1857)—Arched Rock—Mackinac—by [John Disturnell after John Wells Foster]. In Disturnell, *A Trip Through the Lakes of North America,* 111. Repeated in Disturnell, *The Great Lakes* (1863), 90, and in Disturnell, *The Great Lakes* (1871). [**Not illustrated**].

June 1849 (published 1860)—Arch Rock—by [after John Wells Foster]. Published in Strickland, *Old Mackinaw,* 84. [**Not illustrated**].

June 1849—[Sugar-Loaf, Mackinac]—by [John Wells Foster]. Original sketch on which the lithograph was based.

June 1849 (published 1851)—Sugar-Loaf, Mackinac—by [John Wells Foster]. Tinted lithograph by Ackerman Lithography. In Foster and Whitney, *Report on the Geology and Topography of a Portion of the Lake Superior Land District,* 2:plate XIX. [**Figure 7.31**].

June 1849 (published 1860)—Sugar-Loaf—Mackinac—by [after John Wells Foster]. Published in Strickland, *Old Mackinaw,* 76. [**Not illustrated**].

June 1849—[Gros Cap of Lake Michigan]—by [John Wells Foster]. Original sketch on which the lithograph was based.

June 1849 (published 1851)—Gros Cap of Lake Michigan—by [John Wells Foster]. Tinted lithograph by Ackerman Lithography. In Foster and Whitney, *Report on the Geology and Topography of a Portion of the Lake Superior Land District,* 2:plate XVII. [**Figure 7.32**].

August 8, 1849—[Diagram of the premises which William B. Ogden desires permission to occupy]—by William Butler Ogden. Enclosed with letter from Ogden to Major Charles H. Larnard, Aug. 8, 1849, RG 92, Consolidated Correspondence File, National Archives and Records Administration. [**Figure 7.34**].

1849–54—[Straits of Mackinac]—by Captain John N. Macomb and others. Manuscript maps on which the published chart of 1854 was based.

June 20, 1850—Fort Mackinac—by Lieutenant John Newton. National Archives and Record Administration (RG 77, Fortifications Map File, Drawer 1, Sheet 12). [**Figure 8.1**].

1850—Mackinac—by Charles Alexander Fuller. In Drake, *A Systematic Treatise,* opp. p. 346. Clements Library (C2-1850-Dr). [**Figure 8.2**].

July 1852—[Straits of Mackinaw]—by [Robert E. Clarke]. Original drawing on which the engraving was based.

July 1852 (published March 1853)—Straits of Mackinaw—by [Robert E. Clarke]. In Clarke, "Notes from the Copper Region," 434. Clements Library (Serials 1). [**Figure 8.3**].

July 1852 (published 1861 and later)—Straits of Mackinaw—by [Robert E. Clarke]. Inset on *Johnson's Michigan and Wisconsin by Johnson & Browning* published in *Johnson's New Illustrated (Steel Plate) Family Atlas* (New York, 1861), no. 46. Clements Library (W-1-B). [**Not illustrated**].

July 1852—[The Arch Rock]—by [Robert E. Clarke]. Original drawing on which the engraving was based.

July 1852 (published March 1853)—The Arch Rock—by [Robert E. Clarke]. In Clarke, "Notes from the Copper Region," 434. Clements Library (Serials 1). [**Figure 8.4**].

July 1852 (published 1865)—Arch Rocks, Lake Superior—by [after Robert E. Clarke]. Inset on *Colton's New Railroad Map of the States of Ohio, Michigan, Indiana* (New York, 1865). Clements Library (Atlas Box M). [**Not illustrated.**]

July 1852 (published 1870)—Arched Rock, Mackinac Island—by [after Robert E. Clarke]. In Winchell, *Sketches of Creation,* 248. [**Not illustrated**].

July 1852 (published 1870 and later)—Arch Rock—by [after Robert E. Clarke]. In Van Fleet, *Old and New Mackinac,* 138. [**Not illustrated**]. Copied from the plate in Winchell.

July 1852—[The Sugar Loaf Rock]—by [Robert E. Clarke]. Original drawing on which the engraving was based.

July 1852 (published March 1853)—The Sugar Loaf Rock—by [Robert E. Clarke]. In Clarke, "Notes from the Copper Region," 435. Clements Library (Serials 1). [**Figure 8.5**].

July 1852 (published 1870)—View of Sugar Loaf, Mackinac Island—by [after Robert E. Clarke]. In Winchell, *Sketches of Creation,* 247. [**Not illustrated**].

July 1852 (published 1870 and later)—Sugar Loaf Rock—by [after Robert E. Clarke]. In Van Fleet, *Old and New Mackinac,* 140. [**Not illustrated**]. Copied from the plate in Winchell.

July 1852—[Arch Rock—distant view]—by [Robert E. Clarke]. Original drawing on which the engraving was based.

July 1852 (published March 1853)—Arch Rock—Distant View—by [Robert E. Clarke]. In Clarke, "Notes from the Copper Region," 436. Clements Library (Serials 1). [**Figure 8.6**].

1852—Round Island and Island of Mackinac—by Lieutenant George W. Rose. National Archives and Records Administration. Not located, but there is a copy in Mackinac State Historic Parks library. [**Not illustrated**]. Mackinac State Historic Parks copy is stamped "Lake Survey."

ca. 1852—[Mackinac Base]—by Lieutenant William F. Raynolds. National Archives and Records Administration (RG 77, Civil Works Map File, O 131 1/2). [**Not illustrated**]. Shows triangulation points from eastern end of Bois Blanc Island into Lake Michigan.

July 27, 1853—[Drawing showing construction details of nine cisterns in Fort Mackinac]—by [Major Thomas Williams]. Enclosed with Williams to Grayson of this date and forwarded from Detroit with Grayson to Jesup of July 31, 1853, RG 92, Consolidated Correspondence File, National Archives and Records Administration.

October 1853—Indian encampment near the British Landing Id of Mackinaw—by Alfred R. Waud. Historic New Orleans Collection (1977.137.38.7). [**Figure 8.10**].

1853—Scotts Farm—Mackinaw—by Alfred R. Waud. Historic New Orleans Collection (1977.137.38.16). [**Figure 8.13**]. Shows two wooden structures.

1853—Scotts Farm—Mackinaw—by Alfred R. Waud. Historic New Orleans Collection (1977.137.38.8). [**Figure 8.14**]. Sketch shows a barn and houses.

1853–54—Sugarloaf rock Mackinaw—by Alfred R. Waud. Historic New Orleans Collection (1977.137.38.11). [**Figure 8.9**]. Second, smaller sketch at bottom.

1853–54—Fort Holmes Mackinaw [at top left:] highest point used for triangulation—by Alfred R. Waud. Historic New Orleans Collection (1977.137.38.9). [**Figure 8.8**].

1853–54—Wigwam of bark and mats—Mackinaw—by Alfred R. Waud. Historic New Orleans Collection (1977.137.38.15). [**Figure 8.11**].

1853–54—Scotts Cave Mackinaw—by Alfred R. Waud. Historic New Orleans Collection (1977.137.38.17i). [**Figure 8.12**].

1853–54—Room where Indians receive their amenities Mackinaw—by Alfred R. Waud. Historic New Orleans Collection (1977.137.38.17ii). [**Not illustrated**]. Very rough sketch showing Native Americans seated at a table.

1853?—[Town of Mackinac, on Lake Huron, State of Michigan]—by [unknown]. Original sketch on which the engraving was based.

1853? (published September 20, 1856)—Town of Mackinac, on Lake Huron, State of Michigan—by [unknown]. In *Frank Leslie's Illustrated Newspaper* 2 (September 20, 1856): 232. Mackinac State Historic Parks (1977.102.1). [**Figure 8.29**].

1853?—[View from the fortifications, Mackinac, Michigan]—by [unknown]. Original sketch on which the engraving was based.

1853? (published September 20, 1856)—View from the Fortifications, Mackinac, Michigan—by [unknown]. In *Frank Leslie's Illustrated Newspaper* 2 (September 20, 1856): 236. Mackinac State Historic Parks (1977.101.1). [**Figure 8.31**].

1853?—[Town and harbor of Mackinac, Michigan]—by [?]. Original sketch on which the engraving was based.

1853? (published September 20, 1856)—Town and Harbor of Mackinac, Michigan—by [unknown]. In *Frank Leslie's Illustrated Newspaper* 2 (September 20, 1856): 237. Mackinac State Historic Parks (1977.100.1). [**Figure 8.32**].

July 7, 1854—[View of Mackanac]—by Aaron Bellangee. Noted in the artist's journal on this date. Aaron Bellangee Memorandum Book, typescript in Mackinac State Historic Parks library. This appears to have been a view of the town or, possibly, the Huron [Island] House hotel.

November 22, 1854—[Plan of Major Williams's quarters]—by Major Thomas Williams. Drawn into body of letter of this date from Williams to Mary Williams. Burton Historical Collection (Williams Family Papers). [**Figure 8.23**].

1854—Mackinaw 1854—by Alfred R. Waud. Historic New Orleans Collection (1977.137.38.10). [**Figure 8.7**]. View from the beach in front of St. Anne's Church toward Fort Mackinac and the town.

1854—Gateway to Ft. Mackinac 1854—by Alfred R. Waud. Historic New Orleans Collection (1977.137.38.12). [**Figure 8.20**].

1854—Straits of Mackinac with the Approaches Thereto from Lakes Huron and Michigan and the Entrance by the Detour Passage to the St. Mary's River. From trigonometrical Surveys under the direction of the Topographical Bureau of the War Department in obedience to Acts of Congress requiring the Survey of the Northern and North Western Lakes under the orders of Lieut. Col. James Kearney Topographical Engineers in 1849 and of Capt. J. N. Macomb Corps Topl Engrs. in 1851, 1852, 1853, and 1854—by Captain John N. Macomb and others. National Archives and Records Administration (RG 77, Civil Works Map File, AMA 158-1). [**Not illustrated**].

1854 (published 1856)—Straits of Mackinac with the Approaches Thereto from Lakes Huron and Michigan and the Entrance by the Detour Passage to the St. Mary's River. From trigonometrical Surveys under the direction of the Topographical Bureau of the War Department in obedience to Acts of Congress requiring the Survey of the Northern and North Western Lakes under the orders of Lieut. Col. James Kearney Topographical Engineers in 1849 and of Capt. J. N. Macomb Corps Topl Engrs. in 1851, 1852, 1853 and 1854—by Captain John N. Macomb and others. National Archives (RG 49, Old Map File, Michigan 62). [**Not illustrated**]. Copies are held by many other institutions.

1854?—[View of the town of Mackinac]—by an officer of the U.S. Army. Original drawing from which the *Ballou's* lithograph was made.

1854? (published May 5, 1855)—View of the Town of Mackinaw—by an officer of the U.S. Army. *Ballou's Pictorial Drawing-Room Companion,* May 5, 1855, 280. Clements Library. [**Figure 8.15**].

1854?—[Arch Rock, Mackinaw]—by an officer of the U.S. Army. Original drawing from which the *Ballou's* lithograph was made.

1854? (published May 5, 1855)—Arch Rock, Mackinaw—by an officer of the U.S. Army. *Ballou's Pictorial Drawing-Room Companion,* May 5, 1855, 280. Clements Library. [**Figure 8.16**]. A view from above.

1854?—[Arch Rock—second view]—by an officer of the U.S. Army. Original drawing from which the *Ballou's* lithograph was made.

1854? (published May 5, 1855)—Arch Rock.—Second View—by an officer of the U.S. Army. *Ballou's Pictorial Drawing-Room Companion,* May 5, 1855, 281. Clements Library. [**Figure 8.17**]. A view from the beach.

1854?—[Sugar Loaf or Pyramid Rock]—by an officer of the U.S. Army. Original drawing from which the *Ballou's* lithograph was made.

1854? (published May 5, 1855)—The Sugar Loaf, or Pyramid Rock—by an officer of the U.S. Army. *Ballou's Pictorial Drawing-Room Companion,* May 5, 1855, 281. Clements Library. [**Figure 8.18**].

January 3, 1855—No. 1 [Buildings destroyed by fire on January 3]—by Major Thomas Williams. Enclosed with letter of this date to Major General Thomas Jesup, RG 92, Consolidated Correspondence File, National Archives and Records Administration. [**Figure 8.19**].

January 29, 1855—No. 2 [Plan for the construction of public buildings at Fort Mackinac]—by Major Thomas Williams. Enclosed with letter of this date to Major General Thomas S. Jesup, RG 92, Consolidated Correspondence File, National Archives and Records Administration. [**Figure 8.21**].

March 19, 1855—[Sketch of a silver plate affixed to coffin of Charlotte O'Brien]—by Major Thomas Williams. Sketched into body of letter of this date from Williams to Mary Williams. Burton Historical Collection (Williams Family Papers). [**Figure 8.27**].

July 25, 1855—Island of Mackinaw, Lake Huron, July 25th, 1855—by Sir Daniel Wilson. Library and Archives Canada (1995-213-2). [**Figure 8.28**].

July 1855—Proposed Improvements. Stone Building as it now stands—by Major Thomas Williams. Enclosed with report on the condition of quarters of this date, RG 92, Consolidated Correspondence File, National Archives and Records Administration. [**Figure 8.22**]. Two elevations showing existing condition and suggested improvements for officers' stone quarters.

July 1855—Ground plan as it now is. Elevation as it now is. Proposed Improvement. Ground Plan—by Major Thomas Williams. RG 92, Consolidated Correspondence File, National Archives and Records Administration. [**Figure 8.24**]. Two elevations and two floor plans showing existing condition and suggested improvements to officers' wooden quarters.

1855—[Island of Mackinac showing surveys of military reserve & government land]—by Captain John Navarre Macomb and others. Manuscript survey map on which later copies were based.

1855 (probably drawn April 1856)—Island of Mackinac Showing Surveys of Military Reserve & Government Land—by Captain John Navarre Macomb and others. National Archives and Records Administration (RG 77, Fortifications Map File, Drawer 137, Sheet 24). [**Not illustrated**]. Probably the finished copy submitted to the Topographical Bureau on April 3, 1856.

1855 (copy drawn June 18, 1857)—Island of Mackinac Showing Surveys of Military Reserve & Government Land—by Captain John Navarre Macomb and others. National Archives and Records Administration (RG 77, Fortifications Map File, Drawer 137, Sheet 25). [**Figure 8.25**].

1855 (copy drawn ca. 1860 or later)—Island of Mackinac Showing Surveys of Military Reserve & Government Land—by Captain John Navarre Macomb and others. National Archives and Records Administration (RG 77, Fortifications Map File, Drawer 137, Sheet 31-2). [**Not illustrated**].

1855 (copy drawn January 16, 1862)—Island of Mackinac Showing Surveys of Military Reserve & Government Land—by Captain John Navarre Macomb and others. National Archives and Records Administration (RG 77, Fortifications Map File, Drawer 137, Sheet 26). [**Not illustrated**].

July 28, 1856—[Sketch of a boundary marker for the Military Reserve]—by Major Thomas Williams. Enclosed with letter of this date from Williams to Colonel Samuel Cooper. Location unknown but probably in RG 94, National Archives and Records Administration.

July 28, 1856—[Sketch of a boundary marker for the Military Reserve]—by Major Thomas Williams. Drawn into retained copy of letter from Williams to Colonel Samuel Cooper of this date. Bentley Historical Library (Fort Mackinac Letterbook, 1855–66, 851251 CA.5c, p. 21). [**Figure 8.26**].

July 29, 1856—[Sketch of a boundary marker for the Military Reserve]—by Major Thomas Williams. Enclosed with letter of this date from Williams to S. P. Brady of Detroit with request for an estimate. Bentley Historical Library (Fort Mackinac Letterbook, 1855–66, 851251 CA.5c, p. 22).

ca. 1856—Fort at Mackinaw—by Edwin Whitefield. Royal Ontario Museum (953.125.4a). [**Figure 8.30**].

1856–60—The Island Makinak—by Franz Holzhuber. Glenbow Museum, Calgary, Alberta (65.38.68). [**Not illustrated**]. A crude and fanciful rendering of the fort and town from the east.

1856–60—The Island of Makinak, Fort Makinak—by Franz Holzhuber. Glenbow Museum, Calgary, Alberta (65.39.69). [**Not illustrated**]. A crude and fanciful rendering of a fort with four blockhouses on a bluff.

1856–60—[Arch Rock]—by Franz Holzhuber. Glenbow Museum, Calgary, Alberta (65.39.70). [**Not illustrated**].

1856–60—[Sioux Camp on Mackinac Island]—by Franz Holzhuber. Glenbow Museum, Calgary, Alberta (65.39.71). [**Not illustrated**].

August 1857—[Mackinaw City]—by Robert C. Phillips. Original survey map from which the lithograph was produced.

August 1857 (published 1857)—Mackinaw City from Actual Survey Made August 1857. [Inset:] Straits of Mackinac and Vicinity from actual survey and other authentic sources by R. C. Phillips, Civil Engineer, Cincinnati Sept. 1857.—by Robert C. Phillips. Lithograph by Middleton, Wallace & Co. Mackinac State Historic Parks (2006.00.58). [**Figure 8.33**].

November 10, 1857—[Mackinac Island showing boundary lines between government and private property]—by George W. Lamson. Survey completed by October 15 and transmitted to Topographical Bureau on November 10. It is described in Meade, *Report . . . 1857*, 28.

June 23, 1858—[Plan of barracks to replace those destroyed by fire]—by [Captain Henry C. Pratt]. Enclosed with letter of June 23, 1858, from Pratt to Assistant Adjutant General, Department of the East. Bentley Historical Library (Fort Mackinac Letterbook, 1855–66, 851251 CA.5c, p. 38. Original letter is in RG 92, Consolidated Correspondence File, National Archives and Records Administration, but the plan has been separated from it.

July 15, 1859—Plan of Proposed Hospital at Fort Mackinac, Michigan—by [Assistant Surgeon John Frazier Head]. Enclosed with letter from Captain Henry C. Pratt to Major General Thomas Jesup of this date. RG 92, Consolidated Correspondence File, National Archives and Records Administration. [**Figure 8.42**].

July 26, 1859—British Landing Mackinac July 26, 1859—by [unknown]. In sketchbook. Detroit Institute of Arts (55.237.15). [**Figure 8.34**].

July 27, 1859—Arched Rock Mackinac July 27, 1859—by [unknown]. In sketchbook. Detroit Institute of Arts (55.237). [**Not illustrated**]. View from the water.

July [27], 1859—[Unfinished sketch of Arch Rock]—by [unknown]. In sketchbook. Detroit Institute of Arts (55.237). [**Not illustrated**].

July 27, 1859—Mackinac July 27 1859—by [unknown]. In sketchbook. Detroit Institute of Arts (55.237.17). [**Figure 8.36**]. View of village from Lover's Leap.

July 27, 1759—Lover's Leap. Mackinac July 27, 1859—by [unknown]. In sketchbook. Detroit Institute of Arts (55.237.21). [**Figure 8.37**]. View from below.

July 29, 1859—Sugarloaf Rock Mackinac July 29, 1859—by [unknown]. In sketchbook. Detroit Institute of Arts (55.237). [**Not illustrated**]. View from west side at ground level.

July 30, 1859—Mackinaw July 30 1859—by [unknown]. In sketchbook. Detroit Institute of Arts (55.237.70). [**Illustrated without number**]. Additional notation: "Young America, my opposite neighbor at table-loq—Guess your legs are pretty long, or else your shoes be."

July 1859—Mackinac—July 1859 Pomeroy Ruminans—by [unknown]. In sketchbook. Detroit Institute of Arts (55.237.13). [**Figure 8.35**]. Man sitting on rock at water's edge, probably along the east shore with St. Martin Islands in the background.

July 1859—[Sketch of large rock]—by [unknown]. In sketchbook. Detroit Institute of Arts (55.237). [**Not illustrated**].

July 1859—The August number of Harpers-Mackinaw July 1859—by [unknown]. In sketchbook. Detroit Institute of Arts (55.237). [**Not illustrated**]. Scene of sleeping man leaning against a tree.

July 1859—Our pretty waiting maid Island House—Mackinac July 1859—by [unknown]. In sketchbook. Detroit Institute of Arts (55.237.80). [**Illustrated without number**].

August 1, 1859—Mackinac Aug 1 1859—by [unknown]. In sketchbook. Detroit Institute of Arts (55.237.37). [**Figure 8.39**]. Study of boats on the beach with two men seated on wheelbarrows.

August 1, 1859—Mackinac Aug 1st 1859—by [unknown]. In sketchbook. Detroit Institute of Arts (55.237). [**Not illustrated**]. Indians with a Mackinaw boat by a wharf.

August 2, 1859—Aug 2 1859—by [unknown]. In sketchbook. Detroit Institute of Arts (55.237.41). [**Figure 8.40**]. Mackinaw boat on beach with people cooking.

August 3, 1859—Mackinac Aug. 3, 1859—by [unknown]. In sketchbook. Detroit Institute of Arts (55.237.45). [**Figure 8.38**]. Study of a Mackinaw boat.

August 1859—[Fort Mackinac from the harbor]—by [unknown]. In sketchbook. Detroit Institute of Arts (55.237.51). [**Figure 8.41**]. View of the fort drawn on brown paper.

August 1859—[Boats & Indian figures]—by [unknown]. In sketchbook. Detroit Institute of Arts (55.237). [**Not illustrated**]. The sketchbook includes a number of unidentified sketches and character studies that might have been made on Mackinac Island.

ca. 1860—Birds Eye View of Straits—by [unknown]. Lithograph by Middleton, Strobridge and Company, Cincinnati, OH. Location of an original example undetermined.

Photograph in State Archives of Michigan (PF 889, Islands—Mackinac—Maps and Illustrations). [**Not illustrated**]. A circular, bird's-eye view focusing on the proposed Mackinaw City and its railroad and ferry connections but also showing St. Ignace and Mackinac Island.

ca. 1860—[Location of stores on Mackinac Island]—by [unknown]. Sketch in an American Fur Company Letterbook. Location of original undetermined. Negative photostats in Burton Historical Collection (Pictures, M/Loc—Mackinac Island and American Fur Company Papers, L5:1820–22). The original sketch might be in a letterbook held by the Stuart House Museum, Mackinac Island. [**Not illustrated**]. The composition is a rough plan of buildings along Astor Street between Main and Market with a number of houses and stores labeled and the "Old Store" (American Fur Company warehouse) and "McLeod House" (Stuart House) identified. The use of the name "McLeod House" dates this to 1860 or later.

APPENDIX B

Descriptive Accounts of Mackinac, 1669 – 1860

The surviving, pre-photographic, visual impressions of the Straits of Mackinac are supported and complemented by numerous written descriptions of the place and its people. These are found in a variety of formats, from letters and reports to journal entries, travel books, and newspaper articles. Each is a unique reflection of its time and the perspective of its author, and each enhances the imagery and expands our understanding of earlier times at the Straits.

The list below offers a chronological compilation of the most useful extended descriptions of the Straits of Mackinac and of the people and events that shaped its history. For the most part, these comprise travelers' accounts or diaries that address a diversity of subjects but provide at least some information on the physical appearance of the writer's surroundings. The majority of individual letters have been excluded unless they contain particularly good or unique descriptions. Very specifically focused documents, such as engineer's reports on fortifications or garrison order books, have also been omitted unless they address broader subjects, such as the local topography. Also absent from this list are the many state or regional gazetteers produced during the nineteenth century. Their entries on the Straits and its settlements and geographical features tend to be largely derivative of other sources and repeat much of the same information. Travel guides and local histories produced before 1861 have been included, however, because they present information that was considered useful to visitors.

The list is not comprehensive, but it is an attempt at a basic bibliography of descriptive narratives of the Straits of Mackinac. Although these accounts have been identified from many sources, particular appreciation for guidance is due to Robert R. Hubach's *Early Midwestern Travel Narratives* (rev. ed., 1998), to Larry Massie, and to the collecting efforts of the staff of Mackinac State Historic Parks. Bibliographic citations and abbreviations are as in the notes to the main text.

1669

November 10–11 (and later)—Father Claude Allouez. Jesuit missionary's description, in the form of a letter, of his passage through the Straits of Mackinac during a voyage to Lake Michigan. The earliest description of the Straits. *JR,* 54:197–203.

1670–71

1670–71—Father Claude Dablon. Jesuit missionary's account of activities at the Straits for the year. *JR,* 55:157–67.

1671–72

1671–72—Father Claude Dablon. Jesuit missionary's account of activities at the mission of St. Ignace for the past year. *JR,* 56:115–19. This narrative was illustrated by Allouez and Dablon's map of Lake Superior identifying missions in the Ottawa country (Fig. 1.5).

1672–73

1672–73—Father Jacques Marquette. Jesuit missionary's account of activities at St. Ignace for the year. *JR,* 57:249–63.

1674–75

1674–75—Father Claude Dablon. Jesuit superior's compiled account of activities at the mission of St. Ignace for the year. *JR,* 59:217–19.

1675–76

1675–76—Father Philippe Pierson. Jesuit missionary's account of activities at the mission of St. Ignace for the year in a letter dated from Michilimackinac, April 25, 1676. *JR,* 60:209–11.

1677–78

1677–78—Father Henri Nouvel. A brief summary of Nouvel's report of activities at the mission of St. Ignace for the year. *JR,* 61:69.

1679

August 27–September 12—René-Robert Cavelier de La Salle. Narrative of his visit to Michilimackinac with the *Griffon,* including a report of the subsequent loss of the vessel. La Salle, *Relation,* 37–47.

August 27–September [12]—Father Louis Hennepin. Narrative of his visit to Michilimackinac with La Salle's party. Hennepin gives September 2 as the date of their departure for Green Bay. Hennepin, *A New Discovery,* 84–88.

August 27–29 and September 17–October 5—Henri de Tonty. Narrative of his visit to Michilimackinac, arriving with La Salle's party and then making a side trip to Sault Ste. Marie. Tonty, *Relation,* 21–22.

1679—Father Jean Enraljan. Summary of his narrative of activities at the mission of St. Ignace over the past year. *JR*, 61:101–47.

1680

Fall 1680 to Easter week **1681**—Father Louis Hennepin. Brief narrative of a winter spent at Michilimackinac during his return voyage to Canada. Hennepin, *A New Discovery*, 260–63.

1680–83

1680–83—Father Thierry Beschefer. Summary narrative of activities of the Jesuit missionaries at St. Ignace over the past three years in a letter dated at Québec, October 21, 1683. *JR*, 62:191–201.

1688

April 18–June 2 and September 10–24—Captain Louis-Armand de Lom d'Arce de Lahontan. Narrative of two visits to Michilimackinac. Lahontan, *New Voyages*, 1:86–90, 101–4. This account was illustrated by the author's map of Michilimackinac (Figs. 1.10–1.12).

1689

May 22–June 8—Captain Louis-Armand de Lom d'Arce de Lahontan. Narrative of a third visit to Michilimackinac on his return from western explorations. Lahontan, *New Voyages*, 1:136–42.

1691

August 1691–Spring **1692**—Father Sébastien Rale. Retrospective account of a visit to Michilimackinac in a letter to his brother dated October 12, 1723. *JR*, 67:153–61.

1695–97

1695–97—Captain Antoine Laumet de Lamothe Cadillac. Retrospective account of his command at Michilimackinac, with a description of the Indians of the region, written about 1718. *WHC*, 16:350–59.

1698

September 14–15—Father Jean-François Buisson de St. Cosme. Account of his departure from Michilimackinac for Lake Michigan by walking from St. Ignace to Gros Cap. Kellogg, *Early Narratives of the Northwest*, 342–43.

1706

August 14—Father Joseph Marest. Jesuit missionary's narrative of events at Michilimackinac during the summer in a letter to Governor Vaudreuil dated August 14, 1708 [*sic*: 1706]. *WHC*, 16:232–38.

1708

August 19–23—François Clairambault d'Aigremont. Official report of his inspection visit to Michilimackinac in a letter dated at Québec, November 14, 1708. *MPHC*, 33:446–52.

1710

1710—Antoine-Denis Raudot. Description of Michilimackinac gathered from other sources and presented in the form of a letter dated at Québec, 1710. Silvy, *Letters from North America*, 161–62.

1712

Summer—Father Gabriel Marest. Narrative of a Jesuit missionary's visit to Michilimackinac in a letter dated November 9, 1712. *JR*, 66:279–85.

1717

June 20–28—Father Dominicus Varlet. Narrative of a visit to Michilimackinac in a letter to his mother dated October 16, 1717. Dominicus Varlet Papers, BHC.

1721

June 28–30—Father Pierre-François-Xavier de Charlevoix. Narrative of his visit to Michilimackinac on his way into Lake Michigan. Presented in the form of a letter dated June 30, 1721. Charlevoix, *Journal*, 2:39–57.

1749

September 22–October 7—Ensign Michel Chartier de Lotbinière. Report of the engineer's visit to Michilimackinac, written to accompany his plan of the fortified village (Fig. 1.15). Gérin-Lajoie, "Fort Michilimackinac in 1749." Original manuscript in Library and Archives Canada.

1754

August 10–September 3—Joseph-Charles "Jolicoeur" Bonin. Narrative of a soldier's visit to Michilimackinac with the Péan expedition. Stevens, Kent, and Wood, *Travels in New France*, 37–47.

1755

ca. 1755—Anonymous. Description of Michilimackinac in a memoir on the route to the Mississippi and Chicago. "Memoire sur la partie occidentale du Canada."

1757

ca. 1757—Captain Louis-Antoine de Bougainville. Description of Michilimackinac by an army officer. Compiled from other sources and included in his memoir on the posts of Canada. *WHC*, 18:172–73, 183.

1761

September–May 15, **1762**—Alexander Henry. British fur trader's narrative of his arrival and first residence at Michilimackinac. Henry, *Travels and Adventures*, 36–57.

September 28–October 1—Lieutenant James Gorrell. Journal of a British officer describing the arrival of British troops at Michilimackinac. "Lieut. James Gorrell's Journal," *WHC*, 1:25.

1762

June 2–7—Ensign Thomas Hutchins. Journal kept by a British officer and cartographer during a tour of the western posts. Chiefly a record of Indian councils at Michilimackinac. In Hanna, *The Wilderness Trail*, 2:363–65, and *SWJP*, 10:523–26. The author drew a map of Michigan's Lower Peninsula that includes details of the Straits of Mackinac (see appendix A).

1763

May–August—Alexander Henry. Narrative of his second residence at Michilimackinac and his captivity by the Ojibwa. Henry, *Travels and Adventures*, 71–126.

Spring?—Mr. Hamburgh. "Minutes" of supposed travels in the Great Lakes. It includes no mention of the Indian uprising and is primarily a description of the country, possibly compiled from other sources. In Mereness, *Travels in the American Colonies*, 360–61.

1764

April 27–May—Alexander Henry. Narrative of his return to Michilimackinac from winter hunting camp and his departure for Fort Niagara. Henry, *Travels and Adventures*, 155–63.

September—Alexander Henry. Brief narrative of his return to Michilimackinac with British troops. Henry, *Travels and Adventures*, 187.

November 3–April 16, **1765**—Captain William Howard. Journal of Indian affairs kept by the commandant. *SWJP*, 11:696–98.

1765

June 17–May 23, **1766**—John Porteous. Journal of a fur trader's residence at Michilimackinac with trips to Sault Ste. Marie and L'Arbre Croche. John Porteous Papers, vol. 3, BHC.

1766

August 28–September 3—Jonathan Carver. Journal of his time at Michilimackinac before departing on his western explorations. Parker, *The Journals of Jonathan Carver*, 71–73.

September 17—John Porteous. Brief journal entry of his departure from Michilimackinac for Detroit. John Porteous Papers, vol. 4, BHC.

September 21–July 3, **1767**—Major Robert Rogers. Journal of Indian affairs kept by the commandant of Michilimackinac. Clements, *Journal of Major Robert Rogers*.

1767

June 6—John Porteous. Brief journal entry of his arrival at Michilimackinac. John Porteous Papers, vol. 6, BHC.

August 16—John Porteous. A long description of Michilimackinac in a letter to his father of this date. John Porteous Papers, BHC.

August 29–May 27, 1768—Jonathan Carver. Brief journal of a winter spent at Michilimackinac. Parker, *The Journals of Jonathan Carver*, 133–34.

December 8–June 17, 1768—Captain Lieutenant Frederick Spiesmacher. Journal of Indian affairs kept by the commandant. Archives du Séminaire de Québec.

1769

November 7–July 2, 1772—Surgeon's Mate Daniel Morrison. Journal of nearly three years at Michilimackinac kept by the post surgeon. Original manuscript in Daniel Morrison Papers, BHC. Published in May, *The Doctor's Secret Journal*.

1771

July 12–25—John Porteous. Journal of a fur trader's trip from Michilimackinac to Sault Ste. Marie and back and then to Detroit. John Porteous Papers, vol. 7, BHC.

1773

Summer–September—Peter Pond. Fur trader's retrospective account of a summer at Michilimackinac. "Journal of Peter Pond," *WHC*, 18:326–29.

1774

April 16–November 18, **1775**—John Askin. Journal of a merchant and farmer at Michilimackinac. Quaife, *The John Askin Papers*, 1:50–58.

July–August—Peter Pond. Retrospective account of a summer of commerce and society at Michilimackinac. "Journal of Peter Pond," *WHC*, 18:341–42.

1775

Summer—Peter Pond. Retrospective account of a summer at Michilimackinac. "Journal of Peter Pond," *WHC*, 18:344–45.

1779

Spring–September 17, **1780**—John Long. Fur trader's narrative of his activities at Michilimackinac, interrupted by a trip to Prairie du Chien, Wisconsin, in June–September 1780. Long, *Voyages and Travels*, 144–52.

October 7—Lieutenant Governor Patrick Sinclair. Report on the advantages of the island of Michilimackinac over the mainland site in a letter of this date to Captain Diedrich Brehm. *MPHC*, 9:523–26. The report includes a sketch map of the proposed fort site and a topographical view of the island (Figs. 2.6 and 2.7).

1783

July 21–August 15—Sergeant John Hay. Journal of a voyage from Montréal to Michilimackinac and return. Contains little detail. No year is noted on the manuscript, and 1783 has been assigned by Library and Archives Canada. Internal evidence suggests that the journal might actually have been written in 1784 or 1785. John Hay Papers, MG23 J5, LAC.

1788

Summer—Captain Gother Mann. Report on the island of Michilimackinac and its defenses submitted December 6, 1788. *MPHC*, 12:33–34. The author mapped Lake Huron and the Straits of Mackinac during this voyage (Fig. 2.14 and appendix A).

1789

July 9—Lord Edward Fitzgerald. Brief account of Michilimackinac in a letter of this date to his mother. Moore, *The Life and Death of Lord Edward Fitzgerald*, 1:148–50.

1792

Summer (20 days)—Sergeant Reuben Reynolds. Account of Michilimackinac given to U.S. authorities by a U.S. soldier taken captive by the Indians in May 1792 and carried to Michilimackinac. His description was taken down at Philadelphia on October 19, 1792, following his return through Montréal. *ASP, Indian Affairs*, 1:244.

1795

October 31–September 3, **1796**—Thomas Duggan. Journal of the Indian Department storekeeper during the last year of British control of Michilimackinac. Thomas Duggan Journal, CL.

1796

September 1—Lieutenant Andrew Foster. Descriptive report of the government buildings at the post of Michilimackinac as turned over to American forces under Major Henry Burbeck. Fort Mackinac Order Book, 3–5, U.S. Military Academy Library.

1797

August 15–22—Major Caleb Swan. Narrative of his visit to Michilimackinac with General James Wilkinson in a letter of October 10, 1797, to Captain Frederick Frye. Published as "Some Account of the Country and Climate of the North-Western Lakes," *Medical Repository* 1, no. 1 (1797): 526–29. Later reprinted in *Magazine of American History* 19 (1888): 74–75. Swan's letter included a rough ground plan of Government House (Fig. 3.4).

1799

June 29–September 25—Father Gabriel Richard. Extracts from his journal kept during a summer at Michilimackinac and vicinity. *MPHC*, 1:484–85.

ca. June (2 days)—Lieutenant George Landmann. Retrospective account of a visit to Michilimackinac by a British engineer. Describes and characterizes the U.S. officers of the garrison. Landmann, *Adventures and Recollections*, 1:78–81.

1800

September—Senator Uriah Tracy. Description of Michilimackinac in a letter of December 20 to Secretary of War Samuel Dexter. RG 77, Buell Collection, NARA. See also Tracy's letters to James McHenry of November 26 and 28, 1800. James McHenry Papers, CL.

1802

June 9–August 1, **1804**—Reverend David Bacon. Accounts in three letters in the *Connecticut Evangelical Magazine* 3 (1802–3): 159–60, 359–60, and 4 (1803–4): 39. Also numerous extracts from his letters for this period in Bacon, *Sketch of the Rev. David Bacon*, 44–65.

October 30—[Surgeon Francis LeBarron]. Long description written as a letter to the editor of this date. "Fort Michilimackinac," *Columbian Centinel* 38, no. 40 (January 15, 1803): 1–2. The correspondent is not named in the letter but has been identified from context.

1804

June 9–ca. July 21—Father Jean Dilhet. Retrospective account by a Catholic priest of his summer ministry at Michilimackinac. Dilhet, *État de l'Église*, 123–28.

August (3 days)—Thomas Verchères de Boucherville. Retrospective account of a Canadian fur trader's visit to Michilimackinac. Quaife, *War on the Detroit,* 42.

October 5–May 19, **1805**—Sally Ellis Kingsbury. Account by the wife of Fort Mackinac's commandant of a winter at Michilimackinac in a letter to her sister of September 10, 1805. General Correspondence, Jacob Kingsbury Papers, BHC.

1807

1807—George Heriot. Description of Michilimackinac and its people, probably compiled from other sources as the author did not visit. Heriot, *Travels Through the Canadas,* 184–86.

1810

July 22–August 12—Wilson Price Hunt. Retrospective account of a fur trader's visit to Michilimackinac as part of an American Fur Company expedition to Oregon. Lee and Frost, *Ten Years in Oregon,* 27–28. See also Washington Irving's account of Hunt's time at Michilimackinac in "Astoria." Irving, *Three Western Narratives,* 282–83.

July 22–August 12—Alexander Ross. Retrospective account of a fur trader's visit to Michilimackinac with an American Fur Company expedition to Oregon. Ross, *Adventures,* 172–74.

1811

May 27–after July 29—Henry Brevoort. Narrative of a summer at Michilimackinac by an agent of John Jacob Astor in four letters to Washington Irving. Hellman, *Letters of Henry Brevoort,* 20–48.

1812

1812–**25**—Elizabeth Thérèse Baird. Reminiscences of childhood on Mackinac Island. Most of her narrative relates to the decade after the War of 1812. *WHC,* 14:17–64.

1812—Anonymous correspondent (probably Josiah Dunham). Description of Mackinac Island published as "Michillimakinak" in *The Washingtonian* of Windsor, Vermont, September 14, 1812. Dunham, who had commanded Fort Mackinac in 1805–7, was editor of the paper. Repeated in the *Plattsburgh Republican* of October 9, 1812.

1814

May 18–October 29—Lieutenant Andrew Bulger. Retrospective account of the defense of Michilimackinac by a British officer. Bulger, *An Autobiographical Sketch,* 8–15.

July 24—Anonymous correspondent. A description of Michilimackinac, probably as it was in 1812, in a letter from Detroit of this date. Printed in the *Columbian Centinel* of August 24, 1814.

July 24–August 7—Surgeon Usher Parsons. Journal of the surgeon of U.S.S. *Lawrence* during the expedition to Michilimackinac. Fredriksen, *Surgeon of the Lakes,* 86–91.

July 24–August 7—Humphrey Howe Leavitt. Reminiscence of the campaign against Michilimackinac by an Ohio volunteer. Leavitt, *Autobiography,* 22–24.

July 24–September—Seaman David Bunnell. Retrospective account of the Michilimackinac campaign by a sailor of U.S.S. *Scorpion.* Bunnell, *Travels and Adventures,* 122–24.

1815

August 15–July **1816**—James H. Lockwood. Reminiscences of a trader at Michilimackinac. Lockwood, "Early Times and Events in Wisconsin," *WHC,* 2:102–3, 107–8.

September 16—Lieutenant Colonel Talbot Chambers. Description of Mackinac Island and its defenses contained in a letter of this date to Major General Jacob Brown. RG 77, Buell Collection, NARA.

October 16–September 8, 1816—Jacob Butler Varnum. Retrospective journal of an Indian factory employee. Original privately owned. Copy in MSHP library.

November 17—Anonymous U.S. officer. Description of Mackinac Island in an extract of a letter of this date published as "Michilimackinac," *Niles Weekly Register* 9 (Supplement, Feb. 24, 1816): 80.

1816

July 12–August 4—Little Wiley. Brief account in a letter from a fur trader to his mother dated August 4, 1816. Little Wiley Papers, Minnesota Historical Society. Photostats in BHC.

1816–1817—James W. Biddle. Reminiscences of an army employee including anecdotes about Mackinac Island. Biddle, "Recollections of Green Bay in 1816–17," *WHC,* 1:49–57.

1817

August 28–September 1 and September 7–9—Judge Advocate Samuel A. Storrow. Long description of Mackinac Island in a letter to Major General Jacob Brown of December 1, 1817. *WHC,* 6:155–60, 163–64.

1818

Spring—Estwick Evans. Brief description of Michilimackinac by a traveler and writer who probably gathered the information while at Detroit. Evans, *A Pedestrious Tour,* 129.

July 4–September 10—Gurdon S. Hubbard. Reminiscences of an American Fur Company clerk of a summer on Mackinac Island. Hubbard, *Autobiography,* 14–28. See also Hubbard, "Journey of Gurdon S. Hubbard," *MPHC,* 3:125, and Hubbard, "A Voyageur of 1818," *MPHC,* 14:544.

1819

May 1—Captain Henry Whiting. Description of Michilimackinac Island in "Geographical Memoranda of the Territory of Michigan." Michigan Collection, CL. Also printed in *Detroit Gazette,* May 7, 1819, 2:3.

mid-May–mid-October—Gurdon S. Hubbard. Reminiscence of an American Fur Company clerk. Hubbard, *Autobiography,* 73–82.

June 19–21—Lieutenant John A. Dix. Journal of an aide to Major General Jacob Brown during an inspection visit to Mackinac Island. New York State Library. Typescript in BHL.

June 19–22, 28–29, and July 9–10—Captain Roger Jones. Journal of an aide to Major General Jacob Brown during three stays on Mackinac Island. Severance, "Gen. Brown's Inspection Tour," 309–12, 315, 318.

October (1 night)—Philander Prescott. Recollection of a traveler's brief stop at Mackinac Island. Parker, *The Recollections of Philander Prescott,* 12–14.

1819 or 1820—Dr. John J. Bigsby. Retrospective account of a visit to Mackinac Island. Bigsby, *The Shoe and Canoe,* 2:145–55. See also Bigsby, "Notes on the Geography and Geology of Lake Huron," *MPHC,* 30:73, 82–83, in which he notes having visited in both years. Bigsby's visits inspired a distant sketch of Mackinac Island (Fig. 4.13).

1820

Spring–Fall—Gurdon S. Hubbard. Reminiscence of his summer's work on Mackinac Island as a clerk of the American Fur Company. Hubbard, *Autobiography,* 107.

May (a few days)—Ebenezer Childs. Reminiscences of a businessman's visit to Mackinac Island. "Recollections of Wisconsin Since 1820," *WHC,* 4:155–59.

June 6–13—James Doty. Journal of a visit to Mackinac Island with the Lewis Cass expedition. *WHC,* 13:176–77.

June 6–13—Captain David Bates Douglass. Journal of a visit to Mackinac Island with the Cass expedition. Jackman and Freeman, *American Voyageur,* 26–33. Six sketches made by Douglass during this trip are known to survive (Figs. 5.4–5.9).

June 6–13—Henry R. Schoolcraft—Journal of a visit to Mackinac Island with the Cass expedition. Schoolcraft, *Narrative Journal,* 109–25. Schoolcraft probably drew views during this visit (see appendix A).

June 6–13—Charles C. Trowbridge—Journal of a visit to Mackinac Island with the Cass expedition. Brown, "With Cass in the Northwest," 142–43.

June 16–after September 11—Surgeon William Beaumont. Journal of his travels from Plattsburgh to Mackinac with a description of the island. Myer, *Life and Letters of Dr. William Beaumont,* 83–85.

June 17–July 3—Jedidiah Morse. Narrative report on Mackinac and its Indians. Morse, *Report,* 14, and appendix, 6–7.

July 31–August 2—Major Joseph Delafield. Journal of an engineer serving with the boundary survey. McElroy and Riggs, eds., *The Unfortified Boundary,* 286–88.

August 29–September 13—Charles C. Trowbridge. Journal of his return voyage through Mackinac. Brown, "With Cass in the Northwest," 347–48.

September 9–13—Captain David Bates Douglass. Journal of his return visit to Mackinac Island. Jackman and Freeman, *American Voyageur,* 112.

September 9–13—Henry R. Schoolcraft. Journal of his return visit to Mackinac Island. Schoolcraft, *Narrative Journal,* 405–8. Schoolcraft probably drew a view of Old Michilimackinac at this time (Figs. 5.10 and 5.11).

1821

May–Autumn—Gurdon S. Hubbard. Reminiscence of a clerk of the American Fur Company working on Mackinac Island. Hubbard, *Autobiography,* 116–17.

June 10—Anonymous correspondent. Description of Indians at Mackinac in a letter to the editor of this date. *Niles Weekly Register* 21 (October 13, 1821): 101.

July?—Albert G. Ellis. Recollections of a visit to Mackinac Island. "Fifty-Four Years' Recollections of Men and Events in Wisconsin," *WHC,* 7:213–15.

1822

June–Autumn—Gurdon S. Hubbard. Reminiscence of a clerk of the American Fur Company. Includes Hubbard's account of the wounding of Alexis St. Martin. Hubbard, *Autobiography,* 131–33.

June 3–7 and 12–20—Major Joseph Delafield. Journal of two visits by an engineer serving with the boundary survey. McElroy and Riggs, *The Unfortified Boundary,* 369–70, 371–72.

July 4—Henry R. Schoolcraft. Narrative of a brief stop at Mackinac Island to pick up a pilot. Schoolcraft, *Personal Memoirs,* 91–92.

July 4–7—Mary Nexsen Thompson. Description by an officer's wife of her first days on Mackinac Island in a letter to Cassandra Smith of July 7, 1822. Duane N. Diedrich Collection, CL.

August—Anonymous mariner. Account, in the form of a letter, of a voyage on Lake Huron and a visit to Mackinac Island. Published in 1836. *Scenes on Lake Huron,* 9–16.

Summer–Autumn—Lieutenant Henry Bayfield. Descriptive account of Mackinac Island contained in a report to Commodore Robert Barrie of November 1, 1822. ADM 1/3445, NA. The author charted the Straits during this time (Fig. 4.15 and appendix A).

1823

May?–Autumn—Gurdon S. Hubbard. Reminiscence by a clerk of the American Fur Company. Hubbard, *Autobiography,* 143–45.

June 13–16 and September 23–October 3—Major Joseph Delafield. Journal of two brief stops at Mackinac Island while working with the boundary survey. McElroy and Riggs, The *Unfortified Boundary,* 379–80, 461.

October 4–7—Major Stephen H. Long. Journal of a visit by a topographical engineer returning from western explorations. Kane, Holmquist, and Gilman, *The Northern Expeditions of Stephen H. Long,* 245–47. Long made a rough map of the Straits (Fig. 5.14), and his party included artist Samuel Seymour, who drew at least four views on Mackinac Island (see appendix A).

October 9–1831—Amanda and William Ferry. Descriptions in letters to family members. C. Anderson, "Frontier Mackinac Island." Amanda mentioned both maps and views that she and her husband had drawn.

1824

May?–Autumn—Gurdon S. Hubbard. Reminiscence by a clerk of the American Fur Company. Hubbard, *Autobiography,* 151–53.

May 29–October 28—Myra Peters Mason. Descriptive accounts in six letters to her sister. Myra Peters Mason Letters, New-York Historical Society. Copies in MSHP library.

July 28–August 2—Thomas Dean. Brief account of his first three days at Mackinac Island in a letter to Philander Hunt dated August 2. Michigan Collection, CL.

1824–33—Martin Heydenburk. Reminiscence of a Protestant missionary in a letter dated October 5, 1880. The writer has confused some dates. "The Old Church and Mission House at Mackinac," *MPHC,* 3:157–58. See also Heydenburk, "Mackinaw Revisited— How it Looked Forty Years Ago," *MPHC,* 7:196–97.

1825

June 25–August 1—Henry R. Schoolcraft. Narrative of a stop at Mackinac Island, a trip to Sault Ste. Marie, and a return to Mackinac. Schoolcraft, *Personal Memoirs,* 213–14.

June 30 and for "some days thereafter"— Anonymous young man traveling with Governor Lewis Cass. Account in two letters published in the *Detroit Gazette* of July 19, 1825, 2:4–3:1 and August 2, 1825, 3:1–2.

September 4–6—Henry R. Schoolcraft. Journal of a brief visit to Mackinac Island. Schoolcraft, *Personal Memoirs,* 230–31.

1826

August 27–30—Thomas L. McKenney. Account of his visit to Mackinac Island presented in the form of a journal and a letter in McKenney, *Sketches of a Tour to the Lakes,* 383–98. McKenney or artists in his party completed at least two Mackinac scenes that were reproduced in his book (Figs. 5.15 and 5.16).

1827

June 20—John A. Granger. Detailed journal entry of a six-hour stop at Mackinac Island. Current location of original unknown. Typescript in John A. Granger Journal, BHL. Granger sketched Arch Rock and Sugar Loaf (see appendix A).

August–Autumn—Gurdon S. Hubbard. Brief reminiscence of part of a summer spent on Mackinac Island. Hubbard, *Autobiography,* 166.

October 24–October 29, 1828—Lieutenant Samuel P. Heintzelman. Journal of an officer of the Fort Mackinac garrison. Interrupted by a trip to Green Bay in June and July 1828. Samuel P. Heintzelman Papers, LC.

1830

July–November **1833**—Father Samuel C. Mazzuchelli. Retrospective account of his time at Mackinac Island, interrupted by many trips to Green Bay and L'Arbre Croche. Mazzuchelli, *Memoirs,* 24–103.

August 8—Calvin Colton. Journal of a brief visit to Mackinac Island by a journalist, politician, and author. Colton, *Tour of the American Lakes,* 91–95.

August 8—James McCall. Journal of a brief stop by an Indian commissioner on his way to Wisconsin. "McCall's Journal of a Visit to Wisconsin in 1830," *WHC,* 12:183–84.

September (1 day)—Juliette A. Kinzie. Retrospective narrative of a brief visit to Mackinac Island. Kinzie, *Wau-Bun,* 9–22.

November 4–12—Elisha Loomis. Journal of a Protestant mission teacher's trip to Mackinac Island. 851699 Aa 1, BHL. Published in Mason, "Rochester to Mackinac Island."

1831

August 7 and 12–13—Gustave-Auguste de Beaumont. Account of a French traveler in the form of a letter to his brother, Achille. Beaumont, *Lettres d'Amérique,* 124–25, 127. There is a partial translation in Pierson, *Tocqueville and Beaumont in America,* 300–307. Beaumont was a companion of Alexis de Tocqueville and made sketches during his visit, at least four of which were extant as of 1938 (Figs. 6.3–6.5 and appendix A).

August 7 and 12–13—Alexis de Tocqueville. Journal of a French traveler and intellectual. Tocqueville, *Journey to America,* 146–48.

August 7 [and 12–13]—Godfrey T. Vigne. Narrative of an English traveler who accompanied Tocqueville and Beaumont. Vigne, *Six Months in America,* 2:109–17. The author made a sketch of Arch Rock from the water (see appendix A).

August 7?—Anonymous correspondent. Letter to the editor of the *Detroit Courier* of September 1, 1831. There is a partial transcription in Pierson, *Tocqueville and Beaumont in America,* 300. Arrived at Mackinac with Beaumont, Tocqueville, and Vigne.

November 20–23—Jeremiah Porter. Journal of a Protestant missionary's last few days on Mackinac Island before departing for Sault Ste. Marie. Original manuscript in Chicago History Museum. Published in C. Anderson, "Mackinac to Sault Ste. Marie by Canoe in 1831," 468–70.

1832

May (before the 15th)—Charles Whittelsey. Reminiscence of a brief stop at Mackinac Island. "Recollections of a Tour Through Wisconsin in 1832," *WHC,* 1:64–67.

June 17–September 18—Eliza Chappell (later Eliza Chappell Porter). Journal of a Protestant missionary teacher on Mackinac Island. Porter, *Eliza Chappell Porter,* 43–68.

October 12–18—Jeremiah Porter. Letter of a Protestant missionary to Mrs. Charlotte Porter dated October 22, 1832. Michigan Collection, CL.

1833

April 22–July 29—Eliza Chappell (later Eliza Chappell Porter). Journal of a Protestant missionary teacher on Mackinac Island and at St. Ignace. Porter, *Eliza Chappell Porter,* 90–98.

May 27–June 10, July 28–October 12, and end of October to July 1, 1834—Henry R. Schoolcraft. Journal of his first summer and winter as Indian agent on Mackinac Island. Includes much local history information collected by the writer. Schoolcraft, *Personal Memoirs,* 442, 443–48, 449–85.

1834

Spring—Harvey Haynes. Reminiscence of a trip to Mackinac Island to escort supplies for the U.S. Army. "Trip from Rome to Mackinaw in Territorial Days with Powder and Clothing for Soldiers at the Fort," *MPHC,* 13:524–25.

July 14–15—Reverend Jackson Kemper. Journal a visit to Mackinac Island. "Journal of an Episcopalian Missionary's Tour to Green Bay, 1834," *WHC,* 14:404–10.

August–September (ten days)—Susan Farley. Letter to her mother, Susan S. Farley, dated Detroit, September 7, 1834. A fine description of Mackinac Island, which Farley visited to escape a cholera outbreak in Detroit. Farley Family Papers, CL.

after September 6–August 17, 1835—Henry R. Schoolcraft. Journal of the Indian agent's second winter on Mackinac Island. Schoolcraft, *Personal Memoirs,* 489–520.

1834?—Anonymous correspondent. Description of Mackinac Island, the town, and the mission school, most likely by a member of Reverend William M. Ferry's mission family. Published as "Mission School at Mackinaw," *Quarterly Papers of the American Board of Commissioners for Foreign Missions* 20 (March 1835): 77–80.

1835

June (early)—Enos Goodrich. Reminiscence of a brief visit to Mackinac Island. "Across Michigan Territory Sixty Years Ago," *MPHC,* 26:233–34.

August 12–17—George W. Featherstonhaugh. Narrative of a British geologist's visit to Mackinac Island. Featherstonhaugh, *A Canoe Voyage,* 137–49. The author made a number of sketches, one of which was engraved to illustrate his book (Fig. 6.10 and appendix A).

August–November 9—Henry R. Schoolcraft. Journal of the Indian agent while on Mackinac Island. Schoolcraft, *Personal Memoirs,* 521–26.

September 4–7—Chandler R. Gilman. Journal of a tourist's visit to Mackinac Island. It includes the earliest record of the romantic version of the Robinson's Folly story. Gilman, *Life on the Lakes,* 1:88–181.

1836

June 15–October 27—Henry R. Schoolcraft. Journal of the Indian agent while on Mackinac Island. Schoolcraft, *Personal Memoirs,* 536–47.

July 4–5—Harriet Martineau. Journal of an English traveler and writer. Martineau, *Society in America,* 2:8–19. Reprinted in Kestenbaum, *The Making of Michigan,* 61–67.

September 19–22 and October 5–9—James Logan. Narrative of a British traveler. Logan, *Notes,* 73–80, 100.

October 6—Anonymous gentleman. Narrative, concentrating largely on the Indians seen at Mackinac. Written in a letter of this date and published as "Letters from the Indian Country," *The Knickerbocker* 20, no. 1 (July 1842): 1–5.

1837

June 4–November 11—Henry R. Schoolcraft. Journal of the Indian agent while on Mackinac Island. Schoolcraft, *Personal Memoirs,* 559–76. The author drew several plans for a proposed Indian dormitory during this time (see appendix A).

July 20—John A. Clark. Journal of a traveler's stop on Mackinac Island. Clark, *Gleanings by the Way,* 123–25.

July 21–26—Anna B. Jameson. Narrative of an English traveler and writer who stayed with the Schoolcrafts on Mackinac Island. Jameson, *Winter Studies,* 2:118–204. The author drew landscapes and portrait sketches during her visit (Figs. 6.6–6.9 and appendix A).

July (1 day)—George Fuller (signs as Timothy Oldbuck). Reminiscence of a visit to Mackinac Island, recorded in 1847 in the minute book of the Nucleus Club. George Fuller Papers, 46–50, 58–65, BHC.

August 1–9—Frederick Marryat. Narrative of an English traveler and writer. Marryat, *A Diary in America*, 51–52, 58–65.

August 3 (and time before and after)—Marshall Chapin. Very brief account of a visit to Mackinac Island in a letter to Mrs. Chapin (his mother?) of this date. Marshall Chapin Papers, BHC.

Autumn?—Count Francesco Arese. Narrative by an Italian traveler. Arese, *A Trip to the Prairies*, 178.

November 14—Thomas Nye. Journal of a traveler's brief refueling stop on Mackinac Island. McLellan, *Journal of Thomas Nye*, 14–15, and letter dated January 10, 1838, in McLellan, *Two Letters of Thomas Nye*, 13.

1838

after April 21–June 2 and June 16–late June—Henry R. Schoolcraft. Journal of the Indian agent while on Mackinac Island. Schoolcraft, *Personal Memoirs*, 593–95, 596–600.

June 21–27—Douglass Houghton. Journal of the geologist in his "Field Notes and Observations, 1837–1841." Douglass Houghton Papers, BHL. The author drew at least one map of the Straits area during this time (Fig. 6.12).

June 21–27—Bela Hubbard. Rough journal of his visit to Mackinac Island with Houghton. Bela Hubbard Papers, 851637, AcAa 2, Box 1, Vol. 2, BHL. The author drew at least two maps of Mackinac Island and the Straits during this time (Figs. 6.13 and 6.14).

July 5—Anonymous correspondent. Letter to the *Detroit Daily Advertiser* reprinted in *The New-Yorker*, September 8, 1838, 391–92.

July 7–28—Reverend Peter Dougherty. Journal of a Protestant missionary while on Mackinac Island. Anderson, "Diaries of Peter Dougherty," 102–13.

July 23–31—Henry R. Schoolcraft. Journal of the Indian agent while on Mackinac Island. Schoolcraft, *Personal Memoirs*, 600.

July 30—Anonymous traveler. Journal entry of a brief stop on Mackinac Island, recorded on July 31. Anonymous Journal, July 19–August 31, 1838, American Travel Collection, CL.

August 25–before October 29—Henry R. Schoolcraft. Journal of the Indian agent while on Mackinac Island. Schoolcraft, *Personal Memoirs*, 604–15.

August 28, September 20–21, and September–October (several days)—François, comte de Castelnau. Narrative of three visits to Mackinac Island. Castelnau, *Vues et Souvenirs*, 104, 106–7, 107–12. The author made drawings while at Mackinac, six of which were produced as lithographs to illustrate his book (Figs. 6.18–6.23).

September 10—John Kingman. Account of a brief visit to Mackinac Island in the form of a letter of this date published in Kingman, *Letters*, 31–38.

October 8–27 and November 5–December 28—Reverend Peter Dougherty. Journal of a missionary preparing to spend the winter on Mackinac Island. Anderson, "Diaries of Peter Dougherty," 187–90.

1839

June 7–11, June 25–July 6, July 26–August 16—Henry R. Schoolcraft. Journal of the Indian agent while on Mackinac Island. Schoolcraft, *Personal Memoirs*, 649, 657–60, 662–64.

August 12–13—Anonymous, male traveler. Anonymous journal of August 5–14, 1839, of a trip through Wisconsin and by steamer to Detroit. American Travel Collection, CL.

August 14—Douglass Houghton. Journal of the geologist while at St. Ignace. In his "Transcript of Field Notes for the Year 1839." Douglass Houghton Papers, BHL.

August 24–September 14 and September 27–before June 1, 1840—Henry R. Schoolcraft. Journal of the Indian agent while on Mackinac Island. *Personal Memoirs*, 664–66, 666–81.

September?—Sir Richard George Augustus Levinge. Narrative of a British army officer's visit to Mackinac Island. Levinge, *Echoes from the Backwoods*, 2:165–68. The author made some sketches of Native American subjects while on Mackinac Island (see appendix A).

1839—James H. Lanman. Extended description of Mackinac Island in his *History of Michigan*, 269–72.

1840

May 18–ca. July—Lieutenant John Wolcott Phelps. Journal of an officer of the Fort Mackinac garrison, with interruptions for trips elsewhere. John Wolcott Phelps Papers, NYPL. Copy in MSHP library.

May 19—Edward Brewster. Journal of a brief unloading stop at Mackinac Island. Beeson, "From New York to Illinois," 288.

May 22–26—Bela Hubbard. Journal of a surveyor's visit to Mackinac Island. Original manuscript in Bela Hubbard Papers, 851637 AcAa 2, Box 1, Vol. 7, BHL. Published in Peters, *Lake Superior Journal*, 15. See also Hubbard, *Memorials of a Half-Century*, 21–24, for a reminiscence of this trip. The author made three sketches of Mackinac subjects in his journal (Figs. 6.15–6.17).

May 22–26—Charles W. Penny. Journal of a visit to Mackinac Island with Hubbard's party. Carter and Rankin, *North to Lake Superior*, 1–6.

June 23—Mr. Brackett. Journal of a traveler's brief stop at Mackinac Island. Brackett Journal, American Travel Collection, CL.

July 3–4—James S. Buckingham. Narrative of a stop at Mackinac Island by an English traveler. Buckingham, *The Eastern and Western States of America*, 3:351–66.

July 4—Eliza Steele. Account of a brief visit to Mackinac Island. Steele, *A Summer Journey in the West*, 106–13.

August 4–7. Bela Hubbard. Journal of the surveyor's return visit to Mackinac Island. Original manuscript in Bela Hubbard Papers, 851637, AcAa 2, Box 1, Vol. 2, BHL. Published in Peters, *Lake Superior Journal*, 90–91.

August 9—Lieutenant William Fairholme. Journal of a brief visit to Mackinac Island by a British officer traveling in the West. Original manuscript in the Huntington Library. Published in Tykal, *Journal of an Expedition*, 36–37. The author made a sketch of Fort Mackinac and the village (Fig. 7.2).

early September–November 1—Henry R. Schoolcraft. Journal of the Indian agent while on Mackinac Island for annuity payments. Schoolcraft, *Personal Memoirs*, 687–89.

October 21?–April 29, 1841—Lieutenant John Wolcott Phelps. Journal of an officer of the Fort Mackinac garrison. John Wolcott Phelps Papers, NYPL. Copy in MSHP library.

1841

May 7 or 10–30—Lieutenant John Wolcott Phelps. Journal of an officer of the Fort Mackinac garrison. John Wolcott Phelps Papers, NYPL. Copy in MSHP library. Phelps sketched a parhelion observed at Mackinac Island on May 16, 1841 (appendix A).

May 22–August 10—Henry R. Schoolcraft. Journal of the Indian agent while on Mackinac Island. Schoolcraft, *Personal Memoirs*, 699–702.

Summer (1–2 days)—"Morleigh" (pseudonym). Narrative of a visit to Mackinac Island by a British traveler. Morleigh, *A Merry Briton in Pioneer Wisconsin*, 38–41.

October 3—Gustaf Unonius. Journal of a
Swedish immigrant on his way to Wisconsin.
Olsson, *A Pioneer in Northwest America,*
1:99–104.

1842

May—Reverend Peter Dougherty. Brief journal
of a Protestant missionary while on Mackinac
Island. Anderson, "Diaries of Peter
Dougherty," 243.

July (1 day?)—James K. Paulding. Narrative
of a visit to Mackinac Island. Paulding,
"Sketch of the Great Western Lakes," 259–62.

Summer—Dr. Daniel Drake. Narrative
description of Mackinac Island and the
Straits. Drake, *The Northern Lakes,* 25–26,
36–44, of typescript copy in University of
Michigan Special Collections. Drake
reputedly drew a topographical map of
Mackinac Island during this time (see
appendix A).

October 11–15—C. Donald MacLeod. Narrative
of a visit to Mackinac Island. MacLeod, "A
Saunter in the North-West," 113–14.

November 6—George R. Laughton. Account
of a brief stop at Mackinac Island with an
interrupted visit to Fort Mackinac in a letter
of November 11, 1842, to F. S. Church.
American Travel Collection, CL.

1843

June?—Sarah M. Fuller. Account of a brief stop
at Mackinac Island, the first of three during
her voyage. Fuller, *Summer on the Lakes,* 19.

August ca. 5–12—Julius T. Clark. An Indian
department employee forced to remain at
Mackinac "a week or more" while on his way
to Wisconsin. Clark, "Reminiscences of Hole
in the Day," *WHC,* 5:378.

August ca. 20–29 and September (2 or 3 days).
Sarah M. Fuller. A description of her second
and third visits to Mackinac Island. Fuller,
Summer on the Lakes, 169–81. The author's
companion during her September visit, Sara
Ann Clarke, made sketches while on Mackinac
Island, three of which were engraved for the
illustrated edition of Fuller's book (Figs. 7.12,
7.13, and 7.15).

August? (1 day)—A. H. Fletcher. Brief account of
a stop at Mackinac Island in a letter of August
27, 1843, to Miss Elizabeth H. Fletcher.
Original probably in Chicago History
Museum. Copy in MSHP library.

ca. August 31–September 4—Reverend John H.
Pitezel. Journal of a Protestant missionary
who visited Mackinac Island. Pitezel, *Lights
and Shades of Missionary Life,* 25–33.

1844

June (3 or 4 days)—Joseph Le Conte. Detailed
reminiscence of a visit to Mackinac Island
while on the way to Lake Superior, written for
presentation on December 30, 1899. Holmquist,
"Frontier Vacation," 84–85. Virtually the same
information is included in Armes, *The
Autobiography of Joseph Le Conte,* 65–68.

August 22–25—Anonymous traveler. Journal of
a visit to Mackinac Island. Anonymous Great
Lakes Trip Diary, 1844, CHL.

August 23–September 2—Reverend James
Beaven. Narrative of visit to Mackinac Island
by an Episcopalian missionary, interrupted by
a trip to Sault Ste. Marie on August 29–30.
Beaven, *Recreations of a Long Vacation,* 108–
45. The author made sketches of scenery and
Indians, some of which were engraved to
illustrate his book (Figs. 7.18–7.20 and
appendix A).

Summer—John H. Forster. Reminiscence by a
surveyor who visited Mackinac Island.
"Reminiscences of the Survey of the
Northwestern Lakes," *MPHC,* 9:102–3.

1845

July (3 weeks)—Paul Kane. Narrative of time
spent by the artist on Mackinac Island. Kane,
Wanderings of an Artist, 26–29. The author
made many sketches and paintings of scenery
and Native Americans (Figs. 7.14, 7.16, 7.23,
and appendix A).

July–August (2 visits)—Francis Parkman.
Journal of the historian's visit to the Straits of
Mackinac. Wade, *The Journals of Francis
Parkman,* 1:303–8. The author's companion,
Lieutenant Henry Whiting, made a rough
ground plan of the ruins of Old
Michilimackinac (see appendix A).

Summer? (1 day)—Philo Everett. Narrative of a
stop at Mackinac Island. This has many
similarities to George W. Thayer's
reminiscences. Brotherton, "Story of Philo
Everett's Trip," 25.

Summer—George W. Thayer. Reminiscence of a
stop at Mackinac Island. This has many
similarities to Philo Everett's narrative. "From
Vermont to Lake Superior in 1845," *MPHC,*
30:555.

September 6—John H. Forster. Journal of the
geologist's brief stop at Mackinac Island. John
Harris Forster Papers, BHL.

1846

May (2 days)—Paul Kane. Narrative of a brief
visit to Mackinac Island on his way to Sault
Ste. Marie. Kane, *Wanderings of an Artist,* 42–45.

July 25, August (1 night), and August 17–19—
William Cullen Bryant. Narrative of two brief
stops and a longer visit on Mackinac Island.
Bryant, *Letters of a Traveller,* 253–55, 273, 294–
302.

August—Charles Lanman. Narrative of a visit to
Mackinac Island. Lanman, *A Summer in the
Wilderness,* 162–66. Repeated in Lanman,
Adventures in the Wilds of the United States,
1:128–31. The author made sketches of points
of interest (see appendix A).

1847

May 16—E. C. Martin. Journal of a surveyor's
brief stop at Mackinac Island while on his way
to Sault Ste. Marie. "Leaves From an Old Time
Journal: Lake Superior in 1847," *MPHC,* 30:405.

June 8 and July 1—Horace Greeley. Narrative of
two visits to Mackinac Island. Greeley, "Lake
Superior and the North-West," in Cary, *The
National Temperance Offering,* 112–14.

July [1]—Lewis G. Clark. Narrative of incidents
during a visit to Mackinac Island with Horace
Greeley. Clark, *Knick-knacks From an Editor's
Table,* 185–87.

July 23–25—S. & Co. [Robert Sears]—Narrative
of a visit to Mackinac Island in four letters to
the *Democratic Free Press* published July 28–
31, 1847. Much of this copy was reprinted in
Sears, *A New and Popular Pictorial
Description,* 520–23.

August 28–September 2 and September 19–21—
John Locke. Journal of two visits to Mackinac
Island. John Locke Diary, 1847, 1849, CHL.

1847 or 1848—"F." Narrative of a visit to
Mackinac Island by an unnamed author. F.,
"A Trip to Buffalo in the St. Louis."

1848

June 23–24—J. Elliot Cabot and Louis Agassiz.
Journal of a visit by Agassiz and his party to
Mackinac Island. Agassiz and Cabot, *Lake
Superior,* 22–26. Agassiz's party included
artists, though no Mackinac views are known
to have been made.

July 13 and July 15–16—Anonymous. Journal of
a visit to Mackinac Island interrupted by a trip
to Sault Ste. Marie. Anonymous Diary, 1848,
1854, CHL.

1849

June—John W. Foster and Josiah D. Whitney.
Report of the geology of the Straits area,
including descriptions of specific features.
Foster and Whitney, *Report on the Geology,*
2:161–66, 248–55, 258–59. The authors made
numerous maps and sketches of subjects of
geological interest (Figs. 7.24–7.32).

July 15–19—Lieutenant Delancey Floyd-Jones. Narrative of a visit to Mackinac Island contained in two letters to his family dated July 15 and 19. Delancey F. Jones Correspondence, CHL.

July 16—John Hospers. Journal, with little content, of a Dutch immigrant who stopped briefly at Mackinac Island. Van Der Zee, "Diary of a Journey from the Netherlands," 380–81.

1850

1850—Dr. Daniel Drake. Extended description of the Straits of Mackinac touting the healthiness of its climate. Drake had made one or more previous trips to the area since 1842. Drake, *A Systematic Treatise*, 346–49.

1851

April 1 and later—Joseph Austrian. Retrospective narrative of his time working in the fishing industry at Mackinac Island. "Joseph Austrian's Autobiographical and Historical Sketches." Current location of original unknown. Typescript in MSHP library.

Summer—Daniel S. Curtiss. Narrative of his visit to Mackinac Island. Curtiss, *Western Portraiture*, 34–37.

1852

July 28–August 1 and August 17–19—Juliette Hanna Starr Dana. Journal of two visits to Mackinac Island. Manuscript in private collection. Published in Dana, *A Fashionable Tour*, 29–35, 66–67.

July [29–August 1]—Robert E. Clarke. Illustrated narrative of a visit to Mackinac Island. Clarke, "Notes from the Copper Region." The author made sketches while in the Straits area, four of which were engraved to illustrate his article (Figs. 8.3–8.6).

Summer—Elizabeth Fries Ellet. Description of Mackinac Island, probably gathered from other sources and not from an actual visit. Ellet, *Summer Rambles*, 241.

1854

July 6–23—Aaron Bellangee. Journal of a trip to Mackinac for the benefit of his wife's health. "Aaron Bellangee: A Memorandum Book, 1854 Journey to the West, or North." Private collection. Copy in MSHP library. The author made at least one view of Mackinac Island during his visit (see appendix A).

November 8–July 8, 1855—Major Thomas Williams. Continuing, journal-style letters written by the commandant of Fort Mackinac to his wife, Mary Bailey Williams. Williams Family Papers, BHC. The author drew two sketches into these letters (Figs. 8.23 and 8.27).

November 18–April 30, 1855—Bishop Frederic Baraga. Journal, mostly pertaining to ecclesiastical matters, kept by Baraga during a winter on Mackinac Island. Walling and Rupp, *The Diary of Bishop Frederic Baraga*, 63–65.

1854—James J. Strang. Extended account of the Straits area and its history, with a description of Mackinac Island and its fishing industry. Strang, *Ancient and Modern Michilimackinac*, 14–31.

1854—Anonymous officer of the U.S. Army (possibly Major Thomas Williams). Illustrated description of Mackinac Island published as "Mackinaw and Its Scenery." *Ballou's Pictorial Drawing-Room Companion,* May 5, 1855, 280–81. The author made four views of Mackinac that were engraved to illustrate his article (Figs. 8.15–8.18).

1855

Spring—Bayard Taylor. Narrative of a fueling stop at Mackinac Island. The author described trillium blooming in the woods, establishing the season of his visit. Taylor, *At Home and Abroad,* 232–34.

August 26—Dr. Robert Hazlett Cummins. Journal entry of a stop at Mackinac Island. Cummins, *Journal*, 30–33.

1855–57—Brayton Saltonstall. Reminiscence of childhood summers spent on Mackinac Island. Saltonstall, "Reminiscences of the Mackinac Country."

1855–58—Constance Saltonstall Patton. Reminiscence of childhood summers spent on Mackinac Island. Patton, "A Glimpse of Life on Mackinac from 1835 to 1863." Original 1915 typescript in MSHP collection.

1856

August 14—I. M. Hinchman. Account of Mackinac written by an eleven-year-old boy in a letter to his mother. T. H. Hinchman Papers, BHC.

1857

Summer?—Warren Isham or George Duffield. Narrative of a visit to Mackinac Island. Published as "Notes on Lake Superior," first in *Magazine of Travel* 1, no. 1 (September 1857): 424–25, and then in *Travels in the Two Hemispheres,* 424–25.

1857—John Disturnell. Guidebook description of Mackinac Island with a brief account of its history. Disturnell, *A Trip Through the Lakes,* 111–13.

1859

Summer—Anonymous correspondent. Descriptive account of Mackinac Island with information about Ambrose Davenport and the War of 1812. Originally published in the *New York Tribune.* Reprinted as "Mackinac (From the *New York Tribune* of 1859)," *MPHC,* 7:198–202.

1860

July 13—Anonymous correspondent. Account of Mackinac Island in the form of a letter of this date published as "From Mackinac," *The World* 1, no. 30 (July 19, 1860): 2:2–3.

1860—William P. Strickland. A combination of history, local lore, tourist information, and boosterism about Mackinac Island and the Straits area. Strickland, *Old Mackinaw.*

** = Existing architectural feature

1615

Samuel de Champlain reaches shores of
Georgian Bay

1634

Jean Nicollet is first European thought to pass
through Straits of Mackinac

1651

Refugee Hurons and Tionontati establish
village at Straits of Mackinac

1652

Huron-Tionontati village abandoned in favor
of one at Green Bay

1669

Earliest description of Straits of Mackinac
(Allouez)

1670

Earliest description of Mackinac Island (Dablon)
Mission of St. Ignace established on Mackinac
Island (Fall?)

1671

Mission of St. Ignace moved to north mainland.
Chapel constructed (Fall?)
Hurons establish village near new mission
(Fall?)

1672

Hurons construct fort near chapel of St. Ignace
(Summer)
Ottawas establish village near chapel of St. Ignace

1674

Missionaries complete a "fine chapel" of St. Ignace

1677

Ottawas establish a second village at Gros Cap
Chapel of St. Francis Borgia built between
Ottawa villages (November)

1679

La Salle visits Michilimackinac with *Griffon*
(August–September)

1682

Ottawas and Hurons given plans to fortify
their villages

1683

Forts of Ottawas, Hurons, and Jesuits
strengthened

1686

Durantaye fortifies Michilimackinac

1688

Ottawas begin new fort at north end of
East Moran Bay

1690, ca.

Fort de Buade constructed

1697

Fort de Buade abandoned by military forces

1702

Hurons and some Ottawas relocate to Detroit

1703

Ottawas who remain at Michilimackinac rebuild
their village

1705

Jesuits abandon and burn mission of St. Ignace
(Fall)

1706

French fortify Michilimackinac in response to
unrest at Detroit (August)
Jesuits thereafter maintain seasonal mission at
Michilimackinac

1708

Major fire damages Ottawa village and fort
(August)

1708–10

Ottawa relocate village to south shore of Straits

1714, ca.

Jesuits reestablish mission of St. Ignace on south
shore of Straits

1715

Fort Michilimackinac constructed on south
shore of Straits (Summer)

1721

Fort Michilimackinac and mission of St. Ignace
described as in decay

1731

Machicolated redoubt designed for
Michilimackinac. Plan rejected in 1732

1733+

Fort Michilimackinac expanded with new,
military layout of buildings
Large powder magazine constructed in
southeast corner of fort?

1742

Ottawas relocate village from Michilimackinac
to L'Arbre Croche
Jesuits relocate mission of St. Ignace near new
Ottawa village

1743

New parish church built at Michilimackinac
and named for St. Anne

1744–48

Fort Michilimackinac repaired and expanded,
probably in 1747–48

1747

Earliest reference to Ojibwa village on
Mackinac Island
Indian unrest and attacks on French at
Michilimackinac and Detroit (July)

1749

Fort Michilimackinac surveyed by Lotbinière
(September—Fig 1.15)

1751

Guardhouse burns and is repaired
Construction of new guardhouse authorized
Expansion of Fort Michilimackinac toward lake
authorized

1755–58

Probable expansion of Fort Michilimackinac
on land side

1760

French troops evacuate Michilimackinac
(October)

1761

British troops occupy Michilimackinac
(September)

1763

Ojibwas capture Fort Michilimackinac (June)
Earliest description of Skull Cave on Mackinac
Island (published in 1809)

1764

British troops reoccupy Michilimackinac
(September)
Garrison begins repairs of bastions and walls
of fort (Fall)
Former French commandant's house removed
(Fall)

1765

Jesuits abandon mission of St. Ignace and farm
near L'Arbre Croche
John Askin acquires Jesuit mission farm near
L'Arbre Croche
Development of Fort Michilimackinac suburb
probably begins
Fort Michilimackinac surveyed by Magra
(late Summer—Fig. 2.2)

1769

Fort Michilimackinac surveyed by Nordberg
(Spring—Fig. 2.5)
Barracks construction begins (Summer).
Completed in 1770
Commandant proposes to construct new
guardhouse

1770

Commanding officer's house reconstructed

1772
Powder magazine repaired
New storehouse begun. Completed in 1773
Considerable repairs made to pickets of Fort
Michilimackinac

1774
John Askin establishes new farm at French
Farm Lake (July)

1774–75
Repairs made to fort's platforms, stairs, pickets,
and gates
Half a curtain of pickets blown down by wind
Old house removed that was too near powder
magazine

1778–79
Internal defenses constructed and barracks
strengthened with a stockade
British lay up sloop *Welcome* in Cheboygan River

1779
Clearing of land begins on Mackinac Island
(October)
Wharf constructed on Mackinac Island
(October)
Blockhouse begun on Mackinac Island
(October–November)
First house moved to Mackinac Island
(November)

1780
First house and farm established on Bois Blanc
Island near Point aux Pins
Ste. Anne's Church and priest's house moved to
island (February)
New fort laid out on Mackinac Island (Spring) **
Movement of houses and construction of village
underway (June)
Biddle House moved to or constructed on
Mackinac Island (ca.) **
McGulpin House moved to or constructed on
Mackinac Island (ca.) **
Part of wharf destroyed in storm (December)

1781
Barracks and storehouse moved to island
(February)
Western half of Fort Mackinac under
construction (Spring)
Mackinac Island formally purchased from
Ojibwa (May—Fig. 2.9)
Western half of Fort Mackinac temporarily
enclosed (May—Fig. 2.11)
Fort Mackinac guardhouse (1) in place (by June)
Storehouse erected and enlarged in Fort
Mackinac (June—Fig. 2.12)

Barracks (1) and magazine under construction
in Fort Mackinac (June)
Officers' stone quarters begun in Fort Mackinac
(July) **
Government House constructed or relocated to
island (Summer?)
Garrison formally transferred from mainland
to Fort Mackinac (October)
Remains of Old Michilimackinac pulled down
and burned

1782
Ravelin and stone walls of Fort Mackinac
constructed **

1783
Fort Mackinac guardhouse (1) burns (April)
Fort Mackinac guardhouse (2) constructed

1784
Wharf badly damaged by ice and subsequently
repaired (May)
Wharf again broken up by gale (September)

1785 ca.
John Campbell begins sawmill at Mill Creek
(claim 334) on mainland
McGulpin farm (claim 335) established on
mainland near old fort

1787 ca.
Jean Bongas, a free black, keeps a tavern on
Mackinac Island. Dies 1795

1790 ca.
Two wharves shown on Smith plan of town
(Fig. 2.13)
First farms established on western end of Bois
Blanc Island (late 1780s?)
Schindler farm (claim 331) in operation on
Mackinac Island (before 1796)
Mitchell farm (claim 110) in operation on
Mackinac Island (before 1796)

1792
Small barrack room constructed in Fort Mackinac

1793
Possible establishment of earliest residents
at St. Ignace

1796
British troops evacuate Fort Mackinac
(September)
U.S. troops occupy Fort Mackinac (September)

1797 ca.
Only garrison wharf shown on "JM" plan of
Michilimackinac (Fig. 3.3)

1798–99
Fort Mackinac repaired and reconfigured
Three Fort Mackinac blockhouses constructed **
Officers' stone quarters completed **

1799
Ste. Anne's Church and cemetery repaired
Protestants granted right of burial without
Catholic ceremony

1800 ca.
Stockade removed from village of
Michilimackinac

1802
First descriptions of Arch Rock, Fairy Arch,
Sugar Loaf, and Skull Cave

1803
David Bacon begins clearing land for Indian
mission and farm (Spring)

1804
Michael Dousman acquires Bacon mission farm
(Summer)

1805
Earliest known use of name "Water Street" for
Main Street

1807
Government House no longer in use as
commandant's quarters (ca.)
Earliest documented houses and properties at
St. Ignace

1808
American Fur Company incorporated in State
of New York (April)
Earliest known use of name "Market Street"
(August)

1809
Distillery and horse mill constructed west of
town by Francis LeBarron
U.S. Indian factory established in Government
House (November)

1810
South West Company warehouse(s) (later
Northern Hotel) built (ca.)
Straits-area claims surveyed by Aaron Greeley
(Summer—Figs. 3.6 and 3.7)
Mackinac Island military reserve resurveyed by
John Anderson (Fall)

1812
British capture Fort Mackinac (July)

1814
Fort George constructed on heights above Fort
Mackinac (Summer) **
Battle of Mackinac Island (August)
British capture blockading schooners *Tigress* and
Scorpion (September)

1815
Circular bastion constructed at north point
of Fort Mackinac (Winter)
British troops evacuate Fort Mackinac (July)
U.S. troops reoccupy Fort Mackinac (July)
Fort George completed and renamed Fort
Holmes (August)
Mackinac Indian Agency established, at first
provisionally (August)
John Dousman acquires Schindler farm
(claim 331) (ca. by 1817)

1816
Mackinac Indian Agency formally established
Ottawa village located near mouth of Cheboygan
River
Officers' wooden quarters constructed in Fort
Mackinac **
Fort Mackinac blacksmith shop (1) constructed
(by August)

1817
Citizens petition for construction of public jail
(February)
Borough of Michilimackinac incorporated
(March–April)
John Jacob Astor acquires South West Company
assets (April)
American Fur Company takes over Pothier
(South West Company) property
Island and forts mapped (Summer–Fall—
Figs. 4.6 and 4.7)
Government House last appears on Eveleth map
(Fall—Figs. 4.7 and 5.13)
Only the garrison wharf shown on Eveleth map
(Fall—Figs. 4.7 and 5.13)
Last seasonal garrison maintained in Fort
Holmes (Fall)

1818
American Fur Company rents Ogilvy property
(Beaumont Museum lot)
W. H. Puthuff authorized to construct wharf
at foot of Astor Street (April)
Puthuff advertises a boarding establishment
(June)
Michilimackinac County established (October)
County seat established at Mackinac Island
(October)
Earliest reference to "Robinson's Folly"
(December)

1819
American Fur Company retail store
(Beaumont Museum) constructed **
Ste. Anne's Church "destroyed"
Borough of Michilimackinac purchases fire
engine by public subscription

Michael Dousman acquires Campbell's mills
(claim 334) on mainland
Commissary storehouse constructed below Fort
Mackinac (Summer)
Fire in Fort Mackinac badly damages a three-
story building (October)

1820
Government House appears to have been
demolished by this time
La Framboise house constructed at Church and
Main streets (ca.) **
Earliest description of Robinson's Folly (June—
Schoolcraft/Doty)
Village has post office, jail, and council house
used for courthouse (June)

1821
Boardinghouse in operation at Mackinac kept
by a "Madame Allen"
American Fur Company warehouse probably
constructed **
Catholic church of stone proposed at east end
of village (August)
New garrison wharf proposed (November)
Fort Holmes blockhouse moved and rebuilt as
stable (Fall–Winter 1822)

1822
American Fur Company house (Stuart House)
constructed **
American Fur Company clerk's quarters
constructed (ca. or later)
Fort Brady and Indian agency established at
Sault Ste. Marie (Summer)

1823
Former LeBarron's distillery described as
Reaume's distillery
Indian Agency House begun; completed in 1824
Reverend Ferry establishes school in courthouse
or La Framboise house (Fall)

1824
American Fur Company acquires Puthuff's
wharf (ca.)
Samuel C. Lasley advertises his boardinghouse
(October)

1825
Mission House begun (Spring) **
Mission House occupied (October)

1826
Possible construction date of limekiln **
First mention of Chimney Rock and Devil's
Kitchen (Aug.—McKenney)

1827
Fort Mackinac hospital (1) dismantled (May)
New Ste. Anne's Church in place at Church and
Main streets (by June)
Road up Mission Hill described in survey of
roads (June)
Reverend Ferry buys John Dousman farm
(claim 331) for the mission (by July)
Fort Mackinac hospital (2) constructed
(Summer–Fall—Fig. 5.21)
Bois Blanc Island surveyed by Lucius Lyon
(Summer—Fig. 5.23)
Fort Mackinac barracks (1) dismantled (Fall)
Fort Mackinac barracks (2) begun (October);
finished in 1828
Fort Mackinac hospital (2) burns (October)
Fort Mackinac officers' wooden quarters roof
changed to hipped form (?)

1828
Fort Mackinac bake house, carpenter shop,
and storehouse begun (Summer)
Old well in Fort Mackinac at least partially
reopened (June)
Fort Mackinac hospital (3) begun (June) **
Fort Mackinac blacksmith shop (1) dismantled
(Summer)
Fort Mackinac blacksmith shop (2) constructed
(Summer)
Fort Mackinac guardhouse (2) dismantled
(Summer)
Fort Mackinac guardhouse (3) constructed
(September) **
Reconstruction of circular bastion
recommended (September)
Mackinac Island lands surveyed by John Mullett
(October—Fig. 5.25)
Lover's Leap appears on Mullett map as "Little
Rock" (October)
St. Ignace properties surveyed by John Mullett
(November—Fig. 5.27)

1829
Bois Blanc lighthouse (1) constructed (Summer)
Last mention of circular bastion in Fort
Mackinac (October)

1830
Mission Church constructed (Winter) **
Mission Church dedicated (March)
Presbyterian "Mission" cemetery established
near Mission Church (ca.)
New well dug outside north gate of Fort
Mackinac (September)
Garrison firewood reserve exhausted on western
Bois Blanc (October)

1831

New government wharf constructed at Bois
Blanc Island (Spring)

Government wharf reconstructed at Mackinac
Island (Spring)

Ste. Anne's Church enlarged and rectory
constructed (Spring–Summer)

1832

Borough petitions War Department for vacant
lot (Borough Lot—March)

Old distillery described only as a place (March)

U.S. troops bring cholera to Mackinac Island
(July)

1833

Samuel C. Lasley authorized to erect a wharf
(February)

American Fur Company authorized to extend
its wharf (February)

Eliza Chappell establishes mission school in
St. Ignace (June)

1834

John Jacob Astor sells American Fur Company

Earliest description of Point Lookout (July—
Kemper)

Officers' quarters (Hill House) begun;
completed in 1835 **

1835

American Fur Company headquarters moved
to La Pointe, Wisconsin

New flagstaff erected in Fort Mackinac (May)

Saginaw to Mackinac road route surveyed
(Summer)

Target range and ninepins alley in use behind
Fort Mackinac (September)

Earliest description of Fort Mackinac Post
Cemetery (September) **

1836

Treaty of Washington extinguishes Indian
claims to mainland lands

Fenced wood yard completed behind Fort
Mackinac

Three taverns and three boardinghouses
operating on Mackinac Island

1837

Church of St. Ignatius Loyola constructed in
St. Ignace **

Mission school and Mission Church closed
(Spring)

Mission farm (claim 331) acquired by
Samuel C. Lasley (by 1838)

Fort Mackinac evacuated (June)

Mission House suggested for use as Indian
dormitory (June)

Bois Blanc lighthouse (1) collapses in storm
(December)

Army wharf on Bois Blanc Island destroyed
in storm (December)

Garrison wharf and boathouse at Mackinac
Island damaged (December)

1838

Bois Blanc lighthouse (2) built

Michael Dousman acquires American Fur
Company wharf (ca.—by 1839)

Indian Dormitory constructed (Summer) **

Earliest definite mention of Fairy Arch
(June—Hubbard)

Earliest mention of Lover's Leap (July—
Dougherty)

1839

Mackinac County Courthouse constructed **

Dousman sawmill on south mainland probably
ceases operation

John Orr authorized to construct wharf (March)

Biddle and Drew authorized to construct wharf
(March)

Michael Dousman lengthens his wharf (July)

Douglass Houghton describes "small dock" at
St. Ignace (August)

Fort Mackinac reoccupied (August) and then
evacuated (September)

American Fur Company buildings stand empty
(Lanman)

1840

Fort Mackinac reoccupied (May)

Mission House occupied by several homeless
families (May)

First description of Scott's Cave (unnamed)
as a "new" attraction (August)

Easternmost of old South West Company
buildings removed (ca.)

False front added to South West Company
building (Northern Hotel) (ca.)

1841

Triangulation station constructed at
Fort Holmes site

Triangulation station constructed on
St. Martin Islands

Mackinac Island surveyed by Israel C. Woodruff
(September—Fig. 7.1)

1842

Matthew Geary House constructed (ca.) **

American Fur Company declares bankruptcy
and dissolves assets

Three "comfortable" rooming houses at
Mackinac (Summer—Drake)

1843

Fort Mackinac drill ground fenced

Mission House described as abandoned (August)

1844

Fort Mackinac stone walls and picketing renovated

Road constructed from rear of Fort Mackinac to
the lake (Fort Hill) **

Ramp to Fort Mackinac resurfaced with cement

Mission House proposed for use as a hotel
(September)

First settler established at mouth of Cheboygan
River (Fall)

1845

Additional settlers move to mouth of Cheboygan
River

Samuel Abbott's Greek Revival house
constructed (ca.)

Lasley farm (claim 331) becomes Scott farm (ca.)
after death of Lasley

Mission House opens as hotel (Spring)

Renovation of Fort Mackinac completed

Fort Mackinac bird's-eye view drawn by
William Brenschutz (Fig. 7.21)

First sawmill established on Cheboygan River
(Fall 1845–Winter 1846)

1846

William Scott authorized to construct a wharf
(January)

Michael Dousman authorized to erect meat and
vegetable market (April)

William Saltonstall authorized to erect meat and
vegetable market (April)

Saltonstall market possibly earliest building on
water side of Main Street

Post office established at Duncan (Cheboygan)

1847

Small-scale shipbuilding begins at Cheboygan
River

Charter of Borough of Michilimackinac revoked
(March)

Mission House managed by one "Harrick" (July)

Foundation of a "large hotel" being "worked
upon" in village (July)

Earliest mention of Giant's Stairway (July—
Sears)

Ice is an item of trade from Mackinac Island
(July)

First steam mill established at Cheboygan (Fall
1847–Winter 1848)

1848

First school established at Cheboygan River
settlement

Village of Mackinac incorporated (March)

Village of Mackinac bylaws approved (June)

Borough Lot leased to Bela Chapman (June)

Schoolhouse stands on part of Borough Lot
(June)

Village of Mackinac has two "principal lodging
houses" (June)

Fort Mackinac evacuated (June) and reoccupied
(November)

Henry Selby authorized to extend the "Lasley
wharf" (September)

William Spencer asks to build "scow dock"
(September)

Joseph B. Hall authorized to build a wharf for
Jay and Webster (November)

1849

St. Helena Island patented to William Belote

Hamel and Metivier authorized to build a wharf
(April)

Charles O'Malley projects hotel (O'Malley
House) to open in July (April)

O'Malley House (Island House) opens as hotel
(July) **

Michael Dousman authorized to extend his
wharf (July)

1850

Docks constructed at Duncan Bay (Cheboygan)

First bridge constructed across Cheboygan River

Main Street laid out in Cheboygan settlement

First possible reference to Dwightwood Spring
(unnamed—Drake)

Lieutenant Newton surveys Fort Mackinac
(June—Fig. 8.1)

1851

Mill complex begun at Duncan (Cheboygan).
Completed in 1853

First hotel established at Cheboygan settlement

Catholic cemetery at Hoban and Market streets
closed (December)

1852

Dousman and Grove buy American Fur
Company buildings (May)

Earliest description of Fort Holmes observatory
(July)

Earliest description of "new" civilian or
Catholic cemetery (July) **

Mackinac and Round islands mapped by
Macomb-Raynolds (not ill.)

William Wendell's wharf possibly constructed

Small building constructed at foot of
Wendell's wharf

1853

Cisterns constructed beneath Fort Mackinac
buildings (Summer)

Grove House or Dousman House probably
opens in Stuart House (ca.)

1854

Champaign and Louisignon farms (claims 2
and 3) owned by Dousman

Mitchell farm (claim 110) owned by Edward
Biddle

Lake Superior House in operation on lot 332

Island House known as Huron House (July—
Bellangee)

Wendell's wharf mentioned (November)

Larger building probably constructed at foot
of Wendell's wharf

1855

Wharf constructed on Cheboygan River

Fort Mackinac barracks (2) burns (January)

Fort Mackinac barracks (3) begun (Spring)

Cistern constructed on hill behind Fort
Mackinac barracks (Summer)

Mackinac Island government lands surveyed
by Macomb (Fig. 8.25)

Charles Grove gains control of Grove House
following Dousman's death

E. A. Franks purchases Mission House from
American Board (November)

Gurdon Hubbard buys eighty acres of Davenport
farm (claim 331)

1856

William Wendell authorized to construct
wharf opposite lot 332 (May)

Alexander Toll acquires "Dousman Wharf"
(June)

Jacob Wendell acquires "Old Mill Lot" (claim
334) on south shore (June)

Talbot Dousman acquires Dousman farms (1–3)
and properties (June)

Islanders participate in driving Mormons from
Beaver Island (July)

Reinhard Wernigk takes earliest known
Mackinac photograph (July)

Josiah Wendell authorized to build wharf
(near Yoder Dock) (October)

Northern Hotel in operation by this time or
earlier (Fig. 8.30)

William Wendell authorized to extend his
"Wendell Dock" (October)

Toll and Rice authorized to extend "Dousman
Wharf" (October)

Chapman and Gray authorized to construct
dock (October)

Mission cemetery ordered closed as public
nuisance (October)

Probable establishment of Protestant cemetery
on Garrison Road **

Fort Mackinac evacuated (October)

William C. Hulbert authorized to construct
wharf by lot 102 (December)

1857

Fort Mackinac reoccupied (May)

Abbott house at head of Hoban Street burns to
ground (July)

Mackinaw City laid out and platted by R. C.
Phillips (August—Fig. 8.33)

Fort Mackinac evacuated (August)

1858

Lake View House built **

Fort Mackinac reoccupied (May)

Fort Mackinac barracks (3) burns (June)

Fort Mackinac office/bake house row and
blacksmith shop (2) burn (June)

Fort Mackinac barracks (4) begun. Completed in
1859 **

Fort Mackinac headquarters and quartermaster
storehouse begun **

Building (blacksmith shop 3?) begun on site of
blacksmith shop (2)

New bake house begun outside northeast wall of
Fort Mackinac

1859

American House (formerly Lake Superior
House) opens (May)

Lasley House still advertised as hotel (August)

1860

McLeods purchase Grove House (February?)

McLeod House advertised as newly renovated
hotel (June)

Fort Mackinac hospital (4) begun outside east
wall (Summer) **

Michael Early acquires Dousman farm (claim 1)

1861

Fort Mackinac evacuated (April)

Fort Mackinac cannon ordered to Chicago
(May)

Mackinac House advertised as hotel (May)

NOTES

Abbreviations

ADM	Admiralty Papers
AHP	Syrett, *The Papers of Alexander Hamilton*
ASP	*American State Papers*
BHC	Burton Historical Collection
BHL	Bentley Historical Library
BL	British Library
CCF	Consolidated Correspondence File on Fort Mackinac, Michigan
CHL	Clarke Historical Library
CL	William L. Clements Library
DAB	Johnson, *Dictionary of American Biography*
DCB	*Dictionary of Canadian Biography*
DRCHSNY	O'Callaghan, *Documents Relative to the Colonial History of . . . New York*
HSP	Historical Society of Pennsylvania
JR	Thwaites, *The Jesuit Relations and Allied Documents*
LAC	Library and Archives Canada
LC	Library of Congress
MPHC	*Michigan Pioneer and Historical Collections*
MSHP	Mackinac State Historic Parks
NA	National Archives (UK)
NARA	National Archives and Records Administration (USA)
NYPL	New York Public Library
SHSW	State Historical Society of Wisconsin
SWJP	Sullivan and Hamilton, *The Papers of Sir William Johnson*
TP	Carter, *The Territorial Papers of the United States*
WHC	*Wisconsin Historical Collections*

Introduction

1. Saltonstall, "Reminiscences of the Mackinac Country"; Patton, "A Glimpse of Life in Mackinac from 1835 to 1863," 1. Wernigk was listed and advertised as a "photographic artist" in the 1855 *Chicago City Directory* compiled by E. H. Hall. Constance was mistaken in her recollection that photography had not yet been introduced to the United States. It had become fairly common by the 1840s.

2. Saltonstall, "Reminiscences of the Mackinac Country." Constance Saltonstall Patton presented her narrative and the copy of the photograph reproduced here to the Mackinac Island State Park Commission in 1915.

3. It is likely that Reinhard Wernigk took other photographs during his visit to Mackinac Island. At the end of the season, however, the Wernigks set out for Chicago aboard the steamer *Niagara*. On September 24, 1856, soon after leaving Sheboygan, Wisconsin, the vessel caught fire and the couple perished in the disaster. If they carried additional photographs of the Mackinac area, they were lost. See both Saltonstall recollections and "Niagara's Final Voyage," http://www.seagrant.wisc.edu/shipwrecks/michigan/niagara.

4. See, for example, Petersen, *Mackinac Island*, and Brisson, *Picturesque Mackinac*.

5. Curtiss, *Western Portraiture*, 35.

6. J. Lanman, *History of Michigan*, 270.

7. McKenney, *Sketches of a Tour to the Lakes*, 385.

8. Andrew Blackbird and others offer different interpretations. See Blackbird, *History*.

9. Haldimand to Sinclair, Aug. 21, 1780, *MPHC*, 9:573–74.

Chapter 1

1. Aigremont to Pontchartrain, Nov. 14, 1708, *MPHC*, 33:446–52.

2. P. Porter, *Mackinac*, 4–5.

3. *Relation* of 1669–70, *JR*, 54:201.

4. Eccles, *The Canadian Frontier*, 46–56.

5. *DCB*, "Jean Nicollet de Belleborne," 1:516–18. The account of Nicollet's voyage survives in an account by Father Vimont published in the Jesuit *Relations* for 1642–43, *JR*, 23:277–79. The long-held attribution of Green Bay as Nicollet's destination, thus requiring a passage through the Straits of Mackinac, and the date of 1634 have been questioned in Eccles, *The Canadian Frontier*, 37. He maintains that Nicollet's trip was to Lake Superior in 1638. Eccles provides an excellent summary of French activities in the West.

6. Tanner, *Atlas*, 30–31 and map 6.

7. Kent, *Rendezvous at the Straits*, 1:16.

8. Lahontan, *New Voyages*, 1:88.

9. Kent, *Rendezvous at the Straits*, 1:119.

10. Ibid., 1:148–51.

11. His instructions are in Louis XIV's orders, June 30, 1707, *WHC*, 16:242–47.

12. Aigremont to Pontchartrain, Nov. 14, 1708, *MPHC,* 33:451.

13. Ibid., 33:447.

14. See Edmunds and Peyser, *The Fox Wars.*

15. For an understanding of trade at Michilimackinac and the involvement of one officer in it, see the text and documents in Peyser, *Jacques Legardeur de Saint Pierre.* See also Eccles, *The Canadian Frontier,* 145–48. Kent, *Rendezvous at the Straits,* reproduces many trade licenses.

16. This layout appears on all four known maps of Michilimackinac and is familiar to visitors to the twentieth-century reconstruction of the post. See Heldman and Grange, *Excavations at Fort Michilimackinac,* 19–24.

17. Parish records identify the first burial in the "new church" as taking place on Aug. 10, 1743. *WHC,* 19:150.

18. Beauharnois and Hocquart to Maurepas, Sept. 22, 1746, *WHC,* 17:450.

19. "Journal of Occurrences in Canada," Aug. 13, 1747, *DRCHSNY,* 10:119.

20. For a concise account of the French and Indian War, see F. Anderson, *Crucible of War.*

21. Gérin-Lajoie, "Fort Michilimackinac in 1749," 9; "Mémoire sur la partie occidentale du Canada."

22. La Jonquière and Bigot to Rouillé, Oct. 5, 1749, *WHC,* 18:32.

23. Stevens, Kent, and Wood, *Travels in New France,* 37.

24. Ibid., 39–40, 47. "Ononthio" was the traditional Native American name for the governor of New France.

25. *DCB,* "Charles-Michel Mouet de Langlade," 4:563–64; Bougainville to Paulmy, Aug. 19, 1757, *DRCHSNY,* 10:608.

26. *Relation* of 1669–70, *JR,* 54:197–203. A summary of Allouez's life is in *DCB,* "Claude Allouez," 1:57–58.

27. Burden, *The Mapping of North America,* 197–98, map no. 160. On Champlain's activities, see *DCB,* "Samuel de Champlain," 1:186–99.

28. This one-of-a-kind example is today held by the John Carter Brown Library, Brown University. See Burden, *The Mapping of North America,* 228–31, map no. 188.

29. Ibid., 395–96, map no. 309.

30. Ibid., 294–97, map no. 237.

31. Champlain, *The Works of Samuel de Champlain,* 6:234.

32. This line of thought owes much to a discussion I had with Helen Hornbeck Tanner in June 2004.

33. See Sanson's *Ameriqve Septentrionale* (Paris, 1650) in Burden, *The Mapping of North America,* 375–77, map no. 294.

34. Ibid., 411–13, map no. 318.

35. Coyne, *Exploration of the Great Lakes,* 69–73.

36. For a more complete discussion of this map, see Dunnigan, *Frontier Metropolis,* 10–11.

37. *Relation* of 1669–70, *JR,* 54:199.

38. Ibid., 54:199–200.

39. The map was reissued the following year, without the proposed alterations, in the *Relation* of 1671–72, *JR,* 56:91. For more on the printing history of this map, see McCoy, *Jesuit Relations of Canada,* 302–3, 306–8.

40. *Relation* of 1670–71, *JR,* 54:255.

41. Kershaw, *Early Printed Maps of Canada,* 1:146–47, map no. 155. See also *DCB,* "Claude Allouez," and *DCB,* "Claude Dablon," 1:244.

42. Travelers on the modern ferry from St. Ignace to Mackinac Island will have much the same impression when Round and Bois Blanc are viewed from East Moran Bay.

43. *Relation* of 1670–71, *JR,* 55:157.

44. Ibid., 55:95. Dablon then proceeds with an enlightening "long description" of the missions and surrounding country on pages 95–103.

45. *Relation* of 1670–71, *JR,* 55:101, 161.

46. Ibid., 55:171.

47. Ibid., 55:159.

48. Ibid., 55:157, 161, 167.

49. Ibid., 55:173–79. Parhelions are known more popularly as "sun dogs."

50. Ibid., 55:169–71.

51. *Relation* of 1671–72, *JR,* 56:117.

52. Accounts of the storm come from La Salle, *Relation,* 37, and Hennepin, *A New Discovery,* 84.

53. Hennepin, *A New Discovery,* 84. The harbor is today East Moran Bay at St. Ignace.

54. *Relation* of 1671–72, *JR,* 56:117.

55. *Relation* of 1672–73, *JR,* 57:249–50, 255.

56. *Relation* of 1675, *JR,* 59:217–19.

57. Coyne, *Exploration of the Great Lakes,* 69.

58. Hennepin, *A New Discovery,* 261.

59. *Relation* of 1679, *JR,* 61:123–25; Tonty, *Relation,* 21. For further discussion of the village at Gros Cap, see Kent, *Rendezvous at the Straits,* 1:39–41.

60. *Relation* of 1670–71, *JR,* 55:159.

61. La Salle, *Relation,* 30–31.

62. Ibid., 27; Hennepin, *A New Discovery,* 65–66.

63. La Salle, *Relation,* 46–47.

64. See Kent, *Rendezvous at the Straits,* 1:65–104.

65. Ibid., 1:65.

66. *DCB,* "Louis-Armand de Lom d'Arce de Lahontan," 2:439–44.

67. Ibid.

68. Ibid., 2:443.

69. Lahontan, *New Voyages,* 1:88.

70. Conference between Frontenac and the Ottawas, Aug. 19–20, 1682, *DRCHSNY,* 9:183.

71. La Barre to Seignelay, Nov. 4, 1683, ibid., 9:202; Merchants to La Barre, Spring 1684, and La Barre to Merchants, Apr. 14, 1684, quoted in Kent, *Rendezvous at the Straits,* 1:66–67.

72. "Relation" of Sieur de Lamothe Cadillac, 1718, *WHC,* 16:352–53.

73. Lahontan, *New Voyages,* 1:88.

74. *Relation* of 1670–71, *JR,* 55:163–65. Lahontan describes the currents in *New Voyages,* 1:89.

75. Lahontan, *New Voyages,* 1:89.

76. Louis XIV to Frontenac and Champigny, July 14, 1690, *DRCHSNY,* 9:454. Kent, *Rendezvous at the Straits,* 1:119, suggests that existing fortifications were expanded around 1690.

77. Callière to Seignelay, Jan. 1689, *DRCHSNY,* 9:405.

78. "Relation" of Sieur de Lamothe Cadillac, 1718, *WHC,* 16:350, 353. Bark-roofed log houses are visible in Reinhard Wernigk's 1856 photograph of Mackinac Island.

79. "Relation" of Sieur de Lamothe Cadillac, 1718, *WHC,* 16:350.

80. Cadillac to Vaudreuil, Aug. 27, 1706, *MPHC,* 33:276.

81. Marest to Vaudreuil, Aug. 14, 1706, *WHC,* 16:232–38; Aigremont to Pontchartrain, Nov. 14, 1708, *MPHC,* 33:448.

82. Aigremont to Pontchartrain, Nov. 14, 1708, *MPHC,* 33:449.

83. See Vaudreuil to Pontchartrain, Oct. 31, 1710, *WHC,* 16: 264–65; Vaudreuil to Pontchartrain, Nov. 6, 1712, *DRCHSNY,* 9:863; and Bégon memorial, Sept. 20, 1713, *WHC,* 16:295–97.

84. Memorial of Lignery, 1720, *WHC,* 16:387. In 1719 Lignery asked for reimbursement for subsistence for the garrison from September 1715 to September 1716. Account of de Lignery, 1719, *WHC,* 16:384.

85. Conference between Vaudreuil and the Indians, Nov. 14, 1703, *DRCHSNY,* 9:750. Armour, *Colonial Michilimackinac,* 17, suggests that they moved west to Gros Cap.

86. Aigremont to Pontchartrain, Nov. 14, 1708, *MPHC,* 33:450–51. Armour, *Colonial Michilimackinac,* 17.

87. Porteous to Porteous, Aug. 16, 1767, John Porteous Papers, BHC.

88. Stone, *Fort Michilimackinac,* 313, describes the earliest stockade (Feature 5) and shows it on the archaeological map reproduced on page 332. An artist's conception of the earliest fort may be found in Armour, *Colonial Michilimackinac,* 19.

89. See, for instance, Aigremont to Pontchartrain, Nov. 14, 1708, *MPHC,* 33:425, and "Memoir on Detroit," 1714, *WHC,* 16:308.

90. "Memoir on the Savages of Canada," 1718, *WHC,* 16:371.

91. Charlevoix, *Journal,* 2:42.

92. Ibid.

93. Ibid., 2:43. Details of the amount of annual trade and licenses may be found for this period in Kent, *Rendezvous at the Straits,* 1:191–289.

94. See *DCB,* "Pierre-François-Xavier de Charlevoix," 3:103–10.

95. Armour, *Colonial Michilimackinac,* 18–19.

96. Léry to President of the Council of Marine, Oct. 15, 1728, in Roy, *Inventaire des papiers de Léry,* 1:193–94; abstract of dispatches, Oct. 1, 1728, *DRCHSNY,* 9:1010–11. For the redoubts actually constructed, see Dunnigan, *Glorious Old Relic,* 14–24.

97. Léry to Maurepas, Oct. 25, 1731, quoted in Roy, *Hommes et choses du Fort Saint-Frédéric.*

98. Maurepas to Beaharnois and Hocquart, Apr. 8, 1732, quoted in Roy, *Hommes et choses du Fort Saint-Frédéric.*

99. Heldman and Grange, *Excavations at Fort Michilimackinac,* 6–7, 19–24.

100. Charlevoix, *Journal,* 2:45–46.

101. See, for example, Gilman, *Life on the Lakes,* 1:90.

102. Charlevoix, *Journal,* 2:46.

103. "Relation" of Sieur de Lamothe Cadillac, 1718, *WHC,* 16:350.

104. "Journal of Occurrences in Canada," Aug. 13, 1747, *DRCHSNY,* 10:119; Gérin-Lajoie, "Fort Michilimackinac in 1749," 9.

105. See Karrow, "Lake Superior's Mythic Isles."

106. "Journal of Occurrences in Canada," 1746–47, *DRCHSNY,* 10:119.

107. Dunnigan, *Frontier Metropolis,* 34.

108. "Journal of Occurrences in Canada," 1746–47, *DRCHSNY,* 10:119.

109. Ibid., 10:120.

110. For the expedition to Detroit, see Dunnigan, *Frontier Metropolis,* 35. For that of Céloron to the Ohio River, see Eccles, *The Canadian Frontier,* 159.

111. Gérin-Lajoie, "Fort Michilimackinac in 1749," 4, 8. This work is a translation of Lotbinière's *mémoire* and includes his comments on the post.

112. Ibid., 4, 6. See also Heldman and Minnerly, *The Powder Magazine at Fort Michilimackinac.*

113. Gérin-Lajoie, "Fort Michilimackinac in 1749," 6.

114. Ibid., 6.

115. The "new church" is mentioned in a record of interment of Marie Coussante, the first person to be buried beneath the building constructed by her father, Joseph Ainse. Mackinac Register, Aug. 10, 1743, *WHC,* 19:150.

116. Heldman and Grange, *Excavations at Fort Michilimackinac,* 19–24.

117. See, for example, Dunnigan, *Frontier Metropolis,* 38–41.

118. La Jonquière to Rouillé, Sept. 17, 1751, *WHC,* 18:82–83.

Chapter 2

1. Today it is known as Goose Island.

2. Henry, *Travels and Adventures,* 34–35, 38–39.

3. Ibid., 39–51.

4. Ibid., 40.

5. See Peckham, *Pontiac and the Indian Uprising,* for an overview of the events of 1763–64.

6. Etherington to Gladwin, June 12, 1763, *MPHC,* 27:631; Henry, *Travels and Adventures,* 78–79; deposition of Solomon, Aug. 14, 1763, *MPHC,* 27:667. For a discussion of casualties in the garrison, see Harburn, *In Defense of the Red Ensign,* 4–7.

7. *DCB,* "Alexander Henry," 6:316–19.

8. Etherington to Langlade, June 10, 1763, *WHC,* 18:253.

9. Long, *Voyages and Travels,* 141.

10. Weld, *Travels,* 353.

11. For barracks practices, see Dunnigan, *The Necessity of Regularity in Quartering Soldiers.*

12. Williams and Shapiro, *A Search for the Eighteenth Century Village at Michilimackinac,* 4–8.

13. See P. Parker, *The Journals of Jonathan Carver.*

14. For Rogers's story and the transcript of his court martial, by which he was acquitted, see Armour, *Treason? At Michilimackinac.* See also *DCB,* "Robert Rogers," 4:679–83.

15. DePeyster to Gage, May 5, 1775, Thomas Gage Papers, vol. 128, CL.

16. Gage to Turnbull, Sept. 18, 1770, ibid., vol. 96.

17. Gage to DePeyster, May 20, 1775, ibid., vol. 129.

18. For the story of Michilimackinac in the American Revolution, see Armour and Widder, *At the Crossroads.*

19. *DCB,* "Patrick Sinclair," 5:759–61.

20. For a study of the construction, see Dunnigan, "The Post of Mackinac."

21. Hope to Robertson, Sept. 20, 1782, *MPHC,* 10:638.

22. Robertson to Mathews, Sept. 7, 1783, ibid., 11:384–85.

23. Robertson to Haldimand, June 10, 1784, ibid., 11:415–16; Mathews to Robertson, Aug. 12, 1784, ibid., 20:243–44.

24. For the diplomacy relating to the Great Lakes posts, see Bowler, "From the Treaty of Paris to Jay's Treaty," 13–21.

25. *The London Magazine,* Feb. 1761, [64].

26. Charlevoix, *Histoire et description*; Charlevoix, *Journal.*

27. *The London Magazine,* Feb. 1761, [64].

28. Census of Indian tribes, 1736, *WHC,* 17:245–46; "Journal of Occurrences in Canada," 1746–47, *DRCHSNY,* 10:119. See also Tanner, *Atlas,* 40–41 (map 9) and 58–59 (map 13).

29. Henry, *Travels and Adventures,* 108–9.

30. Ibid., 110–13.

31. "Fort Michilimackinac," Oct. 30, 1802, *Columbian Centinel,* 38, no. 40 (Jan. 15, 1803): 1–2; Schoolcraft, *Narrative Journal,* 112.

32. Henry, *Travels and Adventures,* 58–59.

33. Ibid., 115–73.

34. Ibid., 186–87; Bradstreet to Howard, Aug. 31, 1764, Thomas Gage Papers, vol. 24, CL; *DCB,* "Minweweh," 3:452–53.

35. Bradstreet to Howard, Aug. 31, 1764, Thomas Gage Papers, vol. 24, CL.

36. Howard to Bradstreet, Oct. 15, 1764, ibid., vol. 28; Howard to Bradstreet, Jan. 6, 1765, ibid., vol. 34.

37. Howard to Bradstreet, Jan. 6, 1765, ibid., vol. 34; Campbell to Gage, Feb. 25, 1765, ibid., vol. 31; Campbell to Gage, May 31, 1765, ibid., vol. 37.

38. Gage to Campbell, July 15, 1765, ibid., vol. 39.

39. Gage to Campbell, Aug. 19, 1765, ibid., vol. 41.

40. See Brun, *Guide to the Manuscript Maps in the William L. Clements Library,* 180–81. All Clements Library catalog records show the date of the Magra plan as "[1766]."

41. Campbell to Gage, Aug. 25, 1765, Thomas Gage Papers, vol. 41, CL.

42. Gage to Campbell, Aug. 19, 1765, ibid., vol. 41; Gordon to Gage, Aug. 27, 1765, ibid., vol. 41.

43. Campbell to Gage, Sept. 15, 1765, ibid., vol. 42; Gordon to Gage, Oct. 21, 1765, ibid., vol. 44. For an account of Gordon's activities at Detroit, see Dunnigan, *Frontier Metropolis,* 60–63.

44. Campbell to Gage, Oct. 14, 1765, Thomas Gage Papers, vol. 44, CL.

45. See, for example, Heldman and Grange, *Excavations at Fort Michilimackinac,* 33–34.

46. Scott Hawley, personal communication with the author, Apr. 15, 2005. Magra appears in the academy's tuition book for 1760–61, which may be viewed online at: http://dewey.lib.upenn.edu/sceti/codex/public/pagelevel/index.cfm?WorkID=904&Page=29.

47. Great Britain. War Office. *A List,* 1763, 70.

48. Ibid., 1766, 69.

49. Entries of Aug. 9–12, Oct. 15 and 19, 1765, John Porteous Papers, Journals, vol. 3, BHC.

50. Gage to Johnson, May 5, 1766, *SWJP,* 5:200.

51. Howard to Bradstreet, Jan. 6, 1765, Thomas Gage Papers, vol. 34, CL.

52. Report, Nov. 1, 1765, enclosed in Campbell to Gage, Oct. 31, 1765, ibid., vol. 45.

53. Gérin-Lajoie, "Fort Michilimackinac in 1749," 6.

54. Porteous to Porteous, Aug. 16, 1767, John Porteous Papers, BHC.

55. DePeyster to Brehm, June 20, 1779, *MPHC,* 9:387. Another analysis of the problem is in Glazier to Gage, June 10, 1769, Thomas Gage Papers, vol. 86, CL.

56. Sinclair to Brehm, May 29, 1780, *MPHC,* 9:552.

57. Journal of Peter Pond, *WHC,* 18:344–45.

58. Carver, *Travels,* 1778, 18.

59. Journal, July 12, 1771, John Porteous Papers, vol. 7, BHC.

60. P. Parker, *The Journals of Jonathan Carver,* 149.

61. Williams and Shapiro, *A Search for the Eighteenth Century Village at Michilimackinac,* 3–8.

62. Roberts to Gage, July 10, 1767, Thomas Gage Papers, vol. 67, CL; Gage to Roberts, Sept. 2, 1767, ibid., vol. 69.

63. Askin to McMurry, Apr. 28, 1778, in Quaife, *The John Askin Papers,* 1:68; Askin to Henry, June 23, 1778, in ibid., 1:144.

64. DePeyster to Haldimand, July 24, 1778, *MPHC,* 9:367.

65. Orders, Oct. 28, 1779, quoted in Williams and Shapiro, *A Search for the Eighteenth Century Village at Michilimackinac*, 6; opinions on removal of the fort, June 21, 1780, *MPHC*, 9:558.

66. Glazier to Gage, June 10, 1769, Thomas Gage Papers, vol. 86, CL.

67. DePeyster to Carleton, May 30, 1778, *MPHC*, 9:366. John Long camped with the Indians at "Chippeway Point" in the spring of 1779. Long, *Voyages and Travels*, 140; Askin to Barthe, June 26, 1778, in Quaife, *The John Askin Papers*, 1:150.

68. Heldman, *Archaeological Investigations at French Farm Lake*, 8–11; permission to build a house, July 7, 1774, in Quaife, *The John Askin Papers*, 1:49.

69. P. Parker, *The Journals of Jonathan Carver*, 71.

70. Heldman and Grange, *Excavations at Fort Michilimackinac*, 33.

71. Stone, *Fort Michilimackinac*, 317–18.

72. La Jonquière to Rouillé, Sept. 17, 1751, *WHC*, 18:83.

73. Glazier to Gage, Nov. 20, 1769, Thomas Gage Papers, vol. 88, CL; Turnbull to Gage, June 21, 1770, ibid., vol. 93.

74. Turnbull to Gage, May 12, 1767, ibid., vol. 64; Turnbull to Gage, May 12, 1768, ibid., vol. 77.

75. The possibility that Diedrich Brehm was the author was raised by Keith R. Widder. A comparison of the handwriting on Figure 2.3 to several of Brehm's letters shows more similarities than differences. See Brehm to Gage, Aug. 6, 1770, Thomas Gage Papers, vol. 94, CL, in which many of the capitals are similar, particularly C, L, and S. Brehm's numerals on the plan are similar to those in Brehm to Brown, June 30, 1768, enclosed in Brown to Gage, July 1, 1768, ibid., vol. 78, and Brehm to Campbell, Nov. 3, 1765, enclosed in Campbell to Gage, Oct. 31, 1765, ibid., vol. 45. The last document is a formal memorial in which the letter M is similar to those found on Figure 2.3.

76. See Dunnigan, *Frontier Metropolis*, 64–65.

77. Howard to Bradstreet, Jan. 6, 1765, Thomas Gage Papers, vol. 34, CL; Campbell to Gage, May 31, 1765, ibid., vol. 37.

78. Gage to Campbell, July 15, 1765, ibid., vol. 39.

79. Campbell to Gage, Aug. 25, 1765, ibid., vol. 41.

80. Glazier to Gage, Oct. 4, 1768, ibid., vol. 81. For a discussion of quartering practices, see Dunnigan, *The Necessity of Regularity in Quartering Soldiers*.

81. Report, Nov. 1, 1765, enclosed in Campbell to Gage, Oct. 31, 1765, Thomas Gage Papers, vol. 45, CL.

82. Gage to Glazier, June 21, 1768, ibid., vol. 78; Glazier to Gage, Oct. 4, 1768, ibid., vol. 81; Gage to Glazier, Dec. 19, 1768, ibid., vol. 83.

83. Gage to Turnbull, Feb. 22, 1769, ibid., vol. 84; Gage to Glazier, Mar. 17, 1769, ibid., vol. 84.

84. Glazier to Gage, June 10, 1769, ibid., vol. 86.

85. Glazier to Gage, Oct. 4, 1768, ibid., vol. 81.

86. Gage to Glazier, Dec. 19, 1768, ibid., vol. 83; Glazier to Gage, June 10, 1769, ibid., vol. 86.

87. It was still privately claimed when the site was suggested as the most convenient spot for a new storehouse. Turnbull to Gage, Sept. 23, 1771, Thomas Gage Papers, vol. 106, CL.

88. Glazier to Gage, Nov. 20, 1769, ibid., vol. 88; Turnbull to Gage, July 31, 1770, ibid., vol. 94. For further details on the project, see Dunnigan, *The Necessity of Regularity in Quartering Soldiers*.

89. Two plans with the first title were cataloged in the Surveyor General's Office at Québec circa 1789 or 1790. Catalog, *MPHC*, 24:43–44. The latter title appears on a circa 1784 "List of Plans" in Frederick Haldimand Papers, Add. Mss 21886, BL.

90. P. Parker, *The Journals of Jonathan Carver*, 71.

91. DePeyster to Gage, May 5, 1775, Thomas Gage Papers, vol. 128, CL.

92. DePeyster to Brehm, June 20, 1779, *MPHC*, 9:387.

93. Gage to DePeyster, May 20, 1775, Thomas Gage Papers, vol. 129, CL.

94. DePeyster to Haldimand, Sept. 21, 1778, *MPHC*, 9:373.

95. Ibid.

96. Glazier to Gage, June 10, 1769, Thomas Gage Papers, vol. 86, CL.

97. For his service, see *DCB*, "Patrick Sinclair," 5:759–61.

98. Sinclair to Brehm, Oct. 7, 1779, *MPHC*, 9:524.

99. Haldimand to DePeyster, Apr. 16, 1780, ibid., 10:390.

100. Sinclair to Brehm, Oct. 7, 1779, ibid., 9:524.

101. Ibid., 9:523–27.

102. Brehm to Sinclair, Apr. 17, 1780, ibid., 9:533–38.

103. Log, Oct. 16, 1779, Harrow Family Papers, BHC; Sinclair to Brehm, Oct. 29, 1779, *MPHC*, 9:530–33; log, Nov. 5–6, 1779, Harrow Family Papers, BHC.

104. Sinclair to Brehm, Feb. 15, 1780, *MPHC*, 9:539.

105. Sinclair to Brehm, May 29, 1780, ibid., 9:552. John R. Bailey, relying on local knowledge, says that the blockhouse stood east of Government House, roughly near the site of the Indian Dormitory. Bailey, *Mackinac, Formerly Michilimackinac*, 147.

106. Memorandum, n.d., Frederick Haldimand Papers, Add. Mss. 21758, f. 368, BL.

107. Brehm to Sinclair, Apr. 17, 1780, *MPHC*, 9:535.

108. Sinclair to Brehm, July 8, 1780, ibid., 9:579.

109. Schoolcraft, *Personal Memoirs*, 446.

110. Details are from the text of the copy of the deed held by the CL with a new transcription by Owen Jansson.

111. Burbeck to Wayne, Sept. 6, 1796, Anthony Wayne Papers, HSP. One of the 1796 copies is now held by MSHP.

112. Bailey, *Mackinac, Formerly Michilimackinac*, 146–47.

113. The contemporary copy is in Frederick Haldimand Papers, Add. Mss. 21774, BL, and is also printed in *MPHC*, 19:633–34.

114. Hope to Haldimand, Oct. 19, 1782, *MPHC*, 10:656.

115. Hope and others to Robertson, Sept. 20, 1782, ibid., 10:638–40.

116. Hockings report, Sept. 20, 1782, ibid., 10:642–45.

117. Gother Mann report, Dec. 6, 1788, ibid., 12:30–37.

118. Sinclair to Brehm, Oct. 7, 1779, ibid., 9:524; Brehm to Sinclair, Apr. 17, 1780, ibid., 9:534.

119. Sinclair to Brehm, May 29, 1780, ibid., 9:552.

120. This belief was common into the 1960s when research by Dr. David Armour and others dispelled it.

121. Sinclair to Brehm, Oct. 15, 1779, *MPHC*, 9:528–29.

122. Brehm to Sinclair, Apr. 17, 1780, ibid., 9:534. Twiss seems to have prepared at least three proposed designs. Copies were in the Surveyor General's Office in Québec about 1790 but have been lost. Catalog, ca. 1790, *MPHC*, 24:43–44. See appendix A for descriptions of these plans.

123. Sinclair to Haldimand, Aug. 3, 1780, *MPHC*, 9:572–73; Haldimand to Sinclair, Aug. 21, 1780, ibid., 9:573–74.

124. Sinclair to Mathews, Feb. 23, 1781, ibid., 9:629; Sinclair to Powell, May 1, 1781, ibid., 19:631–32.

125. Sinclair to Powell, May 1, 1781, ibid., 19:631–32.

126. Log of *Welcome*, Feb. 12, 1781, Harrow Family Papers, BHC.

127. Sinclair to Powell, June 6, 1781, *MPHC*, 19:638–39.

128. Sinclair to [Haldimand], July 8, 1781, ibid., 10:495; Sinclair to Haldimand, July 31, 1781, ibid., 10:502–3; Sinclair to Haldimand, Oct. 22, 1781, ibid., 10:529–30.

129. Sinclair to Haldimand, Apr. 29, 1782, ibid., 10:572–73.

130. Hockings report, Sept. 20, 1782, ibid., 10:642–45.

131. The plan reproduced with Hockings's report in *MPHC* is actually a redrawing of Sinclair's plan of June 15, 1781. The letters keyed to Hockings's report have been applied inaccurately. For a proper identification of the areas described by Hockings, see the plan in Dunnigan, "The Post of Mackinac," 246–50.

132. The plan, section, and drafts showing the magazine and officers' quarters are described on a list of plans in the Surveyor General's Office at Québec about 1790 in *MPHC*, 24:43–44. The barracks plan is included in a list of circa 1784 in the Frederick Haldimand Papers, Add. Mss. 21886, BL. See appendix A.

133. Hockings report, Sept. 20, 1782, *MPHC*, 10:642–45.

134. Opinions regarding removal of the fort, June 21, 1780, ibid., 9:556–58.

135. Sinclair to Brehm, Oct. 29, 1779, ibid., 9:530–33.

136. Sinclair to Brehm, Feb. 15, 1780, ibid., 9:539.

137. Sinclair to Haldimand, June 8, 1780, ibid., 9:556.

138. Log of *Welcome*, May 17, 1781, Harrow Family Papers, BHC. This describes towing "Mr. Gotier's" raft to the island in five hours.

139. Schoolcraft, *Personal Memoirs*, 445.

140. Sinclair to Brehm, Feb. 15, 1780, *MPHC*, 9:540. The contribution of stockade pickets was a civic duty at Detroit during the French and British regimes. See Dunnigan, *Frontier Metropolis*, 36.

141. Sinclair to Mathews, Feb. 23, 1781, Frederick Haldimand Papers, Add. Mss. 21758, BL.

142. Robertson to Haldimand, Aug. 5, 1784, *MPHC*, 11:442; Robertson to Mathews, ibid., 11:449–50.

143. Standing orders for the guard, May 19, 1789, Dorchester Papers, BHC.

144. Brehm to Sinclair, Apr. 17, 1780, *MPHC*, 9:535.

145. Sinclair to Brehm, July 8, 1780, ibid., 9:579; Brehm to Sinclair, Aug. 10, 1780, Frederick Haldimand Papers, Add. Mss. 21758, BL.

146. See, for example, a land grant to Pierre Grignon, Aug. 10, 1782, *WHC*, 18:432–33.

147. Petition to Captain Daniel Robertson, Oct. 27, 1783, *MPHC*, 11:393–95.

148. Sinclair to DePeyster, Feb. 15, 1780, ibid., 19:499–501; Sinclair to Brehm, Oct. 29, 1779, ibid., 9:530–33; Robertson to Schank, Apr. 28, 1781, ibid., 9:642.

149. Logbook of *Welcome*, Dec. 10, 1780, Harrow Family Papers, BHC; Robertson to Schank, Apr. 28, 1781, *MPHC*, 9:642.

150. Robertson to Mathews, May 26, 1784, *MPHC*, 11:413–14; Robertson to Mathews, Sept. 7, 1784, ibid., 11:452–53.

151. Robertson to Schank, Apr. 26, 1781, ibid., 9:643.

152. Doyle to England, May 16, 1793, ibid., 12:48–49. Campbell was at Michilimackinac as early as the fall of 1783, when he signed the petition requesting confirmation of Sinclair's land grants. For a history of the site, see Martin, *The Mill Creek Site*.

Chapter 3

1. Burbeck to Porter, Sept. 7, 1796, Moses Porter Papers, BHC. See also Burbeck to Wayne, Sept. 6, 1796, Anthony Wayne Papers, HSP.

2. Wayne to Burbeck, Aug. 17, 1796, Fort Mackinac Orderly Book, 1, U.S. Military Academy Library, West Point, NY.

3. The establishment of U.S. control of Mackinac between 1796 and 1802 is detailed in P. Porter, *The Eagle at Mackinac*.

4. Beckwith to post commandants, June 1, 1796, *MPHC*, 25:120–21.

5. Report, Sept. 1, 1796, Fort Mackinac Orderly Book, 3–5, U.S. Military Academy Library, West Point, NY.

6. Sargent to Pickering, Sept. 30, 1796, *TP*, 3:457. See also P. Porter, *The Eagle at Mackinac*, 17–19.

7. Major Burbeck had this duplicated on Sept. 4, 1796, and one copy is now in the collections of MSHP.

8. Sargent to Pickering, Sept. 30, 1796, *TP*, 3:457.

9. Burbeck to Porter, Sept. 7 and 11, 1796, both in Moses Porter Papers, BHC.

10. Swan to Frye, Oct. 10, 1797, *Medical Repository* 1, no. 1 (1797): 527–28.

11. Tracy to McHenry, Nov. 26, 1800, James McHenry Papers, CL; "Fort Michilimackinac," Oct. 30, 1802, *Columbian Centinel*, 38, no. 40 (Jan. 15, 1803): 1–2. LeBarron's authorship of the latter piece has been assumed from context. The letter was clearly written by a post surgeon who had arrived not long before it was written. The second arch mentioned by the writer might have been Fairy Arch (demolished in 1953) or the smaller "Sanilac Arch" at the base of the column supporting Arch Rock. Alexander Henry's account of Skull Cave did not appear in print until 1809.

12. Wayne to Wolcott, Sept. 4, 1796, *TP*, 2:569–72.

13. Wilkinson to Wilkins, Sept. 9, 1797, *MPHC*, 35:629.

14. Burbeck to Hamilton, June 18, 1799, *AHP*, 13:195–96.

15. Tracy to Dexter, Dec. 20, 1800, RG 77, Buell Collection, NARA.

16. Wilkinson to Burbeck, Aug. 19, 1797, Fort Mackinac Orderly Book, 6, U.S. Military Academy Library, West Point, NY; Rivardi to Hamilton, May 2, 1799, *AHP*, 23:92. Rivardi was an elegant draftsman, but he never visited Michilimackinac and must have worked from information provided to him. The plans once in Burbeck's possession might be those believed to be in the collections of the Fraunces Tavern Museum in New York City. See appendix A.

17. McNiff to Wayne, Dec. 19, 1796, Anthony Wayne Papers, CL. McNiff's plan probably showed the island since his Detroit cartography of this time, also produced for Wayne, focused on private land claims. Rivardi to Hamilton, Mar. 21, 1799, *AHP*, 22:573; Howard to Eustis, Oct. 1, 1810, *TP*, 10:333; Burbeck memorandum, n.d. (ca. 1810), Henry Burbeck Papers, U.S. Military Academy Library, West Point, NY.

18. Hamilton to Strong, May 22, 1799, *AHP*, 23:127.

19. Wilkinson to Hamilton, Sept. 6, 1799, ibid., 23:381.

20. Hamilton to Washington, Sept. 9, 1799, ibid., 23:405; Hamilton to Washington, Oct. 12, 1799, ibid., 23:516–17; P. Porter, *The Eagle at Mackinac*, 26–27.

21. Tracy to McHenry, Nov. 28, 1800, James McHenry Papers, CL. See also Tracy to Dexter, Dec. 20, 1800, RG 77, Buell Collection, NARA.

22. Swan to Frye, Oct. 10, 1797, *Medical Repository* 1, no. 1 (1797): 528.

23. Dilhet, *État de l'Église*, 124.

24. Duggan to Selby, Jan. 10, 1796, *MPHC*, 12:192; "Fort Michilimackinac," Oct. 30, 1802, *Columbian Centinel*, 38, no. 40 (Jan. 15, 1803): 1–2.

25. Ross, *Adventures*, 171.

26. Mason to Varnum, Sept. 10, 1808, *TP*, 10:233–36; Varnum to Eustis, Nov. 10, 1809, ibid., 10:284–85.

27. LeBarron to Kingsbury, Nov. 10, 1809, Jacob Kingsbury Papers, L5:1809–10, vol. 14, BHC; Mitchell to Kingsbury, Sept. 30, 1810, ibid.

28. For a history of the American Fur Company, see Lavender, *The Fist in the Wilderness*.

29. Brevoort to Irving, June 28, 1811, in Hellman, *Letters of Henry Brevoort*, 26–31.

30. For a summary of this situation, see Sambrook, "Historical Lineaments."

31. See Rezek, *History of the Diocese of Sault Ste. Marie*, 2:168–74.

32. For Richard's visit, see *MPHC*, 1:484–85. Dilhet's account is in his *État de l'Église*, 123–28.

33. Bacon, *Sketch of the Rev. David Bacon*, 15–19.

34. Ibid., 44–65.

35. Brevoort to Irving, June 28, 1811, in Hellman, *Letters of Henry Brevoort*, 32–33.

36. Burbeck to Porter, Sept. 7, 1796, Moses Porter Papers, BHC.

37. "Report on the nature and state of the works," Sept. 1, 1796, Fort Mackinac Orderly Book, 3–5, U. S. Military Academy Library, West Point, NY.

38. Mathews to Robertson, Aug. 12, 1784 (2 letters), *MPHC*, 20:243–44, 244–45.

39. Robertson to Mathews, Sept. 19, 1784, ibid., 11:453–54.

40. Robertson to Mathews, Aug. 26, 1784, ibid., 11:449–50.

41. Mann report, Dec. 6, 1788, ibid., 12:30–37; Mann report, Sept. 22, 1789, ibid., 23:372–74; Mann to Clarke, Jan. 1, 1791, ibid., 23:375–76.

42. Doyle to England, May 16, 1793, ibid., 12:48–49.

43. Burbeck to Porter, Sept. 11, 1796, Moses Porter Papers, BHC.

44. Burbeck to Wayne, Oct. 25, 1796, Anthony Wayne Papers, HSP.

45. "Report on the nature and state of the works," Sept. 1, 1796, Fort Mackinac Orderly Book, 3–5, U. S. Military Academy Library, West Point, NY; Sterrett field notes, enclosed in Burbeck to Wayne, Oct. 25, 1796, Anthony Wayne Papers, HSP.

46. Robertson to Mathews, Apr. 20, 1783, *MPHC*, 11:358.

47. All these buildings are fully described in "Report on the nature and state of the works," Sept. 1, 1796, Fort Mackinac Orderly Book, 3–5, U.S. Military Academy Library, West Point, NY.

48. Mann report, Dec. 6, 1788, *MPHC*, 12:30–37.

49. Wilkinson to Burbeck, Aug. 19, 1797, Fort Mackinac Orderly Book, 6–7, U.S. Military Academy Library, West Point, NY.

50. Burbeck to Hamilton, June 18, 1799, *AHP*, 23:195–96.

51. Ibid. See also Dunnigan, "The Post of Mackinac," 51–58, 61–88, and P. Porter, *The Eagle at Mackinac*, 24–27.

52. Tracy to Dexter, Dec. 20, 1800, RG 77, Buell Collection, NARA.

53. Swan to Frye, Oct. 10, 1797, *Medical Repository* 1, no. 1 (1797): 527.

54. Rindge, "National Park Service Report on Fort Mackinac Restoration," 14.

55. Ibid., 14, 22.

56. P. Porter, *The Eagle at Mackinac,* 51.

57. Swan to Frye, Oct. 10, 1797, *Medical Repository* 1, no. 1 (1797): 527.

58. Ibid.

59. "Report on the nature and state of the works," Sept. 1, 1796, Fort Mackinac Orderly Book, 5, U.S. Military Academy Library, West Point, NY.

60. Dilhet, *État de l'Église,* 123–24.

61. Richard to Carroll, 1799, *MPHC,* 1:484; Dilhet, *État de l'Église,* 125, 128.

62. Dilhet, *État de l'Église,* 127.

63. Parr to Harris, June 6, 1790, C930, 76, LAC, mentions regulations for use of the house as early as August 1787. Lieutenant Colonel Jacob Kingsbury and his wife resided there until leaving Mackinac Island in May 1805. Kingsbury to her sister, Sept. 10, 1805, Jacob Kingsbury Papers, BHC.

64. "Report on the nature and state of the works," Sept. 1, 1796, Fort Mackinac Orderly Book, 4, U.S. Military Academy Library, West Point, NY.

65. Swan to Frye, Oct. 10, 1797, *Medical Repository* 1, no. 1 (1797): 527.

66. Tracy to Dexter, Dec. 20, 1800, RG 77, Buell Collection, NARA.

67. Kingsbury to her sister, Sept. 10, 1805, Jacob Kingsbury Papers, BHC.

68. Lieutenant Presley O'Bannon sold locks taken from the house in 1807–8. Deposition of Daniel Dunham, Sept. 20, 1808, Solomon Sibley Papers, BHC; Eustis to Varnum, Apr. 26, 1809, *WHC,* 19:334.

69. Burbeck to Porter, Sept. 11, 1796, Moses Porter Papers, BHC; Swan to Frye, Oct. 10, 1797, *Medical Repository* 1, no. 1 (1797): 527; Richard to Carroll, 1799, *MPHC,* 1:484; "Fort Michilimackinac," Oct. 30, 1802, *Columbian Centinel,* 38, no. 40 (Jan. 15, 1803): 1–2.

70. Dilhet, *État de l'Église,* 123.

71. "Fort Michilimackinac," Oct. 30, 1802, *Columbian Centinel,* 38, no. 40 (Jan. 15, 1803): 1–2; LeBarron to Kingsbury, Feb. 15, 1810, L5:1810, vol. 15, Jacob Kingsbury Papers, BHC.

72. Dilhet, *État de l'Église,* 123.

73. Sambrook, "Historical Lineaments," 39–41.

74. Pothier to Sibley, Aug. 12, 1805, Solomon Sibley Papers, BHC.

75. Dickson et al. to Sibley, with enclosure, Sept. 2, 1805, ibid.

76. Sambrook, "Historical Lineaments," 41–52.

77. Dilhet, *État de l'Église,* 124.

78. Duggan to Selby, Jan. 10, 1796, *MPHC,* 12:193.

79. Kingsbury to her sister, Sept. 10, 1805, Jacob Kingsbury Papers, BHC.

80. LeBarron to Kingsbury, Feb. 15, 1810, L5:1810, vol. 15, Jacob Kingsbury Papers, BHC.

81. Bacon to Bayley, Feb. 11, 1803, in Bacon, *Sketch of the Rev. David Bacon,* 47.

82. Bacon to Beaumont, July 31, 1802, Bacon Family Papers, copies in MSHP library.

83. Ibid.; Bacon to Bayley, Feb. 11, 1803, in Bacon, *Sketch of the Rev. David Bacon,* 47.

84. Twelve affidavits sworn before Samuel Abbott, Sept. 20, 1808, Henry Burbeck Papers, U.S. Military Academy Library, West Point, NY. Another set of these affidavits may be found in Solomon Sibley Papers, BHC, with transcripts in the William F. Lawler Papers, BHC. O'Bannon had resigned from the Marine Corps in 1807 and took a commission in the army's Regiment of Artillerists. He commanded Fort Mackinac for a year. No record has been found of any action on the affidavits, which covered a wide variety of allegations of improper behavior. O'Bannon's exploits during the Tripolitan War were the inspiration for the reference to "the shores of Tripoli" in the Marine Corps Hymn and the "Mameluke hilt" sword still worn by Marine Corps officers.

85. "Fort Michilimackinac," Oct. 30, 1802, *Columbian Centinel,* 38, no. 40 (Jan. 15, 1803): 1–2.

86. See Carheil to Callière, Aug. 30, 1702, *JR,* 65:189–99.

87. "Fort Michilimackinac," Oct. 30, 1802, *Columbian Centinel,* 38, no. 40 (Jan. 15, 1803): 1–2.

88. For an account of the history of the territory, see Gilpin, *The Territory of Michigan.*

89. For biographical information, see Quaife, "Detroit Biographies."

90. Greeley to Mansfield, Nov. 3, 1809, *TP,* 10:283.

91. Greeley to Mansfield, Apr. 12, 1810, ibid., 10:312.

92. Graustein, "Nuttall's Travels into the Old Northwest," 64; Voss, *Botanical Beachcombers,* 4–5; Ross, *Adventures,* 174. During his short time on Mackinac Island, Nuttall described the dwarf lake iris, today Michigan's state wildflower. Voss, *Michigan Flora,* 11, 431.

93. Aaron Greeley, "Survey of the Island of Michilli-mackinac in August 1810 . . . Survey of the Island of Bois Blanc . . . Survey of a tract on the main including the old Fort at Michill," RG 49, Old Map File, Michigan 10, NARA.

94. Sambrook, "Historical Lineaments," 52. For the legislation, see "An Act Regulating Land Grants," Mar. 3, 1807, *TP,* 10:86–90.

95. The claims are recorded in *ASP, Public Lands,* 1:332–34 (claims 101–10), 391–94 (claims 279–98), 405–9 (claims 323–26), 494 (claim 596), 512 (claim 637), 544–46 (claims 697–714), and 547 (claim 717). These are listed in Sambrook, "Historical Lineaments," 379–81.

96. Pothier et al. to Sibley, Sept. 21, 1805, Solomon Sibley Papers, BHC. See also transcript of same in William F. Lawler Papers, BHC.

97. *ASP, Public Lands,* 1:332–33. Claim 101 is most easily identified today as the location of Doud Mercantile at the corner of Main and Fort streets and, at its Market Street end, by the historic McGulpin house preserved by Mackinac State Historic Parks.

98. The area is described as "an open space denominated the public square" in Crooks to Astor, [Apr.] 1817, American Fur Company Papers, L5:1816–18, 11, BHC.

99. "Astoria: Or Anecdotes of an Enterprize Beyond the Rocky Mountains," in Irving, *Three Western Narratives,* 282.

100. "An Act Regulating Land Grants," Mar. 3, 1807, *TP,* 10:89. Plats of individual properties might survive in the records of the Treasury Department.

101. Hull to Mansfield, Feb. 2, 1811, *TP,* 10:338.

102. Meigs to Audrain, July 24, 1816, ibid., 10:660–61.

103. Claim 324, *ASP, Public Lands,* 1:406, 478.

104. Howard to Eustis, Sept. 4, 1810, *MPHC,* 40:318–19.

105. Claim 324, *ASP, Public Lands,* 1:406, 478.

106. Dousman to Eustis, Sept. 25, 1811, *TP,* 10:370.

107. Extract of Burbeck's instructions, Feb. 2, 1808, enclosed in Howard to Kingsbury, Sept. 5, 1810, Jacob Kingsbury Papers, L5:1810–11, vol. 17, BHC.

108. Howard to Land Board, Sept. 4, 1810, *MPHC,* 40:319–22.

109. Dousman to Eustis, Sept. 25, 1811, *TP,* 10:370.

110. Howard to Kingsbury, Sept. 12, 1810, Jacob Kingsbury Papers, L5:1810–11, vol. 17, BHC.

111. Howard to Kingsbury, Nov. 15, 1810, ibid.

112. Kingsbury to Howard, Oct. 17, 1810, ibid.; Burbeck memorandum (ca. 1810), Henry Burbeck Papers, U.S. Military Academy Library, West Point, NY.

113. Eustis to Howard, Dec. 10, 1810, *MPHC,* 40:324–25; Kingsbury to Hanks, Feb. 28, 1811, Jacob Kingsbury Papers, L5:1810–11, vol. 17, BHC.

114. Hanks to Kingsbury, Jan. 27, 1811, and LeBarron to Kingsbury, Jan. 28, 1811, both in Jacob Kingsbury Papers, L5:1810–11, vol. 17, BHC.

115. Dousman to Eustis, Sept. 25, 1811, *TP,* 10:370.

116. Kearsley to Graham, Dec. 2, 1829, William F. Lawler Papers, BHC.

117. See Bacon, *Sketch of the Rev. David Bacon,* 44–67, for his experience at Mackinac. Mention of the house and land is in Bacon to Missionary Society, May 1803, ibid., 50.

118. Bacon to Missionary Society, Nov. 4, 1803, ibid., 58.

119. Burbeck memorandum (ca. 1810), Henry Burbeck Papers, U.S. Military Academy Library, West Point, NY.

120. Bacon, *Sketch of the Rev. David Bacon,* 64–65.

121. Dousman's claim 324 was first considered on Oct. 5, 1808, *ASP, Public Lands,* 1:406. Twelve affidavits of Sept. 20, 1808, concerning Lieutenant O'Bannon's irregular activities are preserved in the Henry Burbeck Papers, U.S. Military Academy Library, West Point, NY, and in the Solomon Sibley Papers, BHC, with transcripts in the William F. Lawler Papers, BHC.

122. Howard to Land Board, Sept. 10, 1810, *MPHC,* 40:320–21.

123. Meigs to Audrain, July 24, 1816, *TP,* 10:660–61.

124. Claim 717, *ASP, Public Lands,* 1:547; claim 596, ibid., 1:494; LeBarron to Kingsbury, Jacob Kingsbury Papers, Nov. 10, 1809, L5:1809–10, vol. 14, BHC.

125. Howard to Eustis, Oct. 1, 1810, *TP,* 10:333; Eustis to Howard, Dec. 10, 1810, *MPHC,* 40:324–25.

126. Anderson to Eustis, Feb. 2, 1811, *TP,* 10:339.

127. Anderson and Roberdeau to Swift, Jan. 15, 1816, RG 77, Buell Collection, NARA.

Chapter 4

1. Hanks to Hull, Aug. 4, 1812, *MPHC,* 40:430–33; Irwin to Mason, Oct. 16, 1812, *TP,* 10:411–15. For a complete account of the event and of Mackinac during the War of 1812, see May, *War 1812,* and Dunnigan, *The British Army at Mackinac.* A narrative of the war in Michigan, with much on events relating to Mackinac is Gilpin, *The War of 1812 in the Old Northwest.*

2. Hanks to Hull, Aug. 4, 1812, *MPHC,* 40:430–33.

3. Ibid.

4. Irwin to Mason, Oct. 16, 1812, *TP,* 10:412.

5. Askin to Askin, July 19, 1812, *MPHC,* 32:482–83; Roberts to Brock, July 17, 1812, ibid., 15:108; Roberts to Hanks, July 17, 1812, ibid., 40:440.

6. Hanks to Hull, Aug. 4, 1812, ibid., 40:430–33; Irwin to Mason, Oct. 16, 1812, *TP,* 10:415; Hanks to Roberts, July 17, 1812, *MPHC,* 40:441; Articles of Capitulation, July 17, 1812, ibid., 15:110; Roberts to Baynes, July 17, 1812, ibid., 15:109.

7. Askin to Askin, July 19, 1812, ibid., 32:482–83.

8. Hull to Eustis, Aug. 26, 1812, ibid., 40:462.

9. Van Fleet, *Old and New Mackinac,* 104.

10. "Mackinac (From the *New York Tribune* of 1859)," 7:200. In 1823 Michael Dousman also stated that Lasley had taken the oath. Deposition, Sept. 23, 1823, *ASP, Public Lands,* 5:245.

11. Puthuff to Cass, June 20, 1816, *WHC,* 19:421; account of Samuel Lasley, ca. 1816–20, Charles Larned Papers, BHC.

12. Dousman to Cass, [Oct. 30, 1819], *MPHC,* 36:417; deposition of Samuel N. Lasley, Oct. 15, 1824, *ASP, Public Lands,* 5:50. Generally, Britain did not recognize the naturalization of its subjects as U.S. citizens, so Dousman's argument might have had some validity.

13. Strang, *Ancient and Modern Michilimackinac,* 17.

14. Irwin to Mason, Oct. 16, 1812, *TP,* 10:414; Roster of sloop *Salina,* [July 1812], Daniel Dobbins Papers, Buffalo and Erie County Historical Society Library; roster of the schooner *Mary,* July 25, 1812, William F. Lawler Papers, BHC.

15. Dunnigan, *The British Army at Mackinac,* 13–17.

16. Chauncey to Perry, July 14, 1813, in Cruikshank, *Documentary History,* 7:278–79; Harrison to Armstrong, Oct. 16, 1813, ibid., 8:71–72.

17. Bullock to Freer, Oct. 23, 1813, *MPHC,* 15:424–25.

18. Bulger account, n.d., ibid., 23:446–49; McDouall to Drummond, July 17, 1814, ibid., 15:616–19.

19. For a summary of the campaign, see Gilpin, *The War of 1812 in the Old Northwest,* 241–45, and Gough, *Fighting Sail on Lake Huron,* 82–116. A narrative of the battle is in Dunnigan, *The British Army at Mackinac,* 22–27.

20. Leavitt, *Autobiography,* 23.

21. McDouall to Bulger, May 2, 1815, *MPHC,* 23:512–13.

22. James to Butler, June 28, 1815, *TP,* 10:555–56; Butler to Dallas, Aug. 6, 1815, ibid., 10:586–87.

23. Gratiot to Swift, Feb. 10, 1816, RG 77, Buell Collection, 111–12, NARA.

24. Cass to Crawford, Oct. 27, 1815, *TP,* 10:606–8.

25. See Puthuff to Cass, May 14, 1816, *WHC,* 19:412.

26. Crooks to Astor, Aug. 21, 1814, ibid., 19:360–64; Sinclair to Jones, Nov. 11, 1814, *Niles Weekly Register* 7 (Nov. 19, 1814): 173. The operation is discussed in Lavender, *The Fist in the Wilderness,* 202–4, 220–21.

27. K. Porter, *John Jacob Astor,* 2:699; Crooks to Astor, [Apr.] 1817, American Fur Company Papers, L5:1816–18, 11, BHC.

28. See Crooks to Astor, [Apr.] 1817, ibid. See also Lavender, *The Fist in the Wilderness.*

29. Puthuff to Cass, June 20, 1816, *WHC,* 19:420; Lavender, *The Fist in the Wilderness,* 228–37.

30. Proclamation, Mar. 15, 1817, *TP,* 10:725. The act is published in the *Detroit Gazette* of May 15, 1818, and in *Laws of the Territory of Michigan,* 564–69. They were also recorded in Township Record Book, 12–18, CHL.

31. Acts, Dec. 4, 1817–Apr. 11, 1818, Township Record Book, 12–27, CHL.

32. Ibid., 28–30. This was at the site of the present "Coal Dock."

33. Proclamation, Oct. 26, 1818, *MPHC,* 2:272.

34. Brown to Calhoun, Feb. 5, 1818, RG 77, Buell Collection, NARA.

35. "Michilimakinak," *The Washingtonian,* Sept. 14, 1812. This was repeated in the *Plattsburgh Republican* of Oct. 9 and no doubt appeared in other American newspapers as well.

36. See entry for "Richard Dillon" in "The Peter Winkworth Collection," Library and Archives Canada Web site, and Harper, *Early Painters and Engravers in Canada,* 90.

37. Storrow to Brown, Dec. 1, 1817, *WHC,* 6:157.

38. Claim 699, *ASP, Public Lands,* 1:544.

39. Burnett to Pothier, Aug. 3, 1794, in Hurlbut, *Chicago Antiquities,* 62–63.

40. Bigsby, *The Shoe and Canoe,* 2:146; Richard to Fenwick, Dec. 22, 1822, quoted in Paré, *The Catholic Church in Detroit,* 339.

41. Ordinances, Dec. 4, 1817, and Apr. 11, 1818, Township Record Book, 12–18, 22–24, CHL.

42. Irwin to Mason, Oct. 16, 1812, *TP,* 10:413.

43. For an account of the voyage to Mackinac, see Fredriksen, *Surgeon of the Lakes,* 79–86.

44. Leavitt, *Autobiography,* 22; Croghan to Armstrong, Aug. 9, 1814, in Crawford, *The Naval War of 1812,* 566.

45. Gratiot to Swift, Feb. 10, 1816, RG 77, Buell Collection, 111–12, NARA.

46. "Mackinac (From the *New York Tribune* of 1859)," 7:200–201.

47. Leavitt, *Autobiography,* 22.

48. Fredriksen, *Surgeon of the Lakes,* 87; Leavitt, *Autobiography,* 22.

49. Croghan to Armstrong, Aug. 9, 1814, in Crawford, *The Naval War of 1812,* 566–68.

50. Fredriksen, *Surgeon of the Lakes,* 86–88.

51. Bulger account, n.d., *MPHC,* 23:447.

52. Dunnigan, *The British Army at Mackinac,* 23–25. McDouall's report to Prevost of Aug. 14, 1814, is in *MPHC,* 25:591–94.

53. Fredriksen, ed., *Surgeon of the Lakes,* 88. Accounts of the battle may be found in Dunnigan, *The British Army at Mackinac,* 22–26, and Dunnigan, "The Battle of Mackinac Island."

54. Fredriksen, *Surgeon of the Lakes,* 90.

55. Ibid.; McDouall to Croghan, Aug. 5, 1814, Michigan Collection, CL.

56. Sinclair to Jones, Aug. 9, 1814, in Crawford, *The Naval War of 1812,* 568–70. Croghan's report uses the identical phrase to describe the thickness of the woods.

57. Croghan to Armstrong, Aug. 9, 1814, ibid., 567.

58. Sinclair to Jones, Aug. 9, 1814, ibid., 568–70.

59. Fredriksen, *Surgeon of the Lakes,* 86; deposition of Samuel Lasley, ca. 1816–20, Charles Larned Papers, BHC.

60. Croghan to Armstrong, Aug. 9, 1814, in Crawford, *The Naval War of 1812,* 566–68; Sinclair to Jones, Aug. 9, 1814, ibid., 568–70.

61. Leavitt, *Autobiography,* 24.

62. Fredriksen, *Surgeon of the Lakes,* 92. In 1871, after Holmes's body had been exhumed for burial in a different cemetery, witnesses to the original interment noted the presence of the cannonballs and described how the coffin had been towed to Detroit behind a schooner. Account, Andrew Hunter Holmes Papers, BHC. Parsons's comment suggests that the remains of Captain Van Horne and Lieutenant Jackson might have been treated in the same fashion.

63. Croghan to McArthur, Aug. 23, 1814, in *Niles Weekly Register* 7 (Sept. 24, 1814): 18; Drummond to unaddressed, *MPHC,* 15:638.

64. Sinclair to Turner, Aug. 15, 1814, in Crawford, *The Naval War of 1812,* 570–71.

65. McDouall to Drummond, Sept. 9, 1814, *MPHC,* 15:643. See also Crookshank to Turquand, Aug. 21, 1814, ibid., 15:636–37.

66. Bulger account, n.d., ibid., 23:446–49.

67. Bulger to McDouall, Sept. 7, 1814, ibid., 15:641; Sinclair to Jones, Nov. 11, 1814, in Crawford, *The Naval War of 1812,* 649.

68. Bulger to McDouall, Sept. 7, 1814, *MPHC,* 15:641.

69. Bunnell, *Travels and Adventures,* 123. Bunnell's recollection of his own prescience had the benefit of fifteen years of hindsight.

70. Bulger to McDouall, Sept. 7, 1814, *MPHC,* 15:641–42. Turner's report to Sinclair is in Crawford, *The Naval War of 1812,* 647–48.

71. McDouall to Drummond, Sept. 9, 1814, *MPHC,* 15:644.

72. Quoted in *DCB,* "Robert McDouall," 7.

73. Heriot, *Travels Through the Canadas.* The woman at left is taken from Heriot's *Costume of Domiciliated Indians of North America* (facing p. 292), while two of the men appear to have been adapted from the same source. The warrior kneeling by the boats is very reminiscent of the figure in Benjamin West's classic *The Death of General Wolfe.*

74. Compare it to the reconstitution of the uniform in Dunnigan, *The British Army at Mackinac,* 29, no. 8.

75. Inventory and Valuation, Oct. 31, 1814, *MPHC,* 25:608–10; Prevost to Bathurst, Dec. 4, 1814, ibid., 25:614–15. The later history of the schooners is described in Malcomson, *Warships of the Great Lakes,* 90, 97.

76. Bunnell, *Travels and Adventures,* 123–33, provides a most interesting account of his trip to Québec and, ultimately, to England.

77. Sinclair to Jones, Nov. 11, 1814, in Crawford, *The Naval War of 1812,* 649.

78. Sinclair to Jones, Oct. 28, 1814, ibid., 646–47. Turner faced a court of inquiry at Boston in the summer of 1815. The court blamed the disaster on other factors and found "that the conduct of lieutenant Turner was that of a discreet and vigiland officer." *Niles Weekly Register* 8 (Aug. 1815): 408–9.

79. For a history of Mackinac's second fort, see Dunnigan, *Fort Holmes.*

80. *Western Spy,* Aug. 25, 1815, transcript in William F. Lawler Papers, BHC.

81. Butler to Dallas, Aug. 6, 1815, *TP,* 10:586.

82. McDouall to Bulger, Mar. 1, 1815, *MPHC,* 23:500–501.

83. The name first appears in Chambers to Brown, Sept. 16, 1815, RG 77, Buell Collection, NARA.

84. See Garrison Orders, Oct. 9, 1815, McNeil Order Books, vol. 1, New Hampshire Historical Society, Concord. Fort Holmes was reoccupied in the spring. See Garrison Orders, May 2, 1816, ibid.

85. Chambers to Brown, Sept. 16, 1815, RG 77, Buell Collection, NARA.

86. Extract of a letter, Nov. 17, 1815, *Niles Weekly Register* 9 (Supplement, Feb. 24, 1816): 80.

87. Dunnigan, *Fort Holmes,* 23.

88. A series of measurements of Fort Holmes, recorded in the post order book in the fall of 1816, probably in November, might reflect preliminary work to prepare a plan. McNeil Order Book, vol. 4, New Hampshire Historical Society, Concord.

89. Storrow to Brown, Dec. 1, 1817, *WHC,* 6:157.

90. Gratiot to Swift, Nov. 25, 1817, RG 77, Buell Collection, 174–75, NARA.

91. Grange, "Excavation of the Wooden Quarters at Fort Mackinac," 3.

92. Chambers to Brown, Sept. 16, 1815, RG 77, Buell Collection, NARA.

93. Tracy to Dexter, Dec. 20, 1800, RG 77, Buell Collection, NARA.

94. Harrison to Stanton, Aug. 15, 1819, RG 92, CCF, NARA. The machine is also discussed in Pierce to Root, May 7, 1819, RG 107, Letters Received, NARA, and Curtis to Stanton, Nov. 2, 1819, RG 92, CCF, NARA.

95. Jackman and Freeman, *American Voyageur,* 30.

96. Bayfield to Barrie, Nov. 1, 1822, enclosed in Barrie to Croker, Nov. 16, 1822, ADM 1/3445, NA.

97. McDouall to Bulger, Mar. 1, 1815, *MPHC,* 23:500–501; Cutler to Jesup, Oct. 28, 1829, RG 92, CCF, NARA.

98. Extract of a letter, Nov. 17, 1815, *Niles Weekly Register* 9 (Supplement, Feb. 24, 1816): 80.

99. Dunnigan, *Fort Holmes,* 23.

100. Journal of an aide, June 19, 1819, Jacob Brown Papers, BHC; Schoolcraft, *Narrative Journal,* 112–13; Jackman and Freeman, *American Voyageur,* 27–28.

101. Bayfield to Barrie, Nov. 1, 1822, enclosed in Barrie to Croker, Nov. 16, 1822, ADM 1/3445, NA; Lyon to Jesup, Jan. 1, 1822, RG 92, CCF, NARA.

102. Gratiot to Swift, Nov. 25, 1817, RG 77, Buell Collection, 174–75, NARA.

103. Extract of a letter, Nov. 17, 1815, *Niles Weekly Register* 9 (Supplement, Feb. 24, 1816): 80.

104. Ibid.

105. James W. Biddle, "Recollections of Green Bay in 1816–17," *WHC,* 1:51.

106. Gratiot to Swift, Feb. 10, 1816, RG 77, Buell Collection, 111–12, NARA.

107. Heitman, *Historical Register,* 1:410.

108. Department Orders, July 2, 1817; Detachment Orders, Nov. 2, 1817; Eveleth to Pierce, Nov. 2, 1817, all in McNeil Order Book, vol. 2, New Hampshire Historical Society, Concord.

109. Gratiot to Swift, Nov. 25, 1817, RG 77, Buell Collection, 174–75, NARA.

110. Chambers to Brown, Sept. 16, 1815, RG 77, Buell Collection, NARA; Extract of a letter, Nov. 17, 1815, *Niles Weekly Register* 9 (Supplement, Feb. 24, 1816): 80.

111. Storrow to Brown, Dec. 1, 1817, *WHC,* 6:158.

112. Claim of Louis Bouisson, Oct. 28, 1823, *ASP, Public Lands,* 5:228; Minutes, Jan. 18, 1832, Township Record Book, 61–62, CHL.

113. Severance, "Gen. Brown's Inspection Tour," 312.

114. Storrow to Brown, Dec. 1, 1817, *WHC,* 6:158–59.

115. Department Orders, Aug. 10, 1817, McNeil Order Book, vol. 2, New Hampshire Historical Society, Concord. Storrow left Detroit on August 17 and followed the same inspection route, leaving Mackinac Island on September 1. See Storrow to Brown, Dec. 1, 1817, *WHC,* 6:154–87.

116. Swift to Smith, May 18, 1818, RG 77, Buell Collection, NARA; Smith to Swift, Aug. 19, 1818, RG 77, Letters Received by the Office of Chief of Engineers, Irregular Series, NARA.

117. Baker to Macomb, Oct. 13, 1818, in *Detroit Gazette,* Nov. 13, 1818, 2:3.

118. Schoolcraft, *Narrative Journal,* 393–94.

119. Storrow to Brown, Dec. 1, 1817, *WHC,* 6:159.

120. Butler to Dallas, Aug. 6, 1815, *TP,* 10:586.

121. Anderson and Roberdeau to Swift, Jan. 15, 1816, RG 77, Buell Collection, NARA. Roberdeau later mentioned a "personal knowledge of the passage from Mackinaw to the rapids of St Marys," something he could only have obtained during his 1815 trip. Roberdeau to Swift, June 16, 1817, "Reports on Fortifications . . . January 1814–October 1823," RG 77, Buell Collection, NARA.

122. Gratiot to Swift, Feb. 10, 1816, RG 77, Buell Collection, 111–12, NARA.

123. Ibid.

124. Gratiot to Swift, Nov. 25, 1817, RG 77, Buell Collection, 174–75, NARA.

125. Estimate from Gratiot's settled account and claim no. 2505, Sept. 1, 1817, RG 217, NARA. A "toise" is an archaic French measurement of 76.71 inches, roughly equivalent to the English "fathom" of six feet.

126. Quoted in W. Robinson, *American Forts,* 77, 84.

127. Gratiot to Swift, Nov. 25, 1817, RG 77, Buell Collection, 174–75, NARA.

128. McDouall to Drummond, July 17, 1814, *MPHC,* 15:616–19.

129. McDouall to Bulger, Mar. 1, 1815, ibid., 23:500–501.

130. Extract of a letter, Nov. 17, 1815, *Niles Weekly Register* 9 (Supplement, Feb. 24, 1816): 80; Schoolcraft, *Narrative Journal,* 120.

131. Cullum, *Biographical Register,* 1:99.

132. Brown to Calhoun, Feb. 5, 1818, RG 77, Buell Collection, NARA.

133. Number 336, Aug. 5, 1843, RG 77, Register of Letters Received, NARA.

134. Bigsby, *The Shoe and Canoe,* 2:153.

135. Severance, "Gen. Brown's Inspection Tour," 308–9.

136. Journal of an aide, June 19, 1819, Jacob Brown Papers, BHC.

137. Severance, "Gen. Brown's Inspection Tour," 311. See Journal of an aide, June 19, 1819, Jacob Brown Papers, BHC.

138. Severance, "Gen. Brown's Inspection Tour," 311–12.
139. Bigsby, *The Shoe and Canoe,* 2:145.
140. Cass to Dallas, July 10, 1815, *TP,* 10:566–67.
141. Macomb to Crawford, June 20, 1816, ibid., 10:652–53.
142. Orders, July 8, 1816, McNeil Order Book, vol. 2, New Hampshire Historical Society, Concord.
143. James H. Lockwood, "Early Times and Events in Wisconsin," *WHC,* 2:103–4.
144. A rough draft is also held in RG 77, Fortifications Map File, Drawer 152, Sheet 4–1, NARA.
145. Biddle, "Recollections of Green Bay in 1816–17," *WHC,* 1:49–50.
146. Dobbins was master of the schooner *Salina,* one of the two vessels sent to Detroit under a flag of truce with paroled American prisoners and the American inhabitants of Michilimackinac who had refused to take the British oath of allegiance. "List of Crew and Passengers," [July 25, 1812], Daniel Dobbins Papers, Buffalo and Erie County Historical Society.
147. For a summary of this earliest organized hydrographic survey of the area, see Dunbabin, "Motives for Mapping the Great Lakes," 22–26. Bayfield mentions his two visits to Mackinac Island in a letter to Barrie, Nov. 1, 1822, enclosed in Barrie to Croker, Nov. 16, 1822, ADM 1/3445, NA.
148. For an example of a published British map of the Straits based on Bayfield's surveys, see *Lake Huron Sheet 1,* published by the Hydrographic Office of the Admiralty, June 3, 1848, V12.13a/410-Huron-1848, LAC.
149. Bigsby, *The Shoe and Canoe,* 2:145.

Chapter 5
1. G. Hubbard, *Autobiography,* 143. Although there is much repetition in his account, Hubbard provides numerous personal details about operations at Mackinac Island and in the field. See also Gurdon Hubbard, "Journey of Gurdon S. Hubbard," *MPHC,* 3:125–27. For a history of the American Fur Company, see Lavender, *The Fist in the Wilderness.*
2. G. Hubbard, *Autobiography,* 143–45. Hubbard describes the sorting and packing of furs at several other points in his reminiscence.
3. K. Porter, *John Jacob Astor,* 2:699; Crooks to Astor, [Apr.] 1817, American Fur Company Papers, L5:1816–18, 11, BHC.
4. Crooks to Abbott, Feb. 26, 1818, 73–75, and Crooks to Abbott, Apr. 3, 1818, 80–81, both in American Fur Company Papers, L5:1816–1818, BHC.
5. Crooks to Stuart, Oct. 17, 1819, ibid., 1819–20, 247–48.
6. Abstract of title to Private Claim 293, Stuart House Museum Archives, Box A, Mackinac Island, MI.
7. Act of Apr. 13, 1818, Township Record Book, 28–30, CHL.
8. Mason to her sister, Aug. 6, 1824, Myra Mason Letters, New York Historical Society. Photocopies at MSHP.
9. See Elizabeth Baird, "Reminiscences," *WHC,* 14:18–19.
10. G. Hubbard, *Autobiography,* 16.
11. Thompson to Smith, July 7, 1822, Duane N. Diedrich Collection, CL.
12. Pierce to Root, May 7, 1819, Letters Received, RG 107, NARA; Harrison to Stanton, Aug. 15, 1819, RG 92, CCF, NARA.
13. Bayfield to Barrie, Nov. 1, 1822, enclosed in Barrie to Croker, Nov. 16, 1822, ADM 1/3445, NA.
14. Cass to Calhoun, Mar. 21, 1825, *TP,* 11:665.
15. Brown to Barbour, Jan. 11, 1826, ibid., 11:932.
16. Macomb to Cass, Aug. 19, 1828, ibid., 11:1198.
17. Township Record Book, 36, 39, 44, 49, CHL. On the fire engine, see Crooks to Stuart, Oct. 17, 1819, American Fur Company Papers, L5:1819–20, BHC.
18. *Detroit Gazette,* June 12, 1818, 2:3. The advertisement ran regularly into 1821.
19. Jackman and Freeman, *American Voyageur,* 26.
20. "Ellis's Recollections," *WHC,* 7:214; *Detroit Gazette,* May 24, 1825, 4:4. Lasley's advertisement was dated at Michilimackinac on October 25, 1824, but did not run until the following spring.
21. Schoolcraft, *Narrative Journal,* 121.
22. Minutes of parish council, Aug. 15, 1821, *WHC,* 19:162.
23. Rezek, *History of the Diocese of Sault Ste. Marie,* 2:177. The church is used as a reference point in a survey of roads done on June 23, 1827, titled "Highways 1827," Michilimackinac County Records, Mackinac County.
24. Mazzuchelli, *Memoirs,* 26.
25. Morse, *Report,* 7.
26. The history of the Mackinac mission is discussed in Widder, *Battle for the Soul.*
27. Sambrook, "Historical Lineaments," 53–54.
28. Schoolcraft, *Personal Memoirs,* 203. In a letter to Douglass of Dec. 16, 1824, Schoolcraft describes these as "sketches of *rock scenery.*" Douglass Papers, CL.
29. Granger Journal, June 20, 1827, BHL.
30. Brown, "With Cass in the Northwest," 142; Jackman and Freeman, *American Voyageur,* 27.
31. McDermott, *Seth Eastman.* See especially the chronology on pages 225–27.
32. Ibid., 241 and plate 92. The oil is described on p. 233. There is a photograph in the library collections of MSHP.
33. McDermott, *Seth Eastman,* 248.
34. Schoolcraft, *Information,* vol. 6, list of illustrations.
35. *DAB,* "David Bates Douglass," 5:405–6.
36. See Schoolcraft to Douglass, Dec. 16, 1824, Douglass Papers, CL, and Schoolcraft, *Personal Memoirs,* 203, concerning Schoolcraft's loan of some of his sketches to Douglass.
37. Cass to Douglass, Sept. 15, 1826, Douglass Papers, CL.
38. Schoolcraft, *Personal Memoirs,* 586. See also May, "The Indian Dormitory," 8, 11, 17.
39. See the chronological list of descriptive accounts in appendix B.
40. Schoolcraft, *Narrative Journal,* 124; Jackman and Freeman, *American Voyageur,* 32.
41. Voss, *Botanical Beachcombers,* 7–12. The Douglass Paper, CL, contain instructions and a drawing sent to Douglass for a device to dry and preserve specimens.
42. Schoolcraft, *Narrative Journal,* 113–14.
43. Morse, *Report,* 7.
44. Schoolcraft, *Narrative Journal,* 122.
45. Legate to Jesup, Nov. 27, 1821, RG 92, CCF, NARA.
46. McElroy and Riggs, *The Unfortified Boundary,* 286.
47. Crooks to Abbott, Feb. 26, 1818, American Fur Company Papers, 73-75, L5:1816–1818, BHC.
48. Kelton, *Annals of Fort Mackinac,* 91. The building survived to be photographed many times.
49. Crooks to Stuart, Oct. 17, 1819, American Fur Company Papers, 247–48, L5:1819–20, BHC.
50. See Widder, *Dr. William Beaumont,* for a brief account of the incident and the doctor's subsequent experiments. A firsthand description of the accident is in G. Hubbard, *Autobiography,* 131–32. A recent study of the doctor's life and work is Horsman, *Frontier Doctor.*
51. Beaumont to Lowell, Nov. 1, 1820, in Myer, *Life and Letters of Dr. William Beaumont,* 89.
52. See Humins, "George Boyd," 26, and Stuart to Boyd, Sept. 1, 1820, George Boyd Papers, SHSW.
53. Jackman and Freeman, *American Voyageur,* 31.
54. Ibid.
55. Journal of an aide, June 19, 1819, 2, Jacob Brown Papers, BHC; John A. Granger journal, June 20, 1827, BHL.
56. Jackman and Freeman, *American Voyageur,* 32.
57. Travel journal, 1820, in Myer, *Life and Letters of Dr. William Beaumont,* 82.
58. Schoolcraft, *Narrative Journal,* 111.
59. McElroy and Riggs, *The Unfortified Boundary,* 287.
60. Schoolcraft, *Narrative Journal,* 111.
61. Schoolcraft, *Personal Memoirs,* 493.
62. See, for instance, Figures 2.14 and 2.15 dating to 1788 and 1785–96, respectively.
63. Storrow to Brown, Dec. 1, 1817, *WHC,* 6:164.
64. Letter, June 30, 1825, *Detroit Gazette,* July 19, 1825, 3:1. "Thus passes the glory of the Hurons."
65. Ibid.
66. Claim 335, *ASP, Public Lands,* 1:408.
67. Dilhet, *État de l'Église,* 126.
68. Treaty of Greenville, Aug. 3, 1795, *TP,* 2:527. The area was surveyed by A. G. Ellis in August 1834 and shown on a map that survives in the Henry Schoolcraft Papers, LC. See appendix A.
69. Burbeck to Wayne, Sept. 6, 1796, Anthony Wayne Papers, HSP.

70. Askin to Askin, Sept. 1, 1807, *WHC,* 19:323.
71. McDermott, *Seth Eastman,* 239.
72. Schoolcraft, *Personal Memoirs,* 493.
73. Wade, *The Journals of Francis Parkman,* 1:306–7. Whiting's sketch is reproduced in facsimile.
74. Journal, May 31, 1828, Samuel P. Heintzelman Papers, LC.
75. Schoolcraft, *Narrative Journal,* 403–4; Jackman and Freeman, *American Voyageur,* 112.
76. *Laws of the Territory of Michigan,* 566.
77. Territorial act, Oct. 6, 1805, *TP,* 10:30.
78. Deposition of Samuel Lasley, Oct. 15, 1824, *ASP, Public Lands,* 5:50.
79. Puthuff to Cass, Feb. 2, 1817, William Woodbridge Papers, BHC; appointment, Apr. 6, 1817, *TP,* 10:725.
80. McKenney, *Sketches of a Tour to the Lakes,* 389–96.
81. "Highways 1827," Michilimackinac County Records, Mackinac County.
82. Minutes, Jan. 18, 1832, Township Record Book, 61–62, CHL.
83. "Highways 1827," Michilimackinac County Records, Mackinac County.
84. Kane, Holmquist, and Gilman, *The Northern Expeditions of Stephen H. Long,* 245–47.
85. Claim 334, *ASP, Public Lands,* 1:408.
86. Martin, *The Mill Creek Site,* 40.
87. Kane, Holmquist, and Gilman, *The Northern Expeditions of Stephen H. Long,* 247.
88. Long to Macomb, Apr. 23, 1825, in ibid., 391–92.
89. McKenney, *Sketches of a Tour to the Lakes,* 383–84.
90. For a biographical sketch, see *DAB,* "Thomas Loraine McKenney," 12:89–90.
91. McKenney, *Sketches of a Tour to the Lakes,* 201.
92. Ibid., 385, 394.
93. Ibid., 385. McKenney also offers the alternate theory that the name came from "Imakinakos," a spirit who once inhabited the island. Ottawa historian Andrew J. Blackbird maintained that white historians had never correctly translated the name of the island, which he said derived from an earlier, extinct tribe that had once lived there. Blackbird, *History,* 19–21.
94. Cass to Douglass, Sept. 15, 1826, Douglass Papers, CL. There is no evidence that Douglass complied with the request.
95. McKenney, *Sketches of a Tour to the Lakes,* 385–86.
96. Ibid., 386–87.
97. Ferry to [White], Aug. 13, 1825 (misdated 1824), in C. Anderson, "Frontier Mackinac Island," 207–8. In the same letter she refers to her "charts, maps, etc." (210).
98. S. Tuttle, *Conversations,* 30, 34.
99. Ibid., 9, 12.
100. Ferry to [White], Nov. 1, 1823, in C. Anderson, "Frontier Mackinac Island," 197–98.
101. Ferry to [White], [Summer 1827], ibid., 103.
102. Ferry to White, July 8, 1825, ibid., 210–11.
103. Ferry to [White], Aug. 13, 1825, ibid., 207.

104. Ferry to [White], [Summer 1827], ibid., 102–3.
105. Legate to Scott, Mar. 8, 1823, William F. Lawler Papers, BHC; "Congress News," Mar. 6, 1826, *Detroit Gazette,* Mar. 28, 1826, 2:2. The secretary of war also allowed the use of public land for a mission at Green Bay in 1829. "Green Bay Mission," *The Churchman* 1, no. 45, Jan. 28, 1832, 1:1.
106. Ferry to Evarts, Sept. 5, 1827, Records of American Board of Commissioners for Foreign Missions, 18.4.8, vol. 1, no. 189, Houghton Library.
107. McKenney, *Sketches of a Tour to the Lakes,* 386–89.
108. Thompson to Smith, July 7, 1822, Duane N. Diedrich Collection, CL.
109. Bayfield to Barrie, Nov. 1, 1822, enclosed in Barrie to Croker, Nov. 16, 1822, ADM 1/3445, NA.
110. Survey of Fort Mackinac, July 15, 1825, RG 92, CCF, NARA.
111. Beaumont to Stanton, Sept. 20, 1824, ibid.
112. Inspection report, July 14, 1826, RG 159, Reports, 1814–1842, NARA.
113. Brown to Barbour, Jan. 11, 1826, *TP,* 11:932.
114. Beaumont to Stanton, Sept. 20, 1824, RG 92, CCF, NARA.
115. Inspection report, July 14, 1826, RG 159, Reports, 1814–1842, NARA.
116. Thompson to Jesup, Nov. 14, 1826, RG 92, CCF, NARA. It is possible that the limekiln Thompson referred to Thompson is the one still barely visible along Lime Kiln Trail in the woods north of Fort Mackinac.
117. Inspection report, July 14, 1826, RG 159, Reports, 1814–1842, NARA.
118. Thompson to Jesup, Jan. 5, 1827, RG 92, CCF, NARA.
119. Thompson to Jesup, May 5, 1827, ibid.
120. Satterlee to Thompson, Dec. 28, 1826, ibid.
121. Thompson to Jesup, May 31, 1827, and Aug. 31, 1827, ibid.
122. Report, Oct. 9, 1827, Quarterly Reports of the Quartermasters, 1826–1848, RG 217, NARA.
123. This is held in the collections of the Clements Library, Print Division. The identification of the subject of this watercolor as the 1827 hospital was made by Phil Porter, then curator of history for MSHP.
124. See Grange, *Excavations at Fort Mackinac,* 48, 53.
125. Ferry to White, Nov. 13, 1827, in C. Anderson, "Frontier Mackinac Island," 108.
126. Sumner to Jesup, Nov. 7, 1827, and Thompson to Jesup, Nov. 7, 1827, both in RG 92, CCF, NARA.
127. Ferry to White, Nov. 13, 1827, in C. Anderson, "Frontier Mackinac Island," 108–9; journal, Oct. 31, 1827, Samuel P. Heintzelman Papers, LC.
128. Thompson to Jesup, Nov. 7, 1827, RG 92, CCF, NARA.
129. Quarterly report, Mar. 31, 1828, ibid.
130. Quarterly report, June 30, 1828, ibid.

131. Inspection report, June 1828, Reports 1814–1842, 145–47, RG 159, NARA.
132. Thompson to Jesup, Sept. 26, 1828, and quarterly report, Sept. 30, 1828, both in RG 92, CCF, NARA.
133. Inspection report, June 1828, Reports 1814–1842, 145–47, RG 159, NARA.
134. Wolcott to Lovell, Nov. 15, 1835, RG 94, Quarterly Reports of Sick and Wounded for Michigan Posts, NARA.
135. Lyon to Tiffin, Sept. 8, 1827, *TP,* 11:1117.
136. For the army, see Harrison to Stanton, Aug. 15, 1819, RG 92, CCF, NARA. G. Hubbard, *Autobiography,* 18–19, describes a party of twenty-five "picked choppers" harvesting firewood on Bois Blanc in the summer of 1818.
137. Schoolcraft, *Narrative Journal,* 408.
138. Baird, "Reminiscences," *WHC,* 14:32.
139. Depositions, 1823, *ASP, Public Lands,* 5:226–28.
140. Depositions, 1808, 1810, ibid., 1:405–6, 547.
141. Depositions, 1823, ibid., 5:221–22.
142. Treaty of Greenville, Aug. 3, 1795, *TP,* 2:527; instructions from Burbeck, Feb. 2, 1808, Jacob Kingsbury Papers, L5:1810–11, vol. 17, BHC.
143. Tanner, *Atlas,* 158–59, map 30.
144. Instructions from Burbeck, Feb. 2, 1808, and Kingsbury to Hanks, Feb. 28, 1811, both in Jacob Kingsbury Papers, L5:1810–11, vol. 17, BHC.
145. Depositions, 1823, *ASP, Public Lands,* 5:226–28.
146. Graham to Tiffin, Mar. 8, 1827, *TP,* 11:1058.
147. Lyon to Tiffin, Dec. 21, 1826, ibid., 11:1019.
148. Graham to Tiffin, May 17, 1827, ibid., 11:1079–80; Lyon to Lyon, Aug. 9, 1827, Box 380F, Lyon Family Papers, BHL.
149. Lyon to Tiffin, Sept. 8, 1827, *TP,* 11:1117–18.
150. Graham to Tiffin, May 17, 1827, ibid., 11:1079–80.
151. Thompson to Jones, Sept. 11, 1827, RG 49, NARA.
152. Widder, *Battle for the Soul,* 120; S. Tuttle, *Conversations,* 34.
153. Petition, [Dec. 20, 1825], *TP,* 11:836–37.
154. Graham to Tiffin, June 13, 1827, ibid., 11:1085.
155. Ward to Ward, Mar. 16, 1829, Ward Family Papers, CHL. See also Hyde, *The Northern Lights,* 98.
156. Deposition, 1823, *ASP, Public Lands,* 5:227.
157. Baird, "Reminiscences," *WHC,* 14:28. Baird describes the process of sugar making in great detail.
158. Ibid., 14:23, 32. "Caraboo" and Nero both appear on a list of dogs compiled by the Borough of Michilimackinac in April 1818. Michael Dousman Papers, BHC.
159. Today, the name "Spring Street" is preserved only beyond the point where the road forks at the top of the hill near Trinity Episcopal Church.
160. The courses and distances of Mullett's survey are recorded on the copies of his map and in his survey notes, a transcript of which is in the SHSW. This was made in 1906 from the original notebook in the Grand Rapids Public Library. A copy of the transcript is in the library of MSHP.

161. Journal, Oct. 22, 1828, Samuel P. Heintzelman Papers, LC.

162. Graham to Eaton, June 15, 1830, *TP*, 12:179.

163. See the list in appendix A. NARA holds three copies. CL and MSHP each hold one, and at least two are in the hands of private owners.

164. Karpinski, *Bibliography*, 247. See also appendix A.

165. Sambrook, "Historical Lineaments," 52–53.

166. Ibid., 53. The claims may be found in *ASP, Public Lands*, 5:220–52.

167. Bailey to Graham, Nov. 10, 1827, *TP*, 11:1119.

168. Ibid.

169. Lasley claim, *ASP, Public Lands*, 5:245.

170. Account of Samuel Lasley, ca. 1816–20, Charles Larned Papers, BHC.

171. Davenport claim, *ASP, Public Lands*, 5:223–24.

172. Dousman claim, ibid., 5:220–21.

173. Ibid.

174. Lasley deposition, ibid., 5:49–50.

175. Dousman's wartime activities saw him barred from the fur trade for several years after the war. See Dousman to Cass, Oct. 30, 1819, *MPHC*, 36:416–19. That Dousman was offered a commission in the Michigan Fencibles demonstrates that Lasley's charges of recruiting for the British were credible. See Dunnigan, *The British Army at Mackinac*, 14–15.

176. Bourrassa claim, *ASP, Public Lands*, 5:229.

177. Bigsby, *The Shoe and Canoe*, 2:145.

178. Schoolcraft, *Personal Memoirs*, 230.

179. The continuous, or at least intermittent occupation of St. Ignace is suggested in Smith, *Before the Bridge*, 53, and in Kent, *Rendezvous at the Straits*, 1:186–87, who notes some occupation there in 1754.

180. M. Porter, *Eliza Chappell Porter*, 95.

181. Jaudron and Lorain claims, *ASP, Public Lands*, 5:224–25.

182. Fredriksen, *Surgeon of the Lakes*, 86–87.

183. The surveys are recorded in *ASP, Public Lands*, 5:224–50. See also Sambrook, "Historical Lineaments," 383–84.

184. Mazzuchelli, *Memoirs*, 71.

185. Treaty of Greenville, Aug. 3, 1795, *TP*, 2:527.

186. A. G. Ellis, "11520 Acres Ceded to the United States . . . ," Aug. 1834, Henry Schoolcraft Papers, LC. See appendix A.

187. St. Andre claim, *ASP, Public Lands*, 5:241.

188. Survey, Sept. 27, 1827, in "Highways 1827," Michilimackinac County Records, Mackinac County.

189. M. Porter, *Eliza Chappell Porter*, 92. Father Samuel Mazzuchelli recalled a population of two hundred Catholic whites and two hundred Indians at this time. Mazzuchelli, *Memoirs*, 71.

190. Rezek, *History of the Diocese of Sault Ste. Marie*, 2:126; Smith, *Michilimackinac*, 29.

191. Karpinski, *Bibliography*, 247.

192. Baird, "Reminiscences," *WHC*, 14:63.

193. U.S. General Land Office, *Report on Michigan Land Claims*, Sen. Doc. 221, 29th Cong., 2nd Sess., 1847. See appendix A.

194. See Voss, "Flora of St. Helena Island," 28, and Smith, *Before the Bridge*, 59.

195. McLellan, *Journal of Thomas Nye*, 15.

196. Puthuff to Cass, May 14, 1816, *WHC*, 19:412.

197. James Doty diary, June 6, 1820, ibid., 13:176.

Chapter 6

1. Vigne, *Six Months in America*, 2:110–11.

2. Schoolcraft, *Personal Memoirs*, 442.

3. Ibid., 522.

4. Ibid., 520.

5. Blois, *Gazetteer of the State of Michigan*, 323. See also John Kingman's comments about his visit in 1838 in his *Letters*, 32.

6. Logan, *Notes*, 74. The Lasleys' establishment was described by a number of visitors of the 1830s.

7. Schoolcraft, *Personal Memoirs*, 522.

8. Martineau, *Society in America*, 2:13.

9. Ordinance, Feb. 2, 1833, Township Record Book, 64, CHL; Dousman to Woodbridge, July 23, 1839, William Woodbridge Papers, BHC.

10. Petition, Jan. 22, 1835, *TP*, 12:853–54. For the Waugoshance lightship, see Hyde, *The Northern Lights*, 103.

11. Martineau, *Society in America*, 2:12.

12. Schoolcraft, *Personal Memoirs*, 91–92.

13. Gilman, *Life on the Lakes*, 1:97.

14. J. Lanman, *History of Michigan*, 271.

15. See Lavender, *The Fist in the Wilderness*, 398–419, particularly 416–19.

16. A summary of Mackinac's transition economy in this period may be found in P. Porter, *Mackinac*, 31–37.

17. Ordinance, Apr. 11, 1818, Township Record Book, 22–24, CHL.

18. Enos Goodrich, "Across Michigan Territory Sixty Years Ago," *MPHC*, 26:234.

19. Featherstonhaugh, *A Canoe Voyage*, 1:144.

20. See the table of fish packed at Mackinac in Sears, *A New and Popular Pictorial Description*, 522. Complaints against fish inspector Ambrose R. Davenport may be found in Dousman to Woodbridge, Nov. 28, 1839, William Woodbridge Papers, BHC.

21. See Vose to Acting Assistant Adjutant General, Dec. 15, 1828, William F. Lawler Papers, BHC, and Cutler to Jesup, Oct. 28, 1829, RG 92, CCF, NARA.

22. Inspection Report, June 21, 1831, RG 159, Reports, 1814–1842, NARA.

23. Barnum to Jesup, Aug. 20, 1835, RG 92, CCF, NARA.

24. Penrose to Jesup, Feb. 2, 1835, ibid.

25. J. Clark, *Gleanings by the Way*, 124.

26. Baird, "Reminiscences," *WHC*, 14:46.

27. Ibid.

28. Rezek, *History of the Diocese of Sault Ste. Marie*, 2:177.

29. Widder, *Battle for the Soul*, 88–90.

30. Stuart to Grant, Sept. 18, 1833, in Marlatt, *Stuart Letters*, 15–16.

31. For a discussion of the confrontations, see Widder, *Battle for the Soul*, 91–101. Mazzuchelli's account of Ferry's sermons and his own defense of the Catholic position is preserved in Mazzuchelli, *Memoirs*, 28–43.

32. Pierson, *Tocqueville and Beaumont in America*, 301, 306–7.

33. Vigne, *Six Months in America*, 2:121.

34. Mazzuchelli, *Memoirs*, 43.

35. Martin Heydenburk, "Mackinaw Revisited—How it Looked Forty Years Ago," *MPHC*, 7:197.

36. Widder, *Battle for the Soul*, 133.

37. Schoolcraft, *Personal Memoirs*, 578–79.

38. Reverend Jackson Kemper, "Journal of an Episcopalian Missionary's Tour to Green Bay, 1834," *WHC*, 14:406, 410. The rumors are mentioned in the diary of Peter Dougherty, another missionary. See C. Anderson, "Diaries of Peter Dougherty," 105–6.

39. Schoolcraft, *Personal Memoirs*, 578.

40. Jameson, *Winter Studies*, 2:141; C. Anderson, "Diaries of Peter Dougherty," 104.

41. Report of the American Board for 1837 quoted in E. Wood, *Historic Mackinac*, 1:669.

42. Jameson, *Winter Studies*, 2:129, 141.

43. Colton, *Tour of the American Lakes*, 93.

44. Ordinance, Feb. 2, 1833, Township Record Book, 64, CHL.

45. Widder, *Battle for the Soul*, 124.

46. Colton, *Tour of the American Lakes*, 91; "M'Call's Journal," *WHC*, 12:183–84.

47. Colton, *Tour of the American Lakes*, 92.

48. Tocqueville, *Journey to America*, 146.

49. Advertisement, Oct. 25, 1824, *Detroit Gazette*, May 24, 1825, 4:4; Farley to Farley, Sept. 7, 1834, Farley Family Papers, CL. Lasley had been permitted to construct a wharf opposite his premises by an ordinance of Feb. 2, 1833, Township Record Book, 64, CHL.

50. See Petersen, *Mackinac Island*, 26–27, 28–29.

51. Baird, "Reminiscences," *WHC*, 14:41, and Pierce to La Framboise, May 14, 1838, Baird Family Papers, SHSW.

52. Colton, *Tour of the American Lakes*, 93.

53. Juliette Kinzie uses the expression in *Wau-Bun*, 11

54. "Mission School at Mackinaw," *Quarterly Papers of the American Board of Commissioners for Foreign Missions* 20 (Mar. 1835): 78.

55. Widder, *Battle for the Soul*, 88–90. This includes the subscription list.

56. Martin Heydenburk, "The Old Church and Mission House at Mackinac," Oct. 5, 1880, *MPHC*, 3:157–58. Heydenburk says that construction continued through 1831 and the church was dedicated on March 4, 1832. In reality this had occurred two years earlier.

57. Provensalles to Greene, July 23, 1830, quoted in Widder, *Battle for the Soul,* 171. See also American Board, *Annual Report* (1830), 94.

58. Farley to Farley, Sept. 7, 1834, Farley Family Papers, CL.

59. Colton, *Tour of the American Lakes,* 91.

60. Susan Farley described the church as that color in 1834. Farley Family Papers, CL.

61. *Detroit Courier,* Sept. 1, 1831, quoted in Pierson, *Tocqueville and Beaumont in America,* 300.

62. Pierson, *Tocqueville and Beaumont in America,* 301.

63. Mazzuchelli, *Memoirs,* 43.

64. Pierson, *Tocqueville and Beaumont in America,* 302.

65. Tocqueville, *Journey to America,* 146; Vigne, *Six Months in America,* 2:113; Pierson, *Tocqueville and Beaumont in America,* 302.

66. Jameson, *Winter Studies,* 2:203–5.

67. Schoolcraft, *Personal Memoirs,* 561.

68. Ibid., 561–62.

69. For an account of Anna Jameson's life and career, see Fowler, *The Embroidered Tent,* 139–75. A briefer summary may be found in Brehm, *The Women's Great Lakes Reader,* 194–95.

70. Jameson, *Winter Studies,* 2:208, 134, 144–45.

71. Ibid., 2:119.

72. Ibid., 2:128.

73. Featherstonhaugh, *A Canoe Voyage,* 1:139.

74. Jameson, *Winter Studies,* 2:118–21.

75. Ibid., 2:134.

76. Ibid., 2:123.

77. Ibid., 2:123–24.

78. Ibid., 2:129.

79. Featherstonhaugh, *A Canoe Voyage,* 1:137–38.

80. Schoolcraft, *Personal Memoirs,* 519.

81. Featherstonhaugh, *A Canoe Voyage,* 1:141–44.

82. Ibid., 1:148–49.

83. Catlin, *Letters and Notes,* 2:161.

84. Martineau, *Society in America,* 2:19, 11.

85. Schoolcraft, *Personal Memoirs,* 651.

86. Gilman, *Life on the Lakes,* 1:103–4.

87. See the comments of James McCall in 1830 in his journal, *WHC,* 12:183.

88. Jackman and Freeman, *American Voyageur,* 32.

89. Houghton field notes, June 21, 1838, Douglass Houghton Papers, BHL; Hubbard Field Notes, June 21, 1838, Bela Hubbard Papers, BHC.

90. Hubbard field notes, June 23, 1838.

91. Ibid., June 25, 1838. The destruction of Fairy Arch is described in an article in the *Island Star* 2, no. 1 (Oct. 26, 1953): 1:1. This was the student newspaper of the Thomas M. Ferry School, and a copy is preserved in folder 5408, Alicia Poole Papers, BHL.

92. Colton, *Tour of the American Lakes,* 93; "Mission School at Mackinaw," *Quarterly Papers of the American Board of Commissioners for Foreign Missions* 30 (Mar. 1835): 78; Goodrich, "Across Michigan Territory Sixty Years Ago," *MPHC,* 27:233; Gilman, *Life on the Lakes,* 1:103, 106.

93. Penrose to Jesup, Aug. 28, 1835, RG 92, CCF, NARA.

94. Gilman, *Life on the Lakes,* 1:104–5.

95. Ibid., 1:90.

96. Carter and Rankin, *North to Lake Superior,* 1–3.

97. Hubbard field notes, June 25, 1838.

98. Carter and Rankin, *North to Lake Superior,* 1–3.

99. C. Anderson, "Diaries of Peter Dougherty," 106.

100. Goodrich, "Across Michigan Territory Sixty Years Ago," *MPHC,* 26:233.

101. Schoolcraft, *Personal Memoirs,* 600.

102. Castelnau, *Vues et Souvenirs,* 106; Schoolcraft, *Personal Memoirs,* 600.

103. Castelnau, *Vues et Souvenirs,* 103–6.

104. Hyde, *The Northern Lights,* 98.

105. Ward to Wendell, Apr. 24, 1833, Ward Family Papers, CHL.

106. Ward to Wendell, Sept. 17, 1837, ibid.

107. "The Falling of the Lighthouse," reminiscence of Emily Ward, n.d., and Ward to Wendell, Dec. 12, 1837, both in ibid.

108. Dunn to Garland, Dec. 12, 1837, and Jan. 2, 1838, Letterbook of Sergeant R. J. Dunn, copy in MSHP library.

109. Hyde, *The Northern Lights,* 98.

110. Castelnau, *Vues et Souvenirs,* 109; anonymous travel journal, July 31, 1838, American Travel Collection, CL.

111. Castelnau, *Vues et Souvenirs,* 107.

112. Jameson, *Winter Studies,* 2:121.

113. Kane, *Wanderings of an Artist,* 27.

114. Gilman, *Life on the Lakes,* 1:117ff.

115. Castelnau, *Vues et Souvenirs,* 110–11. See also Carter and Rankin, *North to Lake Superior,* 1.

116. McKenney, *Sketches of a Tour to the Lakes,* 389; Bela Hubbard field notes, June 25, 1838. A biography of the commandant may be found in *DCB,* "Daniel Robertson," 5:714–16.

117. Castelnau, *Vues et Souvenirs,* 110.

118. Ibid.

119. Ibid., 103.

120. George Fuller account, [1847], Minutes of the Nucleus Club, 49–50, George Fuller Papers, BHC.

121. Hubbard field notes, June 22, 1838, Bela Hubbard Papers, BHL; Martineau, *Society in America,* 2:12.

122. Castelnau, *Vues et Souvenirs,* 109; George Fuller account, [1847], Minutes of the Nucleus Club, 59, George Fuller Papers, BHC.

123. Goodrich, "Across Michigan Territory Sixty Years Ago," *MPHC,* 26:234.

124. Gilman, *Life on the Lakes,* 1:112.

125. Ibid.; Goodrich, "Across Michigan Territory Sixty Years Ago," *MPHC,* 26:234.

126. Dunnigan, *Frontier Metropolis,* 192.

127. "Caleb F. Davis," manuscript collection card file, BHC; Lossing, *The Pictorial Field Book of the War of 1812,* 267n. Lossing was told that Davis had made the Mackinac view in August 1839.

128. Proclamation, Oct. 26, 1818, *MPHC,* 2:272; Schoolcraft, *Narrative Journal,* 121.

129. Dousman to Woodbridge, Feb. 2, 1838, William Woodbridge Papers, BHC.

130. Carter and Rankin, *North to Lake Superior,* 4; Journal of John Wolcott Phelps, Nov. 17, 1840, John Wolcott Phelps Papers, NYPL.

131. The best account of the history of the building is May, "The Indian Dormitory." A copy is in the MSHP library. The passage is quoted on page 4.

132. Ibid., 7–10, 15. See the plans described in appendix A.

133. Ibid., 17–20.

Chapter 7

1. L. Clark, *Knick-knacks From an Editor's Table,* 186.

2. Horace Greeley, "Lake Superior and the North-West," in Cary, *The National Temperance Offering,* 113.

3. C. Lanman, *A Summer in the Wilderness,* 165.

4. [Sears], "Two Days at Mackinaw, No. 2."

5. Beaven, *Recreations of a Long Vacation,* 146–47.

6. P. Porter, *Mackinac,* 41–42.

7. [Sears], "Two Days at Mackinaw, No. 2"; F. "A Trip to Buffalo in the *St. Louis,*" 151.

8. [Sears], "Two Days at Mackinaw, No. 2." Sears offers a comprehensive analysis of the fishing industry at Mackinac and its chief competitors, Beaver Island, Thunder Bay, and Sault Ste. Marie. Some of this information is repeated in Sears, *A New and Popular Pictorial Description,* 522–23.

9. Dousman to Woodbridge, July 23, 1839, William Woodbridge Papers, BHC.

10. Acts of Mar. 4, 1839 (Orr; Biddle and Drew), Jan. 4, 1846 (William Scott), Sept. 23, 1848 (Lasley Wharf, William Spencer), Nov. 22, 1848 (Joseph Hall), Apr. 13, 1849 (Hamel and Metivier), and July 27, 1849 (Dousman), Township Record Book, 68, 82, 2/14, 2/16, 2/20, 2/21, CHL.

11. Bylaws of Village of Mackinac, June 8, 1848, Township Record Book, 2/2–5, CHL.

12. Irvin to Cass, Apr. 3, 1832, *TP,* 12:462; undated statement, ca. 1890, Early Family Collection, MSHP.

13. Paulding, "Sketch of the Great Western Lakes," 261.

14. M. Fuller, *Summer on the Lakes,* 172–73.

15. [Sears], "Two Days at Mackinaw, No. 3."

16. Kane, *Wanderings of an Artist,* 28.

17. Pitezel, *Lights and Shades of Missionary Life,* 25.

18. Beaven, *Recreations of a Long Vacation,* 111.

19. Drake, *The Northern Lakes,* 38.

20. Farley to Farley, Sept. 7, 1834, Farley Family Papers, CL.

21. Holmquist, "Frontier Vacation," 84.

22. Diary, Aug. 22, 1844, Anonymous Great Lakes Trip Diary, CHL.

23. The bears are mentioned in ibid., Aug. 23, 1844, and in 1841 in Morleigh, *A Merry Briton in Pioneer Wisconsin,* 38. The latter thought himself ill-treated at the Lasley House and described Mrs. Lasley as a "fat frowsy old woman" and the proprietor "a stupid old boor."

24. Holmquist, "Frontier Vacation," 84–85.

25. Drake, *The Northern Lakes,* 38; Beaven, *Recreations of a Long Vacation,* 144.

26. In a flurry of correspondence with representatives of the Quartermaster General's Department late in 1844, the American Board confirmed that its building occupied military reserve land at the pleasure of the army. This exchange was probably related to plans to lease the Mission House for use as a hotel. See Stuart to Whiting, Nov. 14, Stuart and Hastings to Whiting, Dec. 18, Whiting to Stuart, Dec. 20, and Whiting to Jesup, Dec. 24, all in RG 92, CCF, NARA.

27. Brotherton, "Story of Philo Everett's Trip"; George W. Thayer, "From Vermont to Lake Superior," *MPHC,* 30:555. It should be noted that these accounts are virtually identical and are thus perhaps suspect in some of their details.

28. Bryant, *Letters of a Traveller,* 294.

29. Agassiz and Cabot, *Lake Superior,* 22; Diary, July 13–16, 1848, Anonymous diary, 1848/1854, CHL.

30. "Mackinaw—Summer Resort," *Detroit Free Press,* Apr. 10, 1849, 2.

31. *Acts of the Legislature . . . 1847,* 68–69.

32. *Acts of the Legislature . . . 1848,* 119–24.

33. Bylaws of the Village of Mackinac, June 8, 1848, Township Record Book, 2/2-5, CHL.

34. Diary, May 19, 1840, John Wolcott Phelps Papers, NYPL.

35. Bryant, *Letters of a Traveller,* 301.

36. Drake, *The Northern Lakes,* 36.

37. Bryant, *Letters of a Traveller,* 296.

38. Larson, *Essayons,* 36–37.

39. Morleigh, *A Merry Briton in Pioneer Wisconsin,* 39.

40. Act, Feb. 2, 1833, Township Record Book, 64, CHL.

41. Acts, Mar. 4, 1839, ibid., 68.

42. Irvin to Cass, Apr. 3, 1832, *TP,* 12:462. Concerning the road and associated surveys and sketch map, see Minutes, Jan. 18, 1832, Township Record Book, 61–62, CHL, and the correspondence in King to McCabe, Jan. 19, 1832, McCabe to King, Jan. 23, 1832, and McCabe to Cutler, Jan. 23, 1832, all in Fort Mackinac Letters Sent, 1829–1836, RG 94, NARA.

43. Minutes, June 8, 1848, Township Record Book, 2/3–5, 12, CHL.

44. P. Porter, "Mackinac Island's Post Cemetery," 3; Gilman, *Life on the Lakes,* 1:110.

45. Bryant, *Letters of a Traveller,* 298–302.

46. Tykal, *Journal of an Expedition,* 36.

47. E. Steele, *A Summer Journey in the West,* 107.

48. A summary of the 83rd's service may be found in Stewart, *The Service of British Regiments,* 350. For a brief biography of Ainslie, see Harper, *Early Painters and Engravers in Canada,* 4.

49. These are from an album titled "Sketches in Canada and the States of Illinois & Michigan. 1841, 42, 43. H. F. Ainslie."

50. MacLeod, "A Saunter in the North-West," 114.

51. Pitezel, *Lights and Shades of Missionary Life,* 31.

52. Drake, *The Northern Lakes,* 40.

53. E. Steele, *A Summer Journey in the West,* 107–8.

54. Baird, "Reminiscences," *WHC,* 14:36.

55. MacLeod, "A Saunter in the North-West," 114.

56. Drake, *The Northern Lakes,* 40.

57. MacLeod, "A Saunter in the North-West," 114.

58. Wade, *The Journals of Francis Parkman,* 1:306–7. A facsimile of Whiting's sketch map is illustrated on the latter page.

59. Tykal, *Journal of an Expedition,* 36.

60. Harper, *Early Painters and Engravers in Canada,* 61. The date of Cayley's death given in the notation with the sketches (1874) disagrees with that in Harper (1890). Cayley has not been found in the 1846–47 and 1850–51 Toronto directories.

61. Buckingham, *The Eastern and Western States of America,* 3:361.

62. Olsson, *A Pioneer in Northwest America,* 1:99.

63. Agassiz and Cabot, *Lake Superior,* 22.

64. Olsson, *A Pioneer in Northwest America,* 1:102.

65. Schoolcraft, *Narrative Journal,* 122.

66. Reverend Jackson Kemper, "Journal of an Episcopalian Missionary's Tour to Green Bay, 1834," *WHC,* 14:410.

67. Gilman, *Life on the Lakes,* 1:106.

68. M. Fuller, *Summer on the Lakes,* 171.

69. Ibid.

70. Ibid., 250–51. See Hubach, *Early Midwestern Travel Narratives,* 96.

71. M. Fuller, *Summer on the Lakes,* 169–70.

72. Ibid., 170, 237.

73. Ibid., 252, 249.

74. MacLeod, "A Saunter in the North-West," 114.

75. Pitezel, *Lights and Shades of Missionary Life,* 30–31.

76. M. Fuller, *Summer on the Lakes,* 250.

77. Ibid., 173–74.

78. Ibid., 175–81.

79. Ibid., 174.

80. Kane, *Wanderings of an Artist,* 26–28.

81. Pitezel, *Lights and Shades of Missionary Life,* 27–28.

82. Kane, *Wanderings of an Artist,* 26–29. For an illustrated catalog of Kane's work, see Harper, *Paul Kane's Frontier.*

83. Phelps Journal, Oct. 23, 1840, John Wolcott Phelps Papers, NYPL.

84. Gilman, *Life on the Lakes,* 1:162–63, describes a service conducted by Schoolcraft in September 1835 in which the Indian agent "read a very good sermon."

85. C. Anderson, "Diaries of Peter Dougherty," 103–4.

86. Pitezel, *Lights and Shades of Missionary Life,* 32.

87. Carter and Rankin, *North to Lake Superior,* 4.

88. Pitezel, *Lights and Shades of Missionary Life,* 29.

89. Rezek, *History of the Diocese of Sault Ste. Marie,* 2:179–84, 126. A list of Ste. Anne's pastors to 1882 is found in Kelton, *Annals of Fort Mackinac,* 56–57.

90. Rezek, *History of the Diocese of Sault Ste. Marie,* 1:359–63.

91. Ibid., 1:366–67.

92. Skolla to Skolla, July 17, 1845, in ibid., 1:363.

93. Rezek, *History of the Diocese of Sault Ste. Marie,* 2:178.

94. Mazzuchelli, *Memoirs,* 43.

95. Phelps Journal, Oct. 23, 1840, John Wolcott Phelps Papers, NYPL.

96. Rezek, *History of the Diocese of Sault Ste. Marie,* 2:185.

97. Pierce to La Framboise, May 14, 1838, Baird Family Papers, SHSW; Burbey, *Our Worthy Commander,* 29–30.

98. Deed, Oct. 26, 1827, in Rezek, *History of the Diocese of Sault Ste. Marie,* 2:177–78.

99. Beaven, *Recreations of a Long Vacation,* 4.

100. Ibid., 144.

101. For an account of O'Brien's years at Mackinac, see Nicholas, *The Chaplain's Lady.*

102. Beaven, *Recreations of a Long Vacation,* 139, 140–41.

103. Ibid., 141, 113.

104. Ibid., 139–40.

105. Ibid., 140.

106. Pitezel, *Lights and Shades of Missionary Life,* 30.

107. See the letterbook of Ordnance Sgt. R. J. Dunn for this period. Photocopy in MSHP library.

108. Phelps Journal, May 19 and 25, 1840, John Wolcott Phelps Papers, NYPL.

109. Report of improvements, Sept. 15, 1843, and Robinson to Jesup, Sept. 11, 1844, both in RG 92, CCF, NARA.

110. See Register of Enlistments, U.S. Army and muster rolls of Captain Martin Scott's company, 5th Infantry, 1844–45, NARA. Photocopies in MSHP library.

111. Lieutenant John Newton's 1850 plan shows only the walls. The next official work that identifies buildings as well was drawn by Walter Griswold in June 1863, Fortification Map File, Drawer 1, Sheet 14, RG 77, NARA. Its date places it outside the scope of this study.

112. Robinson to Jesup, Sept. 11, 1844, RG 92, CCF, NARA.

113. Holmquist, "Frontier Vacation," 85.

114. Sachse, "Frontier Legend," 165.

115. Kinzie, *Wau-Bun,* 305.

116. Register of Enlistments, U.S. Army and muster rolls of Captain Martin Scott's company, 5th Infantry, 1844–45, NARA. Photocopies in MSHP library.

117. "Journal of a Voyage from Green Bay to Buffalo," Sept. 6, 1845, John Harris Forster Papers, BHL.

118. Sachse, "Frontier Legend," 167–68.

119. [Sears], "Two Days at Mackinaw, No. 1."

120. Foster and Whitney, *Report on the Geology,* 2:248.

121. Schoolcraft, *Narrative Journal,* 119–20, 113–14. Geological descriptions are scattered throughout his account as well as that of Captain Douglass, who accompanied him. Hubbard and Houghton's comments may be found in their journals and field notebooks from 1838–40 preserved in the BHL.

372   NOTES

122. Voss, *Botanical Beachcombers*, 26–27, 76.
123. G. Fuller, *Geological Reports of Douglass Houghton*, 584.
124. Foster and Whitney, *Report on the Geology*, 2:161–65, is their discussion of the limestone composition of Mackinac Island.
125. Disturnell, *A Trip Through the Lakes*, 111; Disturnell, *The Great Lakes* (1863), 89; Disturnell, *The Great Lakes* (1871), 76; Strickland, *Old Mackinaw*, 76.
126. Foster and Whitney, *Report on the Geology*, 2:248–50.
127. Ibid., 2:249–50.
128. Ibid., 2:250–51.
129. Ibid., 2:251, 253.
130. See Stanley, *Pre-Historic Mackinac Island*, for its geological history. A more concise explanation of area geology may be found in Porter and Nelhiebel, *The Wonder of Mackinac*.
131. Foster and Whitney, *Report on the Geology*, 2:258–59.
132. Ibid., 2:164–65.
133. Ibid., 2:165.
134. Ibid., 2:164; "Transcript of Field Notes for the Year 1839," Aug. 14, 1839, Douglass Houghton Papers, BHL.
135. The track along the East Bluff, today called Huron Road, appears as a path on the Eveleth maps of 1817 (Figs. 4.7 and 5.13) but is not shown on the 1841 Woodruff survey (Fig. 7.1). An indication of Mission Hill and Huron Road may be seen in Hannah White's bird's-eye view of 1833–34 (Fig. 6.1).
136. Ogden to Larnard, Aug. 8, 1849, RG 92, CCF, NARA.
137. Bryant, *Letters of a Traveller*, 301–2; Drake, *The Northern Lakes*, 36–37.
138. Horace Greeley, "Lake Superior and the Northwest" in Cary, *The National Temperance Offering*, 114.
139. Agassiz and Cabot, *Lake Superior*, 22; Journal, July 13–16, 1848, Anonymous Diary 1848, 1854, CHL.
140. "Mackinaw—Summer Resort." It is depicted as the "Huron House" in Alfred Waud's sketch of 1854 (Fig. 8.7) and was known as the "Island House" by the time an anonymous artist stopped there in 1859 (Figs. 8.34–8.39).
141. Buckingham, *The Eastern and Western States of America*, 3:366.
142. Drake, *The Northern Lakes*, 38.
143. *DAB*, "William Butler Ogden," 13:644–45.
144. Ogden to Larnard, Aug. 8, 1849, RG 92, CCF, NARA.
145. Marcy to Jesup, n.d., written on the back of ibid.
146. Larnard to Jesup, Aug. 23, 1849, RG 92, CCF, NARA.
147. Jesup to Crawford, Jan. 2, 1850, docketed on ibid.
148. Crawford to Jesup, Jan. 5, 1850, docketed on ibid.
149. See Widder, *Mackinac National Park*, and P. Porter, *View from the Veranda*.

Chapter 8

1. Floyd-Jones to his father and sister, July 19, 1849, Delancey F. Jones Correspondence, CHL.
2. Cullum, *Biographical Register*, 2:171–72. Floyd-Jones was a lieutenant of the 4th Infantry Regiment and a veteran of the Mexican War, who served as aide-de-camp to Brigadier General Hugh Brady at Detroit from 1848 to 1850.
3. Floyd-Jones to his father and sister, July 15, 1849, Delancey F. Jones Correspondence, CHL.
4. Floyd-Jones to his father and sister, July 19, 1849, Delancey F. Jones Correspondence, CHL.
5. Drake, *A Systematic Treatise*, 347.
6. Letter from Mann, Aug. 7, 1856, in Van Fleet, *Old and New Mackinac*, 163.
7. Aaron Bellangee Journal, July 7, 1854, Aaron Bellangee Memorandum Book, typescript copy in MSHP library.
8. Curtiss, *Western Portraiture*, 34. Bellangee makes a similar statement in his journal.
9. Hale, "The Man Without a Country," 665. This first appeared in *The Atlantic Monthly* of December 1863.
10. Woolson, "Fairy Island."
11. The Grove House is mentioned in Strang, *Ancient and Modern Michilimackinac*, 21. The original version of this text appeared in January 1854. Charles C. Grove and Michael Dousman purchased the building in May 1852. Abstract of title, Private Claim 293, copy in Stuart House Museum Archives, Box A, Mackinac Island, MI.
12. Two issues of this extremely rare paper are held by the BHL and a third is held by the CHL.
13. Williams to Jesup, Aug. 17, 1855, RG 92, CCF, NARA.
14. Journal, July 8, 1854, Aaron Bellangee Memorandum Book, typescript copy in MSHP library.
15. "Joseph Austrian's Autobiographical and Historical Sketches," 17–18, typescript in MSHP library.
16. Clarke, "Notes from the Copper Region," 437.
17. "The wharf at Wendells" is mentioned in Williams to Williams, Nov. 15, 1854, Williams Family Papers, BHC.
18. P. Porter, *Mackinac*, 33–37.
19. Clarke, "Notes from the Copper Region," 437.
20. Strang, *Ancient and Modern Michilimackinac*, 24–25.
21. Ibid., 20–21.
22. Ibid., vii–x.
23. Woolson, "Fairy Island," 66–67.
24. Strang, *Ancient and Modern Michilimackinac*, ix–x.
25. Saltonstall, "Reminiscences of the Mackinac Country."
26. Woolson, "Fairy Island," 67.
27. Williams to Jesup, May 29, 1856, Fort Mackinac Letterbook, 1855–66, BHL.
28. Williams to Williams, Jan. 3, 1855, Williams Family Papers, BHC.
29. Williams to Jesup, June 21, 1853, RG 92, CCF, NARA.
30. Dana, *A Fashionable Tour*, 30; Cummins, *Journal*, 32.
31. Williams to Jesup, July 15, 1853, RG 92, CCF, NARA.
32. Williams to Williams, Nov. 20, 1854, Williams Family Papers, BHC.
33. Williams to Cooper, Apr. 1, 1853, and Williams to Jesup, July 15, 1853, both in RG 92, CCF, NARA.
34. Williams to Cooper, Apr. 1, 1853, Cobb to Floyd, Feb. 23, 1858, and Floyd to Cobb, Mar. 5, 1858, all in ibid.
35. May, "The Indian Dormitory," 53–54.
36. C. Lanman, *A Summer in the Wilderness*, 165.
37. Ibid., 165–66.
38. Larnard to commandant, Department of the East, Nov. 23, 1848, William F. Lawler Papers, BHC.
39. Estimate of funds required, Mar. 31, 1849, RG 92, CCF, NARA.
40. Larnard to Jesup, May 6, 1849, ibid.
41. Totten to Jesup, May 22, 1850, ibid.
42. Newton to Totten, June 20, 1850, Letters Received, N119, RG 77, NARA.
43. Ibid.
44. Ibid.
45. Ibid. See also Williams to Jesup, May 29, 1856, Fort Mackinac Letterbook, 1855–66, BHL.
46. "From Mackinac," *The World*, July 19, 1860, 2:3.
47. Johnston to Floyd, Aug. 27, 1857, RG 92, CCF, NARA.
48. Ibid. See also Strickland, *Old Mackinaw*, 202. The developer for the proposed "Mackinaw City" had suggested that he would donate land to the government for this purpose.
49. Russell to Jesup, Apr. 25, 1851, and Aug. 12, 1851, both in RG 92, CCF, NARA.
50. Williams to Jesup, June 21, 1853, RG 92, CCF, NARA.
51. Williams to Grelaud, May 29, 1856, RG 92, CCF, NARA; Williams to Jesup, May 29, 1856, Fort Mackinac Letterbook, 1855–66, BHL.
52. Lawson, *Statistical Report*, 74–77.
53. Martineau, *Society in America*, 2:17. Ironically, Clitz died that fall of cancer and was buried in the fort's graveyard. P. Porter, "Mackinac Island's Post Cemetery," 4.
54. Marryat, *A Diary in America*, 52.
55. Drake, *A Systematic Treatise*, 346–47.
56. Ibid., 348.
57. Clarke, "Notes from the Copper Region," 434.
58. Dana, *A Fashionable Tour*, 30. One of these was certainly Clarke's vessel.
59. Ibid., 30, 66.
60. Clarke, "Notes from the Copper Region," 434–45.
61. Ibid., 435–36. Juliette Starr Dana also describes a voyage around Mackinac Island in August 1852 in a boat rowed by six soldiers. Dana, *A Fashionable Tour*, 66–67.
62. F., "A Trip to Buffalo in the *St. Louis*." See also Dana, *A Fashionable Tour*, 33–34.
63. Clarke, "Notes from the Copper Region," 437.
64. Ibid., 434.

65. F., "A Trip to Buffalo in the *St. Louis*," 150. He added that the Mackinac potatoes had "as yet escaped the rot," which was then causing terrible famine in Ireland.

66. Dana, *A Fashionable Tour*, 32.

67. Clarke, "Notes from the Copper Region," 437. He left on the same boat as Juliette Starr Dana, who was "almost frozen to death" by the time she was able to board the *London*. Dana, *A Fashionable Tour*, 35.

68. Biographical information on Waud has been taken from Ray, *"Our Special Artist"* and *Alfred R. Waud: Special Artist on Assignment*.

69. Ray, *"Our Special Artist,"* 12; *The New-York City Directory, for 1854–1855*, 739.

70. *Alfred R. Waud: Special Artist on Assignment*, 1, 5.

71. The last is titled "Room where Indians received their amenities Mackinaw" and is listed in appendix A. The drawing depicts a group of figures seated at a table, probably in the Indian Agency House.

72. "Mackinaw—Summer Resort."

73. Journal, July 7, 1854, Aaron Bellangee Memorandum Book, typescript in MSHP library.

74. The hotel is not mentioned in the surviving copies of the *Mackinac Herald* for 1859–61.

75. See Woodford, *Charting the Inland Seas*, 22–25.

76. Clarke, "Notes from the Copper Region," 435; Dana, *A Fashionable Tour*, 29; Cummins, *Journal*, 30.

77. Strickland, *Old Mackinaw*, 99.

78. Clarke, "Notes from the Copper Region," 435.

79. Van Fleet, *Old and New Mackinac*, 142.

80. Peters, *Lake Superior Journal*, 91.

81. Van Fleet, *Old and New Mackinac*, 142.

82. *Island Star* 2, no. 1 (Oct. 26, 1953): 1:1.

83. Strickland, *Old Mackinaw*, 88; Van Fleet, *Old and New Mackinac*, 142. Edwin O. Wood associates it with Captain Thomas Scott, Fort Mackinac's British commandant in 1787–88. *Historic Mackinac*, 1:591–92.

84. Bryant, *Letters of a Traveller*, 299.

85. Williams to Williams, Apr. 5, 1855, Williams Family Papers, BHC.

86. For an analysis, see Ford, "Architectural Record of the John Dousman House."

87. Photo taken and published by W. S. White of Kalamazoo, MSHP photo collection, File F-6-U.

88. "Mackinaw and Its Scenery," 280.

89. Cullum, *Biographical Register*, 1:526–27.

90. "Mackinaw and Its Scenery," 280.

91. Strang, *Ancient and Modern Michilimackinac*, 16.

92. Williams to Williams, Nov. 15, 1854, Williams Family Papers, BHC; Minutes, Oct. 4, 1856, Township Record Book, 2/49–50, CHL.

93. Williams to Williams, Nov. 15, 1854, Williams Family Papers, BHC.

94. "Mackinaw and Its Scenery."

95. Taylor, *At Home and Abroad*, 234.

96. "Mackinaw and Its Scenery," 281.

97. Ibid.; Taylor, *At Home and Abroad*, 233–34.

98. Williams to Jesup, June 1, 1853, and Williams to Grayson, June 9 and July 27, 1853, all in RG 92, CCF, NARA.

99. Williams describes the entire event in great detail in a letter to his wife, Jan. 3, 1855, Williams Family Papers, BHC.

100. Williams to Jesup, Jan. 4, 1855, and enclosed proceedings of a board of survey, RG 92, CCF, NARA.

101. Williams to Williams, Jan. 3, 1855, Williams Family Papers, BHC.

102. Williams to Jesup, Jan. 29, 1855, RG 92, CCF, NARA.

103. For a record of his service at Fort Mackinac, see Nicholas, *The Chaplain's Lady*.

104. Beaven, *Recreations of a Long Vacation*, 140–41.

105. Journal, July 9, 1854, Aaron Bellangee Memorandum Book, copy in MSHP library.

106. "Report on the Condition of Public Quarters," July 1855, RG 92, CCF, NARA.

107. Proceedings of a board of survey, June 10, 1858, ibid.

108. Bailey to Jesup, May 25, 1857, ibid.

109. Williams to Williams, July 2, 1855, Williams Family Papers, BHC.

110. "Report on the Condition of Public Quarters," July 1855, RG 92, CCF, NARA.

111. Williams to Williams, Nov. 22, 1854, Williams Family Papers, BHC. Major Williams's father was John R. Williams (1782–1854), first mayor of Detroit.

112. Williams to Williams, Feb. 3, 1855, ibid.

113. Williams to Cooper, Oct. 12, 1856, Fort Mackinac Letterbook, 1855–1866, BHL.

114. Irvin to Cass, Apr. 3, 1832, *TP*, 12:462.

115. Cutler to Jones, Apr. 14, 1830, Letters Sent, 1829–1836, RG 94, NARA.

116. Graham to Eaton, June 15, 1830, *TP*, 12:179.

117. Whiting to Jesup, May 1, 1843, William F. Lawler Papers, BHC.

118. Larnard to Jesup, Dec. 6, 1851, RG 92, CCF, NARA.

119. Meade, *Report . . . 1857*, 27.

120. Ibid.

121. A rough topographical map of Mackinac Island had been completed in 1841 (Fig. 7.1). Work resumed in earnest at the Straits in 1849. See Woodford, *Charting the Inland Seas*, 21, 30–37. In 1852 Lieutenant G. W. Rose drew a map titled "Round Island and Island of Mackinac," a copy of which is in the MSHP collection, though the original was not located at NARA. It and a related map are described in appendix A. The efforts of the Lake Survey resulted in a finished chart, "Straits of Mackinac . . . ," published in 1854 and also described in appendix A. See also Meade, *Report . . . 1857*, 12.

122. Meade, *Report . . . 1857*, 27.

123. Ibid.

124. Macomb's original orders were dated May 21, 1855. See notes on Macomb, "Island of Mackinac . . . ." 1855, RG 77, Fortification Map File, Drawer 137, Sheet 24, NARA.

125. A notation at the upper right on Figure 8.25 credits the town and shore to Lieutenant William F. Raynolds and J. A. Potter. See also Lieutenant George W. Rose, "Round Island and Island of Mackinac," 1852, in appendix A.

126. Williams to Cooper, June 23, 1856, Fort Mackinac Letterbook, 15–16, BHL; Williams to Cooper, July 28, 1856, ibid., 21.

127. Williams to Brady, July 29, 1856, ibid., 22; Williams to Brady, Aug. 7, 1856, ibid., 23.

128. "Statement of the Condition of Fort Mackinac," May 25, 1857, RG 92, CCF, NARA; Elzey to Cooper, July 12, 1857, Fort Mackinac Letterbook, 33, BHL.

129. Elzey to Cooper, July 12, 1857, and Elzey to Short, July 13, 1857, ibid., 34.

130. Meade, *Report . . . 1857*, 28. Six years later, Meade would lead federal troops to victory at Gettysburg.

131. A number of the 1857 markers remain in place, and three of them had been located by the summer of 2006 by Larry Rickley, Larry Rickley, Jr., and James Dunnigan.

132. Ordinance, Dec. 22, 1851, Township Record Book, 2/31, CHL.

133. Dana, *A Fashionable Tour*, 33.

134. See Nicholas, *The Chaplain's Lady*, 4.

135. Minutes, Oct. 4, 1856, Township Record Book, 2/50–51, CHL.

136. Taylor, *At Home and Abroad*, 233.

137. Cummins, *Journal*, 30–33.

138. *Mackinac Herald*, Aug. 20, 1859, 3:4.

139. Norton, *Edwin Whitefield*, 22, 18. See also Harper, *Early Painters and Engravers in Canada*, 330.

140. Taylor, *At Home and Abroad*, 233. The pier on the site of the original Dousman wharf is still called the "Coal Dock."

141. "From Mackinac," *The World* 1, no. 30 (July 19, 1860): 2:2.

142. Ibid., 2:3.

143. Williams to Williams, Nov. 15, 1854, Williams Family Papers, BHC.

144. Patton, "A Glimpse of Life in Mackinac," 6.

145. Strang, *Ancient and Modern Michilimackinac*, 21. Patton, "A Glimpse of Life in Mackinac," 3, remembers it as the Dousman House, and both names seem to have been used in the 1850s.

146. Williams to Jesup, June 16, 1853, and July 15, 1853, both in RG 92, CCF, NARA.

147. The building was standing at the time of Abbott's death in 1851 but does not appear on Francis Cayley's view of the town (Fig. 7.10) of ca. 1840–43.

148. Patton, "A Glimpse of Life in Mackinac," 1. The site is today occupied by the Cloghaun bed and breakfast, which reportedly utilized the foundation of the Abbott house.

149. King to Abbott, May 5, 1851, describes Samuel Abbott's death on April 26. Details on its value are in King to Abbott, Oct. 25, 1852, and inventory of the late Samuel Abbott, Dec. 6, 1852. All are in Abbott Family Papers, BHC.

150. Saltonstall to Abbott, July 24, 1856, and June 9, 1857, ibid.

151. Saltonstall, "Reminiscences of the Mackinac Country."

152. Details of the fire are in Saltonstall to Abbott, July 3, 1857, Abbott to Saltonstall, July 13, 1857, Saltonstall to Abbott, July 16, 1857, and "Account of Sale," July 21, 1857, all in Abbott Family Papers, BHC. The reminiscences of both Brayton and Constance Saltonstall discuss the fire in great detail but place the event in July 1856.

153. Patton, "A Glimpse of Life in Mackinac," 3.

154. Strang, *Ancient and Modern Michilimackinac,* 20–22.

155. Ibid., 20–21.

156. Blois, *Gazetteer of the State of Michigan,* 344; Houghton field notes, Aug. 14, 1839, Douglass Houghton Papers, BHL.

157. See Smith, *Before the Bridge,* 57–63. For a visitor's description, see Bryant, *Letters of a Traveller,* 300.

158. Strickland, *Old Mackinaw,* 100.

159. Smith, *Before the Bridge,* 66.

160. See Martin, *The Mill Creek Site,* for a summary of the documentation of these mills.

161. Ware, *The Centennial History of Cheboygan County and Village,* 28–30. Ellis Olson offers an account with somewhat different details in "Cheboygan County—Early Settlement" in Ranville and Campbell, *Memories of Mackinaw,* 20–23.

162. Ware, *The Centennial History of Cheboygan County and Village,* 31–39; Strang, *Ancient and Modern Michilimackinac,* 25.

163. Ware, *The Centennial History of Cheboygan County and Village,* 31–44, 29.

164. Strickland, *Old Mackinaw,* 200.

165. Ferris, *The States and Territories of the Great West,* quoted in ibid., 173–74.

166. Much of the text of this is also available in Strickland, *Old Mackinaw,* 200–204, and in Ranville and Campbell, *Memories of Mackinaw,* 9–11.

167. Mansfield, *Exposition,* 4–7, 8–10.

168. Strickland, *Old Mackinaw,* 200.

169. G. Robinson, *History of Cheboygan and Mackinac Counties,* 15.

170. Its specific call number is: Security File/EC 2 M158.5 M287 1857a S.F.

171. See Conkling, *Exposition of Mackinaw City and Its Surroundings.*

172. Ranville and Campbell, *Memories of Mackinaw,* 11–12.

173. "Mackinac (From the *New York Tribune* of 1859)," 7:198, 201–2.

174. Ibid., 202.

175. Diary, July 16, 1848, Anonymous Diary 1848, 1854, CHL.

176. Beaven, *Recreations of a Long Vacation,* 143.

177. Rezek, *History of the Diocese of Sault Ste. Marie,* 2:126; Woolson, "Fairy Island," 65. The sketch is clearly titled "Father Pirett's House, Chenau," so it is not his residence in St. Ignace. The sketchbook includes no identified St. Ignace views.

178. "Mackinac (From the *New York Tribune* of 1859)," 7:202; "From Mackinac," *The World* 1, no. 30 (July 19, 1860): 2:2.

179. Bryant, *Letters of a Traveller,* 298.

180. Woolson, "Fairy Island," 63.

181. "Mackinac (From the *New York Tribune* of 1859)," 7:202.

182. Dana, *A Fashionable Tour,* 34.

183. Johnston to Floyd, Aug. 27, 1857, RG 92, CCF, NARA.

184. Strang, *Ancient and Modern Michilimackinac,* 21.

185. "Statement of the Condition of Fort Mackinac," May 25, 1857, RG 92, CCF, NARA.

186. Pratt to Jesup, June 10, 1858, and "Proceedings of a Board of Survey," June 10, 1858, both in ibid.

187. "Proceedings of a Board of Survey," June 10, 1858.

188. Pratt to Assistant Adjutant General, June 23, 1858, Fort Mackinac Letterbook, 1855–66, 38, BHL.

189. Pratt to Assistant Adjutant General, July 29, 1858, and Pratt to Wendell, Aug. 5, 1858, both in ibid., 40–41.

190. Pratt to Jesup, Apr. 23, 1859, and Report of Annual Inspection, June 30, 1859, both in RG 92, CCF, NARA. The latter was sent under cover of a letter of July 27, 1859.

191. See Pratt to Jesup, Apr. 23, 1859, and Report of Annual Inspection, June 30, 1859, both in RG 92, CCF, NARA.

192. Griswold, "Fort Mackinac," June 1863, RG 77, Fortification Map File, Drawer 1, Sheet 14, NARA.

193. Head to Pratt, July 15, 1859, and Pratt to Jesup, July 27, 1859, both in RG 92, CCF, NARA.

194. The notes and estimate are filed with the plan and Pratt's covering letter of July 27, 1859, in RG 92, CCF, NARA.

195. Hartsuff to Johnston, July 2, 1860, and Hartsuff to Johnston, Aug. 10, 1860, both in RG 92, CCF, NARA.

196. It is shown in this location and labeled "New Hospital" in Griswold's 1863 plan. "Fort Mackinac," June 1863.

197. Sharp to Quartermaster General, July 1, 1874, RG 92, CCF, NARA.

Epilogue

1. *Mackinac Herald,* May 18, 1861, 2.

2. Ibid., 1.

3. For an account of Mackinac during the Civil War years, see P. Porter, *Mackinac,* 45–49.

BIBLIOGRAPHY

Manuscript, Map, and Graphic Collections

Archives du Séminaire de Québec (Archives Nationales
    de Québec), Québec
    Frederick Spiesmacher journal of Indian Affairs
Archives of the Archdiocese of Baltimore
    Bishop John Carroll Correspondence
Bentley Historical Library, Ann Arbor, MI
    Francis S. Belton Collection
    Campau Family Papers, Joseph Campau Letters,
        1828–1855
    Fort Mackinac Letterbook, 1855–66
    John Harris Forster Papers
    Journal of John A. Granger, 1827 (typescript of
        lost original)
    Douglass Houghton Papers
    Bela Hubbard Papers
    Journal of One of the Aides on Tour of General
        Jacob Brown in 1819 (typescript)
    Lyon Family Papers
    Alicia Poole Papers
British Library, London
    Frederick Haldimand Papers
Buffalo and Erie County Historical Society, Buffalo, NY
    Daniel Dobbins Papers
Burton Historical Collection, Detroit Public Library
    Abbot Family Papers
    American Fur Company Papers
    Jacob Brown Papers (typescripts)
    Marshall Chapin Papers
    Ramsay Crooks Papers (photostats)
    Dorchester Papers
    Michael Dousman Papers
    George Fuller Papers
    Harrow Family Papers
    T. H. Hinchman Papers
    Andrew Hunter Holmes Papers
    Edward Jacker Papers
    Jacob Kingsbury Papers
    Charles Larned Papers
    William F. Lawler Papers (typescripts)
    Daniel Morrison Papers
    Benjamin K. Pierce Papers
    John Porteous Papers
    Moses Porter Papers (photostats of originals in
        Essex Institute)
    Solomon Sibley Papers
    Dominicus Varlet Papers (typescripts)
    Little Wiley Papers (photostats of originals in
        Minnesota Historical Society)
    Williams Family Papers
    William Woodbridge Papers
Clarke Historical Library, Central Michigan University,
    Mount Pleasant
    An act to prevent ston'd horses from running at
        large. . . . 1818
    Anonymous diary, 1848, 1854
    Great Lakes trip diary, 1844
    Delancey F. Jones Correspondence, 1848–1849
    Samuel C. Lasley Affidavit, 1824

John Locke Diary, 1847, 1849
    Township Record Book, Borough of
        Michilimackinac, 1817–1858
    Ward Family Papers (typescripts)
Historical Society of Pennsylvania, Philadelphia
    Simon Gratz Collection (photocopies at MSHP)
    Anthony Wayne Papers
Houghton Library, Harvard University, Cambridge, MA
    Records of American Board of Commissioners for
        Foreign Missions
The Huntington Library, San Marino, CA
    James D. Doty, "Notes on the Northwest"
    William Fairholme Journal
Library and Archives Canada, Ottawa, ON
    Graphics Collection
    MG 23 J5. John Hay, Miscellaneous Papers
    National Map Collection
Library of Congress, Washington, DC
    Samuel P. Heintzelman Papers
    Henry R. Schoolcraft Papers
    Mackinac County, St. Ignace, MI
    Michilimackinac County Records
    Mackinac State Historic Parks, Mackinac Island, MI
    Ordnance Sgt. R. J. Dunn Letterbook (photocopy—
        source of original unknown)
    Early Family Collection
    Graphics Collection
    Myra Peters Mason Letters (photocopies from New-
        York Historical Society)
    Patton, Constance Saltonstall (Mrs. William
        Ludlow), "A Glimpse of Life in Mackinac from
        1835 to 1863." Typescript dated October 1915
National Archives, Kew, London
    ADM 1, Admiralty Papers
    WO 34, Jeffery Amherst Papers
    Map Collection
National Archives and Records Administration,
    Washington, DC, and College Park, MD
    RG 49, Records of the Bureau of Land Management
    RG 75, Records of the Bureau of Indian Affairs
    RG 77, Records of the Chief of Engineers
        Letters Received
        Entry 221, Buell Collection of Historic Documents
            Relative to the Corps of Engineers, 1801–1819
        Entry 222, Reports on Fortifications and
            Topographical Surveys, January 1814–October
            1823
    RG 92, Records of the Office of the Quartermaster
        General
        Consolidated Correspondence File, Fort
            Mackinac, Michigan
    RG 94, Records of the Office of the Adjutant General
        Fort Mackinac, Letters Sent, 1829–1836
        Quarterly Reports of Sick and Wounded for
            Michigan Posts
    RG 107, Records of the Secretary of War
        Letters Received, Main Series
        Letters Received, Unregistered Series

RG 159, Inspection Reports of the Office of the
    Inspector General
    Reports, 1814–1842
RG 217, Records of the 3rd Auditor's Office, Treasury
    Department
    Quarterly Reports of the Quartermasters, 1826–1848
New Hampshire Historical Society, Concord
    John McNeil Orderly Books, 1813–1825
New-York Historical Society, New York
    Myra Peters Mason Letters (photocopies at MSHP)
New York Public Library
    John Wolcott Phelps Papers (photocopies at MSHP)
Olin Library, Greenslade Special Collections and
    Archives, Kenyon College, Gambier, OH
    David Bates Douglass Papers
Private Collections
    Joseph Austrian's Autobiographical Sketches
        (photocopy at MSHP)
    Bacon Family Papers (photocopies at MSHP)
    Aaron Bellangee Memorandum Book (photocopies
        at MSHP)
    Incidents in the Life of Jacob Butler Varnum, 1809–
        1823 (copies at MSHP)
Ste. Anne's Church, Mackinac Island, MI
    Financial Record Book, 1828–1838 (microfilm copy
        at MSHP)
State Historical Society of Wisconsin, Madison
    Baird Family Papers (photocopies at MSHP)
    James D. Doty, "Memorandum of Travels in
        Northern Michigan and Wisconsin, July 10–
        August 8, 1822"
Stuart House Museum, Mackinac Island, MI
    Manuscript Collection
United States Military Academy Library, West Point, NY
    Henry Burbeck Papers
Western Reserve Historical Society, Cleveland, OH
    Elisha Whittlesey Papers, MSS 1529
William L. Clements Library, Ann Arbor, MI
    American Travel Collection
    Jacob Brown Papers
    Duane N. Diedrich Collection
    David Bates Douglass Papers
    Thomas Duggan Journal
    Farley Family Papers
    Thomas Gage Papers
    Henry C. Gilbert Papers
    James McHenry Papers
    Michigan Collection
    Northwest Territory Collection
    Wayne Family Papers

Printed Primary Sources

*Acts of the Legislature of the State of Michigan, Passed
    at the Annual Session of 1842: with an Appendix,
    Containing the Treasurer's Annual Report, and the
    Annual Report of the Auditor General.* Detroit: Bagg
    and Harmon, printers, 1842.
*Acts of the Legislature of the State of Michigan, Passed
    at the Annual Session of 1843: with an Appendix,*

Containing the Treasurer's Annual Report. Detroit: Ellis and Briggs, printers to the Legislature, 1843.

Acts of the Legislature of the State of Michigan, Passed at the Annual Session of 1847: with an Appendix, Containing the Treasurer's Annual Report, &c. Detroit: Bagg and Harmon, printers to the state, 1847.

Acts of the Legislature of the State of Michigan, Passed at the Annual Session of 1848: with an Appendix, Containing the Treasurer's Annual Report, &c. Detroit: Bagg and Harmon, printers to the state, 1848.

Agassiz Louis, and J. Elliot Cabot. *Lake Superior: Its Physical Character, Vegetation, and Animals, Compared With Those of other and Similar Regions.* Boston: Gould, Kendall and Lincoln, 1850.

American Board of Commissioners for Foreign Missions. *Annual Report.* Boston: American Board of Commissioners for Foreign Missions, 1830.

American State Papers. Documents, Legislative and Executive of the Congress of the United States . . . Indian Affairs . . . Volume 1. Washington, DC: Gales and Seaton, 1832.

American State Papers. Documents, Legislative and Executive of the Congress of the United States . . . Public Lands . . . Volume 1. Washington, DC: Gales and Seaton, 1832.

American State Papers. Documents of the Congress of the United States, in Relation to Public Lands . . . Volume 5. Washington, DC: Gales and Seaton, 1860.

American Tract Society. *Eliza: The Indian Sorceress.* N.p.: n.p., [1830].

Anderson, Charles A., ed. "Diaries of Peter Dougherty." *Journal of the Presbyterian Historical Society* 30, no. 2 (June 1952): 95–114; no. 3 (September 1952): 175–92; no. 4 (December 1952): 236–53.

———, ed. "Frontier Mackinac Island, 1823–1834: Letters of William Montague and Amanda White Ferry." *Journal of the Presbyterian Historical Society* 25, no. 4 (December 1947): 192–222; 26, no. 2 (June 1948): 101–27; no. 3 (September 1948): 181–91.

———, ed. "Mackinac to Sault Ste. Marie by Canoe in 1831." *Michigan History* 30, no. 3 (July–September 1946): 466–75. Journal of Jeremiah Porter.

Arese, Count Francesco. *A Trip to the Prairies and in the Interior of North America [1837–1838].* Trans. Andrew Evans. New York: Harbor Press, 1934.

Armes, William Dallam, ed. *The Autobiography of Joseph Le Conte.* New York: D. Appleton and Company, 1903.

Armour, David A., ed. *Treason? At Michilimackinac: The Proceedings of a General Court Martial Held at Montreal in October 1768 for the Trial of Major Robert Rogers.* Rev. ed. Mackinac Island, MI: Mackinac Island State Park Commission, 1972.

Bacon, Leonard. *Sketch of the Rev. David Bacon.* Boston: Congregational Publishing Society, 1876.

Bacqueville de La Potherie, Claude-Charles Le Roy. *Histoire de l'Amérique Septentrionale.* Rouen: J. Nion and F. Didot, 1722.

Barber, John, and Henry Howe. *All the Western States and Territories from the Alleghenies to the Pacific and from the Lakes to the Gulf. . . .* Cincinnati: Howe's Subscription Book Concern, 1867.

———. *Our Whole Country; or, The Past and Present of the United States, Historical and Descriptive. . . .* 2 vols. Cincinnati: H. Howe, 1861.

Beaumont, Gustave-Auguste de. *Lettres d'Amérique, 1831–1832.* Paris: Presses Universitaires de France, 1973.

Beaven, James. *Recreations of a Long Vacation; or a Visit to Indian Missions in Upper Canada.* London: James Burns; Toronto: H. and W. Bowsell, 1846.

Beeson, Lewis, ed. "From New York to Illinois by Water in 1840." *Michigan History* 37, no. 3 (September 1948): 270–89. Diary of Edward Brewster.

Bigsby, John J. *The Shoe and Canoe.* 2 vols. London: Chapman and Hall, 1850.

Blois, John T. *Gazetteer of the State of Michigan, in Three Parts, Containing a General View of the State. . . .* Detroit: Sydney L. Rood and Company, 1838.

Blowe, Daniel. *A Geographical, Commercial, and Agricultural View of the United States of America: Forming a Complete Emigrant's Directory Throughout Every Part of the Republic, Particularly the Western States and Territories. . . .* Liverpool: Printed for the editor by Henry Fisher, 1820.

Brehm, Victoria, ed. *The Women's Great Lakes Reader.* Duluth, MN: Holy Cow! Press, 1998.

Brotherton, R. A., ed. "Story of Philo Everett's Trip from Jackson, Michigan, to Marquette in 1845." *Inland Seas* 1, no. 4 (October 1945): 23–28.

Brown, Ralph H., ed. "With Cass in the Northwest in 1820: The Journal of Charles C. Trowbridge." *Minnesota History* 23 (June–December 1942): 347–48.

Bryant, William Cullen. *Letters of a Traveller; Or, Notes of Things Seen in Europe and America.* New York: G. P. Putnam, 1850.

———, ed. *Picturesque America; or the Land We Live In.* 2 vols. New York: D. Appleton and Company, 1872–74. In vol. 1 (1872) is Constance F. Woolson, "Mackinac With Illustrations by J. Douglas Woodward," 279–91.

Buckingham, James Silk. *The Eastern and Western States of America.* 3 vols. London: Fisher, Son, and Company, 1842.

[Bulger, Andrew]. *An Autobiographical Sketch of the Services of the Late Captain Andrew Bulger of the Royal Newfoundland Fencible Regiment.* Bangalore: Regimental Press, 2nd Battalion 10th Regiment, 1865.

Bunnell, David C. *The Travels and Adventures of David C. Bunnell During Twenty-three Years of a Sea-faring Life; Containing an Accurate Account of the Battle on Lake Erie, Under the Command of Com. Oliver H. Perry Together with Ten Years' Service in the Navy of the United States Also Service Among the Greeks, Imprisonment Among the Turks, &c. &c.* Palmyra, NY: J. H. Bortles, 1831.

Carter, Clarence Edwin, ed. *The Correspondence of General Thomas Gage with the Secretaries of State, 1763–1775.* 2 vols. New Haven: Yale University Press, 1931.

———. *The Territorial Papers of the United States.* 27 vols. Washington, DC: GPO, 1934–54.

Carter, James L., and Ernest H. Rankin, eds. *North to Lake Superior: The Journal of Charles W. Penny, 1840.* Marquette, MI: John M. Longyear Research Library, 1970.

Carver, Jonathan. *Travels Through the Interior Parts of North America, in the Years 1766, 1767, and 1768.* London: Printed for the author, 1778.

———. *Travels Through the Interior Parts of North America, in the Years 1766, 1767, and 1768.* London: C. Dilly, 1781.

Cary, Samuel Fenton, ed. *The National Temperance Offering and Sons and Daughters of Temperance Gift.* New York: R. Vandien, 1850.

Castelnau, François, comte de. *Vues et Souvenirs de l'Amérique du Nord.* Paris: A. Bertrand, 1842.

Catlin, George. *Letters and Notes on the Manners, Customs, and Condition of the North American Indians.* 2 vols. London: By the author, 1841.

Champlain, Samuel de. *The Works of Samuel de Champlain in Six Volumes.* Ed. H. P. Biggar. Toronto: Champlain Society, 1936.

Charlevoix, Pierre-François-Xavier de. *Histoire et description générale de la Nouvelle France, avec le journal historique d'un voyage fait par ordre du roi dans l'Amérique Septentrionale.* 3 vols. Paris: Didot, 1744.

———. *Journal of a Voyage to North America. Undertaken by Order of the French King. Containing the Geographical Description and Natural History of that Country, particularly Canada. Together with an Account of the Customs, Characters, Religion, Manners and Traditions of the original Inhabitants.* 2 vols. London: R. and J. Dodsley, 1761.

Clark, John A. *Gleanings by the Way.* Philadelphia: W. J. and J. K. Simon, 1842.

Clark, Lewis Gaylord. *Knick-knacks From an Editor's Table.* New York: D. Appleton and Company, 1852.

Clarke, Robert E. "Notes from the Copper Region." *Harper's New Monthly Magazine* 6, no. 34 (March 1853): 434–37.

Clements, William L., ed. *Journal of Major Robert Rogers.* Worcester, MA: American Antiquarian Society, 1918.

Colton, Calvin. *Tour of the American Lakes, and Among the Indians of the North-West Territory, in 1830.* London: F. Westley and A. H. Davis, 1833.

Conkling, Edgar. *Exposition of Mackinaw City and its Surroundings.* Cincinnati: Caleb Clark, printer, 1865.

Coyne, James H., ed. *Exploration of the Great Lakes, 1669–1670, by Dollier de Casson and De Bréhant de Galinée: Galinée's Narrative and Map with an English Version, Including All the Map Legends.* Toronto: Ontario Historical Society, 1903.

Crawford, Michael J., ed. *The Naval War of 1812: A Documentary History, Volume III, 1814–1815.* Washington, DC: Naval Historical Center, 2002.

Cruikshank, Ernest A., ed. *The Documentary History of the Campaign Upon the Niagara Frontier.* 9 vols. Welland, ON: Lundy's Lane Historical Society, 1896–1908.

Cummins, Robert Hazlett. *Journal of Dr. Robert Hazlett Cummins Written During a Tour of the Great Lakes in August, 1855.* N.p.: De Vinne Press, 1895.

Curtiss, Daniel S. *Western Portraiture, and Emigrant's Guide: A Description of Wisconsin, Illinois and Iowa; With Remarks on Minnesota, and Other Territories.* New York: J. H. Colton, 1852.

Dana, David T., III, ed. *A Fashionable Tour Through the Great Lakes and Upper Mississippi: The 1852 Journal of Juliette Starr Dana.* Detroit: Wayne State University Press, 2004.

Davenport, Bishop. *A New Gazetteer, or Geographical Dictionary, of North America and the West Indies.* Baltimore: G. M'Dowell and Son, 1833.

DePeyster, Arent Schulyer. *Miscellanies by an Officer.* Dumfries: C. Munro, 1813.

Dilhet, Jean. *État de L'Église Catholique ou Diocèse des États-Unis de L'Amérique Septentrionale.* The Catholic University of America Studies in American Church History, Vol. 1. Trans. and annot. by Patrick William Browne. Washington, DC: Salve Regina Press, 1922.

Disturnell, John. *The Great Lakes, or Inland Seas of America; Embracing a Full Description of Lakes Superior, Huron, Michigan, Erie, and Ontario; Rivers St. Mary, St. Clair, Detroit, Niagara, and St. Lawrence: Lake Winnipeg, etc.: Together With the Commerce of the Lakes and Trips Through the Lakes: Giving a Description of Cities, Towns, etc. Forming Altogether a Complete Guide for the Pleasure Traveller and Emigrant.* New York: Charles Scribner, 1863.

———. *The Great Lakes, or Inland Seas of America; Embracing a Full Description of Lakes Superior, Huron, Michigan, Erie, and Ontario; Rivers St. Mary, St. Clair, Detroit, Niagara, and St. Laurence: Commerce of the Lakes, etc. etc. Together with a Guide to the Upper Mississippi River. . . .* Philadelphia: W. B. Zeiber, 1871.

———. *A Trip Through the Lakes of North America; Embracing a Full Description of the St. Lawrence River, Together with All the Principal Places on its Banks, From its Source to its Mouth: Commerce of the Lakes, etc. Forming Altogether a Complete Guide for the Pleasure Traveler and Emigrant.* New York: J. Disturnell, 1857.

Drake, Daniel. *The Northern Lakes: A Summer Residence for Invalids of the South.* Louisville, KY: J. Maxwell, Jr., 1842.

———. *A Systematic Treatise, Historical, Etiological, and Practical of the Principal Diseases in the Interior Valley of North America, as They Appear in the Caucasian, Indian, and Esquimaux Varieties of its Population.* Cincinnati: W. B. Smith and Company, 1850.

Eastman, Mrs. Mary H. *The American Annual: Illustrative of the Early History of North America.* Philadelphia: J. B. Lippincott, 1855.

Ellet, Elizabeth Fries. *Summer Rambles in the West.* New York: J. C. Riker, 1853.

Evans, Estwick. *A Pedestrious Tour, of Four Thousand Miles, Through the Western States and Territories, During the Winter and Spring of 1818. . . .* Concord, NH: Joseph C. Spear, 1819.

F. "A Trip to Buffalo in the *St. Louis:* Return in the *St. Louis,* Number XIX." *Western Literary Messenger* 9 (1848): 150–51.

Featherstonhaugh, George W. *A Canoe Voyage up the Minnay Sotor; with an Account of Lead and Copper Deposits in Wisconsin. . . .* 2 vols. London: R. Bentley, 1847.

Ferris, Jacob. *The States and Territories of the Great West. . . .* New York: Miller, Orton, and Mulligan, 1856.

Foster, John Wells, and Josiah Dwight Whitney. *Report on the Geology and Topography of a Portion of the Lake Superior Land District in the State of Michigan.* 2 vols. Washington, DC: House of Representatives, 1850–51.

Fredriksen, John C., ed. *Surgeon of the Lakes: The Diary of Dr. Usher Parsons, 1812–1814.* Erie, PA: Erie County Historical Society, 2000.

Fuller, George N., ed. *Geological Reports of Douglass Houghton, First State Geologist of Michigan, 1837–1845.* Lansing: Michigan Historical Commission, 1928.

Fuller, Margaret. *Summer on the Lakes, in 1843.* Boston: Charles C. Little and James Brown, 1844.

Gérin-Lajoie, Marie, trans. and ed. "Fort Michili-mackinac in 1749: Lotbinière's Plan and Description." *Mackinac History* 2, no. 5. Mackinac Island: Mackinac Island State Park Commission, 1976.

Gilman, Chandler Robbins. *Life on the Lakes: Being Tales and Sketches Collected During a Trip to the Pictured Rocks of Lake Superior.* 2 vols. New York: G. Dearborn, 1836.

Graustein, Jeannette E., ed. "Nuttall's Travels into the Old Northwest: An Unpublished 1810 Diary." *Chronica Botanica* 14, nos. 1–2 (1950–51):3–86.

Great Britain. War Office. *A List of the Colonels, Lieutenant Colonels, Majors, Captains, Lieutenants, and Ensigns of His Majesty's Forces on the British and Irish Establishments. . . .* London: J. Millan, 1763 and 1766.

Hall, E. H. *The Chicago City Directory, and Business Advertiser.* Chicago: Robert Fergus, 1855.

Hanna, Charles A. *The Wilderness Trail or the Ventures and Adventures of the Pennsylvania Traders on the Allegheny Path.* 2 vols. New York: G. P. Putnam's Sons, 1911.

Hellman, George S., ed. *Letters of Henry Brevoort to Washington Irving Together with Other Unpublished Brevoort Papers.* New York: G. P. Putnam's Sons, 1918.

Hennepin, Louis. *Aenmerkelyke Voyagie Gedaan na't Gedeelte van Noorder America. . . .* Leyden: Pieter vander Aa, 1704.

———. *A New Discovery of a Vast Country in America, Extending Above Four Thousand Miles, Between New France & New Mexico.* London: M. Bentley et al., 1698.

Henry, Alexander. *Travels and Adventures in Canada and the Indian Territories Between the Years 1760 and 1776.* New York: I. Riley, 1809.

Heriot, George. *Travels Through the Canadas, Containing a Description of the Picturesque Scenery. . . .* London: R. Phillips, 1807.

Holmquist, June Drenning, ed. "Frontier Vacation: Joseph Le Conte's Early Geological Excursion." *Minnesota History* 32, no. 2 (Summer 1951): 81–99.

Howe, Henry. *The Great West, Containing Narratives of the Most Important and Interesting Events in Western History, Remarkable Individuals, Adventurous Sketches of Frontier Life, Descriptions of Natural Curiosities.* New York and Cincinnati: Henry Howe, [1851].

Hubbard, Bela. *Memorials of a Half-Century.* New York: G. P. Putnam's Sons, 1887.

Hubbard, Gurdon S. *The Autobiography of Gurdon Saltonstall Hubbard.* Chicago: R. R. Donnelley and Sons, 1911.

Hurlbut, Henry H., ed. *Chicago Antiquities.* Chicago: By the editor, 1881. Contains "Wilderness Letters of William Burnett, the Fur Trader, 1786–1803."

Irving, Washington. *Three Western Narratives.* New York: Library of America, 2004.

Jackman, Sydney W., and John F. Freeman, eds. *American Voyageur: The Journal of David Bates Douglass.* Marquette, MI: Northern Michigan University Press, 1969.

Jameson, Mrs. Anna. *Winter Studies and Summer Rambles in Canada.* 2 vols. New York: Wiley and Putnam, 1839.

Kane, Lucile, June D. Holmquist, and Carolyn Gilman, eds. *The Northern Expeditions of Stephen H. Long: The Journals of 1817 and 1823 and Related Documents.* St. Paul: Minnesota Historical Society Press, 1978.

Kane, Paul. *Wanderings of an Artist Among the Indians of North America from Canada to Vancouver's Island and Oregon Through the Hudson's Bay Company's Territory and Back Again.* London: Longman, Brown, Green, Longmans, and Roberts, 1859.

Kellogg, Louise Phelps, ed. *Early Narratives of the Northwest, 1634–1699.* New York: Barnes and Noble, 1917. Reprint, 1967.

Kestenbaum, Justin L., ed. *The Making of Michigan, 1820–1860.* Detroit: Wayne State University Press, 1990.

Kingman, John. *Letters Written by John Kingman While on a Tour to Illinois and Wisconsin in the Summer of 1838*. Hingham, MA: Jedidiah Farmer, 1842.

Kinzie, Juliette A. *Wau-Bun: The "Early Day" in the North-West*. Ed. Milo M. Quaife. Chicago: R. R. Donnelley and Sons, 1932.

Lahontan, Louis-Armand de Lom d'Arce de. *New Voyages to North-America*. 2 vols. London: H. Bonwicke, T. Goodwin, M. Wotton, B. Took, and S. Manship, 1703.

———. *Nouveaux voyages de Mr. le Baron de Lahontan dans l'Amérique Septentrionale*. 2 vols. La Haye: Chez les Frères l'Honoré, 1703.

———. *Nouveaux voyages de Mr. le Baron de Lahontan dans l'Amérique Septentrionale*. 2 vols. La Haye: Chez les Frères l'Honoré, 1703. Smaller format, pirated edition.

[Landmann, George]. *Adventures and Recollections of Colonel Landmann, Late of the Royal Engineers*. 2 vols. London: Colburn and Company, 1852.

Lanman, Charles. *Adventures in the Wilds of the United States and British American Provinces*. 2 vols. Philadelphia: J. W. Moore, 1856.

———. *A Summer in the Wilderness; Embracing a Canoe Voyage up the Mississippi and Around Lake Superior*. New York: D. Appleton and Company, 1847.

Lanman, James H. *History of Michigan, Civil and Topographical, in a Compendious Form; With a View of the Surrounding Lakes*. New York: E. French, 1839.

La Salle, René-Robert Cavelier de. *Relation of the Discoveries and Voyages of Cavelier de La Salle from 1679 to 1681: The Official Narrative*. Trans. Melville B. Anderson. Chicago: Caxton Club, 1901.

Laws of the Territory of Michigan. Detroit: Sheldon and Wells, 1827.

Lawson, Thomas. *Statistical Report on the Sickness and Mortality in the Army of the United States Compiled from the Records of the Surgeon General's and Adjutant General's Offices—Embracing a Period of Twenty Years from January, 1819, to January, 1839*. Washington, DC: Printed by Jacob Gideon, Jr., 1840.

Leavitt, Humphrey Howe. *Autobiography of the Hon. Humphrey Howe Leavitt Written for his Family*. New York: n.p., 1893.

Lee, Daniel, and Joseph H. Frost. *Ten Years in Oregon*. New York: By the authors, 1844.

"Letters from the Indian Country." *The Knickerbocker* 20, no. 1 (July 1842): 1–5. Long and detailed letter from Mackinac dated October 6, 1836, signed "E. W. J.," describing Indian treaty payments.

Levinge, Sir Richard George Augustus. *Echoes from the Backwoods; or, Sketches of Transatlantic Life*. 2 vols. London: Colburn, 1846.

Logan, James. *Notes of a Journey Through Canada, the United States of America, and the West Indies*. Edinburgh: Fraser and Company, 1838.

Long, John. *Voyages and Travels of an Indian Interpreter and Trader, Describing the Manners and Customs of the North American Indians. . . .* London: For the author, 1791.

McAfee, Robert B. *History of the Late War in the Western Country, Comprising a Full Account of all the Transactions in that Quarter, from the Commencement of Hostilities at Tippecanoe, to the Termination of the Contest at New Orleans on the Return of Peace*. Lexington, KY: Worsley and Smith, 1816.

McElroy, Robert, and Thomas Riggs, eds. *The Unfortified Boundary: The Diary of the First Survey of the Canadian Boundary Line from St. Regis to the Lake of the Woods by Major Joseph Delafield*. New York: Privately printed, 1943.

McKenney, Thomas L. *History of the Indian Tribes of North America, With Biographical Sketches and Anecdotes of the Principal Chiefs. Embellished With One Hundred and Twenty Portraits, from the Indian Gallery in the Department of War at Washington*. 3 vols. Philadelphia: Edward C. Biddle, 1836–44.

———. *Sketches of a Tour to the Lakes of the Character and Customs of the Chippeway Indians and of Incidents Connected with the Treaty of Fond du Lac*. Baltimore: Fielding Lucas, Jr., 1827.

"Mackinac." *Frank Leslie's Illustrated Newspaper* 2 (September 20, 1856): 231–32, 236–37.

"Mackinaw and Its Scenery." *Ballou's Pictorial Drawing-Room Companion*, May 5, 1855, 280–81.

McLellan, Hugh, ed. *Journal of Thomas Nye Written during a Journey between Montreal and Chicago in 1837*. Champlain, NY: By the editor, 1932.

———, ed. *Two Letters of Thomas Nye Relating to a Journey from Montreal to Chicago in 1837*. Champlain, NY: By the editor, 1931.

MacLeod, C. Donald. "A Saunter in the North-West." *Brother Jonathan* 6, no. 5 (September 30, 1843): 113–17.

Mansfield, Edward Deering. *Exposition of the Natural Position of Mackinaw City and the Climate, Soil, and Commercial Elements of the Surrounding Country*. Cincinnati: Wrightson, printers, 1857.

Marlatt, Helen Stuart Mackay-Smith, ed. *Stuart Letters of Robert and Elizabeth Sullivan Stuart and Their Children, 1819–1864*. [New York?]: Privately printed, 1961.

Marryat, Frederick. *A Diary in America, With Remarks on Its Institutions*. New York: William H. Colyer, 1839.

Marshall, Thomas Maitland, ed. *The Life and Papers of Frederick Bates*. 2 vols. St. Louis: Missouri Historical Society, 1926.

Martineau, Harriet. *Society in America*. 3 vols. London: Saunders and Otley, 1837.

Mason, Philip P., ed. "Rochester to Mackinac Island." *Michigan History* 37, no. 1 (March 1953): 39–41. Journal of Elisha Loomis.

May, George S., ed. *The Doctor's Secret Journal*. Mackinac Island, MI: Mackinac Island State Park Commission, 1960. Journal of Daniel Morrison.

———, and Herbert Brinks, eds. *A Michigan Reader: 11,000 B.C. to A.D. 1865*. Grand Rapids, MI: William B. Eerdmans, 1974.

Mazzuchelli, Samuel Charles. *Memoirs Historical and Edifying of a Missionary Apostolic of the Order of Saint Dominic among Various Indian Tribes and among the Catholics and Protestants in the United States of America*. Trans. M. Benedicta Kennedy. Chicago: W. F. Hall Printing, 1915.

Meade, George G. *Report of the Survey of the North and Northwest Lakes, by Capt. George G. Meade . . . being Appendix G of the Report of the Chief Topographical Engineer, Accompanying Annual Report of the Secretary of War, 1857*. Washington, DC: C. Alexander, 1858.

———. *Report of the Survey of the North and Northwest Lakes by Capt. George G. Meade, Being Appendix I of the Report of the Chief Topographical Engineer, Accompanying Annual Report of the Secretary of War, 1858*. Washington, DC: L. Towers, 1859.

———. *Report of the Survey of the North and Northwest Lakes by George G. Meade; Being Appendix B, of the Report of the Chief Topographical Engineer, Accompanying Annual Report of the Secretary of War, 1859*. Detroit: Daily Free Press Steam Print House, 1859.

"Mémoire sur la partie occidentale du Canada, depuis Michillimakinac jusqu'au fleuve du Mississipi." *Bulletin des Recherches Historiques* 26 (January 1920): 25–32.

Mereness, Newton D., ed. *Travels in the American Colonies*. New York: Macmillan, 1916.

Michigan Pioneer and Historical Collections. 40 vols. Lansing: Michigan Historical Commission, 1877–1929.

Moore, Thomas. *The Life and Death of Lord Edward Fitzgerald*. 2 vols. London: Longman, Rees, Orme, Brown and Green, 1831.

Morleigh. *A Merry Briton in Pioneer Wisconsin: A Contemporary Narrative Reprinted from Life in the West: Back-Wood Leaves and Prairie Flowers: Rough Sketches on the Borders of the Picturesque, the Sublime, and Ridiculous. Extracts from the Note Book of Morleigh in Search of an Estate. Published in London in the Year 1842*. Madison: State Historical Society of Wisconsin, 1950.

Morse, Jedidiah. *A Report to the Secretary of War of the United States, on Indian Affairs, Comprising a Narrative of a Tour Performed in the Summer of 1820, Under a Commission from the President of the United States, for the Purpose of Ascertaining, for the Use of the Government, the Actual State of the Indian Tribes in our Country*. New Haven: S. Converse, 1822.

Myer, Jesse S. *Life and Letters of Dr. William Beaumont*. St. Louis: C. V. Mosby Company, 1939.

The New-York City Directory, for 1854–1855. New York: Charles R. Rode, [1854].

O'Callaghan, E. B., et al., eds. *Documents Relative to the Colonial History of the State of New York.* 15 vols. Albany: Weed, Parsons and Company, 1856–77.

Olney, Jesse. *A Practical System of Modern Geography. . . .* 55th ed. New York: Pratt, Woodford and Company, 1847.

Olsson, William, ed. *A Pioneer in Northwest America, 1841–1858: The Memoirs of Gustaf Unonius.* 2 vols. Minneapolis: University of Minnesota Press, 1950.

Parker, Donald Dean, ed. *The Recollections of Philander Prescott: Frontiersman of the Old Northwest, 1819–1862.* Lincoln: University of Nebraska Press, 1966.

Parker, John, ed. *The Journals of Jonathan Carver and Related Documents, 1766–1770.* St. Paul: Minnesota Historical Society Press, 1976.

Paulding, James Kirk. "Sketch of the Great Western Lakes." *The Columbian Lady's and Gentleman's Magazine* 1 (1844): 258–66.

Peters, Bernard C., ed. *Lake Superior Journal: Bela Hubbard's Account of the 1840 Houghton Expedition.* Marquette, MI: Northern Michigan University Press, 1983.

Peyser, Joseph L., ed. *Jacques Legardeur de Saint Pierre: Officer, Gentleman, Entrepreneur.* East Lansing: Michigan State University Press, 1996.

Pitezel, John H. *Lights and Shades of Missionary Life Containing Travels, Sketches, Incidents, and Missionary Efforts, During Nine Years Spent in the Region of Lake Superior.* Cincinnati: By the author, 1860.

Porter, Mary H., ed. *Eliza Chappell Porter: A Memoir.* Chicago: Fleming H. Revell Company, 1892.

Quaife, Milo M., ed. *The John Askin Papers.* 2 vols. Detroit: Detroit Library Commission, 1928–31.

———, ed. *War on the Detroit: The Chronicles of Thomas Verchères de Boucherville and the Capitulation by an Ohio Volunteer.* Chicago: Lakeside Press, 1940.

———, ed. *The Western Country in the 17th Century: The Memoirs of Lamothe Cadillac and Pierre Liette.* Chicago: Lakeside Press, 1947.

Quarterly Papers of the American Board of Commissioners for Foreign Missions 20 (March 1835).

[Raudot, Antoine Denis]. *Letters from North America by Father Antoine Silvy, S.J.* Trans. Ivy Alice Dickson. Belleville, ON: Mika Publishing, 1980.

Relation de ce qui c'est passé de plus remarquable aux Missions de Peres de la Compagnie de Jesus en la Nouvelle France, les années 1670 & 1671. Paris: Chez Sebastien Mabre-Cramoisy, 1672.

Report from the Secretary of War, in Compliance with a Resolution of the Senate of the 19th Instant, Transmitting a Report of the Survey of the Military Road from Saginaw to Mackinaw. Washington, DC: U.S. Congress, 1838.

Ross, Alexander. *Adventures of the First Settlers on the Oregon or Columbia River: Being a Narrative of the Expedition Fitted Out by John Jacob Astor, to Establish the "Pacific Fur Company."* London: Smith, Elder, and Company, 1849.

Roy, Pierre-Georges, ed. *Inventaire des papiers de Léry conservés aux Archives de la Province de Québec.* 3 vols. Archives de la Province de Québec, 1939–40.

Saltonstall, Brayton. "Reminiscences of the Mackinac Country." *Michigan History* 2 (April 1918): 383–86.

Scenes on Lake Huron; A Tale; Interspersed with Interesting Facts, in a Series of Letters. By a North American. Lake Mariners, Listen to This Tale. New York: By the author, 1836.

Schoolcraft, Henry R. *Information Respecting the History, Condition and Prospects of the Indian Tribes of the United States. . . .* 6 vols. Philadelphia: Lippincott, Grambo and Company, 1851–57.

———. *Narrative Journal of Travels Through the Northwestern Regions of the United States Extending from Detroit Through the Great Chain of American Lakes to the Sources of the Mississippi River Performed as a Member of the Expedition Under Governor Cass in the Year 1820.* Albany: E. and E. Hosford, 1821.

———. *Personal Memoirs of a Residence of Thirty Years With the Indian Tribes on the American Frontier With Brief Notices of Passing Events, Facts, and Opinions, A.D. 1812 to A.D. 1842.* Philadelphia: Lippincott, Grambo and Company, 1851.

Sears, Robert, ed. *A New and Popular Pictorial Description of the United States: Containing an Account of the Topography, Settlement, History, Revolutionary and Other Interesting Events, Statistics, Progress in Agriculture, Manufactures, and Population, &c., of Each State in the Union.* 3rd ed. New York: Robert Sears, 1848.

[———]. "Two Days at Mackinaw, No. 1, No. 2, No. 3, No. 4." *Democratic Free Press,* July 28, 29, 30, 31, 1847. Author signs as "S. & Co."

Severance, Frank H., ed. "Gen. Brown's Inspection Tour Up the Lakes in 1819." *Publications of the Buffalo Historical Society, Volume XXIV.* Buffalo: Buffalo Historical Society, 1920.

Sketches of the War, Between the United States and the British Isles: Intended as a Faithful History of all the Material Events from the Time of the Declaration in 1812, to and Including the Treaty of Peace in 1815: Interspersed with Geographical Descriptions of Places, and Biographical Notes of Distinguished Military and Naval Commanders. Rutland, VT: Fay and Davison, 1815.

Spooner, Harry, ed. "At Fort Mackinac a Century Ago." *Michigan History* 12 (1928). Selections from the post order book for 1833–36.

Steele, Eliza. *A Summer Journey in the West.* New York: John S. Taylor and Company, 1841.

Steele, Oliver Gray. *Steele's Western Guide Book, and Emigrant's Directory. Fourth Edition. Greatly Improved and Enlarged.* Buffalo: Oliver G. Steele, 1836.

———. *Steele's Western Guide Book, and Emigrant's Directory. Tenth Edition, Greatly Improved and Enlarged.* Buffalo: Steele and Peck, 1838.

———. *The Traveller's Directory, and Emigrant's Guide.* Buffalo: Steele and Faxon, 1832.

Stevens, Sylvester K., Donald H. Kent, and Emma Edith Wood, eds. *Travels in New France by J. C. B.* Harrisburg: Pennsylvania Historical Commission, 1941.

Strang, James Jesse. *Ancient and Modern Michilimackinac, Including an Account of the Controversy between Mackinac and the Mormons.* Ed. George S. May. Mackinac Island, MI: W. S. Woodfill, 1959.

Strickland, William P. *Old Mackinaw; or, the Fortress of the Lakes.* Philadelphia: James Challen and Son, 1860.

Sullivan, James, and Milton W. Hamilton, eds. *The Papers of Sir William Johnson.* 14 vols. Albany: University of the State of New York, 1921–65.

Swan, Caleb. "The Northwestern Country in 1797." *Magazine of American History* 19 (1888): 74–75.

Syrett, Harold C., ed. *The Papers of Alexander Hamilton.* 27 vols. New York: Columbia University Press, 1961–.

Taylor, Bayard. *At Home and Abroad: A Sketch-Book of Life, Scenery, and Men.* New York: G. P. Putnam, 1860.

Thwaites, Reuben Gold, ed. *The Jesuit Relations and Allied Documents.* 73 vols. Cleveland: Burrows Bros. Company, 1896–1901.

Tocqueville, Alexis de. *Journey to America.* Trans. George Lawrence. Ed. J. P. Mayer. New Haven: Yale University Press, 1960.

Tonty, Henri de. *Relation of Henri de Tonty Concerning the Explorations of LaSalle from 1678 to 1683.* Trans. Melville B. Anderson. Chicago: Caxton Club, 1898.

Travels in the Two Hemispheres. . . . Detroit: Doughty, Straw and Company, and Raymond and Selleck, 1858. Compilation of issues of *Magazine of Travel* from 1857. Contains "Notes from Lake Superior," probably by Warren Isham.

Tuttle, Sarah. *Conversations on the Mackinaw and Green-Bay Indian Missions.* Boston: T. R. Marvin for the Massachusetts Sabbath School Union, 1831.

Tykal, Jack, ed. *Journal of an Expedition to the Grand Prairies of the Missouri, 1840.* Spokane, WA: Arthur H. Clark Company, 1996. Journal of Lieutenant William Fairholme.

Van Der Zee, Jacob, trans. and ed. "Diary of a Journey from the Netherlands to Pella, Iowa, in 1849." *Iowa Journal of History and Politics* 10, no. 3 (July 1912): 363–82. Diary of John Hospers.

Vigne, Godfrey T. *Six Months in America.* 2 vols. London: Whittaker, Treacher, and Company, 1832.

Wade, Mason, ed. *The Journals of Francis Parkman*. 2 vols. New York: Harper and Brothers, 1947.

Walling, Regis M., and N. Daniel Rupp, eds. *The Diary of Bishop Frederic Baraga*. Detroit: Wayne State University Press, 1990.

Weld, Isaac. *Travels Through the States of North America, and the Provinces of Upper and Lower Canada, During the Years, 1795, 1796, and 1797*. London: J. Stockdale, 1800.

Wisconsin Historical Collections. 31 vols. Madison: State Historical Society of Wisconsin, 1855–1931.

Wood, W. H., ed. *Select Documents of the Canadian War of 1812*. 3 vols. Toronto: Champlain Society, 1920–26.

Woolson, Constance Fenimore. "Fairy Island." *Putnam's Monthly Magazine* 16, no. 31 (July 1870): 62–69.

Secondary Sources

Alfred R. Waud: Special Artist on Assignment. New Orleans: Historic New Orleans Collection, 1979.

The American Sketchbooks of Franz Holzehübe: An Austrian Visits America, 1856–1860. An Exhibition of Watercolor Sketches Lent by Mr. and Mrs. Oscar Salzer of Los Angeles, California, Presented and Published for the First Time. Topeka: University of Kansas Museum of Art, 1959.

Anderson, Fred. *Crucible of War: The Seven Years' War and the Fate of Empire in British North America, 1754–1766*. New York: Alfred A. Knopf, 2000.

Andrews, Roger. *Old Fort Mackinac on the Hill of History*. Menominee, MI: Herald-Leader Press, 1938.

Armour, David A. *Colonial Michilimackinac*. Mackinac Island, MI: Mackinac State Historic Parks, 2000.

———. "David and Elizabeth: The Mitchell Family of the Straits of Mackinac." *Mackinac History*, 2, no. 6. Mackinac Island, MI: Mackinac Island State Park Commission, 1982.

———, and Keith R. Widder. *At the Crossroads: Michilimackinac during the American Revolution*. Mackinac Island, MI: Mackinac Island State Park Commission, 1978.

Bailey, John R. *Mackinac, Formerly Michilimackinac*. 3rd Neosho ed. Lansing, MI: Robert Smith Printing, 1897.

"Biographical Sketches of 1827 5th Infantry Officers." Unpublished training aid, Fort Snelling Historic Site, St. Paul, MN.

Blackbird, Andrew J. *History of the Ottawa and Chippewa Indians of Michigan; a Grammar of Their Language, and Personal and Family History of the Author*. Ypsilanti, MI: Ypsilanti Job Printing House, 1887.

Bowler, R. Arthur. "From the Treaty of Paris to Jay's Treaty: The Western Posts in British and American Policy." In Brian Leigh Dunnigan, ed., *Niagara 1796: The Fortress Possessed*. Youngstown, NY: Old Fort Niagara Association, 1996.

Boynton, James. *Fishers of Men: The Jesuit Mission at Mackinac, 1670–1815*. Mackinac Island, MI: Ste. Anne's Church, 1996.

Brisson, Steven C. *Picturesque Mackinac: The Photographs of William H. Gardiner, 1896–1915*. Mackinac Island, MI: Mackinac State Historic Parks, 2006.

Brun, Christian. *Guide to the Manuscript Maps in the William L. Clements Library*. Ann Arbor: University of Michigan, 1959.

Burbey, Louis H. *Our Worthy Commander: The Life and Times of Benjamin K. Pierce in Whose Honor Fort Pierce Was Named*. Fort Pierce, FL: Indian River Community College Historical Data Center, 1976.

Burden, Philip D. *The Mapping of North America*. Rickmansworth, England: Raleigh Publications, 1996.

Bushnell, David I., Jr. *Sketches by Paul Kane in the Indian Country, 1845–1848*. Washington, DC: Smithsonian Institution, 1940. Smithsonian Miscellaneous Collections, vol. 99, 1941.

Callahan, Edward W. *List of Officers of the Navy of the United States and of the Marine Corps from 1775 to 1900*. 1901. Reprint, New York: Haskell House Publishers, 1969.

Chartrand, René. *Canadian Military Heritage, Volume 1, 1000–1754*. Montréal: Art Global, 1993.

Clinton, George W. *The Late Com. Stephen Champlin: A Paper Read by Judge Clinton Before the Buffalo Historical Society, December 5, 1870*. [Buffalo: Buffalo Historical Society, ca. 1870].

Cullum, George W. *Biographical Register of Officers and Graduates of the U.S. Military Academy at West Point, from its Establishment, March 16, 1802, to the Army Reorganization of 1866–67*. 2nd ed. 2 vols. New York: D. Van Nostrand, 1868.

Davis, Marion Morse. *Island Stories: Straits of Mackinac*. Lansing: F. DeKleine Company for the author, 1947.

Dictionary of Canadian Biography. 12 vols. Toronto: University of Toronto Press, 1966–1991.

Donnelly, Joseph P. *Jacques Marquette*. Chicago: Loyola University Press, 1968.

Dunbabin, J. P. D. "Motives for Mapping the Great Lakes: Upper Canada, 1782–1827." *Michigan Historical Review* 31, no. 1 (Spring 2005): 1–43.

Dunnigan, Brian Leigh. "The Battle of Mackinac Island." *Michigan History* 59, no. 4 (Winter 1975): 239–54.

———. *The British Army at Mackinac, 1812–1815*. Mackinac Island, MI: Mackinac Island State Park Commission, 1980.

———. *Fort Holmes*. Mackinac Island, MI: Mackinac Island State Park Commission, 1984.

———. *Frontier Metropolis: Picturing Early Detroit, 1701–1838*. Detroit: Wayne State University Press, 2001.

———. *Glorious Old Relic: The French Castle and Old Fort Niagara*. Youngstown, NY: Old Fort Niagara Association, 1987.

———. *King's Men at Mackinac: The British Garrisons, 1780–1796*. Mackinac Island, MI: Mackinac Island State Park Commission, 1973.

———. *The Necessity of Regularity in Quartering Soldiers: The Organization, Material Culture and Quartering of the British Soldier at Michilimackinac*. Mackinac Island, MI: Mackinac State Historic Parks, 1999.

———. "The Post of Mackinac, 1779–1812." Thesis submitted to the State University College of New York at Oneonta, Cooperstown Graduate Programs, 1979. Copy in the collections of Mackinac State Historic Parks.

Eccles, W. J. *The Canadian Frontier, 1534–1760*. Rev. ed. Albuquerque: University of New Mexico Press, 1983.

Edmunds, R. David, and Joseph L. Peyser. *The Fox Wars: The Mesquakie Challenge to New France*. Norman: University of Oklahoma Press, 1993.

Ford, Thomas B. "Architectural Record of the John Dousman House, Mackinac Island, Michigan." Unpublished report, October 1979, in the collections of Mackinac State Historic Parks.

Fowler, Marian. *The Embroidered Tent: Five Gentlewomen in Early Canada*. Toronto: Anansi, 1982.

Gilpin, Alec. *The Territory of Michigan, 1805–1837*. East Lansing: Michigan State University Press, 1970.

———. *The War of 1812 in the Old Northwest*. East Lansing: Michigan State University Press, 1958.

Gough, Barry. *Fighting Sail on Lake Huron and Georgian Bay: The War of 1812 and Its Aftermath*. Annapolis: Naval Institute Press, 2002.

Grange, Roger. T. "Excavation of the Wooden Quarters at Fort Mackinac: An Interim Report." Unpublished report in collections of Mackinac State Historic Parks.

———. *Excavations at Fort Mackinac, 1980–1982: The Provision Storehouse*. Mackinac Island, MI: Mackinac Island State Park Commission, 1987.

Gravier, Gabriel. *Carte des Grands Lacs de l'Amérique du Nord dressée en 1670 par Bréhab de Gallinée Missionaire Sulpicien*. Rouen: E. Cagniard, 1895.

Groce, George C., and David H. Wallace. *The New-York Historical Society's Dictionary of Artists in America, 1564–1860*. New Haven: Yale University Press, 1957.

[Hale, Edward Everett]. "The Man Without a Country." *Atlantic Monthly* 12, no. 74 (December 1863): 665–79.

Harburn, Todd. *In Defense of the Red Ensign at Michilimackinac, 1763*. Okemos, MI: Michilimackinac Society Press, 2000.

———. *The King's Quiet Commandant at Michilimackinac: A Biographical Sketch of Captain George Etherington of the 60th Royal American Regiment*. Okemos, MI: Michilimackinac Society Press, 1999.

Harper, J. Russell. *Early Painters and Engravers in Canada.* Toronto: University of Toronto Press, 1970.

———, ed. *Paul Kane's Frontier: Including Wanderings of an Artist among the Indians of North America by Paul Kane.* Fort Worth, TX: Amon Carter Museum, 1971.

Heitman, Francis B. *Historical Register and Dictionary of the United States Army, from Its Organization, September 29, 1789 to March 2, 1903.* 2 vols. Washington, DC: GPO, 1903.

Heldman, Donald P. *Archaeological Investigations at French Farm Lake in Northern Michigan, 1981–1982.* Mackinac Island, MI: Mackinac Island State Park Commission, 1983.

———, and Roger T. Grange, Jr. *Excavations at Fort Michilimackinac, 1978–1979: The Rue de la Babillarde.* Mackinac Island, MI: Mackinac Island State Park Commission, 1981.

———, and William L. Minnerly. *The Powder Magazine at Fort Michilimackinac: Excavation Report.* Mackinac Island, MI: Mackinac Island State Park Commission, 1977.

Horsman, Reginald. *Frontier Doctor: William Beaumont, America's First Great Medical Scientist.* Columbia: University of Missouri Press, 1996.

Hubach, Robert R. *Early Midwestern Travel Narratives: An Annotated Bibliography, 1634–1850.* Detroit: Wayne State University Press, 1998.

Humins, John Harold. "George Boyd: Indian Agent of the Upper Great Lakes, 1819–1842." Ph.D. diss., Michigan State University, Department of History, 1975. Copy in the collections of Mackinac State Historic Parks.

Hyde, Charles K. *The Northern Lights: Lighthouses of the Upper Great Lakes.* Lansing, MI: Two Peninsulas Press, 1986.

Johnson, Allen, and Dumas Malone, eds. *Dictionary of American Biography.* 20 vols. New York: Scribner, 1931.

Karpinski, Louis C. *Bibliography of the Printed Maps of Michigan, 1804–1880.* Lansing: Michigan Historical Commission, 1931.

Karrow, Robert W., Jr. "Lake Superior's Mythic Isles: A Cautionary Tale for Users of Old Maps." *Michigan History* 69, no. 1 (Jan.–Feb. 1985): 24–31.

Kelton, Dwight H. *Annals of Fort Mackinac.* Chicago: Fergus Printing, 1882.

Kent, Timothy J. *Rendezvous at the Straits: Fur Trade and Military Activities at Fort de Buade and Fort Michilimackinac, 1669–1781.* 2 vols. Ossineke, MI: Silver Fox Enterprises, 2004.

Kershaw, Kenneth A. *Early Printed Maps of Canada.* 4 vols. Ancaster, ON: Kershaw Publishing, 1993–98.

La Rue, Carl D. "The Lilacs of Mackinac Island." *American Midland Naturalist* 39, no. 2 (March 1948): 505–8.

Larson, John W. *Essayons: A History of the Detroit District U.S. Army Corps of Engineers.* Detroit: U.S. Army Corps of Engineers Detroit District, 1981.

Lavender, David. *The Fist in the Wilderness.* New York: Doubleday, 1964.

Lossing, Benson J. *The Pictorial Field Book of the War of 1812; or Illustrations, by Pen and Pencil, of the History, Biography, Scenery, Relics, and Traditions of the Last War for American Independence.* New York: Harper and Brothers, 1869.

McCoy, James C. *Jesuit Relations of Canada, 1632–1673: A Bibliography.* Paris: Arthur Rau, 1937.

McDermott, John Francis. *Samuel Seymour: Pioneer Artist of the Plains and the Rockies.* Washington, DC: GPO, 1951.

———. *Seth Eastman: Pictorial Historian of the Indian.* Norman: University of Oklahoma Press, 1961.

Malcomson, Robert. *Historical Dictionary of the War of 1812.* Lanham, MD: Scarecrow Press, 2006.

———. *Warships of the Great Lakes, 1754–1834.* Annapolis: Naval Institute Press, 2001.

Martin, Patrick Edward. *The Mill Creek Site and Pattern Recognition in Historical Archaeology.* Mackinac Island, MI: Mackinac Island State Park Commission, 1985.

May, George S. "The Indian Dormitory." Unpublished manuscript, ca. 1966, in the collections of Mackinac State Historic Parks.

———. "John C. Pemberton: A Pennsylvania Confederate at Fort Mackinac." *Mackinac History* 1, no. 11. Mackinac Island, MI: Mackinac Island State Park Commission, 1968.

———. "Reconstruction of the Church of Ste. Anne de Michilimackinac: A Pictorial Story." *Mackinac History* 1, no. 6. Mackinac Island, MI: Mackinac Island State Park Commission, 1964.

———. *War 1812: The United States and Great Britain at Mackinac, 1812–1815.* 2nd rev. ed. Mackinac Island, MI: Mackinac State Historic Parks, 2004.

Nicholas, Edward. *The Chaplain's Lady: Life and Love at Fort Mackinac.* Mackinac Island, MI: Mackinac Island State Park Commission, 1987.

Norton, Bettina A. *Edwin Whitefield: Nineteenth-Century North American Scenery.* Barre, MA: Barre Publishing, 1977.

Paré, George. *The Catholic Church in Detroit, 1701–1888.* Detroit: Gabriel Richard Press, 1951.

Peckham, Howard H. *Pontiac and the Indian Uprising.* New York: Russell and Russell, 1947.

Petersen, Eugene T. *Mackinac Island: Its History in Pictures.* Mackinac Island, MI: Mackinac Island State Park Commission, 1973.

Pierson, George Wilson. *Tocqueville and Beaumont in America.* New York: Oxford University Press, 1938.

Porter, Kenneth Wiggins. *John Jacob Astor, Business Man.* 2 vols. Cambridge, MA: Harvard University Press, 1931.

Porter, Phil. *The Eagle at Mackinac: The Establishment of United States Military and Civil Authority on Mackinac Island, 1796–1802.* Mackinac Island, MI: Mackinac Island State Park Commission, 1991.

———. *Mackinac: An Island Famous in These Regions.* Mackinac Island, MI: Mackinac State Historic Parks, 1998.

———. "Mackinac Island's Post Cemetery." *Mackinac History* 3, no. 3. Mackinac Island, MI: Mackinac State Historic Parks, 1999.

———. *View from the Veranda: The History and Architecture of the Summer Cottages on Mackinac Island.* Mackinac Island, MI: Mackinac Island State Park Commission, 1981.

———, and Victor R. Nelhiebel. *The Wonder of Mackinac: A Guide to the Natural History of the Mackinac Area.* Mackinac Island, MI: Mackinac Island State Park Commission, 1984.

Porter, Whitworth. *History of the Corps of Royal Engineers.* 7 vols. London: Longmans, Green, and Company, 1889.

Prucha, Francis Paul. *The Sword of the Republic: The United States Army on the Frontier, 1783–1846.* Bloomington: Indiana University Press, 1977.

Quaife, Milo M. "Detroit Biographies: Aaron Greeley." *Burton Historical Collection Leaflet* 5, no. 5 (March 1927): 49–64.

Ranville, Judy, and Nancy Campbell. *Memories of Mackinaw.* Mackinaw City, MI: Mackinaw City Public Library, 1976.

Ray, Frederic E. *"Our Special Artist": Alfred R. Waud's Civil War.* Mechanicsburg, PA: Stackpole Books, 1994.

Rezek, Antoine Ivan. *History of the Diocese of Sault Ste. Marie and Marquette Containing a Full and Accurate Account of the Development of the Catholic Church in Upper Michigan.* 2 vols. Houghton, MI: Antoine Ivan Rezek, 1906–7.

Rindge, Warren L. "National Park Service Report on Fort Mackinac Restoration, Mackinac Island, Michigan." Unpublished report dated November 1, 1934. Copy in collections of Mackinac State Historic Parks.

Robinson, George. *History of Cheboygan and Mackinac Counties.* Detroit: Union Job Printing Company, 1873.

Robinson, Willard B. *American Forts: Architectural Form and Function.* Urbana: University of Illinois Press, 1977.

Roy, Pierre-Georges. *Hommes et choses du Fort Saint-Frédéric.* Montréal: Les Éditions Dix, 1946.

Sachse, Nancy D. "Frontier Legend; Bennington's Martin Scott." *Vermont History* 34, no. 3 (1966): 157–68.

Sambrook, Richard Alan. "Historical Lineaments in the Straits of Mackinac: An Investigation of Cultural Cartography." Master's thesis, Department of Geography, Michigan State University, 1980. Copy in the collections of Mackinac State Historic Parks.

———. "Maps of Fort Michilimackinac: Images of the Colonial Frontier." Unpublished paper presented at North American Cartographic Information Society, Fifth Annual Meeting, November 10–13, 1985. Copy in the collections of Mackinac State Historic Parks.

[Smith, Emerson R.]. *Before the Bridge: A History and Directory of St. Ignace and Nearby Localities.* St. Ignace, MI: Kiwanis Club of St. Ignace, 1957.

———. *Michilimackinac: Compiled by Members of the Michilimackinac Historical Society.* St. Ignace, MI: Mackinac County Chamber of Commerce, 1958.

Stanley, George M. *Pre-Historic Mackinac Island.* Lansing: State of Michigan, Department of Conservation, 1945.

Stewart, Charles H. *The Service of British Regiments in Canada and North America: A Resume.* Ottawa: Department of National Defence Library, 1964.

Stone, Lyle M. *Archaeological Investigation of the Marquette Mission Site, St. Ignace, Michigan, 1971: A Preliminary Report.* Mackinac Island, MI: Mackinac Island State Park Commission, 1972.

———. *Fort Michilimackinac, 1715–1781: An Archaeological Perspective on the Revolutionary Frontier.* East Lansing: Michigan State University Museum, 1972.

Sundberg, Trudy J., and John K. Gott. *Valiant Virginian: Story of Presley Neville O'Bannon, 1776–1850, First Lieutenant U.S. Marine Corps, 1801–1807.* Westminster, MD: Heritage Books, 1994.

Sutherland, Stuart. *His Majesty's Gentlemen: A Directory of Regular British Army Officers of the War of 1812.* Toronto: Iser Publications, 2000.

Tanner, Helen Hornbeck, ed. *Atlas of Great Lakes Indian History.* Norman: University of Oklahoma Press, 1987.

Tuttle, Charles Richard. *General History of the State of Michigan with Biographical Sketches, Portrait Engravings, and Numerous Illustrations.* Detroit: R. D. S. Tyler and Company, 1873.

Van Fleet, James A. *Old and New Mackinac.* Ann Arbor, MI: Courier Steam Printing House, 1870.

———. *Summer Resorts of the Mackinaw Region and Adjacent Localities.* Detroit: Lever Print, 1882.

Voss, Edward G. *Botanical Beachcombers and Explorers: Pioneers of the 19th Century in the Upper Great Lakes.* Ann Arbor: University of Michigan Herbarium, 1978.

———. "Flora of St. Helena Island (Straits of Mackinac), Michigan." *Michigan Botanist* 40, no. 2 (2001): 27–47.

———. *A History of Floristics in the Douglas Lake Region (Emmet and Cheboygan Counties), Michigan, with an Account of Rejected Records.* N.p.: n.p., 1956.

———. *Michigan Flora: A Guide to the Identification and Occurrence of the Native and Naturalized Seed-Plants of the State.* Bloomfield Hills, MI: Cranbrook Institute of Science, 1972.

Ware, W. H. *The Centennial History of Cheboygan County and Village.* Cheboygan, MI: Northern Tribune Print, 1876.

Widder, Keith R. *Battle for the Soul: Métis Children Encounter Evangelical Protestants at Mackinaw Mission, 1823–1837.* East Lansing: Michigan State University Press, 1999.

———. "The Cartography of Dietrich Brehm and Thomas Hutchins and the Establishment of British Authority in the Western Great Lakes Region, 1760–1763." *Cartographica* 36, no. 1 (1999): 1–23.

———. *Dr. William Beaumont: The Mackinac Years.* Mackinac Island, MI: Mackinac Island State Park Commission, 1975.

———. *Mackinac National Park, 1875–1895.* Mackinac Island, MI: Mackinac Island State Park Commission, 1975.

———. *Reveille Till Taps.* Mackinac Island, MI: Mackinac Island State Park Commission, 1972.

Williams, J. Mark, and Gary Shapiro. *A Search for the Eighteenth Century Village at Michilimackinac: A Soil Resistivity Survey.* Mackinac Island, MI: Mackinac Island State Park Commission, 1982.

Winchell, Alexander. *Sketches of Creation: A Popular View of Some of the Grand Conclusions of the Sciences in Reference to the History of Matter and of Life. . . .* New York: Harper and Brothers, 1870.

Wood, Edwin O. *Historic Mackinac: The Historical, Picturesque and Legendary Features of the Mackinac Country.* 2 vols. New York: Macmillan, 1918.

Woodford, Arthur M. *Charting the Inland Seas: A History of the U.S. Lake Survey.* Detroit: Wayne State University Press, 1994.

Woodford, Frank B., and Albert Hyma. *Gabriel Richard: Frontier Ambassador.* Detroit: Wayne State University Press, 1958.

Woolson, Constance Fenimore. *Castle Nowhere: Lake Country Sketches.* New York: Harper and Brothers, 1886. Primarily useful for the reminiscences of the island contained in the short story "Jeannette."

INDEX